HOLT
Literature
&Language
Arts

HOLT
Handbook

Grammar • Usage • Mechanics • Sentences

Introductory Course
ANNOTATED TEACHER'S EDITION

 Mastering the CALIFORNIA STANDARDS
in English-Language Conventions

Instructional Framework by

John E. Warriner

HOLT, RINEHART AND WINSTON

A Harcourt Classroom Education Company

Austin • New York • Orlando • Atlanta • San Francisco • Boston • Dallas • Toronto • London

AUTHOR **JOHN E. WARRINER** taught for thirty-two years in junior and senior high schools and in college. He was a high school English teacher when he developed the original organizational structure for his classic *English Grammar and Composition* series. The approach pioneered by Mr. Warriner was distinctive, and the editorial staff of Holt, Rinehart and Winston have worked diligently to retain the unique qualities of his pedagogy in the *Holt Handbook*. John Warriner also co-authored the *English Workshop* series and edited *Short Stories: Characters in Conflict*.

STAFF CREDITS

EDITORIAL

Manager of Editorial Operations
Bill Wahlgren

Executive Editor
Robert R. Hoyt

Program Editor
Marcia L. Kelley

Project Editor
Kathryn Rogers

Writing and Editing
David Bradford, Gabrielle Field, Karen H. Kolar, Theresa Reding

Copyediting
Michael Neibergall, *Copyediting Manager;* Mary Malone, *Copyediting Supervisor;* Christine Altgelt, Joel Bourgeois, Elizabeth Dickson, Emily Force, Julie A. Hill, Julia Thomas Hu, Jennifer Kirkland, Millicent Ondras, Dennis Scharnberg, *Copyeditors*

Project Administration
Marie Price, *Managing Editor;* Lori De La Garza, *Editorial Operations Coordinator;* Heather Cheyne, Mark Holland, Marcus Johnson, Jennifer Renteria, Janet Riley, Kelly Tankersley, *Project Administration;* Ruth Hooker, Joie Pickett, Margaret Sanchez, *Word Processing*

Editorial Permissions
Janet Harrington, *Permissions Editor*

ART, DESIGN, AND PHOTO

Book Design
Diane Motz, *Senior Design Director;* Sally Bess, Tim Hovde, *Designers;* Charlie Taliaferro, *Design Associate*

Graphic Services
Kristen Darby, *Manager*

Image Acquisitions
Joe London, *Director;* Jeannie Taylor, *Photo Research Supervisor;* Rick Benavides, *Photo Researcher;* Sarah Hudgens, *Assistant Photo Researcher;* Elaine Tate, *Art Buyer Supervisor*

Cover Design
Preface, Inc.

PRODUCTION
Belinda Barbosa Lopez, *Senior Production Coordinator*
Nancy Hargis, *Media Production Supervisor*
Beth Prevelige, *Prepress Manager*

MANUFACTURING/ INVENTORY
Shirley Cantrell, *Supervisor of Inventory and Manufacturing*
Wilonda Ieans, *Manufacturing Coordinator*
Mark McDonald, *Inventory Planner*

For acknowledgments, see page 479, which is an extension of the copyright page.

Printed in the United States of America

ISBN 0-03-065288-X

1 2 3 4 5 6 7 8 9 048 05 04 03 02 01

CONTENTS IN BRIEF

CONTENTS

The Parts of a Sentence
Subject and Predicate, Kinds of Sentences

CHAPTER 1

Standards Focus

Sentence Structure 1.1 Use effective coordination and subordination of ideas to express complete thoughts.

Parts of Speech Overview

Noun, Pronoun, Adjective 24

CHAPTER 2

Standards Focus

Grammar 1.2 Identify and properly use indefinite pronouns.

Capitalization 1.4 Use correct capitalization.

Parts of Speech Overview

Verb, Adverb, Preposition, Conjunction, Interjection **48**

Standards Focus

Sentence Structure 1.1 Use effective coordination and subordination of ideas to express complete thoughts.

The Phrase and the Clause

Prepositional Phrases, Independent and Subordinate Clauses, Sentence Structure 74

Complements

Direct and Indirect Objects, Subject Complements 104

 Standards Focus

Language Convention 1.0 Students write and speak with a command of standard English conventions appropriate to this grade level.

Agreement

Subject and Verb, Pronoun and Antecedent 122

Standards Focus

Grammar 1.2 Identify and properly use indefinite pronouns, and ensure that verbs agree with compound subjects.

Using Verbs Correctly

CHAPTER 7

Principal Parts, Regular and Irregular Verbs, Tense 146

Standards Focus

Grammar 1.2 Identify and properly use present perfect, past perfect, and future perfect verb tenses.

Using Pronouns Correctly

CHAPTER

8

Standards Focus

Language Convention 1.0 Students write and speak with a command of standard English conventions appropriate to this grade level.

Using Modifiers Correctly

CHAPTER

Comparison and Placement **196**

Standards Focus

Language Convention 1.0 Students write and speak with a command of standard English conventions appropriate to this grade level.

Punctuation

  Standards Focus

Punctuation 1.3 Use colons after the salutation in business letters, semicolons to connect independent clauses, and commas when linking two clauses with a conjunction in compound sentences.

Punctuation

  Standards Focus

Language Convention 1.0 Students write and speak with a command of standard English conventions appropriate to this grade level.

Spelling

CHAPTER

14

Standards Focus

Spelling 1.5 Spell frequently misspelled words correctly (e.g., *their, they're, there*).

Correcting Common Errors

Key Language Skills Review

CHAPTER

15

 Standards Focus

Language Convention 1.0 Students write and speak with a command of standard English conventions appropriate to this grade level.

16

Standards Focus

Sentence Structure 1.1 Use simple, compound, and compound-complex sentences; use effective coordination and subordination of ideas to express complete thoughts.

Sentence Diagramming 412

 Standards Focus

Sentence Structure 1.1 Use simple, compound, and compound-complex sentences.

Why should I study grammar, usage, and mechanics?

Many people would say that you should study grammar to learn to root out errors in your speech and writing. Certainly, the *Holt Handbook* can help you learn to avoid making errors and to correct the errors you do make. More importantly, though, studying grammar, usage, and mechanics gives you the skills you need to take sentences and passages apart and to put them together, to learn which parts go together and which don't. Instead of writing sentences and passages that you hope sound good, you can craft your sentences to create just the meaning and style you want.

Knowing grammar, usage, and mechanics gives you the tools to understand and discuss your own language, to communicate clearly the things you want to communicate, and to develop your own communication style. Further, mastery of language skills can help you succeed in your other classes, in future classes, on standardized tests, and in the larger world, including, eventually, the workplace.

How do I use the *Holt Handbook*?

The *Holt Handbook* is part of the Holt Literature and Language Arts program. The skills taught in the *Holt Handbook* are important to your success in the reading, writing, speaking, and listening components of this program.

Not only can you use this book as a complete grammar, usage, and mechanics textbook, but you can also use it as a reference guide when you work on any piece of writing. Whether you are writing a personal letter, a report for your social studies class, or some other piece of writing, you can use the *Holt Handbook* to answer your questions about grammar, usage, capitalization, punctuation, and spelling.

How is the *Holt Handbook* organized?

The *Holt Handbook* is divided into three main parts:

PART 1 The **Grammar, Usage, and Mechanics** chapters provide instruction on and practice using the building blocks of language—words, phrases, clauses, capitalization, punctuation, and spelling. Use these chapters to discover how to take sentences apart and put them together. The last chapter, **Correcting Common Errors**, provides additional practice on key language skills as well as standardized test practice in grammar, usage, and mechanics.

PART 2 The **Sentences** chapters include Writing Effective Sentences and Sentence Diagramming. **Writing Effective Sentences** provides instruction on and practice with writing correct, clear, and interesting sentences. **Sentence Diagramming** teaches you to analyze and diagram sentences so you can see how the parts of a sentence relate to each other.

PART 3 The **Resources** section includes **History of English**, a concise history of the English language; **Test Smarts**, a handy guide to taking standardized tests in grammar, usage, and mechanics; and **Grammar at a Glance**, a glossary of grammatical terms.

How are the chapters organized?

Each chapter begins with a Diagnostic Preview, a short test that covers the whole chapter and alerts you to skills that need improvement, and ends with a Chapter Review, another short test that tells you how well you have mastered that chapter. In between, you'll see rules, which are basic statements of grammar, usage, and mechanics principles. The rules are illustrated with examples and followed by exercises and reviews that help you practice what you have learned.

What are some other features of this textbook?

- **Oral Practice**—spoken practice and reinforcement of rules and concepts
- **Writing Applications**—activities that let you apply grammar, usage, and mechanics concepts in your writing
- **Tips & Tricks**—easy-to-use hints about grammar, usage, and mechanics

- **Meeting the Challenge**—questions or short activities that ask you to approach a concept from a new angle
- **Style Tips**—information about formal and informal uses of language
- **Help**—pointers to help you understand either key rules and concepts or exercise directions

Holt Handbook on the Internet

As you move through the *Holt Handbook*, you will find the best online resources at **go.hrw.com.**

What are the California standards?

The California State Board of Education has adopted a set of standards for achievement in Written and Oral English Language Conventions. You will be expected to master these standards during the school year. Each chapter of the *Holt Handbook* begins with a box listing the California standards that you will cover in that chapter.

1.0 Written and Oral English Language Conventions

Students write and speak with a command of standard English conventions appropriate to this grade level.

Sentence Structure

1.1 Use simple, compound, and compound-complex sentences; use effective coordination and subordination of ideas to express complete thoughts.

Grammar

1.2 Identify and properly use indefinite pronouns and present perfect, past perfect, and future perfect verb tenses; ensure that verbs agree with compound subjects.

Punctuation

1.3 Use colons after the salutation in business letters, semicolons to connect independent clauses, and commas when linking two clauses with a conjunction in compound sentences.

Capitalization

1.4 Use correct capitalization.

Spelling

1.5 Spell frequently misspelled words correctly (e.g., *their, they're, there*).

Teaching Strands

This teaching-strand chart shows you some ways to connect grammar instruction and writing instruction.

The *Holt Handbook* is designed to be a flexible teaching tool that accommodates many teaching philosophies and styles. For example, some teachers will prefer to use the handbook as a reference source, having students refer to it only as the need for explicit grammar instruction arises. Others will use the handbook as a teaching text, having their classes work through the instruction, examples, and exercises in a more methodical fashion. Your personal teaching style and the needs of your students will determine the best way for you to teach this material.

GO TO: go.hrw.com
KEYWORD: HLLA

All resources for this handbook are available for preview on the *One-Stop Planner CD-ROM*. All worksheets and tests may be printed from the CD-ROM.

Workshop numerals refer to workshops found in *Holt Literature and Language Arts, Introductory Course.*

Writing Assignments	Rationale
WORKSHOP 1: NARRATION	Narrative writing calls for using pronouns correctly, which requires understanding case, pronoun-antecedent agreement, and subject-verb agreement. Using quotations and contractions in dialogue to show informal speech patterns is common. Consistent verb tense and clue words advance the story coherently.
WORKSHOP 2: EXPOSITION	"How-to" instructions create images through precise adjectives and adverbs, while words or phrases indicating location complete the mental picture. Transitional words can indicate the order of steps. Commas separate a series of steps or parts of a list; a colon may precede the list.
WORKSHOP 3: RESPONSE TO LITERATURE	To describe a plot and offer an opinion when writing a short story interpretation, writers rely on carefully chosen positive and negative words, fresh descriptions, and words signaling order of events. Correct pronoun case must be used to show the author's point of view. Appositives can provide additional information.
WORKSHOP 4: RESEARCH	Because research reports require a sophisticated writing style, students need to use correctly spelled, formal language to incorporate information and quotations from many sources. Writing a report demands attention to sentence structure, capitalization, and punctuation. Phrases and clauses create sentence variety, but sentence fragments should be avoided.
WORKSHOP 5: PERSUASION	Strong, clear action verbs and their objects help a writer to emphasize points and to build a case in a persuasive essay. Challenging questions and exclamations help clarify the writer's stance. Careful capitalization, clearly punctuated sentences, and correctly used words help to eliminate ambiguity and confusing points.

Links to Grammar	Links to Usage	Links to Mechanics
personal and possessive pronouns (Ch. 2)	pronoun-antecedent agreement (Ch. 6); pronoun case (Ch. 8)	
verbs, adverbs (Ch. 3)	agreement (Ch. 6); tense (Ch. 7)	punctuating contractions (Ch. 13)
sentences classified by purpose (Ch. 1)		punctuating quotations (Ch. 13)
adjectives (Ch. 2); adverbs and prepositions (Ch. 3)	comparison of modifiers (Ch. 9); *between, among; good, well; than, then* (Ch. 10)	using commas to separate two or more adjectives (Ch. 12); using colons with a list (Ch. 12)
adjective and adverb phrases (Ch. 4)	using modifiers (Ch. 9)	commas with interrupters (Ch. 12)
adjectives (Ch. 2); adverbs (Ch. 3)	comparison of modifiers, double negatives (Ch. 9)	
pronouns (Ch. 2); complements (Ch. 5)	pronoun-antecedent agreement (Ch. 6); pronoun case (Ch. 8)	apostrophes with contractions and possessives (Ch. 13)
clauses and phrases (Ch. 4)		commas with interrupters (Ch. 12)
independent and subordinate clauses, sentence structure (Ch. 4)	formal, standard usage (Ch. 10)	punctuating compound and complex sentences (Ch. 12); spelling (Ch. 14)
sentences, fragments, subjects, predicates (Ch. 1); adverb and adjective phrases (Ch. 4)	subject-verb agreement with intervening phrases, with indefinite pronouns, with compound subjects, and with subjects after verbs (Ch. 6)	capitalization of titles (Ch. 11); punctuation of direct quotations (Ch. 12 & Ch. 13); capitalizing and punctuating sources (Ch. 11–13)
transitive and intransitive verbs (Ch. 3); direct and indirect objects, subject complements (Ch. 5)	principal parts of verbs (Ch. 7)	apostrophes with contractions (Ch. 13); words often confused (Ch. 14); capitalizing the first word in a sentence (Ch. 11)
kinds of sentences (Ch. 1)	pronouns, including *whom,* as objects; nominative case pronouns (Ch. 8)	end marks (Ch. 12)

By Amy Benjamin

Dispelling the Myths about Grammar Instruction

because those lessons in syntax, placement, word classification, and the subtleties of style helped them to be better writers, more efficient readers, clearer thinkers.

It is not uncommon for English teachers as well as their trainers and supervisors to hold that the teaching of grammar is quaint and unnecessary at best, prejudicial and exclusionary at worst.

I know an excellent English teacher whose students, many years after graduation, remember her for her grammar lessons. Unfortunately, instead of being proud of this, she is chagrined. . . . "*Grammar*!? Of all things in my class to remember! Why *grammar*? Why can't they remember me for all the wonderful literature I taught them? for what I taught them about composition? expression? creativity? Why just *grammar*? I don't even teach *grammar* anymore. I teach the *writing* process."

Perhaps these students remembered their grammar lessons because of the usefulness of those lessons or because of the satisfaction that they derived from learning challenging material. Perhaps they remembered

How lamentable it is that teaching writing through a process approach has become an orthodoxy in which the grammatical strand of English language arts is pitted against the literary strand, as if the two are not intertwined. Who set up this false dichotomy? The notion that grammar instruction is antithetical to the writing process is specious. My purpose in this essay is to debunk some of the myths about grammar instruction and to refurbish its tarnished reputation.

It is not uncommon for English teachers as well as their trainers and supervisors to hold that the teaching of grammar is quaint and unnecessary at best, prejudicial and exclusionary at worst. The problem begins with muddy terminology. Some people conflate the terms *grammar, usage,* and *mechanics,* as well as the terms *correct/incorrect* and *standard/ nonstandard.* Before I turn my fire extinguisher on the grammar myths, let me clarify my terms: By *grammar,* I refer to the rules which govern how words function in a sentence to make meaning. That *man bites dog* means something different from *dog bites man* is a function of grammar. By *usage,* I refer to the social conventions that determine what is considered standard. By *standard,* I do not mean *correct.* I mean that style of the English language which most educated people accept in formal circumstances. By *mechanics,* I refer to physical manifestations of language such as spelling, punctuation, capitalization and other conventions. In the case of *mechanics,* the terms *correct* and *incorrect* are more appropriate than they are when we are talking about matters of usage, but even spelling is not without gray areas.

Reasonable people can disagree over matters of content and methodology in teaching. However, I think everyone would agree that to under-stand a complicated system we need to know the names of its parts, their forms and functions, how the parts relate to the whole, and where these parts belong if the system is to operate at maximum efficiency. That said, here's what some people say about grammar instruction, and why I disagree with them.

Myth #1:

The explicit teaching of grammar does not improve writing ability, so time spent on grammar is time not spent on more worthy pursuits in the English classroom.

Think about it. Suppose my car is making a funny noise. Suppose I have no better understanding of what is going on under the hood than that. I take it to my mechanic, trusting his knowledge, integrity, and skill. He'll figure out what's wrong with my car and fix the problem. I'll pay the bill, and if all is not well, I'll get either another mechanic or another car. That is how many car owners (myself included) operate. We don't have the time or the inclination to learn the taxonomy, nomenclature, and anatomy of our cars.

When we don't speak explicitly to students about grammar, syntax, diction, and coherence, we have to resort to the "funny noise" method: We have to say "This part just doesn't sound right here," or "You're not saying this clearly." We may be able to help writers fix the sentence, but we haven't given them the generality that will allow them to apply what they've learned to similar circumstances.

On the other hand, I can know the names of all the tools in my toolbox, what each is for, and how they relate to one another; but if I don't use them to facilitate an actual job in progress, then my knowledge does not fulfill its intended purpose. For many of us, the grammar lessons that we learned in school were about "picking out." We'd "pick out" all kinds of structures: the parts of speech, subjects and predicates, simple subjects, helping verbs. Later, we'd hunt down adverbial clauses, subject complements, infinitives. We'd underline and double underline. We'd diagram. The trouble with our instruction was not that it was misguided, but that it was unfinished. Having learned to spot prepositional phrases, we may not have learned why doing so could improve our discourse.

How can we *use* our ability to identify grammatical structures such as prepositional phrases in our own reading and writing? We may have learned that the object of a preposition must be in the objective case, and that the object of a preposition is never the subject of the sentence. This knowledge helps us solve some usage problems, but that is not its main value. Knowing how to discern the subject and verb can help us read dense prose. When reading dense prose, the reader needs strategies. One such strategy is to reduce the sentence to its subject and verb. That done, the reader sees prepositional phrases for what they are: details. Beyond that, knowing about prepositions helps writers add sentence variety, as they learn not to begin sentence after sentence with the subject. Beginning a sentence with a prepositional phrase can set the stage for the action, but we have to be judicious: Sometimes, that prepositional phrase can be distracting or redundant. As modifiers, prepositional phrases can be movable, and their placement affects meaning, rhythm, and emphasis. Prepositional phrases, "time and place words," add detail and dimension. The novice writer who has difficulty fleshing out a topic can do well to consciously add more prepositional phrases. It is knowing what prepositional phrases can and can't do for you that makes being able to identify them worthwhile. Selecting standard pronoun case, creating purposeful variety in sentence structure, adding detail and dimension, and eliminating redundancy are some good reasons for being able to recognize prepositional phrases.

> It is knowing what prepositional phrases can and can't do for you that makes being able to identify them worthwhile.

Recognition of a grammatical structure is only the beginning. If we think of grammar instruction as building an awareness of language choices available to the careful writer, then we view such instruction in two phases: recognition and application. Too often, the application phase does not happen. When it does not, the recognition phase seems to lack practicality. Thus does grammar instruction fall out of favor.

Myth #2:
Grammar instruction applies only to the editing phase of the writing process.

When people operate under this myth, they are confusing grammar with usage and mechanics. Usage and mechanics may be seen as "touchups," part of the finishing-off of a written piece. As such, they are not essential to the real intellectual work of the process, although no one should minimize their importance. Usage and mechanics can determine the first and last impressions that the reader gets of the writer's work. The point is that we should not limit our understanding of grammar to the surface features of usage and mechanics.

Along with diction and rhetoric, grammar (unlike usage and mechanics) is *organic* to the crafting of sentences and text. Writers with an awareness of grammar can make informed choices about how word order affects meaning. Picture a

carpenter. He doesn't just blindly reach into his toolbox, pull out a screwdriver, try to make it do the work of a wrench, and figure he'll just sand down the rough spots later. We can make our students better writers if we teach them to use grammatical knowledge consciously as they match their syntax to their intentions.

We understand the power of graphic organizers in both reading and writing for many learners. We teach students to map their ideas as a prewriting strategy. We teach them to make Venn diagrams to show similarities and differences, and flowcharts to express sequence. Sentence structures are patterns. We can think in terms of certain grammatical templates, containers, that work well for certain types of ideas. Parallel structure and compound sentences or simple sentences with compound constituents are good containers for *like* elements bearing equal importance. Complex sentences are good containers to use when we need to show the backgrounding and foregrounding of elements that do not bear equal importance. Sentence structure selections occur in the drafting and revision stages of the writing process, as the writer searches for the clearest, most efficient way to express thoughts.

Many writers have an intuitive sense of what kinds of containers work best with what kinds of ideas. When we bring this underlying awareness of grammar to the conscious level, we help students manage inchoate ideas in the same way that a graphic organizer, such as a Venn diagram, might. Indeed, there is much to be said for using one of the many versions of graphic organizers *along with* sentence structure templates. The writer can then look at a branch diagram or a cluster, decide how the ideas are related, and then consider an array of syntactical containers to suit them.

What I've described is a way of understanding the role of grammar in the writing process that is deeper than what is commonly thought, i.e., that grammatical thinking enters the picture only as the cleanup man. In fact, we already make intuitive grammatical choices as we compose our thoughts. Those intuitive choices may or may not be the best ones for the purpose. By building awareness of sentence and textual structure, we can increase our chances that our message is clear, efficient, and graceful.

Myth #3:
Grammar is boring.

There are many ways to make our classrooms boring. We can "cover material" in a perfunctory way, "going over" the exercises done for homework or as seatwork. We can convey to students that their language is "wrong" and ours is "right." We can be language prudes, fainting and blanching at every double negative or misplaced modifier that dares to show its face in our presence. We can insist that the answer key is always the authority and that grammar is a "no

discussion" subject. We can isolate the study of grammar, treat it as something we "have to get through" before moving on to literature. We can fail to make any connection between grammar and journalism, grammar and advertising, grammar and novels, grammar and drama, grammar and music, grammar and poetry. These are ways to make grammar boring.

I've heard teachers claim that grammar instruction interferes with creativity.

I've heard teachers claim that grammar instruction interferes with creativity. "Grammar is boring," they say. "And writing should be fun and interesting." This is a misguided notion, because creativity thrives within structure. The sonneteer works within a strictly prescribed structure, choosing that structure because it is the best container for particular ideas. The sonnet form is not constraining but liberating: The format frees the writer from decisions about rhythm and rhyme scheme. Because of the structure, half the work is done. I can't think of any creative pursuit—music, fine arts, dance, photography, drama, writing—that does not demand mastery of technique. I can't think of any creative pursuit in which there is no terminology, no anatomy, no structure, no tradition, no rules. Why would learning any kind of writing, much less creative writing, be

detached from the fundamentals? Knowledge of structure is not a hindrance, but a guide that enables, rather than impedes, creativity.

Sometimes, grammar instruction is thought of as "drill and kill." This pejorative implies that the instruction will consist of lower level thinking skills, mindless repetition, and lack of application to authentic language. We picture fill-in-the-blank workbook-type questions in which there is one right answer. The book that you have in your hands is an extremely useful, in fact indispensable, tool for the teaching of language. However, any grammar text is most effective when used *along with*, not in place of, literature and student writing. It might seem that students would naturally make the crossover from what they learn in grammar exercises to their own language use, but such is not necessarily the case. As teachers, we have to make that crossover happen very deliberately, pointing out structures that students have learned and how those structures are used to make meaning in authentic contexts. Thus does grammar instruction transcend the practice exercises that illustrate targeted concepts.

Everybody loves language; children and teenagers love it especially, because they are in the process of defining their own culture by laying claim to words and expressions all their own. When we invite students to analyze their own neologisms, grammatical idiosyncrasies, and dialectical styles, we enliven grammar lessons immeasurably. As English teachers, we embrace all forms of the English language even while we recognize that mastery of standard English is essential for success in certain precincts of society.

Another way to make grammar instruction interesting is to let students discover how language changes right before our eyes. Movies and novels set in various pockets of the English-speaking world are museums of linguistic anthropology. Compare the idioms of *To Kill A Mockingbird* to those of *The Color Purple*. Analyze the language of a movie set in New Orleans and compare it to the language of a movie set in Los Angeles.

There are many ways to make our classrooms interesting. Our love of the subject is contagious. Grammar is exciting and rewarding to learn not because we get the answers right, but because we've applied logic and found patterns, and because there may be more than one answer, depending on the circumstances, audience, and purpose. Contrary to myth, a good grammar lesson can invite a lively discussion about ambiguities in meaning and the best way to express thought in a particular context. It can even ignite a discussion about social power structures, prejudices, and immigration. This is not boring stuff.

Myth #4:
Grammar applies only to English classes.

For lack of a better term, we refer to subjects other than English as "content areas." Aside from the obvious expectation that we use standard English in school, how can students apply grammar to their content area classes?

Every teacher wants students to be better readers. A law student told me recently that she was glad that she knew something about grammar, because she needed it to read complex materials in her courses. She found that by mentally pulling out the subject and verb, she could follow the lines of technical text.

Needless to say, grammatical knowledge of the English language is essential for learning another language. Just as grammar has fallen out of favor in many English classes, it has suffered a similar blow in the pedagogy of learning other languages as well, where grammar instruction has been supplanted by "conversation." The predictable consequence has been much confusion and frustration for both teachers, who feel that their hands are tied, and students, many of whom are bewildered by the gymnastics of the French verb when they don't even know how English verbs behave.

What about science, math, social studies, the arts? All teachers love words. The biology teacher is fussy about the difference between *osmosis* and *diffusion.* Getting students to make fine distinctions is an important part of teaching students to think like scientists. Teachers want to give away the words of their subject areas the way grandmothers want to give away food. We want to invite our students into the professional conversation of our subject areas.

> # Teachers want to give away the words of their subject areas the way grandmothers want to give away food.

As English teachers, we love words about words, language about language. To us, there is a vast difference between an action verb and a linking verb, a predicate nominative and a direct object, a transitive verb and an intransitive verb. In teaching students to talk the talk, we turn them into licensed operators, not just amateurs. A licensed operator can make the machinery run more efficiently, can anticipate potential problems, and can fix what is wrong. An amateur *hopes* that the sentence "sounds good."

Grammar should be the permeable membrane that allows knowledge learned in English class to transform into skill in the content area classes. Active voice may be preferable in English classes where the subject is often *people doing things* (S-V-O). In composing a lab report, however, passive voice may be the better choice. *The difference in pressure was recorded* might sound more scientific than *I recorded the difference in pressure.* In the language of lab reports, the fact that the technician did the action is irrelevant. A radiologist writes her report in the passive voice: *No abnormalities were found*, rather than *I found no abnormalities*. In English class, we show students the difference in tone between active and passive voice.

It is important to learn to think in action verbs in all subject areas. A student who is writing about the Reformation needs to focus on who did what: *Martin Luther <u>translated</u> the Bible into the German vernacular. His translation <u>enabled</u> more people to read the Bible.* The action verbs tell the story. They give students a starting point when writing and a focus when reading. All subject areas use this concept; it is we English teachers who actually teach it in our grammar lessons.

The social studies teacher and the science teacher may not know it, but the benefits of grammar instruction are carried through the student's entire day.

Myth #5:
Grammar instruction is ethnocentric and prejudicial.

As English teachers, we need to avoid giving the impression that we are the designated Keepers of the Language. We can teach the etiquette of standard English without denying a student the right to his or her own dialect.

An educated person has that social thermostat that linguists call code-switching. The metaphor of table manners is apt: What we are expected to do at an outdoor barbecue differs from what we're expected to do at Thanksgiving dinner. Those of us who can't tell the difference, who can't code-switch, are socially awkward. This is not to say that standard English is better than any particular dialect. Standard English is not more expressive, more poetic, or even more accurate. It is simply the expected currency of mainstream society in formal situations. We don't have to use it all of the time, but if we *can't* use it when it is expected, then we are at a cultural disadvantage that our education should remedy.

We are constantly making impressions that indicate our understanding of our social context. Those who are successful in their chosen fields,

indeed, those for whom a chosen field is an option in the first place, know how to control the impression that others have of them. People judge our status and education levels not only through language, but also through dress, manners, and gesture.

Once we acknowledge that standard English is just another form of English that is appropriate for certain situations but not for all, then we are free to enjoy the dialects of English that we find in authentic literature, regional speech, song lyrics, and casual conversation. We can look at new coinages, popular metaphors, slang, and jargon with the interest of a linguist rather than the arrogance of a pedant.

We can teach the etiquette of Standard English without denying a student the right to his or her own dialect.

That language is a changing social contract is evidenced by grammar books of yore. Even in one generation, the *who/whom* distinction has attenuated, as has the use of the past perfect tense of verbs. Certain usages, such as the nominative case after a linking verb, sound stuffy. We have yet to solve the problem that exists because we lack a generic singular pronoun: *He,* once preferred, is thought to be sexist; *one* sounds stilted and British; *they* is a grammatical mismatch. That leaves *he or she*, which can seem awfully conspicuous. It's interesting to have students compare the style guides of various publications on sensitive points such as this.

Myth #6:
As native speakers, we don't have to learn grammar.

It is true that we already know grammar intuitively. Native speakers learn, quite naturally, how to put words together to make meaning. What we don't learn naturally is the metalanguage, that is, the language of language. Absent that, we can't explain what we mean about what we are trying to say, and others are at a loss to help us.

Terminology is powerful.

Recently, I worked with a group of elementary school teachers who were looking for teaching strategies that would improve their students' writing skills. When I suggested that they develop a scope and sequence in grammar skills, they were skeptical. "They already know how to use adjectives, nouns, and verbs," one teacher said. "Why do they have to know the *names* of these things?" "That just isn't the way we teach anymore," said another with a wave of her hand. "We don't want to interfere with the children's creativity. Teaching them grammar would interrupt their flow." A fourth-grade teacher added, "But that isn't on the state test, and we really don't have time for anything that doesn't get the scores up." Here's what I would answer:

Terminology is powerful. We can't improve our sentences until we understand the crucial role played by verbs. We certainly can't understand that role until we know how to identify verbs in context and that verbs come in various flavors: finite verbs, infinitives, participles, gerunds.

Further, creativity and "flow" are enhanced, not impeded, by knowledge of language structure and what certain kinds of phrases and sentences can and can't do. When the reader has to stumble over and re-read awkward, redundant, convoluted, or misplaced structures within sentences, does it matter how creative the writer was? Doesn't the logic of grammar *improve* the flow of prose?

To answer the last objection, the statewide tests may or may not have explicit questions regarding grammar. Some do; some don't, and the nature of those tests can and will change. What will not change is that a writer who knows where commas belong makes the job easier on the reader, as does the writer who understands subordination, agreement, and overall

sentence management. If we acknowledge that the whole purpose of writing is to communicate, and that communication is accomplished by writing clearly, then we can see the application of grammar to writing. Of course, if grammar instruction never makes the leap from identification of a structure to its effective application, then these teachers are right to reject it as largely irrelevant.

What Knowing Grammar Can Do for Writers

Finally, here is a list of what you can do when you know a few things about grammar:

- If you know how to use parallel structure, you can make your message smoother, clearer, easier on the reader, more logical, and more memorable.

- If you know when to use active voice and when to use passive voice, you can control the directness or indirectness of your message. You control the power and impact of your words. You can also avoid the trouble that comes from being too direct or accusatory.

- If you know how to use verb tense consistently, you can guide your reader through the tangle of time in your narrative.

- If you know how to vary the grammatical constructs in your sentence structure, you can make your flow of sentences more musical, more nuanced, less choppy.

- If you know the difference between a phrase, a clause, and a sentence, you can guide your reader by using well-placed punctuation.

Like poetry, grammar is about the beauty of expressing exactly what we mean by placing the words just right.

Understanding how grammar works puts the writer on the right path. When writers begin a definition by saying "Osmosis is *when* . . ." they are failing to apply the concept that a subject complement, not an adverbial clause, must follow a linking verb. The "*is when* . . ." definition is going to fall on its face because the key term has not been handled properly in the sentence. Definitions call for classification. First, we must place the term in its proper realm: "Osmosis is a . . . process? means? phenomenon?" The writer must stop and think about what *kind* of thing osmosis is. Such categorical thinking is absolutely essential to the scientist, but it does not happen with the ungrammatical ". . . *is when*" structure. This example demonstrates the relationship between grammar and the logical progression of ideas.

Knowing grammar is useful, but even if it weren't, learning it would still be worthwhile because it is interesting. Like chess, grammar is about how power and proximity govern relationships and possibilities. Like engineering, grammar is about structure, balance, efficiency and strength. Like mathematics, grammar is about patterns and forms. Like geology, grammar is at once eternal and dynamic. Like poetry, grammar is about the beauty of expressing exactly what we mean by placing the words just right. ∎

Amy Benjamin is an English teacher at Hendrick Hudson High School in Montrose, New York. In addition, she is a consultant to teachers, administrators, staff developers, and people in the business world. Amy specializes in showing people how to use clear, concise language. She has written several books about teaching literacy skills in all subject areas, as well as two plays (Romeo and Juliet Will Not Be Performed Tonight *and* Romeo and Juliet: Still Not Dead) *and a young adult novel* (Russell Kim: My Real Name). *Amy lives in Fishkill, New York, with her husband Howard and son Mitch.*

By Brock Haussamen

Grammar: Why Teach It?

Why should students learn—and teachers teach—grammar? Simply memorizing the parts of speech doesn't, by itself, make students better writers. Worrying about errors can quickly dampen student enthusiasm for a writing project. Over the past three decades, grammar's reputation has suffered. Is grammar useful? Why teach it?

I believe the central reason for teaching and learning grammar is that it gives all of us a language for talking about language, and certainly the ability to talk about language is a fundamental educational goal. It is difficult to discuss sentences without knowing basic grammar in the same way that it is difficult to talk about a sport or a science or politics without knowing the names of its elements and how they are organized. Knowing basic grammar is what enables students to discuss the sentences in a book they are reading or in a paper they are writing, and to discuss their native language or a second language.

Think of grammar as having two faces. One is its public face, which can be quite formal. The other face is private and more friendly.

The Two Faces of Grammar

To teach grammar effectively, we need to show students how to put it to use. The language of grammar—the names for the parts of speech and other sentence components that appear in the grammar section of this textbook—has two distinct kinds of uses. Think of grammar as having two faces. One is its public face, which can be quite formal. The other face is private and more friendly.

Public Grammar

The public face of grammar consists of all the rules we teach students to follow in their writing and all the errors we tell them to avoid making. In this textbook it is the material in the sections on usage and mechanics. I call usage and mechanics "public grammar" because they identify the conventions of the standard American dialect in which our society carries on its formal writing and speaking. There are many good reasons to teach these conventions. Such a standard dialect helps people from different places and different backgrounds to communicate clearly. The conventions of public grammar help sustain the uniformity of our writing system, on which our society depends utterly. Finally, they reflect the language of economic power. In general, people who can write and speak according to the standard conventions have a better chance at participating in the influential core of our society. People who do not master those conventions will likely face obstacles at every turn.

It is important for us to remember and to remind our students that public grammar is different from, not inherently better than, the language students normally use. The do's and don'ts of public grammar create an illusion that they are rigorously logical, like the rules of mathematics, and that they are permanent. Neither of these claims is true. The do's and don'ts are sometimes illogical, and they change. Just a few decades ago, grammar textbooks like this one would have insisted on the distinction between *will* and *shall*; today that distinction is all but gone. A few decades into the future, a book such as this will probably simplify and may even omit the distinction between *who* and *whom*, which is already fading in informal English.

The "right" clothes, like the "right" grammar, depend on what is appropriate or expected in a given situation.

Try explaining to your students that their grammar is like the clothes they wear. The "right" clothes, like the "right" grammar, depend on what is appropriate or expected in a given situation. Around their friends, students talk and dress in particular ways. At formal occasions or in the workplace, they will be required to dress, to talk, and to write in other ways. This approach will less likely demean those students who do not routinely hear and use standard English. It also gives grammatical correctness a practical value and encourages your students to see language differences as an example of social diversity and opportunity.

Private Grammar

The other face of grammar is much more personal. By "private grammar," I mean the language structure that all of us already carry around in our heads and put to use when we communicate or think. In contrast to the study of public grammar, which has evolved over centuries, the description of our inherent language ability has grown from the work of linguists over the last several decades. Such grammar is private in the sense that it operates inside our heads, so quickly we are not even conscious of it. You won't find questions about private grammar on standardized tests; it is what students possess in order to read the tests in the first place.

If using public grammar can be compared to wearing socially acceptable formal clothes, private grammar can be compared to doing what comes naturally, to physical skills such as walking or running or throwing. Ask students to take a statement and turn it into a question in their native language. They can do it easily. They can fit new slang words into sentences fluidly. They know quickly when the language they hear or read sounds confusing or clear, choppy or smooth. They do all this with their private grammar.

Private grammar can be compared to doing what comes naturally, to physical skills such as walking or running or throwing.

If they can do all this already, how will studying grammar help them do more? The answer is that any skill that already comes somewhat naturally, like throwing a ball or making music, will improve if we learn about it and practice it. Students will be using the language of grammar to some degree when they revise and combine sentences in the section on "Writing Effective Sentences" in this textbook. They will do so to a greater degree whenever you show them how to improve the style of their writing by finding active verbs or expanding sentences with participles or prepositional phrases.

Putting Grammar to Use

As you can see from these descriptions of public and private faces, the language of basic grammar has many uses. Nonetheless, it is a difficult language for students to grow com-

fortable with; its vocabulary looks large and forbidding; many of the terms combine with each other in ways that seem strange to students ("adjective clause"); and because it is a language about language, it strains the verbal skills of many of its students, both children and adults. So, like any language it must be practiced often and put to use in a variety of contexts. Here are some general suggestions.

Use Private Grammar to Teach Public Grammar

As language users, we all have an intuitive sense that sentences are made up of sections. Give students a sentence and ask them to divide it into chunks and to group the words that go together. This approach can remain basic or can become more refined as students divide and cluster clauses and phrases.

This sort of activity easily leads to sentence diagramming. If you are not familiar with diagramming, see Chapter 00. I teach students not the whole of it but just the basic components; even elementary diagrams help many students see the subject-predicate core of a sentence more clearly. If you choose to teach diagramming more thoroughly, students will be able to analyze difficult sentences that they encounter in reading and will build their comprehension. Many students enjoy constructing the diagrams; the activity taps students' visual and spatial skills in addition to their verbal ones.

Another way to draw on students' private grammatical ability is to provide them with practical shortcuts for getting at the essential points of grammar. Grammarians over the years have assembled a number of these simple methods, and your students will love you for telling them about these methods. One good book on the subject is Rei Noguchi's *Grammar and the Teaching of Writing: Limits and Possibilities* (NCTE). Students find the shortcuts practical, and they also appreciate the positive reinforcement of their grammatical instincts.

Use Grammar for Reading

Although grammar is most closely associated with writing, students can put grammar to use when they read.

Knowing grammatical terminology gives students the tools they need to discuss a difficult sentence in a story or a poem. Ask students to pick out the main verb and then the simple subject; finding these can help them figure out the rest of the sentence. Poets bend sentences around a good deal, but most poetry consists of recognizable sentences and sentence parts. Often you can help students move beyond their perplexity about a poem by reminding them to look for the sentences and their basic parts.

In discussing with students what they enjoy or don't enjoy about a writer's style, look for the grammatical characteristics of the writer's sentences. What parts of speech stand out in the sentences? Some writers specialize in strong, active verbs, with few forms of the verb *be*. In other writers' texts, *is* and *are* abound, but the nouns stand out. In still others', the adjectives and adverbs catch the reader's attention.

Another approach is to ask students how long a writer's sentences are, on average. What characteristic sentence lengths do students notice among types of writers, or the writers of different periods? This approach can lead to a discussion of the different structures that make up a writer's sentences. Some writers like to add modifiers, phrases, and clauses; other writers keep sentences short to highlight the main nouns and verbs. Some start a sentence with long introductory word groups; others go right to the subject.

Bring grammar into the reading of advertisements, political language, and the World Wide Web. Advertisements provide good examples of sentence fragments, imperative verbs, and words that look like nouns but act like adjectives ("a Labor Day sofa sale"). Political speeches and slogans make interesting use of *we* and other personal pronouns. E-mail seems to encourage sentences that are variously clipped, casual, funny, skillful, and careless. Ask students to bring in examples for discussion.

Use Grammar for Revision

When students write, help them use grammar not just in the final editing stage, when they hunt out their violations of public grammar, but in the revising stage as well, when they can experiment with private grammar to develop their style as writers.

This textbook shows students how to combine sentences by inserting words or using conjunctions. Students can use some of the same methods to build a single sentence. They can build their sentences by adding participles (especially –*ing* participles that function half as an active verb, half as an adjective) and also by adding appositives. "A spider, **a repulsive, hairy creature, no bigger than a tarantula,** crawled into the room. . . . **Hands trembling, sweat dripping from his face,** he flung the magazine left and right, **trying to kill the spiders,** but there were too many." That example of an eighth-grader's work is from Harry Noden's *Image Grammar: Using Grammatical Structures to Teach Writing,* an excellent source for these and other techniques. Students can also add phrases, especially prepositional phrases, and clauses to a sentence, expanding the information about their main point, giving more details in order to paint a picture, building, and penetrating further into their topic. (The sentence that you just read is one example; you can find more—and better ones—in the work of most accomplished writers.) Students may think at first that they are merely making sentences longer, but they will quickly find that they are also saying more.

Conclusion

The suggestions in this essay are only a sample of the good ideas for using the language of grammar to help students become better readers and writers. The books I have mentioned will lead you to other ideas. And your colleagues in language arts can provide you with many other suggestions for using grammar in the classroom. If you think of grammar as a language for talking about language and you keep in mind the differences

Weaver, Constance. *Teaching Grammar in Context*. Portsmouth: Boynton/Cook, 1996.

William, Joseph M. Style: *The Lessons in Clarity and Grace*. 6th ed. New York: Longman, 2000. ■

Brock Haussamen has taught at Raritan Valley Community College in New Jersey since 1968. He is the author of Revising the Rules: Traditional Grammar and Modern Linguistics *(Kendall/Hunt) and also of a book on the history of the local New Jersey railroads. He began serving as president of the Assembly for the Teaching of English Grammar in 2000. His hobby and passion recently is playing ragtime piano.*

between public and private grammar, you can make grammar a valuable part of your students' language education.

For Further Reading

Assembly for the Teaching of English Grammar. www.ateg.org.

Berk, Lynn M. *English Syntax: From Word to Discourse*. New York: Oxford UP, 1999.

Haussamen, Brock. *Revising the Rules: Traditional Grammar and Modern Linguistics*. 2nd ed. Dubuque: Kendall/Hunt, 2000.

Kolln, Martha. *Rhetorical Grammar: Grammatical Choices, Rhetorical Effect*. 3rd ed. Boston: Allyn and Bacon, 1998.

Kolln, Martha, and Robert Funk (contributor). *Understanding English Grammar*. 5th ed. Needham: Allyn and Bacon, 1998.

Noden, Harry R. *Image Grammar: Using Grammatical Structures to Teach Writing*. Portsmouth: Heinemann/Boynton Cook, 1999.

Noguchi, Rei. *Grammar and the Teaching of Writing: Limits and Possibilities*. Urbana: NCTE, 1991.

By Rei R. Noguchi

Getting Down to Basics:
Using What Students Already Know

Like sentences, subjects and verbs are among the most basic elements of grammar and writing instruction.

Too often we struggle in teaching basic grammar to our students. Yet what really are the basics and how should we teach them? The most basic—the rock-bottom minimum—are sentence, verb, and subject. Surprisingly, we can teach these three basic elements by taking advantage of the unconscious linguistic knowledge that students already possess, their private grammar, so to speak. By tapping this

unconscious knowledge, we can help students identify more easily the three basic elements, and, more important, help them better understand subsequent instruction in grammar, usage, and mechanics.

Why are the sentence, verb, and subject the very basics of grammar instruction? Take the notion of sentence. The sentence constitutes the most important unit in written texts, particularly in writing for school. A shaky grasp of what counts as a written sentence inevitably and unintentionally leads to distracting sentence fragments, fused sentences, and comma splices. Clearly, to master formal written English, students need to differentiate between a genuine sentence and an inappropriate nonsentence. Like sentences, subjects and verbs are among the most basic elements of grammar and writing instruction. Besides helping to define a sentence, subjects and verbs constitute elements on which a great deal of grammar and writing instruction builds. Without a reliable way of identifying subject and verb, students can almost certainly expect rough going.

How can we teach the concepts of subject, verb, and sentence so that students can identify them easily? I would suggest that, rather than relying solely on semantic definitions, we take fuller advantage of what we often ignore or downplay in our teaching of grammar, namely, the tremendous unconscious knowledge that all fluent or near-fluent speakers of English bring to the classroom every day. Put more bluntly, our students know a great deal more about grammar than many of us think. This grammar is not school grammar but their "private grammar," the system of rules unconsciously learned and unconsciously used by all fluent speakers of English in everyday conversation. We cannot teach this personal underlying grammar for the simple reason that our students already know it. All we can do is bring this knowledge to the surface and exploit it to the fullest.

Identifying the Sentence

Exploiting the unconscious linguistic knowledge of students is the key to teaching the very basics of grammar. For students unaccustomed or resistant to working with abstract definitions, identifying sentences and fragments may prove difficult. To identify fragments, students must, at minimum, understand that a fragment is an "incomplete sentence"; to apply this definition, however, students must understand what a sentence is. To understand what a sentence is, students must understand such terms as subject, predicate, and independent clause. Each of these terms may require further definitions yet.

Exploiting the unconscious linguistic knowledge of students is the key to teaching the very basics of grammar.

To avoid the chain of seemingly endless definitions to identify sentences and fragments, teachers can take advantage of their students' unconscious knowledge of what constitutes a complete sentence. Teachers can, for example, use the following frame to help students tap what they already know.

Sentence Frame:
They liked the idea that

_____.

Many word groups will fit in the frame, but whatever they are, they will all be genuine declarative sentences. Students can try out fragments you provide, such as *Thinking of joining the team* or *Because he joined the team,* as well as any suspicious word groups they themselves may write. If students discover a fragment, they can add or delete words to make it fit into the frame and thereby change the fragment into a genuine sentence. There is no need to define a sentence formally at this stage. If students can perform the simple test given here, they already unconsciously know what a sentence is, and with that knowledge they can easily identify fragments, which are just parts of sentences. With a bit of guidance and exploration, students will discover that fused sentences and comma splices won't fit in the empty slot either.

Identifying Verbs

If we tap the private grammar of our students, we can also help them identify specific and important parts of the sentence. Below are two frames that will help students identify words that can serve as main verbs.

Main-Verb Frame 1:
They might _____ (it) now.

Main-Verb Frame 2:
They aren't _____-ing (it) now.

Any word that fits in the empty slots above will be the base form (infinitive) of the main verb, the form listed in the dictionary (e.g., *eat, collect, finish, sleep*). There is no need here to define *main verb*. If the word fits in the empty slot, it's a word that English speakers and writers can and do use as a main verb in sentences.

Because verbs don't always occur in the base form in actual sentences, students need other strategies to identify verbs, especially in the sentences they compose. Here again, we can take advantage of the unconscious linguistic knowledge of students, this time their uncanny ability to produce negative sentences and yes-no questions, to assist students in identifying helping verbs.

If we examine the following sentences, we see that a helping verb is a word that immediately precedes the negative element (*–n't* or *not*) in negated sentences or the word that gets fronted in yes-no questions.

EXAMPLES

1. Jim should go to the football game. *[Transform this into a negative sentence or a question.]*

   Jim **should**n't go to the football game.

   Should Jim go to the football game?

2. Jim went to the football game.

   Jim **did**n't go to the football game.

   Did Jim go to the football game?

If we have students transform declarative sentences into either negative sentences or yes-no questions, we can help them identify helping verbs. Again, there is no need to define *helping verb* formally. Though students may have never heard of the term *helping verb* (or *auxiliary verb*) before, they already unconsciously know what it is if they can produce a corresponding negative sentence or a corresponding yes-no question from a declarative sentence. Making such transformations requires complex linguistic knowledge. Yet, remarkably, we don't have to teach students how to do this. If students are fluent or near-fluent in spoken English, they already know it, as amply demonstrated in their daily speech. What we need to do, however, is to

take advantage of this knowledge in teaching the basics of grammar.

Main Verb *Be*

The main verb *be* (as in *They were friends*) is especially tricky because, unlike other main verbs, it moves to the front in yes-no questions (*Were they friends?*). It also takes the negative element in negative sentences (*They weren't friends*). The main verb *be* can thus masquerade as the helping verb *be* (compare *They were friends* to *They were running*). To make matters worse, the main verb *be* appears frequently in student writing. Indeed, when we complain that our students write with too many *be* verbs, we really mean the main verb *be*, not the helping verb *be*. This gives all the more reason for students to be able to identify the

main verb *be*. Teaching students to use the main-verb frames and the helping-verb transformations can reduce confusion over the function of *be* in a sentence. Further, having students memorize the main-verb forms of *be* can reduce the confusion even more.

Identifying Subjects

Once students have identified the verb of a sentence, they can easily identify the subject. To identify the latter, they can insert the verb in the question frame below and then answer the question.

> Simple-Subject Frame:
> Who or what _____?

In most cases, the answer to the question will be the subject of the sentence.

non-native, bring to the language arts classroom every day.

Further References

DeBeaugrande, Robert. "Forward to the Basics: Getting Down to Grammar." *College Composition and Communication* 35 (1984): 358–67.

Noguchi, Rei R. *Grammar and the Teaching of Writing: Limits and Possibilities.* Urbana, IL: National Council of Teachers of English. 1991. ■

Rei R. Noguchi, Professor of English and Linguistics at California State University, Northridge, has taught courses in linguistics to practicing and prospective language arts teachers for over seventeen years. He is the author of Grammar and the Teaching of Writing: Limits and Possibilities *(NCTE). When not teaching or writing, he enjoys reading, bicycling, and following various kinds of sports, particularly baseball.*

Applying Knowledge of Subjects and Verbs

Being able to identify subjects and verbs brings considerable payoffs. It will help students understand *clause*, which, in turn, will help them understand *independent* (or *main*) *clause* and *subordinate* (or *dependent*) *clause*. Understanding these terms will help them better understand the notion of *sentence*, which, in turn, will help them better understand and correct any unintentional fragment or run-on sentence. (Think also of all the punctuation rules that directly or indirectly refer to these structures.) Being able to identify subjects and verbs will certainly help students identify errors in subject-verb agreement, errors in verb-tense consistency, and even the overuse of main verb *be*. This skill can also help students identify verbs in the passive voice and can help students choose the correct case of personal pronouns. In short, knowing how to identify subjects and verbs leads to an understanding of a host of other concepts.

Conclusion

For many language arts teachers, teaching grammar is both a labor of love and a love of labor. Many of us like the notion of grammar as a system, the wholes and parts fitting into place. Yet too often we struggle with difficult concepts and often with indifferent students. We can make the labor of teaching grammar less—and, hopefully, the love of grammar more for both teacher and student—if we take advantage of the prodigious private linguistic knowledge that all fluent speakers of English, native and

By Billy T. Boyar, Ph.D.

Raising Expectations:
The Importance of Teaching Grammar to ESL Students

In the sixth grade, my class was taught sentence diagramming. Trying to superimpose our simple schoolbook diagrams on the infinity of language felt mysterious. Studying grammar in such a systematic way was like mapping the stars: We named unidentified words and charted their relationships. Words and phrases depended on other words like moons held to planets by gravity, and verbs sparkled like stars. I was not surprised, years later, to learn that the word *grammar* is etymologically related to *glamour* and *gramarye*,

> **S**tudying grammar in such a systematic way was like mapping the stars: We named unidentified words and charted their relationships.

suggesting magic. To me, the study of grammar has always been interesting and provocative in its own right. There are, however, important practical reasons for studying grammar and even more important practical reasons for ESL students to study it.

In the past, some people have disparaged the formal, systematic teaching of grammar to the ESL student. When people emphasize the importance of the natural way of learning language, beginning with hearing and mimicking, I agree with them. When they stress the necessity of creating a relaxed noncritical environment in which the ESL student feels free to practice speaking his or her new language, I agree with them. I agree that the study of literature and written composition is crucial. I even agree that grammar, if taught to young children or to ESL beginners of any age, should be fun and games, or should not be taught at all. However, when people advocate such approaches to the exclusion of a formal program of grammar for ESL students who are at least on an intermediate level and at least in the sixth grade, their argument is extreme, and I disagree with them.

Why is the study of grammar, usage, and mechanics important for appropriately mature and advanced ESL students?

Avoiding False Analogies

A study of English grammar, usage, and mechanics helps ESL students to avoid developing English language habits based on false analogies with the rules for their primary language. A comparative study of different languages shows that the basic patterns of grammar, conventions such as punctuation and capitalization, and the special uses of words can be vastly different. For example, a Spanish sentence doesn't necessarily need a subject (the subject can be implied by the verb); Spanish uses the present tense where English would sometimes use the past tense; question marks and exclamation points are placed both at the beginning and at the end of sentences; and a double negative is considered standard usage. English is even further from the grammatical expectations of Chinese and other non-Western ESL students.

In the past, some people have disparaged the formal, systematic teaching of grammar to the ESL student.

In my composition class, a Mexican American student submitted an essay that contained this sentence: "The Christmas party resulted well." The cognates *to result* (English) and *resultar* (Spanish) have confusingly similar meanings, yet their usage is distinctly different. Here, *resultar* could be translated *to turn out*. My student meant that the party turned out well, but she was basing her English usage on a false analogy with Spanish usage.

Not only does the ESL student tend to base English grammar rules on such false analogies, but also he or she often hears nonstandard usage repeated by friends and family. Being continually reinforced, the false analogy becomes an ingrained habit. Without the formal, systematic study of English grammar, usage, and mechanics, the ESL student may always have difficulty with standard English.

Promoting Academic Success

Teaching grammar to ESL students will help them succeed academically, especially if they plan to attend college. I have taught ESL and English at both high school and college. In composition classes, which also often contain ESL students, I frequently need to explain a point of grammar in order to help students understand why I am asking them to revise their papers. I want them to understand the principle so that they can avoid committing the same error over and over in future essays. For example, I ask them not to separate the subject and verb with only one comma (as in *Sara, who lives nearby is on my soccer team.*). This comment inevitably requires a further explanation: "Here you have inserted a nonessential clause between the subject and verb."

"But Mister," asks one ESL student, "what do you mean . . . *nonessential?*"

"A nonessential clause is a clause that can be removed. . . ."

"But what's a clause?"

"A clause contains a subject and a verb—it can be independent or subordinate. There are three kinds of subordinate . . ."

"What do you mean *subordinate?*"

"I mean that they have a subject and verb but that they cannot stand . . ."

"So what's a subject?"

"A subject is the noun or pronoun doing the . . ."

"Noun?"

The problem is that trying to teach a little bit of grammar is like trying to paint a little bit of a wall: It doesn't work.

I encounter situations like this all the time—and of course, ESL students aren't the only ones who don't know formal English grammar. The problem is that trying to teach a little bit of grammar is like trying to paint a little bit of a wall: It doesn't work. In a college composition class, instructors typically explain points of grammar, usage, and mechanics as they are related to essays submitted by students. However, it would not be appropriate to stop the composition class in order to devote the rest of the course to the basics of grammar. The result is that the ESL student who knows no formal English grammar is poorly served because he or she cannot take full advantage of the instructor's explanations.

Like many a native English speaker's, the ESL student's grammar and usage may never be perfect. Rather than perfection, the goal is a workable compromise. If students can communicate effectively in English, does it matter that they speak with an accent? The lives of ESL students will not be destroyed, for example, if they do not master the subjunctive mood. As teachers, we must demand excellence, but at the same time, we should carefully consider what exactly we want students to master.

Supporting Career Success

Studying grammar will help ESL students succeed professionally. Recently, a city employee asked me to tutor him in English. He had started out as a garbage collector, but after a few years his bosses recognized his ability and promoted him, then promoted him again. He suddenly found himself having to write memos and job descriptions. Now, in order to keep

the job, he was required to improve his English grammar, usage, and mechanics.

The reality is that proficiency in standard English is a badge required for acceptance in many careers and professions in the United States. Teachers, lawyers, doctors, and so forth may not be given the respect and trust they deserve if their use of language departs too far from the standard. Beyond this country, English has become the foremost international language. The dialect of the neighborhood, rightly cherished, will not succeed very well in commerce on the World Wide Web. The formal, systematic study of grammar, usage, and mechanics helps the ESL student separate neighborhood dialect from public language, in order to develop that public language in a clear and conscious way. Being truly bilingual, of

countless others, a refined bilingualism can open doors to wider possibilities.

Increasing Language Ownership

ESL students will benefit from the formal study of English because a better understanding of language patterns, a confidence in punctuation, and a command of the special uses of words will help them internalize English as a language of their own. Language ownership is an important topic. Language is a huge part of personal identity. It is a major reference point in our understanding of who we are. However, it should be emphasized that we can own more than one language; we can have two or more languages and dialects as expressions of our identity. It is helpful, healing, and sane for ESL students whose home is the United States to adopt English and care for it as their own. The problem is that immigrants have not always been welcomed with open arms, which is ironic in a land of immigrants. Our ESL students may therefore feel somewhat alien and sense that the English language is the language of others. One category of ESL students speaks English most of the time. They speak English in school; they speak it in their after-school jobs; and they even speak it most of the time at home: with brothers and sisters nearly all of the time, with parents some of the time, but with grandparents not at all. Even though these students speak English

The reality is that proficiency in standard English is a badge required for acceptance in many careers and professions in the United States.

course, is more than merely owning a badge. Coupling a career or professional training with authentic bilingualism will broaden opportunities in ways that are numerous and unforeseen: as a police officer, nurse, doctor, lawyer, salesperson, diplomat, translator, flight attendant, psychotherapist, teacher, construction supervisor, municipal work supervisor, governor, or president. In any of these careers and professions and most of the time, they paradoxically still consider English their second language. In addition, since they use their "primary" (home) language less and less, it does not grow.

The knowledge of grammar, usage, and mechanics is one tool in many, but we should not underestimate its importance.

These ESL students can be left in a world of little language indeed. A systematic study of grammar, usage, and mechanics in a friendly environment will tend to cut through the cycle of alienation. In the same way that we may feel better about our own cars when we learn how they work and can repair them ourselves, ESL students can learn how English works and can feel the pride of ownership.

Conclusion

Finally, ESL students are in the advantageous position of having a head start on bilingualism. If they continue to grow in their first language and if we give them the tools that they need for their second language, they will become truly bilingual. They need many tools in their language tool kits: the training to hear English phonemes, so that they can be good listeners; the skill of pronunciation, so that they can speak clearly; the knowledge of literature, so that they can contemplate the values of English-language cultures and the cultures of the rest of the world; and the art of writing compositions, so that they can express their own truths. The knowledge of grammar, usage, and mechanics is one tool in many, but we should not underestimate its importance. For ESL students, grammatical knowledge is a *sine qua non* of becoming bilingual on a professional level. On this level of bilingualism, the advantages are many, but it seems we and our students sometimes set our sights too low. Perhaps we have been guilty of not expecting our ESL students to accomplish as much as other students. They can aspire to the same—or better—careers and professions and can partake richly of the larger culture. Beyond these avenues, however, from the point of view of those of us who love language, ESL students will be able to look at language from a higher vantage point. From this aerial view, perhaps some will even rediscover the old meaning of grammar: magic. ∎

Billy Boyar has taught composition, literature, and ESL in high schools and community colleges for twenty years. Billy lives in Austin, Texas, where he teaches at Austin Community College. He has worked with juvenile offenders, volunteered with Hospice, and mediated as an ombudsman in nursing homes. In his free time, he enjoys studying Spanish and reading philosophy and finds his garden rewarding and a great way to unwind. He believes that a formal, systematic study of grammar is an important part of an ESL program.

Holt Handbook

> ## Your **California Roadmap** to Grammar, Usage, and Mechanics Mastery

Now more than ever before, there is a demand for students at all grade levels to develop competence in the language arts and facility with the English language. Students need to be able to access information with ease, to appreciate the literary arts, and perhaps most importantly, to apply their language skills at levels demanded in the twenty-first century.

GIVING MIDDLE SCHOOL STUDENTS ACCESS TO LANGUAGE SKILLS

Students in each classroom—including English language learners, special education students, students with learning difficulties, and advanced learners—are at varying levels of preparation and have different strengths and needs. Giving these students the tools they need to succeed is no easy task. That's where the *Holt Handbook* comes in.

Designed specifically for middle school teachers and students in California, the *Holt Handbook* is an integral part of a comprehensive, balanced language arts program called *Holt Literature and Language Arts*. This program leads the charge in providing a carefully researched method for not only helping your students meet and master the California standards in the language arts, but also helping them to embrace the power of the English language in all its forms.

The motivating force behind the organization and instructional delivery of the *Holt Handbook* is the desire to offer teachers and students a method to focus on the written and oral English language conventions required by the standards— to provide a compelling and effective way to teach and learn grammar, usage, and mechanics skills. Based on John Warriner's time-tested model for instruction, the *Holt Handbook* can also stand alone as a powerful tool for giving students access to the language skills they need most.

Covering All Your Students Need to Know About **Grammar, Usage, and Mechanics**

THREE MAIN PARTS COVER THE BASICS

PART I: GRAMMAR, USAGE, AND MECHANICS chapters help students use and practice using the building blocks of language—words, phrases, clauses, capitalization, punctuation, and spelling. The last chapter, **Correcting Common Errors,** gives students more practice building key language skills and taking tests in standardized formats.

PART II: The **SENTENCES** section is divided into two main areas of instruction: The **Writing Effective Sentences** chapter focuses on building grammatically correct, clear, and interesting sentences; the **Sentence Diagramming** chapter teaches students how the parts of a sentence relate to each other.

PART III: The **RESOURCES** chapters include **History of English,** a concise history of the English language; **Test Smarts,** a guide to taking standardized tests in grammar, usage, and mechanics; and **Grammar at a Glance,** a glossary of grammatical terms.

Pupil's Edition

Instructional Delivery
That Keeps Students on Track

Each chapter in the **Holt Handbook** is carefully sequenced so
that students are introduced to and taught new rules and skills
at the right time. Each chapter includes entry-level diagnosis, direct
instruction of the rules followed immediately by exercises, ongoing
assessment, and application of new knowledge through writing.
This direct and practical instructional approach allows you to keep
track of your students' pace, progress, and degree in mastering each
California standard.

DIAGNOSTIC PREVIEW
**Short tests that cover the whole
chapter let you pretest for the most
essential knowledge and skills.**

RULE, EXAMPLE, EXERCISE
**The introduction of
a new rule is followed
immediately by examples
and exercises.**

CHAPTER

2

1.0 Written and Oral English Language Conventions
Students write and
speak with a command
of standard English con-
ventions appropriate to
this grade level.
1.4 Edit written manu-
scripts to ensure that
correct grammar is used.
1.5 Use correct capitalization.

Numerals in brackets
refer to rules tested
by the items in the
Diagnostic Preview.

1. [2p]
2. [2p]
3. [2h, o, a, b]
4. [2h, l, a, g]
5. [2h, m, l]
6. [2h, j, a]
7. [2h, i, p]
8. [2h, i, a]
9. [2h, o, a]
10. [2a, d]

Parts of Speech Overview
Noun, Pronoun, Adjective

Diagnostic Preview

A. Identifying Nouns, Pronouns, and A...

Tell whether each italicized word or word group i...
sentences is used as a *noun*, a *pronoun*, or an *adjec...*

EXAMPLE   **1.** *Each* student is required to take a for...
language.
1. *Each—adjective; language—noun*

1. *That* drummer is the *best* performer.
2. That *German shepherd* puppy is a sweet-natur...
rascal.
3. *Everybody* says that *high school* will be more w...
fun, too.
4. *This* is the greatest year the junior varsity volle...
ever had.
5. *Who* can tell me whose bicycle *this* is?
6. Jenna prepared a special breakfast for her pare...
this *morning*.
7. This is their fault because *they* ignored all the ...
8. *We* received word that they aren't in *danger*.
9. *Each* of these clubs decorated a float for the Ci...
parade.
10. The runner *Carl Lewis* won several Olympic *medals.*

Common Nouns and Proper Nouns

2c. A *common noun* names any one of a group of
persons, places, things, or ideas.

A common noun generally does not begin with a capital letter.

2d. A *proper noun* names a particular person, place,
thing, or idea.

A proper noun begins with a capital letter.

Common Nouns	Proper Nouns
poem	"The Raven," *I Am Joaquín*
country	Spain, Ivory Coast
athlete	Joe Montana, Zina Garrison
ship	*Mayflower*, U.S.S. Constitut...
newspaper	*The New York Times, USA T...*
river	Rio de la Plata, Ohio River
street	Market Street, University A...
day	Friday, Independence Day
city	Los Angeles, New Delhi, Ho...
organization	National Forensic League, ... of America

Exercise 3 **Identifying Nouns**

Identify the nouns in each of the following sentences, and label
them *common* or *proper*.

EXAMPLE   **1.** My family likes to visit California when we are
vacationing.
1. *family—common; California—proper*

1. My whole family visited San Francisco during our vacation
last year.
2. The city is famous for its hilly landscape.
3. Some of the steepest streets in the world can be found in the
downtown area.
4. The city is also well-known for its system of streetcars.
5. San Francisco and Oakland, which is across the bay, have a
number of teams that play professional sports.

Review A Writing the Past and Past Participle Forms of Irregular Verbs

Write the correct past or past participle form of the italicized verb given before each of the following s[...]

EXAMPLE **1.** *tell* Has Alameda ____ y[...]
Indian Tipi: Its Histor[...]

1. told

1. *write* Reginald and Gladys Laubin [...] others about American Indi[...]

2. *build* The Laubins ____ their own [...]

3. *stand* Tepees of various sizes once [...] Great Plains. **3.** stood

4. *see* I have ____ pictures of camp[...] decorated tepees. **4.** seen

5. *make* For many years, American I[...] out of cloth rather than buffa[...]

6. *come* The word *tepee*, or *tipi*, has [...] the Sioux language. **6.** com[...]

Review B Writing the Past and Past Participle Forms of Irregular Verbs

Write the correct past or past participle form of the italicized verb given before each of the following sentences.

EXAMPLE **1.** *write* I ____ a report on Jim Thorpe.

1. wrote

1. *blow* Yesterday the wind ____ the leaves into our yard.
2. *break* My pen pal from Australia has never ____ his promise to write once a week.
3. *bring* I ____ the wrong book to class.
4. *burst* The children almost ____ with excitement.
5. *choose* The director ____ James Earl Jones for the role.
6. *come* My aunt and her friend ____ to dinner last night.
7. *do* I have always ____ my homework right after supper.
8. *drink* The guests ____ fruit punch and lemonade.
9. *fall* One of Julian's Russian nesting dolls has ____ off the shelf.
10. *freeze* Has the pond ____ yet?
11. *go* We have never ____ to see the Parthenon in Nashville.
12. *know* Had I ____, I would have called you sooner.
13. *ring* Suddenly the fire alarm ____.
14. *run* Joan Samuelson certainly ____ a good race.
15. *see* I ____ you in line at the movies.
16. *shrink* The apples we dried in the sun have ____.
17. *speak* After we had [...] to play domi[...]
18. *swim* We ____ out [...]

REVIEW EXERCISES

Short reviews after practice exercises offer cumulative assessment so that you can plan future instruction to help all students meet or master the standards.

Chapter Review

A. Using Irregular Verbs

Write the correct past or past participle form of the italicized irregular verb provided before each sentence.

1. *break* The thunder ____ the silence.
2. *ring* Who ____ the fire alarm so quickly?
3. *shrink* This shirt must have ____ in the dryer.
4. *throw* You've ____ the ball out of bounds!
5. *lead* Julio ____ the parade last year, so now it's my turn.
6. *rise* The sun ____ over the pyramids of Giza in Egypt.
7. *swim* We have ____ only three laps.
8. *choose* Vera was ____ as captain of the volleyball team.
9. *go* I have ____ to visit the Grand Canyon twice.
10. *sit* The tiny tree frog ____ motionless.
11. *write* Joan has ____ a story about aliens from the Andromeda galaxy.
12. *do* During class, Jorge ____ the first five problems of his homework assignment.
13. *steal* Three runners ____ bases during the first inning.
14. *break* This summer's heat wave has ____ all records.
15. *drink* Have you ____ all of the tomato juice?
16. *sink* The log had slowly ____ into the quicksand.
17. *lie* The old postcards have ____ in the box for years.
18. *drive* Have you ever ____ across the state of Texas?
19. *begin* Our local PBS station ____ its fund-raising drive.
20. *set* Have you ____ the paper plates and napkins on the picnic table?

CHAPTER REVIEWS

These tests offer additional practice and opportunities for ongoing assessments.

Writing Application
Using Verbs in a Story

Verb Forms and Tenses A local writers' club is sponsoring a contest for the best "cliffhanger" opening of an adventure story. Write an exciting paragraph to enter in the contest. Your paragraph should leave readers wondering "What happens next?" In your paragraph, use at least five verbs from the lists of Common Irregular Verbs in this chapter.

Prewriting First, you will need to imagine a suspenseful situation to describe. Jot down several ideas for your story opening. Then, choose the one you like best. With that situation in mind, scan the lists of irregular verbs. Note at least ten verbs you can use. Include some lively action verbs like *burst*, *swing*, and *throw*.

Writing As you write your rough draft, think of your readers. Choose words that create a suspenseful, believable scene. Remember that you have only one paragraph to catch your readers' interest.

Revising Ask a friend to read your paragraph. Does your friend find it interesting? Can he or she picture the scene clearly? If not, you may want to add, delete, or revise some details.

Publishing Check your spelling, usage, punctuation, and grammar. Check to make sure the forms of verbs are correct and the tenses are consistent. You may want to exchange your cliffhanger with a partner, and complete each other's stories. With your teacher's permission, you can then read the completed stories aloud to the class.

WRITING APPLICATIONS

These end-of-chapter activities guide students in applying new grammar, usage, and mechanics skills in their writing.

1.0 Written and Oral English Language Conventions

1.2 Understand sentence construction (e.g., parallel structure, subordination, proper placement of modifiers) and proper English usage (e.g., consistency of verb tenses).

1.3 Demonstrate an understanding of proper English usage and control of grammar, paragraph and sentence structure, diction, and syntax.

Instruction Based on California Standards

CALIFORNIA STANDARDS

At the beginning of each chapter, students are alerted to the California standards that will be covered. They understand immediately what they are expected to learn.

Pupil's Edition

Instruction Based on **Warriner's** Model

An English teacher for thirty years, John Warriner developed the original instructional approach used throughout the grammar, usage, and mechanics chapters in the **Holt Handbook** *Pupil's Edition*. His logical model of instruction is based on a three-step process: Teach students the rule, show examples of the rule in action, and provide immediate practice to reinforce the skill or concept. This model has been the authoritative standard for teaching grammar, usage, and mechanics skills for over fifty years.

RULE
Clearly stated rules are always presented in red.

EXERCISE
Exercises give immediate practice for rules.

EXAMPLES
A variety of student-friendly examples illustrate the language skill or concept being taught.

─HELP─

Most regular verbs that end in e drop the e before adding –*ing*. Some regular verbs double the final consonant before adding –*ing* or –*ed*.

EXAMPLES
shake—shak**ing**
hug—hu**gged**

Reference Note

For more about **spelling rules**, see Chapter 16. For information on **standard and nonstandard English**, see page 245.

USAGE

Regular Verbs

9b. A *regular verb* forms its past and past participle by adding –*d* or –*ed* to the base form.

Base Form	Present Participle	Past	Past Participle
clean	[is] cleaning	cleaned	[have] cleaned
hope	[is] hoping	hoped	[have] hoped
inspect	[is] inspecting	inspected	[have] inspected
slip	[is] slipping	slipped	[have] slipped

One common error in forming the past or the past participle of a regular verb is to leave off the –*d* or –*ed* ending.

NONSTANDARD   Our street use to be quieter.
STANDARD   Our street **used** to be quieter.

Another common error is to add unnecessary letters.

NONSTANDARD   The swimmer almost drownded in the riptide.
STANDARD   The swimmer almost **drowned** in the riptide.

NONSTANDARD   The kitten attackted that paper bag.
STANDARD   The kitten **attacked** that paper bag.

Using Regular Verbs

owing sentences aloud, stressing the

o meet at the

ed to buy the

called me about

used to live in

ould go to the

WOOF
WOOFS
WOOFING
WOOFED

© 1992 by Sidney Harris.

176   Chapter 9   Using Verbs Correctly

---

6. The chairs have been *moved* into the hall for the dance.
7. That salesclerk has *helped* my mother before.
8. Eli may not have *looked* under the table for the cat.

Exercise 1   **Writing the Forms of Regular Verbs**

Write the correct present participle, past, or past participle form of the italicized verb given before each of the following sentences.

EXAMPLES   **1.** *learn*   Many people today are _____ folk dances from a variety of countries.

   1. learning

   2. *hope*   Dad and I had _____ to take lessons in folk dancing this summer.

   2. hoped

1. *practice*   These Spanish folk dancers must have _____ for a long time.
2. *perform*   Notice that they are _____ in their colorful native costumes.
3. *wish*   Have you ever _____ that you knew how to do any folk dances?
4. *use*   Virginia reels _____ to be popular dances in the United States.
5. *promise*   Mrs. Stamos, who is from Greece, _____ to teach her daughter the Greek chain dance.
6. *lean*   The young Jamaican dancer _____ backward before he went under the pole during the limbo dance competition.
7. *start*   The group from Estonia is _____ a dance about a spinning wheel.
8. *request*   Someone in the audience has _____ an Irish square dance called "Sweets of May."
9. *dance*   During the Mexican hat dance, the woman _____ around the brim of the sombrero.
10. *fill*   The Jewish wedding dance _____ the room with both music and movement.

USAGE

Principal Parts of Verbs   177

Features That Help Students Along the Way

Oral Practice 5 · Using Forms of *Rise* and *Raise* Correctly

Read the following sentences aloud, stressing the italicized verbs.

1. Mount Everest *rises* over 29,000 feet.
2. He *raises* the flag at sunrise.
3. The TV reporter *raised* her voice to be heard.
4. She *rose* from her seat and looked out the window.
5. The constellation Orion had not yet *risen* in the southern sky.
6. They had *raised* the piñata high in the tree.
7. I hope the bread is *rising*.
8. He will be *raising* the bucket from the well.

ORAL PRACTICE
Spoken practice and reinforcement of rules and concepts

TIPS & TRICKS

Sometimes a fragment is really a part of a nearby sentence. You can correct the fragment by attaching it to the sentence that comes before or after it.

SENTENCE WITH FRAGMENT
Mark is practicing his hook shot. Because he wants to try out for the basketb

SENTENC
Mark is
hook sh
wants
the bas

When you
ment to a
to check y
for correc
capitaliza

TIPS & TRICKS
Easy-to-use hints that help students master language skills

STYLE TIP

The verb *lie* can also mean "to tell an untruth." Used in this way, *lie* still does not take an object.

EXAMPLE
Don't **lie** to her, Beth.

The past and past participle forms of this meaning of *lie* are *lied* and [*have*] *lied*.

STYLE TIPS
Information that guides students in making sound decisions about style and usages.

MEETING THE CHALLENGE

Write a poem, correctly using each of the six troublesome verbs, *sit, set, rise, raise, lie*, and *lay*. Be sure to check your poem for correct usage of the troublesome verbs.

MEETING THE CHALLENGE
Questions and short activities that ask students to approach a concept from a new angle

HELP

Some of the subjects and verbs in Review B are compound.

HELP
Pointers that help students understand key rules or exercise directions

T51

Annotated Teacher's Edition

Unique Strategies Make
Planning Lessons Easy

The **Holt Handbook** *Annotated Teacher's Edition* helps you organize your lessons into manageable segments—preteaching, direct teaching, and reteaching, for example—so that students build skills in a systematic, accessible way. Suggestions for differentiating instruction are integrated with lessons to help you support students with special learning needs, including advanced learners, students with learning difficulties, and English-language learners. Features that direct you to program resources for each chapter and lesson are also there to help you along the way.

STANDARDS FOCUS

Grade-Level Standards
(Boldface indicates concepts that are taught and tested in this chapter.)

■ Language Conventions 1.0: **Students write and speak with a command of standard Engli** conventions appropriate to grade level.

■ **Grammar 1.2: Identify and p** erly use indefinite pronoun and present perfect, past pe fect, and future perfect verb tenses; ensure that verbs ag with compound subjects.

■ Capitalization 1.4: **Use corre capitalization.**

Prerequisite/Review Standards

■ Grammar 1.2: Identify and correctly use verbs that are often misused (e.g., *lie/lay, rise/raise, sit/set*), modifiers, and pronouns.

■ Capitalization 1.4: Use correct capitalization.

Standards Coming Up in the Next Grade Level

■ Grammar 1.3: Identify all parts of speech and types and structure of sentences.

■ Capitalization 1.6: Use correct capitalization.

STANDARDS FOCUS

Each chapter opens with a clearly presented summary of standards that will be taught and tested in the chapter, including **Grade-Level Standards, Prerequisite/Review Standards**, and **Standards Coming up in the Next Grade Level**.

PRETEACHING

Lesson Starter

Prior Knowledge. Ask students to supply words that describe the similarities and differences between an orange and a baseball. Students might begin by saying that both objects are round. You mi[g]
Venn diagram
ask students to

PRETEACHING

Located at the beginning of each chapter, these strategies help you identify prerequisite skills and build on the prior knowledge of your students.

DIRECT TEACHING

Modeling and Demonstration

Identifying Nouns. Model how to identify nouns by using the example *self-esteem*. First, ask whether the word names a person, place, thing, or idea. [*idea*] *Self-esteem* names an idea; therefore, *self-esteem* is a noun. Now, have a voluntee[r]
another example from this c[hapter]
demonstrate how to identify

DIRECT TEACHING

Direct teaching strategies to help you present content include modeling and demonstrating new concepts.

RETEACHING

Pronouns

Activity. Ask students to write five descriptive sentences about a celebrity without ever mentioning the celebrity's name. Have two or three volunteers read their sentences, and let classmates try to guess the celebrity. Then, lead students to see that a common word in many of the sentences is *he* or *she*. Point out that pronouns like *he* and *she* are used in place of a noun, common or proper.

RETEACHING

Reteaching strategies offer techniques to help you present material from a fresh perspective.

EXTENSION

Activities and strategies ask students to apply grammar, usage, and mechanics concepts to the other language arts.

DIFFERENTIATING INSTRUCTION

These activities and suggestions help you reinforce language skills with learners having difficulty, English-language learners, advanced learners, and special education students.

CHAPTER RESOURCES

This handy feature lists all materials that support each chapter lesson.

Teaching Suggestions That Help Students Make Connections

Because language arts skills are so interconnected, the *Annotated Teacher's Edition* provides a variety of extension and application strategies that help students make connections between the grammar, usage, and mechanics skills you're teaching them and the writing, science, and social studies skills they need to succeed in other classes. In addition, the *Annotated Teacher's Edition* gives you suggestions for integrating an invaluable element of your students' learning experience—their families and communities.

MINI-LESSON

These practical lessons help students link various grammar, usage, and mechanics skills to one another.

LEARNING FOR LIFE

These real-world suggestions help students relate grammar, usage, and mechanics skills to their own lives and to workplace skills they'll need in the future.

CONTENT-AREA CONNECTIONS

These extension activities reinforce the notion that language arts skills are relevant to other disciplines like science, and social studies.

FAMILY/COMMUNITY ACTIVITY

These activities offer a real-world forum for students' language arts skills.

Teaching Resources

Additional **Practice** and **Strategies** to Help Students Succeed

LANGUAGE & SENTENCE SKILLS PRACTICE

These worksheets provide practice, reinforcement, and extension for topics covered in the *Holt Handbook*. Traditional worksheets offer additional practice for every rule taught in the *Pupil's Edition*. **Language in Context** worksheets let students apply and extend their study of grammar, usage, and mechanics to other areas in the language arts and to content in other disciplines. These worksheets include **Choices** worksheets, **Proofreading Application** worksheets, **Literary Model** worksheets, and **Writing Application** worksheets.

UNIVERSAL ACCESS: DEVELOPMENTAL LANGUAGE & SENTENCE SKILLS

These remedial worksheets provide instruction, practice, and reinforcement to supplement lessons in the *Holt Handbook* and in *Language & Sentence Skills Practice*. Targeted to those students who have not yet mastered specific concepts taught in the *Holt Handbook*, special features of this workbook include **Tips** that help students grasp abstract concepts with mnemonic devices, identification tests, and recognition strategies; **Points of Instruction** that explain how the rule applies to the examples provided; and **Guided Practice** that helps students with the first items of each exercise by asking guiding questions.

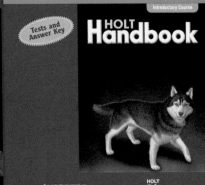

PROGRESS ASSESSMENT FOR THE HOLT HANDBOOK

This booklet contains chapter tests in standardized test format for the grammar, usage, mechanics, and sentences chapters in the *Holt Handbook.* Presented in multiple-choice format, each test offers a sound means of assessing your students' grasp of key English language conventions and, at the same time, offers students opportunities to practice their test-taking skills. The answer key provides useful references to specific rules that tie the answers to relevant instruction in the *Holt Handbook* and helps you pinpoint which skills and concepts students have mastered and which need further attention.

DIAGNOSTIC & SUMMATIVE ASSESSMENTS

These assessments test students' knowledge of language conventions in a multiple-choice format and in the context of students' written work. The diagnostic test given at the beginning of the year is for essential background knowledge and skills that students will need throughout the year. The quarterly tests (summative assessments) include questions related to sentence structure, grammar, punctuation, spelling, and capitalization.

AT HOME: A GUIDE TO STANDARDS MASTERY

Because the support of parents and guardians is essential to students' success in mastering the California standards (and language skills in general), this booklet contains a number of letters that invite parents and guardians to participate in what students are learning. Each of these letters gives suggestions on how parents can integrate grammar, usage, or mechanics instruction into students' lives at home, and prompts them to consider relationships between the skills required by the California guidelines and everyday applications of those skills.

DAILY LANGUAGE ACTIVITIES

This binder contains transparencies that help students practice vocabulary, reading, analogy, and sentence-combining skills. Reinforcing grammar, usage, and mechanics skills covered in the *Holt Handbook,* the proofreading warm-up transparencies offer quick, five- to ten-minute proofreading activities. Sentence-combining transparencies include activities that direct students to combine sentences by inserting a word or phrase, to combine sentences in order to create a particular meaning, and to combine three sentences in different ways.

SPELLING LESSONS AND ACTIVITIES

This component focuses on both sound-pattern and word-analysis strategies. The worksheets provide both instruction and practice in spelling strategies such as determining word parts from other languages, learning related words, and understanding prefixes and suffixes. Review tests are included for each unit, as well as creative games and activities for reviewing the words.

CD-ROM Technology
Reinforces Learning— and Helps You Teach

with Test Generator

CD-ROM for Macintosh® and Windows®

ONE-STOP PLANNER CD-ROM WITH TEST GENERATOR
(for Macintosh® and Windows®)

Planning and managing lessons has never been easier than with the *One-Stop Planner CD-ROM with Test Generator*. This convenient, all-in-one planning tool includes all the teaching resources for the **Holt Handbook,** as well as valuable planning and assessment tools. The *One-Stop Planner* includes

- an easy-to-use test generator that lets you find test items quickly
- previews of all teaching resources, including assessments and worksheets directly linked to the *Pupil's Edition*
- printable program resources
- a direct launch to the **go.hrw.com** Internet site

Teaching resources are presented in easy-to-understand, point-and-click formats. To preview a transparency or to print out tests and worksheets for your students, simply make your selection and click your mouse.

Extend Grammar, Usage, and Mechanics Learning to the **Internet**!

GO.HRW.COM

Internet references in the *Pupil's Edition* part openers direct students to **go.hrw.com**, a Web site that links students to resources related to concepts, rules, and assignments in the *Holt Handbook.*

HOW IT WORKS

When students see the **go.hrw.com** logo and a keyword in the textbook, they can go to the **go.hrw.com** site, enter the keyword, and link instantly to resources that support the grammatical concept or rule they are studying.

INTERACTIVE EXERCISES IN GRAMMAR, USAGE, AND MECHANICS

Among the resources available to students on the **go.hrw.com** site are interactive exercises in grammar, usage, and mechanics. Students can practice skills with short assignments and then complete chapter tests and other assessments—scored immediately—so that students have immediate feedback on their progress.

California Standards Correlation Chart

This chart outlines the chapters of the *Holt Handbook*, the California standards those chapters cover, and the resources available in the *Holt Literature and Language Arts* program to help you teach those standards. The chart lists materials appropriate for use with on-level students, advanced students, learners having difficulty, special education students, and English-language learners. Many of these resources are available on the *One-Stop Planner*®, on other CD-ROMs, or at go.hrw.com.

Holt Handbook Chapter	California Written and Oral English-Language Standards	Differentiating Instruction	
		Advanced Learners	**On-Level Learners**
1 The Parts of a Sentence	**1.0** Students write and speak with a command of standard English conventions appropriate to this grade level. **1.1** Use effective coordination and subordination of ideas to express complete thoughts.	• Teacher's Edition, pp. 9, 14 • Language & Sentence Skills Practice, pp. 21–23	• Teacher's Edition, pp. 2–23 • Language & Sentence Skills Practice, pp. 1–23
2 Parts of Speech Overview: Noun, Pronoun, Adjective	**1.0** Students write and speak with a command of standard English conventions appropriate to this grade level. **1.2** Identify and properly use indefinite pronouns. **1.4** Use correct capitalization.	• Teacher's Edition, pp. 27, 42 • Language & Sentence Skills Practice, pp. 41–43	• Teacher's Edition, pp. 24–47 • Language & Sentence Skills Practice, pp. 24–43
3 Parts of Speech Overview: Verb, Adverb, Preposition, Conjunction, Interjection	**1.0** Students write and speak with a command of standard English conventions appropriate to this grade level. **1.1** Use effective coordination of ideas to express complete thoughts.	• Teacher's Edition, pp. 53, 62, 65 • Language & Sentence Skills Practice, pp. 65–67	• Teacher's Edition, pp. 48–73 • Language & Sentence Skills Practice, pp. 44–67

Differentiating Instruction		Assessment	Additional Resources
Learners Having Difficulty	**English-Language Learners & Special Education Students**		
• Teacher's Edition, pp. 8, 9, 14, 20 • Developmental Language & Sentence Skills, pp. 1–6	• Teacher's Edition, (ELL) pp. 8, 12, 19; (SE) p. 14 • Lesson Plans for Language Development • Supporting Instruction in Five Languages	• Diagnostic & Summative Assessments, Entry-Level Diagnostic Test • Progress Assessment for the Holt Handbook, pp. 1–2 • Test Generator (One-Stop Planner CD-ROM)	• Daily Language Activities Transparencies • Spelling Lessons & Activities • go.hrw.com (keyword: HLLA) • Vocabulary Development
• Teacher's Edition, p. 32 • Developmental Language & Sentence Skills, pp. 7–16	• Teacher's Edition, (ELL) pp. 26, 28, 39, 43; (SE) p. 28 • Lesson Plans for Language Development • Supporting Instruction in Five Languages	• Progress Assessment for the Holt Handbook, pp. 3–4 • Test Generator (One-Stop Planner CD-ROM)	• Daily Language Activities Transparencies • Spelling Lessons & Activities • go.hrw.com (keyword: HLLA) • Vocabulary Development
• Teacher's Edition, pp. 52, 55, 56, 64, 65 • Developmental Language & Sentence Skills, pp. 17–26	• Teacher's Edition, (ELL) pp. 51, 53, 55, 63, 69; (SE) p. 64 • Lesson Plans for Language Development • Supporting Instruction in Five Languages	• Progress Assessment for the Holt Handbook, pp. 5–6 • Test Generator (One-Stop Planner CD-ROM)	• Daily Language Activities Transparencies • Spelling Lessons & Activities • go.hrw.com (keyword: HLLA) • Vocabulary Development

(continued on next page)

Holt Handbook Chapter	California Written and Oral English-Language Standards	Differentiating Instruction	
		Advanced Learners	**On-Level Learners**
4 The Phrase and the Clause	**1.0** Students write and speak with a command of standard English conventions appropriate to this grade level. **1.1** Use simple, compound, and compound-complex sentences; use effective coordination and subordination of ideas to express complete thoughts. **1.3** Use semicolons to connect independent clauses and commas when linking two clauses with a conjunction in compound sentences.	• Teacher's Edition, pp. 78, 81, 87 • Language & Sentence Skills Practice, pp. 90–92	• Teacher's Edition, pp. 74–103 • Language & Sentence Skills Practice, pp. 68–92
5 Complements	**1.0** Students write and speak with a command of standard English conventions appropriate to this grade level.	• Teacher's Edition, p. 118 • Language & Sentence Skills Practice, pp. 107–109	• Teacher's Edition, pp. 104–121 • Language & Sentence Skills Practice, pp. 93–109
6 Agreement	**1.0** Students write and speak with a command of standard English conventions appropriate to this grade level. **1.2** Identify and properly use indefinite pronouns, and ensure that verbs agree with compound subjects.	• Teacher's Edition, p. 129 • Language & Sentence Skills Practice, pp. 128–131	• Teacher's Edition, pp. 122–145 • Language & Sentence Skills Practice, pp. 110–131

Differentiating Instruction		Assessment	Additional Resources
Learners Having Difficulty	**English-Language Learners & Special Education Students**		
• Teacher's Edition, pp. 83, 87, 91 • Developmental Language & Sentence Skills, pp. 27–42	• Teacher's Edition, (ELL) pp. 78, 80, 83, 92, 98; (SE) p. 78 • Lesson Plans for Language Development • Supporting Instruction in Five Languages	• Diagnostic & Summative Assessments, First-Quarter Test • Progress Assessment for the Holt Handbook, pp. 7–8 • Test Generator (One-Stop Planner CD-ROM)	• Daily Language Activities Transparencies • At Home: A Guide to Standards Mastery, p. 27 • At Home: In Five Languages • Spelling Lessons & Activities • go.hrw.com (keyword: HLLA) • Vocabulary Development
• Teacher's Edition, pp. 110, 116 • Developmental Language & Sentence Skills, pp. 43–46	• Teacher's Edition, (ELL) pp. 108, 111, 114, 115, 116; (SE) p. 106 • Lesson Plans for Language Development • Supporting Instruction in Five Languages	• Progress Assessment for the Holt Handbook, pp. 9–10 • Test Generator (One-Stop Planner CD-ROM)	• Daily Language Activities Transparencies • Spelling Lessons & Activities • go.hrw.com (keyword: HLLA) • Vocabulary Development
• Teacher's Edition, pp. 130, 136 • Developmental Language & Sentence Skills, pp. 47–56	• Teacher's Edition, (ELL) pp. 126, 128, 129, 138; (SE) p. 130 • Lesson Plans for Language Development • Supporting Instruction in Five Languages	• Progress Assessment for the Holt Handbook, pp. 11–12 • Test Generator (One-Stop Planner CD-ROM)	• Daily Language Activities Transparencies • At Home: A Guide to Standards Mastery, pp. 28–29 • At Home: In Five Languages • Spelling Lessons & Activities • go.hrw.com (keyword: HLLA) • Vocabulary Development

(continued on next page)

Holt Handbook Chapter	California Written and Oral English-Language Standards	Differentiating Instruction	
		Advanced Learners	**On-Level Learners**
7 Using Verbs Correctly	**1.0** Students write and speak with a command of standard English conventions appropriate to this grade level. **1.2** Identify and properly use present perfect, past perfect, and future perfect verb tenses.	• Teacher's Edition, p. 159 • Language & Sentence Skills Practice, pp. 150–153	• Teacher's Edition, pp. 146–175 • Language & Sentence Skills Practice, pp. 132–153
8 Using Pronouns Correctly	**1.0** Students write and speak with a command of standard English conventions appropriate to this grade level.	• Teacher's Edition, p. 189 • Language & Sentence Skills Practice, pp. 167–170	• Teacher's Edition, pp. 176–195 • Language & Sentence Skills Practice, pp. 154–170
9 Using Modifiers Correctly	**1.0** Students write and speak with a command of standard English conventions appropriate to this grade level.	• Teacher's Edition, p. 216 • Language & Sentence Skills Practice, pp. 195–198	• Teacher's Edition, pp. 196–219 • Language & Sentence Skills Practice, pp. 171–198
10 A Glossary of Usage	**1.0** Students write and speak with a command of standard English conventions appropriate to this grade level. **1.5** Spell frequently misspelled words correctly (e.g., *their, they're, there*).	• Teacher's Edition, p. 226 • Language & Sentence Skills Practice, pp. 208–211	• Teacher's Edition, pp. 220–237 • Language & Sentence Skills Practice, pp. 199–211

Differentiating Instruction		Assessment	Additional Resources
Learners Having Difficulty	**English-Language Learners & Special Education Students**		
• Teacher's Edition, pp. 151, 152 • Developmental Language & Sentence Skills, pp. 57–72	• Teacher's Edition, (ELL) pp. 151, 154, 162; (SE) p. 156 • Lesson Plans for Language Development • Supporting Instruction in Five Languages	• Progress Assessment for the Holt Handbook, pp. 13–14 • Test Generator (One-Stop Planner CD-ROM)	• Daily Language Activities Transparencies • At Home: A Guide to Standards Mastery, p. 30 • At Home: In Five Languages • Spelling Lessons & Activities • go.hrw.com (keyword: HLLA) • Vocabulary Development
• Teacher's Edition, pp. 186, 190, 191 • Developmental Language & Sentence Skills, pp. 73–80	• Teacher's Edition, (ELL) pp. 180, 181, 182, 184, 185, 186; (SE) p. 181 • Lesson Plans for Language Development • Supporting Instruction in Five Languages	• Diagnostic & Summative Assessments, Midyear Test • Progress Assessment for the Holt Handbook, pp. 15–16 • Test Generator (One-Stop Planner CD-ROM)	• Daily Language Activities Transparencies • Spelling Lessons & Activities • go.hrw.com (keyword: HLLA) • Vocabulary Development
• Teacher's Edition, pp. 207, 210 • Developmental Language & Sentence Skills, pp. 81–90	• Teacher's Edition, (ELL) pp. 202, 212; (SE) p. 200 • Lesson Plans for Language Development • Supporting Instruction in Five Languages	• Progress Assessment for the Holt Handbook, pp. 17–18 • Test Generator (One-Stop Planner CD-ROM)	• Daily Language Activities Transparencies • Spelling Lessons & Activities • go.hrw.com (keyword: HLLA) • Vocabulary Development
• Teacher's Edition, p. 222 • Developmental Language & Sentence Skills, pp. 91–94	• Teacher's Edition, (ELL) pp. 224, 229, 232; (SE) p. 234 • Lesson Plans for Language Development • Supporting Instruction in Five Languages	• Progress Assessment for the Holt Handbook, pp. 19–20 • Test Generator (One-Stop Planner CD-ROM)	• Daily Language Activities Transparencies • At Home: A Guide to Standards Mastery, p. 31 • At Home: In Five Languages • Spelling Lessons & Activities • go.hrw.com (keyword: HLLA) • Vocabulary Development

(continued on next page)

Holt Handbook Chapter	California Written and Oral English-Language Standards	Differentiating Instruction	
		Advanced Learners	On-Level Learners
11 Capital Letters	**1.0** Students write and speak with a command of standard English conventions appropriate to this grade level. **1.4** Use correct capitalization.	• Teacher's Edition, p. 251 • Language & Sentence Skills Practice, pp. 232–235	• Teacher's Edition, pp. 238–261 • Language & Sentence Skills Practice, pp. 212–235
12 Punctuation: End Marks, Commas, Semicolons, Colons	**1.0** Students write and speak with a command of standard English conventions appropriate to this grade level. **1.3** Use colons after the salutation in business letters, semicolons to connect independent clauses, and commas when linking two clauses with a conjunction in compound sentences.	• Teacher's Edition, p. 274 • Language & Sentence Skills Practice, pp. 255–258	• Teacher's Edition, pp. 262–287 • Language & Sentence Skills Practice, pp. 236–258
13 Punctuation: Underlining (Italics), Quotation Marks, Apostrophes, Hyphens, Parentheses	**1.0** Students write and speak with a command of standard English conventions appropriate to this grade level.	• Teacher's Edition, p. 291 • Language & Sentence Skills Practice, pp. 281–284	• Teacher's Edition, pp. 288–315 • Language & Sentence Skills Practice, pp. 259–284
14 Spelling	**1.0** Students write and speak with a command of standard English conventions appropriate to this grade level. **1.5** Spell frequently misspelled words correctly (e.g., *their, they're, there*).	• Teacher's Edition, pp. 329, 334 • Language & Sentence Skills Practice, pp. 306–309	• Teacher's Edition, pp. 316–345 • Language & Sentence Skills Practice, pp. 285–309

Differentiating Instruction		Assessment	Additional Resources
Learners Having Difficulty	**English-Language Learners & Special Education Students**		
• Teacher's Edition, pp. 255, 257 • Developmental Language & Sentence Skills, pp. 95–104	• Teacher's Edition, (ELL) pp. 242, 244, 246; (SE) p. 243 • Lesson Plans for Language Development • Supporting Instruction in Five Languages	• Progress Assessment for the Holt Handbook, pp. 21–22 • Test Generator (One-Stop Planner CD-ROM)	• Daily Language Activities Transparencies • At Home: A Guide to Standards Mastery, pp. 32–33 • At Home: In Five Languages • Spelling Lessons & Activities • go.hrw.com (keyword: HLLA) • Vocabulary Development
• Teacher's Edition, pp. 266, 272, 282 • Developmental Language & Sentence Skills, pp. 105–110	• Teacher's Edition, (ELL) pp. 265, 267, 269, 280; (SE) pp. 265, 269 • Lesson Plans for Language Development • Supporting Instruction in Five Languages	• Diagnostic & Summative Assessments, Third-Quarter Test • Progress Assessment for the Holt Handbook, pp. 23–24 • Test Generator (One-Stop Planner CD-ROM)	• Daily Language Activities Transparencies • At Home: A Guide to Standards Mastery, p. 34 • At Home: In Five Languages • Spelling Lessons & Activities • go.hrw.com (keyword: HLLA) • Vocabulary Development
• Teacher's Edition, p. 293 • Developmental Language & Sentence Skills, pp. 111–118	• Teacher's Edition, (ELL) pp. 293, 301, 302, 306; (SE) pp. 293, 301 • Lesson Plans for Language Development • Supporting Instruction in Five Languages	• Progress Assessment for the Holt Handbook, pp. 25–26 • Test Generator (One-Stop Planner CD-ROM)	• Daily Language Activities Transparencies • Spelling Lessons & Activities • go.hrw.com (keyword: HLLA) • Vocabulary Development
• Teacher's Edition, pp. 330, 337 • Developmental Language & Sentence Skills, pp. 119–130	• Teacher's Edition, (ELL) pp. 321, 323, 324, 326, 330; (SE) p. 328 • Lesson Plans for Language Development • Supporting Instruction in Five Languages	• Progress Assessment for the Holt Handbook, pp. 27–28 • Test Generator (One-Stop Planner CD-ROM)	• Daily Language Activities Transparencies • At Home: A Guide to Standards Mastery, p. 35 • At Home: In Five Languages • Spelling Lessons & Activities • go.hrw.com (keyword: HLLA) • Vocabulary Development

(continued on next page)

Holt Handbook Chapter	California Written and Oral English-Language Standards	Differentiating Instruction	
		Advanced Learners	**On-Level Learners**
15 **Correcting Common Errors**	**1.0** Students write and speak with a command of standard English conventions appropriate to this grade level.	• Language & Sentence Skills Practice, pp. 344–348	• Teacher's Edition, pp. 346–381 • Language & Sentence Skills Practice, pp. 310–348
16 **Writing Effective Sentences**	**1.0** Students write and speak with a command of standard English conventions appropriate to this grade level. **1.1** Use simple, compound, and compound-complex sentences; use effective coordination and subordination of ideas to express complete thoughts.	• Teacher's Edition, p. 388 • Language & Sentence Skills Practice, pp. 359–360, 371–374	• Teacher's Edition, pp. 384–411 • Language & Sentence Skills Practice, pp. 349–374
17 **Sentence Diagramming**	**1.0** Students write and speak with a command of standard English conventions appropriate to this grade level. **1.1** Use simple, compound, and compound-complex sentences.	• Teacher's Edition, pp. 412–427	• Teacher's Edition, pp. 412–427

Differentiating Instruction		Assessment	Additional Resources
Learners Having Difficulty	**English-Language Learners & Special Education Students**		
• Developmental Language & Sentence Skills, pp. 131–132	• Lesson Plans for Language Development • Supporting Instruction in Five Languages	• Progress Assessment for the Holt Handbook, pp. 29–30 • Test Generator (One-Stop Planner CD-ROM)	• Daily Language Activities Transparencies • Spelling Lessons & Activities • go.hrw.com (keyword: HLLA) • Vocabulary Development
• Teacher's Edition, pp. 387, 392, 398 • Developmental Language & Sentence Skills, pp. 133–142	• Teacher's Edition, (ELL) pp. 394, 398, 405; (SE) p. 393 • Lesson Plans for Language Development • Supporting Instruction in Five Languages	• Diagnostic & Summative Assessments, End-of-Year Test • Progress Assessment for the Holt Handbook, pp. 31–34 • Test Generator (One-Stop Planner CD-ROM)	• Daily Language Activities Transparencies • At Home: A Guide to Standards Mastery, p. 36 • At Home: In Five Languages • Spelling Lessons & Activities • go.hrw.com (keyword: HLLA) • Vocabulary Development
• Teacher's Edition, pp. 412–427	• Teacher's Edition, (ELL) pp. 412–427 • Lesson Plans for Language Development	• Test Generator (One-Stop Planner CD-ROM)	• Daily Language Activities Transparencies • go.hrw.com (keyword: HLLA)

PART 1

Grammar, Usage, and Mechanics

Grammar

Usage

Mechanics

GO TO: go.hrw.com
KEYWORD: HLLA

Grammar, Usage, and Mechanics   1

CHAPTER

STANDARDS FOCUS

Grade-Level Standards

(Boldface indicates concepts that are taught and tested in this chapter.)

- Language Convention 1.0: **Students write and speak with a command of standard English conventions appropriate to this grade level.**

- Sentence Structure 1.1: **Use simple, compound, and compound-complex sentences; use effective coordination and subordination of ideas to express complete thoughts.**

Prerequisite/Review Standard

- Sentence Structure 1.1: Identify and correctly use prepositional phrases, appositives, and independent and dependent clauses; use transitions and conjunctions to connect ideas.

Standard Coming Up in the Next Grade Level

- Grammar 1.3: Identify all parts of speech and types and structure of sentences.

▼

INTRODUCING THE CHAPTER

- This chapter begins by explaining the difference between a complete sentence and a sentence fragment. Then, subjects and predicates and compound subjects and compound verbs are discussed. The chapter ends with a brief explanation of the four kinds of sentences: declarative, imperative, interrogative, and exclamatory. *(continued)*

1.0 Written and Oral English Language Conventions
Students write and speak with a command of standard English conventions appropriate to this grade level.
1.1 Use effective coordination and subordination of ideas to express complete thoughts.

Numerals in brackets refer to rules tested by the items in the Diagnostic Preview.

1. sent. [1a]
2. sent. [1a]
3. Sara [1a]
4. sent. [1a]
5. Are you [1a]

The Parts of a Sentence
Subject and Predicate, Kinds of Sentences

Diagnostic Preview

A. Identifying Sentences

If a word group is a sentence fragment, rewrite it to make it a complete sentence. If a word group is a sentence, write *sentence*. Some answers will vary.

EXAMPLES
1. Followed the trail on the map.
   1. *I followed the trail on the map.*

2. The López twins come from Nuevo Laredo, Mexico.
   2. *sentence*

1. We read the postcards from our Asian pen pals.
2. Our school has a homework hot line.
3. definitely mailed the invitations yesterday.
4. Will you practice guitar before dinner?
5. going to the Washington Monument?

B. Identifying Simple Subjects and Simple Predicates

Identify the simple subject and the simple predicate in each of the following sentences.

CHAPTER RESOURCES

Internet
- go.hrw.com (keyword: HLLA)

go.hrw.com

Planning
- *One-Stop Planner CD-ROM*
- *On Course: Mapping Instruction*

Practice & Review
- *Language & Sentence Skills Practice,* pp. 2–16; 17–20
- *Developmental Language & Sentence Skills,* pp. 1–6

Application & Enrichment
- *Language & Sentence Skills Practice,* pp. 23;1, 21–22

EXAMPLES **1.** Last year my family traveled to Mecca, Saudi Arabia.

  1. family—simple subject; traveled—simple predicate

  2. The crowded corner market is having a sale.

  2. market—simple subject; is having—simple predicate

 6. My grandmother plays mah-jongg with my friends and me every Saturday.
 7. The farmers have plowed the fields and will plant potatoes.
 8. At night you can rent roller skates for half price at the rink near my house.
 9. On the sand lay a beautiful seashell.
10. On Saturday, Amy, Theo, and I walked through Chinatown and took pictures.
11. Many students in our class have volunteered for the charity softball game.
12. Where did you put Isabella's fuzzy, green wool sweater?
13. *Island of the Blue Dolphins* by Scott O'Dell is one of my favorite books.
14. Beyond the large rocks at the far end of the beach is a small cave.
15. During the last week of vacation, my brother, sister and I hiked through the rain forest.

┌ H E L P ─
A subject or a predicate in Part B may be compound.

6.–15. [1c, e]

C. Punctuating and Classifying Sentences by Purpose

For each of the following sentences, add the appropriate end mark. Then, classify each sentence as *declarative, interrogative, imperative,* or *exclamatory.*

EXAMPLES **1.** Have you read this poem by José Garcia Villa

  1. Have you read this poem by José Garcia Villa?—interrogative

  2. We sampled a Cuban dish at the international fair

  2. We sampled a Cuban dish at the international fair.—declarative

16. Please answer the phone.
17. What a good time we had!
18. Has anyone seen the cat?
19. They sat on a bench and played checkers.
20. Whose book is this?

16. imp. [1i]
17. exc. [1k]
18. int. [1j]
19. dec. [1h]
20. int. [1j]

■ The chapter closes with a **Chapter Review** including a **Writing Application** feature that asks students to create a comic strip using at least one of each of the following sentence types: declarative, imperative, interrogative, and exclamatory.

■ For help in integrating this chapter with writing assignments in *Holt Literature and Language Arts,* use the **Teaching Strands** chart on pages T22–T23.

ASSESSING

Entry-Level Assessment
Diagnostic Preview. You can use the **Diagnostic Preview** to determine your students' understanding of the difference between sentences and sentence fragments, of simple subjects and simple predicates, and of punctuating and classifying sentences by purpose. Because the preview is divided into three separate parts, you may want to use one part at a time to determine the areas in which students are having problems.

Differentiating Instruction
■ *Lesson Plans for Language Development*
■ *Supporting Instruction in Five Languages*
Assessment
■ *Diagnostic & Summative Assessments, Entry-Level Diagnostic Test*
■ *Progress Assessment for the Holt Handbook,* pp. 1–2, 41

■ *Test Generator (One-Stop Planner CD-ROM)*
Other Language Resources
■ *Spelling Lessons & Activities*
■ *Vocabulary Development*
■ *Daily Language Activities Transparencies*

21. imp. [1i]
22. exc. [1k]
23. dec. [1h]
24. imp. [1i]
25. int. [1j]

21. Hang that jacket in the hall closet.
22. How we laughed!
23. Water is composed of oxygen and hydrogen.
24. Call this number in case of an emergency.
25. Did you say to turn left here?

Reference Note

For information on the **understood subject,** see page 18.

---HELP---

To tell whether a group of words is a sentence or a sentence fragment, ask yourself these three questions:

1. What is the subject?
2. What is the verb?
3. What is the complete thought the word group expresses?

If you cannot answer any one of these questions, the word group may not be a sentence.

Sentence or Sentence Fragment?

1a. A *sentence* is a word group that contains a subject and a verb and that expresses a complete thought.

A sentence begins with a capital letter and ends with a period, a question mark, or an exclamation point.

EXAMPLES   **O**ctavio Paz won a Nobel Prize in literature.
[The subject is *Octavio Paz,* and the verb is *won.*]

     Stop. [The understood subject is *you,* and the verb is *Stop.*]

     Do you collect coins? [The subject is *you,* and the verb is *Do collect.*]

     I actually rode on an elephant! [The subject is *I,* and the verb is *rode.*]

A *sentence fragment* is a word group that looks like a sentence but either does not contain both a subject and a verb or does not express a complete thought.

SENTENCE FRAGMENT	Visited an old Spanish mission in San Diego. [The subject is missing. Who visited the mission?]
SENTENCE	My family visited an old Spanish mission in San Diego.
SENTENCE FRAGMENT	Alonzo's sisters and brothers. [The verb is missing. What did Alonzo's sisters and brothers do?]
SENTENCE	Alonzo's sisters and brothers planned a surprise party for his birthday.

RESOURCES

Sentence or Sentence Fragment?
Practice
- *Language & Sentence Skills Practice,* pp. 2–4, 17
- *Developmental Language & Sentence Skills,* pp. 1–2

SENTENCE FRAGMENT	As I walked to school yesterday. [This thought is not complete. What happened as I walked to school yesterday?]
SENTENCE	As I walked to school yesterday, I saw Mr. Saunders walking his dog.

NOTE A word group that has a subject and a verb and that expresses a complete thought is called an **independent clause.** An independent clause can stand alone as a sentence. A word group that has a subject and a verb but does not express a complete thought (such as *As I walked to school yesterday*) is called a **subordinate clause.**

Exercise 1 Identifying Sentences

Identify each of the following word groups as a *sentence* or a *sentence fragment*. If a word group is a sentence fragment, rewrite it to make it a complete sentence. Some answers will vary.

EXAMPLE   1. My aunt and uncle raise shar-peis.
           1. *sentence*

1. My aunt, my uncle, and my cousins at their house in the country last weekend.   1. frag.—I visited
2. After dinner, Aunt Marie told me about the history of the shar-pei breed.   2. sent.
3. Bred these dogs in China.   3. frag.—People
4. Just look at all that loose, wrinkled skin.   4. sent.
5. Protects them from injury during fights.   5. frag.—It
6. Gentle with children.   6. frag.—They are usually
7. Playing catch with Queenie.   7. frag. —is fun
8. The little balls of fur were Queenie's new puppies.   8. sent.
9. Have you ever seen such a sight as these puppies?   9. sent.
10. What a good time we had!   10. sent.

Reference Note
For more about **independent and subordinate clauses,** see page 89.

STYLE   TIP

In speech, people often use sentence fragments. Such fragments usually are not confusing because the context and the speaker's tone of voice and expressions help to complete the meaning.

Professional writers, too, may use sentence fragments to create specific effects in their writing. However, in your writing at school, you should use complete sentences.

Reference Note
For more information on **revising sentence fragments,** see page 386.

DIRECT TEACHING

Correcting Misconceptions
Sentence Fragments. Some students may show little interest in differentiating between sentences and sentence fragments if they feel that a message can be easily communicated without using a complete sentence. Remind students that writing is an important form of communication and that to be competent writers, they must use complete sentences.

APPLICATION

Forming Sentences
Activity. Arrange students in pairs to practice forming sentences. Each student will write a different verb on each card in a set of five index cards and five different subjects on another set of cards. Each partner will take turns selecting subject and verb cards at random and writing a sentence using the cards. Partners will continue forming sentences until each card has been used.

PRACTICE

Guided and Independent
You may wish to have the class work through **Exercise 1** once as guided practice. Then, you could have each student write his or her own sentences as independent practice.

HOMEWORK

MINI-LESSON   **Grammar**

Understood *You* as Subject. Write the following words on the chalkboard, and ask students to identify them as complete sentences or sentence fragments.
1. Run! [*sentence*]
2. The broken stairs. [*fragment*]
3. Be quiet. [*sentence*]
4. For her. [*fragment*]

Remind students that a sentence can consist of a verb and the understood subject *you* (as in items 1 and 3).

Exercise 2 Identifying and Revising Sentences and Sentence Fragments

POSSIBLE ANSWERS

1. Having been introduced to the guest of honor, we took our places at the table.
2. sentence
3. Dragonflies were dancing in the air around the garden.
4. sentence
5. sentence
6. This sculpture is one of the only examples of this type of Aztec art in this area.
7. His pocket contained three pennies, a quarter, a bus token, and four acorns.
8. sentence
9. Along with an electric guitar, a mandolin, and kettledrums, the group played an instrument popular in Africa, the kalimba.
10. sentence

Review A Writing Complete Sentences

POSSIBLE ANSWERS

1. Grandmother sent us a postcard from the Philippines.
2. It was cold at the skating rink.
3. My brother helped me with my science project.
4. A surfer on a huge wave was having an exciting ride.
5. I was hungry at lunchtime.
6. It is too late for a game of checkers.
7. Is that the American Falls or the Horseshoe Falls?
8. The Cuban family next door has lived there for many years.
9. What time is your mom picking us up?
10. The governor of my state is running for president.

COMPUTER TIP

If sentence fragments are a problem in your writing, a computer may be able to help you. Some style-checking programs can find fragments for you. Such programs are useful, but they are not perfect. It is best to check each sentence yourself. Make sure each sentence has a subject and a verb and expresses a complete thought.

Exercise 2 Identifying and Revising Sentences and Sentence Fragments

Some of the following word groups are sentences, and others are sentence fragments. If a word group is a sentence, write *sentence.* If a word group is not a sentence, add words to make the word group a sentence.

EXAMPLE   1. A common custom worldwide.
            1. *Weddings are a common custom worldwide.*

1. Having been introduced to the guest of honor.
2. Hold your horses there, young fellow.
3. Dancing in the air around the garden.
4. It will be on your right.
5. Just how does a fire extinguisher work?
6. One of the only examples of this type of Aztec art in this area.
7. Three pennies, a quarter, a bus token, and four acorns.
8. He called Sunday night.
9. An instrument popular in Africa, the kalimba.
10. How we laughed at that movie!

Review A Writing Complete Sentences

Some of the following word groups are sentences. If a word group is a sentence, rewrite it, adding a capital letter and end punctuation. If a word group is not a sentence, rewrite it, adding a subject or a verb, a capital letter, and end punctuation to make it a sentence.

EXAMPLE   1. wrote a play
            1. *Our language arts class wrote a play.*

1. sent us a postcard from the Philippines
2. it was cold at the skating rink
3. helped me with my science project
4. a surfer on a huge wave
5. was hungry at lunchtime
6. it is too late for a game of checkers
7. is that the American Falls or the Horseshoe Falls
8. the Cuban family next door
9. what time is your mom picking us up
10. the governor of my state

Subject and Predicate

Sentences consist of two basic parts: *subjects* and *predicates*.

The Subject

1b. The *subject* tells *whom* or *what* the sentence is about.

EXAMPLES   **Lois Lenski** wrote *Strawberry Girl.*

              The tooth with a point is called a canine.

To find the subject, ask yourself *who* or *what* is doing something or *about whom* or *what* something is being said.

EXAMPLES   **My best friend** sits next to me in science class.
[*Who* sits? My best friend sits.]

              Science class is very interesting this year. [*What* is interesting? Science class is.]

The Position of the Subject

The subject may come at the beginning, in the middle, or even at the end of a sentence.

EXAMPLES   After school, **Theresa** went to band practice.

              Under our house was **a tiny kitten.**

Exercise 3   Identifying Subjects

Identify the subject in each of these sentences.

EXAMPLE   **1.** The final score was tied.
               1. *The final score*

   1. Many games use rackets or paddles.
   2. Tennis can be an exhausting sport.
   3. Badminton rackets don't weigh very much.
   4. Table-tennis paddles are covered with rubber.
   5. Racquetball uses special rackets.
   6. In Florida, citrus trees grow an important crop.
   7. After three to five years, fruit grows on the new trees.
   8. Does Florida grow all of the citrus fruit in the nation?
   9. California also grows oranges and other citrus fruit.
  10. From Texas comes the Star Ruby grapefruit.

Subject and Predicate
Rules 1b–e *(pp. 7–12)*

O B J E C T I V E S

- To identify complete subjects and simple subjects in sentences
- To identify predicates in sentences
- To complete sentences by providing predicates
- To identify complete predicates and verbs in sentences

DIRECT TEACHING

Modeling and Demonstration

Subject and Predicate. Model how to identify which word or word group in a sentence is the subject by using the example *After school, Theresa went to band practice.* First, ask *Who went to band practice?* [*Theresa*] Then, note that *Theresa* is whom the sentence is about and is the subject of the sentence. Now, have a volunteer use another example from this chapter to demonstrate how to identify the subject of a sentence.

RESOURCES

Subject and Predicate
Practice

- *Language & Sentence Skills Practice,* pp. 5–9, 13–14, 18–19
- *Developmental Language & Sentence Skills,* pp. 3–6

DIFFERENTIATING INSTRUCTION

Learners Having Difficulty

Tell students to imagine they are writing the script for a movie. Ask each student to write one sentence about the topic of his or her film. Students' sentences should name the main character of the film and tell what the main character does. After students have written their sentences, have the students write the sentences on the chalkboard. Then, point out that their main character is the subject of their sentence and the predicate is what the character does.

English-Language Learners

General Strategies. One potentially problematic rule for students is the rule that complete sentences must have stated subjects (except, of course, imperative sentences). In some languages, such as Spanish, the subject may be indicated only by an inflectional ending on a verb and not by a separate word. Students may need extra coaching to help them see that neglecting to state the subjects of their sentences can be confusing to their audience. Tell students that a sentence should not leave an audience wondering who or what is being discussed.

TIPS & TRICKS

If you leave the simple subject out of a sentence, the sentence will not make sense.

EXAMPLES
The Korean . . . is closed today.

A brightly colored . . . sat on the windowsill.

Complete Subject and Simple Subject

The **complete subject** consists of all the words needed to tell *whom* or *what* the sentence is about. The **simple subject** is part of the complete subject.

1c. The **simple subject** is the main word or word group that tells *whom* or *what* the sentence is about.

EXAMPLES **The Korean market** is closed today.

    complete subject   The Korean market

    simple subject   market

A brightly colored blue jay sat on the windowsill.

    complete subject   A brightly colored blue jay

    simple subject   blue jay

Sometimes the same word or words make up both the simple subject and the complete subject.

EXAMPLES In the canyon, **we** saw hawks. [*We* is both the complete subject and the simple subject.]

Little Rascal is the story of a boy and his pet raccoon. [The title *Little Rascal* is both the complete subject and the simple subject.]

NOTE In this book, the term *subject* generally refers to the simple subject unless otherwise indicated.

Exercise 4 Identifying Complete Subjects and Simple Subjects

Identify the complete subject of each of the following sentences. Then, underline the simple subject.

EXAMPLE **1.** From the chimney came a thick cloud of smoke.

    1. a thick cloud of smoke

1. Several tents were set up in the park.
2. Have you heard the new CD by Gloria Estefan?
3. News travels fast in our town.
4. Above the fort, the flag was still flying.
5. Beyond those distant mountains lies an ancient American Indian village.

6. <u>Those newspaper reporters</u> have been interviewing the mayor all morning.
7. On the shelf was <u>a beautiful blue bowl</u>.
8. According to folklore, <u>Pecos Bill</u> made the Grand Canyon.
9. <u>The light in the lighthouse</u> shone all night long.
10. In the drawer were <u>some chopsticks</u>.

The Predicate

1d. The *predicate* of a sentence tells something about the subject.

EXAMPLES   Lois Lenski **wrote *Strawberry Girl*.**

The tooth with a point **is called a canine.**

Exercise 5 **Identifying Predicates**

Identify the <u>predicate</u> in each of the following sentences.

EXAMPLE   **1.** Many people would like to have a robot.
   1. would like to have a robot

1. Robots <u>are machines with "brains."</u>
2. The robot's brain <u>is a computer</u>.
3. Not all robots <u>look like humans</u>.
4. Some robots <u>look like toy cars</u>.
5. One robot <u>explored some of the surface of Mars</u>.
6. Many companies <u>use robots</u>.
7. Cars of the future <u>may be guided by robots</u>.
8. Some household jobs <u>can be done by robots</u>.
9. A robot <u>could clean your room</u>.
10. You <u>might like to have a robot to help with your daily chores</u>.

The Position of the Predicate

The predicate usually comes after the subject. Sometimes, however, part or all of the predicate comes before the subject.

EXAMPLES   **Quickly** we **learned the layout of the small Hopi village.**

At the entrance to the science fair were maps of the exhibits.

Subject and Predicate   **9**

Exercise 6 Identifying Predicates

Write each of the following sentences. Then, underline the predicate.

EXAMPLE 1. At noon we went to a Mexican restaurant.
         1. *At noon we went to a Mexican restaurant.*

1. Our family likes different kinds of food.
2. Last night Dad prepared spaghetti and a salad for supper.
3. Sometimes Mom makes chow mein.
4. With chow mein she serves egg rolls.
5. At the Greek bakery we buy fresh pita bread.
6. Tomorrow Erica will make German potato salad.
7. Lately, tacos have become my favorite food.
8. Carefully, I spoon grated lettuce and cheese into a tortilla.
9. After that come the other ingredients.
10. In the United States, people enjoy a wide variety of foods.

Exercise 7 Writing Predicates

Make a sentence out of each of the following words or word groups by adding a predicate to fill the blank or blanks.

EXAMPLE 1. ____ everyone ____
         1. *With a shout of joy, everyone took a paddle and began to row.*

                              or

         As the waves crashed against the raft, everyone grabbed for the sides.

1. Foamy white water ____.
2. The hot summer air ____.
3. A strong current ____.
4. ____ the eyes of every person on board ____.
5. The lightweight paddles ____.
6. ____ dangerous rocks and swirls ____.
7. Quick action by everyone ____.
8. A sleek, blue rubber raft ____.
9. The man in the white helmet and blue life jacket ____.
10. ____ the people in this photograph ____.

┌HELP─

Although the example in Exercise 7 shows two possible answers, you need to give only one answer for each item.

Exercise 7 Writing Predicates

POSSIBLE ANSWERS

1. Foamy white water roared through the canyon.
2. The hot summer air chapped my skin.
3. A strong current pulled the raft.
4. Suddenly, the eyes of every person on board widened in amazement.
5. The lightweight paddles floated down the river.
6. Around the bend, dangerous rocks and swirls threatened the raft.
7. Quick action by everyone prevented a disaster.
8. A sleek, blue rubber raft almost overturned.
9. The man in the white helmet and blue life jacket saved the little girl's life.
10. Despite all the problems, the people in this photograph arrived safely on shore.

Complete Predicate and Simple Predicate

The **complete predicate** consists of a verb and all the words that describe the verb and complete its meaning.

1e. The **simple predicate,** or **verb,** is the main word or word group in the complete predicate.

EXAMPLES   The nurse **lifted the patient carefully.**

       complete predicate   lifted the patient carefully
       simple predicate (verb)   lifted

       I **saw a picture of a Siberian tiger.**

       complete predicate   saw a picture of a Siberian tiger
       simple predicate (verb)   saw

Exercise 8   **Identifying Complete Predicates and Verbs**

Identify the complete predicate of each of the following sentences. Then, underline the verb.

EXAMPLE   **1.** For several reasons, space travel fascinates me.

       1. For several reasons *fascinates* me

1. My class traveled by train to Houston, Texas.
2. In Houston my classmates and I visited the Lyndon B. Johnson Space Center.
3. The center displays moon rocks.
4. At the center, astronauts train for their flights.
5. In one room we saw several unusual computers.
6. Some chambers reproduce conditions like those on the moon.
7. Do see the films about the space program in the visitors' center.
8. We also toured the San Jacinto Battleground State Historical Park.
9. There, in 1836, Texas won its independence from Mexico.
10. Actually, I had more fun at the space center.

The simple predicate may be a single verb or a **verb phrase** (a verb with one or more helping verbs).

EXAMPLES   Yoshi **went** to Japan last summer. [single verb]

       The park **is located** near a lake. [verb phrase]

       We **should have planned** a picnic. [verb phrase]

┌─ H E L P ─
In this book, the simple predicate is generally called the *verb*.

Reference Note
For information on **helping verbs,** see page 49.

GRAMMAR

GRAMMAR

Exercise 9

DISTRIBUTED REVIEW

Have students review parts of speech by finding the following items in sentences 1, 3, 5, and 8:

1. a pronoun [*I*]

3. a preposition [*in*]

5. three nouns [*patriots, bell, army*]

8. three adjectives [*This, many, historic*]

DIFFERENTIATING INSTRUCTION

English-Language Learners

Vietnamese. For the most part, Vietnamese uses S+V+O word order as English does, so students will expect verbs to follow subjects. However, Vietnamese does not use *it* as the subject in weather, time, and distance expressions such as "It's raining" or "It's 11:00" or in expressions such as "It is easy to . . . " or "It's necessary to. . . . " Remind students that *it* can be used as a subject in English sentences without referring to an antecedent. Then, have students practice the form by responding to questions or activities requiring *it* in the answers.

What time is it? It's 10:00.

How far is it? It's two miles.

Tell us the time now.
It is 2:30.

What's the weather today?
It's sunny and warm.

NOTE   The words *not* and *never* and the contraction *–n't* are not verbs. They are never part of a verb or verb phrase.

EXAMPLE   Kendra **should**n't **have added** another hot pepper to the sauce.

Exercise 9 Identifying Complete Predicates and Verbs

Identify the complete predicate in each of the following sentences. Then, underline the verb.

EXAMPLE   1. The Liberty Bell was made in England.
1. *was made in England*

1. I am writing a report on the Liberty Bell.
2. The Pennsylvania Assembly ordered the Liberty Bell.
3. Thomas Lester had made the bell in London.
4. In 1752, the bell was cracked by its own clapper.
5. American patriots hid the bell from the British army.
6. The bell was not brought back to Philadelphia until 1778.
7. The Liberty Bell cracked again in 1835.
8. This bell has been rung on many historic occasions.
9. The bell is exhibited in the Liberty Bell Pavilion.
10. We will be seeing it on our field trip to Philadelphia.

Finding the Subject

Sometimes it may be difficult to find the subject of a sentence. In such cases, find the verb first. Then, ask yourself *Who?* or *What?* before the verb.

EXAMPLES   Next semester you may take art or music. [The verb is *may take. Who* may take? *You* may take. *You* is the subject of the sentence.]

Can your sister drive us to the park? [The verb is *Can drive. Who* can drive? *Sister* can drive. *Sister* is the subject of the sentence.]

Please read the first chapter. [The verb is *read. Who* should read? *You* should read. *You* is the understood subject of the sentence.]

Reference Note

For more information on **understood subjects,** see page 18.

Compound Subject and Compound Verb

Compound Subject

1f. A *compound subject* consists of two or more subjects that are joined by a conjunction and that have the same verb.

The parts of a compound subject are most often connected by *and* or *or*.

EXAMPLES **Minneapolis** and **St. Paul** are called the "Twin Cities." [The two parts of the compound subject have the same verb, *are called.*]

Will **Mrs. Jones** or **Ms. Lopez** chaperone our field trip? [The two parts of the compound subject have the same verb, *Will chaperone.*]

Flutes, clarinets, and **oboes** are all woodwind instruments. [The three parts of the compound subject have the same verb, *are.*]

Exercise 10 Identifying Compound Subjects

Identify the <u>compound subjects</u> in each of the following sentences.

EXAMPLE **1.** October and June are my favorite months.

     1. October, June

1. Wild <u>ducks</u> and <u>geese</u> migrate south each year.
2. <u>Stars</u> and <u>planets</u> form a galaxy.
3. Someday <u>dolphins</u> and <u>people</u> may be able to communicate with each other.
4. <u>Baseball</u> and <u>soccer</u> are the two most popular sports at my sister's school.
5. <u>Eggs</u> and <u>flour</u> are two ingredients in pancakes.
6. Every year <u>bugs</u> and <u>rabbits</u> raid our vegetable garden.
7. <u>Pizza</u> or <u>ravioli</u> will be served.
8. At a party, <u>balloons</u> or <u>horns</u> make the best noisemakers.
9. <u>Dachshunds</u>, <u>Chihuahuas</u>, <u>Lhasa apsos</u>, and <u>Pekingese</u> ran around in the yard.
10. In the Tower of London are famous <u>jewels</u> and <u>crowns</u>.

Reference Note

| Notice that **commas** are **used to separate three or more parts of a compound subject.** For more about this use of commas, see page 268.

Subject and Predicate   **13**

Compound Subject and Compound Verb

Rules 1f, g *(pp. 13–16)*

OBJECTIVES

- To identify compound subjects in sentences
- To identify compound verbs in sentences
- To complete sentences by supplying compound subjects and compound verbs

DIRECT TEACHING

Modeling and Demonstration

Compound Subject and Compound Verb. Model how to identify compound subjects and compound verbs by using the example *Mrs. Jones and Ms. Lopez will drive the vans and chaperone our field trip.* First, ask *What two people or things is the sentence about?* [*Mrs. Jones, Ms. Lopez*] Then, point out that they are the two parts of the compound subject and that they are connected by *and.* Then, ask *What about Mrs. Jones and Ms. Lopez?* [*They will drive and chaperone.*] Then, point out that the two subjects share the same verbs and that those two verbs are also connected by *and.* Now, have a volunteer use another example in this chapter to demonstrate how to identify compound subjects and compound verbs.

GRAMMAR

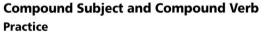

RESOURCES

Compound Subject and Compound Verb

Practice

- *Language & Sentence Skills Practice,* pp. 10–12, 18–19

Special Education Students

Ask students to use a tape recorder to dictate short descriptive paragraphs about their favorite books or TV programs. Have them use as many compound subjects and compound verbs as possible.

Learners Having Difficulty

Some students may benefit from working through the exercises with advanced students. Assign an exercise to groups of two or three students. Encourage them to talk about the sentences and to analyze the problems they have with the sentences. You may want to walk about the room to verify that the information is being explained adequately.

Advanced Learners

Point out to students that using compound subjects and compound verbs is one way to make their writing more interesting and effective. Have students revise a past or current writing project by adding some compound subjects and compound verbs.

Exercise 12 Writing Compound Subjects and Compound Verbs

POSSIBLE ANSWERS

1. Jake and Max are beginning a stamp collection.

Compound Verb

1g. A *compound verb* consists of two or more verbs that are joined by a conjunction and that have the same subject.

A connecting word such as *and* or *but* is used to join the parts of a compound verb.

EXAMPLES   Ben **overslept** but **caught** his bus anyway.

Conchita **hums, sings,** or **listens** to the radio all day.

My father **bought** a Chinese wok and **cooked** vegetables in it.

Exercise 11 Identifying Compound Verbs

Identify the compound verbs in the following sentences.

EXAMPLE   1. I have proofread my paper and made a final copy.
      1. have proofread, made

1. Mai and her parents left Vietnam and arrived in California in 1994.
2. Julie received good grades and made the honor roll.
3. Every week, our band practices together and writes songs.
4. Before supper I usually set the table or peel the vegetables.
5. Floyd asked for a watch but received a bike instead.
6. We gathered firewood and headed back to camp.
7. Last week everyone gave a speech or recited a poem.
8. The referee will call a rain delay or postpone the game.
9. I remembered the bread but forgot the milk.
10. The Greek restaurant has closed but will reopen soon.

Exercise 12 Writing Compound Subjects and Compound Verbs

Make sentences by adding compound subjects or compound verbs to fill in the blanks in the following word groups.

EXAMPLES   1. _____ are coming to the party.
      1. Fran and Terry are coming to the party.

      2. At the mall, we _____.
      2. At the mall, we ate lunch and went to a movie.

1. _____ are beginning a stamp collection.

HELP

Remember to include helping verbs when you are identifying verbs in Exercise 11.

MINI-LESSON Grammar

Finding Compound Subjects and Compound Verbs. Write the following sentences on the chalkboard:

1. Marco and Anna played their guitars.

2. Anna played her guitar and sang for us.

3. Marco and Anna played their guitars and sang for us.

Ask the class to identify the verb in the first sentence [*played*] and to find the compound subject by asking who played [*Marco, Anna*].

2. _____ were my favorite teachers last year.
3. The creature from outer space _____.
4. At the end of the play, the cast _____.
5. Last week _____ were interviewed on a talk show.
6. In the garage are _____.
7. During the storm, we _____.
8. At the front door were _____.
9. After school, my friends _____.
10. He _____ before the birthday party.

Review B Identifying Subjects and Verbs

Identify the <u>subjects</u> and <u>verbs</u> in each of the following sentences.

EXAMPLE   **1.** In the history of African American music are many unforgettable names.

 1. names—subject; are—verb

1. You may recognize the man in the picture on this page.
2. Most people immediately think of his deep, raspy voice.
3. Ray Charles is called the father of soul music.
4. He lost his sight at the age of seven and became an orphan at fifteen.
5. However, misfortune and trouble did not stop Ray Charles.
6. His musical genius turned his troubles into songs.
7. Today, the songs of Ray Charles are heard all over the world.
8. Do his songs contain different musical styles?
9. Gospel, jazz, blues, and even pop are all part of his sound.
10. His special style and powerful performances have drawn fans to Ray Charles for nearly fifty years.

┌─HELP─┐

Some of the subjects and verbs in Review B are compound.

A sentence may have both a compound subject and a compound verb.

```
          S       S  V            V
EXAMPLES  Zina and I bought corn and fed the ducks.

          S           S   V            V
          Carrots and celery are crunchy and satisfy your
          appetite.
```

Subject and Predicate   **15**

Exercise 12 Writing **Compound Subjects and Compound Verbs**

POSSIBLE ANSWERS continued

2. Mr. Wu and Ms. Jones were my favorite teachers last year.
3. The creature from outer space stepped forward and hugged me.
4. At the end of the play, the cast bowed and waved to the audience.
5. Last week actors and directors were interviewed on a talk show.
6. In the garage are tools and tires.
7. During the storm, we drank apple cider and talked about our vacation.
8. At the front door were Lou and Nell.
9. After school, my friends play tennis or fly kites.
10. He blew up balloons and hung crepe paper streamers before the birthday party.

Then, ask students to identify the compound verb in the second sentence [*played, sang*] and the compound subject and compound verb in the third sentence [*Marco, Anna; played, sang*].

Finally, ask students to compose their own sets of sentences in the same pattern: one with a compound subject, one with a compound verb, and one with both. Have them label the compound parts.

EXTENSION

Relating to Writing

Tell students that using compound subjects and compound verbs is one way to combine sentences. Demonstrate the point by asking students to make one sentence from the following two sentences:

Juan plays piano.
Donna plays piano.

Point out that the resulting sentence *Juan and Donna play piano* contains a compound subject, *Juan* and *Donna*.

Reference Note

For more information about **compound, complex,** and **compound-complex sentences,** see page 97.

───

STYLE ✏️ TIP

In your own writing, you can combine ideas by creating compound subjects and verbs. Combining sentences in this way will help make your writing smoother and easier to read. Compare the examples below.

CHOPPY
Susan went hiking in the mountains. Mark went hiking, too. Aunt Connie went with them.

REVISED
Susan, Mark, and Aunt Connie went hiking in the mountains.

Reference Note

For more information on **combining sentences,** see page 396.

───

NOTE   Sometimes a sentence will contain more than one subject and verb, but neither the subject nor verb will be compound.

EXAMPLES **I like** apples, but my **sister prefers** oranges. [S V / S V]
[compound sentence]

In San Antonio, **we toured** the Alamo, while our **friends visited** the Riverwalk. [S V / S V]
[complex sentence]

David wipes the table, and **Cindy dries** the dishes that **Dad has washed.** [S V / S V / S V]
[compound-complex sentence]

Exercise 13 Identifying Compound Subjects and Compound Verbs

Identify the compound subject and the compound verb in each of the following sentences.

EXAMPLE   1. Tina and Julia washed the dog and dried it.
    1. *Tina, Julia—subject; washed, dried—verb*

1. Alice and Reiko sang and played the piano.
2. Either Dwayne or I will find the coach and ask his advice.
3. Patrick and she read the same biography of Dr. Martin Luther King, Jr., and reported on it.
4. Roses and lilacs look pretty and smell good.
5. The dentist or her assistant cleans and polishes my teeth.
6. In many traditional Japanese homes, doors or partitions are framed in wood, left open in the middle, and then covered with rice paper.
7. Larry and she washed the dishes but did not dry them.
8. The lamb and its mother had leapt the fence but were still inside the yard.
9. Fish, rays, turtles, and dolphins live in the Gulf of Mexico and often swim near the shore.
10. Did Uncle Ted or his children call or visit you on their way through town?

Learning for Life 🌐

Creating an Advertisement. Point out to students that one well-written sentence can have a stronger effect than a series of weaker sentences. Advertisers often use one powerful sentence to get their audience's attention.

Ask students to collect examples of effective advertisements that use a single, powerful sentence. You may want students to focus on advertising that supports a specific cause or relays an important message. Students can post examples of effective

Review C · Identifying Subjects and Predicates

Identify the complete subject and the complete predicate in each of the following sentences. Then, underline the simple subject and the verb.

EXAMPLE 1. Reports and legends of huge apelike creatures fascinate many people.

1. *subject—Reports and legends of huge apelike creatures; predicate—fascinate many people*

1. These creatures are known as *Yeti* in the Himalayas and as *Rakshas* in Katmandu.
2. American Indians of the Northwest call them *Mammoth*.
3. *Sasquatch* and *Bigfoot* are other common names for these mysterious creatures.
4. Since 1818, they have been seen and described by people in the United States and Canada.
5. According to most accounts, Bigfoot adults are very strong and large and smell very bad.
6. Their huge footprints have been measured and cast in plaster by eager searchers.
7. However, these reports and bits of evidence generally do not convince scientists.
8. Not one live Bigfoot has ever been captured by either scientists or the general public.
9. As a result, the Bigfoot is simply a fantasy to most people.
10. Still, in pockets of deep wilderness across the country might live whole families of these shy creatures.

Review D · Writing Sentences

Tell whether each of the following sentence parts can be used as a *subject* or a *predicate.* Then, use each sentence part in a sentence. Begin each sentence with a capital letter, and end it with the correct mark of punctuation. Use a variety of subjects and verbs in your sentences.

EXAMPLE 1. will drive us home

1. *predicate—Will your mother drive us home?*

1. my favorite book
2. watched a good mystery

┌─HELP─┐

Some of the subjects and verbs in Review C are compound.

Subject and Predicate   **17**

---

advertisements on the class bulletin board.

Have students design their own ads that feature a single sentence as a slogan or attention-grabber.

Students can create ads for a student election or a school event such as a play or bazaar.

After students have written their sentences, have them meet with partners to evaluate their ads' effectiveness. Partners should also proofread each other's work.

3. the flying saucer
4. the oldest house in town
5. prepares delicious Korean food
6. growled and bared its teeth
7. the shiny red car and the bicycle
8. caught a huge fish
9. can borrow your skates
10. the best tacos and enchiladas in town

Kinds of Sentences

Sentences may be classified according to purpose.

1h. A *declarative sentence* makes a statement and ends with a period.

EXAMPLES   Our media center has several computers**.**

Patrick Henry lived in Virginia**.**

1i. An *imperative sentence* gives a command or makes a request. Most imperative sentences end with a period. A strong command ends with an exclamation point.

EXAMPLES   Please pass the potatoes**.** [request]

Sit down**.** [command]

Stop shouting**!** [strong command]

The subject of a command or a request is always *you*, even if the word *you* never appears in the sentence. In such cases, *you* is called the **understood subject.**

EXAMPLES   [**You**] Please pass the potatoes**.**

[**You**] Stop shouting**!**

1j. An *interrogative sentence* asks a question and ends with a question mark.

EXAMPLES   Did the Apollo 13 spacecraft reach the moon**?**

How old are you**?**

Reference Note
For information on **how sentences can be classified according to structure,** see page 96.

Review D   Writing Sentences
POSSIBLE ANSWERS
continued

3. subject: The flying saucer is the subject of my little brother's drawing.
4. subject: The oldest house in town is being made into a museum.
5. predicate: My neighbor prepares delicious Korean food.
6. predicate: The tiger growled and bared its teeth.
7. subject: The shiny red car and the bicycle belong to my dad.
8. predicate: Juan caught a huge fish.
9. predicate: No one can borrow your skates.
10. subject: The best tacos and enchiladas in town are served at Washington Middle School.

Kinds of Sentences
Rules 1h–k *(pp. 18–20)*

OBJECTIVE

■ To classify sentences as declarative, imperative, interrogative, or exclamatory and to provide the correct punctuation

RESOURCES
Kinds of Sentences
Practice
■ *Language & Sentence Skills Practice,* pp. 15–16, 20

1k. An *exclamatory sentence* shows excitement or expresses strong feeling and ends with an exclamation point.

EXAMPLES   What a difficult assignment that was!

             I got her autograph!

Oral Practice   Classifying Sentences by Purpose

Read each of the following sentences aloud, and say which end mark—a period, a question mark, or an exclamation point—should be added. Then, identify each sentence as *declarative*, *interrogative*, *imperative*, or *exclamatory*.

EXAMPLE   1. What a funny show that was

            1. *What a funny show that was!—exclamatory*

1. Please help me find my umbrella.   **1.** imp.
2. How happy I am!   **2.** exc.
3. Have you and your sister been to the new video store on Congress Avenue?   **3.** int.
4. Go east for three blocks, and look for a yellow mailbox next to a red door.   **4.** imp.
5. My father and I are cleaning the attic together later this afternoon.   **5.** dec.
6. What a delicious salad this is!   **6.** exc.
7. During our last summer vacation, we toured the garment district in New York City.   **7.** dec.
8. Do you like barbecued chicken?   **8.** int.
9. My surprise visit last month pleased both my grandmother and Aunt Gabriela.   **9.** dec.
10. When is your next piano lesson?   **10.** int.

Review E   Classifying Sentences by Purpose

For each of the sentences on the following page, add an appropriate end mark. Then, identify each sentence as *declarative*, *imperative*, *interrogative*, or *exclamatory*.

EXAMPLE   1. Have you ever seen the Grand Canyon

            1. *Have you ever seen the Grand Canyon?*
            —interrogative

STYLE   TIP

Be careful not to overuse exclamation points in your writing. Save them for sentences that really do show strong emotion. When used too much, exclamation points lose their effect.

OVERUSED

For her birthday, Katy's parents threw her a bowling party! About twenty friends and family members attended, and we all had a great time! I had two strikes in one game!

IMPROVED

For her birthday, Katy's parents threw her a bowling party. About twenty friends and family members attended, and we all had a great time. I had two strikes in one game!

DIRECT TEACHING

Modeling and Demonstration

Kinds of Sentences. Model how to identify imperative sentences by discussing the following examples: *Please pass the potatoes* and *Watch out for that car!* First, point out that an imperative sentence gives a command or makes a request. Then, ask whether *Please pass the potatoes* is a request or command. [*request*] Point out that most imperative sentences, especially requests, end with a period. Then, ask whether *Watch out for that car!* is a request or a command. [*command*] Point out that many commands end with a period, but strong commands such as this one end with an exclamation point. Then, have a volunteer use another example from this chapter to demonstrate how to classify a sentence.

DIFFERENTIATING INSTRUCTION

English-Language Learners

General Strategies. Students might be able to create different kinds of sentences more easily if you give them a simple declarative sentence and ask them to form the other three types of sentences starting from this base.

EXAMPLE

The game was exciting.

Was the game exciting?

Please tell me whether the game was exciting.

How exciting the game was!

DIFFERENTIATING INSTRUCTION

Learners Having Difficulty

To give extra practice in using the four sentence types, cut out magazine pictures that are colorful, vivid, and suitable for writing prompts. Give one to each student, along with instructions to write a short descriptive paragraph based on what is in the picture. Tell each student to use one interrogative, one imperative, one exclamatory, and at least two declarative sentences in the paragraph.

MEETING THE CHALLENGE

In any kind of writing, correct end punctuation is important. However, it is especially important in written dialogue. The punctuation helps a reader know how a speaker says something. A sentence can mean very different things when its end punctuation is changed.

Write a short dialogue that includes the same sentence used three times—each time with different punctuation and different meaning.

ANSWER
Dialogues will vary.

1. We enjoyed our vacation in the Southwest. 1. dec.
2. Dad took these photographs when our family visited the Grand Canyon. 2. dec.
3. Our guide spoke both Spanish and English. 3. dec.
4. How pretty the sunset is! 4. exc.
5. Don't stand so close to the edge. [or !] 5. imp.
6. Did you buy any turquoise-and-silver jewelry? 6. int.
7. It was quite chilly at night. 7. dec.
8. What a great movie we saw about the canyon! 8. exc.
9. Did you take the short hike or the long one? 9. int.
10. Look at us riding on mules in this canyon. 10. imp.

Terms and numerals in brackets refer to concepts and rules tested by the items in the Chapter Review.

1. The light [1a]
2. sent. [1a]
3. sent. [1a]
4. It looks eerie [1a]
5. , the human population has grown. [1a]
6. sent. [1a]
7. sent. [1a]
8. , the guard looked up. [1a]
9. sent. [1a]
10. Did you see [1a]

11.–20. [complete subject and complete predicate]

Chapter Review

A. Identifying Sentences

For each of the following word groups that is a sentence fragment, revise the word group to make it a complete sentence. If a group is a sentence, write *sentence.*   Some answers will vary.

1. Burned brightly throughout the night.
2. He studies computer programming after school.
3. The band sounds so wonderful tonight!
4. Whenever the mountains are covered with fog.
5. Over the past two thousand years.
6. Be seated.
7. Behind us barked the dogs.
8. Just as I neared the castle's drawbridge.
9. Should we sand the wood now?
10. The artist carving the totem pole?

B. Identifying the Complete Subject and the Complete Predicate

Write each of the following sentences. Then, underline the complete subject once and the complete predicate twice.

11. *Black Beauty* is a story about a horse.
12. Sometimes bats fly into our chimney.
13. A wonderful smell of baking bread came from the kitchen and filled the house.
14. The chief will speak to you now.
15. Milk and cheese can help you develop strong bones.
16. Two eagles and a hawk live near our house.
17. Adele peeled and ate the orange.
18. Several knights guarded the castle and drove off the dragon.
19. Under the lettuce was my tomato.
20. Will Ahmad and Nadim set the table before lunch?

Monitoring Progress
Chapter Review. To assess student progress, you may want to compare the types of items missed on the **Diagnostic Preview** with those missed on the **Chapter Review.** If students have not made significant progress, you may want to refer them to **Chapter 15: Correcting Common Errors, Exercises 1** and **2,** for additional practice.

Chapter Review   **21**

C. Identifying Simple Subjects and Simple Predicates

┌HELP──

Sentences in Part C may contain compound subjects and compound verbs.

For each of the following sentences, write the simple subject and the simple predicate.

21. The winner is Mr. Otis Kwan!
22. Suddenly, the clock stopped.
23. Many cactuses have grown in the garden.
24. Have you ever eaten yakitori?
25. Yancy and Rollo will meet us at the shopping mall.
26. When did they reach the summit of Mount Fairweather?
27. Yellow, orange, and red have always been my favorite colors.
28. Prince and Princess jumped the fence and barked at my brother's friend.
29. The sports banquet will be held on April 4.
30. We bought milk and bread but forgot the eggs.

21.–30. [1c, e]

D. Punctuating and Classifying Sentences by Purpose

Write each sentence, adding an appropriate end mark. Then, classify each sentence as *declarative, imperative, interrogative,* or *exclamatory.*

31. imp. [1i]   31. Listen to them! [or .]
32. exc. [1k]   32. What music they make!
33. dec. [1h]   33. My name is Lucy.
34. imp. [1i]   34. Tell me more about your trip to Romania.
35. int. [1j]   35. How long has Marlon played the zither?
36. dec. [1h]   36. I will ask her to come over for dinner.
37. int. [1j]   37. Who is the star of the film?
38. imp. [1i]   38. Stop it now!
39. exc. [1k]   39. I'm so happy to see you!
40. int. [1j]   40. Which pair of shoes did you decide to buy?

Writing Application
Using Sentence Variety

Sentences Classified by Purpose As a special project, your social studies class is creating a comic book. Each class member will contribute a comic strip about a particular historical event or historical person. In your comic strip, include at least one of each of the four kinds of sentences—declarative, imperative, interrogative, and exclamatory.

Prewriting First, jot down some ideas for the characters and story line of your comic strip. You may want to look through your social studies book for ideas. Then, plan the frames of your comic strip. Think about how you could include the four types of sentences in your characters' dialogue. For example, what request or command could a character make?

Writing Use your prewriting notes to help you make a draft of your comic strip. Use word balloons to add the dialogue to the pictures. As you write, you may decide to add details. Keep in mind that you will be able to add details in the pictures that go with the words.

Revising Ask a friend to read your cartoon. Are your characters' conversations clear? Can your friend follow the story line? If not, you may need to add, revise, or rearrange sentences.

Publishing Check your comic strip for errors in grammar, spelling, and punctuation. Make sure that you have used all four kinds of sentences and that you have used periods, question marks, and exclamation points correctly for each kind of sentence. You and your classmates may want to photocopy all the comic strips and gather them in a folder for each member of the class.

APPLICATION

Writing Application

Prewriting Tip. Some students may prefer to draw their cartoon panels before they attempt to create a verbal story line.

Writing Tip. One way students can use each of the four kinds of sentences is to present them in dialogue. Point out to students that interrogative and declarative sentences can be used to ask and answer questions on their topics. Exclamatory sentences can be used to express their enthusiasm for the subject. Imperative sentences can be used to tell the reader to take some action.

Scoring Rubric. While you will want to pay particular attention to students' use of complete sentences and of types of sentences, you will want to evaluate the students' overall writing performance. You may want to give a split score to indicate development and clarity of the composition as well as grammar skills.

CHAPTER

2

STANDARDS FOCUS

Grade-Level Standards

(Boldface indicates concepts that are taught and tested in this chapter.)

- Language Conventions 1.0: **Students write and speak with a command of standard English conventions appropriate to this grade level.**

- Grammar 1.2: **Identify and properly use indefinite pronouns** and present perfect, past perfect, and future perfect verb tenses; ensure that verbs agree with compound subjects.

- Capitalization 1.4: **Use correct capitalization.**

Prerequisite/Review Standards

- Grammar 1.2: Identify and correctly use verbs that are often misused (e.g., *lie/lay, rise/raise, sit/set*), modifiers, and pronouns.

- Capitalization 1.4: Use correct capitalization.

Standards Coming Up in the Next Grade Level

- Grammar 1.3: Identify all parts of speech and types and structure of sentences.

- Capitalization 1.6: Use correct capitalization.

▼

INTRODUCING THE CHAPTER

- This chapter should help students use nouns, pronouns, and adjectives effectively in their writing. The first part of the chapter defines the noun and

(continued)

1.0 Written and Oral English Language Conventions
Students write and speak with a command of standard English conventions appropriate to this grade level.
1.2 Identify and properly use indefinite pronouns.
1.4 Use correct capitalization.

Parts of Speech Overview
Noun, Pronoun, Adjective

Diagnostic Preview

Identifying Nouns, Pronouns, and Adjectives

Identify each of the italicized words in the following sentences as a *noun*, a [*pronoun*], or an *adjective*.

Numerals in brackets refer to rules tested by the items in the Diagnostic Preview.

1. [2a, b]
2. [2a, c]
3. [2b]
4. [2c]
5. [2c]
6. [2b, a]
7. [2c, b]
8. [2b, a]
9. [2a]
10. [2c, b]

EXAMPLE   **1.** Her older *brother* has an *important* test today.
   1. brother—noun; important—adjective

1. The *Romans* built a huge system of roads, [*some*] of which are still used.
2. Last summer we visited *Alaska*, which is our *largest* state.
3. [*Which*] of the projects does [*that*] illustrate?
4. The *Hawaiian* dancers wore *colorful* costumes.
5. *The* bubbling volcano, *inactive* for years, is now a popular tourist attraction.
6. The campers enjoyed [*themselves*] as they watched the sun set behind the *mountains*.
7. "*That* notebook is [*mine*]," Angela said.
8. [*They*] made a touchdown just before the final *whistle*.
9. *Colombo* is the capital *city* of Sri Lanka.
10. The pen with the *blue* ink is [*hers*].

CHAPTER RESOURCES

Internet
- go.hrw.com (keyword: HLLA)

go. hrw .com

Planning
- *One-Stop Planner CD-ROM*
- *On Course: Mapping Instruction*

Practice & Review
- *Language & Sentence Skills Practice*, pp. 25–37; 38–40
- *Developmental Language & Sentence Skills*, pp. 7–16

Application & Enrichment
- *Language and Sentence Skills Practice*, pp. 43; 24, 41–42

The Noun

2a. A *noun* is a word or word group that is used to name a person, place, thing, or idea.

Persons	parents, Scott, teacher, Ms. Theresa Vargas, sister, linebackers, baby sitter
Places	White House, states, Nairobi, school
Things	rocket, desks, ocean, hamster, computer, Newbery Medal, Golden Gate Bridge
Ideas	danger, freedom, kindness, fears, dream

Notice that some nouns are made up of more than one word. A *compound noun* is a single noun made up of two or more words used together. The compound noun may be written as one word, as a hyphenated word, or as two or more words.

One Word	daydream, Iceland
Hyphenated Word	self-esteem, sister-in-law
Two Words	Rita Rodriguez, family room

Exercise 1 Identifying Nouns

Identify the nouns in the following sentences.

EXAMPLE
1. Clara Barton was the founder of the American Red Cross.
1. *Clara Barton, founder, American Red Cross*

1. Clara Barton was born in Massachusetts.
2. She was educated in a rural school and grew up with a love of books.
3. She began her career as a teacher.
4. During the Civil War, however, she distributed medicine and other supplies.
5. Later she helped find soldiers who were missing in action.

explains the difference between proper nouns and common nouns. Next, the chapter focuses on pronouns and their antecedents and discusses the different types of pronouns. Then the chapter explains adjectives, including proper and demonstrative adjectives.

■ The chapter closes with a **Chapter Review** including a **Writing Application** feature that asks students to write a plot summary and a description of the characters for a short science fiction movie spoof.

■ For help in integrating this chapter with writing assignments in *Holt Literature and Language Arts,* use the **Teaching Strands** chart on pp. T22–T23.

ASSESSING

Entry-Level Assessment
Diagnostic Preview. You can use the **Diagnostic Preview** to determine students' knowledge of nouns, pronouns, and adjectives, but even students who can identify these parts of speech may not use them effectively in their writing. Evaluating writing samples should reveal weaknesses.

The Noun
Rule 2a *(pp. 25–26)*

OBJECTIVES

■ To identify nouns in sentences

■ To classify nouns in sentences as common or proper

■ To revise sentences by substituting proper nouns for common nouns

■ To answer questions with complete sentences and to identify each proper noun used in the sentences

Differentiating Instruction
■ *Lesson Plans for Language Development*
■ *Supporting Instruction in Five Languages*
Assessment
■ *Progress Assessment for the Holt Handbook,* pp. 3–4, 41

■ *Test Generator* (One-Stop Planner CD-ROM)
Other Language Resources
■ *Spelling Lessons & Activities*
■ *Vocabulary Development*
■ *Daily Language Activities Transparencies*

Lesson Starter

Prior Knowledge. Ask students to supply words that describe the similarities and differences between an orange and a baseball. Students might begin by saying that both objects are round. You might want to draw a Venn diagram on the chalkboard and ask students to suggest words that describe both items and words that apply to only one item or the other. Tell students that the words listed in the diagram are all adjectives.

DIRECT TEACHING

Modeling and Demonstration

Identifying Nouns. Model how to identify nouns by using the example *self-esteem*. First, ask whether the word names a person, place, thing, or idea. [*idea*] *Self-esteem* names an idea; therefore, *self-esteem* is a noun. Now, have a volunteer use another example from this chapter to demonstrate how to identify a noun.

DIFFERENTIATING INSTRUCTION

English-Language Learners

Spanish. In Spanish, some proper nouns differ from those in English. When discussing an absent person, a Spanish speaker will insert a definite article before a title. For example, "Dr. Hernandez is retired" translates as *El doctor Hernández está jubilado.* Also, titles such as *doctor* (Dr.), *señor* (Mr.), *señora* (Mrs.), and *general* (General) are not capitalized preceding a name. Therefore, Spanish speakers may say "I saw the general Powell" instead of "I saw General Powell." You may want to emphasize that the article is omitted in English and that the title is capitalized.

6. She organized the <u>American Red Cross</u> and was its <u>president</u> for many <u>years</u>.
7. She raised <u>money</u> for the <u>Red Cross</u> and worked with <u>victims</u> of <u>floods</u> and other <u>disasters</u>.
8. Her <u>kindness</u> touched the <u>lives</u> of countless <u>men</u>, <u>women</u> and <u>children</u>.
9. Her <u>life</u> has been an <u>inspiration</u> to many <u>people</u> who have followed in her <u>footsteps</u>.
10. What a remarkable <u>career</u> and <u>legacy</u> she left the <u>people</u> of the <u>world</u>!

Proper Nouns and Common Nouns

Reference Note

For information about **capitalizing proper nouns,** see page 241.

A **proper noun** names a particular person, place, thing, or idea and begins with a capital letter. A **common noun** names any one of a group of persons, places, things, or ideas. It is usually not capitalized.

Common Nouns	Proper Nouns
woman	Aunt Josie
teacher	Jaime Escalante
city	Los Angeles
country	Germany
continent	Asia
monument	Lincoln Memorial
team	Karr Cougars
book	*Barrio Boy*
holiday	Chinese New Year
religion	Judaism
language	Swahili

Exercise 2 Identifying Common and Proper Nouns

Identify the nouns in the following sentences, and label them *common* or *proper*.

EXAMPLE   1. The people of Japan celebrate many holidays.
           1. *people—common; Japan—proper; holidays—common*

RESOURCES

The Noun
Practice
■ *Language & Sentence Skills Practice,* pp. 25–27, 38–40
■ *Developmental Language & Sentence Skills,* pp. 7–8

1. The <u>picture</u> below is of the <u>Snow Festival</u> in <u>Sapporo</u>.
2. Many <u>groups</u> work together to build these giant <u>sculptures</u> of <u>snow</u>.
3. Do you recognize any of the <u>statues</u> or <u>buildings</u>?
4. Is that the <u>Statue of Liberty</u> made out of <u>snow</u>?

5. In the historic <u>city</u> of <u>Kyoto</u> each <u>June</u>, you can see a <u>parade</u> of <u>spears</u>.
6. A popular <u>fair</u> in <u>Tokyo</u> offers pickled <u>radishes</u>.
7. Many <u>villages</u> are colorfully decorated for the <u>Feast of the Lanterns</u>.
8. <u>Toshiro</u> said that his <u>town</u> enjoys the <u>Star Festival</u> every <u>summer</u>.
9. Several <u>flowers</u>, among them the <u>iris</u> and the <u>lily</u>, have their own special <u>days</u>.
10. The <u>birthday</u> of <u>Buddha</u> is observed in <u>April</u>.

Exercise 3 **Substituting Proper Nouns for Common Nouns**

In the sentences on the next page, substitute a proper noun for each italicized common noun. You will need to change or leave out some other words in each sentence. You may also make up proper names to use. Answers will vary.

Exercise 2

DISTRIBUTED REVIEW
Ask students to identify the complete subject and the complete predicate in sentences 2, 3, and 6.

2. complete subject—Many groups; complete predicate—work together to build these giant sculptures of snow

3. complete subject—you; complete predicate—Do recognize any of the statues or buildings

6. complete subject—A popular fair in Tokyo; complete predicate—offers pickled radishes

DIFFERENTIATING INSTRUCTION

Advanced Learners
Have students read and discuss John Gardner's "Dragon, Dragon" or another folk tale that uses common nouns rather than proper names for its characters. Ask students to consider why the author uses common nouns rather than proper ones for the characters in the story. [*Students may say that there are so many characters in the story that it is easier for the reader to remember them with descriptive common nouns than with proper ones. Common nouns may also make the characters seem more universal.*]

English-Language Learners

Hmong. Hmong places a plural classifier, *cov*, before nouns in order to make them plural. Explain that many English nouns are made plural by adding an *s* or *es* to the end of the word. This addition, except for its placement and attachment to the noun itself, is much like the use of a plural classifier. If necessary, review and practice with students the creation of plurals in English.

Special Education Students

You may wish to use the chapter exercises in a variety of tutoring situations, such as cross-age tutoring, peer tutoring, and community volunteer tutoring. Because student expectations and success are directly related, tutors should establish specific time lines and goals for student performance. Clear, prompt feedback along with measurable, valid criteria for evaluation will help build trust and mutual respect and will boost students' self-esteem.

EXAMPLE 1. The *principal* awarded the *student* the prize for the best creative essay.

1. *Ms. Chen awarded Paula Perez the prize for the best creative essay.*

1. The *student* is from a *city*.   1. Marc/San Francisco
2. Usually, my *uncle* looks through the *newspaper* after we finish dinner.   2. Uncle Dean/*The Washington Post*
3. The *child* watched a *movie*.   3. Ali/*The Wizard of Oz*
4. A *teacher* asked a *student* to talk about growing up in Mexico.   4. Ms. Miller/Imelda
5. My *cousin* read that *book*. 5. Sarah/*Island of the Blue Dolphins*
6. Surrounded by newspaper reporters, the *mayor* stood outside the *building*.   6. Mayor Bose/City Hall
7. Does the *girl* go to this *school*?   7. Rosie/Central Middle School
8. That *singer* wrote the *song*.   8. Loretta Lynn/"Coal Miner's Daughter"
9. My *neighbor* bought her husband a new *car* for his birthday last Saturday.   9. Mrs. Berkowitz/Ford
10. When he was a college student, the *coach* played for that *team*.   10. Coach Johnson/the Pirates
11. The *painting* is in a *museum*.11. La Calunnia/the Uffizi Gallery
12. Officer Potts/ Congress Avenue Bridge
12. The *officer* directed us to the *bridge*.
13. My relatives, who are originally from a *town*, now live in a *city*.   13. Eureka/San Diego
14. The librarian asked my *classmate* to return the *book* as soon as possible.   14. Jorge/*The Wind in the Willows*
15. That *newspaper* is published daily; this *magazine* is published weekly.   15. *The New York Times/The Nation*
16. Ted read a *poem* for the *teacher*.   16. "The Raven"/Mrs. Long
17. That *state* borders the *ocean*.17. Massachusetts/Atlantic Ocean
18. Italy/May
18. The owner of that store visited a *country* during a *month*.
19. A *man* flew to a *city* one day.   19. Mr. Kim/Paris
20. Last week the *president* talked about the history of our *nation*.   20. President Clinton/the United States

Exercise 4 **Using Proper Nouns**

Developers are planning to build a new shopping mall in your neighborhood. They are trying to find out what kinds of stores and other attractions the community would like at the mall. The developers have prepared the following survey.

CONTENT-AREA CONNECTIONS

Social Studies
Places and Names. To give students practice in naming proper nouns, have students complete a team race on a social studies topic that they are studying. Divide the class into groups of four. Give each group a social studies category, and have the groups write as many proper nouns as they can in five minutes. All group members are responsible for generating answers. (Possible categories include states and their capitals, continents, oceans, rivers, countries, presidents, and

Answer each question with a complete sentence. Underline each proper noun that you use.

EXAMPLE   **1.** When would you be most likely to go to the mall?

     1. I would be most likely to visit the mall on Saturdays, especially in August and November.

New Mall Questionnaire
1. What stores would you most like to see at the mall?
2. What would you be most likely to buy at the mall?
3. What types of movies would you prefer to see at the mall theater?
4. What restaurants would you like to have in the mall's food court?
5. Would you go to the mall arcade? If so, what games would you play?
6. What brands of clothes do you prefer?
7. Would you purchase books or magazines at the mall? If so, what books or magazines interest you?
8. To what clubs, organizations, or associations do you belong?
9. What special or seasonal events would attract you to the mall?
10. At what nearby malls do you sometimes shop?

Review A   **Identifying and Classifying Nouns**

Identify the nouns in the following sentences, and label them *common* or *proper*.

EXAMPLE   **1.** In 1989, President George Bush gave General Colin Powell a big job.

     1. 1989—common; President George Bush—proper; General Colin Powell—proper; job—common

ANSWERS
Exercise 4
Responses will vary, but each response should be a complete sentence and all proper nouns should be underlined.

The Noun   **29**

---

battles.) Have one student in each group record the group's ideas, one student make sure the answers are proper nouns, and two students act as prompters. One prompter can mention letters in the alphabet not yet used as initial letters in the group's ideas. The other prompter can mention areas in the category overlooked by the group (for example, state capitals of Western states).

1. He appointed Powell leader of the Joint Chiefs of Staff.
2. Powell became one of the top military officers in the United States.
3. In the photo here, he is shown talking with soldiers during the Persian Gulf War.
4. Do you think the troops were excited to meet the general?
5. Powell grew up in the Bronx, a neighborhood in New York City.
6. His parents came to the United States from Jamaica.
7. Powell graduated from the City College of New York.
8. There he joined the Reserve Officers' Training Corps.
9. Did you know that Powell was awarded the Purple Heart during the Vietnam War?
10. In his speeches, he often encourages students to graduate from high school.

The Pronoun

2b. A *pronoun* is a word that is used in place of one or more nouns or pronouns.

In each of the following examples, an arrow is drawn from a pronoun to the noun or nouns it stands for in the sentence.

EXAMPLES   When Cindy Davis came to the bus stop, **she** was wearing a cast.

The trees and bushes are dry; **they** should be watered.

This stable is large. **It** has stalls for thirty horses.

The word or word group that a pronoun stands for is called its ***antecedent.***

EXAMPLES   My **aunt** sold her car. [*Aunt* is the antecedent of *her*.]

Anthony, call your mother. [*Anthony* is the antecedent of *your*.]

Reference Note

For information about choosing **pronouns that agree with their antecedents,** see page 137.

30   Chapter 2   Parts of Speech Overview

GRAMMAR

The Pronoun

Rule 2b *(pp. 30–37)*

OBJECTIVES

- To revise sentences, replacing nouns with pronouns

- To identify pronouns in sentences

- To identify pronouns as personal, reflexive, or intensive

- To identify pronouns as indefinite or demonstrative

- To identify pronouns as relative or interrogative

DIRECT TEACHING

Modeling and Demonstration

Identifying Antecedents. Model how to identify the antecedent of a pronoun by using the example *Bill lent Tina his book.* First, ask students to identify the pronoun. [*his*] Then, list the information the pronoun provides. [*The pronoun refers to one person. The person is male.*] Next, find the word to which the pronoun logically refers. [*The one male person in the sentence is Bill.*] *Bill* is the antecedent of *his.* Now, have a volunteer use an example from this chapter to demonstrate how to identify the antecedent of a pronoun.

RESOURCES

The Pronoun

Practice

- *Language & Sentence Skills Practice,* pp. 28–32, 38–40
- *Developmental Language & Sentence Skills,* pp. 9–14

Sometimes the antecedent is not stated because the reader can understand the meaning of the sentence without it.

EXAMPLES   Call **your** mother. [The antecedent of *your* is clearly the person to whom the sentence is directed.]

          They beat **us** fair and square. [The antecedent of *They* is clearly the team that the speaker played against. The antecedent of *us* is clearly the team of which the speaker is a member.]

Oral Practice **Substituting Pronouns for Nouns**

Read each of the following sentences aloud, replacing the repeated ~~nouns~~ with pronouns.

EXAMPLE   **1.** Viviana set up Viviana's game on the table.
          1. Viviana set up her game on the table.

1. The passengers on the departing ocean liner waved to ~~the passengers'~~ friends on shore. **1.** their
2. The test was so long that I almost didn't finish ~~the test~~. **2.** it
3. Rachel's neighbors asked ~~Rachel~~ to baby-sit. **3.** her **4.** he/his
4. Carlos said that ~~Carlos~~ had already cleaned ~~Carlos's~~ room.
5. The directions were long, but ~~the directions~~ were clear.
6. Mom was born in Nigeria, and ~~Mom~~ speaks French, **5.** they
English, Spanish, and Italian. **6.** she
7. Ask those police officers if ~~the police officers~~ know the way to Alhambra Avenue. **7.** they
8. The twins saved ~~the twins'~~ money; now, that new bicycle built for two is ~~the twins'~~. **8.** their/theirs
9. Did Warren's aunt fix some tacos for ~~Warren~~? **9.** him
10. Our whole family spent the weekend at home, but ~~our whole family~~ had the best time ever. **10.** we

Personal Pronouns

A **personal pronoun** refers to the one speaking (**first person**), the one spoken to (**second person**), or the one spoken about (**third person**). Personal pronouns have both singular and plural forms.

EXAMPLE   **I** am sure **he** told **you** about **their** plans.

┌─**HELP**─
When you use a pronoun, always be sure that its antecedent is clear to the reader. If the pronoun could possibly refer to one of two or more antecedents, revise the sentence to make the meaning more clear.

UNCLEAR
My aunt called my sister after she won the talent contest. [Who won the talent contest, my aunt or my sister?]

CLEAR
After my sister won the talent contest, my aunt called her.

Learners Having Difficulty

Have students work at the chalk-board as you dictate sentences containing pronouns. Ask students to circle the pronouns and to draw arrows to the pronouns' antecedents. Students can also point to them-selves, other students, and objects around the classroom to act out different types of pronouns. These activities may aid students' under-standing of the relationships between pronouns and their antecedents.

─HELP─

Do not confuse the possessive pronoun *its* with the contraction *it's*. The pronoun *its* means "belonging to it." The con-traction *it's* means "it is" or "it has." The apostrophe shows that letters have been left out.

Some other possessive pronouns that are often confused with contractions are *their*, meaning "belong-ing to them," (confused with *they're*, meaning "they are") and *your*, meaning "belonging to you" (confused with *you're*, meaning "you are").

Reference Note

For more information about **words that are often confused,** see page 329.

Personal Pronouns		
	Singular	Plural
First person	I, me, my, mine	we, us, our, ours
Second person	you, your, yours	you, your, yours
Third person	he, him, his, she, her, hers, it, its	they, them, their, theirs

The ***possessive pronouns***—*my, mine, our, ours, your, yours, her, hers, his, its, their,* and *theirs*—are personal pronouns that are used to show ownership or possession.

EXAMPLES   Nina stored **her** suitcase under **her** bed.

Is that paper **yours** or **mine**?

NOTE   Some teachers prefer to call some possessive forms of pronouns (such as *my, your,* and *our*) adjectives. Follow your teacher's instructions regarding possessive forms.

Reflexive and Intensive Pronouns

A ***reflexive pronoun*** refers to the subject and is necessary to the basic meaning of the sentence. An ***intensive pronoun*** emphasizes its antecedent and is unnecessary to the basic meaning of the sentence.

Reflexive and Intensive Pronouns	
First person	myself, ourselves
Second person	yourself, yourselves
Third person	himself, herself, itself, themselves

REFLEXIVE   They chose new books for **themselves**.

She gave **herself** the day off from practicing.

INTENSIVE   David **himself** bought a sandwich.

The award will be presented by the principal **herself**.

Exercise 5 Identifying Pronouns

Identify all of the pronouns in each of the following sentences.

EXAMPLE 1. I lent her my camera.

1. *I, her, my*

1. The dentist asked me several questions before examining my teeth.
2. Dad asked the mechanics working on his car to call him about his bill.
3. Our cousins have decided they will visit Peru.
4. She asked herself where she could have put her book.
5. He washed the mats thoroughly and put them out in the sun to dry.
6. Here is a postcard from Egypt for you and me.
7. We helped ourselves to tacos and beans.
8. You gave us your support when we needed it.
9. He had to do his social studies homework before playing soccer with us.
10. I found the weak battery and replaced it myself.

Exercise 6 Identifying Types of Pronouns

In each of the following sentences, identify the italicized pronoun as *personal*, *reflexive*, or *intensive*.

EXAMPLE 1. Eric gave *her* a flower.

1. *personal*

1. Darren *himself* did not know where the gifts were hidden.
2. Did Teri offer *them* directions to the community center?
3. Elena is a very good actress, and *she* always learns her lines very quickly.
4. Kara treated *herself* to a short nap after a long day.
5. Although *it* fell from the top branches of the elm tree, the chipmunk was not injured.
6. Have *you* told Dennis about the new sports complex?
7. Tracy and Ed carried the aquarium to the car *themselves*.
8. Brian and Erin just arrived home, so *they* have not started their homework assignment yet.
9. Rosalia congratulated *herself* on meeting her goal.
10. The dog made *itself* dizzy by chasing its own tail.

MEETING THE CHALLENGE

If you are not sure whether a pronoun is reflexive or intensive, use this test: Read the sentence aloud, omitting the pronoun. If the meaning of the sentence stays the same, the pronoun is intensive. If the meaning changes, the pronoun is reflexive.

Identify the boldface pronoun in each of the following sentences as *reflexive* or *intensive*. Use the test described above to explain how you made your choice.

1. The children enjoyed **themselves** at the park.
2. Jeremy repaired the tire **himself.**

ANSWERS
1. The pronoun is reflexive. Without *themselves,* the sentence doesn't make sense.
2. The pronoun is intensive. Without *himself,* the meaning stays the same.

Demonstrative Pronouns

A *demonstrative pronoun* points out a specific person, place, thing, or idea.

Demonstrative Pronouns			
this	that	these	those

EXAMPLES   What is **that**?

                This is the uniform once worn by Satchel Paige.

                These are the shoes he used to wear.

                Are **those** really his autographs?

Reference Note

For information on **adjectives,** see page 38.

NOTE   *This*, *that*, *these*, and *those* can also be used as adjectives. When these words are used to modify a noun or pronoun, they are called *demonstrative adjectives.*

PRONOUN   **This** is a delicious papaya. [*This* refers to *papaya.*]

ADJECTIVE   **This** papaya is delicious. [*This* modifies *papaya.*]

PRONOUN   **That** is the stamp my cousin sent from Sweden. [*That* refers to *stamp.*]

ADJECTIVE   **That** stamp was the first in my collection. [*That* modifies *stamp.*]

Indefinite Pronouns

Reference Note

For more information on **indefinite pronouns,** see page 129.

An *indefinite pronoun* refers to a person, a place, a thing, or an idea that may or may not be specifically named.

Common Indefinite Pronouns			
all	each	more	one
any	either	much	other
anybody	everybody	neither	several
anyone	everyone	nobody	some
anything	few	none	somebody
both	many	no one	something

EXAMPLES   **Everyone** in the class was invited to the party.

None of the boys knew **much** about camping.

> NOTE Most words that can be used as indefinite pronouns can
> also be used as adjectives.
>
> PRONOUN   **Some** are bored by this movie.
> ADJECTIVE   **Some** people are bored by this movie.

Exercise 7   Identifying Pronouns

Identify the italicized pronoun in each of the following
sentences as *indefinite* or *demonstrative*.

EXAMPLE   **1.** *Someone* has been sitting in my chair.
        1. *indefinite*

1. Are you asking *anyone* to the dance this weekend?
2. *This* is my jacket; that one must be yours.
3. *Something* is different about your hair.
4. *That* was the funniest thing I have ever seen a kitten do!
5. *This* is good, but Chrissy's report is better.
6. The armadillo paused at the puddle and drank *some* of
   the water.
7. Are *those* the socks you are wearing with those shoes?
8. We have to choose between *these* and the ones we looked
   at yesterday.
9. Linda did more sit-ups than *several* who tried before her.
10. *Nobody* knows the answer to that.

Review B   Identifying Pronouns

Identify the pronoun or pronouns in each of the following
sentences.

EXAMPLE   **1.** Everyone in my class likes going on field trips.
        1. *Everyone; my*

1. Last week, we really enjoyed ourselves at the National
   Museum of African Art.
2. It has been part of the Smithsonian Institution in
   Washington, D.C., since 1979.

CONTENT-AREA CONNECTIONS

Math
Number Line. Point out to students the
connection between numbers and indefinite
pronouns: Both name quantities. Most indefinite pronouns name a vague quantity, but
some, such as *one* and *none,* are very precise.
Discuss this connection with students.
Students can even arrange the pronouns

according to quantity, from *none* to *all,* along
a number line such as the following one:

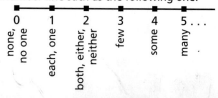

TEACHING **TIP**

Review B If you have instructed students to classify possessive pronouns as adjectives, the following pronouns should not be included in the answers: *its* in sentence 3, *our* in sentences 4 and 7, *her* in sentence 8, and *my* in sentence 9.

EXTENSION

Critical Thinking

Metacognition. Point out to students that there are probably too many pronouns to memorize all of them by type. Ask students what their strategies are for remembering the different types of pronouns. Have students describe and rate the effectiveness of their strategies. Students having trouble with pronouns should develop new strategies. Have students meet in groups to share and compare their ideas.

3. In 1987, the museum's collection was moved to its present underground facility.
4. Our teacher, Ms. Martinez, told us about the museum before we went there.
5. She said the entrance is made of pink granite.
6. I was surprised by the six domes on top.
7. Everyone had at least one question to ask our museum guide.
8. We enjoyed hearing her lively explanations of the artwork.
9. This is a photograph of one of my favorite objects at the museum.
10. Do you like it?

Mask, Bassa Peoples, Liberia. Wood, pigment, bone or ivory, iron (9 ½ " X 5 ¾ " X 4 ½ "). National Museum of African Art, Eliot Elisofon Archives, Smithsonian Institution, #88-5-1. Photo Credit: Franko Khoury.

Interrogative Pronouns

An *interrogative pronoun* introduces a question.

Interrogative Pronouns				
what	which	who	whom	whose

EXAMPLES   **What** is the first event in the contest?

Who is going to represent our team?

To **whom** is the e-mail addressed?

Which of the books are you reading?

Whose is the car in the driveway?

Relative Pronouns

A *relative pronoun* introduces an adjective clause.

Common Relative Pronouns				
that	which	who	whom	whose

Reference Note

For information on **adjective clauses,** see page 91.

EXAMPLES   Harry S. Truman, **who** became president when Franklin D. Roosevelt died, surprised many people with his victory over Thomas Dewey in 1948.

              Robins are among the birds **that** migrate south for the winter.

Exercise 8 Identifying Relative and Interrogative Pronouns

Identify the italicized pronouns in each of the following sentences as *relative* or *interrogative.*

EXAMPLE   **1.** *Which* of those snow sculptures do you think will win the prize?

         1. interrogative

1. The only student *that* could complete the obstacle course was Sophia.
2. *What* was the name of the volcano that erupted in Washington?
3. *What* was causing that sound outside your room at night?
4. "*Who* left all of those markers on the floor yesterday?" asked Ms. Jackson.
5. Lilacs, *which* are known throughout the world for their fragrant flowers, grow best in northern climates.
6. The new teacher, *whom* we have not yet met, will start Monday.
7. *Which* of you remembers the name of the author of "The Celebrated Jumping Frog of Calaveras County"?
8. *Whose* turn is it to take out the trash?
9. The light bulb, *which* had been flickering for a few days, finally burned out.
10. To *whom* did you lend your textbook?

The Adjective

Rule 2c (pp. 38–41)

OBJECTIVES

- To identify adjectives and the words they modify in sentences
- To complete a story by adding appropriate adjectives
- To identify adjectives, including proper adjectives, in sentences
- To change proper nouns into proper adjectives and to use the adjectives in sentences
- To distinguish between demonstrative pronouns and demonstrative adjectives

GRAMMAR

DIRECT TEACHING

Modeling and Demonstration

Words That Adjectives Modify.
Model how to identify the word an adjective modifies by using the example *The sea, blue and sparkling, stretched out before us invitingly.* First, ask students to identify the adjectives. [*The, blue, sparkling*] Then, ask them what stretched out. [*sea*] Next, ask what is blue and sparkling. [*sea*] The adjectives *The, blue,* and *sparkling* modify the noun *sea.* Now, have a volunteer use another example from this chapter to demonstrate how to identify what word an adjective modifies.

PRACTICE

Guided and Independent

You may wish to have students complete **Exercise 9** as guided practice and **Exercise 10** as independent practice. **HOMEWORK**

| STYLE | TIP |

Some adjectives are more specific and vivid than others. You can make your writing more interesting by replacing dull adjectives with more vivid ones.

ORIGINAL
Mr. Sato is a **nice** man. [The adjective *nice* is dull and doesn't really say much about Mr. Sato.]

REVISED
Mr. Sato is a **generous** man. [The adjective *generous* is more specific about Mr. Sato.]

Reference Note
For information on using **predicate adjectives,** see page 114.

Reference Note
For information on using **a** and **an,** see page 222.

The Adjective

2c. An *adjective* is a word that is used to modify a noun or a pronoun.

To *modify* a word means to describe the word or to make its meaning more definite. An adjective modifies a noun or pronoun by telling *what kind, which one, how many,* or *how much.*

What Kind?	Which One or Ones?	How Many or How Much?
gentle dog	**sixth** grade	**two** tickets
Irish town	**these** books	**full** pitcher
scary movie	**other** people	**most** players
purple shoes	**any** CD	**no** work

Adjectives usually come before the words they modify. Sometimes, however, an adjective comes after the word it modifies.

EXAMPLES The dog is **gentle.** [The predicate adjective *gentle* modifies *dog.*]

The sea, **blue** and **sparkling,** stretched out before us invitingly. [The adjectives *blue* and *sparkling* modify the noun *sea.*]

NOTE The adjectives *a, an,* and *the* are called **articles.**

Exercise 9 Identifying Adjectives

Identify each adjective in the following sentences. Do not include *a, an,* or *the.*

EXAMPLE 1. The sky was clear, and the night was cold.
1. *clear, cold*

1. A silvery moon rode down the western sky.
2. It shed a pale light on the quiet countryside.
3. Long meadows spread out between two hills.
4. The smell of the wild onion was strong.
5. The only sound we heard was the sharp crackle of the fire.

RESOURCES

The Adjective

Practice

- *Language & Sentence Skills Practice,* pp. 33–40
- *Developmental Language Sentence & Skills,* pp. 15–16

6. Suddenly, <u>several</u> stars came out.

7. I watched until the <u>entire</u> sky glowed with <u>bright</u> stars.

8. I was <u>lonely</u> and <u>happy</u> at the <u>same</u> time.

9. I finally became <u>sleepy</u> and longed for my <u>warm</u> bed.

10. Soon I went indoors and fell into a <u>deep</u> sleep.

Exercise 10 Identifying Adjectives and the Words They Modify

Identify the adjectives and the words they modify in the following sentences. Do not include *a, an,* or *the.*

EXAMPLE 1. It costs five dollars to go to that movie.

       1. five—dollars; that—movie

1. I have a <u>free</u> ticket for the <u>last</u> game.

2. We ate <u>spicy</u> crawfish, and they were delicious.

3. The <u>new</u> neighbor is helpful and nice.

4. The bear, angry and hungry, surprised the campers.

5. <u>Many</u> students compete in the <u>regional</u> events.

6. Will <u>country</u> musicians play at the <u>county</u> fair?

7. Despite the <u>long</u> delay, we remained cheerful.

8. A <u>shiny</u> coin stared up at me from the the <u>icy</u> sidewalk.

9. Take <u>one</u> booklet and pass the rest to the <u>next</u> row.

10. A <u>few</u> colorful birds perched in the <u>tall</u>, <u>green</u> trees on the bank of the river.

Exercise 11 Writing Adjectives for a Story

The following story is about a cave exploration. Copy the sentences, adding an appropriate adjective for each blank. Underline the adjectives you add.
Adjectives will vary.

EXAMPLE 1. Exploring caves is ____ on ____ days.

      1. Exploring caves is <u>fun</u> on <u>hot</u> days.

1. Have you ever been in a ____ cave like the one shown at right? **1.** real

2. Would you say it looks ____ and ____? **2.** dark/scary

3. My father and I explored this ____ cave once. **3.** huge

4. It was ____ but ____, too. **4.** frightening/fun

5. We found some ____ rock formations. **5.** strange

6. We also heard ____ sounds. **6.** weird

COMPUTER TIP

Some software includes a thesaurus feature. You can use the computer thesaurus to find synonyms to replace dull or overused adjectives in your writing. Always check the meaning of an unfamiliar adjective in a dictionary, though, to make sure it is just the right word.

TEACHING TIP

Exercise 9 Students might identify *my* in sentence 9 as an adjective, depending upon your instructions regarding the **Note** on p. 32.

DIFFERENTIATING INSTRUCTION

English-Language Learners

Spanish. In Spanish most adjectives are placed after the nouns they modify. The words *the beautiful woman,* for example, are expressed as *la mujer bella.* When the adjective modifies a plural noun in Spanish, the adjective changes form to agree with the noun. For example, *the beautiful women* is expressed as *las mujeres bellas.* Reinforce the correct positioning of adjectives in English, and remind students that in English the forms of almost all adjectives remain the same even when they modify plural nouns.

English-Language Learners

Hmong. Because Hmong speakers are accustomed to a complex system of more than one hundred noun classifiers, each of which can be used only with nouns of the same class, shape, group, or form, English-language learners may be uncomfortable with the relative simplicity of English article usage. Remind students that English relies on its indefinite articles, *a* and *an,* and its definite article, *the,* as its primary noun "classifiers."

The Adjective **39**

MINI-LESSON Mechanics *Continued on p. 40*

Punctuating Adjectives in a Series.
Often two or more adjectives are used before a noun to make its meaning more specific. Remind students of the rules regarding comma usage with series of adjectives.

1. Use commas to separate two or more adjectives before a noun.

    Try this healthful, tasty snack.

2. Do not place a comma between an adjective and the noun directly following it.

APPLICATION

Relating to Vocabulary

Adjectives. Give students practice in choosing adjectives that can make their writing more interesting. Write the following sentences on the chalkboard. Have students replace the underlined adjectives with more vivid adjectives without changing the basic meanings of the sentences.

1. The <u>cold</u> wind made us shiver.

2. Our neighbor has a <u>cute</u> kitten.

3. We all think he is a <u>nice</u> person.

4. It's a <u>pretty</u> night.

5. She is a <u>good</u> soccer player.

[Possible responses are given.]

1. *icy, north, gusty*

2. *fuzzy, playful, frisky*

3. *funny, trustworthy, helpful*

4. *starry, clear, calm*

5. *talented, skillful, aggressive*

Reference Note

For information on **capitalizing proper adjectives,** see page 250.

┌HELP┐

Some proper nouns, such as *Easter* and *Sioux*, do not change spelling when they are used as proper adjectives.

7. My father took some ____ photographs.   **7.** interesting

8. We looked up and saw ____ bats flying above our heads.

9. After exploring for about ____ hours, we were ready to see the sky again.   **9.** three   **8.** black

10. Spelunking, as cave exploring is called, can be a very ____ experience, if you have a ____ guide.   **10.** fascinating/good

Proper Adjectives

A *proper adjective* is formed from a proper noun and begins with a capital letter.

Proper Nouns	Proper Adjectives
Japan	**Japanese** islands
Easter	**Easter** Sunday
Queen Victoria	**Victorian** drama
Sioux	**Sioux** customs

Exercise 12 Identifying Adjectives

Identify all of the <u>adjectives</u> in the following sentences. Then, underline each <u>proper adjective</u>. Do not include the articles *a*, *an*, or *the*.

EXAMPLE   **1.** The Navajo weaver made a blanket on a wooden loom.

   1. *Navajo, wooden*

1. Music can express <u>sad</u> or <u>happy</u> feelings.

2. The quartet sang <u>several</u> <u>Irish</u> songs.

3. The <u>gold</u> watch with the <u>fancy</u> chain was made by a <u>famous</u> <u>Swiss</u> watchmaker.

4. She is a <u>Balinese</u> dancer.

5. On vacation, Mom enjoys <u>long</u>, <u>quiet</u> breakfasts.

6. <u>Many</u> <u>Australian</u> people are of <u>British</u> origin.

7. The <u>Egyptian</u> mummies are on display on the <u>first</u> floor.

8. We are <u>proud</u> of Joshua.

9. The movie is based on a <u>popular</u> <u>Russian</u> novel.

10. In <u>Canadian</u> football, a team has <u>twelve</u> players on the field at <u>one</u> time.

40   Chapter 2   Parts of Speech Overview

MINI-LESSON Mechanics   *Continued from p. 39*

Jameel's gift to me was a colorful, hand-woven basket. (no comma before *basket*)

Write the following sentences on the chalkboard, and ask volunteers to add the necessary commas.

1. The ripe[,] juicy apples are ready to eat.

2. Would you enjoy a cool[,] refreshing swim in the lake?

3. Winston is a cute[,] affectionate[,] playful dog.

Exercise 13 — Writing Proper Adjectives

Change the following proper nouns into proper adjectives. Then, use each proper adjective in a sentence.

EXAMPLE   **1.** France

          1. French—We bought French bread at the bakery.

1. England
2. Inca
3. Hinduism
4. Celt
5. Alaska
6. Thanksgiving
7. Shakespeare
8. Korea
9. Navajo
10. Boston

┌HELP┐

You may want to use a dictionary to help you spell the adjectives in Exercise 13.

Demonstrative Adjectives

This, that, these, and *those* can be used both as adjectives and as pronouns. When they modify nouns or pronouns, they are called **demonstrative adjectives.** When they are used alone, they are called **demonstrative pronouns.**

ADJECTIVE   What are **these** skates doing in the living room?

PRONOUN   What are **these** doing in the living room?

ADJECTIVE   I prefer **that** brand of frozen yogurt.

PRONOUN   I prefer **that.**

Reference Note

For more information on **demonstrative pronouns,** see page 34.

Exercise 14 — Identifying Demonstrative Pronouns and Demonstrative Adjectives

In each of the following sentences, identify the italicized word as a *demonstrative pronoun* or a *demonstrative adjective.*

EXAMPLE   **1.** Who gave you *those* beautiful flowers?

          1. demonstrative adjective

1. *That* is the strangest hot-air balloon I have ever seen!
2. Will *those* squirrels find enough to eat during the winter?
3. My dog, Manda, has been chewing on *this* piece of rawhide for three weeks.
4. *These* are the only shoes I can find that will fit you.
5. According to the guidebook, *those* are the largest trees in North America.

The Adjective   **41**

Exercise 13

Writing Proper Adjectives

ANSWERS

Responses will vary. Here are some possibilities:

1. English
   I like English tea sets.
2. Incan
   I would like to see some Incan ruins.
3. Hindu
   My uncle studied Hindu beliefs.
4. Celtic
   Do you know anyone who has studied a Celtic language?
5. Alaskan
   Manuel is writing a report on the Alaskan pipeline.
6. Thanksgiving
   We enjoyed the Thanksgiving dinner.
7. Shakespearean
   Are Shakespearean sonnets always love poems?
8. Korean
   Is the Korean language similar to Japanese?
9. Navajo
   Was that a Navajo blanket we saw in the museum?
10. Boston
    My favorite salad involves Boston lettuce and avocados.

TECHNOLOGY TIP

Many word-processing programs include a thesaurus feature. If students compose on the computer, encourage them to use the thesaurus to find synonyms for adjectives that may be bland or overused. Remind students to check the definitions of synonyms in a dictionary to be sure they are using words with the correct connotations.

DIRECT TEACHING

Correcting Misconceptions

Demonstrative Pronouns and Demonstrative Adjectives. It is easy for students to confuse demonstrative pronouns with demonstrative adjectives since the words *this, that, these,* and *those* are used for both parts of speech. To help students differentiate between the two, tell students that like personal pronouns (*I, you, he, she, it, they*), demonstrative pronouns are just one word (*this, that, these, those*) and don't modify another word. Similarly, demonstrative adjectives are just like regular adjectives in that they must modify a noun or pronoun (*this hat, red hat, that one, first one*).

DIFFERENTIATING INSTRUCTION

Advanced Learners

Have students read and discuss a story such as "What Do Fish Have to Do with Anything?" by Avi, in which descriptive adjectives are used to create a mood or describe a character. Ask students what mood is created or how a character is described in the story and which adjectives help convey the mood or description.

TEACHING TIP

Review D Students might identify *my* in items 4, 6, and 7 as an adjective, depending upon your instructions regarding the **Note** on p. 32.

PRACTICE

Guided and Independent

You may wish to use **Review D** as guided practice. Then, have students complete **Review E** as independent practice. **HOMEWORK**

6. Is *that* your final offer?
7. The geese always return to *these* same lakes.
8. What do you plan to do with *that* lump of clay?
9. I'm afraid she's gone too far *this* time.
10. Can *this* be the same person I knew back in third grade?

Review C Identifying Adjectives

Identify the adjectives in the following sentences. Do not include *a, an,* or *the.*

EXAMPLE 1. I enjoy visiting the large railroad museum in our city.
1. *large, railroad*

1. Museums can be interesting.
2. Large cities have different kinds of museums.
3. Some museums display sculpture and paintings.
4. These museums may focus on one special kind of art.
5. For example, they might specialize in Chinese art or Mexican art.
6. Other museums feature birds, sea creatures, dinosaurs, and other animals.
7. A curator holds an important job in a museum.
8. A curator needs to know many facts about a particular display.
9. Some valuable objects must be displayed in a stable environment.
10. Some people prefer displays of modern art, while others enjoy exhibits of folk art.

Review D Identifying Nouns, Pronouns, and Adjectives

Identify all of the nouns,[pronouns, and adjectives in each of the following sentences. Do not include *a, an,* or *the.*

EXAMPLE 1. I think models make a great hobby.
1. *I—pronoun; models—noun; great—adjective; hobby—noun*

1. Do[you]have a favorite hobby?
2. Models are enjoyable and educational.

42 Chapter 2 Parts of Speech Overview

FAMILY/COMMUNITY ACTIVITY *Continued on pp. 43–45*

Writing a Letter to the Editor. A responsible citizen will have opinions on current issues and should be able to express those opinions clearly and convincingly. Have students write a letter to the editor of their school or classroom newspaper on a topic of their choice. Point out that the careful use of nouns, pronouns, and adjectives will make their opinions clearer and their arguments more effective.

Bring copies of student newspapers to class, and have students select several good

3. [They] require little space.

4. [I] keep [mine] on a bookshelf [my] dad and [I] built [ourselves].

5. Models are packaged in kits.

6. [My] favorite models are historic ships and antique planes.

7. On [my] last birthday, [my] parents gave [me] two model kits of biplanes.

8. [They] came with directions in several languages.

9. [Many] of the tiny parts are designed for an exact fit.

10. Do [you] think the bright decals add a realistic look?

Review E Identifying Nouns, Pronouns, and Adjectives

Identify all of the nouns, [pronouns], and adjectives in each of the following sentences. Do not include *a, an,* or *the*.

EXAMPLE **1.** Pueblos are practical housing for people in hot, dry regions.

1. *Pueblos—noun; practical—adjective; housing— noun; people—noun; hot—adjective; dry— adjective; regions—noun*

1. The brown building in the photograph contains several individual homes.

2. *Pueblo* is a Spanish word for a structure like [this] and for a town.

3. This building is located at the Taos Pueblo in New Mexico.

The Adjective **43**

examples of letters to the editor to display on the class bulletin board. Students can use these as inspiration and as models for their own letters.

Arrange students in small groups to brainstorm for possible topics. Each group member should decide on his or her own topic and position and should write a list of at least three points to support the argument. Students can then work individually on their letters.

Caution students to keep their letters

4. Can [you] tell how <u>pueblos</u> are made?
5. [They] are built of <u>adobe</u>.
6. <u>People</u> make <u>adobe</u> by mixing <u>mud</u> with <u>grass</u> or <u>straw</u>.
7. [They] shape the <u>mixture</u> into <u>bricks</u> and let [them] bake in the <u>sun</u>.
8. <u>Buildings</u> made with <u>this</u> <u>material</u> stay <u>cool</u> during the <u>summer</u> <u>months</u>.
9. [Anyone] on a <u>visit</u> to the <u>Southwest</u> can find <u>other</u> <u>pueblos</u> like <u>this</u> [one].
10. <u>Old</u> <u>pueblos</u> built by the <u>Hopi</u> and the <u>Zuni</u> fascinate [me].

Review F Writing Sentences Using Nouns, Pronouns, and Adjectives

Write ten original sentences using the parts of speech given below. In each sentence, underline the word that is the listed part of speech.

EXAMPLE   **1.** an adjective that comes after the word it describes
       1. Our guide was very helpful.

1. a proper noun
2. a possessive pronoun
3. an adjective that tells *how many*
4. a reflexive pronoun
5. a proper adjective
6. an article
7. a third-person pronoun
8. a demonstrative adjective
9. an indefinite pronoun
10. a noun that names an idea

Review F Writing Sentences Using Nouns, Pronouns, and Adjectives

POSSIBLE ANSWERS
Sentences will vary.

1. Did you know that <u>Chicago</u> is very windy?
2. Iris asked me to name <u>my</u> favorite color.
3. I bought <u>eight</u> apples at the fruit stand.
4. John gave <u>himself</u> a bruise on his shin when he bumped into the open dishwasher door.
5. Uncle Otis and Aunt Dottie enjoyed the <u>Hawaiian</u> luau.
6. Where did you put <u>the</u> vases for the flowers?
7. I believe <u>they</u> said she would be here in twenty minutes.
8. <u>This</u> sweater fits better than the other one.
9. <u>Everybody</u> thought the assignment was easy.
10. There can never be too much <u>kindness</u> in the world.

FAMILY/COMMUNITY ACTIVITY   *Continued from p. 43*

under two hundred words in length. Remind them to use pronouns and nouns to refer clearly to their topics and their arguments. Also, point out that precise adjectives can make their writing clear and vivid.

After students have finished writing, pair them to evaluate each other's work. Peer evaluators should be able to name the topic and position of the letter and identify the supporting reasons and conclusion. Partners can share ideas to make each other's arguments more convincing.

2

Terms and numerals in brackets refer to concepts and rules tested by the items in the Chapter Review.

1. [2c, a]
2. [2b, a]
3. [2b, c]
4. [2c, a]
5. [2c]
6. [2b, a]
7. [2b]
8. [2c]
9. [2b, a]
10. [2c]

11.–15. [2a]

16.–18. [2b]

Chapter Review

A. Identifying Nouns, Pronouns, and Adjectives

Identify each italicized word or word group in the following sentences as a _noun_, a [pronoun], or an _adjective_.

1. My _best_ friend plays _soccer_.
2. [We] went to _Boston_ last summer.
3. Help [yourself] to some _Chinese_ food.
4. What a _beautiful_ garden _Mrs. Murakami_ has!
5. _These_ directions were _accurate_.
6. [That] is a fast _merry-go-round_.
7. Juana invited [us] to [her] fiesta.
8. _Sharp_ tools are _necessary_ for making a wood carving.
9. Almost [everyone] in the band takes private music _lessons_.
10. _This_ story is my _favorite_ one.

B. Identifying Common and Proper Nouns

Identify the nouns in the following sentences, and label each _common_ or _proper_.

11. The religion our family practices is Islam.
12. Was Spanish the first language your mother spoke?
13. The musicians in the band play guitars, keyboards, and drums.
14. My favorite movie is _Willy Wonka and the Chocolate Factory_.
15. Many American tourists visit London in the summer.

C. Identifying Pronouns

Identify all of the pronouns in each of the following sentences.

16. My cat ate all of its food this morning.
17. Each of the girls said someone had already told her about the band concert.
18. I brought a casserole to the potluck dinner and put it in the oven.

Chapter Review **45**

ASSESSING

Monitoring Progress
Chapter Review. To assess student progress, you may want to compare the types of items missed on the **Diagnostic Preview** with those missed on the **Chapter Review.** You may want to work on specific goals with individual students who are still having difficulty mastering essential information.

TEACHING TIP

Review A Students might identify _her_ in item 7 as an adjective, depending upon your instructions regarding the **Note** on p. 32.

TEACHING TIP

Review C Students might identify _My_ and _its_ in item 16, _his_ in item 19, and _our_ in item 24 as adjectives, depending upon your instructions regarding the **Note** on p. 32.

GRAMMAR

Once students have finished revising their letters, ask for volunteers to read their letters aloud. Discuss with the class each letter's position and support and also each letter's use of nouns, pronouns, and adjectives. Students can publish their letters in the class or school newspaper or present their ideas in an open forum in which their classmates can offer well-reasoned, constructive feedback.

19.–25. [2b]

19. The doctor <u>herself</u> removed <u>his</u> bandages.
20. Did <u>anyone</u> notice the person <u>who</u> delivered the package?
21. "I think this winter is going to be long and cold," he said to <u>himself</u>.
22. Didn't <u>you</u> ask <u>him</u> not to do <u>that</u>?
23. That book is not the <u>one</u> <u>that</u> I wanted to read.
24. We asked <u>ourselves</u> if <u>he</u> really intended to come to <u>our</u> party.
25. <u>Which</u> of the sweaters is <u>yours</u>?

D. Identifying Proper and Demonstrative Adjectives

Identify the <u>adjectives</u> in the following sentences. Do not include the articles *a, an,* or *the.* Then, label each [*proper adjective*] and each ⟨*demonstrative adjective*⟩.

26.–30. [2c]

26. The [Easter] holiday lasted for <u>one</u> <u>short</u> week.
27. The apple, <u>glossy</u> and <u>red</u>, rolled out of the bag and across the <u>smooth</u> table.
28. The rain was <u>steady</u> throughout ⟨that⟩ <u>gloomy</u> afternoon.
29. Would you like ⟨these⟩ [French] posters, or would you rather have those?
30. The [Siamese] cat is <u>playful</u>, but ⟨that⟩ <u>old</u> tabby is <u>aloof</u>.

E. Identifying Nouns, Pronouns, and Adjectives

Identify each *noun,* [*pronoun*], and *adjective* in the following sentences. Do not include the articles *a, an,* and *the.*

31. [2b, a]
32. [2a–c]
33. [2a, c]
34. [2a, b]
35. [2a–c]
36. [2a–c]
37. [2a–c]

31. [Someone] told [me] about the <u>movie</u>.
32. [We] are moving to <u>Belgium</u>, a <u>European</u> <u>country</u>.
33. J. S. <u>Bach</u>, a <u>German</u> <u>composer</u>, wrote <u>many</u> <u>pieces</u> for the <u>harpsichord</u>.
34. "Is [this] the <u>tape</u> [you] wanted?" asked <u>Mr. Imagi</u>.
35. <u>Ted</u> talked [himself] into the <u>purchase</u> of a <u>new</u> <u>computer</u>.
36. [Some] of the <u>old</u> <u>songs</u> are <u>lovely</u>.
37. These <u>colors</u> are <u>brighter</u> than [those].

RESOURCES

Parts of Speech Overview

Review
- *Language & Sentence Skills Practice,* pp. 38–40

Assessment
- *Progress Assessment for the Holt Handbook,* pp. 3–4, 41
- *Test Generator (One-Stop Planner CD-ROM)*

38. Professor Auerbach [herself] will present the award to [us].

39. The Swedish car in the driveway is [ours].

40. Does [anybody] know when the city of San Antonio was founded?

38. [2a, b]

39. [2a–c]

40. [2a, b]

Writing Application
Using Pronouns in a Plot Summary

Pronouns and Antecedents   You are in a filmmaking class at the community center and need ideas for a project. The theme of the project is science fiction movie spoofs. Write a plot summary for a short movie. Explain the plot of the movie, and describe the characters. Be sure that the pronouns you use refer clearly to their antecedents.

Prewriting   In a spoof, a writer imitates and makes fun of another work. Imagine several science fiction movie spoofs— for example, *There's an Alien in My Soup* or *Nerds from Neptune.* Choose the idea that you like the best. Then, brainstorm some ideas for a simple plot. Jot down brief descriptions of the setting and the characters in the movie.

Writing   Use your notes to help you write your first draft. Summarize what happens in the movie from beginning to end. Describe each character as you introduce him or her. Keep the props and costumes simple—you are working on a low budget.

Revising   Ask a friend to read your movie idea. Is the plot interesting? Is it funny? Can your friend tell which character is performing each action? If not, you may need to revise some details. Check to make sure each pronoun refers clearly to its antecedent.

Publishing   Read your summary one more time to catch other errors in spelling, grammar, and punctuation. You may want to develop one scene from your plot summary. With the help of several classmates, dramatize this scene in front of the class. Use simple masks and props to create the effect of science fiction.

APPLICATION

Writing Application

Writing Tip. As students write their first drafts, they will be working on plots, character descriptions, costumes, and props. Because of the sophisticated level of thinking and organizational skills in this task, encourage students not to be concerned with punctuation or spelling errors at this stage. Ask students to develop their own plans for completing the project, basing their plans on the steps in the writing cycle.

Scoring Rubric. While you will want to pay particular attention to students' use of pronouns and antecedents, you also will want to evaluate overall writing performance. You may want to give a split score to indicate development and clarity of the composition as well as grammar skills.

Grade-Level Standards

(Boldface indicates concepts that are taught and tested in this chapter.)

- Language Conventions 1.0: **Students write and speak with a command of standard English conventions appropriate to this grade level.**

- Sentence Structure 1.1: Use simple, compound, and compound-complex sentences; **use effective coordination** and subordination of ideas to express complete thoughts.

Prerequisite/Review Standards

- Sentence Structure 1.1: Identify and correctly use prepositional phrases, appositives, and independent and dependent clauses; use transitions and conjunctions to connect ideas.

- Grammar 1.2: Identify and correctly use verbs that are often misused *(e.g., lie/lay, sit/set, rise/raise)*, modifiers, and pronouns.

Standard Coming Up in the Next Grade Level

- Grammar 1.3: Identify all parts of speech and types and structure of sentences.

▼

INTRODUCING THE CHAPTER

- This chapter should help students recognize and understand the functions of verbs, adverbs, prepositions, conjunctions, and interjections.

(continued)

1.0 Written and Oral English Language Conventions
Students write and speak with a command of standard English conventions appropriate to this grade level.
1.1 Use effective coordination of ideas to express complete thoughts.

Parts of Speech Overview
Verb, Adverb, Preposition, Conjunction, Interjection

Diagnostic Preview

Identifying Verbs, Adverbs, Prepositions, Conjunctions, and Interjections

Identify each of the italicized words or word groups in the following sentences as a *verb*, an *adverb*, a *preposition*, a *conjunction*, or an *interjection*.

Numerals in brackets refer to rules tested by the items in the Diagnostic Preview.

1. v./.prep. [3a, c]
2. adv. [3b]
3. conj./prep. [3d, c]
4. adv./prep. [3b, c]
5. conj./conj./v. [3d, a]
6. adv./adv. [3b]

EXAMPLE   1. A tornado *is* a terrible *and* violent storm.
   1. is—verb; and—conjunction

1. The tornado *struck* our neighborhood *without* warning.
2. We do *not* have a basement in our house.
3. I grabbed my dog Muffin *and* ran *into* the bathroom, the safest room in the house.
4. Muffin and I were *tightly* wedged *between* the sink and the bathtub.
5. *Either* the house was shaking *or* I was, and the air *became* very cold.
6. *Suddenly,* a siren went *off.*

CHAPTER RESOURCES

Internet
- go.hrw.com (keyword: HLLA)

go.
hrw
.com

Planning
- *One-Stop Planner CD-ROM* 💿
- *On Course: Mapping Instruction*

Practice & Review
- *Language & Sentence Skills Practice,* pp. 45–61; 62–64
- *Developmental Language & Sentence Skills,* pp. 17–26

Application & Enrichment
- *Language & Sentence Skills Practice,* pp. 67; 44, 65–66

7. A tornado *had been sighted* right *in* the area.
8. Then everything suddenly *grew* calm—it seemed almost *too* calm.
9. I *was* ready for the worst, *but* the tornado did not touch my house *or* any other home in the area.
10. *Well,* I was frightened, *but* I was not hurt.

7. v./prep. [3a, c]
8. v./adv. [3a, b]
9. v./conj./conj. [3a, d]
10. int./conj. [3e, d]

The Verb

3a. A *verb* is a word that expresses action or a state of being.

EXAMPLES We **went** to Boston last April.

Is a firefly a kind of beetle?

Every complete sentence has a verb. The verb says something about the subject.

In this book, verbs are classified in three ways — (1) as *main* or *helping* verbs, (2) as *action* or *linking* verbs, and (3) as *transitive* or *intransitive* verbs.

Main Verbs and Helping Verbs

In many sentences, a single word is all that is needed to express the action or the state of being.

EXAMPLES The dog **barked** all night.

Brett **throws** the ball a long way.

Mr. Rivera **is** the new English teacher.

In other sentences, the verb consists of a main verb and one or more helping verbs.

A ***helping verb*** (also called an *auxiliary* verb) helps the **main verb** to express action or a state of being.

EXAMPLES **can** speak

will learn

should have been fed

Reference Note

For more information about **verbs,** see page 146.

┌HELP──

Remember, a verb cannot be a helping verb unless there is another verb for it to help. If a verb such as *was* or *had* is the only verb in a sentence, it is not a helping verb.

EXAMPLES

I **had** called my grandmother already. [*Had* is helping the main verb, *called.*]

They **had** a good time at the nature center. [*Had* is the only verb; there is no other verb for it to help.]

The Verb 49

GRAMMAR

- The chapter closes with a **Chapter Review** including a **Writing Application** feature that asks students to write ten sentences using the verb *be* at least twice as a helping verb and at least three times as a linking verb.

- For help in integrating this chapter with writing assignments in *Holt Literature and Language Arts,* use the **Teaching Strands** chart on pages T22–T23.

ASSESSING

Entry-Level Assessment
Diagnostic Preview. You could use the **Diagnostic Preview** to gauge students' familiarity with verbs, adverbs, prepositions, conjunctions, and interjections. You may want to assign only the exercises students are likely to find troublesome.

The Verb
Rule 3a *(pp. 49–58)*

OBJECTIVES

- **To identify verb phrases and helping verbs**

- **To use helping verbs in original sentences**

- **To identify action verbs and linking verbs in sentences**

- **To distinguish between action verbs and linking verbs**

- **To distinguish between transitive verbs and intransitive verbs**

- **To use transitive verbs and intransitive verbs in sentences**

Differentiating Instruction
- *Lesson Plans for Language Development*
- *Supporting Instruction in Five Languages*

Assessment
- *Progress Assessment for the Holt Handbook,* pp. 5–6, 41

- *Test Generator (One-Stop Planner CD-ROM)* 🌐

Other Language Resources
- *Spelling Lessons & Activities*
- *Vocabulary Development*
- *Daily Language Activities Transparencies*

GRAMMAR

PRETEACHING

Lesson Starter

Motivating. Write on the chalkboard the words *Maria, Tranh, their dogs, the park,* and *sunny day.* Ask students to suggest ways the words could be combined in a story. As students share their ideas, write the verbs they mention to the side on the chalkboard. Then, ask students what type of word carries all the action in their story ideas. Lead students to see that words that express action or a state of being are verbs.

DIRECT TEACHING

Modeling and Demonstration

Identifying Verbs and Helping Verbs. Model how to identify main verbs and helping verbs by using the examples *I do wash the dishes* and *I will do the dishes.* First, ask which word in *do wash* tells you what action is being performed. [*wash*] Ask which word helps the word *wash.* [*do*] Then, ask students which word in *will do* expresses most of the verb's meaning [*do*] and which word helps *do.* [*will*] Point out that some words can be a helping verb in some sentences and a main verb in others. Now, have a volunteer use other examples from this chapter to demonstrate how to identify a main verb and a helping verb.

─HELP─

The word *not* and its contraction, *–n't,* are adverbs telling *to what extent;* neither is part of a verb phrase.

Together, the main verb and its helping verb or verbs are called a *verb phrase.*

EXAMPLES   Many students **can speak** Spanish.

I **will be learning** all the state capitals tonight.

The dog **should have been fed** by now.

Commonly Used Helping Verbs					
am	being	do	have	must	were
are	can	does	is	shall	will
be	could	had	may	should	would
been	did	has	might	was	

NOTE   Some words can be used as both helping verbs and main verbs.

HELPING VERB   I **do** wash the dishes.

MAIN VERB   I will **do** the dishes.

Sometimes a verb phrase is interrupted by another part of speech.

EXAMPLES   Suzanne **should** not **call** so late at night. [The verb phrase *should call* is interrupted by the adverb *not.*]

The scientists **did**n't **think** the asteroid would hit the earth. [The verb phrase *did think* is interrupted by *–n't,* the contraction for *not.*]

Did you **watch** the new video? [The verb phrase *Did watch* is interrupted by the subject *you.*]

Exercise 1   Identifying Verb Phrases and Helping Verbs

Identify the verb phrase in each of the following sentences. Then, underline the helping verb or verbs.

EXAMPLE   1. We are going to Arizona this summer.
1. *are going*

1. The Petrified Forest has long attracted many tourists.

RESOURCES

The Verb
Practice
- *Language & Sentence Skills Practice,* pp. 45–51, 62–64
- *Developmental Language & Sentence Skills,* pp. 17–20

2. Its spectacular beauty has captured their imaginations.
3. Visitors can see the Painted Desert at the same time.
4. The colors of the desert do not remain the same for long.
5. Specimens of petrified wood are exhibited at the tourist information center.
6. Have you ever seen a piece of petrified wood?
7. A guide will gladly explain the process of petrification.
8. Visitors can purchase the fossilized wood as a souvenir.
9. Tours of the Petrified Forest are not recommended for amateur hikers.
10. Hikes must be arranged with park rangers.

Exercise 2 Using Verb Phrases in Original Sentences

Use each of the following word groups as the subject of a sentence with a verb phrase. Make some of your sentences questions. Underline each helping verb and the main verb in each sentence.

EXAMPLE   1. your neighbor's dog
          1. *Can your neighbor's dog do tricks?*

1. my bicycle
2. the astronauts
3. a tiny kitten
4. the hard assignment
5. a famous singer
6. some strange footprints
7. my grandmother
8. the subway
9. a funny costume
10. the refreshments
11. our softball team
12. his favorite movie
13. the bird watchers' club
14. the new computer chip
15. Queen Elizabeth
16. her school picture
17. today's newspaper
18. a slice of bread
19. the pencil sharpener
20. my calendar

Review A Identifying Verbs

Identify the verbs in each of the following sentences. Be sure to include helping verbs.

EXAMPLE   1. Fairy tales are sometimes called folk tales.
          1. *are called*

1. Long ago, many people could not read.

DIFFERENTIATING INSTRUCTION

English-Language Learners

Cantonese. Because Cantonese does not use helping verbs for questions or negatives, the use of *do* as a helping verb may be particularly puzzling for Cantonese speakers. Students may use regular verb forms and avoid inserting a helping verb: *How much money you have?*

Since the helping verb is unstressed in English sentences, students may have difficulty perceiving its use. Emphasizing the use of *do* and other helping verbs when speaking to students may focus their attention on and assist them in using helping verbs.

PRACTICE

Guided and Independent

Exercise 2 You may want to have students complete items 1 through 10 as guided practice and items 11 through 20 as independent practice. **HOMEWORK**

Exercise 2 Using Verb Phrases in Original Sentences

ANSWERS
Sentences will vary. Make sure that students use a verb phrase in each sentence and that some of the sentences are questions. Check that students have underlined each helping verb as well as the main verb in each sentence.

<table>
<tr><td>

DIFFERENTIATING INSTRUCTION

Learners Having Difficulty

If you are teaching more than one part of speech at one time, a permanent classroom display or poster will probably help students remember the names of the parts of speech. Include the names of the parts of speech being covered, lists of examples from the textbook, and model sentences.

Exercise 3

DISTRIBUTED REVIEW

Have students review nouns and pronouns by finding the following items in the first three sentences.

1. one proper noun and one common noun [*Maricopa, pottery*]

2. three nouns and one pronoun [*pottery, kinds, clay; they*]

3. one pronoun [*itself*]

</td><td>

2. Instead, they <u>would memorize</u> stories.
3. Then they <u>would tell</u> the stories to their family members and friends.
4. In this way, the people, or folk, <u>passed</u> the tales on from generation to generation.
5. Finally, some people <u>wrote</u> the collected stories.
6. Two German brothers, Jakob and Wilhelm Grimm, <u>published</u> a famous collection of German folk tales.
7. The brothers <u>had heard</u> many of the tales from their older relatives.
8. Their collection of stories <u>became</u> extremely popular all over the world.
9. "Sleeping Beauty," "Cinderella," and "Rumpelstiltskin" <u>were</u> all <u>preserved</u> by the brothers Grimm.
10. In your library, you <u>can</u> probably <u>find</u> these tales and many others, too.

Action Verbs

An ***action verb*** expresses either physical or mental activity.

PHYSICAL ACTIVITY   I **have used** a computer in math class.

         Please **cook** dinner, Jerome.

MENTAL ACTIVITY   Fran **understands** the science assignment better than anyone else does.

         The magician **is thinking** of a number.

Exercise 3   Identifying Action Verbs

Identify the <u>action verb</u> in each of the following sentences.

EXAMPLE   **1.** The Maricopa people live in Arizona.
      1. live

1. The Maricopa <u>make</u> unusual pottery.
2. For this pottery they <u>use</u> two kinds of clay.
3. One kind of clay <u>forms</u> the bowl or platter itself.
4. The other kind of clay <u>colors</u> the pottery.
5. First, the potters <u>mold</u> the clay by hand.
6. Then, they <u>shape</u> it into beautiful bowls and vases.
7. With the second type of clay, the potters <u>create</u> designs.

</td></tr>
</table>

8. They often <u>etch</u> designs on the pottery with a toothpick.
9. Each family of potters <u>has</u> its own special designs.
10. These designs <u>preserve</u> Maricopa traditions from generation to generation.

Linking Verbs

A *linking verb* connects, or links, the subject to a word or word group that identifies or describes the subject.

EXAMPLES   Sandra Cisneros **is** a writer. [The verb *is* connects *writer* with the subject *Sandra Cisneros.*]

The firefighters **had appeared** victorious. [The verb phrase *had appeared* connects *victorious* with the subject *firefighters.*]

The new superintendent **was** she. [The verb *was* connects *she* with the subject *superintendent.*]

Some Linking Verbs Formed from the Verb *Be*		
am	has been	may be
is	have been	might be
are	had been	can be
was	will be	should be
were	shall be	would have been

Other Linking Verbs			
appear	grow	seem	stay
become	look	smell	taste
feel	remain	sound	turn

Some verbs may be either action verbs or linking verbs, depending on how they are used.

ACTION   They **sounded** the bell for a fire drill.

LINKING   Mom **sounded** happy about her new job. [The verb *sounded* links *happy* with the subject *Mom.*]

The Verb   **53**

STYLE   TIP

In the sentence *The new superintendent was she,* the pronoun *she* after the linking verb may sound strange. Many people would use *her* in informal speech. However, in formal, standard English, *she* is the correct form in this sentence.

Reference Note

For more about **pronouns following linking verbs,** see page 113. For information on **formal and informal language,** see page 221.

For more about **pronouns following linking verbs,** see page 113. For information on **formal and informal language,** see page 221.

EXTENSION

Relating to Literature

To help students understand the power of action verbs and the function of linking verbs in descriptions, have them read the song "John Henry" if it is available in their literature book. Ask students to identify each verb as an action verb or a linking verb, and discuss how the verb choice affects the meaning and rhythm of the song.

DIFFERENTIATING INSTRUCTION

Advanced Learners

To give further practice in identifying action and linking verbs, have students choose five verbs from the **Other Linking Verbs** chart. Challenge students to use each verb (except *become* and *seem*) first as an action verb and then as a linking verb.

English-Language Learners

Hmong. In Hmong, the verb *to be* is implied by, rather than used with, predicate adjectives; therefore, Hmong speakers may see the verb as redundant when it's used with a predicate adjective. Students may sometimes omit the verb entirely, writing, "I happy," "she tall," or "he busy," rather than "I am happy," "she is tall," or "he is busy." Remind English-language learners that verbs are necessary in complete sentences in English, and offer practice with the use of *to be,* stressing the verb's presence in posed questions and answers: *Are* you happy? I *am* happy. *Is* she tall? She *is* tall. *Is* he busy? He *is* busy.

CONTENT-AREA CONNECTIONS

Social Studies. Point out to students that linking verbs are very useful in creating a sense of person and place, two important ingredients in historical accounts. Have students use linking verbs in sentences about a person, place, or event they are studying in social studies. Students can use their descriptive paragraphs as study notes for their social studies class.

EXTENSION

Relating to Writing

For students who understand the difference between action and linking verbs, assign independent writing for further practice. Have each student write one paragraph describing someone's personality. Students can consider happiness, sense of humor, friendliness, talents, and other traits. Have each student use and underline at least three different linking verbs and three different action verbs.

TIPS & TRICKS

If you are not sure whether a verb is being used as a linking verb or an action verb, try substituting *is* or *are* for the verb. If the sentence still makes sense, the verb is probably a linking verb. If the sentence does not make sense, the verb is probably an action verb.

EXAMPLES

James **looks** taller. [*James is taller* makes sense; here, *looks* is a linking verb.]

James **looks** out the window. [*James is out the window* does not make sense; here, *looks* is an action verb.]

—HELP—

Remember to include helping verbs in your answers to Exercise 5.

ACTION   The judge **will look** at my science project.

LINKING   Ann **will look** funny in her gorilla costume. [The verb phrase *will look* links *funny* with the subject *Ann*.]

Exercise 4 **Identifying Linking Verbs**

Identify the <u>linking verbs</u> or <u>verb phrases</u> in the following sentences.

EXAMPLE   1. Peanut soup made from fresh roasted peanuts tastes good.

   1. *tastes*

1. Peanuts <u>remain</u> an important crop around the world.
2. The peanut, which <u>is</u> high in protein, <u>is</u> native to South America.
3. Peanuts <u>grow</u> ripe underground.
4. The seeds <u>are</u> the edible part of the plant.
5. The peanut <u>has become</u> an important ingredient in more than three hundred common products, such as wood stains, shampoo, printer's ink, and soap.
6. Of course, roasting peanuts <u>smell</u> wonderful.
7. Peanut butter <u>was</u> the invention of a St. Louis doctor in 1890.
8. Before then, thanks to George Washington Carver, the peanut <u>had become</u> one of the major crops of the South.
9. Carver, a scientist who experimented with peanuts and other plants, <u>had been</u> a slave.
10. It may <u>seem</u> strange, but Carver once prepared an entire dinner out of peanuts.

Exercise 5 **Identifying Action Verbs and Linking Verbs**

Identify the verb in each of the following sentences as an *action verb* or a *linking verb*.

EXAMPLES   1. One of the most successful business leaders in the United States is John Johnson.

   1. *is—linking verb*

   2. Johnson publishes many popular magazines.

   2. *publishes—action verb*

---

1. The photograph at right <u>shows</u> John Johnson as a success.
2. Johnson's life <u>has</u> not always <u>been</u> easy.
3. The small Arkansas town of his childhood <u>had</u> no high school.
4. Therefore, Johnson's mother <u>moved</u> to Chicago.
5. In Chicago, Johnson <u>attended</u> high school with classmates Redd Foxx and Nat "King" Cole.
6. During the Great Depression of the 1930s, Johnson's family <u>grew</u> very poor.
7. However, Johnson <u>studied</u> hard.
8. He <u>became</u> an honor student, the class president, and the editor of the high school newspaper.
9. Johnson <u>started</u> his first magazine with a loan.
10. Now he <u>is</u> the owner of a group of companies worth $200 million per year.

Transitive and Intransitive Verbs

A **transitive verb** is a verb that expresses an action directed toward a person, place, thing, or idea. With transitive verbs, the action passes from the doer—the subject—to the receiver of the action. Words that receive the action of a transitive verb are called **objects**.

EXAMPLES   Tamisha **entertained** the child. [The object *child* receives the action of the verb *entertained*.]

Felipe **visited** San Juan. [The object *San Juan* receives the action of the verb *visited*.]

An **intransitive verb** tells something about the subject or expresses action without the action passing to a receiver, or object.

EXAMPLES   The children **smiled.**

The horses **galloped** across the prairie.

I **am** here.

Reference Note
For more about **objects in sentences,** see page 107.

The Verb   **55**

 Grammar   *Continued on p. 56*

Transitive and Intransitive Verbs.
Students often have difficulty differentiating between transitive and intransitive verbs. Emphasize to students the meaning of the prefix *trans–* by brainstorming for related words, such as *transit* and *transcontinental*.

Point out that *trans–* indicates action *through* or *across.* A transitive verb, then, expresses an action from the subject to the object *through* the verb, whereas an intransitive verb does not take a direct object.

DIFFERENTIATING INSTRUCTION

Learners Having Difficulty
You may want to omit for the moment the concepts of transitive and intransitive verbs. Students may grasp these concepts more easily in connection with **Chapter 5: Complements.**

English-Language Learners
General Strategies. Because many languages use different sentence structures, students may need to be reminded that the basic order of English sentences is subject-verb-object. Languages such as Japanese and Korean follow a subject-object-verb pattern, and Arabic follows a verb-subject-object pattern. You may want to monitor students' work to ensure that they generally use the English subject-verb-object pattern.

APPLICATION

Transitive Verbs

Have students work in groups of three to write sentences with transitive verbs. One student can provide the subject, one can provide a transitive verb, and the third can supply the object of the verb. Each group member can then write the sentence and check to make sure it is correct. After every sentence, have the group members change roles so that after six sentences each student has thought of two subjects, two transitive verbs, and two objects. Challenge each group to keep their sentences on a single topic. Ask for volunteers to share their group's sentences with the class.

DIFFERENTIATING INSTRUCTION

Learners Having Difficulty

Have pairs of students write a paragraph describing a real or imaginary event. Students can act out the verbs in their paragraphs, such as by miming a batter hitting a baseball and a spectator cheering. Tell students to use transitive and intransitive verbs in their paragraphs, to underline each verb, and to identify it as transitive or intransitive.

NOTE Not everything that follows a verb is an object. Many words or word groups that come after the verb give more information without receiving the action of the verb.

EXAMPLES   Tameka writes **poetry.** [The object *poetry* receives the action of the transitive verb *writes.*]

Tameka writes **daily.** [The word *daily* tells when she performs the action of the intransitive verb *writes,* but *daily* does not receive the action and is not an object.]

Tameka writes **in the morning.** [The word group *in the morning* tells when she performs the action of the verb *writes,* but *in the morning* does not receive the action and is not an object.]

Some action verbs may be either transitive or intransitive, depending on how they are used in a sentence.

EXAMPLES   My cousin Julio **plays** baseball on a Caribbean League team. [transitive]

My cousin Julio **plays** every week. [intransitive]

Kanani **studies** Chinese each day after school. [transitive]

Kanani **studies** hard. [intransitive]

NOTE Linking verbs are intransitive.

EXAMPLES   This soup **tastes** too salty. [The linking verb *tastes* does not express any action for an object to receive. When used as a linking verb, *tastes* is intransitive.]

Does the box **seem** heavier than it should be? [The linking verb *Does seem* does not express any action for an object to receive. *Does seem* is intransitive.]

Exercise 6 Identifying Transitive and Intransitive Verbs

For each of the following sentences, identify the italicized verb as *transitive* or *intransitive*.

MINI-LESSON Grammar   *Continued from p. 55*

Students can practice using the following graphic with different subjects, verbs, and objects to explore the differences between transitive and intransitive verbs.

Students can discuss their examples in small groups.

SUBJECT → TRANSITIVE VERB → OBJECT

EXAMPLE   **1.** Computers *affect* our lives every day.

        1. transitive

1. Computers *make* calculations incredibly quickly.
2. They *perform* many tasks that people often find boring and difficult.
3. Many businesses *benefit* from these machines.
4. Home computers *work* in similar ways.
5. They *do* word processing, a very useful operation for writers.
6. They also *run* programs for thousands of challenging games.
7. Handy pocket computers *fit* easily into a purse, bag, or backpack.
8. My mother *bought* a tiny computer not much larger than a credit card.
9. The information in its memory *appears* on the screen at the touch of a button.
10. Addresses, phone numbers, notes, and other information on the screen *help* my mother with her work.

Oral Practice   **Using Transitive and Intransitive Verbs**

Think of an appropriate verb for each of the following sentences, and read the completed sentence aloud. Then, identify each verb as *transitive* or *intransitive*.

EXAMPLE   **1.** He _____ my older brother's best friend.

        1. is—intransitive

           or

        knows—transitive

1. Aunt Teresa _____ us about some Cherokee traditions.
2. Our experiment with plants and photosynthesis _____.
3. Billy and I _____ green beans and carrots.
4. By noon, the hot sun _____ the ice.
5. Everything _____ fine to me.
6. In the twilight, a shrimp boat _____ into the bay.
7. _____ these hurdles, Jason.
8. _____ Bogotá the capital of Colombia?
9. Wow! What a crazy tie that _____!
10. Several African nations _____ elections this year.

Answers may vary.
1. told—t
2. ended—i
3. picked—t
4. melted—t
5. seems—i
6. cruised—i
7. Jump—t
8. Is—i
9. is—i
10. held—t

Relating to Speaking

Have students work in groups of six to review the types of verbs they have studied (main, helping, action, linking, transitive, and intransitive). Each group member should choose a different type of verb to review and should then take a turn presenting a lesson to the group on that verb type. The lesson should include a definition of the verb type, a list of verbs of that type, and three example sentences using that type of verb. Group members are responsible for answering other students' questions on their type of verb.

Relating to Writing

Point out to students that using a variety of verb types helps make a piece of writing more interesting and engaging. Encourage students to include in their revision step in the writing cycle a quick check of the verb types in their drafts. Students can use the quick check to vary their verbs.

a
b
c
d
e
f
g
h
i
j
k
l
m
n
o
p
q
r
s
t
u
v
w
x
y
z

Review B **Identifying Verbs**

Identify the <u>verb</u> in each of the following sentences. Be sure to include helping verbs. Then, tell whether the verb is used as an *action* or *linking verb*. Then, tell whether it is *transitive* or *intransitive*.

EXAMPLE   1. Can you form the letters of the sign language alphabet?

    1. *Can form—action, transitive*

1. The alphabet chart at left <u>is</u> helpful.   1. link./int.
2. Perhaps you and a friend <u>could practice</u> together.   2. act./int.
3. At first, it <u>may be</u> a challenge.   3. link./int.
4. Many people <u>communicate</u> with these letters as well as thousands of other signs.   4. act./int.
5. Many people <u>use</u> forms of sign language.   5. act./tran.
6. For example, referees, coaches, and football players sometimes <u>give</u> signals in sign language.   6. act./tran.
7. Some stroke victims <u>must learn</u> sign language during their recovery period.   7. act./tran.
8. Scientists <u>have taught</u> very simple signs to gorillas and chimpanzees.   8. act./tran.
9. These animals <u>have been talking</u> to people and to each other in sign language.   9. act./int.
10. In the picture below, the gorilla on the left and the woman <u>are having</u> a conversation in sign language.   10. act./tran.

The Adverb

3b. An *adverb* is a word that modifies a verb, an adjective, or another adverb.

Just as an adjective makes the meaning of a noun or a pronoun more definite, an adverb makes the meaning of a verb, an adjective, or another adverb more definite.

EXAMPLES   Reporters **quickly** gather the news. [The adverb *quickly* modifies the verb *gather.*]

The route is **too** long. [The adverb *too* modifies the adjective *long.*]

Our newspaper carrier delivers the paper **very early.** [The adverb *very* modifies another adverb, *early.* The adverb *early* modifies the verb *delivers.*]

Adverbs answer the following questions:

Where?	How often?	To what extent?
When?	*or*	*or*
How?	How long?	How much?

EXAMPLES   Please put the package **there.** [*There* modifies the verb *put* and tells *where.*]

I will call you **later.** [*Later* modifies the verb phrase *will call* and tells *when.*]

Softly, I shut my door. [*Softly* modifies the verb *shut* and tells *how.*]

Alannah **always** reads science fiction novels. [*Always* modifies the verb *reads* and tells *how often.*]

Would you please **briefly** explain what you mean? [*Briefly* modifies the verb phrase *Would explain* and tells *how long.*]

An owl hooted **very** late last night. [The adverb *very* modifies the adverb *late* and tells *to what extent.*]

The lemonade was **too** sour. [*Too* modifies the adjective *sour* and tells *how much.*]

—HELP—

Often, adverbs can be recognized by the suffix *–ly.* Remember, however, that not all adverbs end in *–ly* and not all words that end in *–ly* are adverbs.

ADVERBS
     swam **quickly**
     left **later**

ADJECTIVES
     only friend
     early flight

The Adverb   **59**

GRAMMAR

The Adverb
Rule 3b *(pp. 59–62)*

OBJECTIVES

- **To identify adverbs and the words they modify**

- **To use appropriate adverbs in sentences**

DIRECT TEACHING

Modeling and Demonstration

Identifying Adverbs. Model how to identify adverbs by using the example *Reporters gather the news.* First, write the example on the chalkboard along with these categories: *Where? When? How? How often?* and *To what extent?* Then, write an appropriate adverb in each of the categories. [*there, now, quickly, daily, more*] Add the words to the example sentence, and draw arrows from the words to the verb *gather.* Point out that each of the words is an adverb modifying the verb in the sentence. Then, have volunteers use other examples from the chapter to demonstrate how to identify an adverb by supplying words for each category, placing them in the sentence, and indicating which word they modify.

DIRECT TEACHING

The Adverb

Activity. Have students work in groups of five to make lists of common adverbs. Each group member can take one of the categories in the **Words Often Used as Adverbs** chart. After each group member has written a number of adverbs for his or her category, have the group discuss which adverbs can be placed in more than one category. Have the groups present their lists to the class.

Correcting Misconceptions

The Adverb. Have students review the adverbs they listed in the activity above to see that many are formed by adding –ly to an adjective (*bad*—*badly*). Then, have the students examine the adverb chart on this page to see that not all adverbs end in –ly (*then, often,* and *very,* for example). Also, point out that not all words ending in –ly are adverbs (*lovely, silly*).

| STYLE | TIP |

In your own writing, try not to overuse the adverb *very.* Replace it with a less common adverb, or revise the sentence so that other words carry more of the descriptive meaning.

EXAMPLE
The runt of the litter is still very small.

REVISED
The runt of the litter is still **quite** small.
or
The runt of the litter **weighs just one pound and is only six inches long.**

┌HELP─

The word *not* and its contraction, *–n't,* are adverbs.

Words Often Used as Adverbs	
Where?	here, there, away, up, outside
When?	now, then, later, soon, ago
How?	clearly, easily, quietly, slowly
How often? *or* **How long?**	never, always, often, seldom frequently, usually, forever
To what extent? *or* **How much?**	very, hardly, almost, so, really most, nearly, quite, less, only

The Position of Adverbs

Adverbs may come before, after, or between the words they modify.

EXAMPLES **Quietly,** she will tiptoe from the stage. [*Quietly* comes before *will tiptoe,* the verb phrase it modifies.]

She will **quietly** tiptoe from the stage. [*Quietly* comes between *will* and *tiptoe,* the verb phrase it modifies.]

She will tiptoe **quietly** from the stage. [*Quietly* comes after *will tiptoe,* the verb phrase it modifies.]

Exercise 7 Identifying Adverbs

Identify the adverb in each of the following sentences. Then, give the word or words each adverb modifies.

EXAMPLE 1. Williamsburg is a very interesting place.
   1. very—interesting

1. Visitors to Williamsburg can truly imagine what life must have been like in the 1700s.
2. As you can see in the photo on the opposite page, Williamsburg was carefully built to resemble a small town of the past.
3. On one street a wigmaker slowly makes old-fashioned powdered wigs.
4. Nearby, a silversmith designs beautiful candlesticks, platters, and jewelry.

5. Down the block the bookbinder <u>skillfully</u> <u>crafts</u> book covers out of leather.

6. His neighbor, the blacksmith, <u>is</u> <u>certainly</u> important because he makes shoes for horses.

7. In colonial times people <u>could</u> <u>seldom</u> <u>afford</u> new shoes for themselves.

8. <u>Nowadays</u>, many curious tourists <u>visit</u> the bootmaker's shop.

9. Another <u>very</u> <u>popular</u> craftsman makes lovely musical instruments.

10. Williamsburg <u>definitely</u> <u>gives</u> tourists the feeling that they have visited the past.

Exercise 8 **Identifying Adverbs and the Words They Modify**

Each of the following sentences contains at least one adverb. Identify each adverb. Then, give the word each adverb modifies. Be prepared to tell whether the word modified is a verb, an adjective, or an adverb.

EXAMPLE   **1.** If you look closely at a world map, you can quite easily find Brazil.

    1. closely—look; quite—easily; easily—can find

1. The nation of Brazil actually covers almost half of the continent of South America.
2. A large portion of the Amazon rain forest grows there.
3. Many people have become more active in the preservation of the rain forest.
4. The loss of the rain forest may seriously affect the planet's climate.
5. Very early in the sixteenth century, Brazil was colonized by the Portuguese.
6. The country later became an independent republic.
7. Brazilians often say *Bom día*, which means "good day" in Portuguese.
8. In Brazil, sports fans can almost always find a soccer game in progress.
9. Brasília, the capital of Brazil, is an extremely modern city.
10. My aunt travels frequently, but she hasn't been to Brasília.

┌─HELP─┐

In the example sentence in Exercise 8, *look* is a verb, *easily* is an adverb, and *can find* is a verb.

Exercise 8 **Identifying Adverbs and the Words They Modify**

ANSWERS

1. actually—covers (verb)
2. there—grows (verb)
3. more—active (adjective)
4. seriously—may affect (verb)
5. Very—early (adverb); early—was colonized (verb)
6. later—became (verb)
7. often—say (verb)
8. almost—always (adverb); always—can find (verb)
9. extremely—modern (adjective)
10. frequently—travels (verb); n't—has been (verb)

DIFFERENTIATING INSTRUCTION

Advanced Learners

To give students further practice using adverbs, have them use adverbs in descriptive paragraphs on such topics as getting a new pet, making dinner, or baby-sitting. Each student should use at least five adverbs to help make the paragraph clear and interesting. Have students underline the adverbs.

The Preposition

Rule 3c *(pp. 62–66)*

OBJECTIVES

- To identify prepositions and their objects
- To use appropriate prepositions in sentences
- To distinguish between adverbs and prepositions

DIRECT TEACHING

Modeling and Demonstration

Identifying Prepositions. Model how to identify prepositions by using the example *Your math book is on the table.* First, ask what word shows the relationship between *book* and *table.* [*on*] Then, read the example aloud, using different prepositions. Point out how different prepositions change the relationship between the book and the table. Now, have a volunteer demonstrate how to identify a preposition. Have the volunteer also supply different prepositions to show how the relationship expressed in the sentence changes.

Exercise 9 **Writing Appropriate Adverbs**

Write the following sentences. Then, fill in each blank with an appropriate adverb. Use a different adverb in each sentence.

EXAMPLE   **1.** ____ I learned some Spanish words.
 1. *Quickly, I learned some Spanish words.*
                          Adverbs will vary.

1. I ____ watch TV after school. **1.** never
2. You will ____ bait a hook yourself. **2.** soon
3. My little sister crept down the stairs ____. **3.** quietly
4. Do you think that you can ____ find the answer to the math problem? **4.** easily
5. She is ____ eager for lunch. **5.** very
6. In the evening, the African drums beat ____. **6.** loudly
7. People in the highest balcony could ____ hear the speakers onstage. **7.** not
8. Does thunder ____ follow lightning? **8.** always
9. Would you dim the light ____ for me? **9.** slightly
10. The sky over Honolulu was ____ clear that I could see for miles. **10.** so

The Preposition

3c. A *preposition* is a word that shows the relationship between a noun or a pronoun and another word in the sentence.

EXAMPLES   Your math book is **underneath** your coat, Allen. [The preposition *underneath* shows the relationship of *coat* to *book.*]

The one **behind** us honked his horn. [The preposition *behind* shows the relationship of *us* to *one.*]

Notice how changing the preposition in the following sentences changes the relationship between *hit* and *net.*

I hit the ball **over** the net.
I hit the ball **into** the net.
I hit the ball **under** the net.
I hit the ball **against** the net.
I hit the ball **across** the net.

| TIPS & TRICKS |

Many prepositions can be remembered as "anywhere a cat can go."

EXAMPLES
up the tree
behind the sofa
under the bed
through the door

RESOURCES

The Preposition
Practice
- *Language & Sentence Skills Practice,* pp. 55–57, 62–64
- *Developmental Language & Sentence Skills,* pp. 23–24

Commonly Used Prepositions		
aboard	between	past
about	beyond	since
above	by	through
across	down	throughout
after	during	till
against	except	to
along	for	toward
among	from	under
around	in	underneath
at	into	until
before	like	up
behind	of	upon
below	off	with
beneath	on	within
beside	over	without

Some prepositions are made up of more than one word. These are called ***compound prepositions.***

Some Compound Prepositions		
according to	in addition to	next to
aside from	in place of	on account of
because of	in spite of	out of

The Prepositional Phrase

A preposition always has at least one noun or pronoun as an object. This noun or pronoun is called the ***object of the preposition.*** The preposition, its object, and any modifiers of the object make up a ***prepositional phrase.*** Generally, the object of the preposition follows the preposition.

EXAMPLES   The pile **of dry leaves** had grown much larger. [The preposition *of* relates its object, *leaves*, to *pile*. The adjective *dry* modifies *leaves*.]

Reference Note

For more information about **prepositional phrases,** see Chapter 4.

The Preposition   **63**

DIFFERENTIATING INSTRUCTION

English-Language Learners
Spanish. In Spanish, the single preposition *a* can be translated as *in, on, at,* and many other English prepositions. Therefore, you may want to give students extra practice in using prepositions of place. The following generalizations and examples may prove helpful.

1. *In* is often used for cities, states, and countries. [*We live* in *Denver,* in *Colorado, and* in *the United States.*]

2. *On* is often used for streets. [*We live* on *Harris Street.*]

3. *At* is often used for addresses that include the number. [*We live* at *112 Harris Street.*]

Have students use the correct prepositions in sentences of their own.

English-Language Learners
Cantonese. Unlike English, Cantonese does not have a large range of prepositions. Since English preposition usage is unpredictable and idiomatic, Cantonese speakers may find prepositions difficult to master. Help students learn the patterns of preposition usage by teaching the prepositions along with the words they generally follow: *go to, come from.* Emphasize the prepositions you use when speaking to students.

*Would you like to go **to** the concert?*

*That jade piece came **from** China.*

Learning for Life

Continued on pp. 64–65

Writing and Performing a Skit. Discuss with students the comedy skits they have seen on TV. Point out that skits can also play a more serious role in education, in training films for the military or for businesses, and in helping people adjust to a new environment, such as a new school.

Brainstorm with students for topics on which a new student at your school might need instruction or advice. Arrange students in groups of four to select a topic and to prepare a skit to perform for the class.

DIFFERENTIATING INSTRUCTION

Learners Having Difficulty

Allow students to use the **Commonly Used Prepositions** list on p. 63 when they are completing **Exercises 10–12**. Make sure students understand that for a word to be a preposition, it must have a noun or pronoun object.

Special Education Students

Students can practice using prepositional phrases in sentences by working as a group to create variations on given sentences. One student will give a sentence with a prepositional phrase, such as "The dog walked by the bushes." Other students will create new sentences by changing the preposition or prepositional phrase. Once they have created several sentences, another student should give a new sentence with a preposition, and the other students can continue the activity.

| TIPS & TRICKS |

When you are looking for the object of a preposition, be careful. Sometimes the object comes before, not after, the preposition.

EXAMPLES
This is the movie that I told you about on Tuesday. [*That* is the object of the preposition *about.*]

| STYLE   TIP |

Ending a sentence with a preposition is becoming more accepted in casual speech and informal writing. However, in formal writing it is generally best to avoid doing so.

He poured sauce **over the pizza.** [The preposition *over* relates its object, *pizza,* to *poured.* The article *the* modifies *pizza.*]

A preposition may have more than one object.

EXAMPLES This flea collar is **for cats** and **dogs.** [The preposition *for* has the two objects *cats* and *dogs.*]

My big sister had to decide **between the University of Wisconsin** and **Carroll College.** [The preposition *between* has the two objects *the University of Wisconsin* and *Carroll College.*]

Exercise 10 Identifying Prepositions and Their Objects

Identify the prepositional phrase in each of the following sentences. Underline the preposition, and circle its object.

EXAMPLE 1. Otters are related to weasels and minks.

1. *to* (weasels) and (minks)

1. Yesterday afternoon, we planted a sapling behind the (garage).
2. I bought a pattern for a (sari).
3. They live near the (airport).
4. For his (birthday), my brother wants a guitar.
5. The pictures won't be developed until (Friday) or (Monday).
6. I received a letter from my (aunt) and (uncle).
7. The largest of all (falcons) is the arctic falcon.
8. What are the answers to the third and fourth (questions)?
9. There are many uses for (peanuts).
10. I think that you might need a graphing calculator for that (problem).

Exercise 11 Using Prepositions

Using the treasure map on the next page, give an appropriate preposition for each of the following sentences. Be sure to use a variety of prepositions. Prepositions may vary.

EXAMPLE 1. Can you find the *X* _____ this map?

1. *on*

1. Our rowboat rests _____ Mournful Beach. **1.** on
2. Follow the path _____ the treasure. **2.** to

Learning for Life   *Continued from p. 63*

Students' skits should last between three and five minutes and should focus on solving a problem related to a common situation at their school. One group member can play the new student; the other group members can offer help and advice.

After each group has written a rough draft of its skit, group members should work together to fine-tune the script, focusing on making the skit both informative and entertaining. Special attention should be paid to the use of the parts of

3. Notice that Skull Rock lies ____ the cliff.   **3.** on
4. A sandy path leads ____ the stone ruins.   **4.** from
5. Did you jump ____ the fallen tree along the cliff?   **5.** over
6. Don't slip ____ the path up Lookout Hill!   **6.** on
7. Walk ____ the river.   **7.** along
8. Go ____ the waterfall!   **8.** under
9. You need not walk ____ the woods.   **9.** through
10. The treasure is ____ the open field and the gnarled oak tree.

10. near

Preposition or Adverb?

Some words may be used as both prepositions and adverbs. Remember that a preposition always has at least one noun or pronoun as an object. An adverb never does. If you can't tell whether a word is used as an adverb or a preposition, look for an object.

PREPOSITION   Clouds gathered **above** us. [*Us* is the object of the preposition *above*.]

ADVERB   Clouds gathered **above**. [no object]

Advanced Learners

Provide students with copies of simple directions found with a recipe, a board game, or a common household product. Have students write *prep.* over the prepositions, *obj.* over the objects of verbs, and *o.p.* over objects of prepositions. Then, discuss how the use of prepositional phrases can make directions more understandable.

Learners Having Difficulty

Have students find pictures that show action scenes. Have each student describe the scene by writing five sentences containing prepositions. Then, have two students exchange pictures and sentences. Students should circle prepositions in their partners' sentences and then discuss what prepositions were used and why.

speech discussed in this chapter.

After allowing some rehearsal time, have each group perform its skit for the class. Groups could also perform their skits as part of an orientation for incoming students at the beginning of the next academic year.

GRAMMAR

The Conjunction

Rule 3d *(pp. 66–68)*

O B J E C T I V E

■ To identify conjunctions in sentences

DIRECT TEACHING

Modeling and Demonstration

Identifying Conjunctions. Model how to identify conjunctions by using the examples *beans and rice, after breakfast but before lunch,* and *The deer ran, for they smelled smoke* (conjunctions joining words, joining phrases, and joining clauses). First, explain to students that a *junction* is the place at which two roads join; similarly, a *conjunction* is a word that joins words, phrases, or clauses. Then, read the examples aloud, emphasizing the conjunctions. Next, have a volunteer demonstrate how to identify a conjunction by following the pattern of the examples and using the same conjunctions to join new words, phrases, and clauses. *(peanut butter and jelly, after class but before supper,* and *The puppy ran, for he was frightened)* Last, have a volunteer use another example from this chapter to demonstrate how to identify a conjunction.

⌐ TIPS & TRICKS ⌐

You can remember the coordinating conjunctions as FANBOYS:

For
And
Nor
But
Or
Yet
So

PREPOSITION	Meet me **outside** the gym tomorrow morning. [*Gym* is the object of the preposition *outside.*]
ADVERB	Meet me **outside** tomorrow morning. [no object]

Exercise 12 Identifying Adverbs and Prepositions

Identify the italicized word in each of the following sentences as either an *adverb* or a *preposition*.

EXAMPLE   **1.** *Above* us, wispy clouds filled the sky.
  1. preposition

1. Before it rains, bring your bike *in*.   **1.** adv.
2. Had you ever seen an authentic Chinese New Year Parade *before*?   **2.** adv.
3. Bright red and green lights sparkled *down* the street.   **3.** prep.
4. Smoke from the campfire quickly disappeared *in* the heavy fog.   **4.** prep.
5. Andy turned the log *over* and found fat, squirming worms.   **5.** adv.
6. A submarine surfaced *next to* an aircraft carrier.   **6.** prep.
7. Will we read a poem by Nikki Giovanni *next*?   **7.** adv.
8. Turn that stereo *down* right now!   **8.** adv.
9. Millicent, did you remember to send a thank-you note *to* Mr. Bernstein?   **9.** prep.
10. What kind *of* dog is that?   **10.** prep.

The Conjunction

3d. A *conjunction* is a word that joins words or groups of words.

A *coordinating conjunction* joins words or word groups that are used in the same way.

Coordinating Conjunctions						
and	but	for	nor	or	so	yet

CONJUNCTIONS	beans **and** rice	movies **or** television
JOINING WORDS	sad **but** true	Egypt, Italy, **and** Spain

RESOURCES

The Conjunction

Practice

■ *Language & Sentence Skills Practice,* pp. 58–59, 62–64
■ *Developmental Language & Sentence Skills,* pp. 25–26

CONJUNCTIONS JOINING PHRASES	could write **or** could telephone
	after breakfast **but** before lunch
	cooking dinner **and** fixing breakfast

CONJUNCTIONS JOINING CLAUSES	I wanted to call, **but** it was late.
	The deer ran, **for** they smelled smoke.
	We knocked on the door, **and** they answered.

Reference Note

For information on using **commas to join words, phrases, or clauses,** see page 268.

NOTE   The word *for* can be used either as a conjunction or as a preposition.

CONJUNCTION	The zebra turned toward the watering hole, **for** it was getting thirsty. [*For* joins the two sentences.]
PREPOSITION	The zebra lay down in the shade **for** a nap. [*For* shows the relationship between the object *nap* and the verb *lay.*]

Reference Note

For more information on using **prepositions,** see page 62.

Correlative conjunctions are pairs of conjunctions that join words or word groups that are used in the same way.

Correlative Conjunctions

both . . . . and	not only . . . but also
either . . . . or	whether . . . or
neither . . . . nor	

EXAMPLES   **Both** Michael Jordan **and** David Robinson planned to play in the charity softball game. [two nouns]

Chris turned **neither** to the west **nor** to the east. [two prepositional phrases]

Not only did Babe Didrikson Zaharias set world records in track and field, **but** she **also** won more than fifty golf tournaments. [two independent clauses]

Exercise 13 **Identifying Conjunctions**

Identify the conjunction in each of the following sentences.

EXAMPLE   **1.** Lena or I will pitch at batting practice.
          1. or

GRAMMAR

The conjunction *so* is often overused. Whenever you can, reword a sentence to avoid using *so*.

EXAMPLE
The scarves were on sale, so Hector bought two.

REVISED
Because the scarves were on sale, Hector bought two.

The Interjection
Rule 3e *(pp. 68–69)*

O B J E C T I V E

■ **To complete sentences by providing interjections**

DIRECT TEACHING

Modeling and Demonstration

Identifying Interjections. Model how to identify interjections by using the example *Aha! I knew you were hiding there.* First, point out to the students that an interjection is a word expressing emotion and that it does not modify any other word or have any grammatical relation to the rest of the sentence. Then, read the example aloud, emphasizing the interjection. Next, have a volunteer substitute a new interjection in the example. Last, have a volunteer use another example from this chapter to demonstrate how to identify an interjection.

MEETING THE CHALLENGE

Write a three-stanza poem in which each stanza consists of only a verb, an adverb, a prepositional phrase, a conjunction, and an interjection. (You can put the parts of speech in any order you choose.)

ANSWER
Poems will vary.

---

1. Julio <u>and</u> Roger joined the soccer team.
2. <u>Whether</u> it rains <u>or</u> not, we will be there.
3. Many Chinese plays include dancing <u>and</u> acrobatics.
4. The squirrels are burying nuts, <u>for</u> the long, cold winter will be here soon.
5. Did Nancy finish her final book report, <u>or</u> is she still working on it?
6. <u>Not only</u> strong <u>but also</u> graceful, the eagle is a beautiful bird.
7. He is not here, <u>nor</u> has he called.
8. The Boys Choir of Harlem will be singing tonight, <u>so</u> we bought tickets.
9. I already addressed the envelope <u>but</u> have not taken it to the post office yet.
10. I have enough money for <u>either</u> popcorn <u>or</u> juice.

The Interjection

3e. An *interjection* is a word that expresses emotion.

An interjection has no grammatical relation to the rest of the sentence.

Often, an interjection is followed by an exclamation point.

EXAMPLES   **Aha!** I knew you were hiding there.

Oops! I punched in the wrong numbers.

Is that a wasp? **Ouch!**

Sometimes an interjection is set off by a comma or a pair of commas.

EXAMPLES   **Well,** what do you think?

The fish weighed, **oh,** about three pounds.

It's time to go, **alas.**

Common Interjections			
aha	hey	ouch	whew
alas	hooray	ow	wow
aw	oh	ugh	yikes
goodness	oops	well	yippee

RESOURCES

The Interjection
Practice

■ *Language & Sentence Skills Practice,* p. 60, 62–64
■ *Developmental Language & Sentence Skills,* pp. 25–26

Exercise 14 Writing Interjections

Have you ever heard the expression "an accident waiting to happen"? How many accidents are waiting to happen in the picture below? Write appropriate interjections to complete the following sentences that the people in the picture might say.

EXAMPLE 1. ____, Vince, have you seen my other roller skate anywhere?

1. *Oh, Vince, have you seen my other roller skate anywhere?*   Interjections will vary.

1. ____! I almost sat on the cat. **1.** Oops
2. ____! Watch out for that book! **2.** Hey
3. ____! Something on the stove is burning. **3.** Uh-oh
4. ____, Lila! Be careful with that milk! **4.** Oh dear
5. ____, we will have to get a new cord for our lamp. **5.** Oh no
6. That smells so bad. ____! **6.** Ugh
7. Down the stairs comes Dad with, ____, the biggest present I've ever seen! **7.** oh my
8. At last the party is over. ____! What a relief! **8.** Whew
9. ____! Look out for the roller skate. **9.** Yikes
10. The party was, ____, interesting to say the least. **10.** well

┌─HELP─
In Exercise 14, use a variety of interjections from the list on the previous page.

GRAMMAR

Determining Parts of Speech

Rule 3f *(p. 70)*

O B J E C T I V E

■ To identify the parts of speech of words

DIRECT TEACHING

Modeling and Demonstration

Determining Parts of Speech. In reviewing parts of speech, emphasize that many words can be used as more than one part of speech. Model this fact by using the examples *Some scientists study bones* and *The professor's study was on the second floor of his house.* Point out that *study* is used as a verb in the first example and as a noun in the second example. Next, have a volunteer demonstrate how a word can be used as different parts of speech by using two other examples from this chapter.

Determining Parts of Speech

Activity. List the following words on the chalkboard, and have students create example sentences showing these words used as different parts of speech.

1. light [*noun, verb, adverb, adjective*]

2. fake [*noun, verb, adjective*]

3. turn [*noun, verb*]

4. well [*noun, adverb, adjective, verb, interjection*]

┌HELP─
You may want to review Chapter 2 before completing Review C.

Determining Parts of Speech

3f. The way a word is used in a sentence determines what part of speech the word is.

Remember that you cannot tell what part of speech a word is until you know how it is used in a particular sentence. The same word may be used as different parts of speech.

VERB	Do you **like** guacamole?
PREPOSITION	That looks **like** guacamole.
ADVERB	The cat climbed **up.**
PREPOSITION	The cat climbed **up** the tree.
NOUN	We threw pennies into the wishing **well.**
ADJECTIVE	Janice isn't feeling **well.**
ADVERB	Did you do **well** on the test?
INTERJECTION	**Well,** what did he say?

Review C Identifying Parts of Speech

Identify the italicized word or words in each of the following sentences as a *noun*, a *pronoun*, an *adjective*, a *verb*, an *adverb*, a *preposition*, a *conjunction*, or an *interjection*.

EXAMPLE   1. Some scientists *study* bones.

      1. study—verb

1. The fans lined up *outside* the stadium. **1.** prep.
2. *She* always drives to work. **2.** pro.
3. Those *plants* grow best in sandy soil. **3.** n.
4. *Either* Rhea *or* Susan bought paper cups for the party.
5. Their parents *own* a card store. **5.** v.   **4.** conj./conj.
6. N. Scott Momaday has written several books, *but* I have read only one of them. **6.** conj.
7. *Oops!* I dropped my backpack. **7.** int.
8. We play *outdoors* every day until dinner time. **8.** adv.
9. This videotape looks *new.* **9.** adj.
10. You don't sound *too* happy. **10.** adv.

RESOURCES

Determining Parts of Speech

Practice

■ *Language & Sentence Skills Practice,* pp. 61–64

Chapter Review

Terms and numerals in brackets refer to concepts and rules tested by the items in the Chapter Review.

1.–5. [verb phrase and helping verb]

A. Identifying Verb Phrases and Helping Verbs

Identify the verb phrase in each of the following sentences. Then, underline each helping verb.

1. Tolbert could not see his brother in the fog.
2. Does Nguyen know the words to the song?
3. Dana might come to the party after all.
4. You should have brought your friend home for our special Chinese dinner last night.
5. Will you join the dance?

B. Identifying Action and Linking Verbs

6. link. [linking verb]
7. act. [action verb]
8. link. [linking verb]
9. act. [action verb]
10. act. [action verb]
11. tran. [transitive verb]
12. int. [intransitive verb]
13. int. [intransitive verb]
14. tran. [transitive verb]
15. int. [intransitive verb]

Identify the verb in each of the following sentences as an *action verb* or a *linking verb*.

6. Ivan will be a superb guitar player someday.
7. Our dog Tadger brought an old bone home yesterday.
8. The whole-wheat bread smelled delicious.
9. Jacqui smelled the exhaust of the huge truck in the next lane of the freeway.
10. Will you look for me in the parade tomorrow?

C. Identifying Transitive and Intransitive Verbs

For each of the following sentences, identify the italicized verb as *transitive* or *intransitive*.

11. Francisco *opened* the door to the cellar.
12. Even the judge *seemed* uncertain about the answer.
13. The piano player *performs* twice each night.
14. We *performed* the play three times that weekend.
15. We *dine* every night at seven.

Chapter Review   **71**

RETEACHING

Determining Parts of Speech

Activity. Arrange students in groups, and have each group use colored construction paper to make eight sets of cards—one set each for nouns, pronouns, adjectives, verbs, adverbs, prepositions, conjunctions, and interjections. Each set of cards should have five examples of that part of speech, each on a separate card. All cards in a set should be the same color. Ask the groups to take a minimum of three cards from each set and to create three complete sentences by stringing the parts of speech together appropriately. Students can use extra words as necessary, but they must make use of all the parts of speech that they select.

ASSESSING

Monitoring Progress

Chapter Review. To assess student progress, you may want to compare the types of items missed on the **Diagnostic Preview** with those missed on the **Chapter Review.** You may want to work on specific goals with individual students who are still having difficulty mastering essential information.

RESOURCES

Parts of Speech Overview
Review
■ *Language & Sentence Skills Practice,* pp. 62–64
Assessment
■ *Progress Assessment for the Holt Handbook,* pp. 5–6, 41
■ *Test Generator (One-Stop Planner CD-ROM)*

D. Identifying Adverbs and the Words They Modify

Identify the adverb or adverbs in each of the following sentences. Then, give the word each adverb modifies.

16.–20. [adverbs]

16. Mr. Chavez never watches television, but he listens to the radio often.

17. Carefully open the dryer, and check to see whether the clothes are too wet.

18. early–Did awake/ very–early

18. Did you awake very early?

19. Our old cat creeps gingerly from room to room.

20. Recently, I received an extremely interesting letter from my pen pal in Italy.

E. Identifying Prepositions and Their Objects

Identify the prepositional phrase in each of the following sentences. Underline the preposition and circle its object.

21.-25. [3c, object of preposition]

21. Tanya's pet hamster likes sleeping behind the computer.

22. Has your house ever lost power during a thunderstorm?

23. Some animals hunt only between dusk and dawn.

24. Bring me the largest head of lettuce, please.

25. According to my father, my uncle was a carpenter.

F. Identifying Verbs, Adverbs, Prepositions, Conjunctions, and Interjections

Identify each italicized word or word group in the following sentences as a *verb*, an *adverb*, a *preposition*, a *conjunction*, or an *interjection*.

26. prep. [3c]

27. v. [3a]

28. int. [3e]

29. v./adv. [3a, b]

30. v./conj. [3a, d]

26. I always have fun *at* a water park.

27. You *can slide* as fast as a sled down the huge water slide.

28. *Wow*! What a truly exciting ride that is!

29. Some parks *rent* inner tubes *inexpensively*.

30. You *may become* tired, *but* you won't be bored.

G. Determining Parts of Speech

Identify the italicized word in each of the following sentences as a *verb*, an *adjective*, an *adverb*, a *preposition*, or an *interjection*.

31. *Well*, I suppose you know what you are doing.

32. Ms. Jefferson will not be back in school until she is *well*.

33. When I sat down on the couch, my sister moved *over*.

34. The bowls are in the cupboard *over* the sink.

35. Did you *test* the batteries before you installed them?

31. int. [3f, e]

32. adj. [3f, 2c]

33. adv. [3f, b]

34. prep. [3f, c]

35. v. [3f, a]

Writing Application
Using Verbs in a List

Helping Verbs and Linking Verbs   You and your classmates have decided to list some goals for the coming year. The theme for your lists is "How I Can Make the World a Better Place." Write a list of ten or more goals or resolutions for yourself. Make each of your resolutions a complete sentence. In your list, use the verb form *be* at least two times as a helping verb and three times as a linking verb.

Prewriting   First, think of some realistic goals you can set for yourself. List as many goals as you can.

Writing   From your list, choose the resolutions that seem the most important and the most manageable. Write each of them as a complete sentence.

Revising   Read through your list. Are your resolutions clear and specific? Will you really be able to keep them? If not, revise or replace some of the resolutions.

Publishing   Be sure that you've used a form of the verb *be* as a helping verb twice and as a linking verb three times. Make sure that all of your sentences are complete. Identify each helping verb and linking verb. Do a final check for errors in grammar, spelling, and punctuation. You and your classmates may want to have everyone in the class submit one or two of their favorite resolutions and compile a list of resolutions for the entire class. Post the list on the bulletin board.

Reference Note

For information on **complete sentences,** see page 386.

APPLICATION

Writing Application

Prewriting Tip. Students may find it helpful to categorize their lists in the prewriting stage so that they can start their writing with specific areas for improvement in mind. For example, they might brainstorm goals having to do with schoolwork, social life, homework, or family obligations.

Scoring Rubric. While you will want to pay particular attention to students' use of *be* as a helping verb and a linking verb, you may also want to evaluate overall writing performance. You may want to give a split score to indicate development and clarity of the composition as well as grammar skills.

Chapter Review   **73**

1.0 Written and Oral English Language Conventions

Students write and speak with a command of standard English conventions appropriate to this grade level.

1.1 Use simple, compound, and compound-complex sentences; use effective coordination and subordination of ideas to express complete thoughts.

1.3 Use semicolons to connect independent clauses and commas when linking two clauses with a conjunction in compound sentences.

Numerals in brackets refer to rules tested by the items in the Diagnostic Preview.

1. adv. [4d]
2. adv. [4d]
3. adj. [4c]
4. adv. [4d]
5. adj. [4c]
6. adj. [4c]

The Phrase and the Clause

Prepositional Phrases, Independent and Subordinate Clauses, Sentence Structure

Diagnostic Preview

A. Identifying Adjective Phrases and Adverb Phrases

Identify the prepositional phrase in each of the following sentences, and tell whether the phrase is used as an *adjective phrase* or an *adverb phrase*. Then, give the word or words that the phrase modifies.

EXAMPLE   1. This newspaper article on weather patterns is interesting.

1. *on weather patterns; adjective phrase—article*

1. The hikers are ready for a break.
2. Yesterday we rode our bikes through the park.
3. That store has something for everyone.
4. The Reverend Jesse Jackson spoke at the convention.
5. Most children like books with colorful pictures.
6. Students from both South America and North America attended the meet.

7. I wear heavy wool socks <u>under my hiking boots</u>.
8. Joel and Tina <u>are participating in the Special Olympics</u>.
9. The <u>door to the secret room</u> is locked.
10. <u>According to the map</u>, Tony's farm is just ahead.

7. adv. [4d]
8. adv. [4d]
9. adj. [4c]
10. adv. [4d]

B. Identifying Independent Clauses and Subordinate Clauses

For each of the following items, identify the italicized word group as either an *independent clause* or a *subordinate clause*.

EXAMPLE   **1.** Marco got the tables ready *while Nestor set up the chairs.*

       1. subordinate clause

11. *When school is out,* these halls seem quite lonely.
12. As far as I can tell, the red piece goes right here, and *the green piece goes under there.*
13. *If you exercise regularly,* your endurance will increase.
14. Just before the train sped across the road, *the bell rang,* and the gate went down.
15. *Geronimo,* who was a leader of the Apache, *died in the early part of the twentieth century.*

11. sub. [4g]
12. ind. [4f]
13. sub. [4g]
14. ind. [4f]
15. ind. [4f]

C. Identifying Types of Sentences

Identify each of the following sentences as <u>simple</u>, <u>compound</u>, <u>complex</u>, or <u>compound-complex</u>.

EXAMPLE   **1.** Mom is late, but she will be here soon.

       1. compound

16. Jaleel learned several African folk tales and recited them.
17. Raccoons and opossums steal our garbage as the dogs bark at them from inside the house.
18. The school bus stopped suddenly, but no one was hurt.
19. The dance committee has chosen a Hawaiian theme, so the volunteers will decorate the gym with flowers and greenery while Todd finds the right music.
20. Luis Gonzalez stepped up to the plate, and the crowd roared enthusiastically.

16. s. [4j]
17. cx. [4l]
18. cd. [4k]
19. cd.-cx. [4m]
20. cd. [4k]

adjective phrases and adverb phrases. The chapter then defines the clause and explains independent and subordinate clauses. The section on subordinate clauses includes treatment of adjective and adverb clauses. Finally, the chapter discusses sentence structure, focusing on simple and compound sentences but also including a look at complex and compound-complex sentences.

- The chapter closes with a **Chapter Review** including a **Writing Application** feature that asks students to write a narrative using adjective and adverb phrases.

- For help in integrating this chapter with writing assignments in *Holt Literature and Language Arts,* use the **Teaching Strands** chart on pages T22–T23.

ASSESSING

Entry-Level Assessment

Diagnostic Preview. You may wish to use the **Diagnostic Preview** to evaluate students' understanding of prepositional phrases, independent and subordinate clauses, and sentence structure. You may want to assess **Parts A, B,** and **C** separately to help you determine which areas might require more emphasis. Going over the answers orally in class may serve as a helpful review for some students.

Differentiating Instruction
- *Lesson Plans for Language Development*
- *Supporting Instruction in Five Languages*
- *At Home: In Five Languages*

Assessment
- *Diagnostic & Summative Assessments, First Quarter Test*

- *Progress Assessment for the Holt Handbook,* pp. 7–8, 41
- *Test Generator (One-Stop Planner CD-ROM)*

Other Language Resources
- *Spelling Lessons & Activities*
- *Vocabulary Development*
- *Daily Language Activities Transparencies*

PRETEACHING

Lesson Starter

Motivating. Ask students to suggest humorous answers to the question "Where would be a bad place to have a picnic?" Start students off by writing on the chalkboard *in traffic* and *on a yak*. Write students' suggestions on the chalkboard, and then point out that the groups of words are all prepositional phrases that tell *where* the action happens. If added to the sentence *Do not have a picnic . . .* , each of the phrases would modify the verb phrase *Do have.*

The Phrase

Rule 4a *(p. 76)*

OBJECTIVE

■ **To determine whether given groups of words are phrases**

DIRECT TEACHING

Modeling and Demonstration

The Phrase. Model how to identify a group of words as a phrase by using the example *could have been looking.* First, ask if the example *could have been looking* has a subject. [*no*] Then, ask whether the example has a verb. [*Yes, it is a verb.*] Then, ask whether the example is used as a single part of speech. [*Yes, it is used as a verb.*] Point out that since the definition of a phrase is "a group of related words that is used as a single part of speech and that does not contain both a verb and its subject," the example is a phrase. Now, have a volunteer demonstrate how to identify a group of words as a phrase, using another example from this chapter.

Reference Note
For more about **clauses,** see page 89.

The Phrase

4a. A *phrase* is a group of related words that is used as a single part of speech and that does not contain both a verb and its subject.

EXAMPLES could have been looking [no subject]

in the backyard [no subject or verb]

to reach the highest shelf [no subject or verb]

NOTE If a word group has both a subject and a verb, it is called a *clause.*

EXAMPLES The coyote howled. [*Coyote* is the subject of the verb *howled.*]

when Al left [*Al* is the subject of the verb *left.*]

Phrases cannot stand alone as sentences. They must be used with other words to make a complete sentence.

PHRASE **in the box**
SENTENCE We put the CD's **in the box.**

Exercise 1 Identifying Phrases

Identify each of the following word groups as *a phrase* or *not a phrase.*

EXAMPLE 1. some people enjoy skiing
1. *not a phrase*

1. not a phrase
2. phrase
3. not a phrase
4. phrase
5. phrase
6. not a phrase
7. phrase
8. phrase
9. not a phrase
10. not a phrase

1. ski lifts are used for Alpine skiing
2. down the snowy hills
3. slalom skiers race through gates
4. during the race
5. before the other skiers
6. skiers love the Colorado slopes
7. with tiny snowflakes on my face
8. for a hot cup of soup
9. we sat beside the cozy fire
10. maybe I can go again next year

RESOURCES

The Phrase
Practice
■ *Language & Sentence Skills Practice,* p. 69

Prepositional Phrases

4b. A *prepositional phrase* includes a preposition, the object of the preposition, and any modifiers of that object.

The prepositional phrase is one kind of phrase. Prepositions show the relationship of a noun or pronoun to another word in the sentence. The noun or pronoun that follows a preposition is called the **object of the preposition.** A preposition, its object, and any modifiers of the object are all part of the prepositional phrase.

EXAMPLES
> The man **from Singapore** was giving a speech. [The preposition *from* shows the relationship between the object *Singapore* and the noun *man.*]
>
> The tree **in front of the window** blocks our view. [The compound preposition *in front of* shows the relationship between the object *window* and the noun *tree. The* modifies *window.*]
>
> Please hand me the book **on the long, green table.** [The preposition *on* shows the relationship between the object *table* and the noun *book.* The adjectives *the, long,* and *green* modify *table.*]

A preposition may have more than one object.

EXAMPLES
> Aaron showed his arrowhead collection to **Tranh** and **her.** [The preposition *to* has two objects.]
>
> The dinner of **baked chicken, salad,** and **two vegetables** also came with dessert. [The preposition *of* has three objects.]

Exercise 2 Identifying Prepositional Phrases and Their Objects

For each of the following sentences, identify the <u>prepositional phrase</u> and circle the (object or objects) of the preposition.

EXAMPLE
> **1.** Dinosaurs and other giant reptiles roamed across the earth sixty-five million years ago.
>
> *1. across the (earth)*

1. Although some of the (dinosaurs) were enormous, others were quite small.

Reference Note

For more about **objects of prepositions,** see page 63.

Prepositional Phrases
Rules 4b–d *(pp. 77–89)*

OBJECTIVES

- To identify prepositional phrases and their objects in sentences

- To complete sentences by using prepositional phrases

- To identify adjective phrases and the words they modify

- To complete sentences by using adjective phrases

- To identify adverb phrases and the words they modify

- To write sentences using adverb phrases

GRAMMAR

DIRECT TEACHING

Modeling and Demonstration

Prepositional Phrases. Model how to identify a prepositional phrase by using the example *Please hand me the book on the long, green table.* First, ask which word is the preposition. [*on*] Then, ask which word is the object of the preposition. [*table*] Ask if there are any modifiers. [*yes; the, long, green*] Then, point out that the preposition, the object of the preposition, and any modifiers make up a prepositional phrase; therefore, *on the long, green table* is a prepositional phrase. Finally, point out that the preposition *on* shows the relationship between the book and the table. Now, have a volunteer use another example from this chapter to demonstrate how to identify a prepositional phrase.

GRAMMAR

DIFFERENTIATING INSTRUCTION

English-Language Learners

General Strategies. In some languages, prepositions come after their objects. For example, *in the house* would be "the house in." Other languages do not always use prepositions, so that *I went to the train station* would be "I go arrive train station." If your English-language learners use similar constructions in English, ask them how the phrases are spoken in their native languages. Then, explain how prepositions are used in English, and point out differences in usage.

Special Education Students

Pair students, and give each pair an object such as a paperweight. Partners can take turns writing prepositional phrases and demonstrating them by using the object. For example, they might position the object "under the desk" or "on my head." Challenge each pair to act out and list at least ten such phrases.

Advanced Learners

Many songs make use of prepositional phrases. You can give students the example of the old Thanksgiving song "Over the River and Through the Woods." Have students compose their own songs, using prepositional phrases to describe a journey. Students can set their songs to well-known melodies or to original tunes and can perform their compositions for the class.

─HELP─

Like some prepositional phrases, an *infinitive* is a word group beginning with the word *to*. However, a prepositional phrase has a noun or pronoun as its object, while an infinitive contains *to* and a verb form.

2. The drawing on this (page) includes a stegosaurus, twenty feet long, and a saltopus, about two feet long.
3. Many dinosaurs fed on (plants) and (vegetables).
4. Dinosaurs with sharp (teeth) ate flesh.
5. Can you imagine seeing this flying reptile, the pterodactyl, above (you)?
6. It once lived in (Europe) and (Africa).
7. Until a few (years) ago, scientists believed that all dinosaurs were coldblooded.
8. According to recent (studies), however, some dinosaurs may have been warmblooded.
9. Many scientists say that birds and crocodiles may be related to (dinosaurs).
10. Some people in (science) even claim that birds are living dinosaurs.

Exercise 3 **Identifying Prepositional Phrases and Their Objects**

Identify the prepositional phrase in each of the following sentences. Underline each preposition, and circle its (object) or objects.

EXAMPLE
1. The package was for my brother and me.
1. *for my (brother) and (me)*

1. The Sahara is a huge desert that lies south of the (Mediterranean).

2. We waited until lunchtime.
3. The house across the street has green shutters.
4. Do not make repairs on the brakes yourself.
5. Maura said that the word *lasso* comes from a Spanish word that means "snare."
6. May I sit between you and him?
7. The woman in the blue uniform is my aunt.
8. The *Cherokee Phoenix* was the first newspaper printed in an American Indian language.
9. He is saving money for a stereo and a guitar.
10. The messenger slipped the note under the door.

Oral Practice **Using Appropriate Prepositional Phrases**

Read the following sentences aloud, filling in each blank with an appropriate prepositional phrase. Answers will vary.

EXAMPLE   **1.** We saw Jason ____.

    1. *We saw Jason at the mall.*

1. My favorite comedian will appear ____.
2. That bus always arrives ____.
3. The fans ____ cheered every score.
4. The children tumbled ____.
5. The light ____ is broken.
6. Our car waited ____.
7. ____ sat a bald eagle.
8. A rich vein of gold ran ____.
9. ____ dashed a frightened squirrel.
10. His grandmother told us a story ____.

1. at the party
2. after five o'clock
3. at the game
4. in the yard
5. over the door
6. at the curb
7. On the branch
8. through the mountain
9. Across the street
10. about Mexico

Adjective Phrases

4c. A prepositional phrase that modifies a noun or pronoun is called an *adjective phrase.*

In other words, an adjective phrase is a prepositional phrase that is used as an adjective.

ADJECTIVE   **Icy** chunks fell from the skyscraper.
ADJECTIVE PHRASE   Chunks **of ice** fell from the skyscraper.

Reference Note

For more information about **adjectives,** see page 38.

EXTENSION

Critical Thinking

Metacognition. After students have completed the exercises, have them think of the strategies they use to identify prepositional phrases. Do they first find the preposition and then the object? How do they determine which other words are part of the prepositional phrase? Do they make sure that what they think is a prepositional phrase does not contain a subject and verb?

Prepositional Phrases   **79**

DIFFERENTIATING INSTRUCTION

English-Language Learners

General Strategies. To help students see how adjective phrases can help make descriptions precise, bring several pictures of the same type of object to class. For example, you could use several magazine advertisements of cars. Ask students to use adjective phrases to identify and distinguish among the objects.

STYLE TIP

You can use adjective phrases to add details to your writing or to combine ideas into one sentence.

ORIGINAL
His favorite pastime is reading books.

REVISED
His favorite pastime is reading books **about space exploration.**

ORIGINAL
The squirrel was in the top of the tree. The squirrel chattered at me.

REVISED
The squirrel **in the top of the tree** chattered at me.

Adjective phrases answer the same questions that single-word adjectives answer.

What kind?	Which one?
How many?	How much?

EXAMPLES   Mr. Arnaud ordered a dinner **of boiled crawfish.**
[The adjective phrase modifies the noun *dinner.* The phrase answers the question *What kind?*]

The one **with the big pockets** costs a little more.
[The adjective phrase modifies the pronoun *one.* The phrase answers the question *Which one?*]

There was enough room **for only three people.** [The adjective phrase modifies the noun *room.* The phrase answers the question *How much?*]

Notice in these examples that an adjective phrase generally follows the word it modifies.

Exercise 4   Identifying Adjective Phrases

Identify the adjective phrase in each of the following sentences. Then, give the word that the phrase modifies.

EXAMPLE   1. Diego Rivera was a famous painter from Mexico.
1. *from Mexico—painter*

1. People throughout the world enjoy Rivera's art.
2. One photograph on the next page shows an indoor mural that he painted.
3. Rivera often painted the walls of buildings.
4. His murals are beautiful examples of popular twentieth-century art.
5. Rivera's artworks often include symbols of Mexican culture.
6. His work with other Mexican artists was also very important.
7. Rivera was a major influence on the mural artist Juan O'Gorman.

8. O'Gorman's <u>mural</u> on the left beautifies a university library.

9. O'Gorman does not paint his murals; instead, he uses tiny <u>pieces</u> of colored tile.

10. The complicated <u>pattern</u> upon the library walls fascinates everyone who sees it.

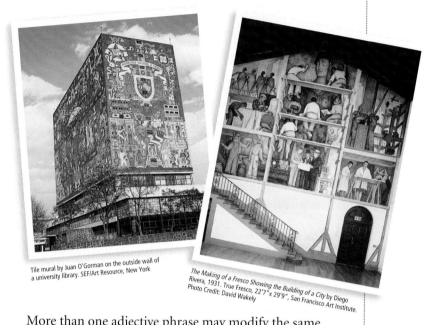

Tile mural by Juan O'Gorman on the outside wall of a university library. SEF/Art Resource, New York

The Making of a Fresco Showing the Building of a City by Diego Rivera, 1931. True Fresco, 22'7"x 29'9", San Francisco Art Institute. Photo Credit: David Wakely

More than one adjective phrase may modify the same noun or pronoun.

EXAMPLE That painting **of sunflowers by van Gogh** is famous. [The two adjective phrases, *of sunflowers* and *by van Gogh,* both answer the question *Which painting?*]

An adjective phrase may also modify the object of another adjective phrase.

EXAMPLE A number **of the paintings by that artist** are landscapes. [The adjective phrase *of the paintings* answers the question *What kind of number?* The adjective phrase *by that artist* answers the question *Which paintings?*]

Prepositional Phrases   **81**

DIFFERENTIATING INSTRUCTION

Advanced Learners
Challenge students to write sentences that contain a second adjective phrase that modifies the object of the first adjective phrase in the sentence. Students can also work in small groups to create sentences containing strings of adjective phrases, each of which modifies the object of the preceding phrase. Have students share their sentences with the class.

┌HELP──── ⊗
Some sentences
in Exercise 5 contain more
than one adjective phrase.

Exercise 5 **Identifying Adjective Phrases**

Identify each <u>adjective phrase</u> in the following sentences. Then, give the <u>noun or pronoun the phrase modifies</u>.

EXAMPLE **1.** This book about birds of North America has won many awards for photography.

1. *about birds—book; of North America—birds; for photography—awards*

[*Of flight* and *in the survival* both modify *importance.*]

1. It explains the <u>importance</u> <u>of flight</u> <u>in the survival</u> <u>of the bird population</u>.

2. The <u>key</u> <u>to successful flight</u> is the <u>structure</u> <u>of the feather</u>.

3. As you can see, the shaft and the vane are the two main <u>parts</u> <u>of a feather</u>.

4. The <u>area</u> <u>inside the quill</u> <u>of a feather</u> is hollow.

5. <u>Barbs</u> <u>on the shaft</u> form a feather's vane.

6. The <u>curves</u> <u>in the vane</u> and the <u>notches</u> <u>of the feather</u> permit easy, quick movement.

7. The <u>wings</u> <u>of airplanes</u> resemble birds' wings.

8. <u>Feathers</u> <u>on the wings and tails</u> <u>of birds</u> often are quite showy.

9. Fast-flying <u>birds</u> <u>like swifts</u> usually have pointed wings.

10. Have you ever seen <u>any</u> <u>of the birds</u> that have these <u>kinds</u> <u>of feathers</u>?

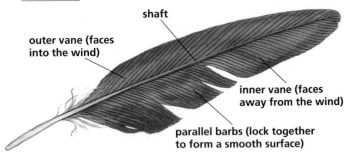

shaft

outer vane (faces into the wind)

inner vane (faces away from the wind)

parallel barbs (lock together to form a smooth surface)

Exercise 6 **Writing Adjective Phrases**

Fill in the blank in each of the following sentences with an appropriate adjective phrase. Answers will vary.

EXAMPLE **1.** That storm _____ might be dangerous.

1. *That storm from the east might be dangerous.*

RETEACHING

Adjective Phrases

You may wish to provide each student with a sample design or picture, and then pairs of students can practice using adjective phrases in conjunction with drawing. Each student can use adjective phrases to describe the design or picture to a partner. The partner then uses the student's description to draw the design or picture without having seen it. Partners can compare the finished drawings with the originals and brainstorm for adjective phrases that would have helped make the drawing more accurate.

CONTENT-AREA CONNECTIONS

Science

Scientific Description. Point out to students that **Exercise 5** shows how adjective phrases can be used in scientific description. Tell students that adjective phrases are an important part of classification, especially in distinguishing one species or substance from another.

Ask each student to write a brief paragraph or two on a scientific topic of his or her choice. (Students who have difficulty choosing a topic may want to discuss possibilities with their science teachers.) Have students describe the topic using at least six adjective phrases, and have them underline the phrases.

1. The shelf _____ is too high to reach.
2. I certainly hope that my gorilla costume wins a prize _____.
3. The girl _____ is one of my best friends.
4. The argument _____ really wasn't very important.
5. My favorite birthday present was the one _____.
6. Give your ticket to the man _____.
7. Did you see a bear on your trip _____?
8. Put the groceries _____ away, please.
9. My sister is the girl _____.
10. As I looked around the house, I noticed that an African design decorated the wall _____.

1. in the kitchen
2. for originality
3. in that picture
4. over tickets
5. from Aunt Rita
6. at the gate
7. to Montana
8. on the counter
9. with blond hair
10. of the living room

Adverb Phrases

4d. **A prepositional phrase that is used to modify a verb, an adjective, or an adverb is called an *adverb phrase*.**

In other words, an adverb phrase is a prepositional phrase that is used as an adverb.

ADVERB	We walk **there** every Saturday.
ADVERB PHRASE	We walk **along the lake** every Saturday.

Adverb phrases answer the same questions that single-word adverbs answer.

When?	Where?	Why?
How?	How often?	How long?

EXAMPLES The statue stands **next to a large oak tree.** [The adverb phrase modifies the verb *stands* and answers the question *Where?*]

Ready **by dawn,** the travelers set out early to reach the capital. [The adverb phrase modifies the adjective *Ready* and answers the question *When?*]

Are these jeans long enough **for you**? [The adverb phrase modifies the adverb *enough* and answers the question *How?*]

Reference Note

For more about **adverbs,** see page 59.

DIFFERENTIATING INSTRUCTION

Learners Having Difficulty
Write the sentence *We rode our bicycles* on the chalkboard. Ask students to suggest adverb phrases to complete the sentence, and write these phrases on the board as well. Remind students that their adverb phrases should modify the verb *rode*. Then, review students' phrases and lead the class to see that the phrases answer the same questions as single-word adverbs: *When? Where? Why? How? How often? How long?*

English-Language Learners
General Strategies. Some students may have problems deciding which preposition to use when writing adverb phrases about transportation. If students are confused about the uses of *in* and *on,* tell them that as a general rule, *on* is used for vehicles that carry only one person: "get *on* a motorcycle or bicycle." For vehicles that carry several people, *in* is used: "get *in* the car or canoe." For vehicles that carry about twenty or more people, *on* is again used: "get *on* the plane or train."

Cantonese. Adverbs usually come before verbs and adjectives in Cantonese, so a Cantonese-speaking student may tend to place all adverbs and adverb phrases at the front of the sentence: *This weekend on Saturday, I played soccer.*

Have students practice sentence variety by placing adverbs and adverb phrases at the beginning and at the end of sentences, and discuss differences in emphasis and meaning.

From Sarah, I received a pretty bracelet.

I received a pretty bracelet from Sarah.

Exercise 7

DISTRIBUTED REVIEW
Have students identify the verb in sentences 1, 2, 7, and 9. Then, have them classify each verb as an action verb or a linking verb. [1. *hung—action verb;* 2. *is—linking verb;* 7. *jogs—action verb;* 9. *were—linking verb*]

EXTENSION

Relating to Literature
If Lloyd Alexander's short story "The Stone" is in students' literature book, ask students to read and discuss it. Then, ask them to identify as many adverb phrases as possible in the first four paragraphs. You may want to read those paragraphs aloud, omitting the adverb phrases to demonstrate how different the story would be without them.

NOTE Adverb phrases may appear anywhere in a sentence. They may come before or after the words they modify. Also, other words may come between an adverb phrase and the word or words it modifies.

EXAMPLES **After swimming lessons,** Aunt Helen drove us home.

Dad has been afraid **of snakes** since he was a boy.

We rode our bikes **over the bridge.**

Exercise 7 **Identifying Adverb Phrases**

Identify the adverb phrase used in each of the following sentences. Then, write the word or words the phrase modifies.

EXAMPLE 1. My hamster disappeared for three days.
1. *for three days—disappeared*

1. That mirror hung in the front hall.
2. The cat is afraid of thunderstorms.
3. The normally graceful acrobat plunged into the net but did not hurt herself.
4. Jimmy Smits will speak at our school.
5. Mom discovered several field mice in the cellar.
6. With great courage, Rosa Parks disobeyed the bus driver.
7. She jogs around the reservoir every morning.
8. In the evenings, they played word games.
9. Soon, my shoes were full of sand.
10. We have planted several new varieties of day lilies along the fence.

As with adjective phrases, more than one adverb phrase can modify the same word.

EXAMPLE Cesar Chavez worked **with the United Farm Workers for many years.** [Both adverb phrases, *with the United Farm Workers* and *for many years,* modify the verb *worked.*]

An adverb phrase may be followed by an adjective phrase that modifies the object of the preposition in the adverb phrase.

EXAMPLE Yesterday we went **to an exhibit of rare coins.** [The adverb phrase *to an exhibit* modifies the verb *went.* The adjective phrase *of rare coins* modifies *exhibit,* the object of the preposition in the adverb phrase.]

Exercise 8 **Identifying Adverb Phrases**

Identify the <u>adverb phrase</u> used in each of the following sentences. After each phrase, give the <u>word or words the phrase modifies</u>.

EXAMPLES 1. On Passover evening, we prepare a Seder, which is a Jewish holiday meal and ceremony.

1. *On Passover evening—prepare*

2. Passover celebrates a time long ago when Jewish slaves freed themselves from their masters.

2. *from their masters—freed*

1. On Passover, many of our relatives visit our home.
2. We always invite them for the Seder.
3. Our whole family helps with the preparations.
4. Soon, everything is ready for this special meal.
5. In this photograph you can see how beautiful our holiday table is.
6. Holding all the special Passover foods, the Seder plate is displayed in the center of the table.
7. On the plate is a roasted egg representing new life.
8. Horseradish, which represents slavery's bitterness, is placed near the egg.
9. The other carefully arranged foods are also used during the Passover feast.
10. Throughout the entire meal, everyone enjoys a variety of delicious foods.

EXTENSION

Looking at Language

Discuss with students the impact that colloquialisms have on the English language. Colloquialisms, the colorful expressions used in everyday conversation, usually have understood meanings that are different from the literal meanings of the words used. Colloquialisms give our speaking and writing a casual, conversational tone. Share with students the following colloquial expressions, each of which contains a prepositional phrase.

Would you **get off my back**?

Is Dan **in the doghouse** again?

Success is **just around the corner.**

Our experiment **went down the tubes.**

He's **gone off the deep end.**

See whether students can come up with other colloquialisms that contain prepositional phrases.

Learning for Life

Continued on pp. 86–87

Writing a Travel Brochure. Bring to class a number of travel brochures, and discuss with students the descriptions and directions found in the texts. You may want to have students circle the prepositional phrases they find.

If possible, have someone from the area visitors' bureau speak to the class about local attractions. Ask the class to suggest their own favorite sites as well, and list the

GRAMMAR

Exercise 9 **Writing Sentences with Adverb Phrases**

POSSIBLE ANSWERS
Sentences will vary. Here are some possibilities:

1. Down the hall walked Mr. Ramond.

2. The mascot stood by them.

3. I saw them in the mall.

4. The ball rolled under the car.

5. She stepped onto the diving board.

6. We held the banners high over our heads.

7. This basket was made by a Navajo woman.

8. Through the sky the rocket rose.

9. I will arrive at five o'clock sharp.

10. Those sculptures were imported from Egypt.

APPLICATION

Relating to Writing

Ask students to examine pieces of their own writing for the use of prepositional phrases. Ask if they can see places where they could add prepositional phrases to make their meanings clearer or to make their writing more detailed and interesting. Have students make revisions and then exchange papers to share constructive feedback.

┌HELP─
To determine if a prepositional phrase is an adjective or an adverb phrase, ask yourself what question the phrase answers. Adjective phrases modify a noun or a pronoun and answer the questions *What kind? How many? Which one?* and *How much?* Adverb phrases modify verbs, adjectives, or adverbs and answer the questions *When? Where? Why? How? How often?* and *How long?*

EXAMPLES
Please hand me the book **on the table**. [The phrase answers the question *Which book?*, so *on the table* is an adjective phrase.]
They bicycled **through the park**. [The phrase answers the question *Where?*, so *through the park* is an adverb phrase.]

Exercise 9 **Writing Sentences with Adverb Phrases**

Write ten sentences using the following word groups as adverb phrases. Underline each phrase. Then, draw an arrow from the phrase to the word or words it modifies.

EXAMPLE   1. for the airport
           1. My grandparents left for the airport.

1. down the hall
2. by them
3. in the mall
4. under the car
5. onto the diving board
6. over our heads
7. by a Navajo woman
8. through the sky
9. at five o'clock sharp
10. from Egypt

Review A **Identifying Adjective and Adverb Phrases**

Each of the following sentences contains a prepositional phrase. Identify each phrase, and label it *adjective phrase* or *adverb phrase*.

EXAMPLES   1. Wilma Rudolph won three gold medals in the 1960 Olympic games.
            1. *in the 1960 Olympic games—adverb phrase*

            2. Rudolph overcame many obstacles in her life.
            2. *in her life—adjective phrase*

1. Wilma Rudolph did not have the childhood you might expect of a future Olympic athlete.
2. She and her twenty-one sisters and brothers were raised in a needy family.
3. Rudolph suffered from polio and scarlet fever when she was four years old.
4. Illnesses like these were often deadly.
5. For many years afterward, Rudolph used a leg brace when she walked.
6. Still, she never lost sight of her dreams.
7. She battled the odds against her.
8. With her family's help, she exercised hard every day.
9. All of her hard work made her strong.
10. Years later, she gained fame as a world-class athlete.

Learning for Life   ***Continued from p. 85***

various places on the chalkboard. Tell students to imagine they are directing a visitor to one of the sites listed. Ask "How would you use prepositional phrases to describe the place and direct someone to it?"

Have students work in groups to create travel brochures for a site (or two or three related sites) listed on the chalkboard. As students write the text for their brochures, encourage them to use adjective and

Review B Identifying Adjective and Adverb Phrases

Each of the following sentences contains at least one prepositional phrase. Identify each prepositional phrase, and label
each one *adjective phrase* or *adverb phrase*.

EXAMPLES 1. In China, farmers are considered the backbone
of the country.
  1. *In China—adverb phrase; of the country—adjective
     phrase*

  2. With over one billion people to feed, China asks
     much from its farmers.
  2. *With over one billion people to feed—adjective
     phrase; from its farmers—adverb phrase*

1. Many of the Chinese people
   are farmers.
2. They generally work their
   farms by hand.
3. Chinese farmers usually
   use hand tools instead of large
   machines.
4. Farmland throughout China is
   carefully prepared, planted,
   and weeded.
5. Farmers also harvest their
   crops with great care.
6. In the hills, the Chinese make
   flat terraces.
7. As you can see, water from
   high terraces can flow to lower
   terraces.
8. Farmers build ridges around the
   terraces so that the terraces can be
   flooded during the growing season.
9. In flat areas, water is pumped
   out of the ground.
10. Another Chinese method of
    irrigation is shown in the
    lower picture.

Prepositional Phrases   **87**

GRAMMAR

adverb phrases in sentences to describe the
place and give directions to it. Students can
research their sites in the library or at the
local visitors' bureau. Students may add

maps, drawings, and photographs to the
guide, but encourage them to focus on
the text.

Review C — Using Prepositional Phrases in Sentences

POSSIBLE ANSWERS

1. Among the papers in the recycling bin, Dani <u>found</u> what she needed.
2. I <u>can see</u> over the fence, but my brother cannot.
3. Where is the <u>package</u> for your sister?
4. The automobile <u>moved</u> toward him.
5. What do you <u>know</u> about the schedule?
6. Tom <u>did</u> not <u>finish</u> his paper before class.
7. The <u>flowers</u> along the wall are orange and red marigolds.
8. No sound <u>came</u> through the door.
9. The dog <u>hid</u> under the table.
10. In the evening we <u>will attend</u> the concert.
11. We <u>walked</u> our bicycles across the narrow bridge.
12. Did the escaped canary <u>fly</u> near you and Anna Maria?
13. The <u>passengers</u> aboard the sailboat waved to Caroline and me.
14. Lori <u>went</u> to the Grand Canyon.
15. Marcus and the kitten <u>slept</u> beneath the handmade quilt.
16. According to the scientist our proposal <u>needed</u> work.
17. What <u>is</u> beyond the farthest planet?
18. His face was <u>pale</u> next to the blue helmet.
19. A flock of birds <u>perched</u> upon the highest tree branch.
20. The <u>present</u> from my brother and me is on that table.

─HELP─

Although two possible answers are shown in the example, you need to write only one sentence for each item in Review C.

Review C — Using Prepositional Phrases in Sentences

Use each of the following prepositional phrases in a sentence. Then, underline the word or word group that the prepositional phrase modifies.

EXAMPLE 1. across the street
1. They <u>live</u> across the street.
or
The <u>store</u> across the street is open.

1. among the papers
2. over the fence
3. for your sister
4. toward him
5. about the schedule
6. before class
7. along the wall
8. through the door
9. under the table
10. in the evening
11. across the narrow bridge
12. near you and Anna Maria
13. aboard the sailboat
14. to the Grand Canyon
15. beneath the handmade quilt
16. according to the scientist
17. beyond the farthest planet
18. next to the blue helmet
19. upon the highest tree branch
20. from my brother and me

Review D — Writing Sentences with Adjective Phrases and Adverb Phrases

Use each of the following phrases in two separate sentences. In the first sentence, use the phrase as an adjective. In the second sentence, use the phrase as an adverb.

EXAMPLE 1. in Indiana
1. The people in Indiana are called "Hoosiers."
We once lived in Indiana.

1. from California
2. in my class
3. along the path
4. under the bridge
5. behind you
6. throughout the summer
7. at the beginning
8. around the corner
9. during dinner
10. on the patio

The Clause

4e. A *clause* is a word group that contains a verb and its subject and that is used as a sentence or as part of a sentence.

Every clause contains a subject and a verb. However, not all clauses express complete thoughts. Clauses that express complete thoughts are called *independent clauses.* Clauses that do not express complete thoughts are called *subordinate clauses.*

Independent Clauses

4f. An *independent* (or *main*) *clause* expresses a complete thought and can stand by itself as a sentence.

EXAMPLES

    S   V
Gertie practices soccer every day.

    S   V
She has improved a great deal.

        S   V
Her team won yesterday's game.

When an independent clause stands alone, it is called a sentence. Usually, the term *independent clause* is used only when such a clause is joined with another clause.

SENTENCE **He worked on the jigsaw puzzle.**

INDEPENDENT CLAUSE After Kevin had fed the cats, **he worked on the jigsaw puzzle.**

RESOURCES

The Clause

Practice

- *Language & Sentence Skills Practice,* pp. 77–82, 87–88
- *Developmental Language & Sentence Skills,* pp. 33–38

GRAMMAR

Review D **Writing Sentences with Adjective Phrases and Adverb Phrases**

POSSIBLE ANSWERS

1. My friend from California is trying out for the Olympics.
   The package came from California.
2. The winner in my class was Tim.
   In my class I met Alice, who became my best friend.
3. The trees along the path are oaks.
   Along the path the baby stumbled.
4. The water under the bridge looks peaceful.
   Under the bridge the boat sailed.
5. The wall behind you has a serious crack.
   Look behind you!
6. The parties throughout the summer are planned for out-of-doors.
   Throughout the summer and into the fall, the flowers bloomed.
7. The chapters at the beginning of the book are the most memorable.
   Did you know at the beginning of the project that you would learn so much?
8. The house around the corner is painted blue.
   Walk to the end of the block and go around the corner to find the shop.
9. Richard's silence during dinner was unusual.
   The phone rang during dinner.
10. Rain interrupted lunch on the patio.
    I saw the missing kitten on the patio.

The Clause

Rules 4e–i *(pp. 89–96)*

OBJECTIVES

- To identify clauses as independent or subordinate
- To identify adjective clauses in sentences
- To write sentences using adjective clauses
- To identify adverb clauses in sentences
- To write sentences using adverb clauses

DIRECT TEACHING

Modeling and Demonstration

The Clause. Model how to identify independent and subordinate clauses by using the example clauses *She has improved a great deal* and *if you finish on time*. First, ask which word is the subject of the first example. [*She*] Then, ask which word or words are the verb. [*has improved*] Then, ask whether the clause expresses a complete thought and can stand by itself. [*yes*] Therefore, since the first example has a subject and a verb, expresses a complete thought, and can stand by itself, it is an independent clause. Then, repeat the procedure with the second clause. The clause *if you finish on time* has a subject (*you*) and a verb (*finish*), but it does not express a complete thought and cannot stand by itself; therefore, it is a subordinate clause. Now, have a volunteer use other examples from this chapter to demonstrate how to identify independent and subordinate clauses.

Correcting Misconceptions

Subordinate Clauses. One way to help students recognize the difference between independent and subordinate clauses is to read clauses aloud in a manner that exaggerates the incomplete nature of the subordinate clause. Here are some examples that you can read to the class:

1. Though the meal was delicious . . .

2. After you mow the lawn . . .

3. While Ray was riding his bike . . .

Ask students to react to what you read. Point out that all three clauses leave the listener wanting information that an independent clause would provide but that a subordinate clause does not.

┌HELP┐

A subordinate clause that is capitalized and punctuated as if it were a sentence is a **sentence fragment.** Avoid using sentence fragments in your writing.

Reference Note

For more on **correcting sentence fragments,** see page 386.

Subordinate Clauses

4g. A *subordinate* (or *dependent*) *clause* does not express a complete thought and cannot stand by itself as a complete sentence.

EXAMPLES
$$\overset{S}{\text{if}}\ \overset{V}{\text{you finish on time}}$$

$$\text{which}\ \overset{S}{\text{we}}\ \overset{V}{\text{found}}\ \text{on the sidewalk}$$

Subordinate means "lesser in rank or importance." A subordinate clause must be joined with at least one independent clause to make a sentence and express a complete thought.

SUBORDINATE CLAUSES	that Dad cooked for us
	if you set realistic goals
	before the sun sets

SENTENCES	We all enjoyed the dinner **that Dad cooked for us.**
	If you set realistic goals, you are more likely to succeed.
	Before the sun sets, I need to mow the lawn.

Notice the words that begin the subordinate clauses: *that*, *if*, and *before*. The chart below lists some other words that can signal the beginning of a subordinate clause.

Words Often Used to Begin Subordinate Clauses			
after	how	unless	which
although	if	until	while
as	since	when	who
as if	so that	whenever	whom
as though	than	where	whose
because	that	wherever	
before	though	whether	

Exercise 10 Identifying Independent and Subordinate Clauses

For each of the following items, identify the italicized word group as either an *independent clause* or a *subordinate clause*.

EXAMPLES
1. I'll do the experiment *if you will record the results.*
1. subordinate clause

2. *Ignacio,* who is an artist, *painted the banner.*
2. independent clause

1. *While Dad was sleeping,* we decorated the house for his birthday party.
2. Just as Terri came in the door, *the phone rang.*
3. Somalis, *who traditionally raise and export livestock,* are nomadic.
4. Before you accept the invitation, *ask your mother.*
5. Do you know *when the train should arrive*?
6. *Although he was better at social studies,* he loved art.
7. Two uniformed soldiers guarded the entrance *where an iron gate stood.*
8. When the snows melt, *these streams will fill and rush down to the valley.*
9. That art paper *that you are using* really soaks up ink.
10. *Toni Morrison,* whose parents were once sharecroppers, *won the Pulitzer Prize.*

1. sub.
2. ind.
3. sub.
4. ind.
5. sub.
6. sub.
7. sub.
8. ind.
9. sub.
10. ind.

Adjective Clauses

4h. An *adjective clause* is a subordinate clause that modifies a noun or pronoun.

Like an adjective or an adjective phrase, an adjective clause may modify a noun or a pronoun. Unlike an adjective phrase, an adjective clause contains both a subject and verb.

ADJECTIVE	a **white** cat
ADJECTIVE PHRASE	a cat **with white fur** [With white fur does not have a subject and verb.]
ADJECTIVE CLAUSE	a cat **that has white fur** [That has white fur has a subject, that, and a verb, has.]

Reference Note

For information about **nouns,** see page 25. For information about **pronouns,** see page 30.

Critical Thinking

Metacognition. After students complete **Exercise 10,** ask them to write brief answers to the following questions:

1. How did the way you read the items in **Exercise 10** help you decide whether the items were independent or subordinate clauses?

2. How did you use the examples on pages 89 and 90 to help you identify subordinate clauses?

Learners Having Difficulty

Write the following sentences on the chalkboard, using a second color of chalk for the adjective clauses. For each sentence, ask a volunteer to draw an arrow from the adjective clause to the word it modifies.

1. The dancer, **who looked familiar,** was my mother's friend. [*dancer*]

2. Let's go to the store **that is having the best sale.** [*store*]

3. We went to the lake on Friday, **which was my birthday.** [*Friday*]

4. The boy **who fell down the stairs** was not hurt. [*boy*]

The Clause   **91**

English-Language Learners

Spanish. Because the Spanish relative pronoun *que* can mean *that, which,* or *who,* Spanish speakers may tend to use *that* even in cases where *who* or *which* would sound more natural in English. You may want to show them some sentences containing *that, which,* and *who* in adjective clauses, allowing them to investigate in which situations each is used.

Spanish. In Spanish it is considered awkward to end a clause with a verb. For example, in an English sentence such as *I like the book that Maria is reading,* the Spanish speaker may invert the subject and the verb in the adjective clause. You may want to give students a list of sentences containing adjective clauses that end in verbs, and emphasize the subject-verb order. Also, suggest that students practice reading the sentences aloud.

An adjective clause usually follows the noun or pronoun it modifies and tells *Which one?* or *What kind?*

EXAMPLES   The runner **who came in second** was Tina. [The adjective clause modifies the noun *runner* and answers the question *Which one?*]

I would like a dog **that I could take for long walks.** [The adjective clause modifies the noun *dog* and answers the question *What kind?*]

Exercise 11 **Identifying Adjective Clauses**

Identify each adjective clause in the following sentences.

EXAMPLE   1. Her coat was lined with fleece that kept her warm.
   1. *that kept her warm*

1. Jordan, whose aunt once rode on the space shuttle, is visiting her this summer.
2. Grandfather gave me that arrowhead, which has been in our family for generations.
3. The doctor looked at the notes that the nurse had written.
4. What was the name of the man who helped us?
5. Panama hats, which are prized far and wide, are woven of jipijapa leaves.
6. We could not have done it without Harry, whose skill saved the day.
7. Have you heard of Sister Juana Ines de la Cruz, the Mexican nun who championed women's rights in 1691?
8. Argentina's pampas, where fine herds of cattle graze, offer ranchers rich and vast grasslands.
9. Since ancient times, Asian ginger has been prized for the tang that it gives many dishes.
10. Ric, whom Doris calls "The Prince," is always a good sport.

Exercise 12 **Using Adjective Clauses in Sentences**

Write ten sentences using the following word groups as adjective clauses.

EXAMPLE   1. where I grew up
   1. *This is the street where I grew up.*

1. which had been imported from Japan
2. who is always on time
3. that live in this ecosystem
4. where the roses grow
5. whose short stories appear in your text
6. whom you talked about yesterday
7. that was having a sale
8. which may or may not be true
9. for whom our school is named
10. whose hard work made this event possible

Adverb Clauses

4i. An *adverb clause* is a subordinate clause that modifies a verb, an adjective, or an adverb.

Like an adverb or an adverb phrase, an adverb clause may modify a verb, an adjective, or another adverb. Unlike an adverb phrase, an adverb clause contains a subject and verb.

ADVERB	**Shyly,** the toddler hid behind her mother.
ADVERB PHRASE	**With a shy smile,** the toddler hid behind her mother. [*With a shy smile* does not have a subject and verb.]
ADVERB CLAUSE	**Since the toddler was shy,** she hid behind her mother. [*Since the toddler was shy* has a subject, *toddler,* and a verb, *was.*]

An adverb clause answers the following questions: *How? When? Where? Why? To what extent? How much? How long?* or *Under what conditions?*

EXAMPLES **After he had moved the books,** Marvin dusted the shelves. [The adverb clause tells *when* Marvin dusted the shelves.]

Then he put the books back **where they belonged.** [The adverb clause tells *where* he put the books.]

He cleaned his room **because it was very messy.** [The adverb clause tells *why* he cleaned his room.]

┌HELP┐

Introductory adverb clauses are usually set off by commas.

EXAMPLES
After we built the camp- fire, we roasted hot dogs.

Although the song is good, it is not one of their best.

Reference Note

For more information on **using commas to set off introductory elements,** see page 274.

Exercise 12 **Using Adjective Clauses in Sentences**

POSSIBLE ANSWERS

1. The TV, which had been imported from Japan, was twenty years old when we replaced it.

2. George, who is always on time, is wearing his cap and gown.

3. In science class we will study endangered organisms that live in this ecosystem.

4. That is the garden where the roses grow.

5. Avi, whose short stories appear in your text, is a popular writer.

6. The new baby, whom you talked about yesterday, is sweet.

7. The store that was having a sale was very crowded.

8. The story, which may or may not be true, is spreading throughout the school.

9. In social studies class we are studying George Washington, for whom our school is named.

10. Mrs. Asher, whose hard work made this event possible, is wearing the pink dress.

GRAMMAR

Exercise 13

DISTRIBUTED REVIEW

For a quick review of parts of speech, ask students to find the following items in the designated sentences:

1. an adjective [*Tiny*]

2. a pronoun [*you*]

4. a verb phrase [*must be fed*]

PRACTICE

Guided and Independent

Exercise 14 You may wish to have students complete the first ten items as guided practice and the last ten items as independent practice. **HOMEWORK**

Exercise 14 **Writing Sentences with Adverb Clauses**

POSSIBLE ANSWERS

1. When I save enough money, I will buy a new CD.

2. Dad will be home soon if things go according to the schedule.

3. Since we have lived here, we have painted the house twice.

4. After the assembly was over, the homecoming parade began.

5. Before school starts, we will choose new shoes.

6. Although we couldn't speak Japanese, our guests could speak English.

7. Melanie is older than she is but younger than Marc.

8. Because they were going to the rink, their ice skates were strung over their shoulders.

9. Until the sun set, we could still read the map.

10. While the lions are drinking from the river, the people on the photo safari take pictures.

STYLE TIP

In most cases, deciding where to place an adverb clause is a matter of style, not correctness.

As he leapt across the gorge, Rex glanced back at his alien pursuers.

Rex glanced back at his alien pursuers as he leapt across the gorge.

Which sentence might you use in a science fiction story? The sentence to choose would be the one that looks and sounds better in the context—the rest of the paragraph to which the sentence belongs.

Exercise 13 **Identifying Adverb Clauses**

Identify each adverb clause in the following sentences.

EXAMPLE **1.** Call when you can.
  1. when you can

1. Tiny wildflowers sprang up wherever they could.
2. Unless you want to sink, do not pull that large plug at the bottom of the boat.
3. Wind blew softly across the sand dunes while the caravan made its way home.
4. As soon as the cows come in, they must be fed.
5. To our surprise, when we entered the woods, a dozen armadillos were foraging right in front of us.
6. Although the piano had not been used for some time, it was still in tune.
7. Unless the shipment arrives today, the order will not be ready on time.
8. Because the airplane had been painted yellow, it was easily seen from the ground.
9. I'm not going if you're not going.
10. I had never heard anyone sing as he did.

Exercise 14 **Writing Sentences with Adverb Clauses**

Write twenty sentences using the following word groups as adverb clauses.

EXAMPLE **1.** as soon as he can
  1. He will be here as soon as he can.

1. when I save enough money
2. if things go according to the schedule
3. since we have lived here
4. after the assembly was over
5. before school starts
6. although we couldn't speak Japanese
7. than she is
8. because they were going to the rink
9. until the sun set
10. while the lions are drinking from the river

11. as long as the band plays
12. whenever the train arrives at the station
13. unless the dog is on a leash
14. wherever you see grasshoppers
15. although the trail was steep
16. when Alexa won the marathon
17. so that we could use the computer
18. while the storm was raging
19. than you are
20. as though they had run ten miles

Review E **Identifying Clauses**

For each of the following sentences, identify the italicized clause as an *independent clause* or a *subordinate clause*. Then, identify each subordinate clause as an *adjective clause* or an *adverb clause*.

EXAMPLE   **1.** Those Japanese sandals *that you are wearing* are zoris.
                 1. subordinate clause—adjective clause

1. *Camels stamped and bellowed in annoyance* when packs were put on them.
2. Aloe plants, *which originated in Africa,* are now widely available in the United States.
3. As far as scientists can tell, *there is no connection between these two events.*
4. *If you adjust the blinds,* you won't have that glare on your monitor.
5. *The castanets,* which were quite old, *had been Melanie's grandmother's.*
6. *You were always singing* when you were little.
7. Three Indian elephants patiently towed the logs *that had just been cut.*
8. Stay with us *as long as you want.*
9. *Southeast Asia depends heavily on the seasonal rain* that the monsoons bring.
10. The Forbidden City, *where China's emperors lived,* is enclosed by walls.

1. ind.

2. sub.—adj.

3. ind.

4. sub.—adv.

5. ind.

6. ind.

7. sub.—adj.

8. sub.—adv.

9. ind.

10. sub.—adj.

GRAMMAR

Exercise 14 **Writing Sentences with Adverb Clauses**

ANSWERS continued

11. I want to stay as long as the band plays.
12. Whenever the train arrives at the station, someone will meet you.
13. Unless the dog is on a leash, it is not welcome on the trail.
14. Wherever you see grasshoppers, there are probably many others hidden in the grass.
15. The climbers were not winded although the trail was steep.
16. When Alexa won the marathon, we all celebrated with her.
17. We signed a list so that we could use the computer in turn.
18. While the storm was raging, the family was cozy by the fire.
19. Hank is taller than you are.
20. The horses looked as though they had run ten miles.

Review F Writing Sentences with Clauses and Prepositional Phrases

POSSIBLE ANSWERS

1. I like the still life of the <u>boots</u> with a cowboy hat.

2. The <u>salesperson</u> who told us about computers works at Computer Magic.

3. Under the surface of the clear lake, we <u>could see</u> the lost mask.

4. Since the club meets in the afternoon, we <u>will</u> not <u>be able</u> to go shopping.

5. Would you like a new <u>outfit</u> for yourself, Bobbie?

6. If you <u>walk</u> through the puddles, your shoes will get wet.

7. Over the treetops, the clouds <u>looked</u> like cotton balls.

8. Before we ate dinner, the light <u>had faded</u>.

9. The <u>sweet peas</u> that grow along the fence smell like perfume.

10. The puppy <u>raced</u> toward us wagging his tail.

Sentence Structure
Rules 4j–m (*pp. 96–100*)

OBJECTIVES

■ To identify sentences as simple or compound

■ To classify sentences according to structure

—HELP—

Although two possible answers are shown in the example, you need to write only one sentence for each item in Review F.

Reference Note

For information about **independent clauses** and **subordinate clauses,** see page 89.

Review F Writing Sentences with Clauses and Prepositional Phrases

Use each of the following phrases and clauses in a sentence. Then, underline the word that the phrase or clause modifies.

EXAMPLE 1. under the flat rock
1. *Under the flat rock <u>lived</u> many odd insects.*
or
The <u>insects</u> under the flat rock wriggled.

1. with a cowboy hat
2. who told us about computers
3. under the surface
4. since the club meets in the afternoon
5. for yourself
6. through the puddles
7. over the treetops
8. before we ate dinner
9. that grow along the fence
10. toward us

Sentence Structure
Simple Sentences

4j. A *simple sentence* has one independent clause and no subordinate clauses.

A simple sentence may have a compound subject, a compound verb, or both. Although a compound subject has two or more parts, it is still considered a single subject. In the same way, a compound verb or verb phrase is considered one verb.

                    S   V
EXAMPLES My **mother belongs** to the Friends of the Library.
[single subject and single verb]

          S   S   V
Argentina and **Chile are** in South America.
[compound subject]

RESOURCES

Sentence Structure
Practice
■ *Language & Sentence Skills Practice,* pp. 83–86, 89
■ *Developmental Language & Sentence Skills,* pp. 39–42

```
      S    V             V
Jeannette read Stuart Little and reported on it.
[compound verb]

          S     S    V
The acrobats and jugglers did amazing tricks and

          V
were rewarded with a standing ovation. [compound
subject and compound verb]
```

Compound Sentences

4k. A *compound sentence* consists of two or more
independent clauses, usually joined by a comma and a
connecting word.

In a compound sentence, a coordinating conjunction (*and, but,
for, nor, or, so,* or *yet*) generally connects the simple sentences.
A comma usually comes before the conjunction in a compound
sentence.

EXAMPLES   I forgot my lunch**,** **but** Dad ran to the bus with it.

            She likes sweets**,** **yet** she seldom eats them.

Notice in the second example above that, usually, a sentence is
compound if the subject is repeated.
    Sometimes the independent clauses in a compound
sentence are joined by a semicolon.

EXAMPLES   The blue one is mine**;** it has my initials on it.

            The spider is not an insect**;** it is an arachnid.

Exercise 15 Identifying Simple Sentences and
              Compound Sentences

Identify each of the following sentences as *simple* or *compound*.

EXAMPLE   **1.** That story by Lensey Namioka is good, and you
              should read it.

          1. *compound*

1. My dad and I like tacos, and we're making them for dinner. **1.** cd.
2. Some trees and shrubs live thousands of years. **2.** s.
3. It rained, but we marched in the parade anyway. **3.** cd.
4. Mr. Edwards will lead the singing, for Ms. Cruz is ill. **4.** cd.

Reference Note

For more information
about **using commas
with conjunctions,** see
page 270. For more about
using **semicolons,** see
page 279.

| STYLE | TIP |

Sometimes you can com-
bine two simple sentences
to make one compound
sentence. Just connect the
two simple sentences by
using a comma and *and,
but, for, nor, or, so,* or *yet.*

ORIGINAL
    The rain has stopped. The
    sky is still dreary and gray.

COMBINED
    The rain has stopped**,** **but**
    the sky is still dreary and
    gray.

Combining sentences this
way can help make your
writing smoother and more
interesting.

Modeling and Demonstration

Sentence Structure. Model how to
identify compound sentences by
using the example *I forgot my lunch,
but Dad ran to the bus with it.* First,
ask how many subjects are in the
sentence. [*two*] Then, ask how many
verbs are in the sentence. [*two*] Ask
if the subjects and verbs are compound and form one clause or if they
form separate clauses. [*They form
two separate clauses.*] Then, ask
whether each clause expresses a complete thought and can stand by itself.
[*yes*] Finally, ask how the two clauses
are joined. [*with a comma and the
conjunction* but] Since the sentence
has two independent clauses joined
with a conjunction, the sentence is a
compound sentence. Now, have a
volunteer use another example from
this chapter to demonstrate how to
identify compound sentences.

MINI-LESSON **Grammar**   *Continued on pp. 98–99*

Creating Compound Sentences.
Students may have no difficulty identifying
compound sentences but may have trouble
forming them. Remind students that if they
want to combine two simple sentences to

make a compound sentence, the two
simple sentences should express related
ideas. Discuss with students the differences
between the following compound
sentences:

DIFFERENTIATING INSTRUCTION

English-Language Learners

General Strategies. Investigate with students the conjunctions that can be used in compound sentences. Write the following paragraph on the chalkboard, and list the conjunctions to one side. Have students fill in each of the blanks with the appropriate conjunction. Discuss with students their choices and the differences between the words.

Mario had an important soccer game early Saturday morning, _____ [so] he decided to go to bed early. He felt confident about the game, _____ [yet or but] he went to bed feeling anxious. The next morning Mario woke up late, _____ [for] he had forgotten to set the alarm. Mario had no time to take a shower, _____ [but or yet] he did manage to eat breakfast. Neither of his parents could give him a ride, _____ [but or yet] Mario didn't panic. He could get a ride with a teammate, _____ [or] he could walk to the game. His team was counting on him.

5. s. **5.** My aunts, uncles, and cousins from Costa Rica visited us last summer.

6. cd. **6.** I had worked hard all morning, yet I had not finished the job by lunchtime.

7. s. **7.** Abe peeled and chopped all of the onions and dumped them into a huge pot.

8. cd. **8.** All ravens are crows, but not all crows are ravens.

9. s. **9.** Chippewa and Ojibwa are two names for the same American Indian people.

10. cd. **10.** I liked this movie best; it was more exciting than the others.

Review G Identifying Simple Sentences and Compound Sentences

Identify each of the following sentences as *simple* or *compound*.

EXAMPLE **1.** Have you or Sandy ever seen the movie *The Bridge on the River Kwai*?

 1. simple

1. My stepbrother is only eight years old, and he is fascinated by bridges. **1.** cd.

2. We buy postcards with pictures of bridges, for he likes to collect them. **2.** cd.

3. He has several cards of stone bridges. **3.** s.

MINI-LESSON **Grammar** *Continued from p. 97*

Jeb is on the soccer team, and his brother Michael plays baseball.

Jeb is on the soccer team, and he has a brother.

Students should recognize that in the first sentence both independent clauses are about sports; the ideas are related. The two independent clauses in the second sentence have no such unifying idea and should be

4. Stone bridges are strong but are costly to build. **4.** s.
5. Many bridges are quite beautiful. **5.** s.
6. The Central American rope bridge shown here is one kind of suspension bridge. **6.** s.
7. The modern bridge on the previous page is another kind of suspension bridge. **7.** s.
8. Suspension bridges may look dangerous, yet most are safe. **8.** cd.
9. Bridges must be inspected regularly. **9.** s.
10. My stepbrother collects postcards of bridges, and I collect postcards of towers. **10.** cd.

Complex Sentences

4l. A *complex sentence* contains one independent clause and at least one subordinate clause.

Subordinate clauses usually begin with a word such as *who, whose, which, that, after, as, if, since,* and *when.* A subordinate clause can appear at the beginning, in the middle, or at the end of a complex sentence.

EXAMPLES   Before Chen planted his garden, he made a sketch of the layout.

                                 S V
independent clause   he made a sketch of the layout

                                     S   V
subordinate clause   Before Chen planted his garden

  When bees collect pollen, they pollinate the plants that they visit.

                                   S V
independent clause   they pollinate the plants

                                   S   V
subordinate clause   When bees collect pollen

                                   S V
subordinate clause   that they visit

Sentence Structure **99**

---

left as two separate sentences.

    Write the following pairs of sentences on the chalkboard, and ask students to tell whether they could be combined to make compound sentences.

1. The house is almost finished.
The family will move in next month. [*yes*]

2. Penguins are my favorite animals.
Karen's family went to the wildlife park. [*no*]

Sentence Structure

Draw on the chalkboard a chart with a column for each type of sentence structure. Ask for a volunteer to write a simple sentence in the first column. Then, show students how clauses can be added to the simple sentence to create the other three structures. Add a second independent clause to make a compound sentence, and write the sentence in the second column. Fill in the other columns in a similar fashion. Then, have another student write a new simple sentence, and repeat the process, asking for volunteers to suggest clauses to add to build the other sentence structures.

MEETING THE CHALLENGE

Write directions telling someone exactly how to get to your favorite place. Use at least five prepositional phrases, three adverb clauses, and two adjective clauses to add details that help your reader follow your directions. When you are finished, underline the prepositional phrases, adverb clauses, and adjective clauses in your directions.

ANSWER
Answers will vary.

Compound-Complex Sentences

4m. A sentence with two or more independent clauses and at least one subordinate clause is a *compound-complex sentence.*

EXAMPLE   I picked up the branches that had fallen during the storm, and Rosa mowed the grass.

	S V
independent clause	I picked up the branches

	S V
independent clause	Rosa mowed the grass

	S V
subordinate clause	that had fallen during the storm

Exercise 16 Classifying Sentences by Structure

Identify each of the following sentences as *simple, compound, complex,* or *compound-complex.*

EXAMPLE   **1.** It was raining, but the sun was shining when we looked out the window.

    1. compound-complex

1. cd.   **1.** Cuba's capital is Havana, and this beautiful city has been the center of Cuban culture since 1552.

2. s.   **2.** The heavy branches of an oak tree hung over our table and shaded us from the sun.

3. cx.   **3.** When you are looking at a work by Monet, stand back at least fifteen or twenty feet.

4. cd.-cx.   **4.** As it happens, you're right and I'm wrong.

5. s.   **5.** Seashells filled Liz's suitcase and spilled onto the floor.

6. cd.   **6.** According to our records, your next appointment isn't until next month, but we do thank you for your call.

7. s.   **7.** The Internet and other forms of electronic communication are shaping the world's future.

8. cx.   **8.** Because opinions are still divided, further discussion will be necessary.

9. cd.   **9.** The clock's minute hand is moving, but the second hand has stopped.

10. cx.   **10.** Between Asia and Africa lies a land bridge that is known as the Sinai Peninsula.

CONTENT-AREA CONNECTIONS

Mathematics
Graph. Hand out copies of an article or paragraph that demonstrates well-developed writing style. You might use a magazine article or part of a selection from your literature textbook.

    Have students analyze the sentence structure in the piece by labeling each sentence *simple, compound, complex,* or *compound-complex.* Then, have them count the number of sentences of each type to come up with four separate totals. Finally, ask students to create a simple bar graph to show how many sentences of each type of structure the piece contains.

Numerals in brackets refer to the rules tested by the items in the Chapter Review.

1. [4d]
2. [4c]
3. [4c]
4. [4c]
5. [4d]
6. [4d]
7. [4c]
8. [4c]
9. [4d]
10. [4d]

11. sub. [4g]
12. sub. [4g]
13. ind. [4f]
14. sub. [4g]
15. ind. [4f]
16. ind. [4f]
17. sub. [4g]
18. ind [4f]

Chapter Review

A. Identifying Adjective and Adverb Phrases

Identify the prepositional phrase in each of the following sentences, and tell whether the phrase is used as an *adjective phrase* or an *adverb phrase*. Then, give the word or words that the phrase modifies.

1. The crowd waved banners during the game.
2. That book about the Underground Railroad is interesting.
3. Have you seen the pictures of the Wongs' new house?
4. The water in my glass was cold.
5. Uncle Eduardo carefully knocked the snow off his boots.
6. You should travel to Utah if you have never seen a beautiful desert.
7. Do you have the new CD by the Three Tenors?
8. The swings in the park are a bit rusty.
9. A clown handed balloons to the children.
10. The mail carrier left a package on the front porch.

B. Identifying Independent and Subordinate Clauses

For each of the following items, identify the italicized word group as either an *independent clause* or a *subordinate clause*.

11. Yamile and her family enjoyed their vacation in Indonesia, *which is a country made up of thousands of islands.*
12. *Whenever he pressed the button,* another buzzer sounded.
13. After Luis worked out on the weight machines and swam ten laps in the pool, *he took a shower.*
14. Bring an extra sweatshirt with you *if you have one.*
15. *Martin enjoys speaking Japanese* when he visits the Nakamuras.
16. Before you leave for school, *do you always remember to brush your teeth*?
17. Is Rena the one *who went to New Zealand*?
18. *Did our grandmother ever tell you* how she came to this country from Latvia?

Chapter Review **101**

ASSESSING

Monitoring Progress

Chapter Review. To assess student progress, you may want to compare the types of items missed on the **Diagnostic Preview** with those missed on the **Chapter Review.** You may want to work on specific goals with individual students who are still having difficulty mastering essential information.

RESOURCES

The Phrase and the Clause

Review

■ *Language & Sentence Skills Practice,* pp. 87–89

Assessment

■ *Progress Assessment for the Holt Handbook,* pp. 7–8, 41

■ *Test Generator Generator (One-Stop Planner CD-ROM)*

19. sub. [4g]
20. ind. [4f]

19. *Unless you don't like getting wet and working outside all day,* we could use your help at the Spanish club car wash on Saturday.

20. *Mr. Boylan,* whom we met several times at school events, *is the author of a novel.*

C. Identifying Clauses

For each of the following sentences, identify each italicized clause as an *adjective clause* or an *adverb clause.*

21. adv. [4i]
22. adj. [4h]
23. adv. [4i]
24. adj. [4h]
25. adj. [4h]

21. *When you have a chance,* send me an e-mail.

22. Anyone *who knows Vita* can tell you how smart she is.

23. *When the Castillo family arrived at the ski lodge that evening,* they went right to bed.

24. The theater company, *which had come to town only that afternoon,* put on a spectacular show.

25. Sherlock Holmes, *whose creator was Sir Arthur Conan Doyle,* is probably the most famous fictional detective in literature.

D. Identifying Types of Sentences

Identify each of the following sentences as *simple, compound, complex,* or *compound-complex.*

26. s. [4j]
27. cd.-cx. [4m]
28. s. [4j]
29. cx. [4l]
30. cx. [4l]
31. cd. [4k]
32. cd.-cx. [4m]

26. Sir Ernest Shackleton was an Antarctic explorer.

27. He wanted to be the first man to reach the South Pole, and in 1908, he led a party that came within ninety-seven miles of the pole.

28. In 1914, he led the British Imperial Trans-Antarctic Expedition to Antarctica.

29. Shackleton intended to cross Antarctica, which no one else had ever crossed before.

30. Before the expedition could land, Shackleton's ship, the *Endurance,* was trapped in the ice of the Weddell Sea for ten months.

31. Finally, the ice crushed the ship, and Shackleton and his men were stranded on the ice for five more months.

32. The men escaped the ice in small boats, and they landed on Elephant Island, where they lived in a makeshift camp.

33. Shackleton and five other men sailed to South Georgia Island, where they sought help from Norwegian whalers.

34. Shackleton's first attempts to return to Elephant Island did not succeed, but he finally rescued his crew on August 30, 1916.

35. Shackleton's expedition failed to cross Antarctica, but he brought all of his men home safely.

33. cx. [4l]

34. cd. [4k]

35. cd. [4k]

Writing Application

Using Prepositional Phrases in a Story

Using Prepositional Phrases to Add Detail   The Friends of Animals Society is having a contest for the best true-life pet story. The winner of the contest will have his or her story published in the local newspaper. Write a brief story to enter in the contest. In your story, tell about an unusual pet that you have heard about or known. Use at least five adjective phrases and five adverb phrases in your story.

Prewriting   First, you will need to choose a pet about which to write. Then, jot down details about how the animal looks and how it acts. In your notes, focus on a specific time when the animal did something funny or amazing.

Writing   Begin your draft with an attention-grabbing paragraph. Introduce and describe your main character. Be sure that you have included any human characters that play a part in the story. Also, describe the story's setting—for example, your kitchen, your neighbor's backyard, or the woods.

Revising   Ask a friend to read your draft. Depending on what your friend tells you, you may need to add, cut, or rearrange details. Make sure you have used at least five adjective phrases and five adverb phrases.

Publishing   Check your story carefully for errors in grammar, spelling, and punctuation. You and your classmates may want to collect your stories into a booklet. Along with your stories, you might include pictures or drawings of the pets you have written about.

Complements
Direct and Indirect Objects, Subject Complements

STANDARDS FOCUS

Grade-Level Standard

(Boldface indicates concepts that are taught and tested in this chapter.)

■ Language Convention 1.0: **Students write and speak with a command of standard English conventions appropriate to this grade level.**

Prerequisite/Review Standard

■ Language Convention 1.0: Students write and speak with a command of standard English conventions appropriate to this grade level.

Standard Coming Up in the Next Grade Level

■ Grammar 1.3: Identify all parts of speech and types and structure of sentences.

▼

INTRODUCING THE CHAPTER

■ The first part of this chapter asks students to look at incomplete sentences and to evaluate when a complement is needed. The second section deals with direct and indirect objects. The last section of the chapter defines subject complements and explains the two types, predicate nominatives and predicate adjectives.

■ The chapter closes with a **Chapter Review** including a **Writing Application** feature that asks students to write a paragraph using direct objects and indirect objects.

(continued)

1.0 Written and Oral English Language Conventions

Students write and speak with a command of standard English conventions appropriate to this grade level.

┌HELP┐

Some sentences in the Diagnostic Preview have more than one complement.

Numerals in brackets refer to rules tested by the items in the Diagnostic Preview.

1. i.o./d.o. [5c, b]
2. p.a. [5f]
3. p.n./p.n. [5e]
4. d.o./d.o. [5b]
5. i.o./i.o./d.o. [5c, b]
6. p.a./p.a. [5f]
7. d.o. [5b]
8. d.o./d.o. [5b]
9. p.a. [5f]
10. i.o./d.o./d.o. [5c, b]
11. p.a. [5f]

Diagnostic Preview

Identifying Complements

Identify each complement in the following sentences as a *direct object*, an *indirect object*, a *predicate nominative*, or a *predicate adjective*.

EXAMPLE   **1.** Many forests are cold and snowy.

    1. cold—predicate adjective; snowy—predicate adjective

1. We made our parents a family tree for their anniversary.
2. The sun disappeared, and the wind suddenly grew cold.
3. The home of the former president is now a library and museum.
4. The newspaper published an article and an editorial about ex-Mayor Sharon Pratt Dixon.
5. My uncle gave my sister and brother ice skates.
6. After the long hike, all of the Scouts felt sore and sleepy.
7. Leaders of the Ojibwa people held a meeting last summer.
8. I wrote my name and address in my book.
9. Your dog certainly appears healthy to me.
10. They always send us grapefruit and oranges from Florida.
11. Most stars in our galaxy are invisible to the human eye.

CHAPTER RESOURCES

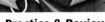

Internet

■ go.hrw.com (keyword: HLLA)

go. hrw .com

Planning

■ *One-Stop Planner CD-ROM* 🎵

■ *On Course: Mapping Instruction*

Practice & Review

■ *Language & Sentence Skills Practice,* pp. 94–103; 104–106

■ *Developmental Language & Sentence Skills,* pp. 43–46

Application & Enrichment

■ *Language & Sentence Skills Practice,* pp. 109; 93, 107–108

12. Did the workers capture an <u>alligator</u> in the sewer system?
13. Our trip on the Staten Island ferry became an <u>adventure</u>.
14. The air show featured <u>balloons</u> and <u>parachutes</u>.
15. The maples are becoming <u>gold</u> and <u>red</u> early this year.
16. My parents bought <u>themselves</u> several Celia Cruz CDs.
17. Aunt Kathleen gave <u>Ricardo</u> and <u>me</u> tickets for the show.
18. The two most popular sports at my school are <u>football</u> and <u>volleyball</u>.
19. The water in the pool looked <u>clean</u> and <u>fresh</u>.
20. My mother's homemade Sabbath bread tastes <u>delicious</u>.

12. d.o. [5b]
13. p.n. [5e]
14. d.o./d.o. [5b]
15. p.a./p.a. [5f]
16. i.o./d.o. [5c, b]
17. i.o./i.o./d.o. [5c, b]
18. p.n./p.n. [5e]
19. p.a./p.a. [5f]
20. p.a. [5f]

Recognizing Complements

5a. A *complement* is a word or word group that completes the meaning of a verb.

Every sentence has a subject and a verb. Sometimes the subject and the verb can express a complete thought all by themselves.

EXAMPLES
    S V
Adriana swam.

      S   V
The puppy was sleeping.

Often, however, a verb needs a complement to complete its meaning.

INCOMPLETE
      S   V
My aunt found [*what?*]

COMPLETE
    S   V   C
My aunt found a **wallet**. [The noun *wallet* completes the meaning of the verb *found*.]

INCOMPLETE
     S   V
Sarah bought [*what?*]

COMPLETE
  S   V   C   C
Sarah bought **herself** a new **jacket**. [The pronoun *herself* and the noun *jacket* complete the meaning of the verb *bought*.]

TIPS & TRICKS

You can remember the difference in spelling between *complement* (the grammar term) and *compliment* (an expression of affection or respect) by remembering that a compl**e**ment compl**e**tes a sentence.

Recognizing Complements **105**

GRAMMAR

■ For help in integrating this chapter with writing assignments in *Holt Literature and Language Arts,* use the **Teaching Strands** chart on pages T22–T23.

ASSESSING

Entry-Level Assessment
Diagnostic Preview. You can use the **Diagnostic Preview** to gauge students' understanding of sentence completeness, especially as it relates to the classification of objects and subject complements. You also might use the preview as a tool to determine which students have problems identifying and using complements correctly.

PRETEACHING

Lesson Starter
Motivating. Write three columns of words on the chalkboard: subjects, verbs, and complements. The words can be based on a topic of your choice, such as school sports or favorite music. You can enlist students' help in coming up with the list of words. Then, have students create as many sentences as they can by combining words from the three columns. (They can add words such as articles and adjectives, if necessary.) The sentences can be silly or humorous, as long as they make sense syntactically and the words are used as subjects, verbs, and complements, as indicated by the columns on the board.

Differentiating Instruction
■ *Lesson Plans for Language Development*
■ *Supporting Instruction in Five Languages*
Assessment
■ *Progress Assessment for the Holt Handbook,* pp. 9–10

■ *Test Generator* (One-Stop Planner CD-ROM)
Other Language Resources
■ *Spelling Lessons & Activities*
■ *Vocabulary Development*
■ *Daily Language Activities Transparencies*

Recognizing Complements
Rule 5a *(pp. 105–107)*
OBJECTIVE

■ **To complete sentences by adding complements**

Recognizing Complements **105**

DIRECT TEACHING

Modeling and Demonstration

Recognizing Complements. Model how to recognize complements by using the example *Dan made himself a sandwich.* First, ask which words are the subject and verb. [*Dan*—subject; *made*—verb] Next, ask whether the subject and verb express a complete thought by themselves. [no] Then, ask what Dan made. [*a sandwich*] Finally, ask for whom Dan made the sandwich. [*himself*] Tell the students that both the noun *sandwich* and the pronoun *himself* complete the meaning of the verb *made;* therefore, both are complements. Now, have a volunteer use an example from this chapter to demonstrate how to recognize complements.

DIFFERENTIATING INSTRUCTION

Special Education Students

Have a helper work with students in a quiet area where they can read the example sentences aloud. Reading aloud might help students hear incomplete sentences and recognize the need for complements. Then, have the helper work with the students to complete **Exercise 1.**

┌─────────────────────┐
│ TIPS & TRICKS │
└─────────────────────┘

To find the complement in a sentence, try this trick. Cross out all the prepositional phrases first. Then, look for the subject, verb, and any complements that are in the rest of the sentence.

EXAMPLE

James threw the ball ~~over the defender~~ and ~~into the receiver's arms.~~ [The subject is *James.* The verb is *threw. Defender* and *arms* cannot be complements because they are both in prepositional phrases. The complement is *ball.*]

Reference Note

For more about **adverbs,** see page 59. For more about **prepositions** and **prepositional phrases,** see page 62.

	S	V	
INCOMPLETE	The longcase clock was [*what?*]		

	S	V	C
COMPLETE	The longcase clock was an **antique.** [The noun *antique* completes the meaning of the verb *was.*]		

	S	V	
INCOMPLETE	The elephant seemed [*what?*]		

	S	V	C
COMPLETE	The elephant seemed **tired.** [The adjective *tired* completes the meaning of the verb *seemed.*]		

An adverb is never a complement.

ADVERB   The koala chews slowly. [The adverb *slowly* modifies the verb by telling *how* the koala chews.]

COMPLEMENT   The koala chews eucalyptus **leaves.** [The noun *leaves* completes the meaning of the verb *chews* by telling *what* the koala chews.]

A complement is never a part of a prepositional phrase.

OBJECT OF PREPOSITION   Hannah is riding to her friend's house. [The noun *house* is the object of the preposition *to.*]

COMPLEMENT   Hannah is riding her **bicycle.** [The noun *bicycle* completes the meaning of the verb phrase *is riding* by telling *what* Hannah is riding.]

Exercise 1   Writing Complements

Write an appropriate complement to complete each of the following sentences.   Answers will vary.

EXAMPLE   **1.** The class seemed _____ to go on the field trip.

       1. happy

1. postcard
2. her
3. programmer
4. fine
5. firefighter
6. cloudy/dark
7. me

1. Yesterday, Uncle Joe sent me a _____ in the mail.
2. Did you lend _____ your calculator?
3. After college, she became a _____ in Chicago.
4. This puppy looks _____ to me, Doctor.
5. Is your brother still a _____ in Montana?
6. The sky was _____ and _____ that winter night.
7. Give _____ a hand, please.

┌──────────────────────────────────────┐
│ **RESOURCES** │
│ │
│ **Recognizing Complements** │
│ **Practice** │
│ ■ *Language & Sentence Skills Practice,* pp. 94, 104–106 │
└──────────────────────────────────────┘

8. Was that ____ in the dinosaur costume?

9. My little brother ran into the house and showed us a ____.

10. Next on the program for the recital, the middle school chorus will sing ____.

8. Elena

9. frog

10. "Oh, Susannah"

Objects of Verbs

Direct objects and *indirect objects* complete the meaning of transitive verbs.

Direct Objects

The direct object is one type of complement. It completes the meaning of a transitive verb.

5b. A *direct object* is a noun, pronoun, or word group that tells *who* or *what* receives the action of the verb.

A direct object answers the question *Whom?* or *What?* after a transitive verb.

EXAMPLES   **My brother bought a model.** [My brother bought *what*? Bought a *model*. The noun *model* receives the action of the verb *bought*.]

    Jan called **somebody** for the assignment. [Jan called *whom*? Called *somebody*. The pronoun *somebody* receives the action of the verb *called*.]

    Corey studied **Mother Teresa** in his history class. [Corey studied *whom*? Studied *Mother Teresa*. The compound noun *Mother Teresa* receives the action of the verb *studied*.]

A direct object may be a compound of two or more objects.

EXAMPLES   Did the car have spoked **wheels** and a **spoiler**? [The compound direct object of the verb *Did have* is *wheels* and *spoiler*.]

    She needed **glue, paint,** and **decals** for her model. [The compound direct object of the verb *needed* is *glue, paint,* and *decals*.]

Reference Note

For more information about **transitive verbs,** see page 55.

Direct Objects

Rule 5b *(pp. 107–109)*

OBJECTIVE

■ **To identify direct objects in sentences**

DIRECT TEACHING

Modeling and Demonstration

Direct Objects. Model how to identify direct objects by using the example *Mary bought milk, eggs, and bread at the supermarket.* First, ask which words are the subject and verb. [*Mary—subject; bought—verb*] Next, ask whether the subject and verb express a complete thought by themselves. [*no*] Point out that the students often can determine the direct object by turning the sentence into a question using *what* or *whom*. [*What did Mary buy?*] The answer [*milk, eggs, bread*] is the direct object because it directly receives the action of the verb *bought*. A direct object often answers the question *What?* or *Whom?* after a transitive verb. Finally, tell students that they can find other direct objects by following the formula *question word + did + subject + verb.* Now, have a volunteer use an example from this chapter to demonstrate how to identify direct objects.

English-Language Learners

General Strategies. To reinforce the idea that a direct object can answer the question *Whom?* as well as *What?*, write the following sentences on the chalkboard and ask students to identify the direct objects and to tell which question they answer.

1. I can't find David anywhere. [*David—Whom?*]
2. Melanie hugged her grandmother. [*grandmother—Whom?*]
3. Don't tickle her! [*her—Whom?*]
4. My dog greeted me and wagged its tail. [*me—Whom?; tail—What?*]

Reference Note
For more about **linking verbs,** see page 53.

A direct object can never follow a linking verb because a linking verb does not express action.

LINKING VERB   Julia Morgan **was** an architect. [The verb *was* does not express action; therefore, *architect* is not a direct object.]

Exercise 2 Identifying Direct Objects

Identify each direct object in the following sentences. Remember that a direct object may be compound.

EXAMPLE   **1.** Do you enjoy books and movies about horses?
              1. books, movies

1. If so, then you probably know some stories by Marguerite Henry.
2. Her books about horses have thrilled readers for more than forty years.
3. Henry has written many popular books, such as *Misty of Chincoteague* and *King of the Wind.*
4. Her book *King of the Wind* won the Newbery Medal in 1949.

Wesley Dennis, illustration from *King of the Wind* by Marguerite Henry. Illustration © 1947; copyright renewed 1976 by Morgan and Charles Reid Dennis.

Action Verbs and Linking Verbs. Remind students that linking verbs do not take objects because they do not express action. Review the differences between action verbs and linking verbs. Unless stu- dents feel confident in recognizing these types of verbs, they may become frustrated when trying to identify direct and indirect objects.

5. The book tells the <u>adventures</u> of the boy Agba and his beautiful Arabian horse.

6. Agba fed <u>milk</u> and <u>honey</u> to the newborn colt.

7. Sometimes the playful colt bit Agba's <u>fingers</u>.

8. The head of the stables often mistreated <u>Agba</u> and the young <u>colt</u>.

9. Later, the boy and the horse left their <u>home</u> and traveled to England.

10. Read *King of the Wind*, and learn <u>more</u> about the adventures of Agba and his horse.

Wesley Dennis, illustration from *King of the Wind* by Marguerite Henry. Illustration © 1947; copyright renewed 1976 by Morgan and Charles Reid Dennis.

Indirect Objects

The indirect object is another type of complement. Like the direct object, the indirect object helps complete the meaning of a transitive verb. If a sentence has an indirect object, it must also have a direct object.

5c. An ***indirect object*** is a noun, pronoun, or word group that usually comes between the verb and the direct object. An indirect object tells *to whom* or *to what* or *for whom* or *for what* the action of the verb is done.

EXAMPLES   I gave that **problem** some thought. [The noun *problem* is the indirect object of the verb *gave* and answers the question "*To what* did I give some thought?"]

Dad bought **himself** some peanuts. [The pronoun *himself* is the indirect object of the verb *bought* and answers the question "*For whom* did Dad buy peanuts?"]

Luke sent **David Robinson** a fan letter. [The compound noun *David Robinson* is the indirect object of the verb *sent* and answers the question "*To whom* did Luke send a fan letter?"]

TIPS & TRICKS

Here is a trick you can use to see whether a word is an indirect object. Move the word from before the direct object to after it, and add either *to* or *for*. If the sentence still makes sense, you know the word is an indirect object in the original sentence.

EXAMPLE
Carol sold Steve her old television.

Carol sold her old television **to** Steve. [The sentence means the same thing either way.]

Objects of Verbs   **109**

Indirect Objects
Rule 5c *(pp. 109–111)*

OBJECTIVES

- **To identify direct and indirect objects in sentences**
- **To complete sentences by adding direct and indirect objects**

DIRECT TEACHING

Modeling and Demonstration

Indirect Objects. Model how to identify indirect objects by using the example *Vinnie made us some lasagna*. First, ask which words are the subject and verb. [*Vinnie—subject; made—verb*] Next, ask whether the subject and verb express a complete thought by themselves. [*no*] Point out that the students often can determine the indirect object by turning the sentence into a question using *to whom* or *to what* or *for whom* or *for what*. (*Vinnie made some lasagna for whom?*) [*us*] Further point out that the indirect object usually comes between the verb and the direct object. [*made* us *lasagna*] Now, have a volunteer use another example from this chapter to demonstrate how to identify indirect objects.

DIFFERENTIATING INSTRUCTION

Learners Having Difficulty

Provide students with a list of sentences containing direct and indirect objects. Ask them to choose one sentence each and to draw a picture that depicts the action described in the sentence and shows the direct and indirect objects.

Exercise 3

DISTRIBUTED REVIEW

Ask students to find the prepositional phrases in sentences 1, 6, 7, and 8, and to identify each as an adjective phrase or an adverb phrase.

[1. *In Ecuador—adverb phrase; of his relatives—adjective phrase;* 6. *about Ecuadoran heroes—adjective phrase;* 7. *into the Andes Mountains—adverb phrase;* 8. *from the train—adverb phrase*]

EXTENSION

Critical Thinking

Analysis. Have each student write two sentences with the same meaning, one with an indirect object and one with a prepositional phrase (for example, *I sent Aunt Mae a gift* and *I sent a gift to Aunt Mae*). Have students trade sentences with a partner and identify the subject, verb, direct object, and indirect object or object of the preposition in each sentence. Discuss with students how to tell indirect objects from objects of prepositions by noting the position of the object in the sentence (indirect objects almost always come between the verb and the direct object) and by noting the presence or absence of a preposition.

Reference Note

For more information about **prepositional phrases** and **objects of prepositions,** see page 77.

HELP

Some sentences in Exercise 3 do not have indirect objects.

If the word *to* or *for* is used, the noun, pronoun, or word group following it is part of a prepositional phrase and cannot be an indirect object.

OBJECTS OF PREPOSITIONS	The ship's captain gave orders to the **crew.**
	Vinnie made some lasagna for **us.**
INDIRECT OBJECTS	The ship's captain gave the **crew** orders.
	Vinnie made **us** some lasagna.

Like a direct object, an indirect object can be compound.

EXAMPLES   She gave **Ed** and **me** the list of summer activities. [*Ed* and *me* are indirect objects of the verb *gave*. They answer the question "*To whom* did she give the list?"]

Did the peacock show **you** and your **sister** its tail feathers? [*You* and *sister* are indirect objects of the verb *Did show*. They answer the question "*To whom* did the peacock show its tail feathers?"]

Exercise 3   Identifying Direct and Indirect Objects

Identify the direct objects and indirect objects in the following sentences. Remember not to confuse objects of prepositions with direct objects and indirect objects.

EXAMPLE   1. Gabriel sent me a postcard from Ecuador.
            1. *me—indirect object; postcard—direct object*

1. In Ecuador, Gabriel visited many of his relatives.
2. His aunt Luz and uncle Rodrigo showed him the railroad in San Lorenzo.
3. They also visited the port in Esmeraldas.
4. Ecuador exports bananas and coffee.
5. Gabriel's cousin showed him some other sights.
6. She told Gabriel stories about Ecuadoran heroes.
7. Gabriel and his relatives rode a train high into the Andes Mountains.
8. They took photos from the train.
9. Gabriel enjoyed his visit to Ecuador.
10. He brought us some unusual souvenirs.

Exercise 4 **Writing Direct and Indirect Objects**

Write an appropriate direct or indirect object to complete each of the following sentences.   Answers may vary.

EXAMPLE   **1.** This weekend we are painting the ____.

         1. kitchen

1. The President made a ____ on television last night.
2. Did your dad teach ____ those magic tricks?
3. Wow! The governor wrote ____ a letter!
4. Then Marianne asked ____ the question in all our minds.
5. A mechanic replaced the truck's ____.
6. Save ____ a place at your table.
7. Are you still studying ____?
8. Okay, I'll owe ____ two hours' use of my skateboard.
9. Have you taken ____ for a walk?
10. Sam made ____ a table in shop class.

1. speech
2. you
3. me
4. Mr. Liu
5. alternator
6. Lenny
7. French
8. Brenda
9. Rex
10. his mom

Review A **Identifying Direct and Indirect Objects**

Identify the <u>direct objects</u> and <u>indirect objects</u> in the following sentences.

EXAMPLE   **1.** Have you ever given board games much thought?

         1. board games—indirect object; thought—direct object

1. For centuries, people have enjoyed <u>games</u> of strategy.
2. Interest in strategy games has given <u>us</u> <u>chess</u> and <u>checkers</u>.
3. My brother showed <u>me</u> a <u>book</u> about different kinds of board games.
4. Board games reflect many different <u>interests</u> and appeal to all kinds of people.
5. Some games teach <u>players</u> <u>lessons</u> useful in careers and sports.
6. Of course, word games can give <u>people</u> <u>hours</u> of fun.
7. During the more difficult word games, Mrs. Hampton sometimes helps <u>Chen</u> and <u>me</u>.
8. Do you like trivia <u>games</u>?
9. Sharon's uncle bought <u>Ronnie</u> and <u>her</u> <u>one</u> of the new quiz games.
10. A popular television show inspired the <u>game</u>.

┌**HELP**─

Some sentences in Review A do not have indirect objects.

DIFFERENTIATING INSTRUCTION

English-Language Learners
Spanish. Before students begin **Review A,** you may want to remind Spanish speakers that in Spanish, the direct object pronoun generally precedes the verb. You might want to ask a student to write on the chalkboard a short sentence in Spanish containing a direct object. Ask the student to label the parts and rewrite the sentence in English. Label the parts of the English sentence, emphasizing the difference in the position of the direct object. Allow students to use the model while working on **Reviews C** and **D.**

Objects of Verbs   **111**

Subject Complements
Rules 5d–f (pp. 112–118)

OBJECTIVES

- To identify predicate nominatives in sentences
- To identify predicate adjectives in sentences

DIRECT TEACHING

Modeling and Demonstration

Subject Complements. Model how to identify subject complements by using the example *Mount Rushmore is a national memorial.* First, ask which words are the subject and verb. [*Mount Rushmore*—subject; *is*—verb] Then, ask whether *is* is an action verb or a linking verb. [*linking verb*] Next, ask which word in the predicate is connected to *Mount Rushmore* by the linking verb *is*. [*memorial*] *Memorial* is the subject complement that identifies or describes the subject. Now, have a volunteer use another example from this chapter to demonstrate how to identify subject complements.

┌HELP┐

To find the subject complement in a question, rearrange the sentence to make a statement.

EXAMPLE

Is Crystal the pitcher for the softball team?

Crystal is the **pitcher** for the softball team.

Reference Note

For more about **linking verbs,** see page 53.

┌TIPS & TRICKS┐

Remember that some linking verbs (such as *appear, feel, grow, smell,* and *taste*) can also be used as action verbs.

LINKING VERB
The yogurt **smells** sour.

ACTION VERB
I **smell** fresh bagels.

In sentences with verbs like these, first decide whether the verb is used as a linking verb or an action verb. Then, determine what kind of complement, if any, the sentence contains.

Subject Complements

5d. A *subject complement* is a word or word group that is in the predicate and that identifies or describes the subject.

A linking verb connects a subject complement to the subject.

EXAMPLES
    Mrs. Suarez is a helpful **neighbor.** [The subject complement *neighbor* identifies the subject *Mrs. Suarez.* The linking verb *is* connects *Mrs. Suarez* and *neighbor.*]

    The airport appears very **busy.** [The subject complement *busy* describes the subject *airport.* The linking verb *appears* connects *airport* and *busy.*]

    What smells so **good**? [The subject complement *good* describes the subject *What.* The linking verb *smells* connects *What* and *good.*]

    He was the **one** in the middle of the line, in fact. [The subject complement *one* identifies the subject *He.* The linking verb *was* connects *He* and *one.*]

    The author of that story is **Anne McCaffrey.** [The subject complement *Anne McCaffrey* identifies the subject *author.* The linking verb *is* connects *author* and *Anne McCaffrey.*]

Subject complements always complete the meaning of linking verbs, not action verbs.

Common Linking Verbs					
appear	become	grow	remain	smell	stay
be	feel	look	seem	sound	taste

The two kinds of subject complements are the *predicate nominative* and the *predicate adjective.*

Predicate Nominatives

5e. A *predicate nominative* is a word or word group that is in the predicate and that identifies the subject or refers to it.

RESOURCES

Subject Complements
Practice

- *Language & Sentence Skills Practice,* pp. 99–106
- *Developmental Language & Sentence Skills,* pp. 45–46

A predicate nominative may be a noun, a pronoun, or a word group that functions as a noun. A predicate nominative is connected to the subject by a linking verb.

EXAMPLES Seaweed is **algae,** as I remember. [The noun *algae* is a predicate nominative following the linking verb *is.* *Algae* identifies the subject *Seaweed.*]

Was the first runner-up really **he**? [The pronoun *he* is a predicate nominative completing the meaning of the linking verb *Was.* *He* identifies the subject *runner-up.*]

NOTE Expressions such as *It's I* and *That was she* may sound awkward even though they are correct. In informal situations, many people use *It's me* and *That was her.* Such expressions may one day become acceptable in formal situations as well. For now, however, it is best to follow the rules of standard, formal English in all formal speaking and writing.

Be careful not to mistake a direct object for a predicate nominative. A predicate nominative always completes the meaning of a linking verb.

DIRECT OBJECT My brother admired the **gymnast.** [*Gymnast* is the direct object of the action verb *admired.*]

PREDICATE NOMINATIVE My brother became a **gymnast.** [*Gymnast* is the predicate nominative completing the meaning of the linking verb *became.*]

A predicate nominative may be compound.

EXAMPLES Maya Angelou is a great **poet** and **storyteller.** [*Poet* and *storyteller* are predicate nominatives. They identify the subject *Maya Angelou* and complete the meaning of the linking verb *is.*]

Is the shark a **fish** or a **mammal**? [*Fish* and *mammal* are predicate nominatives. They refer to the subject *shark* and complete the meaning of the linking verb *Is.*]

Yesterday was my **birthday, Labor Day,** and the first **day** of the week! [*Birthday, Labor Day,* and *day* are predicate nominatives. They identify the subject *Yesterday* and complete the meaning of the linking verb *was.*]

Reference Note

For more about **formal and informal English,** see page 221.

MEETING THE CHALLENGE

Metaphors A metaphor is a kind of figurative language that says that one thing *is* another (for instance, *My little brother is such a monkey!*). Many metaphors use predicate nominatives. In the example in parentheses, *monkey* is a predicate nominative for *brother.* Look in a collection of poems or stories to find an example of a metaphor that uses a predicate nominative. Write down the metaphor, and underline the predicate nominative. Make sure to also write down the title of the poem or story in which you found the metaphor.

ANSWER
Metaphors will vary.

Subject Complements **113**

DIRECT TEACHING

Subject Complements
Activity. Write the following sentences on the chalkboard, and ask students what the sentences have in common.

Corinna is enthusiastic.
The president of the club is Victor.
My dog is tired.

Lead students to see that the sentences each include the linking verb *is* and a word in the predicate that identifies or describes the subject of the sentence. Discuss with students which words in the predicates are adjectives (*enthusiastic, tired*) and which is a noun (*Victor*). Point out that these words are all subject complements because they identify or describe the subject.

EXTENSION

Looking at Language
Metaphors. Most metaphors use the *subject + linking verb + predicate nominative* pattern to make a comparison. Explain to students that a metaphor is a figure of speech that describes one thing by comparing it to another, unrelated thing. Share with students the following metaphors, pointing out the *subject + linking verb + predicate nominative* pattern:

Your smile is a beam of sunlight.
The ocean was an angry monster.
Fear is a gray veil.

Challenge students to come up with their own metaphors to share with the class.

PRACTICE

Guided and Independent

Exercise 5 You may wish to have students complete the first ten items as guided practice and the last ten items as independent practice.

HOMEWORK

DIFFERENTIATING INSTRUCTION

English-Language Learners

Spanish. Because English has one verb *be* while Spanish has both *estar* and *ser,* Spanish-speaking students may have difficulty reading sentences using forms of *be,* such as those in **Exercises 5** and **6.** Before students can find subject complements in the exercises, you may need to focus on forms of *be* with them.

DIRECT TEACHING

Correcting Misconceptions

Predicate Nominatives and Predicate Adjectives. If students are confusing direct objects with predicate nominatives, you could give them some practice identifying linking verbs. Bring newspaper or magazine articles to class, and assign each student a page or two in which to find linking verbs. Have students underline the linking verbs, circle any predicate nominatives, and put brackets around any predicate adjectives. Remind students that adverbs cannot be predicate nominatives or predicate adjectives.

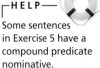

┌HELP┐

Some sentences in Exercise 5 have a compound predicate nominative.

│ S T Y L E   T I P │

Be careful not to overuse the linking verb *be* in your writing. Read your writing. Do you get the feeling that nothing is happening, that nobody is doing anything? If so, you may have used too many *be* verbs. When possible, replace a dull *be* verb with a verb that expresses action.

BE VERB
   My father **is** a cabinet maker.

ACTION VERB
   My father **makes** cabinets.

Exercise 5 Identifying Predicate Nominatives

Identify the <u>predicate nominative</u> in each of the following sentences.

EXAMPLES   **1.** Mount Rushmore is a national memorial.
   1. *memorial*

   2. Is that bird a finch or a sparrow?
   2. *finch, sparrow*

1. San Juan is the <u>capital</u> of Puerto Rico.
2. Her mother will remain <u>president</u> of the P.T.A.
3. Athens, Greece, has long been a <u>center</u> of art and drama.
4. The platypus and the spiny anteater are <u>mammals</u>.
5. The object of Juan Ponce de León's quest was the <u>Fountain of Youth</u>.
6. The peace pipe, or calumet, is a <u>symbol</u> of honor and power among American Indians.
7. Quebec is the largest <u>province</u> in Canada.
8. In 1959, Hawaii became our fiftieth <u>state</u>.
9. That bird must be an <u>eagle</u>.
10. The fourth planet from the sun is <u>Mars</u>.
11. Didn't she eventually become a <u>senator</u>?
12. He remained an <u>umpire</u> for over thirty years.
13. You are not the only <u>one</u> in the room.
14. Hiawatha was a real <u>person</u>.
15. Aren't you the oldest <u>daughter</u> in your family?
16. Could the problem with the engine be an empty gas <u>tank</u>?
17. Lucy Craft Laney was the <u>founder</u> of the Haines Normal and Industrial Institute.
18. For more information about Sadaharu Oh, Japan's great baseball star, a good source is "<u>Move Over for Oh-San</u>" in *Sports Illustrated.*
19. Was the author <u>Chaim Potok</u> or <u>Amy Tan</u>?
20. Be an <u>example</u> for others.

Predicate Adjectives

5f. A *predicate adjective* is an adjective that is in the predicate and that describes the subject.

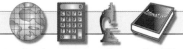

CONTENT-AREA CONNECTIONS

Science
Scientific Descriptions. Point out to students that predicate adjectives are useful in scientific descriptions. Have students write a few sentences in which they use a series of predicate adjectives to describe a scientific topic, such as the characteristics of a species or the symptoms of a disease. Students can share their sentences in small groups.

A predicate adjective is connected to the subject by a linking verb.

EXAMPLES By 9:30 P.M., I was very **tired.** [The adjective *tired* describes the subject *I.*]

I believe that Jacob is **Nigerian.** [The adjective *Nigerian* describes the subject *Jacob.*]

Like a predicate nominative, a predicate adjective may be compound.

EXAMPLES The blanket felt **soft** and **fuzzy.** [Both *soft* and *fuzzy* describe the subject *blanket.*]

The cave looked **cold, damp,** and **uncomfortable.** [*Cold, damp,* and *uncomfortable* all describe the subject *cave.*]

Exercise 6 Identifying Predicate Adjectives

Identify the <u>predicate adjective</u> in each of the following sentences.

EXAMPLES **1.** The porpoise seemed friendly.
1. friendly

2. Does that alligator look hungry?
2. hungry

1. Everyone felt <u>ready</u> for the test.
2. Those fresh strawberries smell <u>delicious</u>.
3. The front tire looks <u>flat</u> to me.
4. Everyone appeared <u>interested</u> in the debate.
5. That scratch may become <u>worse</u>.
6. She is <u>talented</u> in music.
7. During the movie, I became <u>restless</u> and <u>bored</u>.
8. Van looks <u>upset</u> about his grades.
9. Queen Liliuokalani was quite <u>popular</u> with the Hawaiian people.
10. The computer program does not seem <u>difficult</u> to Dana.
11. After a two-hour nap, the baby was still <u>sleepy</u>.
12. These ants are <u>quick</u> and <u>industrious</u>.
13. Even in winter, pine trees stay <u>green</u>.
14. Remain <u>calm</u> in an emergency, and do not panic.
15. This machine has always been <u>inexpensive</u> but <u>efficient</u>.

COMPUTER TIP

If you do overuse *be* verbs in your writing, a computer can help you fix the problem. Use the computer's search function to find each occurrence of *am, are, is, was, were, be, been,* and *being* in a piece of your writing. For each case, decide whether you need to use the *be* verb. If possible, replace it with an action verb, or revise the sentence some other way to add variety.

HELP

Some sentences in Exercise 6 have a compound predicate adjective.

RETEACHING

Predicate Nominatives and Predicate Adjectives

To help students learn the difference between predicate nominatives and predicate adjectives, divide the class into groups of two and ask each pair to make a list of words that would complete the sentence *The room is. . . .* One student can write adjectives, the other articles and nouns. Partners can check each other's lists and suggest further items for each category. Ask each student to share one of his or her subject complements, and have the class identify the word as a predicate adjective or a predicate nominative.

DIFFERENTIATING INSTRUCTION

English-Language Learners

Vietnamese. Vietnamese rarely uses the equivalent of the English verb *be.* Therefore, Vietnamese speakers of English sometimes drop forms of *be* in sentences having subject complements: *I very tired.*

Because the verb *be* is often contracted in conversation, it is especially difficult to hear. Model correct forms, and allow students time for quick drill and repetition.

Teacher: *I'm hungry. Are you?*
Student: *Yes, I'm hungry, too.*
Teacher: *Is Emily hungry?*
Student: *Yes, she's hungry, too.*

GRAMMAR

Learning for Life

Continued on pp.116–117

Writing Instructions. Bring some recipes to class, and have students study them for their use of complements. Discuss with the class the importance of complements in clearly written instructions.

Then, ask students to think about how they would give instructions on how to prepare their favorite food or how to play a favorite sport or game, and have them write a set of instructions. Students could meet in small groups to choose a process that can be performed in four or five steps.

DIFFERENTIATING INSTRUCTION

English-Language Learners

General Strategies. You may want to write the following sentences on the chalkboard to remind students that a few of the linking verbs in the box on p. 112 (for example, *smell, sound, taste, look,* and *feel*) can also be used as action verbs:

1. She smelled fresh bread in the kitchen.
2. They sounded the gong at dinner time.
3. Taste this sauce!
4. I looked at the picture.
5. I could feel a cool breeze.

Learners Having Difficulty

Have students use graphic organizers such as the following to show how word order can help them identify complements in a declarative sentence. Tell them that these graphic organizers leave out all adjectives, adverbs, and prepositional phrases.

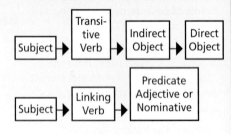

16. A giraffe's legs are very skinny.
17. The hikers were hot and thirsty after the long trek.
18. Isn't that statue African?
19. Don't be jealous of Tiger, the new kitten.
20. Is that myth Greek or Roman?

┌─HELP─
A sentence in Review B may have a compound subject complement.

Review B   Identifying Subject Complements

Identify each subject complement in the following sentences, and label it a *predicate nominative* or a *predicate adjective.*

EXAMPLE   1. The character Jahdu is a trickster.

   1. *trickster—predicate nominative*

1. A trickster is a character who plays tricks on others.
2. Tricksters have been popular in many folk tales throughout the world.
3. Jahdu, however, is the creation of Virginia Hamilton.
4. Her collections of folk tales, such as *The Time-Ago Tales of Jahdu* and *In the Beginning*, are very enjoyable.
5. Jahdu may be her most unusual hero.
6. He certainly seems clever and playful.
7. Even Jahdu's home, a forest on the Mountain of Paths, sounds mysterious.
8. Jahdu can stay invisible, a very useful skill.
9. He can become any object, from a boy to a taxicab.
10. Why are tricksters like Jahdu always such entertaining characters?

┌─HELP─
Some sentences in Review C have more than one complement or a compound complement.

Review C   Identifying Complements

Identify each complement in the following sentences, and label it a *direct object,* an *indirect object,* a *predicate nominative,* or a *predicate adjective.*

EXAMPLE   1. One pet of President Theodore Roosevelt's family was Algonquin, a pony.

   1. *Algonquin—predicate nominative*

1. Some presidents' pets have become famous.   **1.** p.a.
2. Someone may have shown you the book by President George Bush's pet, Millie.   **2.** i.o./d.o.
3. Millie, a spaniel, became an author.   **3.** p.n.

Learning for Life   *Continued from p. 115*

Remind students to write the steps in chronological order and to imagine the reader of their instructions performing the steps.

After students have finished writing, have them meet with a partner for peer evalua-

tion. Students should make sure the instructions are clear and should pay particular attention to whether complements have been used effectively. Partners may find it beneficial to mime the actions of each other's directions.

4. With the help of Mrs. Bush, Millie told a great <u>deal</u> about her days at the White House.   **4.** d.o.
5. President Richard Nixon's best-known pet was <u>Checkers</u>, a cocker spaniel.   **5.** p.n.
6. President Bill Clinton had both a <u>cat</u> named Socks and a <u>dog</u> named Buddy.   **6.** d.o./d.o.
7. President William Howard Taft kept a pet <u>cow</u>.   **7.** d.o.
8. Some presidential pets looked quite <u>strange</u> at the White House.   **8.** p.a.
9. A pet mockingbird was a favorite <u>companion</u> of Thomas Jefferson.   **9.** p.n.
10. Calvin Coolidge's raccoon, Rebecca, appeared <u>comfortable</u> at the White House.   **10.** p.a.

Review D   **Identifying Complements**

Identify each <u>complement</u> in the following sentences as a *direct object*, an *indirect object*, a *predicate nominative*, or a *predicate adjective*.

EXAMPLE   1. Have you ever seen a sari or a bindi?
   1. sari—direct object; bindi—direct object

1. Many women from India wear these <u>items</u>.   **1.** d.o.
2. A sari is a traditional Indian <u>garment</u> of cotton or silk.   **2.** p.n.
3. Women wrap the sari's long, brightly printed <u>cloth</u> around their bodies.   **3.** d.o.
4. As you can see, the softly draped sari is both <u>graceful</u> and <u>charming</u>.   **4.** p.a./p.a.
5. Some women buy <u>themselves</u> <u>cloth</u> woven with golden threads for an elegant look.   **5.** i.o./d.o.
6. As you might imagine, sari wearers can become quite <u>chilled</u> in the winter.   **6.** p.a.
7. In cold climates, Indian women wear their beautiful, lightweight <u>garments</u> under sturdy winter coats.
8. Another traditional ornament for many Indian women is the colored <u>dot</u> in the middle of their foreheads.   **7.** d.o.   **8.** p.n.
9. The word for the dot is *bindi*.   **9.** p.n.
10. The bindi gives the <u>wearer</u> a <u>look</u> of beauty and refinement.   **10.** i.o./d.o.

┌─HELP─
Some sentences in Review D have more than one complement or a compound complement.

Subject Complements   **117**

APPLICATION

Relating to Speaking

Activity. Arrange students in groups of four. Each group member will review one of the four types of complements covered in the chapter and will write five sentences, each containing an example of that type of complement. Then, have each student present a brief lesson to the group on his or her type of complement and read his or her sentences aloud. Tell students to use their voices to stress the complements of their sentences. Other group members can ask questions at the end of each minipresentation.

After students have revised their sets of instructions, you may want to assemble the instructions in a class manual organized by category.

DIFFERENTIATING INSTRUCTION

Advanced Learners

As an alternative to the **Oral Practice,** you might want to tell students to imagine they are writing letters to new pen pals they have never met in person. Have students reflect on how they would describe themselves in their letters. Encourage students to focus on their personality traits, likes and dislikes, goals, hobbies, and so on. Then, have each student write eight sentences he or she could use in the letter: two with direct objects, two with indirect objects and direct objects, two with predicate nominatives, and two with predicate adjectives. Ask students to underline the complements and to label each one by type.

Oral Practice **Creating Sentences with Complements**

Think of an example of each of the following kinds of complements. Then, create a sentence aloud, using your example. Use a variety of subjects and verbs in your sentences.

EXAMPLES **1.** a compound predicate nominative
1. *My aunt is a swimmer and a jogger.*

2. a direct object
2. *Lindsey tossed Sabra the softball.*

3. a pronoun used as a predicate nominative
3. *The winner of the science fair is she.*

1. a predicate adjective
2. an indirect object
3. a direct object
4. a predicate nominative
5. a compound predicate adjective
6. a compound predicate nominative
7. a compound direct object
8. a compound indirect object
9. a pronoun used as an indirect object
10. a pronoun used as a direct object

Answers will vary. Possible responses are given.
1. My pen is blue.
2. Give Melanie a hand with that box.
3. Did you lend Ray that book?
4. Her father is a dentist.
5. Flannel feels soft and warm.
6. The finalists are Leila, Ryan, and she.
7. Mrs. Cuomo made lasagna and manicotti.
8. We should take Todd and Sheila a housewarming present.
9. Please paint us a picture, Mr. Sato.
10. Bake it at 350° for one hour.

Chapter Review

A. Identifying Direct and Indirect Objects

Identify the *direct objects* and *indirect objects* in the following sentences.

1. James Baldwin wrote <u>stories</u>, <u>novels</u>, and <u>essays</u>.
2. Vita made her <u>mother</u> a <u>scarf</u> for her birthday.
3. He handed <u>Amy</u> and <u>me</u> an <u>ad</u> for the concert.
4. A park ranger told <u>Mike</u> the <u>story</u> of Forest Park.
5. Tropical forests give <u>us</u> many helpful <u>plants</u>.
6. Did she tell <u>you</u> about the bear?
7. The senator read the <u>crowd</u> a rousing <u>speech</u>.
8. The tourist gave the <u>pigeons</u> in Trafalgar Square <u>some</u> of his sandwich.
9. On the ferry to Ireland, Mr. McCourt told <u>us</u> the <u>history</u> of Dublin.
10. Bring <u>me</u> the <u>wrench</u> from the workbench, please.

B. Identifying Subject Complements

Identify the subject complements in the following sentences, and label each a *predicate nominative* or a *predicate adjective*.

11. Tuesday is the last <u>day</u> for soccer tryouts.
12. These peaches taste <u>sweet</u> and <u>juicy</u>.
13. Two common desert creatures are the <u>lizard</u> and the <u>snake</u>.
14. My cousin Tena has become an excellent <u>weaver</u> of Navajo blankets.
15. The soil in that pot feels <u>dry</u> to me.
16. The hero of the movie was a <u>songwriter</u> and a <u>singer</u>.
17. Why is Bill Gates so <u>famous</u> and so <u>successful</u>?
18. The three Brontë sisters were <u>Charlotte</u>, <u>Emily</u>, and <u>Anne</u>.
19. *The Adventures of Huckleberry Finn* is probably Mark Twain's best-known <u>book</u>.
20. The movie is <u>shallow</u>, <u>silly</, and <u>boring</u>.

─HELP─

Not all sentences in Part A have indirect objects.

Numerals in brackets refer to rules tested by the items in the Chapter Review.

1. [5b]
2. [5c, b]
3. [5c, b]
4. [5c, b]
5. [5c, b]
6. [5b]
7. [5c, b]
8. [5c, b]
9. [5c, b]
10. [5c, b]
11. [5e]
12. [5f]
13. [5e]
14. [5e]
15. [5f]
16. [5e]
17. [5f]
18. [5e]
19. [5e]
20. [5f]

C. Identifying Complements

Identify the <u>complements</u> in the following sentences, and label each a *direct object*, an *indirect object*, a *predicate nominative*, or a *predicate adjective*.

21. p.n. [5e]	**21.** Madrid is the <u>capital</u> of Spain.
22. i.o./d.o. [5c, b]	**22.** Did you give <u>me</u> your new <u>address</u>?
23. p.a. [5f]	**23.** These sketches of yours are <u>wonderful</u>!
24. d.o. [5b]	**24.** Dr. Jonas Salk developed a <u>vaccine</u> to prevent polio.
25. p.n. [5e]	**25.** Pam Adams is my best <u>friend</u>.
26. i.o./i.o./d.o. [5c, b]	**26.** My father sent his <u>mother</u> and <u>father</u> two <u>tickets</u> to Mexico.
27. p.a./p.a. [5f]	**27.** Your handwriting is <u>neat</u> and <u>readable</u>.
28. p.n. [5e]	**28.** The longest play by Shakespeare is *Hamlet*.
29. i.o./d.o. [5c, b]	**29.** Hugo handed his <u>teacher</u> the <u>papers</u>.
30. i.o./d.o. [5c, b]	**30.** My father tossed the <u>dog</u> an old <u>bone</u>.
31. p.n. [5e]	**31.** That new country performer is my favorite <u>singer</u>.
32. i.o./d.o. [5c, b]	**32.** Thunder sometimes gives <u>me</u> a <u>headache</u>.
33. p.a. [5f]	**33.** Are these toys <u>safe</u> for children?
34. i.o./d.o. [5c, b]	**34.** My dad is buying my <u>mother</u> a <u>bicycle</u>.
35. p.n. [5e]	**35.** Light reflectors for a bike are a good <u>idea</u>.
36. i.o./d.o. [5c, b]	**36.** The king granted <u>them</u> three <u>wishes</u>.
37. p.a./p.a. [5f]	**37.** Our trip to Villahermosa was <u>short</u> but <u>exciting</u>.
38. d.o. [5b]	**38.** Angelo painted a beautiful <u>picture</u> of his mother.
39. d.o. [5b]	**39.** Have you eaten <u>lunch</u> yet?
40. p.n. [5e]	**40.** Miki is <u>one</u> of the best spellers in the class.

Writing Application
Using Complements in a Paragraph

Direct Objects and Indirect Objects   For National Hobby Month, students in your class are making posters about their hobbies. Each poster will include drawings or pictures and a written description of the hobby. Write a paragraph about your hobby to go on your poster. Use at least three direct objects and two indirect objects in your paragraph.

Prewriting   Choose a topic for your poster project. You could write about any collection, sport, craft, or activity that you enjoy in your free time. You could also write about a hobby that you are interested in starting. Freewrite about the hobby. Be sure to tell why you enjoy it or why you think you would enjoy it. If the hobby is new to you, find out more about it from another hobbyist or from the library.

Writing   Begin your paragraph with a main-idea sentence that clearly identifies the hobby or special interest. Check your prewriting notes often to find details you can use in describing the hobby.

Revising   Read your paragraph aloud. Does it give enough information about your hobby? Would someone unfamiliar with the hobby find it interesting? Add, cut, or rearrange details to make your paragraph easier to understand. Identify the transitive verbs in your paragraph. Have you used at least three direct objects and two indirect objects? You may need to revise some sentences.

Publishing   Read over your paragraph for spelling, grammar, and punctuation errors, and correct any you find. You and your classmates may want to make posters using your paragraphs and some pictures. Cut pictures out of magazines and brochures, or draw your own. Then, attach your writing and art to pieces of poster board and display the posters in the classroom.

APPLICATION

Writing Application
Prewriting Tip. The assignment requires that students write paragraphs about their hobbies. Students may need further elaboration on what constitutes a hobby. You can tell them that a hobby is anything someone does on a regular basis for enjoyment and not for profit.

Writing Tip. For students to write paragraphs about their hobbies, they will need to analyze the processes they go through when practicing their hobbies. For example, if they collect things, they will need to discuss where or how the things are obtained and how the collections are kept or displayed.

Scoring Rubric. While you will want to pay particular attention to students' use of direct objects and indirect objects, you will also want to evaluate overall writing performance. You may want to give a split score to indicate development and clarity of the composition as well as grammar skills.

Agreement
Subject and Verb, Pronoun and Antecedent

Diagnostic Preview

A. Choosing Verbs That Agree in Number with Their Subjects

Find the subject of each of the following sentences. Then, choose the form of the verb in parentheses that agrees with the subject.

EXAMPLE **1.** Janelle and Brad (*are, is*) in the drama club.

    1. Janelle, Brad—are

Numerals in brackets refer to rules tested by the items in the Diagnostic Preview.

  1. [6j]
  2. [6b(2), k]
  3. [6b(1), c]
  4. [6b(2), k]
  5. [6g]
  6. [6g]
  7. [6b(2), k]
  8. [6g, k, l]
  9. [6b(2), c]

1. Neither the passengers nor the pilot (*was, were*) injured.
2. There (*are, is*) two exciting new rides at the amusement park.
3. That book of Spanish folk tales (*is, are*) selling out.
4. (*Here are, Here's*) some books about Hawaii.
5. Shel Silverstein and Ogden Nash (*appeal, appeals*) to both children and grown-ups.
6. Velma and her little sister (*was, were*) reading a story by Gyo Fujikawa.
7. (*Was, Were*) your parents happy with the results?
8. Why (*doesn't, don't*) she and Megan bring the lemonade with them to the picnic?
9. The dishes on that shelf (*look, looks*) clean.

CHAPTER RESOURCES

Internet
■ go.hrw.com (keyword: HLLA)

Planning
■ *One-Stop Planner CD-ROM*
■ *On Course: Mapping Instruction*
■ *At Home: A Guide to Standards Mastery,* pp. 28, 29

Practice & Review
■ *Language & Sentence Skills Practice,* pp. 111–123; 124–127
■ *Developmental Language & Sentence Skills,* pp. 47–56

Application & Enrichment
■ *Language & Sentence Skills Practice,* pp. 128, 131; 110, 129–130

10. Either the <u>cats</u> or the <u>dog</u> (*has*, *have*) upset the plants.
11. There (*go*, *goes*) two more <u>deer</u>!
12. I (*am*, *is*) crocheting an afghan.
13. Why (*wasn't*, *weren't*) <u>you</u> at the scout meeting yesterday?
14. Several <u>paintings</u> by that artist (*are*, *is*) now on exhibit at the mall.
15. <u>They</u> (*doesn't*, *don't*) know how to find their way to the family reunion.

10. [6j]
11. [6b(2), k]
12. [6b(1)]
13. [6b(1), k]
14. [6b(2), c]
15. [6l]

B. Choosing Pronouns That Agree with Their Antecedents

For each of the following sentences, identify the <u>pronoun that agrees with its antecedent</u>.

EXAMPLES
  1. Either Eileen or Barbara will bring (*her*, *their*) notes.
    1. her

  2. When Dennis and Aaron were younger, (*he*, *they*) rode the same bus to school.
    2. they

16. A student should proofread (*his or her*, *their*) work carefully before turning in the final copy.
17. Carlos and Andrew finally watched the videos (*he*, *they*) had borrowed.
18. Everyone on the girls' volleyball team has picked up (*her*, *their*) equipment.
19. The cat had batted its toy under the sofa and couldn't reach (*it*, *them*).
20. Jennifer or Sharon will leave early so that (*she*, *they*) can prepare the display.
21. Most of the trees in the park had lost (*its*, *their*) leaves.
22. If you aren't going to finish those crossword puzzles, may I do (*it*, *them*)?
23. Each of the drawings was hung on the wall in (*its*, *their*) frame.
24. When Martin and Stephanie were not rehearsing onstage, (*he or she*, *they*) studied their lines in the hall.
25. Did one of the chickens lose (*its*, *their*) feathers?

16. [6o, n]
17. [6o(5)]
18. [6n,o(1)]
19. [6o]
20. [6o(4)]
21. [6o(3)]
22. [6o]
23. [6o(1)]
24. [6o(5)]
25. [6o(1)]

Differentiating Instruction

■ *Lesson Plans for Language Development*
■ *Supporting Instruction in Five Languages*
■ *At Home: In Five Languages*

Assessment

■ *Progress Assessment for the Holt Handbook,* pp. 11–12, 41

■ *Test Generator (One-Stop Planner CD-ROM)* 🔘

Other Language Resources

■ *Spelling Lessons & Activities*
■ *Vocabulary Development*
■ *Daily Language Activities Transparencies*

are covered. Finally, the chapter teaches agreement between pronouns and antecedents.

■ The chapter closes with a **Chapter Review** for checking students' mastery of agreement. Also, a **Writing Application** feature asks students to use correct subject-verb and pronoun-antecedent agreement in a note about tending pets.

■ For help in integrating this chapter with writing assignments in *Holt Literature and Language Arts,* use the **Teaching Strands** chart on pp. T22–T23.

ASSESSING

Entry-Level Assessment

Diagnostic Preview. You may wish to use the **Diagnostic Preview** to gauge students' understanding of subject-verb and pronoun-antecedent agreement. If only a few students are unable to demonstrate mastery, you could have them read the definitions and work the exercises together.

The preview can also be used to determine the exact nature of problems for students who fail to use correct agreement in their writing.

PRETEACHING

Lesson Starter

Prior Knowledge. Draw stick figures on the chalkboard in three groups: one single figure, one pair, and one group of three. Tell students the figures are students, and ask volunteers to say how many students are in each group. Then, ask *Would you say "three student" or "three students"?* Lead the class to see that nouns are either singular (one item) or plural (more than one item).

Number and Agreement of Subject and Verb

Rules 6a, b *(pp. 124–127)*

OBJECTIVES

- To identify words as singular or plural
- To identify subjects and verbs as singular or plural
- To change the number of subjects and verbs
- To choose verbs that agree in number with their subjects

USAGE

DIRECT TEACHING

Modeling and Demonstration

Number and Agreement of Subject and Verb. Model how to determine that the subject and verb agree in number by using the example *Latrice has been studying Arabic.* First, ask students to identify the subject. [*Latrice*] Then, ask whether this subject is singular or plural. [*singular*] Then, ask which word or words make up the verb in this sentence. [*has been studying*] Ask whether this verb phrase is singular or plural. [*singular*] Point out that singular subjects take singular verbs and that plural subjects take plural verbs. Also, point out that in a verb phrase, the helping verb agrees with the subject in number. Now, have a volunteer use another example from this chapter to demonstrate how to determine whether the subject and verb agree in number.

┌─ **HELP** ─

Most nouns that end in *–s* are plural (*igloos, sisters*). Most verbs that end in *–s* are singular (*sings, tries*).

EXAMPLES
My sister**s** sing.
My sister sing**s**.

However, verbs used with the singular pronouns *I* and *you* do not end in *–s*.

EXAMPLES
I sing.
You sing.

Reference Note

The plurals of some nouns do not end in *–s* (*mice, Chinese, aircraft*). For more about **spelling the plural forms of nouns,** see page 325.

Number

Number is the form a word takes to show whether the word is singular or plural.

6a. Words that refer to one person, place, thing, or idea are generally *singular* in number. Words that refer to more than one person, place, thing, or idea are generally *plural* in number.

Singular	tepee	I	baby	mouse
Plural	tepees	we	babies	mice

Exercise 1 **Identifying Singular and Plural Words**

Identify each of the following words as *singular* or *plural*.

EXAMPLE   **1.** activities
            1. plural

1. peach 1. s
2. libraries 2. p
3. highway 3. s
4. knife 4. s
5. shelves 5. p
6. children 6. p
7. they 7. p
8. enchiladas 8. p
9. women 9. p
10. America 10. s

11. dirt 11. s
12. dress 12. s
13. someone 13. s
14. feet 14. p
15. fantasy 15. s
16. society 16. s
17. potatoes 17. p
18. people 18. p
19. several 19. p
20. fathers-in-law 20. p

Agreement of Subject and Verb

6b. A verb should agree in number with its subject.

A subject and verb *agree* when they have the same number.

(1) Singular subjects take singular verbs.

EXAMPLES   The **ocean roars** in the distance. [The singular verb *roars* agrees with the singular subject *ocean*.]

She plays the violin well. [The singular verb *plays* agrees with the singular subject *She.*]

┌─ **RESOURCES**

Number and Agreement of Subject and Verb
Practice
- *Language & Sentence Skills Practice,* pp. 111–112, 124
- *Developmental Language & Sentence Skills,* pp. 47–48

(2) Plural subjects take plural verbs.

EXAMPLES   **Squirrels eat** the seeds from the bird feeder. [The plural verb *eat* agrees with the plural subject *Squirrels.*]

            They practice after school. [The plural verb *practice* agrees with the plural subject *They.*]

When a sentence contains a verb phrase, the first helping verb in the phrase agrees with the subject.

EXAMPLES   **Latrice has** been studying Arabic.
            They have been studying Arabic.

For information on **verb phrases,** see page 50.

Exercise 2 **Identifying the Number of Subjects and Verbs**

Identify each of the following subjects and verbs as either <u>singular</u> or *plural*.

EXAMPLE   **1.** flag waves
         1. singular

┌HELP┐

All verbs in Exercise 2 agree with their subjects.

1. socks match **1.** p
2. lightning crackles **2.** s
3. leaves rustle **3.** p
4. mosquitoes buzz **4.** p
5. Lyle baby-sits **5.** s
6. bands march **6.** p
7. Richelle knits **7.** s
8. they listen **8.** p
9. singer practices **9.** s
10. horses whinny **10.** p
11. crows fly **11.** p
12. Shannon chooses **12.** s
13. boat floats **13.** s
14. we learn **14.** p
15. leg aches **15.** s
16. Roger guesses **16.** s
17. poets write **17.** p
18. cells divide **18.** p
19. he knows **19.** s
20. ice cube melts **20.** s

Exercise 3 **Changing the Number of Subjects and Verbs**

All of the subjects and verbs in the following sentences agree in number. Rewrite each sentence, changing the subject and verb from singular to plural or from plural to singular.

EXAMPLE   **1.** Lions roar on the plains of Kenya.
         1. A lion roars on the plains of Kenya.

1. Maps show the shape of a country.

Agreement of Subject and Verb   **125**

USAGE

DIRECT TEACHING

Subject-Verb Agreement
Activity. To introduce subject-verb agreement to students, write these two nonsense sentences on the chalkboard:

1. The ama (*plin, plins*) the corb.
2. The amas (*plin, plins*) the corb.

Ask students to select the correct "verbs" and to explain how they were able to make the correct choices. [*Some students will probably say that they chose what "sounded" right.*]

Ask volunteers to replace the non-sense words in each sentence with real words. Tell students to notice how the –s endings in sentence 1 are different from those in sentence 2.

1. The <u>horse jumps</u> the fence.
2. The <u>horses jump</u> the fence.

APPLICATION

Subject-Verb Agreement
Activity. To provide students with practice in subject-verb agreement, have them develop subject-verb pairs like those in **Exercise 2.** You can pair students and have one student in each pair suggest subjects and the other suggest verbs that agree with those subjects. For added practice, have students create complete sentences from their subject-verb pairs as well as from the word pairs in **Exercise 2.**

MINI-LESSON **Grammar**   *Continued on p. 126*

Finding the Subject. To determine correct agreement of the subject and verb, students must be able to locate the subject of a sentence. Write the following sentences on the chalkboard, and have volunteers find the subjects by asking *Who?* or *What?*

before the verbs.

1. The tired <u>campers</u> built a campfire.

2. <u>Leonie</u> enjoyed her hike through the canyon.

Agreement of Subject and Verb   **125**

Exercise 3   Changing the Number of Subjects and Verbs

ANSWERS

1. The (or A) map shows the shape of a country.

2. What country is highlighted on the map below?

3. Do oceans form Kenya's eastern border?

4. A (or The) visitor enjoys Kenya's beautiful scenery.

5. Mount Kenya's peak is covered with snow.

6. A wildlife park has been created in Kenya.

7. In the picture below, a (or the) ranger patrols a park to protect the animals.

8. He certainly has unusual transportation.

9. An industry is located in Kenya's capital, Nairobi.

10. A (or The) Kenyan farmer grows such crops as wheat, corn, and rice.

DIFFERENTIATING INSTRUCTION

English-Language Learners

Cantonese. Cantonese students may sometimes omit s from plurals for two reasons. First, Cantonese speakers do not generally use grammatical devices to express plurality. Second, Cantonese speakers sometimes find it difficult to pronounce final consonant clusters. Students may need some practice hearing and pronouncing the final s.

Focus students' attention by using exercises in which they look for and underline plural words. Irregular plurals must be memorized and practiced, as students might generalize the plural s to all nouns: *The childs (or childrens) found their lost dog.*

2. What countries are highlighted on the map below?

3. Does an ocean form Kenya's eastern border?

4. Visitors enjoy Kenya's beautiful scenery.

5. Mount Kenya's peaks are covered with snow.

6. Wildlife parks have been created in Kenya.

7. In the picture below, rangers patrol a park to protect the animals.

8. They certainly have unusual transportation.

9. Many industries are located in Kenya's capital, Nairobi.

10. Kenyan farmers grow such crops as wheat, corn, and rice.

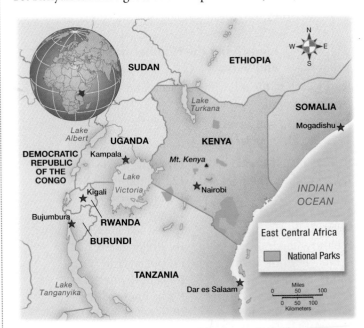

MINI-LESSON   Grammar   *Continued from p. 125*

3. On the calm waters, the <u>boat</u> rocked gently.

4. My <u>tent</u> offered shelter from the rain.

For additional information and practice, refer students to **Chapter 1: The Sentence,** p. 7.

Exercise 4 Choosing Verbs That Agree in Number with Their Subjects

For each of the following sentences, choose the form of the verb in parentheses that agrees with the subject.

EXAMPLE   **1.** The kitten (*pounces, pounce*) on the ball.

      1. *pounces*

1. Firefighters (*risks, risk*) their lives to save others.
2. The snowplow (*clears, clear*) the road quickly.
3. Some dancers (*like, likes*) reggae music best.
4. St. Augustine, Florida, (*has, have*) many old buildings.
5. Some students (*chooses, choose*) to play volleyball.
6. At the science fair, the winner always (*receives, receive*) a savings bond.
7. Strong winds (*whistles, whistle*) through the old house.
8. Each Saturday, club members (*picks, pick*) up the litter in the park.
9. The principal (*makes, make*) announcements over the loudspeaker each day.
10. Doctors (*says, say*) that listening to loud music can harm people's hearing.

Problems in Agreement
Phrases Between Subject and Verb

6c. The number of a subject is not changed by a phrase following the subject.

EXAMPLES   These **shades** of blue **are** my favorite colors.

      The **ballerina** with long black braids **has** been my sister's ballet teacher for two years.

However, if the subject is the indefinite pronoun *all, any, more, most, none,* or *some,* its number may be determined by the object of a prepositional phrase that follows it.

EXAMPLES   **Some** of the oranges **are** gone. [*Some* refers to the plural noun *oranges.*]

      Some of the fruit **is** gone. [*Some* refers to the singular noun *fruit.*]

Reference Note

For information on **phrases,** see Chapter 4.

┌ HELP ┐

The subject of a sentence is never in a prepositional phrase.

EXAMPLE

The **apples** in the refrigerator are not cold yet. [*Apples* is the subject. *Refrigerator* cannot be the subject because it is part of the prepositional phrase *in the refrigerator.*]

Problems in Agreement   **127**

USAGE

Problems in Agreement
Rules 6c–m *(pp. 127–137)*

O B J E C T I V E S

- To choose verbs that agree in number with their subjects when an intervening phrase separates the subject and verb

- To choose verbs that agree in number with indefinite pronouns used as subjects

- To choose verbs that agree with compound subjects

- To read aloud sentences with compound subjects joined by *or* or *nor*

- To choose verbs that agree with subjects that come after the verb

- To read aloud sentences containing *don't* and *doesn't*

- To write *don't* and *doesn't* to agree with subjects in sentences

DIRECT TEACHING

Modeling and Demonstration

Problems in Agreement. Using the example *These shades of blue are my favorite colors,* model how a subject's number is not changed by the prepositional phrase following it. Ask whether the subject *shades* is singular or plural. [*plural*] Then, ask what the verb's number is. [*plural*] Show that the phrase *of blue* does not change the subject's number, even though *blue,* the object of the preposition, is singular. Explain, however, that the number of the indefinite pronouns *all, any, more, most, none,* and *some* may be determined by the prepositional phrase that follows. Now, have a volunteer use another example from this chapter to demonstrate how a subject's number is not changed by a prepositional phrase following it.

DIRECT TEACHING

Correcting Misconceptions

Agreement and Compound Prepositions. Students may erroneously think that compound prepositions such as *along with, as well as, in addition to,* and *together with* change the number of the subject from singular to plural. Encourage students to disregard phrases with compound prepositions when they are trying to determine correct subject-verb agreement.

RETEACHING

Agreement of Subject and Verb

Activity. Another approach to teaching subject-verb agreement is to have students isolate the subject and the verb. Write sentences from **Exercise 5** on the chalkboard. Then, have volunteers come to the board and erase all but the subject and correct verb from each sentence.

DIFFERENTIATING INSTRUCTION

English-Language Learners

Spanish. In Spanish, *la gente* (people) is a singular noun, so Spanish-speaking students might use sentences such as "The people is going to the game." Provide some practice in subject-verb agreement using *people* as the subject.

NOTE   *As well as, along with, together with,* and *in addition to* are compound prepositions. Phrases beginning with compound prepositions do not affect the number of a subject or verb.

EXAMPLE   **Myra,** along with her brothers, **helps** with household chores each evening. [The prepositional phrase *along with her brothers* does not affect the number of the subject *Myra. Myra* is singular and takes a singular verb, *helps.*]

Exercise 5 Choosing Verbs That Agree in Number with Their Subjects

In each of the following sentences, choose the form of the verb in parentheses that agrees with the subject.

EXAMPLE   1. Islands off the coast (*has, have*) a life of their own.
            1. *have*

1. The second-largest island of the United States (*is, are*) located in the Gulf of Alaska.
2. The thirteen thousand people on Kodiak Island (*is, are*) mostly of Scandinavian, Russian, or Native Arctic descent.

3. The citizens of Kodiak (*calls, call*) Alaska the mainland.
4. Sacks of mail (*is, are*) flown there from the mainland.
5. Industries in the community, originally known as Kikhtak, (*includes, include*) farming, fishing, and mining.
6. One cannery on the island (*cans, can*) salmon eggs, or roe.
7. Many residents on the mainland (*considers, consider*) roe a delicacy.
8. Bears like this one (*catch, catches*) fresh salmon.
9. However, their search for leftovers often (*create, creates*) problems for Kodiak.
10. The officials of one town (*has, have*) had to put a special bear-proof fence around the garbage dump.

128   Chapter 6   Agreement

Indefinite Pronouns

Personal pronouns refer to specific people, places, things, or ideas. A pronoun that does not refer to a definite person, place, thing, or idea is called an **indefinite pronoun.**

Personal Pronouns	she	you	we	them
Indefinite Pronouns	each	many	anyone	all

6d. The following indefinite pronouns are singular: *anybody, anyone, anything, each, either, everybody, everyone, everything, neither, nobody, no one, nothing, one, somebody, someone,* and *something.*

EXAMPLES **One** of the supergiant stars **is** Antares.

Each of the tourists **was** given a souvenir.

Does everybody in the restaurant like pita bread?

Exercise 6 Choosing Verbs That Agree in Number with Their Subjects

In the following sentences, choose the form of the verb in parentheses that agrees with the subject.

EXAMPLE **1.** Neither of the teams (*is, are*) on the field.
   1. is

 1. Nearly everybody in Ruby Lee's family (*enjoy, enjoys*) tomato soup.
 2. Neither of them (*was, were*) wearing a hat.
 3. Somebody in the class (*speaks, speak*) French.
 4. Nobody in the first two rows (*want, wants*) to volunteer to be the magician's assistant.
 5. Each of these songs (*is, are*) by the Beatles.
 6. Someone in the crowd (*is, are*) waving a pennant, but I can't tell whether it's Nick.
 7. Everyone in those exercise classes (*has, have*) lost weight.
 8. One of the band members (*play, plays*) lead guitar and sings backup vocals.
 9. No one (*was, were*) listening to the music.
10. (*Do, Does*) either of them know how?

┌─HELP─┐

The words *one, thing,* and *body* are singular. The indefinite pronouns that contain these words are singular, too.

EXAMPLES
Was every**one** there?

Some**body has** answered.

No**thing works** better.

┌─HELP─┐

Remember that the subject is never part of a prepositional phrase.

DIFFERENTIATING INSTRUCTION

Special Education Students

Learning-disabled students often have difficulty focusing their attention. To help them understand agreement rules, create exercises in which students match subjects and predicates to form complete sentences. You may also want to have students skip the chapter's more difficult content.

To provide additional practice, write verbs on flashcards and have the students create sentences by adding subjects that agree with the verbs.

Learners Having Difficulty

Encourage students to read their work aloud before submitting it. Hearing the sentence may help students hear mistakes they might miss visually.

COMPUTER TIP

Using indefinite pronouns correctly can be tricky. To help yourself, you may want to create an indefinite pronoun guide. First, summarize the information in Rules 6d–6f. Then, choose several example sentences to illustrate the rules.

If you use a computer, you can create a help file with these rules and examples. Call up your help file whenever you have trouble with indefinite pronouns in your writing. If you don't use a computer, you can keep your guide in a writing notebook.

HELP

The pronouns listed in Rule 6f aren't always followed by prepositional phrases.

EXAMPLES

All are here.

Some has spilled.

In such cases you should look at the **context**—the sentences before and after the pronoun—to see if the pronoun refers to a singular or a plural word.

6e. The following indefinite pronouns are plural: *both, few, many, several.*

EXAMPLES **Both overflow** occasionally.

Few of the guests **are** wearing formal clothes.

Many of the newer houses **have** built-in smoke detectors.

Several in the group **say** yes.

6f. The indefinite pronouns *all, any, more, most, none,* and *some* may be singular or plural, depending on their meaning in a sentence.

Often, the object of a preposition that follows the pronoun indicates whether the pronoun is singular or plural. If the object of the preposition is singular, the pronoun usually is singular. If the object is plural, the pronoun usually is plural.

EXAMPLES **All** of the snow **has** melted. [*All* is singular because *snow* is singular. The helping verb *has* is singular to agree with *All.*]

All of the snowflakes **have** melted. [*All* is plural because *snowflakes* is plural. The helping verb *have* is plural to agree with *All.*]

Some of the birdseed **is** left in the feeder. [*Some* is singular because *birdseed* is singular. The helping verb *is* is singular to agree with *Some.*]

Some of the sunflower seeds **are** left in the feeder. [*Some* is plural because *seeds* is plural. The helping verb *are* is plural to agree with *Some.*]

Exercise 7 **Choosing Verbs That Agree in Number with Their Subjects**

Choose the <u>correct form of the verb</u> in parentheses in each of the following sentences.

EXAMPLE 1. Many of these puppies (*needs, need*) a good home.
1. *need*

1. Most of the balloons (*has, <u>have</u>*) long strings.
2. All of the girls wearing purple uniforms (*plays, <u>play</u>*) on the softball team.

3. Both of the sneakers (*gives*, *give*) me blisters.
4. Most of these recipes (*requires*, *require*) ricotta cheese.
5. Some of the artists (*paint*, *paints*) landscapes.
6. Few of those songs (*was*, *were*) composed by Duke Ellington.
7. None of the apartments (*has*, *have*) been painted.
8. All of the jewels (*is*, *are*) in the safe.
9. Many in the crowd (*waves*, *wave*) signs.
10. All of the writing (*is*, *are*) upside down.

Compound Subjects

A compound subject is made up of two or more subjects that are connected by the conjunction *and, or,* or *nor.* These connected subjects share the same verb.

6g. **Subjects joined by *and* generally take a plural verb.**

EXAMPLES **Red** and **blue are** the school's colors.

New **uniforms** and **instruments were ordered** for the marching band.

Mr. Lewis, Mrs. Kirk, and **Ms. Jefferson have applied** for new jobs.

(Exercise 8) **Choosing Verbs That Agree in Number with Their Subjects**

Identify the compound subject in each of the following sentences. Then, choose the form of the verb in parentheses that agrees with the compound subject.

EXAMPLE   **1.** Volcanoes and earthquakes (*is, are*) common in that area.

   1. Volcanoes, earthquakes—are

1. The blanket and the robe (*has, have*) Navajo designs.
2. Wind, hail, and freezing rain (*is, are*) predicted for Thursday.
3. A desk and a bookcase (*were, was*) moved into Ella's room.
4. Savannas and velds (*is, are*) two kinds of grasslands found in Africa.

┌HELP─

Some indefinite pronouns, such as *both*, *each*, and *some*, can also be used as adjectives. When an indefinite adjective comes before the subject of a sentence, the verb agrees with the subject as it normally would.

EXAMPLES
   Children love playing in the park.

   Both children love playing in the park.

   The **child loves** playing in the park.

   Each child loves playing in the park.

Reference Note

For information on **conjunctions,** see page 66.

EXTENSION

Critical Thinking

Metacognition. Have students analyze their results from **Exercise 7**. Students should take note of each sentence they missed or had difficulty with and write an example sentence of their own for each problematic indefinite pronoun. Then, have students answer the following questions:

■ What about agreement of subjects and verbs in **Exercise 7** causes you trouble?

■ Why do you have difficulty in this area?

■ How can you improve your understanding in this area?

TEACHING (TIP)

(Exercise 8)   Remind students that compound subjects can be made up of more than two elements. A series of three or more elements can make up a compound subject. No matter how many subjects there are, though, a coordinating conjunction will generally be used before the last item in a series.

Looking at Language

Dialects. Explain that some dialects of American English frequently omit the *–s* ending from verbs. [*He work hard. She like mysteries.*] Suggest that students take turns reading aloud the following subjects and verbs to hear examples of standard English. You may want to have students work together to expand the list and then read aloud their subjects and verbs.

1. horse jumps
2. girls leave
3. apple tastes
4. Marie talks
5. telephone rings

6. soldier waits
7. sisters want
8. teacher gives
9. car stops
10. Bill works

5. A delivery <u>truck</u> and a <u>car</u> with a trailer (*were, was*) stalled on the highway.
6. A <u>raccoon</u> and a <u>possum</u> (*raid, raids*) our vegetable garden every night.
7. <u>Mandy</u> and her <u>aunt</u> (*goes, go*) to the Chinese market every Saturday.
8. <u>Eric</u> and <u>Jarvis</u> (*were, was*) asked to introduce the speaker.
9. <u>Mosquitoes</u> and <u>earwigs</u> (*has, have*) invaded our backyard.
10. <u>Ketchup</u>, <u>onions</u>, and <u>mustard</u> (*goes, go*) well on many sandwiches.

6h. Singular subjects that are joined by *or* or *nor* take a singular verb.

EXAMPLES   A new marble **statue** or a **fountain has been planned** for the park.

On Mondays, either **Manuel** or **Stephie baby-sits** the children.

6i. Plural subjects joined by *or* or *nor* take a plural verb.

EXAMPLES   Either **potatoes** or **beans are served** with the baked chicken.

Tulips or **pansies make** a lovely border for a sidewalk.

6j. When a singular subject and a plural subject are joined by *or* or *nor,* the verb agrees with the subject nearer the verb.

EXAMPLES   Either the **engineers** or their **boss has made** this mistake. [The singular helping verb *has* agrees with the nearer subject, *boss.*]

Either the **boss** or the **engineers have made** this mistake. [The plural helping verb *have* agrees with the nearer subject, *engineers.*]

A soft **blanket** or some warm **booties make** a baby comfortable. [The plural helping verb *make* agrees with the nearer subject, *booties.*]

Some warm **booties** or a soft **blanket makes** a baby comfortable. [The singular verb *makes* agrees with the nearer subject, *blanket.*]

Oral Practice 1 Using Correct Verbs with Compound Subjects Joined by *Or* or *Nor*

Read each of the following sentences aloud, stressing the words in italics.

1. A *desert* or a *jungle is* the setting for the play.
2. The *table* or the *bookshelves need* dusting first.
3. Neither the *bus* nor the *train stops* in our town.
4. Neither *jokes* nor funny *stories make* Gordon laugh.
5. *Flowers* or a colorful *picture makes* a room brighter and more cheerful.
6. Either the *story* or the *poems are* by Langston Hughes.
7. At this restaurant, *rice* or *potatoes come* with the tandoori chicken dinner.
8. Neither the *Carolinas* nor *Illinois borders* Texas.

Review A Choosing Verbs That Agree in Number with Their Subjects

For each of the following sentences, choose the form of the verb in parentheses that agrees with the subject.

EXAMPLE **1.** Tara and Chen (*are, is*) reading the same book.
    1. are

1. Many vegetables (*grow, grows*) quite large during Alaska's long summer days.
2. His mother (*teach, teaches*) math.
3. All of the boats in the harbor (*belong, belongs*) to the village.
4. You and your cousins (*are, is*) invited to the party.
5. Either the wall clock or our wristwatches (*tell, tells*) the correct time.
6. The new magazines on the kitchen table (*are, is*) for the hospital waiting room.
7. My list of favorite foods (*include, includes*) vegetable lasagna and wonton soup.
8. Both my big brother and my sister (*deliver, delivers*) the morning newspaper.
9. Neither pencils nor an eraser (*are, is*) permitted.
10. The clowns and jugglers (*has, have*) always been my favorite circus performers.

STYLE TIP

Compound subjects that have both singular and plural parts can sound awkward even though they are correct. Try to avoid such constructions by revising the sentence.

AWKWARD
Jewelry or flowers make a nice Mother's Day gift.

REVISED
Jewelry makes a nice Mother's Day gift, and **flowers do,** too.

Review A

DISTRIBUTED REVIEW
To review the parts of the sentence, have students find the following types of words in the designated sentences from **Review A.**

1. object of a preposition [*days*]
2. direct object [*math*]
10. predicate nominative [*performers*]

1. celebrate
2. knows
3. C
4. enjoy
5. dresses
6. C
7. have
8. is
9. wears
10. C

APPLICATION

Subject-Verb Agreement

To help students improve their understanding of subject-verb agreement, have each student write nine sentences: three sentences with the subject following the verb, three sentences with the subject followed by a prepositional phrase, and three sentences with indefinite pronouns as subjects. Then, have students exchange sentences with partners. Have partners circle each subject and draw an arrow from it to the verb with which it agrees. Finally, have students review their marked sentences.

┌──────────────────────┐
│ TIPS & TRICKS │
└──────────────────────┘

When the subject of a sentence comes after the verb, the word order is said to be *inverted.* To find the subject of a sentence with inverted order, restate the sentence in normal subject-verb word order.

INVERTED
How much time **has he spent** at the lake?

NORMAL
He has spent how much time at the lake?

INVERTED
Here **are** the **toys.**

NORMAL
The **toys are** here.

Review B   Proofreading a Paragraph for Errors in Subject-Verb Agreement

Most sentences in the following paragraph contain a ~~verb that does not agree in number with its subject.~~ If a sentence is incorrect, give the ∧correct verb form. If a sentence is already correct, write *C*.

EXAMPLE   **[1]** Holiday customs throughout the world is fun to study.

    1. are

   [1] In Sweden, adults and children ∧~~celebrates~~ St. Lucia's Day. **[2]** Everyone there ∧~~know~~ St. Lucia as the Queen of Light. **[3]** Many people eagerly look forward to the December 13 holiday. **[4]** Girls especially ∧~~enjoys~~ the day. **[5]** By tradition, the oldest girl in the family ∧~~dress~~ as St. Lucia. **[6]** The girl in the picture above is ready to play her part. **[7]** You surely ∧~~has~~ noticed the girl's headdress. **[8]** A crown of lighted candles ∧~~are~~ hard to miss! **[9]** Each of the young Lucias also ∧~~wear~~ a white robe. **[10]** Early in the morning, the costumed girls bring breakfast to the adults of the household.

Subject After the Verb

6k. When the subject follows the verb, find the subject and make sure that the verb agrees with it.

The subject usually follows the verb in questions and in sentences that begin with *there* and *here.*

EXAMPLES   **Are** the **birds** in the nest?
            Is the **nest** on a high branch?

            There **go** the **dragons.**
            There **goes** the **dragon.**

NOTE   The contractions *there's* and *here's* contain the verb *is.* These contractions are singular and should be used only with singular subjects.

EXAMPLES   There**'s Uncle Max.**

            Here**'s** your **allowance.**

Choosing Verbs That Agree in Number with Their Subjects

Identify the <u>subject</u> of each sentence. Then, choose the <u>form of the verb</u> in parentheses <u>that agrees with the subject</u>.

EXAMPLE **1.** There (*was, were*) a baby <u>rabbit</u> hiding in the grass.

     1. rabbit—was

1. There (*are, is*) a new foreign-exchange <u>student</u> at my brother's high school.
2. (*Was, Were*) the <u>fans</u> cheering for the other team?
3. (*Has, <u>Have</u>*) the <u>Washingtons</u> moved into their new home?
4. Here (<u>*stand*</u>, *stands*) one brave, young <u>woman</u> and her only <u>son</u>, Dale.
5. (*Has, Have*) the <u>bees</u> left the hive?
6. (*There's, <u>There are</u>*) several correct <u>answers</u> to that tough question.
7. How long (*has, have*) the Huang <u>family</u> owned this tai chi studio?
8. (*Here are, <u>Here's</u>*) the <u>shells</u> that we collected from Driftwood Beach.
9. (*There's, <u>There are</u>*) a <u>pint</u> of fresh strawberries on the <u>kitchen</u> table.
10. There (<u>*were*</u>, *was*) <u>Amy</u> and <u>Wanda</u> in the doorway.

The Contractions *Don't* and *Doesn't*

6l. The word *don't* is the contraction of *do not.* Use *don't* with all plural subjects and with the pronouns *I* and *you.*

EXAMPLES   **I don't** have my keys.   **Dogs don't** meow.

             You don't care.   **Don't they** know?

             We don't agree.   The **boots don't** fit.

6m. The word *doesn't* is the contraction of *does not.* Use *doesn't* with all singular subjects except the pronouns *I* and *you.*

EXAMPLES   **He doesn't** know you.   **Don doesn't** like thunder.

             She doesn't see it.   **Doesn't** the **car** run?

             It doesn't work.   A **penguin doesn't** fly.

MEETING THE CHALLENGE

Your little brother or sister will be attending a movie with your family for the first time Saturday afternoon. To ensure that the outing is a pleasant experience for everyone, you have offered to make a list of good theater manners. Write a list of five rules about how to behave in the theater. Use *don't* or *doesn't* correctly as needed, and be sure your rules use correct subject-verb and pronoun-antecedent agreement.

ANSWER
Rules will vary, but they should reflect correct subject-verb and pronoun-antecedent agreement.

Reference Note

For more information on **contractions,** see page 304.

Finding the Subject
For sentences in which the subject comes after the verb, tell students that they can often find the subject by changing the order of the sentence. For example:

    There are the shoes.

    The shoes are there.

EXTENSION

Subject-Verb Agreement
Activity. To give students experience identifying correct subject-verb agreement in literature, ask them to read a short story such as Mary Whitebird's "Ta-Na-E-Ka" and to find examples of the following constructions:

- sentences with phrases between the subjects and verbs
- sentences with indefinite pronouns used as subjects
- sentences with compound subjects
- sentences with subjects following verbs
- sentences using *don't* and *doesn't*

USAGE

TECHNOLOGY **TIP**

If you have access to tape recorders, you may wish to have students tape each other reading **Oral Practice 2**. Students could then listen to the tapes of themselves to reinforce standard usage of *don't* and *doesn't*.

DIFFERENTIATING INSTRUCTION

Learners Having Difficulty

Pair students, and have each pair construct flashcards with which to review the rules covered so far in the chapter. Each flashcard should have an incomplete rule on one side and the word missing from the rule on the other. For example, the front of the flashcard for **Rule 6b** could read *A verb should agree in _____ with its subject.* The back should supply the missing word, *number.* Each pair should have a full set of matching cards to which they can add **Rules 6c–m** individually. Before students take the **Chapter Review**, allow partners to meet again to quiz each other with their flashcards. You may want to grade partners together on the **Chapter Review**, adding their scores and dividing by two.

Oral Practice 2 Using *Don't* and *Doesn't* Correctly

Read each of the following sentences aloud, stressing the words in italics.

1. *He doesn't* want us to give him a party.
2. *Margo* and *Jim don't* have any juice left.
3. *Lynna doesn't* remember the punchline.
4. The *bus doesn't* stop here.
5. *They don't* believe that old story.
6. *It doesn't* snow here in October.
7. *You don't* sing the blues anymore.
8. That Zuni *vase doesn't* look very old.

Exercise 10 Writing *Don't* and *Doesn't* with Subjects

Identify the <u>subject</u> in each of the following sentences. Then, choose the contraction, either *don't* or *doesn't*, that agrees with the subject.

EXAMPLE   **1.** Our cats _____ like catnip.
                    1. cats—don't

1. don't
2. don't
3. doesn't
4. doesn't

5. don't
6. doesn't
7. don't
8. doesn't

9. don't
10. doesn't

1. My <u>parents</u> _____ listen to rap music.
2. <u>I</u> _____ have much homework tonight.
3. <u>Jerome</u> _____ play the guitar as well as Angela does.
4. The <u>pizza</u> _____ have enough onions, mushrooms, green peppers, or cheese.
5. <u>They</u> _____ permit diving into the pool.
6. This <u>bedroom</u> _____ look very neat.
7. My ski <u>boots</u> _____ fit me this year.
8. Matthew enjoys playing lacrosse, but <u>he</u> _____ like to play soccer.
9. <u>You</u> _____ live on this street anymore.
10. <u>It</u> _____ seem possible that Leon grew an inch in one month.

Review C Proofreading for Errors in Subject-Verb Agreement

Most of the following sentences contain a verb that does not agree in number with its subject. Correct each ~~incorrect verb~~. If a sentence is already correct, write *C*.

EXAMPLE   **1.** Is the people in the picture worried?

         1. Are

1. There ~~is~~ sharks swimming all around them. **1.** are

2. However, the people ~~doesn't~~ seem to care. **2.** don't

3. ~~Has~~ they lost their senses? **3.** Have

4. No, there ~~aren't~~ anything for them to worry about in this shark exhibit. **4.** isn't

5. There's a transparent tunnel right through the shark pool. **5.** C

                            6. rides

6. Everyone who visits the exhibit ~~ride~~ a moving walkway through the tunnel.

7. The sharks don't seem to mind the people. **7.** C

8. Actually, sharks in the wild ~~doesn't~~ attack people very often. **8.** don't

9. Of course, sharks ~~does~~ eat almost anything. **9.** do

10. Caution and respect, therefore, ~~is~~ necessary in shark-inhabited waters.

                           10. are

Agreement of Pronoun and Antecedent

A pronoun usually refers to a noun or another pronoun called its **antecedent.** When you use a pronoun, make sure that it agrees with its antecedent.

6n. **A pronoun should agree in gender with its antecedent.**

Some singular personal pronouns have forms that indicate gender. Feminine pronouns refer to females. Masculine pronouns refer to males. Neuter pronouns refer to things (neither male nor female) and sometimes to animals.

Feminine	she	her	hers
Masculine	he	him	his
Neuter	it	it	its

Reference Note

For more information on **antecedents,** see page 30.

Agreement of Pronoun and Antecedent   **137**

RESOURCES

Agreement of Pronoun and Antecedent
Practice

■ *Language & Sentence Skills Practice*, pp. 119–123, 125–127

■ *Developmental Language & Sentence Skills*, pp. 53–56

USAGE

Agreement of Pronoun and Antecedent
Rules 6n, o *(pp. 137–142)*

O B J E C T I V E

■ **To proofread for pronoun-antecedent agreement**

DIRECT TEACHING

Modeling and Demonstration

Agreement of Pronoun and Antecedent. Model how a pronoun agrees in gender and number with the noun or pronoun to which it refers, using the example *Rosa said she lost her glasses.* First, ask which words are pronouns. [*she, her*] Then, ask whether these pronouns refer to a noun. [*yes—Rosa*] Then, ask what the gender and number of this noun are. [*feminine, singular*] Ask whether the pronouns have the same gender and number. [*yes*] Point out that pronouns and antecedents should agree in number and gender. Now, have a volunteer use another example from this chapter to demonstrate how a pronoun agrees in gender and number with its antecedent.

APPLICATION

Agreement of Pronoun and Antecedent

Activity. Have students practice using pronouns that agree in gender with their antecedents by asking volunteers to create sentences about people or objects in the classroom. For example:

This *chalkboard* looks clean because I washed *it* yesterday.

Miguel passed the test because *he* studied hard.

You might want to list on the chalkboard the people or objects you want students to refer to in creating their sentences. After each student recites a sentence, ask the rest of the class to identify the pronoun, its antecedent, and its gender.

DIFFERENTIATING INSTRUCTION

English-Language Learners

Asian Languages. Students whose native languages use pronouns differently from the way English uses them may have difficulty with pronoun-antecedent agreement in English. In Korean, for example, pronouns do not refer to gender. Japanese has no number agreement, and the languages of Vietnam and Laos have no neuter pronouns. To prevent confusion, you can explain which personal pronouns refer to which sorts of antecedents, with special emphasis on the use of *he, she,* and *it.*

STYLE TIP

To avoid the awkward use of *his or her,* try to rephrase the sentence.

AWKWARD
Each of the actors had memorized **his or her** lines.

REVISED
All of the actors had memorized **their** lines.

Reference Note

For more information about **indefinite pronouns,** see page 34.

EXAMPLES **Rosa** said **she** lost **her** glasses.

Hank took **his** journal to the beach with **him.**

Manny chose that **bike** because of **its** color and styling.

The antecedent of a personal pronoun can be another kind of pronoun. In such cases, you can often look in a phrase that follows the antecedent to tell which personal pronoun to use.

EXAMPLE **One** of those **ladies** left **her** scarf in the car.

Each of the **boys** brought **his** own softball mitt.

Some singular antecedents may be either masculine or feminine. In such cases, use both the masculine and feminine forms of the pronoun.

EXAMPLE **Nobody** in the class finished **his or her** paper early.

NOTE In informal speech and writing, people often use a plural pronoun to refer to a singular antecedent that may be either feminine or masculine.

INFORMAL   Every actor in the play had already memorized their lines.

Such usage is grammatically incorrect and should be avoided, especially in formal situations.

6o. A pronoun should agree in number with its antecedent.

A pronoun that refers to a singular antecedent is singular in number. A pronoun that refers to a plural antecedent is plural in number.

EXAMPLES   Please put the lawn **mower** away after you have finished using **it.**

These **tools** will last longer if you take good care of **them.**

(1) Use a singular pronoun to refer to the indefinite pronouns *anybody, anyone, anything, each, either, everybody, everyone, everything, neither, nobody, no one, nothing, one, somebody, someone,* and *something.*

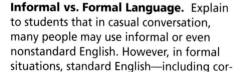

Learning for Life

Informal vs. Formal Language. Explain to students that in casual conversation, many people may use informal or even nonstandard English. However, in formal situations, standard English—including correct agreement—is required.

Tell students that they will be writing letters to obtain information about a summer camp, hobby class, or club. Each student should explain what he or she wants to know about the camp, class, or club, and why. For example, an athlete might want

EXAMPLES Has **one** of the hamsters hurt **its** leg?

Someone left **his or her** jacket on the bus.

Everyone on the girls' team has **her** own locker.

(2) Use a plural pronoun to refer to the indefinite pronouns *both, few, many,* **and** *several.*

EXAMPLES **Both** of the birds had hidden **their** nests well.

Several of the spiders continue to live under that log; it is where **they** hatched.

On a night like this, **few** of the travelers will reach **their** destinations on schedule.

(3) The indefinite pronouns *all, any, more, most, none,* **and** *some* **may be singular or plural, depending on their meaning in a sentence.**

EXAMPLES **None** of the cereal has lost **its** crunch. [*None* is singular because it refers to the singular noun *cereal.*]

None of the cereal flakes have lost **their** crunch. [*None* is plural because it refers to the plural noun *flakes.*]

(4) Use a singular pronoun to refer to two or more singular antecedents joined by *or* **or** *nor.*

EXAMPLES Either **Miguel or Randall** has **his** paintings on display.

Neither **Karli nor Marta** will lend you **her** book.

Using a pronoun to refer to antecedents of different numbers may create an unclear or awkward sentence.

UNCLEAR Neither the kittens nor their mother liked her new food. [*Her* agrees with the nearest antecedent, *mother.* However, it is unclear if the kittens disliked their own new food or if they disliked their mother's new food.]

UNCLEAR Neither the kittens' mother nor the kittens liked their new food. [*Their* agrees with the nearest antecedent, *kittens.* However, it is unclear if the mother disliked her own new food or if she disliked her kittens' new food.]

AWKWARD Neither the kittens nor their mother liked their or her new food.

| STYLE   TIP |

Sentences with singular antecedents joined by *or* can sound awkward if the antecedents are of different genders. If a sentence sounds awkward, revise it to avoid the problem.

AWKWARD
  Mark or Sherrie will bring his or her flashlight.

REVISED
  Either **Mark** will bring **his** flashlight, or **Sherrie** will bring **hers.**

EXTENSION

Relating to Writing

Explain to students that using unclear pronoun references will cause confusion in their writing. Write the following sentences on the chalkboard to show how sentences can be revised to correct unclear pronoun references.

Unclear: Colleen called Alicia while she was doing her homework. [*The antecedent of* she *and* her *is unclear. Who was doing her homework, Colleen or Alicia?*]

Clear: While Colleen was doing her homework, she called Alicia.

Clear: While Alicia was doing her homework, Colleen called her.

Ask each student to choose a piece of writing that he or she has completed and to work with another student to revise any sentences that have unclear pronoun references. Suggest that students highlight all pronouns and then identify the antecedents to which the pronouns refer. Remind students that in paragraphs, pronouns often refer to antecedents in previous sentences.

information about a sports camp that can provide training by professional athletes or coaches. An artist might want to know about a summer art class at a local museum.

Remind students to check their letters to make sure subjects and verbs agree in number and that pronouns agree in gender and number with their antecedents.

It is best to revise sentences to avoid unclear and awkward constructions like the ones on the previous page.

REVISED   Neither the kittens nor their mother liked **the** new food.

                None of the cats liked **their** new food.

(5) Use a plural pronoun to refer to two or more antecedents joined by *and*.

EXAMPLES   When **Tyrell and Davis** get home, **they** will be surprised.

                Have **Chelsea and Susan** tried on **their** new outfits?

Exercise 11   **Proofreading for Pronoun-Antecedent Agreement**

Most of the following sentences contain errors in pronoun-antecedent agreement. Identify the ~~incorrect pronoun~~, and write the ‸correct pronoun. If a sentence is already correct, write *C*.

EXAMPLE   1. Colby and everybody else brought his or her calculators.

          1. *his or her—their*

1. Neither Chile nor Argentina has given ‸~~their~~ consent to the project. **1.** its
2. These tools are sharp; be careful with ‸~~it~~!   **2.** them
3. Of course, Mrs. Chin and her daughters will give us ‸~~her~~ assistance. **3.** their
4. Everyone needs to take ‸~~their~~ project home by Friday. **4.** his or her
5. Many of the houses were decorated with ribbons on ‸~~its~~ doors for the holidays. **5.** their
6. Neither Frank nor Paul has had ‸~~their~~ hair cut recently. **6.** his
7. Every one of the dogs is required to have a numbered tag attached to ‸~~their~~ collar. **7.** its
8. That song on the radio sounds familiar, but I can't remember its title. **8.** C
9. Roseanne and Kimberly, I believe, recently lost ‸~~her~~ glasses. **9.** their
10. Have any of the horses escaped ‸~~its~~ corral? **10.** their

HELP

Remember that a pronoun should refer clearly to its antecedent. If a pronoun could possibly refer to one of two or more antecedents, revise the sentence to make the pronoun's meaning obvious.

UNCLEAR
Marcia wrote Sharon while she was on vacation. [Who was on vacation—Marcia or Sharon?]

CLEAR
When Marcia was on vacation, she wrote Sharon.

Guided and Independent

Exercises   You may wish to use **Exercise 11** as guided practice and have students complete **Exercise 12** as independent practice.

HOMEWORK

USAGE

Exercise 12 Proofreading for Pronoun-Antecedent Agreement

Most of the following sentences contain pronouns that do not agree with their antecedents. Identify each ~~incorrect pronoun~~, and write the˄correct pronoun. If a sentence is already correct, write *C*.

EXAMPLE   **1.** On the first day, no one knew their partner.

    1. their—his or her

1. Somebody in the back row left˄~~their~~ umbrella behind.
2. At last, all of the kittens were having their nap.
3. Several of the students had large scholarships given to˄him or her by local businesses.
4. Anybody in the sixth grade should know˄their mother's maiden name.
5. Neither of the antique cars had˄~~their~~ original paint job.
6. Did many of the apprentices later change˄his or her trade?
7. Yes, anyone can enter˄~~their~~ pet in the contest.
8. Few of the boys know the procedure, but˄he will learn it quickly.
9. None of the girls brought their books.
10. Both of the packages had been opened, and˄it sat forgotten on the floor.

1. his or her
2. C
3. them
4. his or her
5. its
6. their
7. his or her
8. they
9. C
10. they

Exercise 13 Proofreading for Pronoun-Antecedent Agreement

Most of the following sentences contain a pronoun that does not agree in number or gender with its antecedent or antecedents. Identify each ~~incorrect pronoun~~, and write the ˄correct pronoun. If a sentence is already correct, write *C*.

EXAMPLE   **1.** Either Abe or Brian will give their speech first.

    1. their—his

1. Gold and silver gain worth from˄its rarity.
2. Ask Mr. Reed or Mr. Steinhauer if˄~~they~~ will lend you a pen or a pencil.
3. The house at the corner and the house next door have flowers growing in front of˄it.

1. their
2. he
3. them

CONTENT-AREA CONNECTIONS

Social Studies
Writing Activity. Work with the social studies teacher to develop a list of topics students might use to write a five-sentence paragraph in which they emphasize pronoun-antecedent agreement. Geographical topics would give students practice using *it*; biographical topics would emphasize other third-person singular or plural pronouns.

4. C

4. The birds and the butterflies have flown south to their winter homes.

5. her

5. Can even a princess or a queen have ^their every wish?

6. itself

6. Pepper tastes good in a recipe, but not all by ^themselves.

7. C

7. A single red rose or a lily does not cost much, and it will look nice on the table.

8. its

8. Each of the grocery stores advertises ^their sales in the Sunday paper.

9. C

9. Neither Dan nor Bob likes onions on his sandwich.

10. them

10. More of the oranges have stickers on ^it than I thought.

Exercise 14 **Proofreading for Pronoun-Antecedent Agreement**

Most of the following sentences contain a pronoun that does not agree in number or gender with its antecedent or antecedents. Identify and ^correct each ~~incorrect pronoun~~. If a sentence is already correct, write *C.*

EXAMPLE   **1.** Delia and Dawn told me about her idea for a neighborhood show.

   1. her—their

1. Both of my parents gave us ^~~his or her~~ permission, so we used my front yard. **1.** their

2. The name of our play, which was actually a rock opera, was *Strange Night,* and I wrote it. **2.** C

3. Two trees lent us ^its trunks for a stage. **3.** their

4. Somebody bought popcorn with ^their allowance and sold it to the audience. **4.** his or her

5. Everyone in the neighborhood brought his or her own chair to the show. **5.** C

6. Either Matt or Freddy practiced his dance routine. **6.** C

7. Lisa and Tanya play guitar, so we asked ^her to be in our band. **7.** them

8. Joan wore a costume with pink flowers and bluebirds on it. **8.** C

9. Of course, a few dogs and one unhappy cat made ^its entrance at an improper moment. **9.** their

10. Tickets were only fifty cents, and we sold all of ^it before the show began. **10.** them

CHAPTER

Chapter Review

A. Choosing Verbs That Agree in Number with Their Subjects

Numerals in brackets refer to rules tested by the items in the Chapter Review.

1. [6b(2), c]
2. [6g]
3. [6h]
4. [6b(2), k]
5. [6f]
6. [6k,g]
7. [6f]
8. [6m]
9. [6b(1), k]
10. [6k,g]
11. [6d,c]
12. [6j]
13. [6m]
14. [6j]
15. [6b(1), k]
16. [6b(2), c]
17. [6g]
18. [6h]
19. [6m]
20. [6b(2), k]

For each of the following sentences, identify the subject. Then, choose the form of the verb in parentheses that agrees with the subject.

1. The flowers in that garden (*need, needs*) water.
2. She and her cousin (*play, plays*) tennis every weekend except in the winter.
3. Either Paulette or Lily (*attend, attends*) all the local performances of the Alvin Ailey dancers.
4. There (*was, were*) several teachers at the game.
5. All of the corn (*has, have*) dried up.
6. (*Was, Were*) Liang and his sister born in Taiwan?
7. None of the trucks (*has, have*) arrived yet.
8. My best friend at school (*doesn't, don't*) live in our neighborhood.
9. (*Was, Were*) you heating some bean and cheese burritos in the microwave?
10. Here (*come, comes*) Elena and James.
11. Only one of my three dogs, my beagle Neptune, really (*enjoy, enjoys*) the beach.
12. Either the students or their teacher (*has, have*) decided on the color of the new bulletin board.
13. (*Doesn't, Don't*) that sweater belong to Ralph?
14. Neither the clerk nor the shoppers (*was, were*) aware of the fire down the street.
15. Where (*was, were*) you last night around supper time?
16. Several houses in our neighborhood (*is, are*) for sale.
17. My brother and I often (*play, plays*) checkers together.
18. Either he or she (*is, are*) next in line.
19. Marilu (*don't, doesn't*) know the name of the author.
20. There (*was, were*) no other people there besides us.

Chapter Review **143**

ASSESSING

Monitoring Progress

Chapter Review. To assess student progress, you may want to compare the types of items missed on the **Diagnostic Preview** to those missed on the **Chapter Review.** If students have not made significant progress, you could refer them to **Chapter 15: Correcting Common Errors, Exercises 6–9,** for additional practice.

USAGE

RESOURCES

Agreement

Review
- *Language & Sentence Skills Practice,* pp. 124–127

Assessment
- *Progress Assessment for the Holt Handbook,* pp. 11–12, 41
- *Test Generator (One-Stop Planner CD-ROM)*

Chapter Review

B. Changing the Number of Subjects and Verbs

ANSWERS

Sentences may vary slightly.

21. A dog barks in the middle of the night.
22. Birds sing in the distance.
23. A book has fallen off the shelf.
24. Camels pass.
25. A car moves down the highway.
26. Does an elephant eat grass?
27. The men have eaten lunch.
28. A person is at the river today.
29. They have an unusual hobby.
30. A police officer protects the people.

B. Changing the Number of Subjects and Verbs

All the subjects and verbs in the following sentences agree in number. Rewrite each sentence, changing the subject and verb from singular to plural or from plural to singular. You may have to add or delete *a*, *an*, or *the*.

21.–30. [6b(1),(2)]

21. Dogs bark in the middle of the night.
22. A bird sings in the distance.
23. Books have fallen off the shelf.
24. A camel passes.
25. Cars move down the highway.
26. Do elephants eat grass?
27. The man has eaten lunch.
28. Many people are at the river today.
29. She has an unusual hobby.
30. Police officers protect the people.

C. Proofreading for Errors in Pronoun-Antecedent Agreement

Most of the following sentences contain a pronoun that does not agree in number or gender with its antecedent or antecedents. Write each ~~incorrect pronoun~~. Then, write the pronoun that agrees with the antecedent. If a sentence is already correct, write *C*.

31. their [6o(5)]
32. its [6n,o(1)]
33. they [6o(5)]
34. C [6n, o(4)]
35. his [6n,o(1)]
36. their [6o(5)]

31. We had to call the parking lot attendant because two cars and one truck had ~~its~~ lights on.
32. Each of the ducks was tagged with an electronic device around ~~their~~ left leg.
33. Tim and Donny promised ~~he~~ would bring some snacks to the party.
34. Frances or Donna will sing her favorite number.
35. I can't remember which one of my grandfathers spent ~~their~~ eighteenth and nineteenth years fighting in World War II.
36. Both my brother and my sister might lend me ~~his or her~~ favorite videos.

37. Somebody left the engine running in ~~their~~ car.
^

38. Did one of the applicants forget to sign his or her forms?

39. Most of the customers complained that ~~his or her~~ food
^
was cold.

40. Neither of the robins had ~~their~~ winter plumage.
^

37. his or her [6o(1), n]
38. C [6n,o(1)]
39. their [6o(3)]
40. its [6n,o(1)]

Writing Application
Using Agreement in Instructions

Subject-Verb Agreement   Your family is going on a
weekend trip. A neighbor has agreed to look after your pets.
Write a note giving your neighbor complete instructions for
tending the animals. To avoid confusing your reader, make sure
the subjects and verbs in your sentences agree.

Prewriting   Think about pets that you have had or that someone you know has had. If you have never cared for a pet, talk to
someone who has. Take notes on caring for each pet.

Writing   Write a draft of your note. Explain the daily care of
the pets step by step. The more specific your instructions are, the
better. With your teacher's permission, you may use informal,
standard English if you are writing to someone you know well.

Revising   Read your note aloud. Can you follow each step of
the instructions? Are all the steps in order? Have you included all
the necessary information? If not, revise your note to make it
clear and complete.

Publishing   After you have revised your note, check each
sentence for subject-verb and pronoun-antecedent agreement.
Take special care with any verb that is part of a contraction.
Check your note for any other errors in grammar, punctuation,
and spelling. Find or make pictures that illustrate each of your
steps. With your teacher's permission, mount the pictures on a
storyboard and display the storyboard in your classroom.

Reference Note

For more about **informal English,** see page 221.

APPLICATION

Writing Application

Prewriting Tip. Depending on their
familiarity with pets, students may
create extensive lists in the prewriting stage. Tell them they must narrow their lists to only those matters
that are essential to the well-being
of the animals. The focus of the
instructions should be on the necessary procedures, not on describing
the animals.

Writing Tip. Because students will
be writing notes that presumably will
include lists of instructions, you may
wish to refer them to a review of
Chapter 12, p. 281, for the rules for
punctuating lists.

Scoring Rubric. While you will
want to pay particular attention to
subject-verb agreement, you will also
want to evaluate overall writing performance. You may want to give a
split score to indicate development
and clarity of the composition as well
as usage skills.

STANDARDS FOCUS

Grade-Level Standards

(Boldface indicates concepts that are taught and tested in this chapter.)

- Language Convention 1.0: **Students write and speak with a command of standard English conventions appropriate to this grade level.**

- Grammar 1.2: **Identify and properly use** indefinite pronouns and **present perfect, past perfect, and future perfect verb tenses;** ensure that verbs agree with compound subjects.

Prerequisite/Review Standard

- Grammar 1.2: Identify and correctly use verbs that are often misused (e.g., *lie/lay, sit/set, rise/raise*), modifiers, and pronouns.

Standard Coming Up in the Next Grade Level

- Grammar 1.3: Identify all parts of speech and types and structure of sentences.

▼

INTRODUCING THE CHAPTER

- The first part of the chapter explains the difference between regular and irregular verbs and shows how to form the principal parts of regular verbs. Examples of the present participle, past, and past participle forms of irregular verbs are given. This chapter also discusses verb tenses, including tenses of six verbs that often give students problems. *(continued)*

1.0 Written and Oral English Language Conventions

Students write and speak with a command of standard English conventions appropriate to this grade level.

1.2 Identify and properly use present perfect, past perfect, and future perfect verb tenses.

Numerals and terms in brackets refer to rules and concepts tested by the items in the Diagnostic Preview.

1. sat [*sit,set*]
2. written [7c]
3. ran [7c, d]
4. gone [7c]
5. C [7b,d]
6. rose [*rise,raise*]
7. began [7c, d]
8. lying [*lie,lay*]

Using Verbs Correctly
Principal Parts, Regular and Irregular Verbs, Tense

Diagnostic Preview

Revising Incorrect Verb Forms in Sentences

Most of the following sentences contain an ~~error in the use of verbs~~. If a verb form is incorrect, write the correct form. If the sentence is already correct, write *C*.

EXAMPLE   **1.** The last movie I seen was terrible.

      1. saw

1. My friends and I recently have ~~set~~ through several bad movies.
2. Has anyone ever ~~wrote~~ a letter to complain about how many bad movies there are?
3. Last Saturday our local theater ~~run~~ two bad movies!
4. My friends J. D. and Carolyn had ~~went~~ with me to the movie theater.
5. We had hoped that we would enjoy *Out of the Swamp*.
6. In the beginning of the movie, a huge swamp creature ~~raised~~ out of the muddy water.
7. It ~~begun~~ to crawl slowly toward a cow in a field.
8. The cow had been ~~laying~~ under a tree.

CHAPTER RESOURCES

Internet

- go.hrw.com (keyword: HLLA)

go. hrw .com

Planning

- *One-Stop Planner CD-ROM* 🎵
- *On Course: Mapping Instruction*
- *At Home: A Guide to Standards Mastery,* p. 30

Practice & Review

- *Language & Sentence Skills Practice,* pp. 133–145; 146–149
- *Developmental Language & Sentence Skills,* pp. 57–72

Application & Enrichment

- *Language & Sentence Skills Practice,* pp. 150, 153; 132, 151–152

9. She never even ~~seen~~ the swamp monster.
10. I had ~~sank~~ back in my seat, expecting the monster to pounce.
11. Then the lights ~~come~~ back on.
12. What a disappointment—the film had ~~broke~~!
13. It ~~taked~~ a long time before the machine came back on.
14. Some people ~~throwed~~ their hands up in disgust.
15. Children ~~drunk~~ noisily through their straws.
16. I had ~~sat~~ my popcorn on the floor by my seat, and some-one accidentally kicked it over.
17. Finally, the theater manager ~~choosed~~ another movie, but it was only a silly cartoon about a penguin and a polar bear.
18. The penguin wore a coat it had ~~stole~~ from a sleeping polar bear.
19. The bear awoke, ~~becomes~~ angry, and chased the penguin all over the place.
20. Finally, the penguin gave back the coat and ~~swum~~ to Miami Beach to get warm.

9. saw [7c, d]
10. sunk [7c]
11. came [7c, d]
12. broken [7c]
13. took [7c]
14. threw [7c]
15. drank [7c, d]
16. set [sit, set]
17. chose [7c]
18. stolen [7c]
19. became [7c, e]
20. swam [7c, d]

Principal Parts of Verbs

The four basic forms of a verb are called the *principal parts* of the verb.

7a. The four principal parts of a verb are the *base form,* the *present participle,* the *past,* and the *past participle.*

Base Form	Present Participle	Past	Past Participle
start	[is] starting	started	[have] started
wear	[is] wearing	wore	[have] worn

NOTE The words *is* and *have* are included in this chart because present participle and past participle verb forms require helping verbs (forms of *be* and *have*) to form tenses.

HELP
Some people refer to the base form as the *infinitive.* Follow your teacher's directions when labeling this form.

Reference Note
For more information about **helping verbs,** see page 49.

Principal Parts of Verbs **147**

The chapter closes with a Chapter Review for checking students' mastery of correct verb forms and tenses. Also, a **Writing Application** feature asks students to use correct verb forms in writing a paragraph.

■ For help in integrating this chapter with writing assignments in *Holt Literature and Language Arts,* use the **Teaching Strands** chart on pp. T22–T23.

USAGE

ASSESSING

Entry-Level Assessment
Diagnostic Preview. You could use the **Diagnostic Preview** to determine students' understanding of correct verb forms. The parts of the test that students have trouble with should indicate the areas in which students need help and the sections of the chapter on which they should concentrate.

PRETEACHING

Lesson Starter
Motivating. Ask students to name the three basic forms of water: solid (ice), liquid, and gas (steam). Briefly discuss how the forms are all water yet are very different.

Explain that verbs also have different forms. Each form has a specific use or purpose. To illustrate the four basic verb forms, write the following sentences on the chalkboard:

I *play.*
He is *playing.*
She *played.*
They have *played.*

Invite students to suggest other examples of things that have various forms.

Differentiating Instruction
■ *Lesson Plans for Language Development*
■ *Supporting Instruction in Five Languages*
■ *At Home: In Five Languages*
Assessment
■ *Progress Assessment for the Holt Handbook,* pp. 13–14, 41

■ *Test Generator (One-Stop Planner CD-ROM)*
Other Language Resources
■ *Spelling Lessons & Activities*
■ *Vocabulary Development*
■ *Daily Language Activities Transparencies*

Regular and Irregular Verbs

Rules 7b, c *(pp. 148–159)*

O B J E C T I V E S

- To read sentences aloud stressing regular verbs
- To form the principal parts of regular verbs
- To use the principal parts of regular verbs in sentences
- To read sentences aloud stressing irregular verbs
- To identify the correct forms of irregular verbs
- To proofread for incorrect verb forms
- To write correct forms of irregular verbs

DIRECT TEACHING

Modeling and Demonstration

Regular and Irregular Verbs.
Model how to identify regular and irregular verbs by using the example verbs *suppose* and *begin.* First, ask whether *suppose* takes either *–d* or *–ed* to form the past tense. [*yes, –d*] Then, ask what the principal parts of *suppose* are. [*suppose, (is) supposing, supposed, (have) supposed*] Ask whether *suppose* is regular or irregular. [*regular*] Next, ask whether *begin* takes either *–d* or *–ed* to form the past tense. [*no*] Ask what the principal parts of *begin* are. [*begin, (is) beginning, began, (have) begun*] Then, ask whether *begin* is regular or irregular. [*irregular*] Now, have a volunteer use other examples from this chapter to demonstrate how to identify regular and irregular verbs.

As you can see from their names, the principal parts of a verb are used to express time.

PRESENT TIME	She **wears** a blue uniform.
	Ray **has been wearing** his baseball cap.
PAST TIME	Yesterday, we **wore** sweaters.
	I **had worn** braces for three months.
FUTURE TIME	Jessica **will wear** her new dress at the party.
	By next spring, Joey **will have worn** holes in those shoes.

A verb that forms its past and past participle by adding *–d* or *–ed* is called a *regular verb.* A verb that forms its past and past participle differently is called an *irregular verb.*

Regular Verbs

7b. A *regular verb* forms its past and past participle by adding *–d* or *–ed* to the base form.

Base Form	Present Participle	Past	Past Participle
wash	[is] washing	washed	[have] washed
hop	[is] hopping	hopped	[have] hopped
use	[is] using	used	[have] used

Reference Note

For more about **spelling rules,** see Chapter 14.

NOTE   Most regular verbs that end in *–e* drop the *–e* before adding *–ing.* Some regular verbs double the final consonant before adding *–ing* or *–ed.*

EXAMPLES   cause   **caus**ing   **caus**ed
drop   **dropp**ing   **dropp**ed

Reference Note

For more about **standard** and **nonstandard English,** see page 221.

One common error in forming the past or past participle of a regular verb is to leave off the *–d* or *–ed* ending.

NONSTANDARD	Josh was suppose to meet us here.
STANDARD	Josh was **supposed** to meet us here.

RESOURCES

Principal Parts of Verbs

Practice

- *Language & Sentence Skill Practice,* p. 133
- *Developmental Language & Sentence Skills,* pp. 57–58

Oral Practice 1 Using Regular Verbs

Read the following sentences aloud, stressing each italicized verb.

1. We *are supposed* to practice sit-ups this morning.
2. With the help of his guide dog, the man *crossed* the street.
3. Carlos and Rita *have ordered* soup and salad.
4. Her family *had moved* from Trinidad to Brooklyn.
5. Some American Indians *used* to use shells for money.
6. Many *called* shell money "wampum."
7. Larry *has saved* most of his allowance for the past two months.
8. My grandmother *worked* at the computer store.

Exercise 1 Forming the Principal Parts of Regular Verbs

Write the four principal parts for each of the following verbs.

EXAMPLE   **1.** hope

        1. hope; [is] hoping; hoped; [have] hoped

1. skate	**8.** rob	**15.** imagine
2. pick	**9.** laugh	**16.** question
3. live	**10.** love	**17.** ask
4. move	**11.** hop	**18.** worry
5. talk	**12.** snow	**19.** turn
6. stun	**13.** cook	**20.** experiment
7. enjoy	**14.** examine	

┌─HELP─

Remember that the spelling of some verbs changes when *–ing* or *–ed* is added.

Exercise 2 Using the Principal Parts of Regular Verbs

Complete each of the following sentences with the correct form of the given italicized verb.

EXAMPLE   **1.** *paint*   Henry Ossawa Tanner _____ many kinds of subjects.

        1. painted

1. *create*   Tanner _____ images showing people, nature,
1. created   history, and religion.

Exercise 1 Forming the Principal Parts of Regular Verbs

ANSWERS

1. skate; (is) skating; skated; (have) skated
2. pick; (is) picking; picked; (have) picked
3. live; (is) living; lived; (have) lived
4. move; (is) moving; moved; (have) moved
5. talk; (is) talking; talked; (have) talked
6. stun; (is) stunning; stunned; (have) stunned
7. enjoy; (is) enjoying; enjoyed; (have) enjoyed
8. rob; (is) robbing; robbed; (have) robbed
9. laugh; (is) laughing; laughed; (have) laughed
10. love; (is) loving; loved; (have) loved
11. hop; (is) hopping; hopped; (have) hopped
12. snow; (is) snowing; snowed; (have) snowed
13. cook; (is) cooking; cooked; (have) cooked
14. examine; (is) examining; examined; (have) examined
15. imagine; (is) imagining; imagined; (have) imagined
16. question; (is) questioning; questioned; (have) questioned
17. ask; (is) asking; asked; (have) asked
18. worry; (is) worrying; worried; (have) worried
19. turn; (is) turning; turned; (have) turned
20. experiment; (is) experimenting; experimented; (have) experimented

Principal Parts of Verbs   **149**

RESOURCES

Regular and Irregular Verbs
Practice

■ *Language & Sentence Skills Practice,* pp. 134–139, 146
■ *Developmental Language & Sentence Skills,* pp. 59–66

DIRECT TEACHING

Regular Verbs

Activity. Draw the following chart on the chalkboard, write in the base form, and have students complete the chart without looking in their books.

BASE FORM	PRESENT PARTICIPLE	PAST	PAST PARTICIPLE
walk	(is) [walking]	[walked]	(have) [walked]

Ask students to identify what is different about each verb form. Then, ask them to formulate rules for making the forms of the verb *walk*. [*Add –ing to form the present participle; add –ed to form the past and past participle.*]

The Banjo Lesson by Henry Ossawa Tanner, 1893. Oil on canvas. Hampton University Museum, Hampton, Virginia.

2. *learn*	What is the boy in this painting
2. learning	____ to do?
3. *title*	Not surprisingly, Tanner ____
3. titled	this painting *The Banjo Lesson.*
4. *live*	The artist, a native of Pittsburgh,
4. lived	____ from 1859 to 1937.
5. *move*	At the age of thirty-two, Tanner
5. moved	____ to Paris to study and work.
6. *visit*	Other African American artists
6. visited	____ Tanner in France.
7. *admire*	For years, people have ____
7. admired	Tanner's paintings.
8. *plan*	Our teacher is ____ to show us
8. planning	more of Tanner's work.
9. *want*	I have ____ to see Tanner's
9. wanted	famous portrait of Booker T. Washington.
10. *praise*	In his book *Up from Slavery,*
10. praised	Washington ____ Tanner's talent.

Irregular Verbs

7c. An *irregular verb* forms its past and past participle in some other way than by adding *–d* or *–ed* to the base form.

An irregular verb forms its past and past participle in one of the following ways:

- changing vowels

Base Form	Past	Past Participle
win	won	[have] won
sing	sang	[have] sung
hold	held	[have] held

- changing consonants

Base Form	Past	Past Participle
make	made	[have] made
lend	lent	[have] lent
hear	heard	[have] heard

- changing vowels *and* consonants

Base Form	Past	Past Participle
catch	caught	[have] caught
draw	drew	[have] drawn
tear	tore	[have] torn

- making no change

Base Form	Past	Past Participle
burst	burst	[have] burst
cut	cut	[have] cut
hurt	hurt	[have] hurt

NOTE If you are not sure about the principal parts of a verb, look up the verb in a current dictionary. Entries for irregular verbs list the principal parts of the verb.

Common Irregular Verbs			
Base Form	Present Participle	Past	Past Participle
become	[is] becoming	became	[have] become
begin	[is] beginning	began	[have] begun
blow	[is] blowing	blew	[have] blown
break	[is] breaking	broke	[have] broken

(continued)

DIFFERENTIATING INSTRUCTION

English-Language Learners

General Strategies. Emphasize that the past and past participle forms of regular verbs are always the same. Once students have learned the past form, they need only add *have* or *has* to use the past participle.

The lists of common irregular verbs here and on the following pages may seem overwhelming to some students. To help students with irregular verbs, have them use the verbs in a personal context. Require students to master only small increments of the material at a time.

Learners Having Difficulty

Remind students that to form the past and past participle forms of most regular verbs, they add –*ed* or –*d* to the base forms. Write the following verbs on the chalkboard, and have students volunteer the past and past participle form for each.

1. look [*looked*], (have) [*looked*]
2. taste [*tasted*], (have) [*tasted*]
3. touch [*touched*], (have) [*touched*]

APPLICATION

Relating to Literature

If the short story "Stray" by Cynthia Rylant is available in students' literature books, have students list the base forms of five verbs that the writer uses in the selection. Then, ask students to indicate whether the verbs are regular or irregular and have them write the past and past participle forms of each one.

Critical Thinking

Challenge students to name irregular verbs that are not listed in the charts in this section. Students can organize their irregular verbs in a chart such as the **Common Irregular Verbs** chart.

DIFFERENTIATING INSTRUCTION

Learners Having Difficulty

It may be easier for some students to learn the correct form of an irregular verb by listening to principal parts of the verb being read aloud in sentences. You may wish to read the **Common Irregular Verbs** list aloud and ask for volunteers to use the verbs in sentences. To hold students' attention, suggest sentences that relate to a theme of interest to them.

(continued)

Common Irregular Verbs

Base Form	Present Participle	Past	Past Participle
bring	[is] bringing	brought	[have] brought
buy	[is] buying	bought	[have] bought
choose	[is] choosing	chose	[have] chosen
come	[is] coming	came	[have] come
do	[is] doing	did	[have] done
drink	[is] drinking	drank	[have] drunk
drive	[is] driving	drove	[have] driven
eat	[is] eating	ate	[have] eaten
fall	[is] falling	fell	[have] fallen
feel	[is] feeling	felt	[have] felt
find	[is] finding	found	[have] found
freeze	[is] freezing	froze	[have] frozen
get	[is] getting	got	[have] gotten *or* got
give	[is] giving	gave	[have] given
go	[is] going	went	[have] gone
grow	[is] growing	grew	[have] grown
have	[is] having	had	[have] had
hear	[is] hearing	heard	[have] heard
hit	[is] hitting	hit	[have] hit
hold	[is] holding	held	[have] held
keep	[is] keeping	kept	[have] kept
know	[is] knowing	knew	[have] known

Oral Practice 2 Using Irregular Verbs

Read the following sentences aloud, stressing each italicized verb.

1. I *have begun* to learn karate.
2. We *chose* to stay indoors.
3. Earline never *had drunk* buttermilk before.
4. We *did* our homework after dinner.
5. Anna and Dee *have* almost *broken* the school record for the fifty-yard dash.

6. The wind *has blown* fiercely for three days.

7. Last Saturday, Isaac *brought* me a tape of reggae music.

8. The water pipes in the laundry room *have frozen* again.

Exercise 3 **Identifying the Correct Forms of Irregular Verbs**

Choose the <u>correct verb form</u> in parentheses in each of the following sentences.

EXAMPLE   **1.** The children have finally (*broke, broken*) the piñata.

        1. broken

1. We had just (*began, <u>begun</u>*) our project when I got sick.

2. The Ruiz family (*<u>drove</u>, driven*) across the country.

3. Has anyone (*brung, <u>brought</u>*) extra batteries for the radio?

4. I have finally (*chose, <u>chosen</u>*) a book to borrow.

5. Last week the lake (*<u>froze</u>, frozen*) hard enough for skating.

6. My brother and I have (*gave, <u>given</u>*) away all our comic books to the children's hospital.

7. My sister, who is learning to ride, has (*fell, <u>fallen</u>*) off her bicycle several times.

8. Everyone (*<u>went</u>, gone*) back to the classroom to watch the videotape of the spelling bee.

9. David's aunt (*<u>came</u>, come*) here to attend his bar mitzvah.

10. Have you (*ate, <u>eaten</u>*) at the new Philippine restaurant?

11. They should not have (*drank, <u>drunk</u>*) so much ice water after playing tennis.

12. After our guests had (*ate, <u>eaten</u>*), we all toured the city.

13. We have (*came, <u>come</u>*) to expect great things from you.

14. By the time Jason arrived, Gina had already (*went, <u>gone</u>*).

15. When they left, Uncle Enrique (*<u>gave</u>, given*) them some Cuban bread.

16. Their team (*<u>chose</u>, chosen*) another topic for the debate.

17. Oh, yes, Chris and I have (*knew, <u>known</u>*) each other since kindergarten.

18. He (*<u>did</u>, done*) the experiment that very afternoon.

19. Lenny had never (*drove, <u>driven</u>*) a tractor before that day.

20. We must have (*blew, <u>blown</u>*) up a hundred balloons for my little brother's birthday party.

RETEACHING

Irregular Verbs

Divide the class into groups of three. Have each group make flashcards of the verbs listed in the **Common Irregular Verbs** chart. Next, group members should shuffle the cards and randomly choose five each. Each group member then presents his or her verbs to the group, giving the four principal parts of the verb and categorizing the formation of its past and past participle as changing vowels, changing consonants, changing vowels and consonants, or making no change. Group members shuffle the cards again and work together to write three sentences using the past or past participle of three randomly chosen verbs. Have groups share their sentences with the class.

PRACTICE

Guided and Independent

Exercise 3 You might wish to use the first ten items in **Exercise 3** as guided practice. Then, have students complete this exercise as independent practice. **HOMEWORK**

DIFFERENTIATING INSTRUCTION

English-Language Learners

General Strategies. As is true in many languages, the verbs that are irregular in English are among the most common. It is especially important, therefore, that your English-language learners learn these verbs well. You may want to pair these students with others who are proficient in English, first for help defining unknown words and learning correct pronunciations (especially of the past and past participle forms, whose pronunciations are often quite different from those of the base forms), and again later for informal quizzing and reteaching of the definitions and pronunciations.

Exercise 4 **Identifying the Correct Forms of Irregular Verbs**

Choose the <u>correct verb form</u> in parentheses in each of the following sentences.

EXAMPLE **1.** Jameel has already (*drank, drunk*) a large glass of orange juice, but he is still thirsty.

    1. drunk

1. The wool sweater (<u>*felt*</u>, *feeled*) scratchy, so I did not buy it.
2. Ramón (<u>*got*</u>, *gotten*) a part in the school play.
3. The new houseplant has already (*grew*, <u>*grown*</u>) several inches since we bought it.
4. Leslie (*become*, <u>*became*</u>) my best friend back in first grade.
5. I (*holded*, <u>*held*</u>) on to the dog's leash tightly.
6. Our neighbors have (*buyed*, <u>*bought*</u>) a new doghouse for their German shepherd.
7. Kani has (<u>*kept*</u>, *keeped*) a log of his study time.
8. Yesterday we finally (*finded*, <u>*found*</u>) a copy of Pat Mora's latest book.
9. In last night's ballgame, Heather (<u>*hit*</u>, *hitted*) another home run.
10. Have you ever (*hear*, <u>*heard*</u>) traditional Japanese music?

More Common Irregular Verbs			
Base Form	Present Participle	Past	Past Participle
lead	[is] leading	led	[have] led
leave	[is] leaving	left	[have] left
lose	[is] losing	lost	[have] lost
pay	[is] paying	paid	[have] paid
put	[is] putting	put	[have] put
read	[is] reading	read	[have] read
ride	[is] riding	rode	[have] ridden
ring	[is] ringing	rang	[have] rung
run	[is] running	ran	[have] run
say	[is] saying	said	[have] said

More Common Irregular Verbs

Base Form	Present Participle	Past	Past Participle
see	[is] seeing	saw	[have] seen
send	[is] sending	sent	[have] sent
shrink	[is] shrinking	shrank *or* shrunk	[have] shrunk
sing	[is] singing	sang	[have] sung
sink	[is] sinking	sank *or* sunk	[have] sunk
speak	[is] speaking	spoke	[have] spoken
stand	[is] standing	stood	[have] stood
steal	[is] stealing	stole	[have] stolen
swim	[is] swimming	swam	[have] swum
take	[is] taking	took	[have] taken
teach	[is] teaching	taught	[have] taught
tell	[is] telling	told	[have] told
throw	[is] throwing	threw	[have] thrown
wear	[is] wearing	wore	[have] worn
write	[is] writing	wrote	[have] written

Oral Practice 3 **Using Irregular Verbs**

Read the following sentences aloud, stressing the italicized verbs.

1. Despite the blinding snowstorm, the Saint Bernard *had led* the rescue party to the stranded hikers.
2. The school bell *rang* five minutes late every afternoon this week.
3. When she visited New York City, Julia *saw* the Ellis Island Immigration Museum.
4. How many sixth-graders would you guess *have ridden* on this school bus?
5. What is the longest distance you *have swum*?
6. George *ran* to the corner to see the antique fire engine.
7. Gloria and Rose *sang* at the talent show.
8. *Have* you ever *written* haiku?

"You don't say 'He taked my chair'...it's 'My chair was tooken'."

FAMILY CIRCUS reprinted with special permission of King Features Syndicate, Inc.

Relating to Writing

Ask students to think about important moments in their lives. Have any of them won prizes, visited interesting places, or switched schools? Have each student write a descriptive paragraph about such a moment. As students write, tell them to pay close attention to the verbs they use. When students have finished, have them circle the verbs in their paragraphs and identify the principal part of each verb form.

USAGE

Exercise 5

DISTRIBUTED REVIEW

To review the parts of speech, have students find the following items in the designated sentences from **Exercise 5.**

2. adjectives [*cute, little*]
3. adverbs [*never, more, beautifully*]
8. nouns [*rabbit, door, Alice, size*]
16. prepositions [*to, about*]

DIFFERENTIATING INSTRUCTION

Special Education Students

Divide the class into small groups, and ask each student to name two verbs. Then, have the group members use each verb in a separate sentence. Group members should compose and read aloud their sentences in turns. Tell students that their sentences can be serious or silly, as long as the verb forms are used correctly.

Exercise 5 Identifying the Correct Forms of Irregular Verbs

Choose the correct verb form in parentheses in each of the following sentences.

EXAMPLE
1. Ms. Toyama (*took, taken*) her new kitten to the veterinarian.
1. *took*

1. Who (*ran, run*) faster, Jesse or Cindy?
2. That cute little puppy has (*stole, stolen*) a dog biscuit.
3. The Boys Choir of Harlem has never (*sang, sung*) more beautifully.
4. Jimmy's toy sailboat had (*sank, sunk*) to the bottom of the lake.
5. Have you (*thrown, throwed*) yesterday's paper into the recycling bin?
6. Maria had (*wore, worn*) her new spring outfit to the party.
7. Until yesterday, no one had ever (*swam, swum*) across Crystal Lake.
8. Before she followed the white rabbit through the tiny door, Alice had (*shrank, shrunk*) to a very small size!
9. The students have (*written, wrote*) a letter to the mayor.
10. I have never (*spoke, spoken*) to a large audience before.
11. An open convertible (*lead, led*) the ticker tape parade.
12. Vulcan's hammer (*rang, rung*) as he worked metal for the Roman gods.
13. Why had the dog (*took, taken*) the portable phone outside?
14. We (*saw, seen*) a whole stack of petri dishes in the back of the lab closet.
15. Not only have I never (*rode, ridden*) a roller coaster, but I probably never will.
16. Have you (*spoke, spoken*) to your parents about taking those tuba lessons?
17. The children simply (*sang, sung*) "The Bear Went over the Mountain" until the baby sitter read them another story.
18. Why have all those people (*swam, swum*) across the English Channel?
19. The detective always (*wore, worn*) a porkpie hat.
20. The clever fox (*threw, throw*) the dog off the trail.

Exercise 6 Identifying the Correct Forms of Irregular Verbs

Choose the <u>correct verb form</u> in parentheses in each of the following sentences.

EXAMPLE   1. Uncle Alberto (*leaded, led*) the parade.
                1. *led*

 1. Justin (*putted, <u>put</u>*) the soy sauce on the table.
 2. Have Grandma and Grandpa (*<u>left</u>, leaved*) already?
 3. The family (*<u>said</u>, sayed*) grace and then ate dinner.
 4. The senator (*<u>stood</u>, standed*) up and waved to the crowd.
 5. Has Leta (*readed, <u>read</u>*) the story "Miss Awful" yet?
 6. After school Angela (*<u>taught</u>, teached*) me the new dance.
 7. Each Christmas, Aunt Arlene has (*sended, <u>sent</u>*) me a classic children's book.
 8. Mom (*<u>paid</u>, payed*) for the groceries, and we went home.
 9. Ms. Cata (*telled, <u>told</u>*) the children a Hopi myth.
10. Lucas has (*losed, <u>lost</u>*) his favorite CD.

Review A Proofreading for Errors in Irregular Verbs

Most of the following sentences contain an ~~incorrect verb form~~. Identify each error, and write the correct form of the verb. If a sentence is already correct, write *C*.

EXAMPLE   1. Many stories have been wrote about the American athlete Jesse Owens.
                1. *wrote—written*

 1. Owens ~~breaked~~ several sports records during his career. **1.** broke
 2. At the Olympic games of 1936, he ~~winned~~ four gold medals. **2.** won
 3. A photographer took this picture of one of Owens's victories. **3.** C

 4. Owens's career ~~begun~~ in an unusual way. **4.** began
 5. As a little boy, Owens had been very sick, and later he ~~run~~ to strengthen his lungs. **5.** ran
 6. In high school, the other boys on the track team ~~done~~ their practicing after school, but Owens had to work. **6.** did

Principal Parts of Verbs   **157**

7. Owens's coach encouraged him to practice an hour before school and ~~brung~~ him breakfast every morning. **7.** brought

8. The coach ~~knowed~~ Owens's parents couldn't afford to send their son to college. **8.** knew

9. The coach ^seen^ that something had to be done, and he helped Owens's father find a job. **9.** saw

10. Later, Owens went to Ohio State University, where he became a track star. **10.** C

Review B **Writing the Past and Past Participle Forms of Irregular Verbs**

For each of the following sentences, write the correct past or past participle form of the italicized verb.

EXAMPLE   1. *take*   Gloria has ____ the last envelope.

            1. *taken*

1. read	**1.** *read*	Has everyone ____ the assignment for today?
2. burst	**2.** *burst*	Suddenly, the door ____ open.
3. driven	**3.** *drive*	We have ____ on Oklahoma's Indian Nation Turnpike.
4. found	**4.** *find*	Have you ____ your socks yet?
5. spoke	**5.** *speak*	Who ____ at this year's Hispanic Heritage awards ceremony?
6. grown	**6.** *grow*	Patricia has ____ two inches in one year.
7. heard	**7.** *hear*	One of the hikers had ____ the distant growl of thunder.
8. gave	**8.** *give*	Mrs. Matsuo ____ me a copy of the book *Origami: Japanese Paper-Folding.*
9. frozen	**9.** *freeze*	The water in the birdbath has ____ again.
10. chosen	**10.** *choose*	Which play have they ____ to perform?
11. worn	**11.** *wear*	The Highland School Band has always ____ Scottish kilts.
12. knew	**12.** *know*	Noriko ____ the way to Lynn's house.
13. taught	**13.** *teach*	Ms. Brook has ____ all of us how to work together.
14. sent	**14.** *send*	My sweater was too small, so I ____ it to my cousin.
15. rang	**15.** *ring*	Who ____ the doorbell a moment ago?
16. held	**16.** *hold*	The puppy ____ up its injured paw.

17. *hit*   David ____ a ball past third base in the ninth inning.
18. *leave*   Have you ____ your towel at the pool?
19. *see*   We had never ____ a koala before.
20. *buy*   Jerome ____ the decorations for the party.

17. hit
18. left
19. seen
20. bought

(Review C) **Proofreading for Incorrect Verb Forms**

Read each of the following sentences. If the ~~form of a verb is wrong~~, write the correct past or past participle form. If the sentence is already correct, write *C*.

EXAMPLE   **1.** Dr. Seuss knowed how to please readers of all ages.
        1. knew

                                                        1. seen
1. Have you ever ~~saw~~ the wacky characters shown here?
                                                        2. C
2. The imagination of Dr. Seuss brought both of them to life.
3. You may have ~~bursted~~ out laughing at the Cat in the Hat, Horton the elephant, or the Grinch.   **3.** burst
4. In one story, the mean Grinch ~~stoled~~ Christmas.   **4.** stole
5. In another, a bird ~~gived~~ Horton an egg to hatch.   **5.** gave
6. The Lorax spoke out in support of the trees and the environment.   **6.** C
7. The Cat in the Hat has always ~~wore~~ his striped hat.   **7.** worn
8. During his lifetime, Dr. Seuss must have ~~wrote~~ about fifty books with unusual characters.   **8.** written
9. Many children have ~~began~~ reading with his books.   **9.** begun
10. Dr. Seuss ~~choosed~~ *The Lorax* as his own favorite book.
                                                        10. chose

Dr. Seuss, *The Lorax.* © 1971 by Theodor S. Geisel and Audrey S. Geisel. Reprinted by permission of Random House, Inc.

Dr. Seuss, *The Cat in the Hat.* © 1957 by Dr. Seuss. Copyright renewed 1985 by Theodor S. Geisel and Audrey S. Geisel. Reprinted by permission of Random House, Inc.

DIFFERENTIATING INSTRUCTION

Advanced Learners
Have students practice using the different verb forms by writing a poem or song. Each poem or song should include at least five irregular verbs. Invite volunteers to perform their poems or songs for the class.

Tense

Rules 7d, e (pp. 160–164)

OBJECTIVES

- To identify verb tenses in sentences
- To revise a paragraph for consistency of verb tense

USAGE

DIRECT TEACHING

Modeling and Demonstration

Tense. Model how to identify and form the past, present, and future tenses by using the example sentence *A trolley noisily rolled down the track.* First, ask what tense the verb is. [*past*] Then, ask what form of this verb indicates action happening now. [*present: rolls*] Finally, ask what form indicates a future action. [*future: will roll*] Now, have a volunteer use another example from this chapter to demonstrate how to form the past, present, and future tenses.

Tense

7d. The *tense* of a verb indicates the time of the action or of the state of being that is expressed by the verb.

The six tenses are *present, past, future, present perfect, past perfect,* and *future perfect.* These tenses are formed from the principal parts of verbs. Each of these six tenses has its own uses. The following time line shows the relationships between tenses.

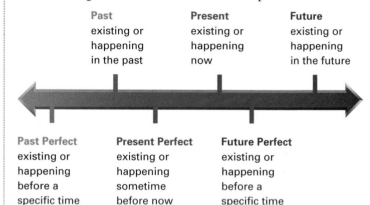

Past	**Present**	**Future**
existing or happening in the past	existing or happening now	existing or happening in the future

Past Perfect	**Present Perfect**	**Future Perfect**
existing or happening before a specific time in the past	existing or happening sometime before now	existing or happening before a specific time in the future

Listing all the forms of a verb is called *conjugating* the verb.

Conjugation of the Verb *Wear*	
Present Tense	
Singular	**Plural**
I wear	we wear
you wear	you wear
he, she, *or* it wears	they wear
Past Tense	
Singular	**Plural**
I wore	we wore
you wore	you wore
he, she, *or* it wore	they wore

RESOURCES

Tense

Practice

- *Language & Sentence Skills Practice,* pp. 140–141, 147
- *Developmental Language & Sentence Skills,* pp. 67–68

Conjugation of the Verb *Wear*	
Future Tense	
Singular	**Plural**
I will (shall) wear	we will (shall) wear
you will (shall) wear	you will (shall) wear
he, she, *or* it will (shall) wear	they will (shall) wear
Present Perfect Tense	
Singular	**Plural**
I have worn	we have worn
you have worn	you have worn
he, she, *or* it has worn	they have worn
Past Perfect Tense	
Singular	**Plural**
I had worn	we had worn
you had worn	you had worn
he, she, *or* it had worn	they had worn
Future Perfect Tense	
Singular	**Plural**
I will (shall) have worn	we will (shall) have worn
you will (shall) have worn	you will (shall) have worn
he, she, *or* it will (shall) have worn	they will (shall) have worn

Progressive Forms

Each of the six tenses also has a form called the ***progressive form.*** The progressive form expresses continuing action or state of being. It is made up of the appropriate tense of the verb *be* plus the present participle of a verb. The progressive is not a separate tense. It is just a different form that each tense can take.

STYLE   TIP

Traditionally, the helping verb *shall* was used only in certain situations. Now, however, *shall* can be used almost any time that you would use *will*.

DIRECT TEACHING

Tense

Activity. Write the following incomplete sentences on the chalkboard. Ask students to fill in the blanks with the tense forms of the verb *eat*.

Before breakfast this morning, I _____ _____ only one bagel in my life. [*had eaten*]

This morning, however, I _____ two. [*ate*]

I _____ _____ many different foods over the years. [*have eaten*]

Usually I _____ different things throughout the day. [*eat*]

Before the day is over, however, I _____ _____ _____ three bagels! [*will have eaten*]

Later tonight I _____ _____ something completely different. [*will eat*]

Point out to students that the verb forms all refer to different times. Tell students that verbs refer to different times by taking different tenses. List the six tenses on the chalkboard: *present, past, future, present perfect, past perfect,* and *future perfect*. Ask students to identify the tense they used in each sentence of the activity.

USAGE

Present Progressive	am, are, is wearing
Past Progressive	was, were wearing
Future Progressive	will (shall) be wearing
Present Perfect Progressive	has, have been wearing
Past Perfect Progressive	had been wearing
Future Perfect Progressive	will (shall) have been wearing

The Verb *Be*

The verb *be* is the most irregular of all the irregular verbs in English. Note the many different forms of *be* in the following conjugation.

Conjugation of the Verb *Be*	
Present Tense	
Singular	**Plural**
I am	we are
you are	you are
he, she, *or* it is	they are
Present Progressive: am, are, is being	
Past Tense	
Singular	**Plural**
I was	we were
you were	you were
he, she, *or* it was	they were
Past Progressive: was, were being	
Future Tense	
Singular	**Plural**
I will (shall) be	we will (shall) be
you will (shall) be	you will (shall) be
he, she, *or* it will (shall) be	they will (shall) be

DIFFERENTIATING INSTRUCTION

English-Language Learners

Vietnamese. Vietnamese expresses time and tense differently from how English does. Therefore, verb tenses may cause much difficulty for Vietnamese students, particularly when the auxiliary verb is used to show tense, as in *John did not complete his work.* Vietnamese students may sometimes rely on context clues, writing "I visit family last night" instead of "I visited family."

Help students practice verb tense forms through focused writing and speaking. For example, introduce the use of *–d* and *–ed* for regular past-tense forms and give students base-form verbs to change to the past tense. Then, have students respond orally to questions using past tense, such as "Tell us something funny that happened to you this past week" or "Did you do something interesting this weekend?" Later, have students practice the form by writing about the same topics. Introduce the other tenses in the same way, but do so one at a time.

USAGE

HELP

The present and past progressive forms of *be* are the most common. The other progressive forms of *be* are hardly ever used.

EXAMPLES

will (shall) be being [future progressive]

has, have been being [present perfect progressive]

MINI-LESSON   Usage

Tense. Students may use the past, present, and future tenses easily but may be confused by the perfect tenses. Write the following sentences on the chalkboard:

I had started camp. [*past perfect*]

I have started camp. [*present perfect*]

I will have started camp. [*future perfect*]

Ask students what each sentence has in common besides the subject *I* and the

Conjugation of the Verb *Be*	
Present Perfect Tense	
Singular	**Plural**
I have been	we have been
you have been	you have been
he, she, *or* it has been	they have been
Past Perfect Tense	
Singular	**Plural**
I had been	we had been
you had been	you had been
he, she, *or* it had been	they had been
Future Perfect Tense	
Singular	**Plural**
I will (shall) have been	we will (shall) have been
you will (shall) have been	you will (shall) have been
he, she, *or* it will (shall) have been	they will (shall) have been

Exercise 7 **Identifying Tenses**

Identify the verb's tense in each of the following sentences.

EXAMPLE   **1.** A trolley noisily rolled down the track.
          1. past

1. Oh, no! Who fed this to the paper shredder?
2. Yes, Mom actually drinks that green stuff from the juicer.
3. Benjamin has left Des Moines.
4. Had you heard Andrés Segovia's music before then?
5. A mosaic of colorful tiles will decorate the entryway.
6. By my twenty-first birthday, I will have qualified for my pilot's license.
7. The committee will notify you of its decision.
8. Will you have saved enough money by then?
9. Evidently, I had thought of every possibility but one.
10. They are using the new modem now.

1. past
2. present
3. pres. perfect
4. past perfect
5. future
6. future perfect
7. future
8. future perfect
9. past perfect
10. pres. progressive

Tense   **163**

USAGE

DIRECT TEACHING

Correcting Misconceptions

Verb Tense. Some students may have difficulty with verb tenses because they do not write or pronounce the endings for present-tense, third-person singular verbs, as in the sentence "She miss the bus almost every day." Similarly, they may have a tendency to omit the *–d* or *–ed* ending for past-tense verbs, as in "She miss the bus yesterday." To give students practice with such endings, create sentences containing present-tense, third-person singular, and past-tense forms. Ask students to underline all of the present-tense endings for third-person verbs. Then, tell students to circle the past-tense endings and to read the sentences aloud. Listen carefully, and model standard pronunciation when necessary.

object *camp.* Lead students to see that each perfect form contains the past participle *started* and the past, present, or future form of the verb *have.* Whether the perfect is past, present, or future depends on the tense of the *have* form. Ask students to label the tense in each example sentence; encourage them to look for a past participle and a form of the verb *have* to identify the perfect tenses.

USAGE

Exercise 8 **Revising a Paragraph for Consistency of Tense**

ANSWERS

Answers will depend on whether students choose to rewrite in the present tense or in the past tense. Corrected verbs are indicated in italics.

Present Tense

1. We trade essays with other English classes.
2. They read and *comment* on our essays, and we read and comment on theirs.
3. We also share reports with other classes in the school.
4. In Spanish I, we are writing letters to students in Argentina.
5. We *practice* our Spanish.
6. They *write* back to us in English.
7. The computer classes *send* a newsletter to all the other classes every week.
8. Every student has e-mail.
9. Students send messages to each other and to teachers.
10. E-mail *makes* it easy to ask questions about assignments.

Past Tense

1. We *traded* essays with other English classes.
2. They read and commented on our essays, and we read and *commented* on theirs.
3. We also *shared* reports with other classes in the school.
4. In Spanish I, we *were* writing letters to students in Argentina.
5. We practiced our Spanish.
6. They wrote back to us in English.
7. The computer classes sent a newsletter to all the other classes every week.
8. Every student *had* e-mail.
9. Students *sent* messages to each other and to teachers.
10. E-mail made it easy to ask questions about assignments.

COMPUTER TIP

Most word processors can help you check your writing to be sure that you have used verbs correctly. For example, a spell-checker will highlight mis-spelled verb forms such as *telled* and *growed*. Some style-checking software can point out inconsistent verb tense.

Remember, though, that the computer is just a tool to help you improve your writing. As a writer, you must make all the style and content choices that affect your writing.

⌐**HELP**⌐

Although the example in Exercise 8 gives two possible revisions, you need to give only one for each sentence.

Consistency of Tense

7e. Do not change needlessly from one tense to another.

To write about events that take place at about the same time, use verbs in the same tense. To write about events that occur at different times, use verbs in different tenses.

INCONSISTENT   The cat jumped onto the counter and steals the sandwich. [The events happen at about the same time, but *jumped* is in the past tense, and *steals* is in the present tense.]

CONSISTENT   The cat **jumped** onto the counter and **stole** the sandwich. [Both verbs are in the past tense.]

CONSISTENT   The cat **jumps** onto the counter and **steals** the sandwich. [Both verbs are in the present tense.]

Exercise 8 **Revising a Paragraph for Consistency of Tense**

Read the following paragraph, and decide whether to rewrite it in the present or the past tense. Then, rewrite all of the sentences, changing the verb forms to correct any needless shifts in tense.

EXAMPLE   **[1]** Since our school has a computer network, we "chatted" with students from other schools.

1. Since our school has a computer network, we "chat" with students from other schools.

or

Since our school had a computer network, we "chatted" with students from other schools.

[1] We trade essays with other English classes. [2] They read and commented on our essays, and we read and comment on theirs. [3] We also share reports with other classes in the school. [4] In Spanish I, we are writing letters to students in Argentina. [5] We practiced our Spanish. [6] They wrote back to us in English. [7] The computer classes sent a newsletter to all the other classes every week. [8] Every student has e-mail. [9] Students send messages to each other and to teachers. [10] E-mail made it easy to ask questions about assignments.

Six Confusing Verbs

Sit and *Set*

The verb *sit* means "to be seated" or "to rest." *Sit* seldom takes a direct object. The verb *set* means "to put (something) in a place." *Set* usually takes a direct object. Notice that *set* has the same form for the base form, past, and past participle.

Base Form	Present Participle	Past	Past Participle
sit	[is] sitting	sat	[have] sat
set	[is] setting	set	[have] set

EXAMPLES   I **will sit** in the easy chair. [no direct object]

I **will set** the cushion in the easy chair. [I will set what? *Cushion* is the direct object.]

The worker **has sat** there. [no direct object]

The workers **have set** their equipment there. [The workers have set what? *Equipment* is the direct object.]

Oral Practice 4   Using the Forms of *Sit* and *Set* Correctly

Read the following sentences aloud, stressing each italicized verb.

1. Before she left, Josie *had set* two loaves of French bread on the table.
2. The clown *sat* on the broken chair.
3. They *are sitting* down to rest awhile.
4. *Has* she *set* her bracelet on the night stand?
5. The Clarks' car *has sat* in the driveway for a week.
6. My little brother *sits* still for only a few seconds at a time.
7. The teacher *is setting* the best projects in the display case in the hall.
8. The librarian *set* the book about Michael Jordan on the large table.

Reference Note

For more about **direct objects,** see page 107.

TIPS & TRICKS

If you do not know whether to use *sit* or *set* in a sentence, try substituting *put.* If the sentence makes sense with *put,* use *set.* If not, use *sit.*

EXAMPLE
Jill (*set, sat*) the CDs on the shelf.

TEST
Jill put the CDs on the shelf. [The sentence makes sense with *put.*]

ANSWER
Jill **set** the CDs on the shelf.

HELP

You may know that the word *set* has meanings that are not given at the top of this page. Check in a dictionary to see if the meaning you intend requires a direct object.

EXAMPLE
The sun **sets** in the west. [Here, *sets* does not take a direct object.]

Six Confusing Verbs
(pp. 165–172)

OBJECTIVES

- To read aloud sentences, stressing the forms of confusing verbs
- To use the verbs *sit* and *set, rise* and *raise,* and *lie* and *lay* correctly in sentences
- To identify the correct forms of *sit* and *set, rise* and *raise,* and *lie* and *lay* in sentences

USAGE

DIRECT TEACHING

Modeling and Demonstration

Six Confusing Verbs. Model how to use the verbs *sit* and *set* correctly by using the examples *I will sit in the easy chair* and *I will set the cushion in the easy chair.* First, ask whether a word in the first sentence receives the action. [no] The verb *sit* takes no direct object; *sit* is correct here because there is no direct object in the sentence. Next, ask whether a word in the second sentence receives the action. [yes: cushion] *Set* does take a direct object; therefore, *set* is correct here. Now, have a volunteer use other examples from this chapter to demonstrate how to determine correct use of the other confusing verbs.

RESOURCES

Six Confusing Verbs
Practice
- *Language & Sentence Skills Practice,* pp. 142–145, 148–149
- *Developmental Language & Sentence Skills,* pp. 69–72

RETEACHING

Six Confusing Verbs

Activity. Consider demonstrating the definitions of the six confusing verbs. To begin, you could stand up and then sit down on a chair. As you sit down, you might say "I sit on the chair." After sitting, you could lift a book and set it on a desk, saying aloud, "I set the book on the desk."

Then, have the students demonstrate the same verbs and describe what they are doing, using the correct verb.

Continue the demonstrations, using the remaining confusing verbs.

┌─HELP─

Use the following short poem to help choose the correct form of *sit* and *set.*

Grandpa Jones **sits** in his chair
And watches the sun **set** in the cool, crisp air.
He **sets** his cup on the nearby table
And looks at the bird that **sits** on the gable.
"**Sit,** Rover," he says to the dog on the floor,
"**Sit** down, neighbor," to the man at the door.
And there they **sat,** two men and a dog,
Sitting together until the fog
Rolled in and made this whole poem—
A **set**up!

┌─HELP─

The verb *raise* has definitions other than the ones given here. Another common definition is "to grow" or "to bring to maturity."

EXAMPLES
They **raise** wheat.

She **raises** sheep.

Notice that both of these uses also take a direct object.

Exercise 9 **Writing the Forms of *Sit* and *Set***

Write the correct form of *sit* or *set* to complete each of the following sentences.

EXAMPLE   **1.** The girls _____ on the porch swing yesterday.

   1. *sat*

1. At the party yesterday, we _____ the birthday presents on the coffee table.   **1.** set

2. Then we _____ on the floor to play a game.   **2.** sat

3. Alana had been _____ next to Rosa.   **3.** sitting

4. The Jiménez twins never _____ together, even though it was their birthday.   **4.** sat

5. Mrs. Jiménez _____ a large cake on the table.   **5.** set

6. Mr. Jiménez had already _____ party hats and favors around the table.   **6.** set

7. He also _____ out the plates.   **7.** set

8. One of the twins _____ on a hat by mistake.   **8.** sat

9. At every party we always _____ quietly while the birthday person makes a wish.   **9.** sit

10. Yesterday, we _____ still twice as long for the Jiménez twins!   **10.** sat

Rise and *Raise*

The verb *rise* means "to go up" or "to get up." *Rise* does not take a direct object. The verb *raise* means "to lift (something) up" or "to cause (something) to rise." *Raise* usually takes a direct object.

Base Form	Present Participle	Past	Past Participle
rise	[is] rising	rose	[have] risen
raise	[is] raising	raised	[have] raised

EXAMPLES   The winner **is rising** to receive his medal. [no direct object]

The winner **is raising** her arms in triumph. [The winner is raising what? *Arms* is the direct object.]

Taxes **rose** quickly. [no direct object]

Congress **raised** taxes. [Congress raised what? *Taxes* is the direct object.]

Learning for Life

Continued on pp. 167–168

Setting Goals for the Future. Discuss with students what they know about contracts. You can bring to class examples of contracts, such as lease agreements or club memberships. Have students take note of the formal language and the use of verb tenses in the contracts. You may want to have students label examples of various tenses in the contracts.

Tell students that they will write a personal contract, entering into an agreement with themselves. The contract should list

Oral Practice 5 Using the Forms of *Rise* and *Raise* Correctly

Read the following sentences aloud, stressing each italicized verb.

1. The audience *had risen* from their seats to applaud the singer.
2. They *raised* the curtains for the play to start.
3. Dark smoke *rose* from the fire.
4. They always *rise* early on Saturday mornings.
5. The wind *had raised* the Chinese dragon kite high above the trees.
6. They *are raising* the banners.
7. The huge crane *can raise* the steel beams off the ground.
8. The temperature *was rising* quickly.

Exercise 10 Writing the Forms of *Rise* and *Raise*

To complete each of the following sentences, supply the correct form of *rise* or *raise*.

EXAMPLE **1.** We will ____ a banner.

   1. raise

   1. raised or raise

1. Before the game the color guards ____ the flag.
2. The fans were ____ for the national anthem. **2.** rising
3. The pitcher ____ his arm to throw the ball. **3.** raised or raises
4. The baseball seemed to ____ above the batter's head. **4.** rise
5. Someone in front of me was ____ a sign that blocked my view. **5.** raising
6. I have ____ my voice to cheer a hundred times during one game. **6.** raised
7. When the sun had ____ too high, the players couldn't see the high fly balls. **7.** risen
8. Whenever someone hits a home run, the fans ____ their mitts to catch the baseball. **8.** raise
9. Yesterday, everyone ____ when the designated hitter hit a home run. **9.** rose
10. As soon as the ninth inning was over, we ____ to leave. **10.** rose

---

USAGE

RETEACHING

Six Confusing Verbs

Activity. Divide the class into groups of three. Have each group member study a different pair of the six confusing verbs in the lesson and present an explanation of the differences between the two verbs to the group. Students' explanations should include strategies for using the verbs correctly and example sentences. Group members should then work together to write a paragraph in which all six of the verbs are used correctly. Invite a group spokesperson to read his or her group's paragraph to the class.

APPLICATION

Six Confusing Verbs

Tenses. Have students expand the charts for each of the verb pairs by writing the six tenses of each verb. Students can then write six sentences for each verb, using each of the tense forms of the verb once.

EXTENSION

Six Confusing Verbs

Comic Strips. Ask students to draw comic strips in which they show the differences between *rise* and *raise*. Have them use the verbs *rise* and *raise* in captions to explain the events taking place. This activity can also be done with the other pairs of confusing verbs.

---

personal goals and resolutions to which each student would like to commit. Have students use a pie chart such as the following to brainstorm for goals and resolutions for each area of their lives.

Lie and Lay

The verb *lie* generally means "to recline," "to be in a place," or "to remain lying down." *Lie* does not take a direct object. The verb *lay* generally means "to put (something) down" or "to place (something)." *Lay* usually takes a direct object.

┌HELP┐

The verb *lie* has definitions other than the ones given here. Another common definition is "to tell an untruth."

EXAMPLE

Little Terry did not **lie** about spilling the milk.

When used this way, *lie* usually does not take a direct object. Its past and past participle forms are *lied* and [have] *lied*.

Base Form	Present Participle	Past	Past Participle
lie	[is] lying	lay	[have] lain
lay	[is] laying	laid	[have] laid

EXAMPLES

The beam **is lying** near the edge. [no direct object]

The workers **are laying** the beams near the edge. [The workers are laying what? *Beams* is the direct object.]

The newspaper **lay** on the kitchen table. [no direct object]

Sara **laid** the newspaper on the kitchen table. [Sara laid what? *Newspaper* is the direct object.]

The beach blanket **has lain** under the umbrella. [no direct object]

They **have laid** the beach blanket under the umbrella. [They have laid what? *Blanket* is the direct object.]

| COMPUTER TIP

If you have trouble using *sit, set, rise, raise, lie,* and *lay* correctly, a computer may be helpful. Use the search function to find and highlight all the uses of these confusing verbs in your writing. Then, look at each case carefully to determine whether you have used the correct form, and revise if necessary.

Oral Practice 6 Using the Forms of *Lie* and *Lay* Correctly

Read the following sentences aloud, stressing each italicized verb.

1. The corrected test paper *lay* on the desk.
2. My teddy bear *lies* on my bed all day.
3. Before the sale, the clerk *laid* samples on the counter.
4. *Have* those toys *lain* outside too long?
5. The Inuit hunter *was laying* his harpoon on the ice.
6. Last night, I *was lying* on the sofa reading a book when the phone rang.
7. I think the hero *has laid* a trap for the villain.
8. *Lay* the baby gently in the crib.

168 Chapter 7 Using Verbs Correctly

Learning for Life **Continued from p. 167**

Have students write their contracts, listing at least five goals and resolutions. Have students pay special attention to the verb tenses they have used. Point out to students that their goals and resolutions should be written in the future tense.

Tell students they do not have to share their contracts, but they should sign and date them and keep them in a safe place. Encourage students to check their contracts periodically to see how well they are pursuing their goals.

Exercise 11 Writing the Forms of *Lie* and *Lay*

To complete each of the following sentences, write the correct form of *lie* or *lay*.

EXAMPLE   **1.** Children often _____ toys in the wrong places.

        1. lay

1. The remote control for the television is _____ under the rocking chair. **1.** lying
2. How long has it _____ there? **2.** lain
3. My brother Ramón probably _____ it there last night. **3.** laid
4. He was _____ on the floor, watching television. **4.** lying
5. Julia, my younger sister, is always _____ her toys in front of the television set. **5.** laying
6. She has _____ little parts from her board games all over the house. **6.** laid
7. Whenever Mom and Dad find one of these parts, they usually _____ it on the bookcase. **7.** lay
8. Yesterday, Dad _____ down on some hard plastic pieces on the sofa. **8.** lay
9. Now those broken bits of plastic _____ at the bottom of the wastebasket. **9.** lie
10. Today, Julia has _____ every single toy safely in the toy chest in her room. **10.** laid

Review D Identifying the Correct Forms of *Sit* and *Set*, *Rise* and *Raise*, and *Lie* and *Lay*

Choose the correct verb from the pair in parentheses in each of the following sentences.

EXAMPLE   **1.** Dad (*sat, set*) the scrapbook from our visit to the Hopi reservation on the table and opened it to the picture shown on the next page.

        1. set

1. The Hopi villages (*lie, lay*) on and around three mesas in the Arizona desert.
2. Waalpi, a village that (*sits, sets*) atop one mesa, was established in 1150.
3. Many Hopi houses and fields have (*laid, lain*) in their present locations for hundreds of years.

Six Confusing Verbs   **169**

USAGE

EXTENSION

Relating to Literature

Verb Tense. After students have read and discussed a poem such as Gary Soto's "Ode to Mi Gato," ask them to list the verbs used in the poem and to identify each verb's tense. Ask students how changing the tense of the verbs would alter the meaning of the poem. ["Ode to Mi Gato" contains mostly present-tense verbs describing the cat and the poem's speaker today and past-tense verbs telling how the speaker found and adopted the cat. Changing the tenses would reduce the sense of the speaker's present love for his cat and the remembrance of their past together.]

4. At the reservation, everyone (*sat*, *set*) quietly during the Hopi Snake Dance.
5. One dancer had (*risen*, *raised*) a snake above his head for the crowd to see.
6. The growing corn (*rises*, *raises*) high in the Hopi country of Arizona.
7. Hot and very tired, I (*lay*, *laid*) on a bench at the Hopi trading post.
8. In a moment, Dad had (*rose*, *raised*) his hat to shade my face.
9. When we entered the pueblo, a Hopi woman (*rose*, *raised*) from her chair to greet us.
10. Smiling, the woman (*sat*, *set*) a beautiful coiled basket on the counter.

Review E Proofreading for Correct Verb Forms

Identify the ~~incorrect verb form~~ in each of the following sentences. Then, write the ∧correct form.

EXAMPLE 1. Lately, everyone in our neighborhood has did more to keep physically fit.
      1. *did—done*

1. No one is ~~setting~~ down anymore—except on stationary bicycles. **1.** sitting
2. My mom has ~~rode~~ 150 miles so far. **2.** ridden
3. In addition, I have never ~~knew~~ so many aerobic dancers. **3.** known
4. Yesterday afternoon, I ~~swum~~ twelve laps in the pool. **4.** swam
5. Last month, a famous exercise instructor ~~choosed~~ our neighborhood for her new fitness center. **5.** chose
6. Many people ~~seen~~ her interviews on local talk shows. **6.** saw
7. All of a sudden, adults and children have ~~began~~ going to the center. **7.** begun
8. Each person is ~~suppose~~ to use different kinds of equipment. **8.** supposed
9. Last night, I ~~rose~~ a fifty-pound weight. **9.** raised
10. So far, no one has ~~broke~~ a leg on the cross-country ski machine. **10.** broken
11. Mom had ~~went~~ to several gyms over the years. **11.** gone
12. After my workout, I just ~~laid~~ on the floor, out of breath. **12.** lay
13. She and I have ~~took~~ several classes at that gym. **13.** taken
14. I must have ~~ran~~ a thousand miles on that treadmill. **14.** run
15. We never ~~worn~~ fancy outfits, only sweat pants and T-shirts. **15.** wore or wear
16. I had ~~chose~~ an hour soaking in the whirlpool as my first exercise plan. **16.** chosen
17. However, I ~~seen~~ the dancers and heard the music. **17.** saw
18. Now I have ~~knowed~~ many of the dancers for a long time. **18.** known
19. My energy level has ~~raised~~, and I'm happier. **19.** risen
20. Don't ~~sit~~ those free weights down; keep at it! **20.** set

Review F Using the Correct Forms of Verbs

Write the correct past or past participle form of the verb in parentheses in each of the following sentences.

EXAMPLE **1.** I have (*grow*) tired of this TV program.
       1. grown

1. Grant (*feel*) proud and happy after winning the chess tournament. **1.** felt
2. Over the years, I have (*keep*) all the postcards from my grandparents. **2.** kept
3. Mother has (*lose*) the sash for her kimono. **3.** lost

Six Confusing Verbs **171**

4. became	**4.** The room quickly (*become*) crowded with curious fans.
5. told	**5.** Mr. Shaw (*tell*) us to read about the life of Harriet Jacobs.
6. made	**6.** Have you (*make*) the hat for your costume yet?
7. stood	**7.** All night the faithful Irish setter (*stand*) watch over the homestead.
8. ridden	**8.** Has Yoshi ever (*ride*) a horse before?
9. heard	**9.** Have you ever (*hear*) the story of Pocahontas?
10. said	**10.** Juanita (*say*) the biscuits would be ready soon.
11. began	**11.** As the sun set, the temperature (*begin*) to drop.
12. eaten	**12.** A squirrel had (*eat*) all the seed we put out for the birds.
13. run	**13.** Has Darius (*run*) ten laps yet?
14. wore	**14.** All the band members (*wear*) the same color socks on Friday.
15. led	**15.** At halftime, our team (*lead*) by two goals.
16. broken	**16.** The secret agent had easily (*break*) the code and deciphered the message.
17. sang	**17.** A whippoorwill (*sing*), crickets chirped, and a breeze rustled the leaves.
18. took	**18.** While I washed the dishes, Diane (*take*) the trash out.
19. fallen	**19.** A baby raccoon had (*fall*) from the tree into the soft pile of pine needles.
20. given	**20.** Have you (*give*) Dad his Father's Day present?

FRANK & ERNEST reprinted by permission of Newspaper Enterprise Association, Inc.

7

Terms and numerals in brackets refer to concepts and rules tested by the items in the Chapter Review.

1. ridden [7a,c]
2. fallen [7a,c]
3. knew [7a,c]
4. blown [7a,c]
5. went [7a,c]
6. brought [7a,c]
7. lay [*lie,lay*]
8. broken [7a,c]
9. wore [7a,c]
10. froze [7a,c]
11. shrunk [7a,c]
12. sang [7a,c]
13. ate [7a,c]
14. rose [rise, *raise*]
15. drank [7a,c]
16. ran [7a,c]
17. began [7a,c]
18. sat [*sit,set*]
19. took [7a,c]
20. come [7a,c]

21. heard [7a,c]
22. broke [7a,c]

Chapter Review

A. Using Correct Forms of Irregular Verbs

For each of the following sentences, write the correct past or past participle form of the verb in parentheses.

1. We had (*ride*) in the car for several hours.
2. Six inches of snow had (*fall*) the night before.
3. I never (*know*) snow was so beautiful.
4. The wind had (*blow*) some of it into high drifts.
5. As we (*go*) past them, they looked like white hills.
6. My brother Ernest had (*bring*) some comics to read.
7. I (*lie*) back and looked at the scenery.
8. Unfortunately, the car heater had (*break*).
9. We all (*wear*) our heavy coats and mittens.
10. However, my ears almost (*freeze*).
11. My favorite wool cap had (*shrink*) to a tiny size in the dryer.
12. During the long ride home, we (*sing*) some songs.
13. At noon, we (*eat*) lunch at a roadside cafeteria.
14. The clerk (*rise*) and asked if we would like some hot chocolate.
15. I (*drink*) two cups of hot cocoa.
16. Mom and I (*run*) around the parking lot to wake up.
17. After lunch, Ernie (*begin*) to feel sleepy.
18. I had never (*sit*) so long in a car before.
19. All warmed up, Ernie (*take*) a long nap.
20. We had (*come*) a long way.

B. Writing the Past and Past Participle Forms of Irregular Verbs

For each of the following sentences, write the correct past or past participle form of the verb in parentheses.

21. Have you (*hear*) the good news about Barbara?
22. The lower branches of the tree (*break*) in the storm.

RESOURCES

Using Verbs Correctly

Review
- *Language & Sentence Skills Practice*, pp. 146–149

Assessment
- *Progress Assessment for the Holt Handbook*, pp. 13–14, 41
- *Test Generator (One-Stop Planner CD-ROM)*

ASSESSING

Monitoring Progress

Chapter Review. To assess student progress, you may want to compare the types of items missed on the **Diagnostic Preview** to those missed on the **Chapter Review.** If students have not made significant progress, you may want to refer them to **Chapter 15: Correcting Common Errors, Exercises 10–13** for additional practice.

USAGE

23. led [7a,c]
24. held [7a,c]
25. lay [*lie,lay*]
26. seen [7a,c]
27. set [*sit,set*]
28. flown [7a,c]
29. wore [7a,c]
30. risen [*rise,raise*]

23. Our current mayor has (*lead*) three successful administrations.
24. The train was crowded, so we stood in the aisle and (*hold*) on to the luggage rack.
25. The tired dog (*lie*) down as soon as it arrived home.
26. As far as I know, they haven't (*see*) that movie.
27. She has always (*set*) the table herself, but tonight she has no time.
28. "So far, children," said Ms. Espinosa, "that robin has (*fly*) all the way from Minnesota on its way to the Gulf Coast for the winter."
29. She (*wear*) her blue parka to the parade.
30. "Time to get up, everyone!" said Mom from the base of the stairs. "The sun has already (*rise*)."

C. Proofreading for Correct Verb Forms

For each of the following sentences, identify the ~~incorrect verb form~~. Then, write the correct form.

31. kept [7c]
32. lay [*lie,lay*]
33. set [*sit,set*]
34. gone [7c]
35. ridden [7c]
36. began [7c, d]
37. hit [7c]
38. raised [*rise,raise*]
39. laid [*lie,lay*]
40. brought [7c]

31. When Dad was a boy in Iowa, he ~~keeped~~ bees.
32. Before I ~~laid~~ down to sleep, I had packed everything I would need for today's trip.
33. Has Everett ~~sit~~ out the food for the picnic?
34. Nobody in our family had ever ~~went~~ to college before Mom did.
35. I have never ~~rode~~ on a camel, but I'd like to someday.
36. Yesterday's class ~~begun~~ with a speed drill.
37. She felt triumphant because she had never ~~hitted~~ a fly ball before.
38. The unit stood at attention as Corporal Martinez ~~rose~~ the flag.
39. The builder ~~lay~~ the plans on the table.
40. Both Leyla and Hussain ~~brung~~ some delicious falafel to the anniversary party.

Writing Application
Using Verbs in a Description

Forms and Tenses of Verbs   Many scientists and writers make predictions about the future. They base their predictions on past and present trends. Write a paragraph or two describing how one everyday item such as a car, a house, a home appliance, or a school might be different one hundred years from now. In your description, be sure to use the correct forms and tenses of verbs.

Prewriting   Choose a topic that interests you, such as video games or skyscrapers. Based on what you already know about the topic, make some predictions about the future. Write down as many details as you can.

Writing   Begin your draft by telling what time period your predictions concern. Then, use your notes to write a clear, vivid description of something in that future time.

Revising   Have a classmate read your composition. How does it sound? Do your predictions sound possible? Add, cut, or revise details to make your description clear and believable.

Publishing   Read your paragraph carefully to check for errors in grammar, spelling, and punctuation. Take special care with the forms of verbs. Use a dictionary to check the forms of any irregular verbs you are not sure about. You may want to present your final draft to the class as a multimedia computer presentation, an illustrated bulletin board, or a three-dimensional mobile.

CONTENT-AREA CONNECTIONS

Science
Writing Predictions. Students may want to combine their predictions with research on a specific area of scientific development, such as robotics or genetic engineering. Students can conduct their research in the school library and provide copies of their sources along with their descriptions. Discuss students' findings with the class.

STANDARDS FOCUS

Grade-Level Standard

(Boldface indicates concepts that are taught and tested in this chapter.)

- Language Convention 1.0: **Students write and speak with a command of standard English conventions appropriate to this grade level.**

Prerequisite/Review Standard

- Grammar 1.2: Identify and correctly use verbs that are often misused (e.g., *lie/lay, rise/raise, sit/set*), modifiers, and pronouns.

Standard Coming Up in the Next Grade Level

- Grammar 1.3: Identify all parts of speech and types and structure of sentences.

▼

INTRODUCING THE CHAPTER

- This chapter first explains the forms of personal pronouns (subject, object, and possessive). Then, subject forms and object forms are discussed in their own sections. Finally, the chapter addresses special problems with the pronouns *who* and *whom* and pronouns used with appositives. All the information, reinforced by multiple exercises and activities, challenges students to use pronouns correctly in their speech and writing.

- The chapter closes with a **Chapter Review** for checking students' mastery of pronoun usage. As part of the Chapter

(continued)

1.0 Written and Oral English Language Conventions
Students write and speak with a command of standard English conventions appropriate to this grade level.

Using Pronouns Correctly
Subject and Object Forms

Numerals and terms in brackets refer to rules and concepts tested by the items in the Diagnostic Preview.

1. I [8b]
2. We [8a,pronoun with appositive]
3. us [8e,pronoun with appositive]
4. Who [8a,*who,whom*]
5. me [8d]
6. us [8e,pronoun with appositive]
7. C [8a]
8. they [8a]
9. C [8a,*who,whom*]

Diagnostic Preview

Revising Incorrect Pronoun Forms in Sentences

Most of the following sentences contain an incorrect pronoun form. If a pronoun is used incorrectly, write the ~~incorrect form~~ of the pronoun and give the correct form. If a sentence is already correct, write *C.*

EXAMPLE 1. The police officer complimented us and they on knowing the rules of bicycle safety.

  1. *they—them*

1. The members of our bicycle club are Everett, Coral, Jackie, and ~~me~~.
2. ~~Us~~ four call our club the Ramblers, named after a bicycle that was popular in the early 1900s.
3. Mrs. Wheeler gave an old three-speed bike to ~~we~~ four.
4. ~~Whom~~ explained the special bicycle safety course?
5. Our cousins gave Coral and ~~I~~ their old ten-speed bikes.
6. Each of ~~we~~ Ramblers rides after school.
7. Sometimes we ride with the members of the Derailers, a racing club.
8. On Saturday mornings, we and ~~them~~ meet at the school.
9. Who told us about the bike trail along the river?

CHAPTER RESOURCES

Internet
- go.hrw.com (keyword: HLLA)

go. hrw .com

Planning
- *One-Stop Planner CD-ROM*
- *On Course: Mapping Instruction*

Practice & Review
- *Language & Sentence Skills Practice,* pp. 155–163; 164–166
- *Developmental Language & Sentence Skills,* pp. 73–80

Application & Enrichment
- *Language & Sentence Skills Practice,* pp. 167, 170; 154, 168–169

10. Everett warned we three about being careful because reckless riders can get hurt.
11. Reckless riders can cause you and they problems.
12. A car almost hit two of them!
13. When the Ramblers ride with the Derailers, it is us who obey all the safety rules.
14. Everett, Coral, Jackie, and I entered a safety contest.
15. Other clubs and us competed for a tandem bike.
16. Everett and her taught Jackie how to ride it and shift gears.
17. One by one, us contestants went through the course.
18. Of all of we riders, the least experienced were the Ramblers.
19. Jackie and me were nervous as the judges were deciding.
20. Finally, the judges announced that the winners of the contest were us Ramblers.

The Forms of Personal Pronouns

The form of a personal pronoun shows how it can be used in a sentence. Pronouns used as subjects and predicate nominatives are in the **subject form.**

EXAMPLES   **He** and **I** went to the post office. [subject]

           The winner of the marathon is **she.** [predicate nominative]

Pronouns used as direct objects and indirect objects of verbs and as objects of prepositions are in the **object form.**

EXAMPLES   Mr. García helped **him** and **me** with yesterday's homework. [direct objects]

           The clerk gave **us** the package. [indirect object]

           When is Theo going to give the flowers to **her**? [object of a preposition]

Possessive forms (*my, mine, your, yours, his, her, hers, its, their, theirs, our, ours*) are used to show ownership or possession.

EXAMPLES   **My** sister had to turn the box on **its** end to get it through the door.

           A mother bear is very protective of **her** cubs.

The Forms of Personal Pronouns   **177**

---

10. us [8c, pronoun with appositive]
11. them [8d]
12. C [8e]
13. we [8b]
14. C [8a]
15. we [8a]
16. she [8a]
17. we [8a, pronoun with appositive]
18. us [8e, pronoun with appositive]
19. I [8a]
20. we [8b, pronoun with appositive]

┌HELP─
The subject form of pronouns is also sometimes known as the **nominative case.** The object form of pronouns is sometimes known as the **objective case.**

Review, the **Writing Application** feature asks students to use correct pronoun forms in writing a paragraph that describes a proposed skit.

■ For help in integrating this chapter with writing assignments in *Holt Literature and Language Arts,* use the **Teaching Strands** chart on pp. T22–T23.

USAGE

ASSESSING

Entry-Level Assessment
Diagnostic Preview. The **Diagnostic Preview** can help you determine areas in which additional instruction may be beneficial. Going over the answers orally may serve as a helpful review for some students, particularly auditory learners.

PRETEACHING

Lesson Starter
Motivating. Introduce pronoun forms by introducing yourself to the class, asking for a book, and noting possession of the book. Emphasize the pronouns: *I* am Ms. Smith. Please, hand *me* that book. This is *his* book.

Then, ask students to identify the function of each pronoun you have used. [*subject; indirect object; shows ownership*] Point out that the pronouns you have used are examples of the subject form, object form, and possessive form of pronouns.

The Forms of Personal Pronouns
(pp. 177–179)

OBJECTIVES

■ To identify pronouns as subject forms, object forms, or possessive forms

■ To identify pronouns in sentences

Differentiating Instruction
■ *Lesson Plans for Language Development*
■ *Supporting Instruction in Five Languages*
Assessment
■ *Diagnostic & Summative Assessments, Midyear Test*

■ *Progress Assessment for the Holt Handbook,* pp. 15–16, 41
■ *Test Generator (One-Stop Planner CD-ROM)* 🎧
Other Language Resources
■ *Spelling Lessons & Activities*
■ *Vocabulary Development*
■ *Daily Language Activities Transparencies*

The Forms of Personal Pronouns   **177**

DIRECT TEACHING

Modeling and Demonstration

The Forms of Personal Pronouns.
Model how forms of personal pronouns are used in a sentence by using the example *I had to turn the box on its end to get it through the door.* First, ask which words are pronouns. [*I, its, it*] Ask how *I* is used in this sentence. [*as a subject*] Next, ask how *its* is used in this sentence. [*to show possession*] Then, ask how *it* is used. [*as a direct object*] *I* is in the subject form. *Its* is in the possessive form, and *it* is the object form. Point out that a pronoun takes different forms depending on how it is used in a sentence. Now, have a volunteer use another example from this chapter to demonstrate how to identify the form of a pronoun.

Exercise 2

DISTRIBUTED REVIEW

To review the parts of a sentence, have students identify the complete subjects, complete predicates, direct objects, and objects of prepositions in the designated sentences from **Exercise 2.** [*Complete subjects are shown in bold, complete predicates are shown in italics, direct objects are underlined once, and objects of prepositions are underlined twice.*]

5. **The young Bannister** *couldn't afford* <u>paper</u>, *so* **he** *drew on barn* <u>doors</u> *and* <u>fences</u>.

6. *Later,* **Bannister** *met* <u>Christiana Carteaux</u> *and married* <u>her</u>.

9. **Bannister** *treasured his* <u>prize</u> *and regarded* <u>it</u> *as a great* <u>honor</u>.

10. <u>What</u> *do* **you** *think of the* <u>painting</u>?

Reference Note
For more information about **possessive pronouns**, see pages 32 and 303.

Personal Pronouns		
	Singular	**Plural**
Subject Form	I you he, she, it	we you they
Object Form	me you him, her, it	us you them
Possessive Form	my, mine your, yours his, her, hers, its	our, ours your, yours their, theirs

Notice that the pronouns *you* and *it* are the same in the subject form and object form.

NOTE   Some authorities prefer to call possessive forms such as *our, your,* and *their* possessive adjectives. Follow your teacher's instructions regarding possessive forms.

Exercise 1   Identifying Pronouns

Identify each of the following pronouns as a *subject form*, an *object form*, or a *possessive form*. If the pronoun can be used as either the subject form or the object form, write *subject or object*.

EXAMPLE   **1.** they
          1. *subject form*

1. him 1. o.   3. it 3. s.o. 5. our 5. p.   7. you 7. s.o. 9. he 9. s.
2. me 2. o.   4. we 4. s.   6. them 6. o.   8. their 8. p. 10. your 10. p.

Exercise 2   Identifying Pronouns in Sentences

For each of the following sentences, identify the pronoun in italics as a *subject form*, an *object form*, or a *possessive form*.

EXAMPLE   **1.** Ever since *he* could remember, Edward Bannister had wanted to be an artist.
          1. *subject form*

RESOURCES

The Forms of Personal Pronouns
Practice
- *Language & Sentence Skills Practice,* p. 155
- *Developmental Language & Sentence Skills,* pp. 73–74

1. He had to work hard to reach *his* goal. **1.** p.
2. Although Bannister was born in Canada, many consider *him* an American artist. **2.** o.
3. Bannister's parents died when *he* was young. **3.** s.
4. The little money they had was left to *their* son. **4.** p.
5. The young Bannister couldn't afford paper, so *he* drew on barn doors and fences. **5.** s.
6. Later, Bannister met Christiana Carteaux and married *her*. **6.** o.
7. She was from Rhode Island, where *her* people, the Narragansett, lived. **7.** p.
8. In 1876, a Philadelphia artistic society recognized Bannister by awarding *him* a gold medal for the painting shown here. **8.** o.
9. Bannister treasured his prize and regarded *it* as a great honor. **9.** o.
10. What do *you* think of the painting? **10.** s.

Edward Bannister, *Under the Oaks* (1876). Oil on canvas. National Museum of American Art, Washington DC/Art Resource, New York.

The Subject Form

Pronoun as Subject

The *subject* tells whom or what the sentence is about.

8a. Use the subject form for a pronoun that is the subject of a verb.

RESOURCES

The Subject Form
Practice
■ *Language & Sentence Skills Practice,* pp. 156–157, 160–161
■ *Developmental Language & Sentence Skills,* pp. 75–76

The Subject Form
Rules 8a, b *(pp. 179–183)*

OBJECTIVES

■ To read sentences aloud and to stress the pronouns used as subjects and predicate nominatives

■ To identify the correct forms of pronouns in sentences

■ To identify pronouns used as predicate nominatives and to write sentences using them correctly

DIRECT TEACHING

Modeling and Demonstration

The Subject Form. Model how a pronoun takes the subject form when it is the subject of a verb by using the example *I walked to school.* First, ask which word or words in this sentence are pronouns. [*I*] Then, ask how this pronoun is used in the sentence. [*as the subject of the verb*] The forms of the pronoun *I* include the subject forms: *I, we;* the object forms: *me, us;* and the possessive forms: *my/mine, our/ours.* Ask which form is used in the sentence. [*subject form*] Now, have a volunteer use another example from this chapter to demonstrate how to identify the subject form of a pronoun.

DIRECT TEACHING

Pronouns

Activity. Write on the board the following sentence:

Juan and _____ will be outside the auditorium.

Ask students how many different pronouns can fit in the blank. Have them work in pairs to list the pronouns and arrive at a number. [*There are seven pronouns that will fit:* I, you, he, she, it, we, they.] Then, ask what these pronouns have in common. [*They can all be used as subjects.*]

EXTENSION

Critical Thinking

Metacognition. Ask students how they figured out which pronouns would work in the sentence above. Ask them whether it is easier for them to rely on position in the sentence or sound. If it is easier for them to use sound, ask students how they can best "hear" the correct form in this sentence. [*It is easier to hear the correct form if the first subject is omitted.*]

DIFFERENTIATING INSTRUCTION

English-Language Learners

Spanish. Because Spanish verbs have endings that indicate the person and number of the subject, pronouns often are omitted in Spanish. For example, in the sentence *Yo hablo español* (*I speak Spanish*), the Spanish speaker typically omits *Yo* (*I*): *Hablo español.* Remind Spanish-speaking students that they should include the subject pronoun in their sentences in English even if to their ears it may sound redundant at first.

USAGE

TIPS & TRICKS

To test whether a pronoun is used correctly in a compound subject, try each form of the pronoun separately.

EXAMPLE
(*She, Her*) and (*I, me*) practiced hard. [*She practiced or Her practiced? I practiced or me practiced?*]

ANSWER
She and **I** practiced hard.

EXAMPLES **I** walked to school. [*I* is the subject of the verb *walked*.]

Did **they** get to the theater on time? [*They* is the subject of the verb *Did get*.]

Dan said that **he** and **she** live on the Tigua reservation near El Paso, Texas. [*He* and *she* are the compound subject of the verb *live*.]

Oral Practice 1 Using Pronouns as Subjects

Read the following sentences aloud, stressing the italicized pronouns.

1. *She* and Ahmed solve crossword puzzles.
2. Are *they* very hard puzzles to solve?
3. Dad and *I* finished putting together a jigsaw puzzle last night.
4. *We* worked for three hours!
5. Finally, *you* and *he* found the missing pieces.
6. *He* and *I* liked the completed picture of flamenco dancers.
7. *They* are from Spain.
8. *We* agreed that *we* would like to see them dance.

Exercise 3 Identifying Correct Pronoun Forms

Choose the correct form of the pronoun in parentheses in each of the following sentences.

EXAMPLE 1. Brad and (*me, I*) wrote a skit based on the myth about Pygmalion.
1. *I*

1. (*Him, He*) and I thought the myth was funny.
2. (*We, Us*) asked Angela to play a part in the skit.
3. Neither (*she, her*) nor Doreen wanted to play a statue that came to life.
4. Finally Brad and (*me, I*) convinced Doreen that it would be a funny version of the myth.
5. (*Him, He*) and I flipped a coin to see who would play the part of Pygmalion.
6. The next day (*we, us*) were ready to perform.
7. Doreen and (*me, I*) began giggling when Brad pretended to be the beautiful statue.

8. In the skit, when Pygmalion returned from the festival of Venus, (*him*, *he*) and the statue were supposed to hug.

9. Instead of hugging, (*they*, *them*) laughed too hard to say the lines correctly.

10. Doreen, Brad, and (*I*, *me*) finally took a bow, and the class applauded.

Pronoun as Predicate Nominative

A *predicate nominative* completes the meaning of a linking verb and identifies or refers to the subject of the sentence.

8b. Use the subject form for a pronoun that is a predicate nominative.

A pronoun used as a predicate nominative usually follows a form of the verb *be* (such as *am*, *are*, *is*, *was*, *were*, *be*, *been*, or *being*).

EXAMPLES The next singer is **she.** [*She* completes the meaning of the linking verb *is* and identifies the subject *singer.*]

The first two speakers might be **he** and **I.** [*He* and *I* complete the meaning of the linking verb *might be* and identify the subject *speakers.*]

Was the winner really **she**? [*She* completes the meaning of the linking verb *Was* and identifies the subject *winner.*]

Oral Practice 2 **Using Pronouns as Predicate Nominatives**

Read the following sentences aloud, stressing the italicized pronouns.

1. The stars of that movie were *he* and *she*.
2. The actors from Australia must be *they*.
3. Of course, the mountain man is *he*.
4. Was the actress really *she*, Jeremy?
5. The director could have been *he*.
6. The villains are *he* and *they*.
7. The movie's biggest fans may be *you* and *I*.
8. The next ones to rent the film will be *we*, I think.

Reference Note

For more information on **predicate nominatives,** see page 112.

┌HELP─

To choose the correct form of a pronoun used as a predicate nominative, try reversing the order of the sentence.

EXAMPLE
   The best gymnast is (*she, her*).

REVERSED
   (*She, Her*) is the best gymnast.

ANSWER
   The best gymnast is **she.**

DIFFERENTIATING INSTRUCTION

English-Language Learners

Hmong. Speakers of Hmong may find pronoun-antecedent agreement, especially in the possessive case, troublesome. Explain that English possessive pronouns have the same function as do combinations of classifiers and pronouns in Hmong. Remind students that pronouns should correctly identify their antecedents and agree with them in gender and number. Tell students that they should review the feminine, masculine, and neuter pronouns along with their cases.

Special Education Students

Some students may have poor decoding skills and may read a different word in place of the one written. The words they insert may be similar in one or more ways to the ones presented: configuration, sound, definition, and linguistic function. Such substitution may or may not affect students' comprehension, but you should listen to each student closely during the **Oral Practice** exercises.

DIRECT TEACHING

Correcting Misconceptions

Students may not know that it is correct to use nominative-case pronouns as predicate nominatives and may think that objective-case pronouns sound less awkward. Assure students that sentences such as *It is I* are correct, and encourage them to practice saying such sentences aloud to help make them more familiar. You can also tell students that they can rewrite sentences to make them sound more natural by flipping the subject and the predicate nominative. For example, *The winner is he* would sound more natural as *He is the winner.*

APPLICATION

Predicate Nominatives

To give students more practice using pronouns correctly as predicate nominatives, have them revise sentences from pieces they have written. Have students rewrite sentences in which pronouns have been used as subjects, making the pronouns predicate nominatives instead.

DIFFERENTIATING INSTRUCTION

English-Language Learners

Cantonese. Cantonese uses fewer pronouns than English and drops them when they are understood: *The nurse put a thermometer in (my) mouth.* Also, there is no difference between the subjective and objective forms in Cantonese. Have students practice the forms of pronouns by relating personal information, such as likes and dislikes, in speech or writing. Practice communication activities. For example, have students interview others in class and report on their findings.

> *Robert likes soccer. He plays on a team.*

During regular classroom conversation, give students opportunities to use forms correctly as they talk about family, classmates, and personal needs.

Teacher: *Did you give **her** the book?*

Student: *Yes, I gave **her** the book.*

Teacher: *What is **his** name?*

Student: ***His** name is _____.*

│ STYLE   TIP │

Expressions such as *It's me* and *That's him* are common in everyday speech. However, these expressions contain the object forms *me* and *him* used incorrectly as predicate nominatives.

Such expressions should be avoided in formal writing and speaking. If the subject form of the pronoun sounds awkward as the predicate nominative, revise the sentence.

AWKWARD
  The next speakers will be **he** and **I.**

REVISED
  He and **I** will be the next speakers.

┌HELP─

Although most of the sentences in Exercise 5 have more than one possible correct answer, you need to give only one for each sentence.

Answers will vary. Here are some possibilities.
  1. he, she
  2. he, she
  3. they, we
  4. she, he
  5. I, he, she
  6. I, he, she
  7. he, she
  8. they, we
  9. he, she
  10. he, she

Exercise 4 Identifying Pronouns Used as Predicate Nominatives

Choose the <u>correct form of the pronoun</u> in parentheses in each of the following sentences.

EXAMPLE   1. The man behind the curtain is (*him, he*).
            1. he

1. The winners are you and (*me, <u>I</u>*).
2. It might have been (*he, him*).
3. The cooks for the traditional Vietnamese meal were (*them, <u>they</u>*).
4. Could it have been (*<u>we</u>, us*)?
5. Every year the speaker has been (*her, <u>she</u>*).
6. That was Carl and (*<u>they</u>, them*) in the swimming pool.
7. The volleyball fans in our family are Dad and (*<u>she</u>, her*).
8. First on the Black History Month program will be (*us, <u>we</u>*).
9. Was that (*<u>he</u>, him*) at the door?
10. Last year, the class treasurer was (*<u>he</u>, him*).

Exercise 5 Writing Sentences with Pronouns Used as Predicate Nominatives

Supply pronouns to complete the following sentences correctly. Use a variety of pronouns, but do not use *you* or *it*.

EXAMPLE   1. The man in the silliest costume was ____.
            1. he

1. The person in the gorilla suit must be ____.
2. The next contestants will be ____ and ____.
3. The winners should have been ____.
4. Can that singer be ____, Samuel?
5. The one sitting in the back row was ____.
6. The first ones in line were my friends and ____.
7. "Excellent interpreters of Shakespeare's characters were ____ and ____," said Mr. Simmons.
8. Are the next entrants on stage ____?
9. The leader of that dragon team is probably ____.
10. Finalists in the contest will be Ted, Lisa, or ____.

Review A **Identifying Correct Pronoun Forms**

Choose the <u>correct form of the pronoun</u> in parentheses in each of the following sentences.

EXAMPLE   **1.** Last summer Carl, Felicia, and (*us, we*) went to San Antonio, Texas.

      1. we

1. Carl and (*she, her*) took these photographs.
2. Early one morning (*him, he*) and (*she, her*) visited the Alamo.
3. That could be (*him, he*) in the crowd outside the Alamo.
4. Felicia and (*I, me*) listened to a mariachi band on the Riverwalk.
5. Of course, the musicians in the picture at right are (*they, them*).
6. Don't (*they, them*) look as though they're having a good time?
7. Carl and (*I, me*) enjoyed visiting the Spanish Governor's Palace in the afternoon.
8. Felicia, Carl, and (*us, we*) particularly liked the palace.
9. In fact, the first guests there that morning were (*us, we*).
10. Maybe you and (*they, them*) will get a chance to visit San Antonio someday.

The Object Form

Pronoun as Direct Object

A ***direct object*** completes the meaning of an action verb and tells *who* or *what* receives the action of the verb.

Reference Note

For more about **direct objects,** see page 107.

The Forms of Personal Pronouns   **183**

The Object Form
Rules 8c–e *(pp. 183–188)*

OBJECTIVES

■ To read sentences aloud and to stress the pronouns used in the objective case

■ To choose the correct forms of pronouns used as direct objects, indirect objects, and objects of prepositions

DIRECT TEACHING

Modeling and Demonstration

The Object Form. Model how a pronoun takes the object form when it is the direct object of a verb by using the example *The teacher thanked me for cleaning the chalkboard.* First, ask which word or words in this sentence are pronouns. [*me*] Then, ask how this pronoun is used in the sentence. [*as the direct object of the verb*] The forms of the pronoun *I* include the subject forms: *I, we;* the object forms: *me, us;* and the possessive forms: *my/mine, our/ours.* Ask which form is used in the sentence. [*object form*] Now, have a volunteer use another example from this chapter to demonstrate how to identify the object form of a pronoun.

DIFFERENTIATING INSTRUCTION

English-Language Learners

Spanish. Some students may have difficulty positioning direct and indirect object pronouns within sentences. For example, "Lalo gave it to me" can be expressed in Spanish as *Lalo me lo dio* (literally, "Lalo me it gave"). Object pronouns can come before verbs in several languages.

RETEACHING

Relating to Literature

Objective Form of Pronouns. To illustrate the value of object pronouns in literature, have your students read "All Summer in a Day" by Ray Bradbury. Then, have them identify as many object pronouns as possible on the first page. You may want to read those paragraphs aloud and replace the object pronouns with their antecedents to demonstrate how different the language would sound without object pronouns. Ask volunteers to express the grammatical value of object pronouns in literature. [*Without object pronouns, the names of the objects would have to be repeated over and over. This repetition would lead to awkward, tedious sentences.*]

| STYLE | TIP |

Just as there are good manners in behavior, there are also good manners in language. In English, it is polite to put first-person pronouns (*I, me, mine, we, us, ours*) last in compound constructions.

EXAMPLES
Veronica showed **Roberto and me** how to use the software program.

She and I arrived early for softball practice.

TIPS & TRICKS

To help you choose the correct pronoun in a compound object, try each pronoun separately in the sentence.

EXAMPLE
Ms. Stone praised Alonzo and (*we, us*). [*Ms. Stone praised we or Ms. Stone praised us?*]

ANSWER
Ms. Stone praised Alonzo and **us.**

8c. Use the object form for a pronoun that is the direct object of a verb.

EXAMPLES The teacher thanked **me** for cleaning the chalkboard. [*Teacher is the subject of the verb thanked. The teacher thanked whom? The direct object is me.*]

The answer surprised **us.** [*Answer is the subject of the verb surprised. The answer surprised whom? The direct object is us.*]

Have you told **him** about the change in plans? [*You is the subject of the verb Have told. You have told whom? The direct object is him.*]

Fred saw **them** and **me** last night. [*Fred is the subject of the verb saw. Fred saw whom? The compound direct object is them and me.*]

Oral Practice 3 Using Pronouns as Direct Objects

Read the following sentences aloud, stressing the italicized pronouns.

1. Kathy found *them* and *me* by the fountain.
2. Mr. Winters took *us* to the concert.
3. Did you see *her* and *him* at the Cajun restaurant?
4. Tyrone frightened *us* with his rubber spider.
5. Ellis invited Luis, Jared, and *me* to his party.
6. The mayor met *them* at Howard University.
7. Uncle Ken thanked *her* for the gift.
8. The fans cheered Anthony and *her*.

Exercise 6 Identifying Pronouns Used as Direct Objects

Choose the <u>correct form of the pronoun</u> in parentheses in each of the following sentences.

EXAMPLE 1. Marcus met Howard and (*I, me*) at the game.
    1. me

1. Mrs. Freeman invited Leroy and (*I, me*) to a Kwanzaa party.
2. The spectators watched (*we, us*) and (*they, them*).
3. The shoes don't fit (*her, she*) or (*I, me*).

MINI-LESSON   Usage

Number of Personal Pronouns. You might want to review with students the singular and plural forms of personal pronouns. Have students alter the sentences in **Oral Practice 3**, changing the singular pronouns to plural and the plural pronouns to singular. Tell them not to change the person of the pronouns.

1. him *or* her, us
2. me
3. them

4. Sean called Marco and (*he*, <u>*him*</u>) on the telephone.

5. Our new neighbors asked (*we*, <u>*us*</u>) for directions to the synagogue.

6. They hired Tía and (<u>*us*</u>, *we*) to rake their yard.

7. The puppy followed Louis and (*he*, <u>*him*</u>) all the way home.

8. Last week, friends from Panama visited (<u>*us*</u>, *we*).

9. Odessa thanked (<u>*her*</u>, *she*) and (<u>*me*</u>, *I*) for helping.

10. The usher showed Greg and (<u>*them*</u>, *they*) to their seats.

Pronoun as Indirect Object

An *indirect object* may come between an action verb and a direct object. An indirect object tells *to whom* or *to what* or *for whom* or *for what* something is done.

For more about **indirect objects,** see page 109.

8d. Use the object form for a pronoun that is the indirect object of a verb.

EXAMPLES   Scott handed **me** a note. [Scott handed what? *Note* is the direct object. To whom did he hand a note? The indirect object is *me*.]

Coretta baked **them** some muffins. [Coretta baked what? *Muffins* is the direct object. For whom did Coretta bake muffins? The indirect object is *them*.]

Elizabeth sent **him** and **me** some oranges from Florida. [Elizabeth sent what? *Oranges* is the direct object. To whom did Elizabeth send oranges? The compound indirect object is *him* and *me*.]

┌HELP┐

Indirect objects do not follow prepositions. If *to* or *for* precedes a pronoun, the pronoun is the object of a preposition, not an indirect object.

Reference Note

For more information about **prepositions and their objects,** see page 63.

Oral Practice 4 **Using Pronouns as Indirect Objects**

Read the following sentences aloud, stressing the italicized pronouns.

1. Mr. Krebs showed Bill and *them* the rock collection.

2. Paco told *me* the answer to the riddle.

3. Mr. Thibaut gives *us* lacrosse lessons.

4. We bought *her* and *him* a present.

5. The artists drew *us* and *them* some pictures.

6. The server brought *me* a bagel with cream cheese.

7. A pen pal in Hawaii sent *her* some shells.

8. My uncle Shannon told *us* a funny story about leprechauns.

The Forms of Personal Pronouns   **185**

DIFFERENTIATING INSTRUCTION

English-Language Learners

Hmong. The objective and subjective uses of Hmong pronouns depend upon their placement within the sentence rather than upon changes to the pronouns themselves, while the possessive case relies upon the use of a possessive classifier. Remind Hmong speakers that English pronouns change form in order to indicate their functions within a sentence, and offer additional review and practice using pronouns in their different cases.

USAGE

DIRECT TEACHING

Pronoun as Indirect Object

Practice. You may want to write the sentences from **Oral Practice 4** on the chalkboard. After the class reads each sentence, use an eraser, book, or other object to cover the pronouns used as indirect objects. Then, have students read the sentences without the covered indirect objects. Help them see that the direct objects are receiving the action of the verb in each sentence. For example: Mr. Krebs showed the rock collection. Mr. Krebs showed what? [*the rock collection*]

Then, uncover the indirect object and ask to whom or to what the action has been done. For example: Mr. Krebs showed the rock collection to whom? [*Bill and them*]

---

4. me

5. us

6. him *or* her

7. them

8. them

DIFFERENTIATING INSTRUCTION

Learners Having Difficulty

You might want to have students work in pairs to complete **Review B.** Have partners alternate writing sentences. As they write each sentence, the partners should work together to identify and circle the subject and object forms of personal pronouns in the sentences, determine the function of each pronoun (subject, predicate nominative, direct object, or indirect object), and identify the relevant rule from the chapter. The partners should note the rule in the margin of their paper and write the correct pronoun form for any incorrect sentences.

APPLICATION

Relating to Writing

Object Form of Pronouns. As an alternative to **Review B,** ask each of your students to write a brief descriptive paragraph about a pet or favorite animal. Students should include object pronouns in each sentence. When they finish their first drafts, tell them to exchange papers with partners, who will check the correctness of the object pronouns.

Review B Revising Incorrect Pronoun Forms in Paragraphs

ANSWERS

1. me—I
2. she—her; I—me
3. C
4. C

Exercise 7 Identifying Pronouns Used as Indirect Objects

Choose the correct form of the pronoun in parentheses in each of the following sentences.

EXAMPLE 1. At the start of class, Mr. Chou assigned (*we, us*) new seats.

1. *us*

1. The store clerk gave (*they, them*) a discount.
2. For lunch, Anthony fixed (*he, him*) and (*she, her*) bean burritos with salsa.
3. Would you please show (*her, she*) and (*me, I*) that Navajo dream catcher?
4. Those green apples made both Christopher and (*he, him*) happy.
5. The waiter brought (*us, we*) some ice water.
6. Why don't you sing (*she, her*) a lullaby?
7. Have they made (*we, us*) the costumes for the play?
8. An usher handed (*me, I*) a program of the recital.
9. The Red Cross volunteers showed (*we, us*) and (*they, them*) a video about first aid.
10. Please send (*me, I*) your new address.

Review B Revising Incorrect Pronoun Forms in Paragraphs

In most of the sentences in the following paragraphs, at least one pronoun has been used incorrectly. Identify each incorrect pronoun, and give the correct form. If all of the pronouns in a sentence are already correct, write *C*.

EXAMPLE [1] Ms. Fisher took several of my friends and I to the museum.

1. *I—me*

[1] At the Museum of Natural History, Luisa and me wanted to see the American Indian exhibit. [2] The museum guide showed she and I the displays of Hopi pottery and baskets. [3] Both she and I were especially interested in the baskets. [4] After half an hour, Ms. Fisher found us.

[5] Then Luisa, her, and I joined the rest of the group. [6] Another guide had been giving Ms. Fisher and they information about the Masai people in Africa. [7] Them and us decided to see the exhibit about ancient Egypt next.

[8] A group of little children passed Ms. Fisher and we on the stairway as we were going to the exhibit. [9] The ones who reached the exhibit first were them. [10] Jeff, the jokester, said that they wanted to find their "mummies." [11] Ms. Fisher and us laughed at the terrible pun. [12] She gave him a pat on the back. [13] We asked her not to encourage him. [14] The museum guide led the children and we to the back of the room. [15] There, he showed us and they a model of a pyramid. [16] Then Ms. Fisher and him explained how the Egyptians prepared mummies. [17] Was it her who asked about King Tutankhamen? [18] Of course, Luisa and me recognized this golden mask right away. [19] As we were leaving, the guide gave the children and we some booklets about King Tut and other famous ancient Egyptians. [20] He handed Luisa and I booklets about the builders of the pyramids.

The golden funerary mask of Egyptian King Tutankhamen. Egyptian National Museum, Cairo, Egypt/SuperStock.

Pronoun as Object of a Preposition

The *object of a preposition* is a noun or a pronoun that follows a preposition. Together, the preposition, its object, and any modifiers of that object make a *prepositional phrase.*

8e. Use the object form for a pronoun that is the object of a preposition.

EXAMPLES above **me**   beside **us**   with **them**

for **him**   toward **you**   next to **her**

Reference Note

For more information about **prepositions,** see page 62.

Oral Practice 5 Using Pronouns as Objects of Prepositions

Read the sentences on the following page aloud, stressing the italicized pronouns.

CONTENT-AREA CONNECTIONS

Social Studies
Pronouns Used in Poetry. Locate a copy of "The New Colossus," a poem by Emma Lazarus that was inscribed on a tablet in the pedestal of the Statue of Liberty in 1903. Tell your students that the Statue of Liberty greeted many of the immigrants who sailed to the United States. Then, write all or some of the poem—particularly the last two sentences—on the chalkboard, and have students identify subject and object pronouns used by the poet.

1. The lemonade stand was built by Chuck and *me*.
2. The younger children rode in front of *us*.
3. Just between *you* and *me*, that game wasn't much fun.
4. Everyone has gone except the Taylors and *them*.
5. Give the message to *him* or *her*.
6. Why don't you sit here beside *me*, Ben?
7. Were those pictures of Amish families taken by *him*?
8. Donna went to the Cinco de Mayo parade with *them*.

Exercise 8

DISTRIBUTED REVIEW

Before students work on **Exercise 8**, you might want to have them identify the prepositions in the designated sentences.

1. In, against
2. with, at
3. to
4. around

Special Pronoun Problems

(pp. 188–192)

OBJECTIVES

- To read sentences aloud and to stress the pronouns *who* and *whom*
- To identify the correct forms of *who* and *whom* and pronouns with appositives

---

DIRECT TEACHING

Modeling and Demonstration

Special Pronoun Problems. Model how to choose correctly between the forms *who* and *whom* by using the example *To (who, whom) did Mike speak?* First, ask how the pronoun is used in this question. [*as the object of the preposition*] Then, ask which form of the pronoun is the object form. [*whom*] The correct sentence is *To whom did Mike speak?* Point out that *who* is used when the pronoun is the subject of a verb, and *whom* is used when the pronoun is the direct or indirect object of a verb, or the object of a preposition. Now, have a volunteer use an example from this chapter to demonstrate how to choose the correct form of *who*.

TIPS & TRICKS

When a preposition is followed by two or more pronouns, try each pronoun alone to be sure that you have used the correct forms.

EXAMPLE

Carrie divided the chores between (*they, them*) and (*we, us*). [*Carrie divided the chores between they or Carrie divided the chores between them? Carrie divided the chores between we or Carrie divided the chores between us?*]

ANSWER

Carrie divided the chores between **them** and **us**.

---

1. The lemonade stand was built by Chuck and *me*.
2. The younger children rode in front of *us*.
3. Just between *you* and *me*, that game wasn't much fun.
4. Everyone has gone except the Taylors and *them*.
5. Give the message to *him* or *her*.
6. Why don't you sit here beside *me*, Ben?
7. Were those pictures of Amish families taken by *him*?
8. Donna went to the Cinco de Mayo parade with *them*.

Exercise 8   Identifying Pronouns Used as Objects of Prepositions

Choose the <u>correct form of the pronoun</u> in parentheses in each of the following sentences.

EXAMPLE   1. Someone else should have sent an invitation to (*they, them*).

      1. them

1. In the first round, Michael Chang played against (*he, him*).
2. Did you sit with Martha or (*her, she*) at the game?
3. Peggy sent homemade birthday cards to Josh, you, and (*them, they*).
4. There is a bee flying around (*he, him*) and you.
5. If you have a complaint, tell it to Mr. Ramis or (*she, her*).
6. Ms. Young divided the projects among (*us, we*).
7. This secret is strictly between you and (*me, I*).
8. Can you believe the weather balloon dropped right in front of (*we, us*)?
9. Please don't ride the Alaskan ferry without Jim and (*me, I*).
10. One of the clowns threw confetti at us and (*they, them*).

Special Pronoun Problems

Who and *Whom*

The pronoun *who* has two different forms. *Who* is the subject form. *Whom* is the object form.

When you are choosing between *who* and *whom* in a question, follow these steps:

RESOURCES

Special Pronoun Problems
Practice
- *Language & Sentence Skills Practice,* pp. 162–166
- *Developmental Language & Sentence Skills,* pp. 79–80

STEP 1   Rephrase the question as a statement.

STEP 2   Identify how the pronoun is used in the statement—as a subject, a predicate nominative, a direct object, an indirect object, or an object of a preposition.

STEP 3   Determine whether the subject form or the object form is correct according to the rules of standard English.

STEP 4   Select the correct form—*who* or *whom*.

EXAMPLE   (*Who, Whom*) rang the bell?

STEP 1   The statement is (*Who, Whom*) *rang the bell*.

STEP 2   The pronoun is the subject of the verb *rang*.

STEP 3   As the subject, the pronoun should be in the subject form.

STEP 4   The subject form is *who*.

ANSWER   **Who** rang the bell?

EXAMPLE   (*Who, Whom*) does Lindsay see?

STEP 1   The statement is *Lindsay does see (who, whom)*.

STEP 2   The pronoun is the direct object of the verb *does see*.

STEP 3   A direct object should be in the object form.

STEP 4   The object form is *whom*.

ANSWER   **Whom** does Lindsay see?

EXAMPLE   To (*who, whom*) did Jo give the gift?

STEP 1   The statement is *Jo did give the gift to (who, whom)*.

STEP 2   The pronoun is the object of the preposition *to*.

STEP 3   The object of a preposition should be in the object form.

STEP 4   The object form is *whom*.

ANSWER   To **whom** did Jo give the gift?

Oral Practice 6   Using Pronouns Correctly in Sentences

Read the following sentences aloud, stressing the italicized pronouns.

1. *Who* owns the sailboat over there?
2. To *whom* did you throw the ball?
3. *Whom* did Miguel marry?

STYLE TIP

The use of *whom* is becoming less common in informal English. Informally, you may begin any question with *who*. In formal written and spoken English, however, you should distinguish between *who* and *whom*. *Who* is used as a subject or a predicate nominative, and *whom* is used as an object.

MEETING THE CHALLENGE

Members of the marching band in your middle school are planning a garage sale to raise money for new uniforms.

Write two spoken announcements: a formal one to be given to a meeting of parents and teachers, and an informal one to be given during a school spirit rally. Describe when and where the garage sale will take place and what types of items are needed. Also, ask for volunteers to help with the sorting, pricing, and selling of items. Use *who* or *whom* twice in each announcement.

ANSWERS

Announcements will vary, but each should contain two uses of who or whom. Informal announcements may use *who* for *whom*.

Special Pronoun Problems   **189**

DIFFERENTIATING INSTRUCTION

Advanced Learners

Have students create their own flowcharts showing the process for choosing between *who* and *whom* in a question, using the list of steps on this page as a model. Have students develop their own example sentences to use within the flowchart.

USAGE

FAMILY/COMMUNITY ACTIVITY   Continued on pp. 190–191

A Letter to the Editor. Explain to students that many people write letters to the editors of newspapers and magazines. The letters typically express an opinion about a newsworthy topic. To make sure the message is clear for readers, the letter writer must take care to use formal, standard English—including the correct use of pronouns.

Have students choose a historical event that they think was important. Students should then imagine that they are writing

4. *Who* was the stranger with the ten-gallon hat?
5. For *whom* did you knit that sweater?
6. *Who* is the author of that book about Jackie Robinson?
7. *Whom* did Josh choose as his subject?
8. By *whom* was this work painted?

Pronouns with Appositives

Reference Note

For more information about **appositives**, see page 272.

Sometimes a pronoun is followed directly by a noun that identifies the pronoun. Such a noun is called an ***appositive.*** To help you choose which pronoun to use before an appositive, omit the appositive and try each form of the pronoun separately.

EXAMPLE   (*We, Us*) Girl Scouts swam laps. [*Girl Scouts* is the appositive identifying the pronoun. *We swam laps* or *Us swam laps*?]

ANSWER   **We** Girl Scouts swam laps.

EXAMPLE   The director gave an award to (*we, us*) actors. [*Actors* is the appositive identifying the pronoun. *The director gave an award to we* or *The director gave an award to us*?]

ANSWER   The director gave an award to **us** actors.

Exercise 9 **Identifying the Correct Forms of Pronouns in Sentences**

Choose the <u>correct form of the pronoun</u> in parentheses in each of the following sentences.

EXAMPLE   **1.** (*Who, Whom*) can do the most jumping jacks?

          1. Who

1. (*We, Us*) baseball players always warm up before practice.
2. (*Who, Whom*) knows how to stretch properly?
3. Coach Anderson has special exercises for (*we, us*) pitchers.
4. To (*who, whom*) did the coach assign thirty sit-ups?
5. (*Who, Whom*) do you favor for tomorrow's game?
6. Would you teach (*we, us*) girls that new batting stance?
7. Please take (*we, us*) fans with you to the next game.

DIFFERENTIATING INSTRUCTION

Learners Having Difficulty
You may want to have students work in pairs for **Exercise 9.** Make one partner responsible for choosing the pronoun and the other for identifying the way the pronoun is used in the sentence. Students should correct any answers that do not follow rules for correct pronoun usage.

FAMILY/COMMUNITY ACTIVITY   ***Continued from p. 189***

letters to the editor, reminding readers about the coming anniversary of that event. Because space in a newspaper is limited, each letter should be no longer than about 250 words.

The letter should identify the event, the anniversary date, and important individuals involved in the event. For example, one student might choose to write about the anniversary of the 1963 March on

8. The ones with the new gloves and jerseys should have been (*we, us*) fielders.

9. (*Who, Whom*) should start the lineup?

10. With (*who, whom*) do you practice after school?

Review C **Revising Incorrect Pronoun Forms in Sentences**

Identify each ~~incorrect pronoun~~ in the following sentences. Then, write the correct pronoun. If a sentence is already correct, write *C*.

EXAMPLE   **1.** At first Karen and me thought that Lucy was imagining things.

        1. me—I

1. Lucy told Karen and ~~I~~ that creatures from outer space had just landed. **1.** me

2. She was certain it was ~~them~~ at the park. **2.** they

3. ~~Whom~~ would believe such a ridiculous story? **3.** Who

4. ~~Us~~ girls laughed and laughed. **4.** We

5. Lucy looked at ~~we~~ two with tears in her eyes. **5.** us

6. Karen and I agreed to go to the park to look around. **6.** C

7. Lucy walked between Karen and me, showing the way. **7.** C

8. In the park she and ~~us~~ hid behind some tall bushes. **8.** we

9. Suddenly a strong wind almost blew ~~we~~ three down. **9.** us

10. A green light shone on Karen and ~~I~~, and a red one shone on Lucy. **10.** me

11. ~~Whom~~ could it be? **11.** Who

12. One of the creatures spoke to us girls. **12.** C

13. Very slowly, Karen, Lucy, and ~~me~~ stepped out from behind the bushes. **13.** I

14. "You almost scared ~~they~~ and me silly!" shouted a creature, pointing at the others. **14.** them

15. Neither Karen nor ~~her~~ could speak, and I could make only a squeaking noise. **15.** she

16. Then the man inside the costume explained to ~~we~~ three girls that a movie company was filming in the park. **16.** us

17. They and we could be in the movie together. **17.** C

18. The equipment hidden in the bushes might have been bumped by one of ~~we~~ girls. **18.** us

Special Pronoun Problems   **191**

19. him

19. Lucy told the director and he about being afraid of the space creatures in the park.

20. we

20. If you see the movie, the short purple creatures under the spaceship are us three girls.

 Review D Replacing Nouns with Pronouns

Revise each of the following sentences, substituting pronouns for the words in italics.

EXAMPLE **1.** The bird hopped lightly into the *bird's* nest.
　　　　　　 1. The bird hopped lightly into its nest.

1. you

1. David, I have already asked *David* several times to clean your room.

2. it

2. The raccoon reached into the water, caught a fish, and ate *the fish.*

3. They

3. *Anne and Paula* should be here in a few minutes.

4. She

4. *Sandra* will be reading my report to the class tomorrow.

5. him

5. Don't forget to return Reginald's book to *Reginald.*

6. he

6. As soon as Willis finishes dinner, *Willis* must leave for play practice.

7. your

7. Diane, did you turn in *Diane's* permission slip yet?

8. our

8. Mario and I have decided to do *Mario's and my* project as a musical skit.

9. him

9. In his locker, Felipe has a photograph of the presidential candidate with *Felipe.*

10. their

10. The dogs came running in as soon as they knew *the dogs'* food dish was filled.

USAGE

Terms and numerals in brackets refer to concepts and rules tested by the items in the Chapter Review.

1. [8b]
2. [8b]
3. [8a]
4. [8a]
5. [8c]
6. [8a, pronoun with appositive]
7. [8a, who, whom]
8. [8d]
9. [8e]
10. [8e, who, whom]
11. [8e]
12. [8a]
13. [8a]
14. [8d]
15. [8a]
16. [8e]
17. [8a]
18. [8d]
19. [8b]
20. [8e]

21.–22. [8b]

Chapter Review

A. Identifying Correct Pronoun Forms

For each of the following sentences, write the <u>correct form of the pronoun</u> in parentheses.

1. Could that be (*she, her*) at the bus stop?
2. The guest speakers were Dr. Lucia Sanchez and (*he, him*).
3. Are you and (*they, them*) going to the basketball game?
4. You and (*I, me*) have been friends for a long time.
5. Sometimes, even our parents cannot tell (*we, us*) apart.
6. (*We, Us*) players surprised the coach with a victory party.
7. (*Who, Whom*) is bringing the holiday turkey?
8. Laura lent my sister and (*I, <u>me</u>*) a new CD.
9. Mr. Lee will divide the money between you and (*I, <u>me</u>*).
10. To (*who, <u>whom</u>*) is the envelope addressed?
11. Please keep this information between you and (*she, her*).
12. Did Maria or (*she, her*) call Grandmother Lopez?
13. Mom and (*they, them*) have gone shopping.
14. Can you show Charlie and (*she, her*) how to fish?
15. Danny and (*I, me*) are practicing woodcraft for camp.
16. Why didn't you tell me about (*he, <u>him</u>*)?
17. Eldon and (*<u>we</u>, us*) were tired of playing checkers.
18. Mom and Dad promised Keith and (*they, <u>them</u>*) a puppy.
19. Was (*<u>he</u>, him*) the only one in the theater?
20. Would you lend your notes to (*we, <u>us</u>*)?

B. Identifying Pronouns Used as Predicate Nominatives

For each of the following sentences, write the <u>correct form of the pronoun</u> in parentheses.

21. The bus driver was (*<u>he</u>, him*).
22. That was Mr. San Miguel and (*they, them*) at the stadium last night.

23.–30. [8b]

23. The most devoted animal-lovers I know are Melanie and (*her*, *she*).
24. The junior racquetball champion last year was (*her*, *she*).
25. Once or twice a month the lifeguard at the local pool is (*he*, *him*).
26. Was that (*they*, *them*) in the parking lot?
27. Second on the program at the concert was (*he*, *him*).
28. It could have been (*her*, *she*), but I doubt it.
29. The devoted baseball fans in our class are Gregorio and (*he*, *him*).
30. The visitors from Taiwan must be (*they*, *them*).

C. Identifying the Correct Forms of Pronouns Used as Subjects, Direct Objects, Indirect Objects, and Objects of Prepositions

For each of the following sentences, choose the correct form of the pronoun in parentheses and tell whether it is used as a *subject*, a *direct object*, an *indirect object*, or an *object of a preposition*.

31. o.p. [8e]
32. o.p. [8e]
33. s. [8a, pronoun with appositive]
34. d.o./d.o. [8c]
35. s. [8a, pronoun with appositive]
36. i.o. [8d]
37. i.o. [8d]
38. o.p. [8e]
39. d.o. [8c]
40. i.o. [8d]

31. The one who cheered loudest was the girl behind (*I*, *me*).
32. Did Isabel travel to Santa Fe with John and (*her*, *she*)?
33. (*We*, *Us*) baseball fans welcomed the decision not to move the team.
34. Peter called (*her*, *she*) and (*I*, *me*) last night.
35. (*We*, *Us*) cousins had a yard sale.
36. Tomas and José gave (*we*, *us*) their addresses in Mexico.
37. Her grandmother in Oregon sent (*her*, *she*) some apples.
38. On the hike, Christie and Maggie walked ahead of (*I*, *me*).
39. The teacher scolded us and (*he*, *him*) for being late.
40. I bought (*they*, *them*) an anniversary present.

Writing Application
Using Correct Pronoun Forms in Writing

Using Pronouns   Health Awareness Week is coming up soon. Your class has been chosen to perform a skit on a health-related topic for the rest of the school. Your teacher has asked each class member to write down an idea for an entertaining, informative skit. Write a paragraph or two describing a skit that your class could perform. Be sure to use correct pronoun forms in your description.

Prewriting   First, you will need to decide on a topic for the skit. Think about the health concerns of people your age. For example, you might plan a skit about the dangers of smoking or the importance of regular dental check-ups. After you choose a topic, brainstorm some ideas for a simple, entertaining skit. Be sure to list any props or costumes your class will need.

Writing   Use your notes to help you write your draft. First, tell what the skit is about and why it is appropriate for Health Awareness Week. Then, explain what happens in the skit from beginning to end. Be sure to tell in a general way what each character does and says. Describe the props and costumes that your class can make or bring from home.

Revising   Ask a classmate to read your paragraph. Is the information given in the skit correct? Does the skit sound entertaining? Is it clear which character does and says what? If not, revise your paragraph. Add details that will make the skit more fun and interesting.

Publishing   Check your sentences to be sure you have used pronouns correctly and clearly. Read through your description carefully to check for errors in grammar, spelling, and punctuation. Use this chapter to help you check for errors in pronoun forms.

Your class may want to hold a contest for the best skit idea. Using the best idea, work together to develop the skit in more detail. Then, with your teacher's permission, give a performance of the skit for other classes.

USAGE

APPLICATION

Writing Application

Prewriting Tip. This writing assignment provides students with an opportunity to develop descriptive paragraphs in which they will use correct pronoun forms. You may want to remind students to review correct pronoun usage before they begin writing their paragraphs and again as they check for errors before publishing.

Writing Tip. Encourage students to be objective about each sentence in their paragraphs. Tell them to examine each sentence separately and to use the following criteria.

1. Does the sentence have a subject and verb and express a complete thought?

2. Does the sentence say exactly what you want it to say?

3. Does it support the topic sentence?

4. Does it contain a subject pronoun or an object pronoun?

Scoring Rubric. While you will want to pay particular attention to students' use of pronouns, you will also want to evaluate overall writing performance. You may want to give a split score to indicate development and clarity of the composition as well as usage skills.

Using Modifiers Correctly
Comparison and Placement

1.0 Written and Oral English Language Conventions

Students write and speak with a command of standard English conventions appropriate to this grade level.

STANDARDS FOCUS

Grade-Level Standard

(Boldface indicates concepts that are taught and tested in this chapter.)

■ Language Convention 1.0: **Students write and speak with a command of standard English conventions appropriate to this grade level.**

Prerequisite/Review Standard

■ Grammar 1.2: Identify and correctly use verbs that are often misused (e.g., *lie/lay, sit/set, rise/raise*), modifiers, and pronouns.

Standard Coming Up in the Next Grade Level

■ Sentence Structure 1.1: Place modifiers properly and use the active voice.

▼

INTRODUCING THE CHAPTER

■ The chapter begins with a discussion of different kinds of modifiers and teaches the degrees of comparison of adjectives and adverbs, both regular and irregular. This section is followed by lessons on the use of *well* and *good,* on the use of adjectives after linking verbs, on avoiding double comparisons and double negatives, and on the correct placement of modifiers.

■ The chapter closes with a **Chapter Review** to help you check students' mastery of the use and placement of modifiers and the correct use of negative

(continued)

Diagnostic Preview

Correcting Errors in the Form, Use, and Placement of Modifiers

Numerals in brackets refer to rules tested by the items in the Diagnostic Preview.

Revisions of double negatives may vary.

1. best [9b, c(3)]
2. faster [9b, c(2)]
3. C [9a, e]
4. anything [9g]
5. that we had planted [9h]
6. regularly [9b, c(1)]
7. [9f]
8. wonderful [9e]
9. with a limp [9h]

Most of the following sentences contain an error in the use of modifiers or negative words. If a sentence has an ~~error,~~ rewrite the sentence correctly. If a sentence is already correct, write *C*.

EXAMPLE   1. The weather looks more worse today.
            1. *The weather looks worse today.*

1. Of the students in class, Odelle writes ~~better.~~
2. Can you type ~~fastest~~ on a computer or on a typewriter?
3. Juan seemed very happy that we had visited him.
4. No one knew ~~nothing~~ about the tornado.
5. The vegetables were eaten by rabbits ~~that we had planted.~~
6. Throughout history, many people have written ~~regular~~ in their diaries.
7. The people who moved in next door are the ~~most~~ friendliest neighbors who have ever lived there.
8. The bread smelled ~~wonderfully.~~
9. Did that armadillo make it across the road ~~with a limp?~~

CHAPTER RESOURCES

Internet

■ go.hrw.com (keyword: HLLA)

Planning

■ *One-Stop Planner CD-ROM*

■ *On Course: Mapping Instruction*

Practice & Review

■ *Language & Sentence Skills Practice,* pp. 172–190; 191–194

■ *Developmental Language & Sentence Skills,* pp. 81–90

Application & Enrichment

■ *Language & Sentence Skills Practice,* pp. 195, 198; 171, 196–197

10. Wynton Marsalis plays the trumpet ~~good~~.
11. If you don't feel well today, you shouldn't go out.
12. ^We read a story written by Mark Twain ~~yesterday~~.
13. Mai is one of the most persistent people I know.
14. I felt ~~sadly~~ at the end of *Old Yeller*.
15. The boy ^ordered a sandwich ~~that was hungry~~.
16. The team ^usually wins the game ~~that has the better defense~~.
17. Tanya is the youngest of my brothers and sisters.
18. It ~~doesn't make~~ no difference to Brian.
19. I'm not sure which I like ~~best~~, CD's or tapes.
20. Arthur's piano playing sounds very ~~nicely~~ to me.
21. The storm came up so ~~sudden~~ that it surprised us.
22. The house looks ~~differently~~ to me.
23. Lena and Ivan are twins, and Lena is the ~~oldest~~ one.
24. We ~~couldn't~~ hardly believe the news!
25. Miyoko looks ~~well~~ in her new school uniform.

10. well [9d(2)]
11. C [9d(2)]
12. Yesterday [9h]
13. C [9a, c(3)]
14. sad [9e]
15. that was hungry [9h]
16. that has the better defense [9h)]
17. C [9a, c(3)]
18. makes [9g]
19. better [9a, c(2)]
20. nice [9e]
21. suddenly [9b]
22. different [9e]
23. older [9a, c(2)]
24. could [9g]
25. good [9d(1)]

Reference Note

For more about **adjectives,** see page 38. For more about **adverbs,** see page 59.

What Is a Modifier?

A *modifier* is a word, a phrase, or a clause that makes the meaning of a word or word group more specific. The two kinds of modifiers are *adjectives* and *adverbs.*

One-Word Modifiers

Adjectives

9a. *Adjectives* make the meanings of nouns and pronouns more specific.

EXAMPLES **That** one is my favorite. [The adjective *That* tells which one.]

Does Stephen know the **secret** combination? [The adjective *secret* tells what kind of combination.]

Estéban has saved **more** money than I have. [The adjective *more* tells how much money.]

Four horses grazed peacefully at the foot of the hill. [The adjective *Four* tells how many horses.]

words. Also, a **Writing Application** feature asks students to use negative words correctly in writing a letter to a friend.

■ For help in integrating this chapter with writing assignments in *Holt Literature and Language Arts,* use the **Teaching Strands** chart on pp. T22–T23.

ASSESSING

Entry-Level Assessment

Diagnostic Preview. You can use the **Diagnostic Preview** to assess your students' skills in recognizing and correcting errors in the form, use, and placement of modifiers. The **Diagnostic Preview** also checks students' skills in recognizing sentences with double negatives. If your students show a particular weakness in one of these areas, you can skip to the relevant part of the chapter.

What Is a Modifier?

Rules 9a, b *(pp. 197–199)*

OBJECTIVE

■ **To identify modifiers as adjectives or adverbs and to tell which word is modified**

Differentiating Instruction

■ *Lesson Plans for Language Development*
■ *Supporting Instruction in Five Languages*

Assessment

■ *Progress Assessment for the Holt Handbook,* pp. 17–18, 41

■ *Test Generator (One-Stop Planner CD-ROM)* 🎧

Other Language Resources

■ *Spelling Lessons & Activities*
■ *Vocabulary Development*
■ *Daily Language Activities Transparencies*

USAGE

Lesson Starter

Motivating. To help students understand how adjectives modify words, consider using the following demonstration. First, identify for the class what you are wearing, using only nouns such as "shirt, pants, shoes." Then, ask students to modify those nouns by using descriptive words called adjectives: "*white* shirt, *blue* pants, *dress* shoes." Invite volunteers to repeat this exercise by describing your classroom, a desk, or another object. Lead students to understand that they are using adjectives to make the meanings of the nouns more specific.

DIRECT TEACHING

Modeling and Demonstration

What Is a Modifier? Model how to identify adjectives and adverbs by using the examples *Does Stephen know the secret combination?* and *The car backfired loudly.* First, ask which word in the first sentence specifies what kind of *combination*. [*secret*] Then, ask what part of speech *combination* is. [*noun*] Point out that since adjectives describe nouns, *secret* is an adjective. Next, ask which word in the second example describes how the car backfired. [*loudly*] Then, ask what part of speech *backfired* is. [*verb*] Since adverbs describe verbs, *loudly* is an adverb. Now, have a volunteer use two other examples from this chapter to demonstrate how to identify adjectives and adverbs.

MEETING THE CHALLENGE

Many adverbs end in *–ly,* but others do not. Also, not all words with the *–ly* ending are adverbs. Some adjectives end in *–ly.* To decide whether a word is an adjective or an adverb, look at how the word is used in the sentence.

In each of the following sentences, identify the highlighted words as an *adjective* or an *adverb.*

1. The **elderly** man **calmly** crossed the street.
2. At first, she did **not** notice that the **holy** relic was missing.

ANSWERS
1. adjective, adverb
2. adverb, adjective

Reference Note

For more about **phrases,** see page 76.

Reference Note

For more about **clauses,** see page 89.

Adverbs

9b. *Adverbs* make the meanings of verbs, adjectives, and other adverbs more specific.

EXAMPLES   The car backfired **loudly.** [The adverb *loudly* makes the meaning of the verb *backfired* more specific.]

The painting is **quite** old. [The adverb *quite* makes the meaning of the adjective *old* more specific.]

The bear traveled **surprisingly** quickly. [The adverb *surprisingly* makes the meaning of the adverb *quickly* more specific.]

Phrases Used as Modifiers

Like one-word modifiers, phrases can also be used as adjectives and adverbs.

EXAMPLES   The cat **with the short tail** is my favorite. [The prepositional phrase *with the short tail* acts as an adjective that modifies the noun *cat.*]

Mr. Rodriguez planted the new bushes **along the fence.** [The prepositional phrase *along the fence* acts as an adverb that modifies the verb *planted.*]

Clauses Used as Modifiers

Like words and phrases, clauses can also be used as modifiers.

EXAMPLES   Spaghetti is the food **that I like best.** [The adjective clause *that I like best* modifies the noun *food.*]

Before Mario went downstairs, he washed his face and hands. [The adverb clause *Before Mario went downstairs* modifies the verb *washed.*]

Exercise 1 **Identifying Modifiers as Adjectives or Adverbs**

Tell whether the italicized word or word group in each of the following sentences is used as an *adjective* or an *adverb*. Then, identify the word that it modifies.

EXAMPLE   **1.** Ms. Olivarez is the woman *on the left.*
1. *adjective—woman*

RESOURCES

What Is a Modifier?
Practice
- *Language & Sentence Skills Practice,* pp. 172–175
- *Developmental Language & Sentence Skills,* pp. 81–82

1. The squirrel darted *quickly* up the tree trunk and hid among the leaves.   **1.** adv.
2. Wang Wei was a talented painter *of landscapes.*   **2.** adj.
3. Gabriela can ski faster *than I can.*   **3.** adv.
4. Is *this* poem the one that you wrote?   **4.** adj.
5. The man *who has curly hair* is my Uncle Thaddeus.   **5.** adj.
6. *Soon* you will need to put the bread in the oven.   **6.** adv.
7. *Before the performance* the actors practiced their lines and gestures.   **7.** adv.
8. Mountain biking is the sport *that I enjoy most.*   **8.** adj.
9. Tasmania is an island *off the coast of Australia.*   **9.** adj.
10. *Because the weather was hot,* we sat with our feet in the stream.   **10.** adv.

Comparison of Adjectives and Adverbs

When adjectives and adverbs are used in comparisons, they take different forms. The specific form they take depends upon how many things are being compared. The different forms of comparison are called *degrees of comparison.*

9c. The three degrees of comparison of modifiers are the *positive,* the *comparative,* and the *superlative.*

(1) The *positive degree* is used when only one thing is being modified and no comparison is being made.

EXAMPLES   *Felita* is a **good** book.

Shawn runs **quickly.**

The horse jumped **gracefully.**

(2) The *comparative degree* is used when two things are being compared.

EXAMPLES   In my opinion, *Nilda* is a **better** book than *Felita.*

Juanita runs **more quickly** than Shawn.

Which of the two horses jumped **more gracefully**?

┌HELP─
Here is a way to remember which form of a modifier to use. When comparing two things, use *–er* (the two-letter ending). When comparing three or more things, use *–est* (the three-letter ending).

Comparison of Adjectives and Adverbs   **199**

USAGE

Comparison of Adjectives and Adverbs
Rule 9c *(pp. 199–204)*

OBJECTIVES

■ **To write the comparative and superlative forms of modifiers**

■ **To use regular and irregular comparative and superlative forms of modifiers correctly in sentences**

DIRECT TEACHING

Modeling and Demonstration

Comparison of Adjectives and Adverbs. Model how to identify the degrees of comparison by using the following examples: Felita *is a good book; In my opinion,* Nilda *is a better book than* Felita; Nilda *is one of the best books I've read.* First, ask which word in the first sentence is an adjective. [*good*] Then, ask if a comparison is made. [*no*] Since no comparison is made, the adjective is in the positive degree. Next, ask whether a comparison is made in the second sentence. [*yes*] Then, ask how many things are compared. [*two;* Nilda *and* Felita] Since only two things are compared, the adjective *better* is in the comparative degree. Finally, ask what is compared in the third sentence. [Nilda *and books*] Since three or more things are compared, *best* is in the superlative degree. Now, have a volunteer use other examples from this chapter to demonstrate how to identify the degrees of comparison.

APPLICATION

Comparison of Adjectives

Activity. Have students practice the use of the positive, comparative, and superlative forms of modifiers by having them describe a character from a popular television program. Have students suggest five adjectives that apply to the character. Then, ask volunteers to write sentences that use each adjective in its comparative and superlative forms by comparing the character to other characters on the program. [*Sample answers:* taller than Bob, more talkative than Julie, funniest of all]

DIFFERENTIATING INSTRUCTION

Special Education Students

You can help students understand the difference between the comparative and superlative degrees by letting them make comparisons using tangible objects. Bring to class a grape, a lemon, and a large orange. Working with students in a small group, ask them to tell which is the biggest [*orange*]. Take away the orange and then ask which is bigger [*lemon*]. Explain that *biggest* is used when there are three or more objects and that *bigger* is used when there are only two.

STYLE TIP

In conversation you may hear such expressions as *Put your best foot forward.* Such uses of the superlative (to compare only two things) are acceptable in informal English. In formal speaking and writing, however, you should follow the rules in this chapter.

STYLE TIP

Many two-syllable modifiers can form their comparative and their superlative forms either way. If adding *–er* or *–est* makes a word sound awkward, use *more* or *most* instead.

AWKWARD carefuller
   BETTER **more careful**

AWKWARD commonest
   BETTER **most common**

(3) The *superlative degree* is used when three or more things are being compared.

EXAMPLES *Nilda* is one of the **best** books I've read.

         Which member of the team runs **most quickly**?

Regular Comparison

Most one-syllable modifiers form the comparative degree by adding *–er* and the superlative degree by adding *–est*.

Positive	Comparative	Superlative
near	near**er**	near**est**
sad	sadd**er**	sadd**est**
cute	cut**er**	cut**est**
bright	bright**er**	bright**est**

Two-syllable modifiers can form the comparative degree by adding *–er* or by using *more*. They can form the superlative degree by adding *–est* or by using *most*.

Positive	Comparative	Superlative
fancy	fanci**er**	fanci**est**
lonely	loneli**er**	loneli**est**
cheerful	**more** cheerful	**most** cheerful
quickly	**more** quickly	**most** quickly

NOTE When you add *–er* or *–est* to some modifiers, you may also need to change the spelling of the base word.

EXAMPLES   sad   **sadd**er   **sadd**est
              [The final *d* is doubled.]

           cute   **cut**er   **cut**est
              [The final *e* is dropped.]

           fancy   **fanci**er   **fanci**est
              [The final *y* is changed to *i*.]

MINI-LESSON   Mechanics

Using Commas Correctly. Tell students to use commas to set off nonessential clauses, but not essential ones.

My oldest brother, **who is in college,** is studying chemistry. [*nonessential clause*]

The car **that Mom bought** is in excellent condition. [*essential clause*]

For more information on punctuating nonessential elements, see **Chapter 12.**

Modifiers that have three or more syllables form the comparative degree by using *more* and the superlative degree by using *most.*

Positive	Comparative	Superlative
difficult	**more** difficult	**most** difficult
interesting	**more** interesting	**most** interesting
skillfully	**more** skillfully	**most** skillfully

Decreasing Comparison

To show a decrease in the qualities they express, modifiers form the comparative degree by using *less* and the superlative degree by using *least.*

Positive	Comparative	Superlative
clean	**less** clean	**least** clean
humorous	**less** humorous	**least** humorous
carefully	**less** carefully	**least** carefully

Exercise 2 Writing Comparative and Superlative Forms

Give the comparative forms and the superlative forms for each of the following modifiers.

EXAMPLES
1. calm
   1. *calmer, calmest; less calm, least calm*

2. happy
   2. *happier, happiest; less happy, least happy*

1. nervous
2. great
3. hot
4. funny
5. noisy
6. easily
7. poor
8. young
9. swiftly
10. intelligent
11. politely
12. efficient
13. old
14. thoughtfully
15. sweet
16. angrily
17. ancient
18. neatly
19. lovely
20. long

Comparison of Adjectives and Adverbs   **201**

┌HELP

A dictionary will tell you when a word forms its comparative or superlative form in some way other than just by adding *–er* or *–est* or *more* or *most.*

Be sure to look in a dictionary if you are not sure whether a word has irregular comparative or superlative forms.

A dictionary will also tell you if you need to double a final consonant (or otherwise change the spelling of a word) before adding *–er* or *–est.*

Reference Note

For more about **how to spell words when adding *–er* or *–est,*** see page 321.

┌HELP

Some words in Exercise 2 may have more than one acceptable comparative and superlative form. You need to give only one comparative and one superlative form for each item.

APPLICATION

Comparative and Superlative Forms

To give students extra practice with comparative and superlative forms, have students in groups of four use the words in **Exercise 2** to create a group story. Have students count off from one to four. Assign students one and three to use comparative forms in the story and students two and four to use superlative forms.

USAGE

Exercise 2 Writing Comparative and Superlative Forms

Decreasing comparisons are formed by using *less* or *least* with the positive or base form of the adjective or adverb.

ANSWERS

1. more nervous, most nervous
2. greater, greatest
3. hotter, hottest
4. funnier, funniest, *or* more funny, most funny
5. noisier, noisiest, *or* more noisy, most noisy
6. more easily, most easily
7. poorer, poorest
8. younger, youngest
9. more swiftly, most swiftly
10. more intelligent, most intelligent
11. more politely, most politely
12. more efficient, most efficient
13. older, oldest
14. more thoughtfully, most thoughtfully
15. sweeter, sweetest
16. more angrily, most angrily
17. more ancient, most ancient
18. more neatly, most neatly
19. lovelier, loveliest, *or* more lovely, most lovely
20. longer, longest

┌─**HELP**───

In Exercise 3, do not use decreasing comparisons.

1. nearest

2. closest

3. brighter

4. smaller

5. more difficult

6. more common

7. more frequently

8. bigger

9. more quickly

10. more slowly

Exercise 3 **Using Comparative and Superlative Forms Correctly in Sentences**

Give the correct form of the italicized modifier for each blank in the following sentences.

EXAMPLE   **1.** *large*   As the illustration below shows, the moon appears _____ during the full-moon phase.

1. *largest*   Answers may vary slightly.

1. *near*   The moon is the earth's _____ neighbor in space.

2. *close*   At its _____ point to the earth, the moon is 221,456 miles away.

3. *bright*   Seen from the earth, the full moon is _____ than the new moon.

4. *small*   The moon appears _____ during the crescent phase than at other times.

5. *difficult* It is _____ to see the new moon than the crescent moon.

6. *common*   The word *crescent* is _____ than the word *gibbous*, which means "partly rounded."

7. *frequently* We notice the moon _____ when it is full than when it is new.

8. *big*   Do you know why the moon appears _____ on some nights than on others?

9. *quickly*   The changes in the moon's appearance take place because the moon travels _____ around the earth than the earth travels around the sun.

10. *slowly*   The moons of some other planets move _____ than our moon.

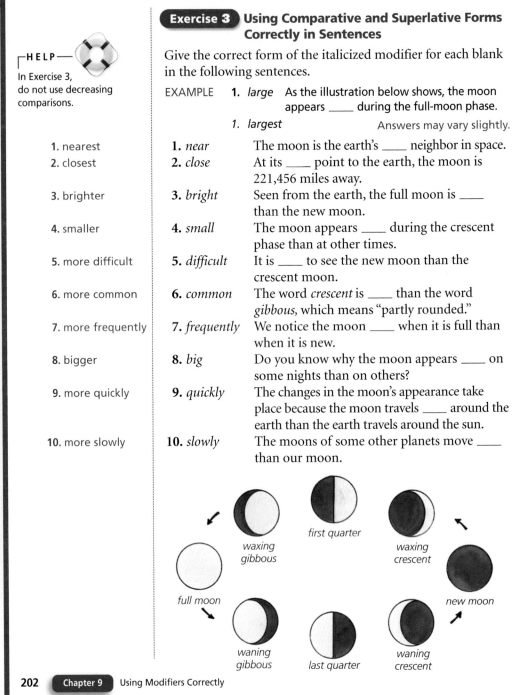

waxing gibbous

first quarter

waxing crescent

full moon

new moon

waning gibbous

last quarter

waning crescent

Irregular Comparison

Some modifiers do not form their comparative and superlative degrees by using the regular methods.

Positive	Comparative	Superlative
good	better	best
well	better	best
bad	worse	worst
many	more	most
much	more	most

NOTE You do not need to add *–er/–est, more/most,* or *less/least* to an irregular comparison. For example, *worse,* all by itself, is the comparative form of *bad. Worser* and *more worse* are non-standard forms.

Exercise 4 Using Irregular Comparative and Superlative Forms

Give the correct form of the italicized modifier for each blank in the following sentences.

EXAMPLE   **1.** *many*   Let's see which of the two teams can wash _____ cars.

       1. more

1. *bad*   This is the _____ cold I have ever had.
2. *much*   We have _____ homework now than we had last year.
3. *well*   Derrick feels _____ today than he did last night.
4. *good*   This peach has a _____ flavor than that one.
5. *well*   Of all the instruments he can play, Shen Li plays the banjo _____.
6. *much*   Catherine ate _____ enchilada casserole on Monday than she had eaten on Sunday.
7. *many*   Of all the volunteers, Doreen has collected the _____ donations for the animal shelter.
8. *bad*   Our team played the _____ game in history.
9. *good*   The judges will now award the prize for the _____ essay.

1. worst
2. more
3. better
4. better
5. best
6. more
7. most
8. worst
9. best

| COMPUTER TIP

A computer can help you find and correct problems with modifiers. A spell-checker will highlight nonstandard forms such as *worser, bestest,* and *gracefuller.*

However, the computer cannot tell you that you have used the superlative form where you should have used the comparative. You will have to look carefully for such errors when you proofread your writing.

USAGE

APPLICATION

Irregular Comparison
Have students write advertising slogans about products they use often. Students should compare their chosen products to other brands and should use modifiers that have irregular comparative and superlative forms. For example: *Acme Toothpaste—The Best Gets Better! Gizmo Marble Set—The Most Marbles for Your Money!* Invite volunteers to share their slogans with the class, identifying modifiers and degrees of comparison.

10. more	10. *many*	I have ____ baseball cards than John does.
11. best	11. *good*	Who is the ____ Japanese chef in town?
12. most	12. *much*	Of all the ranchers, she knows the ____ about lambs and sheep.
13. worst	13. *bad*	Wow! That was the ____ storm I have ever seen.
14. better	14. *well*	I think that another variety of blackberry might grow ____ than these do.
15. most	15. *many*	Who got the ____ signatures for the petition?
16. best	16. *well*	In my opinion, out of all the artists in the world, these Chinese masters paint landscapes ____.
17. worse	17. *bad*	Traffic is always ____ at this time of day than at any other time.
18. more	18. *many*	This year, ____ people attended the ceremony at the reservation than last year.
19. best	19. *good*	Of the book, the movie, and the play, which was ____?
20. more	20. *much*	Of these two containers, which holds ____ juice?

Special Problems in Using Modifiers

9d. The modifiers *good* and *well* have different uses.

(1) Use *good* to modify a noun or a pronoun.

EXAMPLES The farmers had a **good** crop this year. [The adjective *good* modifies the noun *crop*.]

The book was **better** than the movie. [The adjective *better* modifies the noun *book*.]

Of all the players, she is the **best** one. [The adjective *best* modifies the pronoun *one*.]

Good should not be used to modify a verb.

NONSTANDARD N. Scott Momaday writes good.

STANDARD N. Scott Momaday writes **well**.

(2) Use *well* to modify a verb.

EXAMPLES The day started **well**. [The adverb *well* modifies the verb *started*.]

Reference Note

For more about **standard usage,** see page 221.

RESOURCES

Special Problems in Using Modifiers
Practice
- *Language & Sentence Skills Practice,* pp. 182–184, 192
- *Developmental Language & Sentence Skills,* pp. 87–88

USAGE

Special Problems in Using Modifiers
Rules 9d–f *(pp. 204–209)*

OBJECTIVES

- To choose the correct modifiers after linking verbs and action verbs
- To revise double comparisons

DIRECT TEACHING

Modeling and Demonstration
Special Problems in Using Modifiers. Model how to use the modifiers *good* and *well* correctly by using the examples *The farmers had a good crop this year* and *The day started well*. First, ask what the modifier *good* describes in the first sentence. [*crop*] Then, ask what part of speech *crop* is. [*noun*] Point out that since *good* is an adjective, it is used to modify the noun. Next, ask what the modifier *well* describes in the second sentence. [*how the day started*] Then, ask what part of speech *started* is. [*verb*] Point out that since *well* is an adverb, it is used to modify the verb. Adverbs also can be used to modify adjectives and other adverbs, but they cannot be used to modify nouns. Now, have a volunteer use other examples from this chapter to demonstrate how to identify the correct use of *good* and *well*.

The team played **better** in the second half. [The adverb *better* modifies the verb *played*.]

Tina Thompson played **best** in the final game. [The adverb *best* modifies the verb *played*.]

Well can also mean "in good health." When *well* has this meaning, it acts as an adjective.

EXAMPLE   Does Sherry feel **well** today? [The adjective *well* modifies the noun *Sherry*.]

9e. Use adjectives, not adverbs, after linking verbs.

Linking verbs, such as *look, feel, seem,* and *become,* are often followed by predicate adjectives. These adjectives describe, or modify, the subject.

EXAMPLES   Mayor Rodríguez should feel **confident** [not *confidently*] about this election. [The predicate adjective *confident* modifies the subject *Mayor Rodríguez*.]

Did Chris seem **sad** [not *sadly*] to you? [The predicate adjective *sad* modifies the subject *Chris*.]

Exercise 5 Choosing Correct Modifiers After Linking Verbs and Action Verbs

Choose the correct modifier of the two in parentheses in each of the following sentences.

EXAMPLE   1. Ellen said that Murray's matzo ball soup tasted (*delicious, deliciously*).

1. *delicious*

1. The band became (*nervous, nervously*) before the show.
2. You may get a higher score if you remain (*calm, calmly*) while taking the test.
3. We (*eager, eagerly*) tasted the potato pancakes.
4. Cheryl sews (*good, well*), so she made all the puppets for the show.
5. The mariachi band appeared (*sudden, suddenly*) at our table.
6. Ooh, these wild strawberries taste (*good, well*).
7. The plums tasted (*sour, sourly*).
8. Mr. Duncan was looking (*close, closely*) at my essay.

┌─ H E L P ─

Some linking verbs can also be used as action verbs. As action verbs, they may be modified by adverbs.

LINKING VERB

Jeanette looked **alert** [not *alertly*] during the game. [*Alert* modifies the subject *Jeanette*.]

ACTION VERB

Jeanette looked **alertly** around the gym. [*Alertly* modifies the verb *looked*.]

Reference Note

For more about **linking verbs,** see page 53.

USAGE

DIRECT TEACHING

Good, Well

Activity. To show students the correct use of *good* and *well*, write the following sentence on the chalkboard:

I am a good listener because I listen well.

Circle *good* and *well,* and ask students which word each modifies and whether that word is a noun or a verb. [*good*—listener, a noun; *well*—listen, a verb] Have students create similar sentences using both *good* and *well*. [*Example: I am a good pitcher because I pitch* well.]

PRACTICE

Guided and Independent

Exercise 5   You may wish to use the first ten items in **Exercise 5** as guided practice and have students complete the exercise as independent practice.   **HOMEWORK**

Exercise 5

DISTRIBUTED REVIEW
To review verbs, you might want students to identify linking and action verbs in the designated sentences.

5. appeared—action verb

7. tasted—linking verb

If some students are having problems, you might want the class to review the sections on action and linking verbs on p. 53 in **Chapter 3.**

Correcting Misconceptions

Linking Verbs. Students may have difficulty choosing correct modifiers because they mistakenly believe that a modifier after a linking verb modifies that verb. Make sure that students understand that a linking verb is followed by an adjective rather than an adverb because the adjective modifies the subject of the verb, not the verb. Linking verbs that are forms of the verb *be* are relatively easy to identify, but some others may not be. You can point out to your students that a verb is a linking verb if the word *seem* can be substituted for it without significantly changing the meaning of the sentence. For example, one could change *This milk tastes sour* to *This milk seems sour. Tastes* is therefore used as a linking verb in this sentence.

9. Those trophies certainly look (*good, well*) up there, Piper.
10. The bicyclist looked (*cautious,* <u>*cautiously*</u>) both ways before crossing the street.
11. Adobe, dried mud brick, stands up (*good,* <u>*well*</u>) under the hot Southwestern sun.
12. Peg looked at her broken skate (*anxious,* <u>*anxiously*</u>).
13. Don't you think vanilla smells as (*good,* <u>*well*</u>) as or better than those expensive perfumes?
14. Akira Kurosawa was (*good, well*) at making Shakespeare's plays into movies.
15. Sylvia certainly looked (<u>*pretty*</u>, *prettily*) in her new outfit.
16. Even for beginners, green beans grow (*good,* <u>*well*</u>), and quickly, too.
17. We didn't know that you could vault so (*good,* <u>*well*</u>).
18. Erica was (*happy, happily*) to help us.
19. Oh, you are too (*good, well*) at chess for me.
20. Some tropical fish don't get along very (*good,* <u>*well*</u>) with each other.

9f. Avoid using double comparisons.

A ***double comparison*** is the use of both *–er* and *more* (or *less*) or both *–est* and *most* (or *least*) to form a single comparison. When you make a comparison, use only one of these forms, not both.

NONSTANDARD	That was Lon Chaney's most scariest role.
STANDARD	That was Lon Chaney's **scariest** role.

NONSTANDARD	The kitten is less livelier than the puppy.
STANDARD	The kitten is **less lively** than the puppy.

NOTE Remember that irregular comparisons do not use *–er/–est, more/most* or *less/least*. Adding these to an irregular modifier is a double comparison.

NONSTANDARD	more better
STANDARD	**better**

NONSTANDARD	worstest
STANDARD	**worst**

Oral Practice Revising Double Comparisons

Each of the following sentences contains a double comparison. Read each sentence aloud, and identify the double comparison. Then, say the sentence again, using a correct comparison.

EXAMPLE   1. Are you feeling more better now?
           1. more better—better

1. That must be the bestest song you've written yet!
2. Hit the ball less harder next time.
3. Dates are one of the most popularest foods in Africa and Asia.
4. Nicki, this was the most liveliest party ever.
5. The ancient Chinese made paper more earlier than any other people.
6. Yikes, this computer game is the most hardest one I've played.
7. The least boringest of the characters was Jo.
8. Sure, I think Spanish is more easier to learn than English.
9. Please do visit us more oftener.
10. Maybe Friday will arrive more sooner this week.

1. best
2. less hard
3. most popular
4. liveliest
5. earlier
6. hardest
7. least boring
8. easier
9. more often
10. sooner

Review A Writing Comparative and Superlative Forms in Sentences

For each blank in the following sentences, give the correct form of comparison of the italicized word.

EXAMPLE   1. noisy   This is the ____ class in school.
           1. noisiest

1. bad   Yesterday was the ____ day of my entire life.
2. good   Tomorrow should be ____ than today was.
3. old   The ____ American Indian tepee in the world can be seen at the Smithsonian Institution.
4. soon   Your party ended ____ than I had hoped.
5. funny   That is the ____ joke I've ever heard.
6. rapidly   Which can run ____, the cheetah or the lion?
7. beautifully This piñata is ____ decorated than the other one.
8. well   I did well on the first half of the test, but I did ____ on the second half.

1. worst
2. better
3. oldest
4. sooner
5. funniest
6. more rapidly
7. more beautifully
8. better

DIFFERENTIATING INSTRUCTION

Learners Having Difficulty

Some students might resist using standard forms in spoken language because of peer pressure. Point out to these students that casual interactions among peers sometimes require a different form of communication than formal situations. Students can express themselves one way with friends and a different way in class.

EXTENSION

Using Correct Modifiers

Have each student write a paragraph describing significant events or important people in their lives. (Tell students they need not write anything they do not want to share with you.) As students write, tell them to pay close attention to comparative forms. When students are finished, have them circle and identify all the comparisons in their paragraphs. Score each correct comparison 1 point; for each use of a double comparison, score 0.

9. most joyfully

10. strangest

9. *joyfully*   Of all the songbirds in our yard, the mocking-birds sing ____.

10. *strange*   This is the ____ book I have ever read!

Review B   **Proofreading a Paragraph for Correct Forms of Modifiers**

Most of the sentences in the following paragraph have errors in English usage. If a sentence contains an error, ~~identify the error~~ and then write the ∧correct usage. If a sentence is already correct, write *C*.

EXAMPLE   **[1]** You may not recognize the man in the picture on the left, but you probably know his more famous characters.

    1.   more famous—most famous

1. popular
2. C

3. quickly

4. cheerful
5. C
6. rapidly

7. more

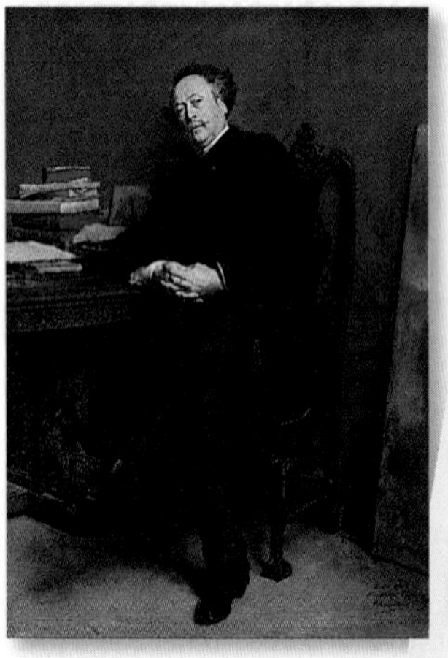

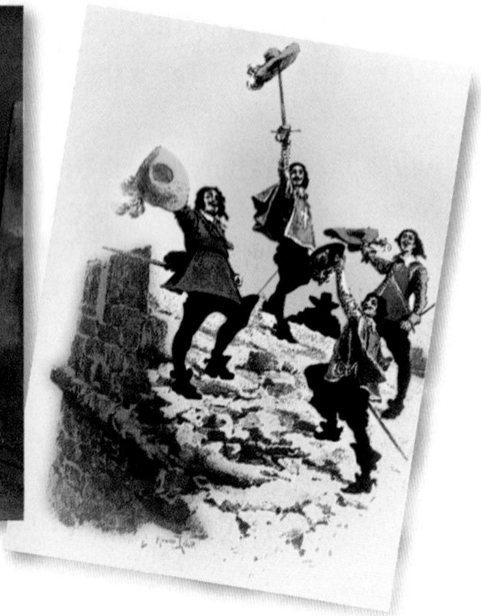

   [1] This man, Alexandre Dumas, wrote two of the most ∧~~popularest~~ books in history—*The Three Musketeers* and *The Count of Monte Cristo.* **[2]** Born in France, Dumas was poor but had a good education. **[3]** As a young playwright, he rose ~~quick~~ to fame. **[4]** In person, Dumas always seemed ~~cheerfully~~.∧ **[5]** Like their author, his historical novels are colorful and full of adventure. **[6]** Their fame grew ~~rapid~~,∧ and the public demanded more of them. **[7]** In response to this demand, Dumas hired many assistants, who probably wrote ∧~~most~~ of his later books than he did. [**8**] Dumas's son, who was also named Alexandre, was a writer, too, and he became ~~famously~~ with the publication of *Camille*. [**9**] At that time, the younger Dumas was often thought of as a ~~more~~ better writer than his father. [**10**] Today, however, the friendship of the three musketeers remains ~~aliver~~ than ever in film, print, and even comic books.

8. famous

10. more alive

Double Negatives

Negative words are a common part of everyday speaking and writing. These words include the modifiers *no, not, never,* and *hardly.* Notice how negative words change the meaning of the following sentences.

POSITIVE   We can count in Spanish.

NEGATIVE   We can**not** count in Spanish.

POSITIVE   They ride their bikes on the highway.

NEGATIVE   They **never** ride their bikes on the highway.

Common Negative Words			
barely	never	none	nothing
hardly	no	no one	nowhere
neither	nobody	not (–n't)	scarcely

9g. Avoid using double negatives.

A *double negative* is the use of two or more negative words to express one negative idea.

NONSTANDARD   Sheila did not tell no one her idea. [The negative words are *not* and *no one*.]

STANDARD   Sheila did **not** tell anyone her idea.

STANDARD   Sheila told **no one** her idea.

NONSTANDARD   Rodney hardly said nothing. [The negative words are *hardly* and *nothing*.]

STANDARD   Rodney **hardly** said anything.

STANDARD   Rodney said almost **nothing.**

| S T Y L E   T I P |

Some fiction writers use double negatives in dialogue. This technique can help make certain characters sound more realistic. However, in your formal speaking and writing, you should avoid using double negatives.

Double Negatives   **209**

USAGE

Double Negatives
Rule 9g *(pp. 209–211)*

OBJECTIVE

■ **To revise sentences by eliminating double negatives**

DIRECT TEACHING

Modeling and Demonstration

Double Negatives. Model how to avoid double negatives by using the incorrect example *Mike did not know nothing about the accident.* First, ask which words in the sentence are negatives. [*not, nothing*] Only one negative is needed to express a negative idea. Ask how the sentence would read with one of the negatives eliminated. [*Mike did not know anything about the accident* or *Mike knew nothing about the accident.*] Point out that either negative can be eliminated to correct a double negative. Now, have a volunteer use an example from this chapter to demonstrate how to identify and correct a double negative.

DIFFERENTIATING INSTRUCTION

Learners Having Difficulty

Some students who use double negatives in speech may be curious about why they should avoid them. You can point out that double negatives may be encountered in informal, everyday speech, but that they're incorrect in formal speech and writing. If read literally, double negatives express the opposite meaning from the meaning intended [*I don't know nothing* means "I know something."] Also, double negatives can sometimes be confusing to readers.

EXTENSION

Relating to Literature

Sometimes authors of stories use double negatives on purpose to give a special flavor to their writing. Ask your students to read the Uncle Remus tale "He Lion, Bruh Bear, and Bruh Rabbit," as retold by Virginia Hamilton (or any of the other Uncle Remus tales of Joel Chandler Harris). As the students read, ask them to make note of the double negatives the narrator and the characters use. What effects do the double negatives have? [*They make the story seem more like a tale that a person is telling orally, and they reflect the speech of the characters in the story.*]

─HELP─

Some double negatives in Exercise 6 may be corrected in more than one way. You need to give just one revision for each sentence.

─HELP─

Some double negatives in Review C may be corrected in more than one way. You need to give just one revision for each sentence.

Exercise 6 Revising Sentences to Correct Double Negatives

Revise each of the following sentences to eliminate the double negative. Revisions may vary.

EXAMPLE   1. Those books don't have no pictures.
1. *Those books don't have any pictures.*
or
Those books have no pictures.

1. The Plains Indians did not waste no part of a bear, deer, or buffalo.   1. any
2. Ms. Wooster never tries nothing new to eat.   2. anything
3. Movie and TV stars from Hollywood never visit nowhere near our town.   3. anywhere
4. Until last summer, I didn't know nothing about Braille music notation.   4. anything
5. By Thanksgiving, the store didn't have none of the silver jewelry left.   5. any
6. I'm so excited that I can't hardly sit still.   6. can
7. No one brought nothing to eat on the hike.   7. anything
8. Strangely enough, Frieda hasn't never tasted our delicious Cuban bread.   8. ever
9. There isn't no more salad in the bowl.   9. any
10. Our dog never fights with neither one of our cats.   10. either

Review C Proofreading Sentences for Correct Use of Modifiers

Most of the following sentences contain errors in the use of modifiers. If a sentence is incorrect, write it correctly. If a sentence is already correct, write *C*.

EXAMPLE   1. Haven't you never made a paper airplane or a paper hat?
1. *Haven't you ever made a paper airplane or a paper hat?*
or
Have you never made a paper airplane or a paper hat?

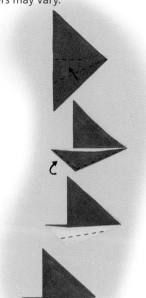

1. Making Japanese origami figures is much ~~more~~ Answers may vary.
   easier than I thought it would be.
2. Origami, the ancient Japanese art of paper folding,
   ~~wasn't hardly known~~ in the United States before
   the 1960s.   **2.** was hardly known
3. Now, many people know how to fold the ~~most~~
   cleverest traditional origami animals.
4. In true origami, artists ~~do not never~~ cut or paste
   the paper.   **4.** do not ever
5. A beginner doesn't need ~~nothing~~ but a sheet of paper
   to create an origami figure.   **5.** anything
6. With a bit of patience, anyone can make a folded-
   paper figure rather ~~quick~~.   **6.** quickly
7. Even kindergartners can do a good job making
   the simple sailboat shown in the diagram.   **7.** C
8. Other origami figures require ~~more~~ greater time and
   patience than this sailboat.
9. Today, there probably ~~isn't no one~~ better at
   origami than Akira Yoshizawa.   **9.** isn't anyone
10. Even the most difficult figure is not too hard for
    him, and he has invented many beautiful new figures.
    10. C

Placement of Modifiers

9h. Place modifying words, phrases, and clauses as close as
possible to the words they modify.

Notice how the meaning of the following sentences changes
when the position of the phrase *from Brazil* changes.

> The singer **from Brazil** gave a radio interview for her fans. [The
> phrase modifies *singer.*]
>
> The singer gave a radio interview for her fans **from Brazil.** [The
> phrase modifies *fans.*]
>
> **From Brazil,** the singer gave a radio interview for her fans.
> [The phrase modifies *gave.*]

A modifer that seems to modify the wrong word in a sentence is called a ***misplaced modifier.***

Placement of Modifiers **211**

RESOURCES

Placement of Modifiers

Practice

- *Language & Sentence Skills Practice,* pp. 186–190, 193–194
- *Developmental Language & Sentence Skills,* pp. 89–90

9 h

USAGE

Placement of Modifiers

Rule 9h *(pp. 211–216)*

OBJECTIVES

- To correct misplaced prepositional phrases

- To correct misplaced adjective clauses

DIRECT TEACHING

Modeling and Demonstration

Placement of Modifiers. Model
how the placement of a modifier can
change the meaning of a sentence
by using the example *The diplomat
from Australia gave a speech for the
visitors.* First, ask what the prepositional phrase *from Australia* modifies. [*diplomat*] Point out that *from
Australia* immediately follows the
noun it describes. Move the phrase
to the beginning of the sentence and
ask what word it modifies. [*gave*]
Point out that moving the phrase
changes the meaning of the sentence. Then, move the phrase to the
end of the sentence and ask what
word it modifies. [*visitors*] The phrase
immediately follows the noun it
modifies. Now, have a volunteer use
an example from this chapter to
demonstrate how the placement of
a modifier can change the meaning
of a sentence.

Placement of Modifiers **211**

DIFFERENTIATING
INSTRUCTION

English-Language Learners

Hmong. As with speakers of many other languages, Hmong English-language learners might display a tendency to place adjectives after the nouns they modify. For example, a Hmong speaker might write "a jacket green" rather than "a green jacket." Be sure to remind your Hmong speakers that in English, single-word adjectives usually precede the words they modify. You may want to offer additional practice in adjective usage and placement.

Reference Note

For more information about **prepositions** and **prepositional phrases,** see pages 62 and 63.

Adjectives and Adverbs

The placement of an adjective or adverb may affect the meaning of a sentence. Avoid placing an adjective or adverb so that it appears to modify a word that you don't mean it to modify.

EXAMPLES   Jackie borrowed some camping equipment **only** for the weekend. [She borrowed the equipment for the weekend, not for any other time.]

Only Jackie borrowed some camping equipment for the weekend. [Jackie—and no one else—borrowed some equipment.]

Jackie borrowed **only** some camping equipment for the weekend. [She borrowed some camping equipment but nothing else.]

Nearly all of the skaters fell. [Most of the skaters fell.]

All of the skaters **nearly** fell. [All of the skaters came close to falling but did not fall.]

Today Randall said he would help me build a birdhouse. [Randall made the statement today.]

Randall said he would help me build a birdhouse **today**. [Randall will help with the birdhouse today.]

Prepositional Phrases

A *prepositional phrase* includes a preposition, the object of the preposition, and any modifiers of that object.

A prepositional phrase used as an adjective generally should be placed directly after the word it modifies.

MISPLACED   Ms. Ruiz got a sweater for her dog with a snowflake pattern.

CLEAR   Ms. Ruiz got a sweater **with a snowflake pattern** for her dog.

MISPLACED   This book describes Nat Turner's struggle for freedom by Judith Berry Griffin.

CLEAR   This book **by Judith Berry Griffin** describes Nat Turner's struggle for freedom.

A prepositional phrase used as an adverb should be placed near the word it modifies.

MISPLACED   Roberto read that some turtles can swim quite fast in a magazine.

CLEAR   Roberto read **in a magazine** that some turtles can swim quite fast.

MISPLACED   I watched a movie that George Lucas produced on Friday.

CLEAR   **On Friday,** I watched a movie that George Lucas produced.

Avoid placing a prepositional phrase where it can modify either of two words. Place the phrase so that it clearly modifies the word you intend it to modify.

MISPLACED   Cynthia Ann said after her ballet class she would take out the trash. [Does the phrase *after her ballet class* modify *said* or *would take*?]

CLEAR   Cynthia Ann said she would take out the trash **after her ballet class.** [The phrase modifies *would take.*]

CLEAR   **After her ballet class** Cynthia Ann said she would take out the trash. [The phrase modifies *said.*]

Exercise 7   **Correcting Misplaced Prepositional Phrases**

Find any misplaced prepositional phrases in each of the following sentences. Then, revise the sentence, placing the phrase near the word it modifies. If a sentence is already correct, write *C*.   Answers may vary.

EXAMPLE   **1.** I read about the car thieves who were caught in this morning's paper.

    1. *I read in this morning's paper about the car thieves who were caught.*

                     or

    In this morning's paper, I read about the car thieves who were caught.

1. Michael went outside to trim the hedges with Bruce.
2. I saw the ants marching through my magnifying glass.

┌HELP──
Some sentences in Exercise 7 may be corrected in more than one way. You need to give just one revision for each.

1. with Bruce
2. Through my magnifying glass,

Placement of Modifiers   **213**

USAGE

FAMILY/COMMUNITY ACTIVITY   *Continued on pp. 214–215*

Writing a Letter of Appreciation. Tell students that sometimes people like to write to businesses or organizations to thank or praise them for carrying a particular product or providing a valuable service. The recipients use those letters to help them determine how well they are doing their jobs. Have each student write a letter of appreciation to a local business or organization that has provided an important product or service or made a welcome change that the student likes. For example, one writer might

USAGE

RETEACHING

Using Modifiers in Sentences

Activity. Break your class into teams of two or three students. Give each team a pencil and a few sheets of paper. On the chalkboard or an overhead transparency, write a short sentence such as *The cheetah ran.* Tell the students that your boring sentence needs help, and it is each team's job to make the sentence more interesting. First, tell the teams that they have fifteen seconds to add an adjective to your sentence. Then, ask for an adverb. Next, ask for a prepositional phrase, and so on. When teams have finished, have volunteers read each team's new, improved sentence to the class.

3. From Kim,
4. with the cellular telephone
5. C
6. in the pond
7. From our back windows
8. In class today
9. in Fred's living room
10. In the attic

Reference Note

For more about **adjective clauses,** see page 91.

COMPUTER TIP

A word-processing program can help you correct misplaced modifiers. First, examine all the modifying words, phrases, and clauses in your writing to make sure they are placed correctly. If you find a misplaced modifier, you can use the cut-and-paste function to place the modifier closer to the word it modifies.

HELP

Some sentences in Exercise 8 may be revised in more than one way. You need to give just one revision for each.

3. Angelo borrowed a radio ~~from Kim~~ with a weather band.
4. That man bought the rare photograph of Geronimo ~~with the cellular telephone~~.
5. The robin sat carefully on the eggs in its nest.
6. The frog seemed to be staring at the moon ~~in the pond~~.
7. We could see the wheat growing ~~from our back windows~~.
8. The sound designer told us about recording a herd of gnus ~~in class today~~.
9. Many people watched the televised ballgame ~~in Fred's living room~~.
10. I found the collection of records your father bought ~~in the attic~~.

Adjective Clauses

An *adjective clause* modifies a noun or a pronoun. Most adjective clauses begin with a relative pronoun—*that, which, who, whom,* or *whose.*

Like adjective phrases, adjective clauses should generally be placed directly after the words they modify.

MISPLACED	Mrs. Chu gives the sculptures to her friends that she carves. [Does Mrs. Chu carve her friends?]
CLEAR	Mrs. Chu gives the sculptures **that she carves** to her friends.
MISPLACED	The students met with a tutor who needed help in math. [Did the tutor need help in math?]
CLEAR	The students **who needed help in math** met with a tutor.

Exercise 8 **Correcting Misplaced Adjective Clauses**

Find any ~~misplaced adjective clauses~~ in each of the following sentences. Then, revise the sentence, placing the clause near the word it modifies. If a sentence is already correct, write *C*.

EXAMPLE	1.	The students wanted to work on a project at the school that they had designed themselves.
	1.	*The students at the school wanted to work on a project that they had designed themselves.*

FAMILY/COMMUNITY ACTIVITY ***Continued from p. 213***

want to thank a business for carrying a particular item of sports equipment or a musical instrument that would be otherwise hard to find. Another writer might want to praise a church or youth organization for organizing a field trip or hosting a party. If a

student cannot think of a topic for a letter of appreciation, have him or her write a letter asking a business or organization to carry a particular product or provide a special service.

The letters should include reasons that a

1. The girl ∧ is from my class ~~that won the spelling bee~~.
2. The blue jay moved carefully ∧ through the snow ~~with small hops~~, which had begun to melt.
3. ∧ I hardly recognized my uncle Ken ~~when he came for a visit~~, whose beard had turned white.
4. Kwanzaa, which was first celebrated in 1966, is an African American holiday developed by Maulana Karenga.
5. The expression "that's the ticket," which means "that's the correct thing," comes from a mispronunciation of the French word *etiquette*.
6. My oldest brother ∧ just graduated from college ~~, who lives in Rhode Island~~.
7. Jason's favorite shirt ∧ already has another stain on it ~~, which was just washed~~.
8. That team ∧ played in front of a sellout crowd ~~, which was having its best season ever~~.
9. "The Rum Tum Tugger" ∧ is a poem about a cat ~~, which we studied in class~~.
10. ∧ We like to watch the many butterflies in the fields ~~on the weekends~~ that are behind our house.

Answers may vary.

1. that won the spelling bee
2. with small hops
3. When he came for a visit,
4. C
5. C
6. , who lives in Rhode Island,
7. , which was just washed,
8. , which was having its best season ever,
9. , which we studied in class,
10. On the weekends,

Review D Proofreading a Paragraph for Correct Placement of Modifiers

Most of the following sentences have misplaced modifying words, phrases, or clauses. If the sentence contains an error, revise the sentence by placing the modifier in the correct place. If the sentence is already correct, write *C*.

EXAMPLE [1] Sometimes the person can be a hero who seems least likely.

1. *Sometimes the person who seems least likely can be a hero.*

[1] J.R.R. Tolkien's *The Hobbit* is a wonderful story that has a very complicated adventure about a simple person. [2] Hobbits are very small, quiet people, and most of the world had never heard of them until a few of them began to have adventures. [3] The hero of the story, Bilbo Baggins, is not a typical hero, who likes nothing more than chatting with his neighbors, sleeping, and eating. [4] Bilbo's quiet life is

┌HELP─
Some sentences in Review D may be correctly revised in more than one way. You need to give just one revision for each.

Review D Proofreading a Paragraph for Correct Placement of Modifiers

ANSWERS
Revisions may vary.

1. J.R.R. Tolkien's *The Hobbit* is a wonderful story about a simple person who has a very complicated adventure.

2. C

3. The hero of the story, Bilbo Baggins, who likes nothing more than chatting with his neighbors, sleeping, and eating, is not a typical hero.

4. Bilbo's quiet life is interrupted when the wizard Gandalf chooses him to help a band of dwarves recover their treasure from a dragon.

USAGE

particular product or service is useful. Encourage students to use different kinds of modifiers, including adjectives, adverbs, and phrases and clauses that act as modifiers. When they have finished, invite volunteers to read their letters aloud to the rest of the class. Have the other students identify modifiers in the letter and check whether or not they have been used correctly.

interrupted when the wizard Gandalf chooses him to help a band of dwarves from a dragon recover their treasure. [5] Bilbo saves the dwarves several times on their way to their old home under the Lonely Mountain, despite being small and shy. [6] Bilbo also finds a magical ring along the way that can make him invisible. [7] Bilbo gets the dwarves out of trouble with the ring and the wizard Gandalf. [8] When they finally reach the mountain, Bilbo tricks the dragon Smaug into revealing a spot in his armor that is weak. [9] The dragon is very angry and attacks a nearby town, but an archer kills Smaug, who has been told about the weak spot. [10] Bilbo goes back to his quiet life, but in *The Lord of the Rings* his nephew Frodo inherits the ring and saves the world.

USAGE

Review D Proofreading a Paragraph for Correct Placement of Modifiers

ANSWERS continued
Revisions may vary.

5. Despite being small and shy, Bilbo saves the dwarves several times on their way to their old home under the Lonely Mountain.

6. Along the way, Bilbo also finds a magical ring that can make him invisible.

7. With the ring and the wizard Gandalf, Bilbo gets the dwarves out of trouble.

8. When they finally reach the mountain, Bilbo tricks the dragon Smaug into revealing a spot that is weak in his armor.

9. The dragon is very angry and attacks a nearby town, but an archer who has been told about the weak spot kills Smaug.

10. In *The Lord of the Rings,* Bilbo goes back to his quiet life, but his nephew Frodo inherits the ring and saves the world.

DIRECT TEACHING

Advanced Learners

Sometimes adjective clauses (particularly those beginning with *that*) can be shortened to prevent wordiness, as in sentence 8:

Retaining the clause: ". . . into revealing a spot **that is weak** in his armor."
Shortening the clause: ". . . into revealing a **weak** spot in his armor."

Have students shorten the adjective clauses in the following sentences:

1. The book that belongs to me is missing. [*My book is missing.*]

2. Do you like the dress that is red? [*Do you like the red dress?*]

Chapter Review

A. Identifying the Correct Forms of Modifiers

Numerals in brackets refer to concepts and rules tested by the items in the Chapter Review.

1. [9e,d(1)]
2. [9b]
3. [9a, c(2)]
4. [9a, c(3)]
5. [9d(2)]
6. [9e]
7. [9b, c(2)]
8. [9a, c(2)]
9. [9c(3)]
10. [9e,d(1)]
11. [9a, c(3)]
12. [9a, c(3)]
13. [9f, c(2)]
14. [9f, c(2)]
15. [9e]

Choose the correct form of the modifier in parentheses in each of the following sentences.

1. Cool water tastes (_good_, well) on a hot day.
2. The wind howled (fierce, _fiercely_) last night.
3. Which twin is (_taller_, tallest), Marcus or Jim?
4. _Forever Friends_ is the (_best_, bestest) book I've read this year.
5. Sergio has always played (good, _well_) during an important match.
6. The roses in the vase smelled (_sweet_, sweetly).
7. They could view the eclipse (more clear, _more clearly_) than we could.
8. Which of these two winter coats is the (best, _better_) value?
9. Of all the days in the week, Friday goes by (more, _most_) slowly for me.
10. Ernesto felt (good, _well_) about volunteering to help collect money for the homeless.
11. Is this the (_darkest_, darker) copy of the three?
12. The (faster, _fastest_) runner is the captain of the track team.
13. Mr. Chen told them to be (_better_, more better) prepared tomorrow.
14. Joni's way of solving the math puzzle was much (more easier, _easier_) than Ken's.
15. We felt (_sleepy_, sleepily) after lunch.

HELP

In some cases, a double negative can be corrected in more than one way. However, you need to give only one revision for each sentence in Part B.

16.–18. [9g]

B. Correcting Double Negatives

Most of the following sentences contain errors in the use of negative words. If the ~~sentence is incorrect~~, write it ⋀correctly. If the sentence is already correct, write _C_.   Answers may vary.

16. None of us knows⋀ ~~nothing~~ about astronomy.   16. anything
17. Wendell can hardly wait to see Serge Laîné in concert.   17. C
18. Kathy⋀ ~~hasn't never~~ heard of the Romanovs.   18. has never

Chapter Review

C. Writing Comparative and Superlative Forms

ANSWERS

21. more difficult, most difficult; less difficult, least difficult

22. newer, newest; less new, least new

23. more quickly, most quickly; less quickly, least quickly

24. colder, coldest; less cold, least cold

25. more fantastic, most fantastic; less fantastic; least fantastic

26. better, best; less good, least good

27. lighter, lightest; less light, least light

28. shorter, shortest; less short, least short

29. more clearly, most clearly; less clearly, least clearly

30. noisier, noisiest or more noisy, most noisy; less noisy, least noisy

USAGE

---

19. could [9g]
20. any [9g]

21.–30. [9c(2),(3)]

┌─HELP─

Remember to include forms showing decreasing comparison in your answers to Part C.

31. On the radio [9h]
32. with the beard [9h]
33. From his friend, [9h]
34. In the backyard, [9h]
35. From our car [9h]
36. that was made of silver [9h]
37. On Tuesday [9h]
38. In the newspaper [9h]
39. At her press conference, [9h]
40. who had on the red hat [9h]

---

19. Last night we couldn't see no stars through the telescope.

20. Whenever I want fresh strawberries, there are never none in the house.

C. Writing Comparative and Superlative Forms

Write the comparative and superlative forms for each of the following modifiers.

21. difficult   **26.** good
22. new   **27.** light
23. quickly   **28.** short
24. cold   **29.** clearly
25. fantastic   **30.** noisy

D. Correcting Misplaced Phrases and Clauses

Find any misplaced phrases and clauses in each of the following sentences. Then, revise each incorrect sentence, placing the phrase or clause near the word it modifies.   Answers may vary.

31. I heard about the bad weather on the radio.

32. The man drove the sports car with the beard.

33. Arthur borrowed a mountain bike from his friend with eighteen speeds.

34. Uncle Mark and Aunt Jennifer were watching the meteor shower in the backyard.

35. We saw the fog rising from our car.

36. I gave a bracelet to my friend that was made of silver.

37. Mom saw a museum exhibit of ancient pottery made in the American Southwest on Tuesday.

38. Una read about the latest political developments in the newspaper.

39. The mayor said she would lead the St. Patrick's Day parade at her press conference.

40. The woman won the CD player who had on the red hat.

Writing Application
Using Negative Words in Description

Negative Words   Everyone has a bad day now and then. Yesterday, it was your turn. You were late for school because your alarm clock did not go off. From then on, things just got worse. Write a letter to a friend giving a funny description of your unlucky day. Make sure that you use negative words correctly.

Prewriting   Write down some notes about a real or imaginary bad day in your life. List at least five things that went wrong during the day. The events can be big or small. Tell how you felt when one thing after another went wrong.

Writing   In your letter, explain the events of your day in the order they happened. Describe each event in detail. Also describe your reactions to the events. You may want to exaggerate some details for a humorous effect.

Revising   Ask a friend to read your letter. Have you described the events clearly? Do your descriptions give a vivid, humorous picture of your day? If not, add or revise details.

Publishing   Be sure that your letter follows the correct form for a personal letter. Proofread your letter carefully for errors in grammar, spelling and punctuation. Read through each sentence one more time to check that negative words are used correctly. With your teacher's permission, you and your classmates may wish to present your descriptions in class and vote on who survived the worst day.

APPLICATION

Writing Application

Prewriting Tip. Most bad days happen because an event, often a mistake, causes another event, which in turn causes another event. Your students will have to analyze the causes of the bad things that happened to them. You can try asking them to start at the end of the day and to think back to what caused the last bad thing to happen, what caused the bad thing before that, and so on.

Scoring Rubric. While you will want to pay particular attention to students' use of negative words, you will also want to evaluate overall writing performance. You may want to give a split score to indicate development and clarity of the composition, as well as usage skills.

USAGE

Chapter Review   **219**

10

A Glossary of Usage
Common Usage Problems

Terms in brackets refer to the concepts tested by the items in the Diagnostic Preview.

Answers may vary.
1. take [*bring*]
2. rather [*kind of*]
3. already [*already*]
4. well [*good,well*]
5. have [*could of*]
6. an [*a,an*]
7. to [*try and*]
8. bad [*bad,badly*]
9. can't [*hardly*]
10. than [*than,then*]
11. [*of*]
12. their
   [*their,there,they're*]

Diagnostic Preview

Correcting Errors in Usage

Each of the following sentences contains an ~~error in the use of formal, standard English~~. Rewrite each sentence correctly.

EXAMPLE   **1.** I knew all the answers accept the last one.
      1. I knew all the answers except the last one.

1. If you're going to the library, would you please ~~bring~~ these books there for me?
2. The water tasted ~~kind of~~ salty.
3. Has Jamila finished the assignment ~~all ready~~?
4. Leon went to the doctor because he didn't feel ~~good~~.
5. They should ~~of~~ asked for directions.
6. We found nothing but a old shoe.
7. Bao will try ~~and~~ fix her bike today.
8. The tuna looked all right but smelled ~~badly~~.
9. Albert ~~can't hardly~~ wait to read that biography of the Olympic star Jesse Owens.
10. Why is this mitt more expensive ~~then~~ that one?
11. He knocked a bowl of plantains off ~~of~~ the table.
12. In rural Vietnam, children often take care of ~~there~~ family's water buffalo.

13. After school we ~~use~~ to have band practice.
14. Tanya made ~~less~~ mistakes after she had started practicing.
15. Do you know ~~who's~~ pencil this is?
16. Mr. Abeyto assigned me to this ~~here~~ seat.
17. A glitch is ~~when~~ a mistake ~~is~~ made by a computer.
18. Did Ann say ~~how come~~ she won't attend the meeting?
19. The food was shared ~~between~~ the families of the village.
20. At one time, Bessie Coleman was the only black woman pilot ~~anywheres~~ in the world.

13. used [*use to, used to*]
14. fewer [*fewer, less*]
15. whose [*whose, who's*]
16. [*this here*]
17. [*when, where*]
18. why [*how come*]
19. among [*between, among*]
20. anywhere [*anywheres*]

About the Glossary

This chapter contains an alphabetical list, or *glossary,* of common problems in English usage. You will notice that some examples in this glossary are labeled *nonstandard, standard, formal,* or *informal.*

The label *nonstandard* identifies usage that is acceptable only in the most casual speaking situations and in writing that attempts to re-create casual speech. *Standard* English is language that is grammatically correct and appropriate in formal and informal situations. *Formal* identifies standard usage that is appropriate in serious speaking and writing situations (such as in speeches and in writing for school). The label *informal* indicates standard usage common in conversation and in everyday writing such as personal letters. When doing the exercises in this chapter, be sure to use only standard English.

The following are examples of formal and informal English.

Reference Note

For a list of **words often confused,** see page 329. Use the **index** at the back of the book to find discussions of other usage problems.

Formal	Informal
angry	steamed
unpleasant	yucky
agreeable	cool
very impressive	totally awesome
accelerate	step on it

A Glossary of Usage   **221**

A, An—How Come

(pp. 222–228)

OBJECTIVES

- To identify correct usage in sentences
- To identify and correct common errors in usage

DIRECT TEACHING

Modeling and Demonstration

A, An. Model how to identify correct usage of commonly misused words by using the example *My father works in an office.* First, ask whether *office* begins with a vowel or a consonant sound. [*vowel sound*] Next, ask whether *an* is used correctly. [*yes*] Then, ask whether *an* could be replaced with *a* here. [*no*] Explain that *a* is used before words beginning with a consonant sound, and *an* is used before words beginning with a vowel sound. Point out that the sound that begins a word, and not the actual letter, is what determines whether *a* or *an* should be used. Now, have a volunteer use another example from this chapter to demonstrate how to identify correct usage of *a* and *an*.

DIFFERENTIATING INSTRUCTION

Learners Having Difficulty

Tell students that one way to remember the difference between *accept* and *except* is by thinking of the *x* in *except* as an X-ing out, or canceling, of something. You might want to use the following example: *All of the dogs* accept/except *hers will eat now.* Ask students which word is appropriate. [*except*]

---

a, an   Use *a* before words beginning with a consonant sound; use *an* before words beginning with a vowel sound. Keep in mind that the sound, not the actual letter, that a word begins with tells you whether *a* or *an* should be used.

EXAMPLES   The airplane was parked in **a** hangar.

She lives on **a** one-way street. [*A* is used because *one* begins with a consonant sound.]

My father works in **an** office.

They arrived **an** hour early. [*An* is used because *hour* begins with a vowel sound.]

accept, except   *Accept* is a verb; it means "to receive." *Except* may be used as either a verb or a preposition. When it is used as a verb, *except* means "to leave out." As a preposition, *except* means "excluding" or "but."

EXAMPLES   The winners of the spelling bee proudly **accepted** their awards. [verb]

Because Josh had a sprained ankle, he was **excepted** from gym class. [verb]

All the food **except** the won-ton soup was ready. [preposition]

ain't   Avoid using this word in speaking and writing; it is nonstandard English.

all right   *All right* can be used as an adjective that means "satisfactory" or "unhurt." As an adverb, *all right* means "well enough." *All right* should be written as two words.

EXAMPLES   This tie looks **all right** with that blue shirt. [adjective]

The baby squirrel had fallen out of its nest, but it was **all right.** [adjective]

Lorenzo and I did **all right** on the pop quiz. [adverb]

"Beats me why I ain't gettin' no better marks in English."

FAMILY CIRCUS reprinted with special permission of King Features Syndicate, Inc.

222   Chapter 10   A Glossary of Usage

RESOURCES

A, An—How Come
Practice
- *Language & Sentence Skills Practice,* pp. 200–201, 205–207
- *Developmental Language & Sentence Skills,* pp. 91–92

a lot   *A lot* should be written as two words.

EXAMPLE   I can make **a lot** of my mom's recipes.

already, all ready   *Already* means "previously." *All ready* means "completely prepared" or "in readiness."

EXAMPLES   We looked for Jay, but he had **already** left.

I had studied for two hours on Sunday night and was **all ready** for the test on Monday.

among   See **between, among.**

anyways, anywheres, everywheres, nowheres, somewheres   These words should have no final *s.*

EXAMPLE   They looked **everywhere** [not *everywheres*] for the missing puzzle piece.

at   Do not use *at* after *where.*

NONSTANDARD   Where is the Chinese kite exhibit at?

STANDARD   Where is the Chinese kite exhibit?

bad, badly   *Bad* is an adjective. It modifies nouns and pronouns. *Badly* is an adverb. It modifies verbs, adjectives, and adverbs.

EXAMPLES   The milk smelled **bad.** [The predicate adjective *bad* modifies *milk.*]

Before I took lessons, I played the piano **badly.** [The adverb *badly* modifies the verb *played.*]

between, among   Use *between* when you are referring to two things at a time even when they are part of a group consisting of more than two.

EXAMPLES   Kim got in line **between** Lee and Rene.

Be sure to weed **between** all ten rows of carrots. [Although there are ten rows of carrots, the weeding is done *between* any two of them.]

Use *among* when you are referring to a group rather than to separate individuals.

EXAMPLE   The four winners divided the prize **among** themselves.

| STYLE | TIP |

A lot sounds vague and boring when it is used too often. When you revise your own writing, try to replace *a lot* with a more exact word or phrase whenever possible.

ORIGINAL   Ernie drinks a lot of water every day.

REVISED   Ernie drinks **at least six large glasses** of water every day.

| STYLE | TIP |

The expression *feel badly* is common in informal English. However, in formal English you should use *feel bad.*

INFORMAL   Beth felt badly about hurting José's feelings.

FORMAL   Beth felt **bad** about hurting José's feelings.

USAGE

EXTENSION

A Lot

To inspire students to use alternatives for the overused *a lot,* bring in a copy of *An Exaltation of Larks* by James Lipton. This illustrated book lists traditional names for groups of animals, such as a "pride of lions." Lipton then coins a series of modern group names such as a "slouch of models" or a "wince of dentists." Have students work in small groups to come up with collective terms for groupings of numerous items in their world: books, teachers, homework, music videos, and so on.

DIRECT TEACHING

Bad, Badly

When discussing the usage of the adjective *bad* and the adverb *badly,* you may want to list some of the verbs they frequently follow, such as *sound, feel, taste, smell,* and *look.* Write a list of such verbs on the chalkboard, emphasizing that when used to show how something is perceived, these verbs are always followed by the adjective *bad,* not the adverb *badly.* Give students extra practice by asking them to complete the following sentences with a sensory verb and adjective(s):

1. Warm, mushy watermelon . . .
2. The thorn on a rosebush . . .
3. Before a thunderstorm, the sky . . .
4. The inside of a garbage dumpster usually . . .
5. During Marie's first piano lesson, her music . . .

DISTRIBUTED REVIEW

Before students attempt to identify the correct words or word groups in **Exercise 1**, ask them to identify the verb *felt* in sentences 6 and 10 as a linking verb or an action verb. [6. *linking.* 10. *linking*]

DIFFERENTIATING INSTRUCTION

English-Language Learners

General Strategies. In presenting *a* and *an*, emphasize the initial sound of the words that *a* and *an* precede so that students understand more clearly which article is appropriate. You might want to have students hold up objects and identify them by saying, "It's a/an . . . ," or you can hold up pictures from a magazine and ask students to identify the objects shown, using *a* or *an* as appropriate.

Cantonese. Cantonese does not use the equivalent of the English articles *a*, *an*, or *the*. Also, Cantonese-speaking students may find the concepts of countable/uncountable and definite/indefinite difficult to grasp. Students may either omit articles (*I like book*), add articles unnecessarily (*She goes to the school every morning*), or confuse the two main types of articles (*Please lend me the pen and the piece of paper*).

Articles are unstressed in English and difficult to hear for those whose language does not use articles. When introducing nouns, use the article with the noun: *This is a noun, and this is an adjective.* Also, have students practice the definite article *the* by using it to point to specific items.

> **Teacher:** *Which book do you want?*
> **Student:** *The one with the red cover.*

For each of the following sentences, choose the word or word group in parentheses that is correct according to the rules of formal, standard usage.

EXAMPLE
1. The picture on this page is titled *After Supper, West Chester,* but the scene could be almost (*anywhere, anywheres*).
1. *anywhere*

1. This colorful work was painted by (*a, an*) artist named Horace Pippin, who lived from 1888 to 1946.
2. By the time Pippin was in elementary school, he was (*already, all ready*) a talented artist.
3. In fact, he had won a drawing contest and had eagerly (*accepted, excepted*) the prize, a box of crayons and a set of watercolor paints.
4. In World War I, Pippin was once caught (*among, between*) U.S. troops and the enemy.
5. During this battle (*somewheres, somewhere*) in France, Pippin's right arm—the arm he used when painting—was seriously wounded.
6. For a long time, Pippin felt quite (*bad, badly*) about his disability, but he was determined to paint again.
7. After Pippin recovered, he tried (*alot, a lot*) of new ways to paint; the most successful was to hold up his right hand with his left arm.

8. It (*ain't, is not*) surprising that one of his first paintings after the war portrayed a battle scene.
9. When Pippin painted *After Supper, West Chester,* in 1935, he was remembering the small town in Pennsylvania (*where he was born, where he was born at*).
10. I think that the painter of this peaceful scene must have felt (*all right, alright*) about his work and about himself.

Horace Pippin, *After Supper, West Chester* (1935). Collection Leon Hecht and Robert Pincus-Witten, New York. © 1991 Gridley/Graves.

224 **Chapter 10** A Glossary of Usage

bring, take   *Bring* means "to come carrying something." *Take* means "to go carrying something." Think of *bring* as related to *come* (*to*) and *take* as related to *go* (*from*).

EXAMPLES   Make sure that you **bring** your book when you come to my house.

Always remember to **take** your coat when you go outside during the winter.

could of   Do not write *of* with the helping verb *could.* Write *could have.* Also avoid *ought to of, should of, would of, might of,* and *must of.*

EXAMPLES   Yvetta wished she **could have** [not *could of*] gone to the movie Saturday night.

We **should have** [not *should of*] asked your mom for permission to go to the park.

don't, doesn't   See page 135.

everywheres   See **anyways,** etc.

except, accept   See **accept, except.**

fewer, less   *Fewer* is used with plural words. *Less* is used with singular words. *Fewer* tells "how many"; *less* tells "how much."

EXAMPLES   This road has **fewer** stoplights than any of the other roads in the county.

This road has **less** traffic than any of the other roads in the county.

good, well   *Good* is an adjective. Do not use *good* to modify a verb; use *well,* which can be used as an adverb.

NONSTANDARD   Heather sings good.

STANDARD   Heather sings **well.**

Although it is usually an adverb, *well* is also used as an adjective to mean "healthy."

EXAMPLE   Keiko went home from school today because she didn't feel **well.**

┌ TIPS & TRICKS ┐

Could of, should of, etc., are common errors because they are mistaken for the contractions of *could have, should have,* etc. When spoken, *could've* sounds like *could of.* The difference is hardly noticeable in speech, but it is very noticeable in writing.

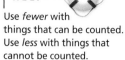

┌ HELP ─

Use *fewer* with things that can be counted. Use *less* with things that cannot be counted.

EXAMPLE
Yolanda has (*fewer, less*) pets than Kristi does.

ASK
Can you count pets? [yes]

ANSWER
Yolanda has **fewer** pets than Kristi does.

EXAMPLE
This car has (*fewer, less*) trunk space than that car.

ASK
Can you count space? [no]

ANSWER
This car has **less** trunk space than that car.

USAGE

NOTE *Feel good* and *feel well* mean different things. *Feel good* means "to feel happy or pleased." *Feel well* means "to feel healthy."

EXAMPLES   I feel **good** when I'm with my friends.

Rashid had a cold, and he still doesn't feel **well**.

had of   See **of.**

had ought, hadn't ought   The verb *ought* should not be used with *had.*

NONSTANDARD   They had ought to be more careful.
STANDARD   They **ought** to be more careful.

NONSTANDARD   You hadn't ought to have said that.
STANDARD   You **oughtn't** to have said that.

or

You **shouldn't** have said that.

hardly, scarcely   *Hardly* and *scarcely* are negative words. They should not be used with other negative words to express a single negative idea.

EXAMPLES   Pedro **can** [not *can't*] **hardly** wait for the fiesta.

The sun **has** [not *hasn't*] **scarcely** shone today.

hisself, theirself, theirselves   These words are nonstandard English. Use *himself* and *themselves.*

EXAMPLES   Mr. Ogata said he would do the work **himself** [not *hisself*], I believe.

They congratulated **themselves** [not *theirselves*] on their victory.

how come   In informal English, *how come* is often used instead of *why.* In formal English, *why* is preferred.

INFORMAL   How come she can leave early?
FORMAL   **Why** can she leave early?

Exercise 2 Identifying Correct Usage

For each of the following sentences, choose the <u>word or word group in parentheses that is correct</u> according to the rules of formal, standard usage.

EXAMPLE   1. There might be (*fewer, less*) accidents if people were more alert around small children.
    1. *fewer*

1. Everyone knows that children are not always as careful as they (*ought, had ought*) to be.
2. However, young children (*can hardly, can't hardly*) be blamed for being curious and adventurous.
3. Just a few days ago, I was involved in a scary situation that (*could of, could have*) led to a serious accident.
4. After I (*brought, took*) my little brother Gerald home from a walk, I called my friend Susan.
5. Gerald quickly wandered off by (*hisself, himself*).
6. I don't know (*how come, why*) he always disappears when I'm on the phone.
7. I found Gerald climbing onto the stove, and in (*fewer, less*) than a second, I lifted him down.
8. I told him that he (*could have, could of*) been burned.
9. He said he would be (*good, well*) from then on.
10. Although the experience was frightening, it turned out (*good, well*).

Oral Practice Proofreading a Paragraph for Correct Usage

Each of the following sentences has at least one error in the use of standard, formal English. Read each sentence aloud, and identify each ~~error~~. Then, say the sentences again, correcting each error.

EXAMPLE   [1] The game of soccer has proved to be more popular than the king of England hisself.
    1. *hisself—himself*

[1] Derby, England, may have been the town where soccer was first played ~~at~~. [2] Sometime around the third century A.D., an early version of the game was played ~~among~~ two towns.

USAGE

Oral Practice Proofreading a Paragraph for Correct Usage

ANSWERS continued

3. Anywhere
4. fewer; well
5. already
6. ought; themselves
7. all right; an
8. didn't obey *or* hardly obeyed
9. bad
10. accept

Its, It's—Them

(pp. 228–231)

OBJECTIVE

■ To identify correct usage in sentences

DIRECT TEACHING

Modeling and Demonstration

Its, It's. Model how to identify correct usage of commonly misused words by using the example *The raccoon washed its face in the shallows of the stream.* First, ask what *its* means in this sentence. [*the raccoon's*] Next, ask whether *its* is the correct word here. [*yes*] Then, ask whether *it's* could be used instead of *its* here. [*no*] Point out that *its* is a possessive pronoun and that *it's* is a contraction meaning *it is*. Now, have a volunteer use another example from this chapter to demonstrate how to identify correct usage of *its* and *it's*.

[3] Anywheres from fifty to several hundred people played in a match. [4] Back then, soccer had less rules than it does today and the participants probably didn't behave very good. [5] By the fifteenth century, the government had all ready outlawed the sport. [6] The king said that young people had ought to be training theirselves in archery instead of playing soccer. [7] According to the king, archery practice was alright because bows and arrows could be used against a enemy. [8] However, many people didn't hardly obey the king's rule, and soccer continued to grow in popularity. [9] Perhaps later kings felt badly about outlawing soccer. [10] Eventually the government had to except that soccer had become the most popular sport in England.

its, it's *Its* is the possessive form of the personal pronoun *it*. *Its* is used to show ownership. *It's* is a contraction of *it is* or *it has*.

EXAMPLES   The raccoon washed **its** face in the shallows of the stream. [possessive pronoun]

My grandparents have a dog; **it's** a collie. [contraction of *it is*]

It's been sunny and warm all day. [contraction of *It has*]

kind of, sort of   In informal English, *kind of* and *sort of* are often used to mean "somewhat" or "rather." In formal English, however, it is better to use *somewhat* or *rather*.

INFORMAL   That story is kind of funny.

FORMAL   That story is **rather** funny.

learn, teach   *Learn* means "to gain knowledge." *Teach* means "to instruct" or "to show how."

EXAMPLES   The students from Vietnam are **learning** English.

Ms. Sanita is **teaching** them.

less   See **fewer, less.**

lie, lay   See page 168.

might of, must of   See **could of.**

RESOURCES

Its, It's—Them
Practice
■ *Language & Sentence Skills Practice,* pp. 201–203, 205–207
■ *Developmental Language & Sentence Skills,* pp. 93–94

nowheres   See **anyways,** etc.

of   Do not use *of* with prepositions such as *inside, off,* and *outside.*

EXAMPLES   Mrs. Cardona stood **outside** [not *outside of*] the office.

The child stepped **off** [not *off of*] the porch.

We heard a noise **inside** [not *inside of*] the engine.

Of is also unnecessary with *had.*

EXAMPLE   If we **had** [not *had of*] known you were hungry, we would have brought some food.

ought to of   See **could of.**

rise, raise   See page 166.

should of   See **could of.**

sit, set   See page 165.

somewheres   See **anyways,** etc.

sort of   See **kind of, sort of.**

suppose to, supposed to   Do not leave the *d* off *supposed* when you write *supposed to.*

EXAMPLE   They were **supposed to** [not *suppose to*] join us at the gate.

take, bring   See **bring, take.**

than, then   *Than* is a conjunction used in making comparisons. *Then* is an adverb meaning "next" or "after that."

EXAMPLES   This cheese is tastier **than** that one.

First the phone rang, and **then** someone knocked on the door.

that there   See **this here, that there.**

their, there, they're   *Their* is the possessive form of *they.* It is used to show ownership. *There* is used to mean "at that place" or to begin a sentence. *They're* is a contraction of *they are.*

Reference Note

For information on **using of with helping verbs,** see **could of,** page 225.

MEETING THE CHALLENGE

Mnemonics are things that aid the memory. They can be short poems, sentences that each start with a certain letter related to what you want to remember, or visual aids, to name just a few. Create a mnemonic to help you remember when to use *between* and *among.* Then, create another mnemonic for a usage problem of your choice.

ANSWER
Mnemonics will vary.

A Glossary of Usage   **229**

DIFFERENTIATING INSTRUCTION

English-Language Learners

Vietnamese. Vietnamese students may confuse words such as *sit* and *set* because Vietnamese does not have the vowel sound found in *sit.* It also does not have the vowel sounds found in *had, fire,* and *hour.* The student may substitute a close sound, but confusion may result with similar sounding words. Practice these vowel sounds with your Vietnamese students.

Students need opportunities to practice spoken English in an encouraging environment that supports their efforts. They should work in groups with native English speakers whenever possible. The teacher may have to model correct pronunciation frequently.

General Strategies. To help students differentiate more clearly between *than* and *then,* point out that *than* always involves a comparison, for example, "Lisa is taller than Alberto." On the other hand, *then* specifies a point in time, for example, "She ate breakfast, and then she went to school."

DIRECT TEACHING

Than, Then

Point out to students that they can remember that *then* is an adverb by thinking of the phrase *then is when.* This phrase can usually be used (though awkwardly) in a sentence that requires *then,* for example, "First the phone rang, and then (is when) someone knocked at the door." *Then* is an adverb; it answers the question *when?*

MINI-LESSON   Mechanics   *Continued on p. 230*

Contractions. Some students might have particular difficulty in distinguishing between possessive pronouns and some contractions. You might want to refer students to the discussion of contractions in **Chapter 13: Punctuation.** Explain that a contraction is a shortened form of a word, number, or group of words. An apostrophe shows where the letters, numerals, or words have been left out. Then, have students identify the full forms of the following contractions:

RETEACHING

Correct Usage

Activity. Have pairs of students create two sets of flashcards. In one set of flashcards, words and groups of words from this section should be used correctly in sentences. The backs of these cards should be labeled *Standard English.* In the second set of cards, the words, groups of words, and nonstandard constructions (such as *theirselves*) should be used in sentences that do not conform to standard English. The backs of these cards should be labeled *Nonstandard English* and, below the label, should have corrected versions of the nonstandard sentences. Have students shuffle the flashcards and then take turns quizzing each other with the cards, alternating roles after each card. Students should tell whether each sentence uses standard English and correct any sentence written in nonstandard English.

PRACTICE

Guided and Independent

Exercises You may wish to use **Exercise 3** as guided practice and have students complete **Review A** as independent practice.

HOMEWORK

Jaguar

Scarf

Lord

Man

EXAMPLES The children played happily with **their** toys. [*Their* tells whose toys.]

We are going over **there** very soon. [*There* tells where we are going.]

There are twelve members in our club. [*There* begins the sentence but does not add to the sentence's meaning.]

They're going to have a Juneteenth picnic. [*They're* is a contraction of *They are.*]

theirself, theirselves See **hisself,** etc.

them *Them* should not be used as an adjective. Use *the, these,* or *those.*

EXAMPLE How much are **those** [not *them*] baseball cards?

Exercise 3 Identifying Correct Usage

For each of the following sentences, choose the <u>word or word group in parentheses that is correct</u> according to the rules of formal, standard English.

EXAMPLE 1. For years, scientists have studied Mayan writing on temples and (*inside of, inside*) caves.
   1. *inside*

1. Some scientists are (*learning, teaching*) themselves how to understand this writing.
2. The Ancient Mayas didn't use an alphabet to write (*there, their, they're*) language.
3. Instead, they drew symbols like (*them, these*) small pictures shown at left.
4. As you can see, the sign for jaguar looked (*somewhat, sort of*) like a jaguar.
5. At times, it could be difficult to tell what a picture was (*suppose, supposed*) to represent.
6. (*Its, It's*) meaning was made clear by the use of another small symbol.
7. (*There, Their, They're*) is an example of this technique in the illustration in the middle.

MINI-LESSON **Mechanics** *Continued from p. 229*

1. it's [*it is* or *it has*]
2. there's [*there is* or *there has*]
3. they're [*they are*]

4. who's [*who is* or *who has*]
5. you're [*you are*]

8. When a scarf symbol was added to the symbol for man, (*then*, *than*) the picture meant "lord."

9. Mayan writing contained other symbols that stood for syllables rather (*then*, *than*) entire words.

10. (*Its*, *It's*) clear we still have a great deal to learn about this beautiful, ancient language.

Review A **Identifying Correct Usage**

Choose the correct word or words in parentheses in each of the following sentences.

EXAMPLE   **1.** Our club will (*accept*, *except*) anyone interested in computers.

     1. accept

1. Well, I (*should of*, *should have*) seen that coming.
2. Few chiefs were more powerful (*than*, *then*) Sitting Bull.
3. Maybe this dog can't find (*its*, *it's*) way home.
4. You didn't do too (*bad*, *badly*) in that last race.
5. David sings pretty (*good*, *well*), doesn't he?
6. Thanks, you've been (*a lot*, *alot*) of help!
7. We (*had ought*, *ought*) to plant our garden next week.
8. That book has (*all ready*, *already*) been checked out.
9. The lenses were dirty, but (*their*, *there*, *they're*) clean now.
10. Would you (*learn*, *teach*) us how to use those castanets?

this here, that there   Do not use *here* and *there* after *this* and *that*.

EXAMPLE   Do you want **this** [not *this here*] book or **that** [not *that there*] one?

try and   In informal English, *try and* is often used for *try to*. In formal English, the correct form is *try to*.

INFORMAL   Pat will try and explain the problem.

FORMAL   Pat will **try to** explain the problem.

use to, used to   Do not leave the *d* off *used* when you write *used to*.

EXAMPLE   Dr. Chang **used to** [not *use to*] live next door to us.

This Here, That There—Your, You're
(pp. 231–234)

OBJECTIVE

- To identify correct usage in sentences

DIRECT TEACHING

Modeling and Demonstration

This Here, That There. Model how to identify and correct common errors in usage by using the incorrect example *Do you want this here book or that there one?* First, ask whether there are any modifiers in this sentence. [*yes; this, that*] Next, ask what these modifiers describe. [*which book, which one*] Then, ask whether the words *here* and *there* are necessary to the meaning of the sentence. [*no*] Point out that *here* and *there* should not be used after *this* and *that*. Now, have a volunteer use another example from this chapter to demonstrate how to identify and correct common usage errors.

APPLICATION

Relating to Writing

You might want to have students review pieces of writing from their notebooks, identifying and correcting any of the common errors in usage listed in this chapter.

USAGE

DIFFERENTIATING INSTRUCTION

English-Language Learners

General Strategies. Some students may need practice in determining the correct use of *used to.* You may want to have them record the following information in their journals:

Used to + verb refers to an action that happened repeatedly in the past but that no longer occurs, or a past condition that no longer exists (for example, *Before I learned English, I used to feel shy around new friends* or *I used to have a red bicycle; now I own a blue one*).

To provide further practice, pair your English-language learners. Have them interview each other about things they used to do before coming to the United States.

DIRECT TEACHING

Who's, You're

Help students determine the correct usage of *who's* and *you're* by writing the following sentences on the chalkboard:

1. (*Whose, Who's*) winning the game?
2. Raise (*your, you're*) hand when (*your, you're*) finished.

Show students how to determine the correct choices by pointing out that the apostrophe in *who's* stands for an *i*, so *who's* means "who is." In *you're*, the apostrophe stands for an *a*, so *you're* means "you are." [1. *Who's*; 2. *your; you're*] Now, have students write several sentences that demonstrate the correct usage of *who's* and *you're*.

| COMPUTER TIP

A computer's spellchecker can identify words that are nonstandard, such as *ain't, hisself,* and *everywheres.* However, the spellchecker cannot tell you when you have used a correctly spelled word in the wrong way. For example, if you use *whose* where you should use *who's,* the computer probably will not find the error. Always proofread your writing carefully to correct such errors in usage.

way, ways   Use *way*, not *ways*, when referring to a distance.

EXAMPLE   We traveled a long **way** [not *ways*] today.

well   See **good, well.**

when, where   Do not use *when* or *where* incorrectly to begin a definition.

NONSTANDARD   A phrase is when a group of words is used as a part of speech.

STANDARD   A phrase is a group of words that is used as a part of speech.

Do not use *where* for *that.*

EXAMPLE   I read **that** [not *where*] the concert has been canceled.

whose, who's   *Whose* is the possessive form of *who.* It shows ownership. *Who's* is a contraction of *who is* or *who has.*

EXAMPLES   **Whose** dog is that? [possessive pronoun]

Who's [*Who is*] the bravest person you know?

He's the only one **who's** [*who has*] turned in a report.

would of   See **could of.**

your, you're   *Your* is the possessive form of *you.* *You're* is the contraction of *you are.*

EXAMPLES   Do you have **your** watch with you? [possessive pronoun]

You're late today. [contraction of *you are*]

Exercise 4   **Identifying Correct Usage**

For each of the following sentences, choose the word or word group in parentheses that is correct according to the rules of formal, standard English.

EXAMPLE   **1.** Take a map on (*your, you're*) next camping trip.

1. *your*

1. A trail map is (*when a map shows, a map that shows*) trails, campsites, and geographical features for a given area.

Continued on pp. 233–234

Learning for Life

Giving Directions. Tell students they will be writing directions that tell a friend how to get from school to a chosen place. To make sure their directions are clear and specific, have students model their directions on the following sentence: "When you get to the corner, a blue house will be on your right." In addition, the directions should answer the following kinds of questions:

- Are there key landmarks along the way, such as big trees or buildings? What

2. For a safe camping trip, a map like (*this here*, *this*) one can be very important.

3. Hikers who are not (*used to*, *use to*) an area often easily lose their way.

4. Every year, rangers report (*where*, *that*) some campers were lost for a day or more.

5. If you don't want to get lost, (*try and*, *try to*) get a good trail map.

6. In fact, every hiker in your group (*who's*, *whose*) able to read a map should have one.

7. With the map, you can choose a (*good*, *well*) location for your campsite.

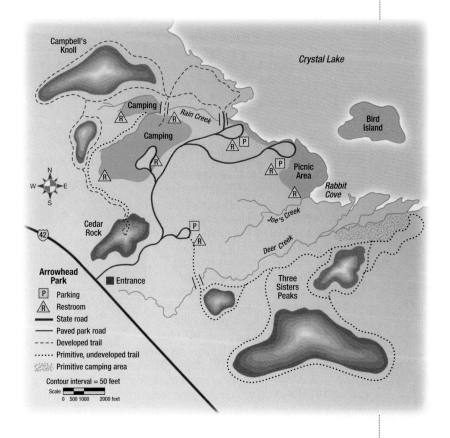

should the visitor do at each landmark?

- How will the visitor know whether he or she is following the directions correctly or has made a wrong turn?

- What does the destination look like? Does it lie between two other structures?

- Are there other routes the visitor could take to reach the destination?

8. When you begin your hike, mark where (*your, you're*) campsite is on the map.
9. If you go quite a (*way, ways*) from your campsite, note your path on the map, too.
10. As (*your, you're*) walking, your trail map can help you figure out exactly where you are.

Review B **Proofreading a Paragraph for Correct Usage**

Most of the sentences in the following paragraph contain errors in the use of formal, standard English. If a sentence is incorrect, rewrite it correctly. If a sentence is already correct, write *C*.

EXAMPLES
[1] Do you know someone who can learn you how to dance the Texas Two-Step?
1. *Do you know someone who can teach you how to dance the Texas Two-Step?*

[2] Well, your in for a real treat!
2. *Well, you're in for a real treat!*

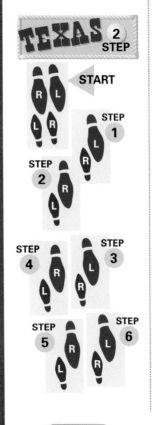

[1] Country music lovers enjoy the two-step because its fun to dance. **[2]** If you don't know anyone who can teach you the two-step, you can use this here diagram to learn the basic steps. **[3]** Grab you're partner and get ready. **[4]** First, listen closely to them musicians. **[5]** Try and catch the rhythm of the music with a small double shuffle step. **[6]** Remember, men, your always starting with the left foot; women, you do just the opposite. **[7]** The man steps to the left, touches his left shoe with his right one, and then steps to the right and does the same thing. **[8]** Then, he takes two kind of quick steps forward followed by two slow shuffle steps. **[9]** Some dancers add variety to there steps by doing a sidestep or a turn. **[10]** Now you've come a long ways toward learning the Texas Two-Step!

1. it's	**5.** to	**8.** rather
3. your	**6.** you're	**9.** their
4. the	**7.** C	**10.** way

Learning for Life

Continued from p. 233

Tell students to use as many of the words from the **Glossary of Usage** as possible in writing their directions. When students are finished, have them exchange directions with a partner. Partners should circle exam-

ples of the correct usage of words discussed in the glossary. They also should mark any sentences that include nonstandard English. Students should then correct their own directions and save them in their notebooks.

Terms in brackets refer to concepts tested by the items in the Chapter Review.

1. your [*your, you're*]
2. bad [*bad, badly*]
3. aren't [*ain't*]
4. an [*a, an*]
5. Fewer [*fewer, less*]
6. all ready [*already, all ready*]
7. take [*bring, take*]
8. [*at*]

Chapter Review

A. Revising Sentences by Correcting Errors in Usage

In each of the following sets of sentences, choose the letter of the sentence that contains an error. Then, write the sentence correctly, using formal, standard English.

1. a. Everyone was at the meeting except Diego.
   b. Does you're dog bite?
   c. Andy waited outside the dentist's office.

2. a. The landfill smelled badly.
   b. No one knew whose knapsack that was.
   c. We could hardly wait for the rain to stop.

3. a. Mr. Catalano says that spiders ain't insects.
   b. I feel rather tired today.
   c. Do you accept personal checks?

4. a. Nina can run faster than he can.
   b. Anna would have finished, but she was interrupted.
   c. Be sure to bring a extra pencil with you.

5. a. The cow and its calf stood in the meadow.
   b. Less students signed up for tutoring this month.
   c. What is the difference between these brands of basketball shoes?

6. a. We did as we were told.
   b. Everyone was already to go.
   c. I used to enjoy playing tennis.

7. a. Penny, bring this book when you go home.
   b. Ms. Michaelson told us that our plan was all right.
   c. Julie said that it's already time to go.

8. a. The team had fewer fouls in the last game.
   b. They looked everywhere for him.
   c. Do you know where he is at?

9. to [*try and*]
10. [*when, where*]

11. [*had of, (of)*]
12. all right [*all right*]
13. among [*between*]
14. a lot [*a lot*]
15. [*this here*]
16. [*of*]
17. supposed to [*suppose to, supposed to*]
18. It's [*its, it's*]
19. those *or* the [*them*]
20. not [*had ought*]
21. all ready [*already*]
22. have [*could of*]
23. well [*good, well*]
24. except [*accept, except*]
25. themselves [*theirselves*]
26. has [*hardly*]
27. their [*their, there, they're*]
28. way [*way, ways*]
29. used [*use to*]
30. You're [*your, you're*]

9. **a.** Water-skiing is more fun than I thought.
   b. We hiked a long way before we pitched camp.
   c. Try ~~and~~ get to the meeting on time, please.
10. **a.** Their team has never beaten your team.
    b. A pop fly is ~~when~~ a ball ~~is~~ batted high into the infield.
    c. I finished my homework; then I called Duane.

B. Revising Sentences by Correcting Errors in Usage

Each of the following sentences contains an ~~error in the use of formal, standard English.~~ Rewrite each sentence correctly.

11. They could have come if the plane had ~~of~~ been on time.
12. My mom said that it is ~~alright~~ for you to have lunch with us.
13. We talked quietly ~~between~~ the three of us.
14. That parade created ~~alot~~ of work for the street cleaners.
15. This ~~here~~ beach is beautiful!
16. When the semi-trailer drove past the house, the picture fell off ~~of~~ Aunt Edna's wall.
17. Jim was ~~suppose to~~ rake the leaves yesterday.
18. ~~Its~~ one of the nicest beaches near Port Aransas.
19. I want to buy some of ~~them~~ crisp, green apples.
20. You ~~hadn't~~ ought to miss the national park.
21. After spending most of the weekend in the library, I was ~~already~~ for the exam.
22. Earlier in the race, I could ~~of~~ caught up with her.
23. "I'm doing ~~good.~~ How are you doing?"
24. Every major country in Western Europe ~~accept~~ Switzerland and Norway belongs to the European Union.
25. Mom and Dad treated ~~theirselves~~ to dinner at a fine restaurant on their anniversary.
26. It ~~hasn't~~ hardly rained all month in west Texas.
27. The birds flew toward ~~there~~ nests.
28. Boston is a long ~~ways~~ from San Francisco.
29. When I was a baby, I ~~use~~ to eat teething biscuits.
30. "~~Your~~ late today," said Ms. Jimenez. "Be on time tomorrow."

USAGE

Writing Application
Using Formal English in a Letter

Formal, Standard Usage You are an after-school helper at a day-care center. The teachers at the center plan to take the children on a field trip. One of the teachers has asked you to write a letter to send to the children's parents. The letter should tell where the children will visit and describe some of the things they will do there. The letter should also list any special items the children need to take with them.

Prewriting First, decide where the children will go on their field trip. They might go to a library, a park, a museum, or a fire station. Then, list the kinds of activities in which the children might participate. Note how the children will travel—for example, by bus or car. Also, note any special clothing or other things they might need for the field trip. List all the details you can imagine.

Writing Begin your draft with a polite greeting to the parents. Then, clearly explain why the children are going on the field trip. Invite the parents to call the day-care center with any questions they might have. In your letter, avoid using any informal or non-standard expressions.

Revising Read over your work carefully, and then ask a friend to read your letter. Does your reader understand the information in the letter? Does the letter follow the guidelines for a proper business letter? Revise any information that is unclear.

Publishing Check your letter for correct spelling, punctuation, and grammar. With your teacher's permission, you may want to discuss the planned field trip with the rest of the class. Post your letter on a class bulletin board or Web page.

┌─ **H E L P** ─
Use the Glossary
of Usage to help you write
the letter in formal,
standard English.

Writing Application

Prewriting Tip. To help students think critically and to help them generate writing ideas, ask them to work together to prepare a questionnaire that focuses on where young children might want to go on a field trip. After students have composed the questionnaire, distribute copies and ask students from another class to fill them out. Read the results to the class, and allow students to use in their letters any of the ideas that they like.

Scoring Rubric. While you will want to pay particular attention to students' usage, you will also want to evaluate overall writing performance. You may want to give a split score to indicate development and clarity of the composition as well as usage skills.

USAGE

STANDARDS FOCUS

Grade-Level Standards

(Boldface indicates concepts that are taught and tested in this chapter.)

- English Language Convention 1.0: **Students write and speak with a command of standard English conventions appropriate to this grade level.**

- Capitalization 1.4: **Use correct capitalization.**

Prerequisite/Review Standard

- Capitalization 1.4: Use correct capitalization.

Standard Coming Up in the Next Grade Level

- Capitalization 1.6: Use correct capitalization.

▼

INTRODUCING THE CHAPTER

- This chapter provides rules for the correct use of capitalization. It includes rules for the capitalization of first words in sentences, the pronoun *I*, and proper nouns and adjectives—including geographical names and names of nationalities, races, and peoples. The chapter also discusses the rules for capitalizing names of school subjects, abbreviations, and titles. Because the chapter emphasizes the importance of capitalization in writing, it can be useful with any writing assignment.

- The chapter closes with a **Chapter Review** including a **Writing Application** feature that

(continued)

1.0 Written and Oral English Language Conventions
Students write and speak with a command of standard English conventions appropriate to this grade level.
1.4 Use correct capitalization.

Capital Letters
Rules for Capitalization

Diagnostic Preview

Correcting Sentences by Capitalizing Words

For each of the following sentences, correctly write each word that should be capitalized but is not. If a sentence is already correct, write *C*.

EXAMPLE   **1.** our guest speaker will be mayor Masella.

      1. Our, Mayor

Numerals in brackets refer to rules tested by the items in the Diagnostic Preview.

1. [11c, h(4)]
2. C [11h(4)]
3. [11d(4)]
4. [11d(2), g, h(1),d(1)]
5. [11g, d(1), h(1)]
6. [11h(1), d(1)]
7. [11d(1), h(4), f]
8. [11f, d(11)]
9. [11h(1), d(1)]
10. [11a, d(3)]
11. [11a, b]

1. Today i learned the song "simple gifts" from my friend.
2. "Hansel and Gretel" is a well-known fairy tale.
3. The kane county fall carnival will be held on saturday, october 19.
4. I believe that the recent trip to japan was organized by dr. alexander.
5. Let's ask the club treasurer, ms. lee.
6. Have you met professor martínez, rondelle?
7. Luis valdez filmed *the shepherd's tale*, a traditional mexican play, for television.
8. The greek god of war was ares.
9. My mother wrote to senator smith about the base closing.
10. members of congress often debate issues.
11. The letter began, "dear Ms. Joy."

CHAPTER RESOURCES

Internet
- go.hrw.com (keyword: HLLA)

Planning
- *One-Stop Planner CD-ROM* 💿
- *On Course: Mapping Instruction*
- *At Home: A Guide to Standards Mastery,* pp. 32–33

Practice & Review
- *Language & Sentence Skills Practice,* pp. 213–226; 227–231
- *Developmental Language & Sentence Skills,* pp. 95–104

Application & Enrichment
- *Language & Sentence Skills Practice,* pp. 232, 235; 212, 233–234

12. Have you seen any of Mary cassatt's paintings?
13. I didn't know that there are mummies in the american museum of natural history.
14. A venezuelan exchange student will be living with our family for eight months.
15. The graduation ceremony was held at Newberry college.
16. When is the jewish holiday yom kippur this year?
17. Grandma asked me what i want for my birthday.
18. Monique said, "that movie is about World war II."
19. Next spring uncle William is going to take me on a hiking trip to mount Elbert.
20. Darnell took a rafting trip on the Colorado River.

12. [11d(1)]
13. [11d(9)]
14. [11f]
15. [11d(3)]
16. [11f, d(4), d(11)]
17. [11c]
18. [11a, d(5)]
19. [11h(3), d(2)]
20. C [11d(2)]

Using Capital Letters

11a. Capitalize the first word in every sentence.

EXAMPLE **M**y sister has soccer practice after school. **T**hen she has to do her homework.

The first word of a directly quoted sentence should begin with a capital letter, whether or not the quotation comes at the beginning of your sentence.

EXAMPLE Reiko asked, "**H**ave you finished your report?"

Traditionally, the first word of every line of poetry begins with a capital letter.

EXAMPLE **L**et the rain kiss you.
Let the rain beat upon your head with silver liquid drops.
Let the rain sing you a lullaby.
The rain makes still pools on the sidewalk.
The rain makes running pools in the gutter.
The rain plays a little sleep-song on our roof at night—
And I love the rain.

Langston Hughes, "April Rain Song"

NOTE Some poets do not follow this style. When you quote from a poem, use capital letters exactly as the poet uses them.

┌HELP─
Capitalize the first word of a sentence fragment used in dialogue.

EXAMPLE
Helena asked, "Have you read Terry Brooks' new novel?"
Jenny answered, "**N**o, not yet."

Reference Note
For more about **direct quotations,** see page 292.

Using Capital Letters **239**

asks students to use proper nouns in writing an essay about a proposed visit to a historical place.

■ For help in integrating this chapter with writing assignments in *Holt Literature and Language Arts,* use the **Teaching Strands** chart on pp. T22–T23.

ASSESSING

Entry-Level Assessment
Diagnostic Preview. You may want to use the **Diagnostic Preview** to identify areas in which students need instruction and practice in capitalization. You may also wish to evaluate actual writing samples to identify specific areas of confusion.

PRETEACHING

Lesson Starter
Prior Knowledge. Ask students what capitalization rules they already know, and write their suggested rules on the chalkboard or on a transparency. Refer to this list as students study the chapter. Add new rules and make necessary revisions. After the students have completed the chapter, have them copy the list of rules.

Using Capital Letters
Rules 11a–d *(pp. 239–250)*

OBJECTIVES

■ To proofread sentences for correct capitalization

■ To write proper nouns, using correct capitalization

Differentiating Instruction
■ *Lesson Plans for Language Development*
■ *Supporting Instruction in Five Languages*
■ *At Home: In Five languages*
Assessment
■ *Progress Assessment for the Holt Handbook,* pp. 21–22, 41

■ *Test Generator (One-Stop Planner CD-ROM)* 🌐
Other Language Resources
■ *Spelling Lessons & Activities*
■ *Vocabulary Development*
■ *Daily Language Activities Transparencies*

MECHANICS

DIRECT TEACHING

Modeling and Demonstration

Using Capital Letters. Model how to proofread sentences for correct capitalization by using the example *on saturday margaret and i drove to yellowstone national park*. First, ask whether the first word in the sentence should be capitalized. [*yes*] Next, ask whether the pronoun *I* should be capitalized. [*yes*] Then, ask what proper nouns are in the sentence. [*Saturday, Margaret, Yellowstone National Park*] Ask whether these proper nouns should be capitalized. [*yes*] Point out that the first word in a sentence, the pronoun *I*, and all proper nouns need to be capitalized. Now, have a volunteer use an example from the chapter to demonstrate how to proofread for capitalization.

Reference Note

For information on using **colons in letters,** see page 281. For information on using **commas in letters,** see page 276.

11b. Capitalize the first word in both the salutation and the closing of a letter.

SALUTATIONS	**D**ear Service Manager:
	Dear Adam,
	My dear Brenda,
CLOSINGS	**S**incerely,
	Yours truly,
	Very truly yours,

11c. Capitalize the pronoun *I.*

EXAMPLE   When **I** returned home, **I** walked the dog.

Exercise 1 **Proofreading Sentences for Correct Capitalization**

If a sentence has one or more errors in capitalization, correctly write each word that should be capitalized. If a sentence is already correct, write *C.*

EXAMPLE   **1.** What time should i call?

        1. I

1. my library report on Edwin Arlington Robinson is due at the end of next month.
2. My sister memorized the limerick that begins, "a tutor who tooted a flute."
3. Aren't you glad that tomorrow is a holiday?   **3.** C
4. Elizabeth said, "we need to buy some more shampoo."
5. My grandparents let me watch television only after i have finished all my chores.
6. I used "yours truly" to close my letter.
7. How many yen did you spend during your vacation in Japan, Alexander?   **7.** C
8. "Everything i need to make the spaghetti sauce is right here," Nanna said.
9. two groups that i like will perform in concert next month in the park.
10. Greg said, "tomorrow is a holiday, so there will be no mail delivery."

RESOURCES

Using Capital Letters (Rules 20a–d) Practice

■ *Language & Sentence Skills Practice,* pp. 213–220, 222–223

■ *Developmental Language & Sentence Skills,* pp. 95–104

11d. Capitalize proper nouns.

A *proper noun* names a particular person, place, thing, or idea. Proper nouns are capitalized. A *common noun* names a kind or type of person, place, thing, or idea. A common noun generally is not capitalized unless it begins a sentence or is part of a title.

Proper Nouns	Common Nouns
Fairview **S**chool	middle school
November	month
Toni **M**orrison	writer
Red **S**ox	team
Kenya	country
Queen **E**lizabeth	queen
Motorola	company

NOTE As you may already have noticed, some proper nouns consist of more than one word. In these names, short words such as prepositions (those of fewer than five letters) and articles (*a, an,* and *the*) are not capitalized.

EXAMPLES **I**sle **o**f **W**ight   **A**ttila **t**he **H**un

(1) Capitalize the names of persons and animals.

Capitalize initials that come before or in the middle of names.

Persons	
Kazue **S**awai	**H**arriet **T**ubman
Harry **S**. **T**ruman	**J**ohn **H**. **C**ole, **J**r.
Heitor **V**illa-**L**obos	**W**. **C**. **H**andy

Animals	
Lassie	**R**over
Shamu	**S**ocks

Reference Note

For more about **proper nouns** and **common nouns,** see page 26.

STYLE TIP

Some names consist of more than one part. The different parts may begin with capital letters only or with a combination of capital and lowercase letters. If you are not sure about the spelling of a name, ask the person with that name, or check a reference source.

EXAMPLES
   du **M**aurier, **D**u**P**ont, **v**an **G**ogh, **V**an **B**uren, **L**a **V**erne, **d**e **l**a **T**our

APPLICATION

Relating to Literature

To support the textbook statement (on page 239) that the first word of a line of poetry usually begins with a capital letter, have students study poems in their literature textbooks. For example, Gwendolyn Brooks in "Cynthia in the Snow" and Langston Hughes in "Poem" begin all lines with capitals. You may want to challenge students to find poems that are exceptions to the statement and that have lines whose first words do *not* begin with capitals.

MECHANICS

DIFFERENTIATING INSTRUCTION

English-Language Learners

General Strategies. In some languages, such as Serbo-Croatian and Vietnamese, it is customary to capitalize only the first word of a geographical name that contains two or more words, while in English we capitalize all the words in the name. For example, *Thai binh duong* means "Pacific Ocean" in Vietnamese. Also, the name of a person's nationality is not capitalized in Spanish, Portuguese, Romanian, or Russian; thus, *a Russian* is *un ruso* in Spanish and *ruskii* in Russian. You may wish to emphasize these two points and give students examples to reinforce these differences between English and their native languages.

Cantonese. Cantonese writers use ideographs, a graphic form of writing that does not use an alphabet and that consequently has no need for capitalization. Therefore, the rules and conventions of English capitalization must be learned and practiced by students who write Cantonese.

COMPUTER TIP

You may be able to use your spellchecker to help you correctly capitalize people's names, geographical names, and other proper nouns. Each time you use a proper noun in your writing, make sure you have spelled and capitalized it correctly. Then, add the name to your computer's dictionary or spellchecker.

(2) Capitalize geographical names.

Type of Name	Examples	
Continents	Asia	North America
	Australia	Europe
Countries	Denmark	Thailand
	Burkina Faso	Costa Rica
Cities, Towns	Minneapolis	New Delhi
	Havana	San Diego
States	Maryland	Mississippi
	West Virginia	Oregon
Islands	Hawaiian Islands	Isle of Wight
	Leyte	Key West
Bodies of Water	Yangtze River	Lake Okeechobee
	Hudson Bay	Caribbean Sea
Streets, Highways	Front Street	Sunset Boulevard
	Fifth Avenue	Interstate 55

NOTE In a hyphenated street number, the second part of the number is not capitalized.

EXAMPLE   Forty-ninth Street

Type of Name	Examples	
Parks	San Antonio Missions	Yellowstone National Park
Mountains	Adirondacks	Mount Kilimanjaro
	Pine Mountain	Andes
Forests	Sherwood Forest	Sierra National Forest
	Black Forest	
Sections of the Country	the South	the Northwest
	Corn Belt	New England

CONTENT-AREA CONNECTIONS

Social Studies

Descriptive Geographical Names. Tell students that the Corn Belt is a region of the midwestern United States where farms produce an abundance of corn as well as other crops. Geographers and others sometimes use names such as this to identify important economic or physical features of a region: the Mountain States, the Wheat Belt, the Sun Belt. You might wish to have students suggest descriptive names for their state or community. Remind students that such names are considered proper nouns and should be capitalized.

NOTE Words such as *east, west, northeast,* or *southwest* are not capitalized when the words indicate a direction.

EXAMPLES Turn **e**ast when you reach the river. [direction]

Mae goes to college in the **E**ast. [section of the country]

Exercise 2 Writing Proper Nouns

For each common noun given below, write two proper nouns that name the same kind of person or thing. Be sure to use capital letters correctly.

EXAMPLE **1.** lake

1. *Lake Louise, Lake Ontario*

1. river	6. singer	11. dog	16. explorer
2. street	7. island	12. politician	17. mountain
3. actor	8. state	13. city	18. lake
4. park	9. country	14. pet	19. continent
5. friend	10. ocean	15. painter	20. athlete

Exercise 3 Proofreading for the Correct Use of Capital Letters

If a sentence has an error in capitalization, correctly write the word that should be capitalized. If the sentence is already correct, write *C*.

EXAMPLE **1.** Huge rigs pump oil from beneath the North sea.

1. *Sea*

1. María Ayala and <u>eileen</u> Barnes are going to Chicago.
2. Our neighbor Ken Oshige recently moved to <u>canada</u>.
3. Midway <u>island</u> is in the Pacific Ocean.
4. We could see <u>mount</u> Hood from the airplane window.
5. After you turn off the highway, head north for three miles. 5. C
6. During the sixteenth century, explorers from Spain brought horses to the <u>west</u>.
7. Several of us went camping near the <u>guadalupe</u> River.
8. My closest friend just moved to Ohio with <u>shadow</u>, her cat.
9. Hawaii Volcanoes National <u>park</u> is in Hawaii.
10. The bookstore is located on Maple <u>street</u> in New Orleans.

┌HELP───

A dictionary and an atlas can help you correctly complete Exercise 2.

Exercise 2 Writing Proper Nouns

ANSWERS
Responses will vary. If possible, have dictionaries, geography books, or atlases available for students to use.

DIRECT TEACHING

Correcting Misconceptions
Capitalizing Direction Words.
Students may mistakenly capitalize words indicating direction, such as *north* and *south.* It may help students understand the difference between words used to indicate direction and the same words used to indicate a section of the country by telling them that an article (*a, an,* or *the*) will be used before a section of the country, such as *the Wild West.* If there is no article, there should be no capital letter.

DIFFERENTIATING INSTRUCTION

Special Education Students
Students with visual-processing deficits may have great difficulty differentiating between a proper noun and a common noun in written text. It may be helpful, when involved in class discussion on this topic, to pay special attention to these students by asking them to make up a proper noun name for a given common noun. Once you are sure they understand the information, read each sentence in **Exercise 3** aloud. Ask the students to state which words are proper nouns and need capitalization. Finally, instruct students to copy the sentence on paper, using correct capitalization. Hearing and speaking proper nouns will help students recognize them visually.

MECHANICS

(3) Capitalize the names of organizations, teams, institutions, and government bodies.

Type of Name	Examples
Organizations	Math Club Oakdale Chamber of Commerce Boy Scouts
Teams	New York Mets Los Angeles Lakers Riverside Raiders
Institutions	University of Oklahoma Kennedy Middle School Mount Sinai Hospital
Government Bodies	League of Arab States Department of Education Federal Bureau of Investigation

NOTE Do not capitalize words such as *hotel, theater,* and *high school* unless they are part of a proper name.

EXAMPLES	Fremont Hotel	the hotel
	Apollo Theater	a theater
	Ames High School	that high school

(4) Capitalize the names of special events, holidays, and calendar items.

Type of Name	Examples	
Special Events	World Series New York Marathon	Parade of Roses Tulip Festival
Holidays	Thanksgiving Labor Day	Martin Luther King, Jr., Day
Calendar Items	Sunday Father's Day	December April Fools' Day

STYLE TIP

The names of government bodies are generally abbreviated.

EXAMPLES
FBI   IRS

Reference Note

For more information on **abbreviations,** see pages 250 and 265.

MECHANICS

DIFFERENTIATING INSTRUCTION

English-Language Learners

General Strategies. In English, the names of days of the week and months of the year are capitalized. In some languages, such as Czech, French, Polish, Portuguese, Romanian, Russian, Spanish, and Vietnamese, those names are written with lowercase letters. For example, *Saturday* is *samedi* in French, *simbata* in Romanian, *sabado* in Spanish, *subbota* in Russian, and *thu bay* in Vietnamese. You may need to remind some students to capitalize these words in English.

NOTE Do not capitalize the name of a season unless it is part of a proper name.

EXAMPLES   a **w**inter storm   the **W**inter **F**estival

(5) Capitalize the names of historical events and periods.

Type of Name	Examples	
Historical Events	**B**oston **T**ea **P**arty **B**attle of **H**astings **W**ar of 1812	**N**ew **D**eal **M**arch on **W**ashington
Historical Periods	**B**ronze **A**ge **R**eformation	**G**reat **D**epression **R**enaissance

Exercise 4 **Correcting Errors in the Use of Capital Letters**

For the following sentences, identify each <u>word that should be</u> <u>capitalized but is not</u>. Then, write the word or words correctly.

EXAMPLE   1. Hart middle school is having a book fair.

　　　　　　 1. *Middle School*

1. Would you like to go to the movies this <u>friday</u>?
2. I think that the <u>special</u> Olympics will be held in our town this year.
3. What plans have you made for <u>easter</u>?
4. My sister and I were born at <u>memorial</u> Hospital.
5. The Rotary <u>club</u> donated equipment for our school's gym.
6. Did dinosaurs live during the <u>stone</u> Age?
7. My favorite baseball team is the Atlanta <u>braves</u>.
8. I always look forward to the first day of <u>springfest</u>.
9. The <u>united states</u> Congress is made up of the <u>senate</u> and the <u>house</u> of <u>representatives</u>.
10. Did you see any fireworks on the <u>fourth</u> of July?
11. Donna's youngest sister is going to join the <u>girl scouts</u> next Wednesday.
12. Our family has a wonderful time at the Alaska <u>renaissance</u> <u>festival</u> each year.

PRACTICE

Guided and Independent
You may wish to use the first ten items in **Exercise 4** as guided practice. Then, have students complete the exercise as independent practice.

HOMEWORK

Exercise 4

DISTRIBUTED REVIEW
After students have corrected the capitalization errors in **Exercise 4**, ask them to identify the prepositional phrases in sentences 3, 4, 15, and 20.

[3. *for Easter;* 4. *at Memorial Hospital;* 15. *during the Middle Ages;* 20. *in May*]

Ask students to identify the function of each proper noun in those sentences. [*object of a preposition*]

EXTENSION

Creative Capitalization

Students who have a firm grasp of **Rules 11a–d** may want to examine some works by writers who use capitalization in creative or unusual ways. As they progress through these rules, students should collect examples of creative capitalization, analyze its effects, and discuss their findings with the class. Students should be prepared to give their opinions about why the authors chose to break or bend the rules. Possible writers to study include Rudyard Kipling and E. E. Cummings. Remind students that creative capitalization is acceptable only in fiction or poetry.

DIFFERENTIATING INSTRUCTION

English-Language Learners

Spanish. Point out to Spanish-speaking students that while adjectives derived from geography, such as those relating to languages, races, peoples, and nationalities, are not capitalized in Spanish, they are capitalized in English. You may wish to ask students about capitalization rules in their native languages and let students discuss how these rules differ from English ones.

STYLE TIP

The words *black* and *white* may or may not be capitalized when they refer to people. Either way is correct.

EXAMPLE
During the Civil War, many **B**lack [or **b**lack] people joined the Union forces.

13. The Grand hotel used to have Roman and Egyptian statues in its lobby.
14. Dave teaches at either the university of Florida or the university of Miami.
15. Why would you like to have lived during the middle ages?
16. If you like baseball games, you will enjoy watching the Texas rangers play.
17. Mrs. Nelson's class prepared the library display about civil rights day.
18. For fifteen years, spring carnival has been our school's main fund-raiser.
19. During the French revolution, people demanded their freedom and rights.
20. We'll be visiting my cousin's high school in may.

(6) Capitalize the names of nationalities, races, and peoples.

Type of Name	Examples	
Nationalities, Races, and Peoples	**M**exican **M**icronesian **C**herokee	**S**wiss **C**aucasian **B**antu

(7) Capitalize the names of businesses and the brand names of business products.

Type of Name	Examples
Businesses	**J.** and **J.** **C**onstruction, **I**nc. **U**ptown **S**hoe **S**tore **G**rommet **M**anufacturing **C**ompany
Business Products	**G**oodyear **A**quatred **N**ikon **P**ronea **F**ord **R**anger

NOTE Names of types of products are not capitalized.

EXAMPLES Goodyear **t**ires, Nikon **c**amera, Ford **t**ruck

(8) Capitalize the names of ships, trains, aircraft, and spacecraft.

Type of Name	Examples	
Ships	*Santa Maria*	*Monitor*
Trains	*Coast Starlight*	*City of Miami*
Aircraft	*Air Force One*	*Spirit of St. Louis*
Spacecraft	*Columbia*	*Lunar Prospector*

(9) Capitalize the names of buildings and other structures.

Type of Name	Examples	
Buildings	**F**latiron **B**uilding **G**allier **H**all	**W**orld **T**rade **C**enter
Other Structures	**H**oover **D**am **A**lamodome	**G**olden **G**ate **B**ridge

(10) Capitalize the names of monuments, memorials, and awards.

Statue of **L**iberty	**L**incoln **M**emorial	**P**ulitzer **P**rize

(11) Capitalize the names of religions and their followers, holy days and celebrations, sacred writings, and specific deities.

Type of Name	Examples	
Religions and Followers	**B**uddhism **T**aoism	**C**hristian **J**ew
Holy Days and Celebrations	**P**urim **C**hristmas	**R**amadan **A**sh **W**ednesday
Sacred Writings	**D**ead **S**ea **S**crolls **B**ible	**K**oran **T**almud
Specific Deities	**A**llah **G**od	**V**ishnu **J**ehovah

Reference Note

For information on using **italics (underlining) for the names of vehicles,** see page 291.

COMPUTER TIP

A computer's spellchecker or style checker might spot some capitalization errors for you.

However, you cannot rely on these programs to find all your mistakes. Since many words are capitalized in some situations but not in others, the computer cannot find every error. Also, the computer might mistakenly highlight a word that is already correct.

Always proofread your writing carefully to make sure you have used capital letters correctly.

RETEACHING

Capitalizing Proper Nouns

Many young students like to create names for things. Read aloud to students the sentences below. Then, ask students to copy the sentences on a sheet of paper and to fill in the blanks.

1. If I discovered a new continent, I would name it _____.

2. If I could rename my school, I would call it _____.

3. If I raised a racehorse, I would name it _____.

4. If I built a sailboat, I would name it _____.

5. If I could rename a favorite holiday, I would call it _____.

6. If I founded my own country, I would name it _____.

7. If I could rename my (town, city, community), I would call it _____.

8. If I could rename the month when I was born, I would call it _____.

Have students check that all of the proper nouns they created are capitalized, circle the proper nouns, and note to the side the relevant capitalization rule and subrule for each one.

MECHANICS

NOTE The words *god* and *goddess* are not capitalized when they refer to deities of ancient mythology. However, the names of specific mythological gods and goddesses are capitalized.

EXAMPLE The Roman **g**od of the sea was **N**eptune.

(12) Capitalize the names of planets, stars, constellations, and other heavenly bodies.

Mars	**P**luto	**North S**tar	**B**etelgeuse
Milky **W**ay	**B**ig **D**ipper	**U**rsa **M**inor	**S**irius

NOTE The word *earth* is not capitalized unless it is used along with the names of other heavenly bodies that are capitalized. The words *sun* and *moon* generally are not capitalized.

EXAMPLES China is home to one fourth of the people on **e**arth.

How far is Saturn from **E**arth?

The **s**un rose at 7:09 this morning.

Oral Practice **Identifying Words That Should Be Capitalized**

Read each of the following sentences aloud, and identify words that should be capitalized.

EXAMPLE 1. We went to the leesburg library to learn more about african american history.

1. *Leesburg Library, African American*

1. The methodist quoted a verse from the bible.
2. Bob has a chevrolet truck.
3. On a clear night you can see venus from earth.
4. My teacher took a cruise on the *song of norway*.
5. Meet me in front of the woolworth building.
6. Pilar received the junior achievement award.
7. Otis made a detailed scale model of the spacecraft *nozomi*.
8. Elena wrote a poem about the greek god zeus.
9. Some navajo make beautiful silver jewelry.
10. Who were the first europeans to settle in mexico?

Review A Correcting Sentences by Capitalizing
Proper Nouns

For each of the following sentences, correctly write the <u>word</u>
<u>or words</u> that should be capitalized.

EXAMPLE **1.** In the late nineteenth century, henry morton
stanley explored an area of africa occupied by
ancestors of the bambuti.

1. *Henry Morton Stanley, Africa, Bambuti*

1. The <u>bambuti</u> people live in the <u>ituri</u> <u>forest</u>, which is
located in the northeast area of the Democratic <u>republic</u>
of the <u>congo</u>.

2. This forest is located almost exactly in the middle of the
continent of <u>africa</u>.

3. It lies north of <u>mungbere</u>, as shown in the boxed area
on the map to the right.

4. The <u>bambuti</u> people, also known as <u>twides</u>,
<u>aka</u>, or <u>efe</u>, have lived there for many
thousands of years.

5. The earliest record of people like the
Bambuti is found in the notes of explorers
from <u>egypt</u> about 2500 B.C.

6. Other early reports of these people are found
on colorful tiles in <u>italy</u> and in the records
of explorers from <u>portugal</u>.

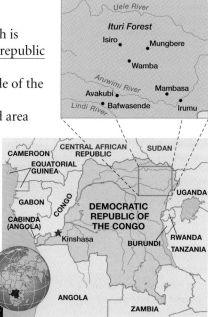

EXTENSION

Review A To emphasize map-
reading skills and the capitalization
of geographical terms, you may want
to use the extension of **Review A**
below as an oral activity or write the
questions on the chalkboard for students to answer in writing. If you use
this exercise as an oral activity, ask
students to indicate which words
should be capitalized.

1. Which city is on the Aruwimi River?
[*Avakubi*]

2. What is the capital of the
Democratic Republic of the Congo?
[*Kinshasa*]

3. What three rivers run through the
Ituri Forest? [*Uele, Aruwimi, and
Lindi*]

4. What two countries border the
Democratic Republic of the Congo
to the south? [*Angola, Zambia*]

5. What city is southeast of Mambasa?
[*Irumu*]

MECHANICS

Using Capital Letters

Rules 11e–h *(pp. 250–258)*

OBJECTIVES

- To correct errors in sentences in the capitalization of school subjects, proper adjectives, abbreviations, and titles

- To write titles for imaginary works and to capitalize them correctly

DIRECT TEACHING

Modeling and Demonstration

Using Capital Letters. Model how to proofread sentences for correct capitalization by using the example *My social studies teacher, mr. cleve, and my english teacher, mrs. brown, both have irish ancestors.* First, ask whether *social studies* should be capitalized. [*no*] Next, ask whether *english* should be capitalized. [*yes*] Point out that school subjects are not capitalized, except (1) course names followed by numbers and (2) language classes. Next, ask whether there are any other proper nouns that should be capitalized. [*yes; Cleve and Brown*] Then, ask whether any abbreviations need to be capitalized. [*yes; Mr. and Mrs.*] Finally, ask whether there are any proper adjectives that need to be capitalized. [*yes; Irish*]. Now, have a volunteer use an example from the chapter to demonstrate how to proofread for capitalization.

MECHANICS

MEETING THE CHALLENGE

Make a list of the school subjects you are taking this year. Then, choose four of the subjects and write a sentence for each. The sentences can be descriptive or can explain why a subject is fun, easy, or difficult. After you have finished your sentences, check to be sure the school subjects you have used correctly follow **Rule 11e**.

EXAMPLE
My last class before lunch is Language Arts I.

ANSWERS
Student answers will vary, but school subjects should be capitalized according to **Rule 11e.**

Reference Note

For more information on **proper adjectives,** see page 40.

Reference Note

For information on using **abbreviations,** see page 265.

7. Stanley met some of the bambuti people, but he didn't write much about them.
8. In the 1920s, paul schebesta went to africa to learn more about the Bambuti people.
9. He learned that the bambuti are very different from the bantu and from other neighbors.
10. In fact, the bambuti were probably the first people in the rain forest that stretches across central africa from the atlantic ocean on the western coast to the eastern grasslands.

11e. Do not capitalize the names of school subjects, except course names followed by a numeral and the names of language classes.

EXAMPLES   social studies, science, health, art, Woodworking II, Consumer Education I, Spanish, English

11f. Capitalize proper adjectives.

A *proper adjective* is formed from a proper noun. Proper adjectives are usually capitalized.

Proper Noun	Proper Adjective
Mexico	Mexican carvings
King Arthur	Arthurian legend
Judaism	Judaic laws
Mars	Martian landscape

11g. Most abbreviations are capitalized.

Capitalize abbreviations that come before and after personal names.

EXAMPLES   Mr., Ms., Mrs., Dr., Gen., M.D., RN, Jr., Sr.

Capitalize abbreviations of the names of organizations, businesses, and government bodies.

EXAMPLES   Inc., Co., Corp., FBI, UN, NAACP, FDA

In addresses, capitalize abbreviations such as those for roads, rooms, and post office boxes.

EXAMPLES   Ave., Dr., Rd., St., Apt., Rm., P.O. Box

250   Chapter 11   Capital Letters

RESOURCES

Using Capital Letters (Rules e–h)
Practice
- *Language & Sentence Skills Practice,* pp. 221–231

Abbreviations of geographical names are capitalized.

EXAMPLES **N.Y.C.**   **S**t. Louis   **N.** America   **O**kla.

> NOTE A two-letter state abbreviation without periods is used when the abbreviation is followed by a ZIP Code. Each letter of the abbreviation is capitalized.
>
> EXAMPLES   Austin, **TX** 78704-6364
>
> New Orleans, **LA** 70131-5140

Some abbreviations, especially those for measurements, are not capitalized.

EXAMPLES   **e**tc., **e.g.**, **v**ol., **c**hap., **in.**, **y**d, **l**b, **cc**, **m**l, **m**m

Exercise 5 Correcting Errors in Capitalization

For each of the following sentences, correctly write each word or abbreviation that should be capitalized.

EXAMPLE   1. I went with mrs. McCain to visit mr. Brennan in the retirement home.
    1. *Mrs., Mr.*

1. The address was p.o. box 32, Green Bay, Wi 54305.   **1.** WI
2. The new student had just moved to our town from st. Petersburg, Florida.
3. Will gen. Scott Quinn be speaking tonight?
4. Mr. Lloyd Mitchell, jr., has been appointed president of Sprockets and Widgets, inc.
5. The next speaker for Career Day will be Chet Patterson, rn, who works at the local hospital.   **5.** RN
6. Blair O'Brien, cpa, has a top-floor office in the Hanley corp. building.   **6.** CPA
7. The Fbi, the Fda, and the Un have decided to cooperate on the investigation.   **7.** FBI/FDA/UN
8. Are you taking art II or spanish?
9. Many scottish people have celtic, scandinavian, and irish ancestors.
10. The Chisholm Trail, which stretched over one thousand miles from San Antonio, tex., to Abilene, kans., was used by cowboys to drive cattle north.

DIRECT TEACHING

Capitalizing Names of School Subjects

Activity. Have your students name all of the school subjects they are taking during the current school year. Using only lowercase letters, list those subjects on the chalkboard. Then, invite volunteers to come to the chalkboard one at a time and to write a sentence about a subject in the list. The sentences can be descriptive or can explain why a subject is fun, easy, or difficult. When each volunteer has finished writing a sentence, have the rest of the class check the sentence to see if **Rule 11e** was correctly followed.

DIFFERENTIATING INSTRUCTION

Advanced Learners

Have students work in small groups to analyze the types of changes made in the spellings of proper nouns converted to proper adjectives. Students could develop categories and give examples of the various types of changes. [*Examples may include adding –n: Cuban, American; adding –ese: Vietnamese, Japanese; and adding –ian: Egyptian, Arabian.*]

After students have completed the activity, have them share their findings with the rest of the class.

RETEACHING

Capitalizing Abbreviations

You might want to have students create a step-by-step process to determine whether a particular abbreviation should be capitalized, as required by **Rule 11g.** Have students write the following five-question process on a sheet of paper:

1. Does the abbreviation come either before or after a personal name?

2. Does the abbreviation stand for the name of an organization, business, or governmental body?

3. Does the abbreviation stand for a geographical name?

4. Is the abbreviation part of an address?

5. Does the abbreviation stand for a measurement?

Point out that if the answer to any of questions 1–4 is *yes,* then the abbreviation should be capitalized. However, if the answer to question 5 is *yes,* then the abbreviation probably should not be capitalized.

Students might want to create a diagram that shows each step (question) in the process and an example for each step. Some students might want to create similar step-by-step processes for other capitalization rules.

Review B **Proofreading a Letter for Correct Capitalization**

Read the following letter. For each numbered word group, identify any words or abbreviations that are not capitalized correctly. Rewrite the words or abbreviations with correct capitalization. If a sentence is already correct, write *C.*

EXAMPLE **[1]** 1066 south Norman st.

1. *South, St.*

March 14, 2003

Mr. Leonard Thornton
1234 Windswept Dr.
1. PA   **[1]** Lancaster, Pa 17601

[2] dear Mr. Thornton:

   [3] I think that the easiest thing you could do to help make lancaster better is to make it safer to ride bicycles here. **[4]** My friend James almost got hit by a car on his way to Memorial middle school. **[5]** As a member of our city's Transportation advisory Board, you can do a lot to encourage cyclists to wear helmets.

6. C   **[6]** Also, in Earth Science I class, we have learned that if more people used bicycles instead of cars, the air would be cleaner. **[7]** One company that I know of, Universal Solutions, inc., rewards people who ride bicycles to work. **[8]** Many cities, such as Boulder, colorado, are building bicycle lanes. **[9]** maybe you could help with programs like these. Thank you for your attention to this matter.

          [10] yours truly,

          Tate Washington

          Tate Washington

11h. Capitalize titles.

(1) Capitalize a person's title when the title comes before the person's name.

EXAMPLES   **J**udge O'Connor   **P**rincipal Walsh

                     Mrs. Santos   **D**octor Ellis

                     Senator Topping   **P**resident Truman

(2) Titles used alone or following a person's name generally are not capitalized.

EXAMPLES   Judy Klein, our club **p**resident, led the meeting.

                     The **s**ecretary gave a speech to Congress.

However, a title used alone in direct address usually is capitalized.

EXAMPLES   Can the cast come off today, **D**octor?

                     Good morning, **M**a'am [or **m**a'am].

(3) Capitalize a word showing a family relationship when the word is used before or in place of a person's name.

EXAMPLES   Are **U**ncle Carlos and **A**unt Rosa here yet?

                     Either **M**om or **D**ad will drive us to the show.

Do not capitalize a word showing a family relationship when the word follows a possessive noun or pronoun.

EXAMPLE   My **c**ousin Dena and her **n**iece Leotie made stew.

Exercise 6 **Correcting Sentences by Capitalizing Words**

For each of the following sentences, correctly write the <u>word or words that should be capitalized</u>. If a sentence is already correct, write *C*.

EXAMPLE   **1.** Thank you, aunt Shirley, for the pretty sweater.

               1. *Aunt*

1. He says that <u>judge</u> Johnson is very strict.
2. Reuben's mother, <u>mrs.</u> Santos, owns the new restaurant.

┌─ **HELP** ─

You may capitalize a title used alone or following a person's name if you want to emphasize the person's high office.

EXAMPLE

   Please come and meet Texas' native daughter and our country's **S**ecretary of **S**tate.

MECHANICS

3. Will your uncle be at the party?　　**3.** C
4. Well, doctor Sakamoto, do I need braces?
5. Did the secretary of state attend the meeting?
6. Is cousin Josie going to Israel?　　**5.** C [*or* Secretary of State]
7. Please accept my apologies, senator.
8. On Saturday, aunt Latisha will arrive from Savannah.
9. Does professor Jones teach American history?
10. I learned to swim at grandpa Brown's cottage on the lake last summer.

Review C **Using Capital Letters Correctly in Sentences**

For each of the following sentences, correctly write the word or words that should be capitalized.

EXAMPLE　　**1.** The Civil war is sometimes called the war between the states.

　　1. War, War Between the States

1. There is a fountain in the middle of lake Eola.
2. dr. jones teaches at York high school.
3. Some of these folk songs are mexican.
4. the atlantic borders the states from maine to florida.
5. Someday i would like to bicycle through europe.
6. all of my friends came to the party.
7. Have you visited the Washington monument?
8. Our history class wrote letters to the secretary-general of the united nations.　　**8.** [*or* Secretary-General]
9. There's a long detour on highway 50 just east of brooksville, dad.
10. Our first fall camping trip will be in october.

(4) Capitalize the first and last words and all important words in titles and subtitles.

Unimportant words in a title include:

- articles (*a, an, the*)

Reference Note

For a list of **prepositions,** see page 63.

- coordinating conjunctions (*and, but, for, nor, or, so, yet*)

- prepositions of fewer than five letters (such as *by, for, into, on, with*)

MINI-LESSON **Mechanics**

Punctuating Titles. Students might ask why some titles are in italics while others are enclosed in quotation marks. Explain that titles of books, plays, periodicals, films, television programs, works of art, long musical works, ships, aircraft, and spacecraft are italicized in print or on a computer or underlined when handwritten or typed. Titles of short works, such as poems or short stories, are enclosed in quotation marks. Then, ask students whether the titles of the following works should be italicized or

Type of Name	Examples	
Books	*The Horse and His Boy*	*Dust Tracks on a Road*
Magazines	*Sports Illustrated for Kids*	*Essence* *Reader's Digest*
Newspapers	*Detroit Free Press* *The Fresno Bee*	*Tulsa Tribune* *The Denver Post*
Poems	"The City Is So Big" "The Sneetches"	"For a Poet" "Steam Shovel"
Short Stories	"The Day the Sun Came Out"	"The Six Rows of Pompons"
Plays	*Once on This Island*	*A Chorus Line*
Comic Strips	*Peanuts*	*Rose Is Rose*
Movies	*Babe: Pig in the City*	*A Bug's Life* *The King and I*
Television Programs	*Touched by an Angel* *Sister, Sister*	*Star Trek: Deep Space Nine*
Videos	*The Lion King II: Simba's Pride*	*Basic Sign Language*
Video Games	*Mario Kart 64*	*Escape Velocity*
Compact Discs	*Bringing Down the Horse*	*Mi Tierra* *Ray of Light*
Audiotapes	*Tiger Woods: The Makings of a Champion*	*My Family Tree: A Recorded History*
Works of Art	*Delfina and Dimas*	*Forever Free*
Musical Works	"Oh, What a Beautiful Morning"	*Peter and the Wolf* "Angel of Mine"

Reference Note

For guidelines on using **italics (underlining)** and **quotation marks with titles,** see pages 290 and 297.

DIFFERENTIATING INSTRUCTION

Learners Having Difficulty

Have students write sentences about titles with which they are familiar. They should each write one sentence about each of the following topics.

1. a favorite television show

2. a favorite book

3. a favorite movie

4. a movie I didn't like

5. a song I like

6. a newspaper

7. a short story I've read

Instruct students to write complete sentences and to capitalize titles correctly. Have students exchange papers with partners, and have partners check the work, referring to **Rule 11h(4).** Allow time for partners to discuss discrepancies in capitalization.

MECHANICS

---

enclosed in quotation marks.

- this textbook [*italics/underlining*]

- a popular movie [*italics/underlining*]

- an article from the front page of the newspaper [*quotation marks*]

For more information on punctuating titles, refer students to **Chapter 13: Punctuation.**

Exercise 7 Writing Titles for Imaginary Works

ANSWERS

Answers will vary. Titles should be capitalized correctly. Here are some possibilities:

1. *Detective Echohawk*
2. *Video Cast*
3. *How to Choose Your Dog*
4. "Save the Trees"
5. *Suburban Gothic*
6. "Baby, Please Come Home"
7. *Amigo in Argentina*
8. *Literary Giggles*
9. "Lost and Found"
10. *Battling Bobcat News*

┌─HELP───

To find out how to correctly word and capitalize the official title of a book, look on the title page of that book. For the official title of a newspaper or periodical, look on the masthead (the section that lists the title, publisher, editors, and other information), which usually appears on the editorial page or in the table of contents. Check to see if the word *the* is included as the first word in the official title. If *the* is not included, do not capitalize the word if you use it in front of the title.

EXAMPLES

My uncle reads **The** *New York Times*.
Do you have a copy of **the** *Detroit Free Press*?

NOTE An article (*a, an,* or *the*) before a title is not capitalized unless it is the first word of the official title.

EXAMPLES   Do you read **t**he *Sacramento Bee*?

Grandmother showed Nehal and me an article in **T**he *Workbasket*.

My mother reads **T**he *Wall Street Journal*.

Coordinating conjunctions and prepositions that begin a title or subtitle are capitalized.

EXAMPLES   I have read **T**hrough *the Looking Glass* three times.

Marcia said that **B**ut *I'll Be Back Again* was very interesting.

Exercise 7 Writing Titles for Imaginary Works

Create a title for each item described below. Be sure each title is capitalized correctly.

EXAMPLE   1. a video about training pet birds
   1. *How to Be Your Bird's Best Friend*

1. a movie about an American Indian detective who solves a murder mystery
2. a magazine for people interested in video games about fly-fishing in Montana
3. a book about choosing the best breed of dog as a pet for your family
4. a song about saving the rain forests
5. a painting about life in a modern suburb somewhere in the United States
6. a poem about a new baby brother or sister coming home for the first time
7. a play about a student's first day at a new school in a South American country
8. a television show about the humorous people who visit the local library
9. a short story about students who go on a field trip to an animal park and get stuck there overnight
10. a newspaper published by the athletics department

Learning for Life

Continued on pp. 257–258

Writing to a Pen Pal. Tell students that many people enjoy writing to pen pals from other parts of the United States or from places around the world. While these pen pals might never meet each other, the correspondence can be a fun way to learn about people and ways of life in other places. Ask your students to each write a letter to a pen pal elsewhere in the United States or in another country. Students can find pen pals by searching appropriate Internet sites or by checking youth-oriented

Correct any incorrect capital or lowercase letters in titles in the following sentences. If a sentence is already correct, write *C*.

EXAMPLE   **1.** Mom gave me an article called "the importance Of fitness."

       1. "The Importance of Fitness"

1. "Heart And Soul" is the only piano duet we can play.
2. Do you read *National geographic World*?
3. My little sister loves *the Cat in the Hat*.
4. I saw *Around the World in Eighty Days* on television.   **4.** C
5. We enjoy watching reruns of *The Cosby show*.
6. My mother likes to work the crossword puzzle in *the New York times*.
7. The children look forward to receiving their copies of *Ranger rick* each month.
8. Tony's short story "a few words about Aunt Frederica's dog Smitty and all his friends" certainly has the longest title of any story written by a member of the class.
9. "A Poem About A Poem" is the title of Mary Elizabeth's funny poem.
10. Julie Andrews' singing is a special feature of the movie *the sound of music*.

Words that should be capitalized or lowercased are underscored.

Review D Proofreading a Paragraph to Correct Errors in Capitalization

Proofread the following paragraph, correcting any errors in the use of capital and lowercase letters.

EXAMPLE   **[1]** what a huge Ship the *titanic* was!

      1. What, ship, Titanic

[1] This magnificent ocean liner sank on april 15, 1912. [2] For more than seventy years, the *Titanic* lay untouched in the icy waters of the atlantic ocean. [3] Then, on September 1, 1985, Dr. Robert Ballard of the woods hole oceanographic institution and his crew found the ship. [4] To view the Ocean floor, the scientists used the remote-controlled vehicle *Argo*, shown on the next page. [5] once they discovered the ship, they attached a special underwater sled to *Argo*. [6] The sled,

Words that should be capitalized or lowercased are underscored.

Learners Having Difficulty
You may want to suggest that students ask family members to think of titles in the following categories:

1. a well-known poem
2. a favorite magazine
3. a newspaper
4. a famous painting
5. a favorite song

Have students use capital letters correctly to record responses.

MECHANICS

magazines. A librarian might be able to help. Caution students never to write to or share personal information with a pen pal unless they have the permission of a parent or guardian. If students are unable to get permission or locate a pen pal, have them write to imaginary pen pals or perhaps a relative or friend in another state or country.

    Each letter should include the name of the writer and his or her age, school, town, state, and country. A writer also may want

with its lights and camera, provided dr. Ballard with more than twenty thousand photographs of the *Titanic*. [**7**] In 1986, Dr. Ballard and his Team returned to explore the wreck of the british ocean liner once more. [**8**] using a minisubmarine, the team was able to explore the sunken ship. [**9**] after years of wondering about the *Titanic*, underwater explorers finally found the Wreck and uncovered the truth about its fate. [**10**] In his book *The discovery of the Titanic*, Dr. Ballard tells about his underwater adventures.

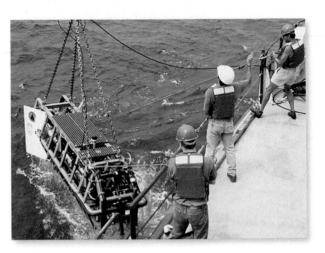

Learning for Life   *Continued from p. 257*

to include information about his or her birthday, favorite books, movies, foods, and other things. When students have finished, have them check their letter for correct capitalization. Afterward, ask students to mail their letters. You also may want them to save a copy for future reference.

1. [11f]
2. [11d(4)]
3. [11d(2)]
4. [11a]
5. [11d(10)]
6. [11c]
7. [11d(3)]
8. [11h(4)]
9. [11g, h(1)]
10. [11d(2)]
11. [11d(7)]
12. [11a, h(4)]
13. [11d(3)]
14. [11d(2)]
15. [11d(5), f]
16. [11d(8)]
17. [11d(11)]
18. [11d(2)]
19. [11a, d(2)]
20. [11e]

21. [11d(2)]

Chapter Review

A. Proofreading Sentences for Correct Capitalization

Words that should be capitalized or lowercased are underscored.

For each of the following sentences, correctly write the word or words that contain an error in capitalization.

1. Sean's dog, Ransom, is a german shepherd.
2. Our Spring vacation begins on march 26.
3. Write to me at 439 Walnut street.
4. Mira asked, "do you know why the *Titanic* sank?"
5. In 1998, David Trimble and John Hume of Northern Ireland jointly won the Nobel peace prize.
6. As soon as i finish my English homework, i'll call you.
7. She would like to go to College someday.
8. We watched a scene from *Romeo And Juliet*.
9. Eric's orthodontist is dr. McCambridge.
10. On Saturday my aunt is taking us to jones beach.
11. Dad used the general Electric waffle iron to make breakfast.
12. have you seen my copy of *newsweek*?
13. The Peace corps volunteers helped build a bridge.
14. The capital of Peru is lima.
15. The French revolution changed european society.
16. The spacecraft *sputnik 2* carried a dog named Laika.
17. Tom's brother is a roman catholic priest.
18. Although I live in Biloxi now, I'm from the north.
19. I answered, "the gulf of Mexico, I think."
20. Are you taking spanish or art this year?

B. Correcting Sentences by Using Capital Letters Correctly

For the following sentences, correctly write each word that contains an incorrect capital or lowercase letter.

21. Malaysia is in the Southeastern part of Asia.

Chapter Review   **259**

ASSESSING

Monitoring Progress
Chapter Review. To assess student progress, you may want to compare the types of items missed on the **Diagnostic Preview** to those missed on the **Chapter Review.** If students have not made significant progress, you may want to refer them to **Chapter 15: Correcting Common Errors, Exercises 22** and **23** for additional practice.

DIRECT TEACHING

Cooperative Learning
Using Correct Capitalization. After students have completed the **Chapter Review,** have them work in small groups to compare their answers. When they have finished discussing the sentences, you may want to have students correct their papers by writing the rule that applies to each error made and then writing the correction. You may want to have them write additional sentences for each type of error that they made.

MECHANICS

22. [11d(6)]
23. [11d(2)]
24. [11d(1, 7, 2)]
25. [11f, d(7)]
26. [11d(2,11)]
27. [11h(2)]
28. [11h(2), d(3)]
29. [11d(1)]
30. [11d(1), h(4)]

22. Its largest ethnic groups are <u>malay</u>, <u>chinese</u>, and <u>indian</u>.
23. The capital and largest city is <u>kuala lumpur</u>.
24. Much of the world's <u>Rubber</u> comes from Malaysia.
25. Other <u>Major</u> products are <u>Tin</u> and <u>Palm Oil</u>.
26. Most inhabitants of <u>malaysia</u> are <u>muslims</u>.
27. Malaysia is a constitutional monarchy headed by a <u>King</u>.
28. The <u>Prime Minister</u> is the <u>Leader</u> of the <u>Government</u>.
29. Many Malays wear the <u>Sarong</u>, a kind of skirt.
30. The <u>Encyclopedia</u> called *World book* can give you more information about Malaysia.

C. Correcting Errors in Capitalization

For the following sentences and word groups, correctly write each <u>word</u> and each <u>abbreviation</u> that should be capitalized.

31. NY [11d(2), g]
32. [11d(2)]
33. [11h(4)]
34. [11g, h(1), d(4)]
35. CIA [11h(3), d(3)]
36. [11a]
37. [11d(2)]
38. [11h(1)]
39. [11h(4)]
40. [11b]

31. Todd's new address is 1240 <u>mud road</u>, Setauket, <u>Ny</u> 11733-2851.
32. The exchange student is from San <u>remo</u>, Italy.
33. My parents' favorite television movie is *Lonesome <u>dove</u>*.
34. We went with <u>mrs.</u> Rigatti to see the floats in the San <u>gennaro</u> Festival.
35. It was a surprise to learn that <u>uncle</u> Elwood had been in the <u>Cia</u> all those years.
36. <u>isn't</u> your aunt Etta here?
37. Mont <u>blanc</u>, the highest peak in the <u>alps</u>, was first climbed in 1786.
38. We sent a petition to <u>mayor</u> Moore.
39. Millie enjoyed reading *Anne of Green <u>gables</u>* so much that she rented the movie.
40. <u>yours</u> sincerely, Beth Tewes

Writing Application
Using Capital Letters in an Essay

Proper Nouns Your social studies teacher has asked you to write about a vacation you would like to take to a historical place. Write an essay telling where you would like to go and why you would like to go there. In your essay, use at least five proper nouns.

Prewriting First, brainstorm a list of historical places that interest you. Which of these places would you most like to visit? Write down notes about what you would do during your visit.

Writing Begin your rough draft by stating where you would like to go and why. Explain what historical event or events happened at that place. Then, tell what particular areas or landmarks you would visit. Be sure to use at least five proper nouns naming places, events, and people.

Revising Ask a friend to read your draft and tell you if any parts seem unclear or uninteresting. Then, revise anything that is confusing or boring.

Publishing Use an encyclopedia or other reference source to check the spelling of any proper nouns you have included. Proofread your essay carefully for any other errors in grammar, spelling, capitalization, and punctuation. Put your essay on poster board, along with pictures or drawings of the place you wrote about in your essay. With your teacher's permission, display your poster in the classroom.

┌─HELP─
An encyclopedia can help you learn more about historical places.

MECHANICS

Grade-Level Standards

(Boldface indicates concepts that are taught and tested in this chapter.)

- Language Convention 1.0: **Students write and speak with a command of standard English conventions appropriate to this grade level.**

- Punctuation 1.3: **Use colons after the salutation in business letters, semicolons to connect independent clauses, and commas when linking two clauses with a conjunction in compound sentences.**

Prerequisite/Review Standard

- Punctuation 1.3: Use a colon to separate hours and minutes and to introduce a list; use quotation marks around the exact words of a speaker and titles of poems, songs, short stories, and so forth.

Standards Coming Up in the Next Grade Level

- Grammar 1.4: Demonstrate the mechanics of writing (e.g., quotation marks, commas at end of dependent clauses) and appropriate English usage (e.g., pronoun reference).

- Punctuation 1.5: Identify hyphens, dashes, brackets, and semicolons and use them correctly.

▼

INTRODUCING THE CHAPTER

- The first part of this chapter discusses end marks and abbrevia-

(continued)

CHAPTER

12

1.0 Written and Oral English Language Conventions
Students write and speak with a command of standard English conventions appropriate to this grade level.
1.3 Use colons after the salutation in business letters, semicolons to connect independent clauses, and commas when linking two clauses with a conjunction in compound sentences.

Numerals in brackets refer to rules tested by the items in the Diagnostic Preview.

1. [12a]
2. [12j(3), e, g, a]
3. [12i(1), a]
4. [12f, a]
5. [12b]
6. [12c]
7. [12m, a]

Punctuation
End Marks, Commas, Semicolons, Colons

Diagnostic Preview

Using Periods, Question Marks, Exclamation Points, Commas, Semicolons, and Colons Correctly

The following sentences lack necessary periods, question marks, exclamation points, commas, semicolons, and colons. Write the letter, word, or words that should be followed by a punctuation mark. Then, add the correct punctuation mark after each word. For numerals, write the entire numeral and insert the correct punctuation mark.
Commas that may be considered optional are underscored.

EXAMPLE   **1.** Mr. Cotton my next-door neighbor asked me to pick up his mail while he is away

    1. Cotton, neighbor, away.

1. The mangos and papayas and avocados will make a good fruit salad.
2. Before the slide presentation began Ms. Jee gave a short, clear history of Korea.
3. Ray Charles a popular singer and musician became blind at the age of seven.
4. I've taken classes in photography, ceramics and weaving.
5. When will dinner be ready?
6. Here comes a tornado!
7. Cheryl will take gymnastics Eddie will take piano lessons.

CHAPTER RESOURCES

Internet
- go.hrw.com (keyword: HLLA)

go. hrw .com

Planning
- One-Stop Planner CD-ROM 💿
- On Course: Mapping Instruction
- At Home: A Guide to Standards Mastery, p. 34

Practice & Review
- *Language & Sentence Skills Practice,* pp. 237–250; 251–254
- *Developmental Language & Sentence Skills,* pp. 105–110

Application & Enrichment
- *Language & Sentence Skills Practice,* pp. 255, 258; 236, 256–257

8. Ted mowed the <u>lawn</u>. cleaned the <u>garage</u>. and painted the <u>shed</u>.

9. Would 6:30 P.M. be too <u>early</u>?

10. This Zuni ring was made in Santa <u>Fe</u>. <u>N</u>. <u>Mex</u>.

11. I finished the <u>letter</u>. but I haven't proofread it <u>yet</u>.

12. Dear Senator <u>Hutchison</u>:

13. We will learn about the federal court <u>system</u>. then we will visit the county courthouse.

14. <u>Sara</u>. <u>Eric</u>. and Manuel can speak both Spanish and <u>English</u>.

15. Hurry, get me some <u>ice</u>!

16. <u>Yes</u>. I did clean my <u>room</u>.

17. When you go cross-country skiing, bring the following <u>items</u>: <u>skis</u>. <u>boots</u>. <u>poles</u>. and ski <u>wax</u>.

18. Shall we leave at 9:00 <u>A.M.</u>?

19. <u>Mr</u>. <u>Pak</u>. when is the Chinese New <u>Year</u>?

20. The Scouts' annual dinner will be held February <u>19</u>. 2003.

8. [12f, a]
9. [12o, e, b]
10. [12k(1), e, a]
11. [12h, a]
12. [12p]
13. [12m]
14. [12f, a]
15. [12d]
16. [12j(1), a]
17. [12n, f, d]
18. [12o, b]
19. [12e, i(2), b]
20. [12k(1)]

End Marks

An **end mark** is a punctuation mark placed at the end of a sentence. *Periods, question marks,* and *exclamation points* are end marks. Periods are also used after some abbreviations.

12a. Use a period at the end of a statement.

EXAMPLES   French is the official language of Haiti, but many people there speak Haitian Creole.

I will write to you soon.

Please let me know when you can visit.

12b. Use a question mark at the end of a question.

EXAMPLES   Have you seen the new science fiction movie?

Where should I meet you?

12c. Use an exclamation point at the end of an exclamation.

EXAMPLES   What a cute puppy that is!

Wow! This egg drop soup is hot!

Reference Note

For more information about **classifying sentences by purpose,** see page 18.

┌ H E L P ─────

Periods (decimal points) are also used to separate dollars from cents and whole numbers from fractions.

EXAMPLES
$6.57 [six dollars and fifty-seven cents]
2.7 [two and seven tenths]

In some countries a comma is used instead of a period in such cases.

End Marks   **263**

tions. Then, comma rules are presented, followed by rules for the use of semicolons and colons.

■ The **Chapter Review** offers students the opportunity to test their mastery of punctuation marks. Finally, the **Writing Application** asks students to write a scene for a television show script, using a variety of end marks.

■ For help in integrating this chapter with writing assignments in *Holt Literature and Language Arts,* use the **Teaching Strands** chart on pp. T22–T23.

ASSESSING

Entry-Level Assessment

Diagnostic Preview. Keep in mind that students who can punctuate the sentences in the **Diagnostic Preview** may not transfer this knowledge to their writing. Therefore, it may be necessary to examine students' writing to determine which punctuation rules students need to practice.

You could use the results of the preview to decide which lessons to teach to the entire class and which ones to assign to small groups.

PRETEACHING

Lesson Starter

Motivating. Explain to students that an exclamation point indicates emotion, but it does not indicate a specific emotion. The emotion that is being expressed is usually indicated by the words in the sentence. Have students compose five exclamatory sentences, each expressing a different emotion such as anger, joy, surprise, disbelief, or love. Ask volunteers to write sentences on the chalkboard. Have other students guess which emotion is being expressed in each sentence.

MECHANICS

End Marks

Rules 12a–e *(pp. 263–267)*

OBJECTIVES

- To correct sentences by adding appropriate punctuation

- To correct paragraphs by adding the proper end marks and capital letters to sentences

MECHANICS

DIRECT TEACHING

Modeling and Demonstration

Punctuating Imperative Sentences. Model how to punctuate imperative sentences by using the example *Please sit down.* First, ask whether the imperative sentence is a request, a mild command, or a strong command. [*request*] Next, ask what mark of punctuation is used at the end of a request. [*period*] Place a period at the end of the sentence. Then, have a volunteer use another example in this chapter to demonstrate how to punctuate an imperative sentence.

STYLE **TIP**

In your own writing, make sure to use exclamation points only when you want to emphasize a strong feeling. Do not overuse exclamation points, or they will lose their effectiveness.

ORIGINAL
The little gray cat looked up at Judy! With one look, Judy knew this was the kitty for her! How lucky that she had visited the animal shelter today!

REVISED
The little gray cat looked up at Judy. With one look, Judy knew this was the kitty for her. How lucky that she had visited the animal shelter today!

┌HELP─

When you finish Exercise 1, you should have ten complete sentences.

12d. Use either a period or an exclamation point at the end of a request or a command (an imperative sentence).

Use a period after an imperative sentence that makes a request or a mild command. Use an exclamation point after a strong command.

EXAMPLES   Please sit down. [a request]

Sit down. [a mild command]

Sit down right now! [a strong command]

Oral Practice   Adding End Marks to Sentences

Read each of the following sentences aloud. Then, say which end mark—a period, a question mark, or an exclamation point—should be added.

EXAMPLE   **1.** What time is it
            1. question mark

1. When does the bus come?
2. What a great game that was!
3. Did you bring your lunch today?
4. Hyo was born in Korea.
5. I don't understand the assignment.
6. Who can identify the subject of this sentence?
7. Pardon me, sir.
8. Imagine me at the White House! 8. [*or* House.]
9. Get the iguana back into your room right now! 9. [*or* now.]
10. The legend for this map is in the lower right-hand corner.

Exercise 1   Correcting a Paragraph by Adding Capital Letters and End Marks

Decide where the sentences in the following paragraph begin and end. Rewrite each sentence, providing the needed capital letters and end marks.

EXAMPLE   what an ancient art weaving is
            What an ancient art weaving is!

have you ever been to Hawaii the first Europeans who landed there found chiefs dressed in beautiful feather cloaks.

RESOURCES

End Marks

Practice

- *Language & Sentence Skills Practice*, pp. 237–239, 251

feathers for cloaks like the one shown here came from thousands of birds̲different-colored feathers were arranged in royal designs̲ the feathers were then attached to a base of woven fibers̲cloaks were worn in battle and for ceremonies̲ most of the islanders did not wear such fine garments̲ colorful prints are worn by all kinds of people on the islands̲every Friday is Aloha Friday̲on that day many people wear Hawaiian prints and live flowers̲

Robert Dampier, *Kamehameha III* (1825). Oil on canvas (24⅛" × 20⅛"). Honolulu Academy of Arts, gift of Mrs. C. Montague Cooke, Jr., Charles M. Cooke III, and Mrs. Heston Wren, in memory of Dr. C. Montague Cooke, Jr., 1951.

12e. Many abbreviations are followed by periods.

Types of Abbreviations	Examples			
Personal Names	I. M. Pei		J. C. Watts	
	Vicki L. Ruíz		M.F.K. Fisher	
Titles Used with Names	Mr.	Mrs.	Ms.	Jr.
	Dr.	Sr.	Ph.D.	D.D.S.
Organizations	Assn.	Co.	Corp.	Inc.

NOTE Abbreviations for government agencies and some widely used abbreviations are written without periods. Each letter of such abbreviations (which are called **acronyms**) is capitalized.

EXAMPLES   CIA (**C**entral **I**ntelligence **A**gency)

NOS (**N**ational **O**cean **S**ervice)

PC (**p**ersonal **c**omputer)

RFD (**R**ural **F**ree **D**elivery)

TV (**tele**vision)

STYLE TIP

When writing the initials of someone's name, place a space between two initials (as in *I. M. Pei*). Do not place a space between three initials (as in *M.F.K. Fisher*).

Reference Note

For more on **using capital letters for abbreviations,** see page 250.

End Marks   **265**

MECHANICS

DIRECT TEACHING

Abbreviations

Activity. Pair students and tell them to make flashcards for the abbreviations in the charts and **Notes** on pp. 265–266, using one side of each card for the abbreviation without periods and the other side for the correctly punctuated abbreviation. (If abbreviations are correct with no punctuation, students should write "Correct as is" on the other side of the card.) Have partners shuffle the cards and then use them to drill each other on the correct punctuation of abbreviations.

DIFFERENTIATING INSTRUCTION

Learners Having Difficulty

Ask students to read aloud sentences 1, 2, 3, 6, 7, 8, 9, and 10 in **Review A,** spelling out the abbreviations as they are written and using a click of the tongue or a snap of fingers to indicate the periods in each.

STYLE TIP

The abbreviations *A.D.* and *B.C.* need special attention. Place *A.D.* before the year and *B.C.* after the year.

EXAMPLES

231 **B.C.**

A.D. 590

There is one exception to this rule. For centuries expressed in words, place both *A.D.* and *B.C.* after the century.

EXAMPLES

fifth century **B.C.**

second century **A.D.**

HELP

If you are not sure whether to use periods with an abbreviation, look up the abbreviation in a dictionary, an encyclopedia, or another reliable reference source.

HELP

Some sentences in Review A need more than one punctuation mark.

Types of Abbreviations	Examples		
Times	A.M.	B.C.	Aug.
	P.M.	A.D.	Sat.
Addresses	Ave.	Blvd.	Ct.
	P.O. Box	Rd.	St.
Geographical Names	Ark.	Colo.	D.C.
	St. Paul	P.R.	U.S.

NOTE A two-letter state abbreviation without periods is used only when it is followed by a ZIP Code. Both letters of the abbreviation are capitalized. No mark of punctuation is used between the abbreviation and the ZIP Code.

EXAMPLES   Washington, **DC** 20013

San Juan, **PR** 00904

Abbreviations for units of measure are usually written without periods and are not capitalized.

EXAMPLES   cc, kg, ml, m, ft, lb, qt

However, you should use a period with the abbreviation *in.* (for *inch*) to prevent confusing it with the word *in.*

When an abbreviation that has a period ends a sentence, another period is not needed. However, a question mark or an exclamation point is used in such situations if it is needed.

EXAMPLES   The game lasted until 8:30 P.M.

Did it start at 5:00 P.M.?

Review A **Correcting Sentences by Adding Punctuation**

Write the following sentences, adding periods, question marks, and exclamation points where they are needed.

EXAMPLE   **1.** Some caterpillars become butterflies

1. Some caterpillars become butterflies.

1. Will Mr.Highwater be teaching the science course?

2. Just after 3:00 P.M., the sun came out.

3. The letter from Ms. E. J. Hunter was dated Fri., Nov. 12.

4. How heavy the traffic was on First Avenue!

5. Do your measuring cups say *ml* or *oz*?

6. Address comments to 7890 E. Kyle Dr., Oswego, New York.

7. By 300 B.C., Chinese cooks already had a philosophy of five tastes.

8. The city of St. Petersburg is situated on a peninsula.

9. Apply at the loading dock at H. J. Movers, Inc.

10. On TV tonight, Dr. Melba West will explain nutrition.

Review B **Using Punctuation Correctly**

For each of the following sentences, write the <u>word or words</u> <u>that should be followed by a period, question mark, or excla-</u> <u>mation point</u>. Add the proper punctuation after each word.

EXAMPLE   1. My neighbor Mr Nhuong showed me this picture of people celebrating the Vietnamese holiday Tet

        1. *Mr., Tet.*

1. Unlike New Year's Day, which is always on <u>Jan.</u>1, Tet can fall on any day in late January or early <u>February.</u>

2. Moreover, Tet isn't just one single day; the celebration lasts a whole <u>week.</u>

3. Wouldn't you like a week-long <u>holiday</u>?

4. Even here at 8420 Beaconcrest <u>Ave,</u> the Nhuong family still enjoy their <u>traditions.</u>

5. According to Mr. Nhuong, the name of the first person to visit a house can bring good or bad luck to the <u>family.</u>

6. Since my nickname is Lucky, the Nhuongs asked me to be their first visitor and to arrive by 7:00 A.M.

7. I tried hard not to be <u>late.</u>

8. One of the Nhuongs' relatives flew in from Santa Barbara, <u>Calif,</u> later that <u>morning.</u>

9. <u>Mrs.</u>Nhuong prepared a huge breakfast, and we all sat down to enjoy <u>it.</u>

10. What a great meal that <u>was</u>!

Guided and Independent

Reviews   You may wish to use **Review A** as guided practice. Then, have students complete **Review B** as independent practice.

HOMEWORK

DIFFERENTIATING INSTRUCTION

English-Language Learners

Hmong. In Hmong, questions often are indicated by the inclusion of the word *puas,* meaning "what," within the body of a sentence rather than through the use of end punctuation. Therefore, some Hmong speakers will use periods where question marks are appropriate or will include the word *what* inappropriately within their sentences. Remind students of the differences between declarative, imperative, and interrogative sentences, and point out that written English relies in part on end punctuation to determine those sentence functions.

MECHANICS

Commas

Rules 12f–l *(pp. 268–278)*

OBJECTIVES

- To proofread sentences for correct use of commas
- To correct compound sentences by adding commas
- To correct errors in the punctuation of sentences with appositives and appositive phrases
- To add commas to sentences with words used in direct address
- To add commas to sentences with introductory elements
- To use commas correctly in conventional situations

DIRECT TEACHING

Modeling and Demonstration

Commas. Model how to proofread sentences for correct use of commas by using the example *I've seen snakes lizards and toads in our yard.* Ask whether there is a series of three or more items in the sentence. [*yes; snakes, lizards, toads*] Next, ask whether all the items in the series are joined by *and, or,* or *nor.* [*no*] Therefore, the items in the series *snakes, lizards, and toads* should be separated by commas. Now, have a volunteer use another example from this chapter to demonstrate how to proofread sentences for correct use of commas.

┌HELP─

Some writers do not use a comma before the conjunction *and, or,* or *nor* when it joins the last two items in a series. However, sometimes such a comma is needed to make the meaning clear. Notice how using a comma before *and* changes the meaning in these examples.

EXAMPLES
Grandma, Mom, and Dad came to the game. [Three people were at the game.]

Grandma, Mom and Dad came to the game. [Grandma is being told who came to the game.]

Including the comma before the conjunction in such a series is not incorrect, so it is best always to use this comma.

Commas

End marks are used to separate complete thoughts. ***Commas,*** however, are generally used to separate words or groups of words within a complete thought. If you fail to use necessary commas, you may confuse your reader.

CONFUSING   The members of the team are Jo Ann Jerry Lee Darrin Marcia and Jeanne. [How many members?]

CLEAR   The members of the team are Jo Ann, Jerry Lee, Darrin, Marcia, and Jeanne. [five members]

Items in a Series

12f. Use commas to separate items in a series.

A ***series*** is three or more items written one after the other. The items may be single words or word groups.

Words in a Series
Sugar cane, bananas, and citrus fruits are grown in Jamaica. [nouns]
Yesterday I dusted, vacuumed, and mopped. [verbs]
The day was wet, cold, and windy. [adjectives]

Word Groups in a Series
At the beach we swam, built sand castles, and played volleyball. [predicates]
I searched for the lost contact lens in the sink, on the counter, and on the floor. [prepositional phrases]
Please punch the time card when you arrive, when you take lunch, and when you leave. [clauses]

When all the items in a series are joined by *and, or,* or *nor,* do not use commas to separate them.

EXAMPLES   I've seen snakes **and** lizards **and** toads in our yard.

Shall we go bowling **or** rent a movie **or** listen to CD's?

RESOURCES

Commas

Practice

- *Language & Sentence Skills Practice,* pp. 240–248, 252
- *Developmental Language & Sentence Skills,* pp. 105–108

Exercise 2 Proofreading Sentences for the Correct Use of Commas

Most of the following sentences need commas. If a sentence needs commas, write the word before each missing comma; then, add the comma. If a sentence is already correct, write *C*. Commas that may be considered optional are underscored.

EXAMPLE   **1.** Beverley DeGale Claire Jackson and Iman won Candace Awards in 1997.

      1. DeGale, Jackson,

1. I finished my dinner, brushed my teeth, combed my hair, and ran out the door.
2. The nurse checked the patient's pulse, took his temperature, and gave him a glass of water.
3. For lunch we had milk, tuna sandwiches, and pears.
4. Cora, Jack, and Tomás entered the contest.
5. Marcus plays golf and football and volleyball.   5. C
6. The U.S. Marine Corps is prepared for battle on land, on the sea, and in the air.
7. For her birthday on September 27, my sister wants a dog and a cat and a hamster and a bird.   7. C
8. Jan told Raul where she had been, where she was, and where she was going.   8. C
9. This project is fun, easy, fast, and inexpensive.
10. Balloons were floating in the living room, the kitchen, the bedrooms, and the dining room.

12g. Use commas to separate two or more adjectives that come before a noun.

EXAMPLES   Pita is a round, flat bread of the Middle East.

              James Earl Jones certainly has a deep, strong, commanding voice.

Do not place a comma between an adjective and the noun immediately following it.

INCORRECT   Alexandra and I found an old, rusty, bicycle in the vacant lot down the street.

CORRECT   Alexandra and I found an old, rusty bicycle in the vacant lot down the street.

┌ H E L P ─

Use a semicolon rather than a comma between phrases in a series when the phrases contain commas.

EXAMPLE
The three sections of this project will be due on Tuesday, March 3; on Thursday, March 19; and on Friday, April 3.

Reference Note
For more information about **semicolons**, see page 279.

Commas   **269**

APPLICATION

Correct Use of Commas

Adjectives in Description. Have each of your students write three or four descriptive sentences about his or her favorite animal. Emphasize the use of vivid, colorful adjectives. Remind students to use commas correctly when separating adjectives in their sentences. Have the students proofread each other's papers for vivid adjectives and the proper use of commas.

RETEACHING

Correct Use of Commas

Activity. Have students divide a piece of paper into six slips by folding and tearing. Tell them to write an adjective on each slip of paper. Collect the slips, shuffle them, and redistribute them. Each student will receive six slips of paper. Tell students to create two sentences using three adjectives from the slips for each sentence. Have several volunteers write their sentences on the chalkboard, and have the other students check the punctuation.

Sometimes the last adjective in a series is thought of as part of the noun. In that case, do not use a comma before the last adjective.

EXAMPLES   The tall pine tree [not *tall, pine tree*] swayed.

Kimchi is a spicy Korean dish [not *spicy, Korean dish*] made with pickled cabbage.

Exercise 3 **Proofreading Sentences for the Correct Use of Commas**

For each of the following sentences, write the word that should be followed by a comma; then, add the comma. If a sentence is already correct, write *C*.

EXAMPLE   1. Mrs. Hirata taught us several beautiful old Japanese folk songs.

1. *beautiful,*

1. His calm,wrinkled face told a story.
2. François Toussaint L'Ouverture was a brilliant,patriotic Haitian leader.
3. The huge,lively,wriggling kingfish dropped from the hook.
4. There's a sleek,shiny bicycle in the store window.
5. The sound of the soft,steady rain put me to sleep.
6. We read Chief Black Hawk's moving farewell speech.   6. C
7. I washed my hands in the cold,clear spring water.
8. May I please have some of that spicy,delicious soup?
9. The old diary had ragged,yellowed pages.
10. The crowded dining room is filled with people celebrating my parents' anniversary.   10. C

Compound Sentences

12h. Use a comma before *and, but, for, nor, or, so,* or *yet* when it joins independent clauses in a compound sentence.

EXAMPLES   Theo will bring the potato salad, and Sarah will bring the apple juice.

Congress passed the bill, but I believe the president vetoed it.

I went to bed early, for I had a big day ahead of me.

NOTE Do not confuse a compound sentence with a simple sentence containing a compound verb. Usually, no comma is needed between the parts of a compound verb.

COMPOUND SENTENCE	We ran relay races first, and then we ate lunch.
SIMPLE SENTENCE	We ran the relay races first and then ate lunch. [The sentence contains a compound verb.]

However, a compound verb made up of three or more verbs generally does require commas.

EXAMPLE   We **ran** the relay races, **ate** lunch, and then **prepared** for the individual races.

Reference Note

For more information on **compound sentences**, see pages 97 and 403. For more information on **compound verbs**, see page 13.

<Exercise 4> **Correcting Compound Sentences by Adding Commas**

Some of the following sentences are compound and need to have commas added. If a sentence needs a comma, write the word or numeral before the missing comma; then, add the comma. If a sentence is already correct, write *C*.

EXAMPLE   **1.** The storm brought heavy rain but a tornado did the most damage.
                   1. rain,

1. At the Native American Heritage Festival, Mary Johns wove baskets from sweet grass and Alice Billie made rings from beads.
2. The sailboat was almost hidden by the fog yet we could see part of the mast.
3. German Silva of Mexico was the fastest male runner in the 1994 and 1995 New York City Marathons and Tegla Loroupe of Kenya was the female winner in both races.
4. Would you like to play checkers or shall we go to the lake instead?
5. I called my friends and told them the news.   5. C
6. Jim practiced the piano piece all month for he wanted to do well at the recital.

Compound Sentence or Compound Verb?

Activity. To help students distinguish a compound sentence from a simple sentence with a compound verb, write the following sentence pairs on the chalkboard:

1. **Fred** *likes* Mexican food yet *dislikes* salsa.
   Fred *likes* Mexican food, yet **he** *dislikes* salsa.
2. **Pam** *swims* often and *jogs* daily.
   Pam *swims* often, and **she** *jogs* daily.
3. **Maria** *reads* books but *sees* no movies.
   Maria *reads* books, but **she** *sees* no movies.

Underline the subjects (shown above in bold) once and underline the verbs (shown above in italics) twice. Circle the comma in each compound sentence, and emphasize that compound sentences have two independent clauses, each of which has a subject and a verb. Therefore, the clauses are separated by a comma and a coordinating conjunction.

MECHANICS

7. Many people are used to celebrating New Year's Day on January 1, but the Chinese New Year begins between January 21 and February 19.

8. The lake contains fish and is home to several alligators. **8. C**

9. The old oak tree shaded the house, but the shade kept the grass from growing.

10. I wanted to buy a camera, so I mowed yards in the neighborhood to earn extra money.

Interrupters

12i. Use commas to set off an expression that interrupts a sentence.

Two commas are used to set off an interrupting expression—one before and one after the expression.

EXAMPLES My favorite gospel singers, BeBe and CeCe Winans, were on TV last night.

As you leave, Jesse, please close the door quietly.

Sometimes an "interrupter" comes at the beginning or the end of the sentence. In such cases, only one comma is needed.

EXAMPLES Yes, I'll call back later.

How did you do in karate class today, Kami?

(1) Use commas to set off appositives and appositive phrases that are not necessary to the meaning of a sentence.

An *appositive* is a noun or a pronoun that identifies or describes another noun or pronoun beside it. An *appositive phrase* is an appositive with its modifiers.

EXAMPLES A gymnast, **Mrs. Shaw,** will coach us. [The appositive *Mrs. Shaw* identifies the gymnast.]

This book is about geology, **the science of the earth and its rocks.** [*The science of the earth and its rocks* is an appositive phrase that identifies *geology*.]

Do not use commas when an appositive is necessary to the meaning of a sentence.

DIFFERENTIATING INSTRUCTION

Learners Having Difficulty

To show students that some phrases are nonessential, write on a large strip of paper a sentence containing an unnecessary appositive phrase. You might want to use one of the examples on this page or p. 273. Fold the strip to hide the appositive phrase to show students that the sentence makes sense without the phrase. Emphasize that when the phrase is reinserted, it must be set off from the sentence by commas.

EXAMPLES   My cousin Roberto lives in Puerto Rico. [I have more than one cousin and am using his name to identify which cousin I mean.]

The character Alice is based on Alice Liddell. [Alice is one of several characters; the appositive tells which character is meant.]

Exercise 5 Punctuating Appositives

Most of the following sentences contain at least one error in the punctuation of appositives and appositive phrases. Write each word that should be followed by a comma, and add the comma. If a sentence is already correct, write *C*.

EXAMPLE   1. Two cold drinks lemonade and punch were available to the guests.

1. *drinks, punch,*

Pierre Auguste Renoir, *Ball at the Moulin de la Galette* (1876). Paris, Musée d'Orsay, Paris, Giraudon/Art Resource, New York.

1. The park a beautiful place for a party was lit by street-lights and had a bandstand.
2. Our hosts Mr. and Mrs. Worthington greeted us at the entrance.
3. Some of the men were wearing boaters straw hats popular at the time.
4. My friend Eliza Wolcott sat in the shade at our table. **4.** C
5. Do you see an empty table a quiet place for conversation?
6. Somehow a puppy the pet of one of the guests got onto the dance floor.
7. Edward Finch, the best dancer has his choice of partners.
8. Music mostly waltzes filled the air.
9. A young woman in a striped dress a new bride, is remembering her wedding.
10. Listen to laughter and lively conversation, the sounds of happy people.   **10.** C

(2) Use commas to set off words used in direct address.

EXAMPLES   Ms. Jacobs, please explain the assignment.

Do you know who Santa Anna was, Beth?

You're right, Inés, to say he was a Mexican general.

In the sentences above, the words *Ms. Jacobs, Beth,* and *Inés* are **nouns of direct address.** They identify the person or persons spoken to or addressed.

┌HELP─

Some sentences in Exercise 6 need more than one comma.

Exercise 6 **Correcting Sentences by Adding Commas**

For each of the following sentences, write each word that should be followed by a comma; then, add the comma.

EXAMPLE   **1.** Are you sure you left your book in the room James?

        1. room,

1. Michi, will you read the haiku you wrote?
2. Carla, please bring me the newspaper when you finish with it.
3. Did you bring the tickets, Jorge?
4. After all the work we've done, Ann, it would be a shame to turn it in late.
5. If you mow the lawn, Kelly, I'll rake the clippings.
6. Please, Mom, can you drive me to rehearsal?
7. Mr. Ferguson, you have a telephone call.
8. You are dismissed, class.
9. How long have you worked here, David?
10. The problem, my friends, is simply lack of effort.

Introductory Words, Phrases, and Clauses

12j. Use a comma after certain introductory elements.

(1) Use a comma after *yes, no,* or any mild exclamation such as *well* or *why* at the beginning of a sentence.

EXAMPLES   **Yes,** you may use my pencil.

Why, it's Arthur!

Well, I think you should apologize.

DIFFERENTIATING INSTRUCTION

Advanced Students

To reinforce comma usage, you may want to have students read a short story such as "President Cleveland, Where Are You?" by Robert Cormier. Have students find examples of compound sentences, introductory expressions, nonessential appositives, and so forth in the story. Then, have students copy in their writer's logs the sentences they find, paying careful attention to correct comma placement. You may want to pair students for this activity and to limit the type of comma usage each pair is searching for. When students have found examples, have them copy their examples onto poster board for a classroom poster. Allow students to write sentences in different colors, but have all students use the same color for commas.

MINI-LESSON **Grammar**

Interjections. Tell students that an interjection is one kind of introductory word. Students will find a list on p. 68 in **Chapter 3: Parts of Speech Overview.** Explain that an interjection is a word used to express an emotion and has no grammatical relationship to the rest of the sentence.

    Often, an interjection is followed by an exclamation point: "Oops! I don't want to make that mistake again." Sometimes an

**(2) Use a comma after two or more introductory preposi-
tional phrases.**

EXAMPLE   **In the valley at the base of the hill,** a herd of
buffalo grazes.

Also, use a comma after a single long introductory
prepositional phrase.

EXAMPLE   **On the winter morning when Kenan discovered
the strange visitor,** the rosebush burst into bloom.

If the introductory prepositional phrase is short, a comma
may or may not be used.

EXAMPLES   **In the morning,** we'll tour the Caddo burial mounds.

In the morning we'll tour the Caddo burial mounds.

On that page, you will see a map of the park.

On that page you will see a map of the park.

(3) Use a comma after an introductory adverb clause.

EXAMPLE   **After the show is over,** we will go out to eat.

NOTE   An adverb clause that comes at the end of a sentence
usually is not preceded by a comma.

EXAMPLE   We will go out to eat **after the show is over.**

Exercise 7 **Using Commas with Introductory Elements**

If a comma is needed in a sentence, write the word before the
missing comma and add the comma. If a sentence is already
punctuated correctly, write *C*.

EXAMPLE   **1.** After he left we noticed that his hat was on
the table.
1. *left,*

1. Before eating the birds were singing noisily.
2. On the table in the kitchen dinner was getting cold.
3. Although he trained hard for a month, Juan could not
   break his own record.   **3.** C
4. Yes that is a cardinal.
5. On her way to school in the morning Roseanne was thinking about her project.

Reference Note

For more about **prepo-
sitional phrases,** see
page 63. For more
about **adverb clauses,**
see page 93.

┌HELP───

Use a comma
after a single short
introductory prepositional
phrase when the comma is
necessary to make the sentence clear.

CONFUSING
  In the evening sunlight
  faded in the western sky.

CLEAR
  In the evening, sunlight
  faded in the western sky.
  [The comma is needed so
  that the reader does not
  read "evening sunlight."]

**MEETING THE
CHALLENGE**

You have seen several
examples of sentences
that require commas to
prevent misreading.
Create five sentences in
which a comma is neces-
sary to prevent humorous
misreading.

ANSWERS
Sentences will vary.

APPLICATION

End Marks and Commas
Activity. Divide the class into
groups, and have each group use a
television and a VCR or a radio and a
tape recorder to tape several small
portions of dialogue from a show.
Have the students write out the dialogue, punctuating it correctly. To
shorten this assignment, you could
also specify that each group concentrate on only one portion of dialogue. Groups can then present their
tapes and punctuated transcripts to
the class.

MECHANICS

Commas   **275**

---

interjection is set off by a comma: "Oh, we
don't have time to see both movies anyway."
    Ask students when they think an interjec-
tion should be followed by an exclamation
point rather than a comma. Lead them to

see that writers use an exclamation point
after an interjection to emphasize a particular emotion the speaker is experiencing,
such as surprise or joy.

Relating to Writing

Social Studies. Have each student check that he or she has correctly used commas in an essay or other writing assignment completed for a social studies class. Students should pay particular attention to sentences that include references to dates and places.

6. When I have time on the <u>weekends</u>, I like to hook rugs.
7. <u>Well</u>, you had better make up your mind soon.
8. With the decorations in the living room in <u>place</u>, Julie was ready for her mother's birthday party.
9. In the corner of the <u>room</u>, a night light showed the way to the door.
10. Because the snow cover was so <u>thin</u>, the deer had no trouble finding food.

Conventional Uses

12k. **Use commas in certain conventional situations.**

(1) Use commas to separate items in dates and addresses.

EXAMPLES   Bill Cosby was born on July 12, 1937, in Philadelphia, Pennsylvania.

Saturday, May 10, will be the day of the soccer playoff.

My aunt has lived at 41 Jefferson Street, Northfield, Minnesota, since 1998.

Notice that a comma separates the last item in a date or in an address from the words that follow it. However, a comma does not separate a month from a day (*July 12*) or a house number from a street name (*41 Jefferson Street*).

NOTE No punctuation is used between the state abbreviation and the ZIP Code.

EXAMPLE   Cerritos, **CA 90701**

┌ S T Y L E   T I P ┐

Business letters use a colon, not a comma, after the salutation.

EXAMPLE
Dear Ms. Hinojosa:

(2) Use a comma after the salutation of a personal letter and after the closing of any letter.

EXAMPLES   Dear Grandma and Grandpa,   Love,

Dear Tyrone,   Sincerely,

Exercise 8 Using Commas Correctly in Conventional Situations

Write the following items and sentences, inserting or deleting commas as needed.

━━━ CONTENT-AREA CONNECTIONS ━━━

History
Direct Address. Have students think of their favorite historical figure. Tell them to write a sentence about this person's life addressed to the person.

Example: Abe Lincoln, I wish you hadn't gone to see that play.

Students may think up serious or humorous sentences. Students could write their sentences under a drawing of that person. Remind them to use commas to set off nouns of direct address. (If the noun of direct address is at the beginning or end of the sentence, only one comma is needed.)

EXAMPLE   1. Friday February 11 is the first day of the fair.
            1. *Friday, February 11, is the first day of the fair.*

1. Yours truly,
2. Shirley Chisholm was born on November 30, 1924, in New York City.
3. The first female principal chief of the Cherokee Nation is Wilma Mankiller, who was born near Rocky Mountain, Oklahoma.
4. Write to me at 327 Adams Way, Darrouzett, TX 79024.
5. The Harvest Carnival is on Friday, October 24, 2003.
6. Dear Uncle Sig,
7. Address orders to Pretty Good Camping Supplies, P.O. Box 528, Southborough, MA, 01772.
8. He made his stage debut on May 25, 1928, in London, England.
9. Friday, July 9, 2004, will be my grandparents' golden wedding anniversary.
10. The main office in Santa Barbara, California, has a new fax number.

┌─ HELP ─

Commas are also used in numbers greater than and including one thousand. Use a comma before every third digit to the left of the decimal point.

EXAMPLE
7,386,149.00 [seven million three hundred eighty-six thousand one hundred forty-nine]

Unnecessary Commas

12l. Do not use unnecessary commas.

Too much punctuation can be just as confusing as not enough punctuation, especially where the use of commas is concerned.

CONFUSING   My friend, Jessica, said she would feed my cat and my dog while I'm away, but now, she tells me, she will be too busy.

CLEAR   My friend Jessica said she would feed my cat and my dog while I'm away, but now she tells me she will be too busy.

Have a reason for every comma or other mark of punctuation that you use. When there is no rule requiring punctuation and when the meaning of the sentence is clear without one, do not insert any punctuation mark.

MECHANICS

Proofreading a Letter for the Correct Use of Commas

The sentences in the following letter each contain an error in the use of commas. Rewrite the letter, adding or deleting commas as needed.

EXAMPLES **[1]** July, 6, 2003
1. *July 6, 2003*

[2] Dear Tom
2. *Dear Tom,*

Optional commas are underscored.

Dear Tom,

    [1] Well, on July 4, 2003, Aunt Lil kept her promise and took me up in her airplane. **[2]** Wow! What a view of the canyons, valleys, and plateaus we had! **[3]** We flew over a hill, and saw a small herd of mustangs. **[4]** Aunt Lil circled above the horses, and the plane's shadow frightened the stallion. **[5]** The whole herd stampeded with tails, and manes and hooves flying in a storm of dust all the way down into the valley. **[6]** One black colt trailed behind, but his mother quickly nudged him onward. **[7]** In a moment, the swift, sturdy mustangs, descendants of the fiery steeds of the Spanish conquistadors, were galloping into the woods. **[8]** I wish you could have seen them, Tom! **[9]** At least I remembered my camera, so here is a picture of those beautiful horses.

        [10] Yours truly,

          Sal

Semicolons

A semicolon is part period and part comma. Like a period, it can separate complete thoughts. Like a comma, it can separate items within a sentence.

12m. Use a semicolon between parts of a compound sentence if they are not joined by *and, but, for, nor, or, so,* or *yet.*

EXAMPLES   Todd's report is about Arizona; mine is about Utah.

The rain clouds are moving in quickly; let's head home.

NOTE Use a semicolon to join independent clauses only if the ideas in the independent clauses are closely related. Otherwise, use a period to make two separate sentences.

EXAMPLES   Do not touch that tree frog; it may be poisonous.
[The two ideas are closely related.]

Do not touch that tree frog. Everyone stay together.
[The two ideas are not closely related.]

Exercise 9 **Proofreading Sentences for the Correct Use of Semicolons**

Most of the following sentences have commas where there should be semicolons. If a sentence needs a semicolon, write the words before and after the missing semicolon; then, insert the semicolon. If a sentence is already correct, write *C.*

EXAMPLE   **1.** Mary Vaux Walcott treasured her box of watercolor paints, she took it with her everywhere she went.

    1. paints; she

Carets indicate placement of semicolons.

1. As a young girl, she visited the Canadian Rockies each year, there she began to paint wildflowers.
2. She loved mountain climbing, she often crossed rugged areas to find new wildflowers.
3. She painted her flowers from life, for she did not like to rely on pencil sketches.   **3.** C
4. You can see five of her paintings on the next page, aren't they beautiful?

┌HELP┐

Use a semicolon rather than a comma between phrases in a series when the phrases contain commas.

EXAMPLE

The acrobats are traveling from Albuquerque, New Mexico; through Phoenix, Arizona; and finally to San Diego, California.

Semicolons
Rule 12m *(pp. 279–280)*

OBJECTIVE

- To proofread sentences for the correct use of semicolons

DIRECT TEACHING

Modeling and Demonstration

Semicolons. Model how to proofread sentences for correct use of semicolons by using the incorrect example *Todd's report is about Arizona, mine is about Utah.* Ask whether there are two independent clauses in this sentence. [*yes; (1) Todd's report is about Arizona; (2) mine is about Utah*] Next, ask whether the two clauses are joined by *and, but, for, nor, or, so,* or *yet.* [*no*] Then, ask whether the ideas in these two clauses are closely related. [*yes*] Point out that these two independent clauses should be joined by a semicolon, placed after *Arizona,* to form a compound sentence. Now, have a volunteer use another example from this chapter to demonstrate how to proofread sentences for correct use of semicolons.

Exercise 9

DISTRIBUTED REVIEW
Before students correct semicolon errors in **Exercise 9,** ask them to identify the subjects and verbs in the sentences designated below.

  6. Painting B, is; it, grows
  8. Painting D, shows; aroma, draws
10. Mary Vaux Walcott, is known; she, painted

Remind students that a semicolon is used between two independent clauses, each of which has a subject and a verb.

MECHANICS

┌ **RESOURCES** ┐

Semicolons
Practice

- *Language & Sentence Skills Practice,* p. 249, 253
- *Developmental Language & Sentence Skills,* pp. 107–108

English-Language Learners

General Strategies. In English, two independent clauses usually cannot be joined by only a comma; two independent clauses must be separated by a semicolon or a comma and a conjunction. However, in some other languages, such as Arabic, Russian, and Turkish, a comma may set off two independent clauses. You may find that some of your English-language learners will use a comma where they should use a semicolon.

RETEACHING

Semicolons

Suggest that students think of the semicolon as "a comma and a dot," with the dot representing a conjunction, or as a "supercomma": If a semicolon (comma under a dot) is used in a compound sentence, the dot indicates that no conjunction is needed. If only a comma is used, the absence of the dot indicates that a conjunction is necessary.

5. Painting A shows a western red lily, such lilies wither quickly when picked.
6. Painting B is of a bottle gentian, a fall flower, it grows in bogs and swamps.   **6.** [*or* flower; it]
7. American wisteria is a climbing plant, and you can see in Painting C that it has many showy flowers.   **7.** C
8. Painting D shows blossoms of the American waterlily opening in early morning, their aroma draws insects.
9. Painting E is of Carolina jessamine, it spreads its fragrant flowers through treetops.
10. Mary Vaux Walcott is known as "the Audubon of North American wildflowers," for she painted more than seven hundred species.   **10.** C

A

B

C

D

E

Mary Vaux Walcott/ National Museum of American Art, Washington, D.C./ Art Resource, New York.

Colons

A colon usually signals that more information follows.

12n. Use a colon before a list of items, especially after expressions such as *the following* and *as follows*.

EXAMPLES   These are the winners of the poetry contest**:** Carmen Santiago, Justin Douglass, and Steven Yellowfeather.

Pack the following items for your overnight trip**:** a toothbrush, toothpaste, and your hairbrush.

The order of the colors seen through a prism is as follows**:** red, orange, yellow, green, blue, indigo, and violet.

NOTE Do not use a colon between a preposition and its object or between a verb and its object. Either omit the colon or reword the sentence.

INCORRECT   My report includes: a table of contents, three chapters, illustrations, and a list of sources.

CORRECT   My report includes a table of contents, three chapters, illustrations, and a list of sources.

CORRECT   My report includes **the following parts:** a table of contents, three chapters, illustrations, and a list of sources.

Colons may also be used to introduce long, formal statements and quotations.

EXAMPLE   Mark Twain had a very definite opinion on happiness**:** "The best way to cheer yourself up is to try to cheer somebody else up."

12o. Use a colon between the hour and the minute when you write the time.

EXAMPLES   8**:**55 A.M.   9**:**15 P.M.   6**:**22 this morning

12p. Use a colon after the salutation of a business letter.

EXAMPLES   Dear Sir or Madam**:**   Dear Mrs. Jordan**:**

Dear Sales Manager**:**   To Whom It May Concern**:**

STYLE	TIP

Personal letters use a comma, not a colon, after the salutation.

EXAMPLE
Dear John**,**

Colons   **281**

MECHANICS

Colons
Rules 12n–p *(pp. 281–282)*

OBJECTIVE

- To correct sentences or salutations by adding colons

DIRECT TEACHING

Modeling and Demonstration
Colons. Model how to proofread sentences for correct use of colons by using the incorrect example *These are the winners of the poetry contest, Carmen Santiago, Justin Douglass, and Steven Yellowfeather.* First, ask whether the sentence contains a list of items. [*yes; Carmen Santiago, Justin Douglass, and Steven Yellowfeather*] Next, ask whether the list is the object of a preposition, since a colon should not come between a preposition and its object. [*no*] Then, ask whether the list is the object of a verb, since a colon should not come between a verb and its object. [*no*] Therefore, a colon should be placed after *contest* to signal that more information follows. Now, have a volunteer use another example from this chapter to demonstrate how to proofread sentences for correct use of colons.

Correcting Misconceptions
Colon Before List. Some students may erroneously think that a colon should be used before all lists of items. Emphasize to students the importance of making sure they do not use a colon after a verb that is followed by a list or series of direct objects. Encourage students to find the verb in a sentence before they use a colon in their writing, and tell them to be especially careful about using a colon after the verb *are.* You can have students check their previous writing samples to correct any errors in colons use.

DIFFERENTIATING
INSTRUCTION

Learners Having Difficulty

Semicolons and Colons. Some students might confuse the colon and the semicolon or think that they are interchangeable. Tell your students that a colon usually indicates the part of the sentence the writer wants to emphasize, whereas a semicolon helps the reader avoid confusion. You may want to have students make and display a poster illustrating the uses of the colon and the semicolon. Students can refer to the poster throughout the year.

Exercise 10 Using Colons Correctly

Most of the following items contain an error in the use of colons. Rewrite each incorrect sentence to correct the error. If a sentence is already correct, write C.

EXAMPLE   1. Bring the following items to class your notebook, a pencil, and your textbook.

1. *Bring the following items to class: your notebook, a pencil, and your textbook.*

1. We visited the following cities:Bayamón, Ponce, and San Juan.
2. A good baby sitter should have the following qualities: promptness, reliability, an interest in children, and common sense.
3. To stay healthy, you should not smoke or chew tobacco. 3. C
4. Add these items to your shopping list:tissues, toothpaste, and shampoo.
5. A good friend should be: loving, loyal, and honest.
6. The first bell rings at 8:10 A.M., and the second bell rings twenty minutes later.
7. Your homework includes: your spelling worksheet, one chapter of reading, and a rough draft of your English composition for Monday.
8. The recipe for Brunswick stew called for these ingredients: lamb, carrots, potatoes, and onions.
9. Every time we see her, Grandmother likes to remind us of her favorite Ben Franklin saying:"Whatever is begun in anger ends in shame."
10. Dear Sir or Madam:

┌HELP┐

Some of the sentences in Review D contain more than one punctuation error.

Review D Proofreading a Letter for the Correct Use of Punctuation

Proofread the following letter for errors in punctuation. Then, rewrite the letter, adding the necessary periods, question marks, commas, semicolons, and colons.

EXAMPLE   **[1]** 1200 E Halifax Avenue

1. *1200 E. Halifax Avenue*

Commas that may be considered optional are underscored.

FAMILY/COMMUNITY ACTIVITY   *Continued on pp. 283–284*

A Short Speech. Tell students that as they get older, there may be various occasions when they will be asked to speak to groups of people. A person may be asked to say a few words about a guest of honor at a birthday party, about the bride and groom at a wedding, or about people at some other celebration.

Have each student write a short speech (no more than one or two minutes) about a friend or family member who is celebrating an important event. The speech should

[1] January 11, 2003

Superintendent of Schools
Baltimore City Board of Education
200 E. North Avenue
Baltimore, MD 21202

[2] Dear Superintendent:

    [3] Would your students be interested in visiting an African American wax museum? **[4]** The only one of its kind is right here in Baltimore. **[5]** The Great Blacks in Wax Museum features life-size wax models of famous African Americans. **[6]** These wax images include leaders in education, civil rights, and science. **[7]** The museum displays statues of the following people: Rosa Parks, Phillis Wheatley, Crispus Attucks, Carter G. Woodson, Dred Scott, Harriet Tubman, Booker T. Washington, Frederick Douglass, and many others.

    [8] Our company offers students and teachers discount tours of the museum during Black History Month; discount tours of other historic attractions are also available then. **[9]** For more information, please call me between 8:30 A.M. and 5:30 P.M.

    [10] Yours truly,

Jane Lee Harper

Jane Lee Harper
President
Uhuru Guided Tours

PRACTICE

Guided and Independent

Reviews You may wish to use **Review D** as guided practice. Then, have students complete **Review E** as independent practice.

HOMEWORK

EXTENSION

Relating to Writing

To reinforce the use of colons in sentences introducing quotations, have students select quotations that they like. If they need help, refer them to a dictionary of quotations. Then, have them write sentences containing the quotations (for example, *I'll never forget Patrick Henry's stirring words: "Give me liberty, or give me death."*).

Have students write their sentences on the chalkboard. Then, ask students to read the quotations and to tell why they like them. Check sentences for correct colon usage.

MECHANICS

recognize the person by name, congratulate him or her on the occasion, and include comments about the person's special qualities. In addition, at least five of the sentences in the speech should include the following punctuation marks and sentence structures:

- an exclamation point
- a series of adjectives
- an appositive
- a colon preceding a list
- a semicolon

HELP

Some of the sentences in Review E contain more than one punctuation error.

Review E Using End Marks, Commas, Semicolons, and Colons Correctly

Each of the following items contains at least one error in the use of end marks, commas, semicolons, or colons. Rewrite the items, adding or changing punctuation to correct each error.

EXAMPLE
1. Mrs. Hunter how long will the leaves remain that color.

1. *Mrs. Hunter, how long will the leaves remain that color?*

Commas that may be considered optional are underscored.

1. Liechtenstein, a country not quite as large as Washington, D.C., is one of the smallest countries in Europe.
2. The students gathered signatures on a petition, and a spokesperson presented their argument for better sidewalks.
3. That must be the biggest fish in the whole lake?. 3. [or lake!]
4. Did you find out which president created the Peace Corps in 1961.?
5. Dear Sir:
6. No, I haven't seen that new movie, but I've heard it's absolutely terrific.
7. Fort Sumter, the site of the first shots fired in the Civil War, is located in Charleston, South Carolina.
8. After the sparrows finished in the birdbath, they flew up to the feeder!.
9. A long, white, shiny limousine pulled into the parking lot,; after that came a bus and a police officer on a motorcycle.
10. Before you may read your mystery novel, you must finish your homework, clean your room, and walk the dog.

FAMILY/COMMUNITY ACTIVITY   *Continued from p. 283*

Tell students that these punctuation marks and sentence structures do not have to be used in the order shown and can be used more than once. However, each punc-tuation mark and sentence structure should be circled and identified in the margin of the speech. Students should save their speeches in their writing notebooks.

CHAPTER

12

Numerals in brackets refer to rules tested by the items in the Chapter Review.

 1. [12i(2), d]
 2. [12e, b]
 3. [12i(1), a]
 4. [12n, f, a]
 5. [12m, a]
 6. [12c, d]
 7. [12h]
 8. [12k(2)]
 9. [12a]
10. [12e, j(3), a]
11. [12k(1), a]
12. [12g, a]
13. [12e, k(1), a]
14. [12h, a]
15. [12k(1), b]
16. [12j(1), i(2), a]
17. [12i(1), a]
18. [12o, e, a]
19. [12j(1), g, a]
20. [12k(1), o, e]

Chapter Review

A. Using Punctuation Correctly

Periods, question marks, exclamation points, commas, semi-colons, and colons are missing in the following items. Write the word or numeral before each missing punctuation mark, and add the correct mark.
Commas that may be considered optional are underscored.

 1. Flora,please pass the pepper.
 2. Did Fred once work for Interactive Corp.?
 3. We are learning about meteorology,the study of weather.
 4. The shirts come in the following four colors:blue,green, brown,and red.
 5. Yasunari Kawabata won the 1968 Nobel Prize in literature;he was the first Japanese writer to win the prize.
 6. Watch out!   6. [or out.]
 7. I wish I could go to camp this summer,but I have to stay home because I caught chickenpox.
 8. Dear Mom and Dad,
 9. I taught Zachary how to swim.
10. While Dr.Sanchez is on jury duty,Dr.Kelley is seeing his patients.
11. My youngest sister was born on April 12,1997.
12. She is a bright,lively child.
13. His address is 2330 River Rd.Sterling,VA 22170-2322.
14. The Mandan and Hidatsa peoples in North Dakota harvested wild rice,and they traded it for buffalo hides and dried meat.
15. Have you ever been to Austin,Texas?
16. Well,Eric,my favorite state in the Northwest is Washington.
17. Tom Brokaw,a national newscaster,was born in South Dakota.
18. I get up at 6:00 A.M. on school days.
19. Yes,a taco is a fried,filled tortilla.
20. The meeting will be held Sunday,February 23,at 2:00 P.M.

Chapter Review   **285**

MECHANICS

ASSESSING

Monitoring Progress
Chapter Review. To assess student progress, you may want to compare the types of items missed on the **Diagnostic Preview** to those missed on the **Chapter Review**. If students have not made significant progress, you may want to refer them to **Chapter 15: Correcting Common Errors, Exercises 24–26,** for additional practice.

RESOURCES

Punctuation
Review
■ *Language & Sentence Skills Practice,* pp. 251–254

Assessment
■ *Progress Assessment for the Holt Handbook,* pp. 23–24, 41
■ *Test Generator (One-Stop Planner CD-ROM)*

B. Using Punctuation Correctly

Periods, question marks, exclamation points, commas, semicolons, and colons are missing in the following items. Write the word or numeral before each missing punctuation mark, and add the correct mark. Commas that may be considered optional are underscored.

21. [12i(2)]
22. [12g, c]
23. [12f]
24. [12h, b]
25. [12e, k(1)]
26. [12m]
27. [12n, b]
28. [12i(1)]
29. [12m]
30. [12i(1)]
31. [12k(1), b]
32. [12f]
33. [12k(1), m]
34. [12g, d]
35. [12m]
36. [12f]
37. [12j(1), i(2)]
38. [12m, e]
39. [12m]
40. [12e, p]

21. Thanks for the new bike, Grandpa.
22. What a friendly, obedient dog you have!
23. Dawn finished her report, read the paper, cooked dinner, and set the table.
24. Can you tell me his address, or should I ask someone else?
25. Write to 637 West Elk Ave., Washington, DC 20015-2602.
26. Our mechanic could not find anything wrong with the water pump; the problem must be somewhere else.
27. Answer the following questions:
    (1) Was Lincoln a successful leader?
    (2) Could the Civil War have ended sooner?
    (3) How important was the naval blockade?
28. One of our troop leaders, Ms. Wells, is teaching us photography.
29. We'll need some minnows; worms aren't good bait in salt water.
30. Ned, the oldest in my family, has many responsibilities.
31. Aren't you going to Glasgow, Scotland, this summer?
32. She hid the lantern, the keys, two maps, and the gold.
33. Before June 1, 1998, I had never heard of Christine; then she was on the front page of every paper.
34. Get those filthy, muddy cowboy boots of yours out of this house now!
35. Chiles rellenos are very spicy; you'll like them.
36. Go to the cave, build a fire, and wait for Sabrina.
37. No, Teresa, there was no TV in those days.
38. Color this one yellow; Mr. Papastratos won't mind.
39. Let's finish this; we'll see about starting something new tomorrow.
40. Dear Mr. President:

MECHANICS

Writing Application
Using End Marks in a Screenplay

Kinds of Sentences   You are a scriptwriter for a popular TV show. You are writing a scene in which one of the characters wins one million dollars in a sweepstakes. Write down the character's response to the good news. Use a variety of end marks to help express the character's feelings.

Prewriting   First, you will need to make up a character or use one from a TV show you have seen. How would that person feel if he or she won a million dollars? Write down some notes on how you think your character would react.

Writing   Using your prewriting notes, write a draft of what your character will say. Make your draft at least one paragraph long. Use end punctuation to help express the character's emotions.

Revising   Read your character's response aloud. Does it sound realistic? Check to make sure you have used a variety of end marks to express your character's feelings.

Publishing   Check your writing for any errors in grammar, spelling, and punctuation. In small groups, exchange papers with another student. Take turns reading the papers to the group as if you each were one of the characters. Use the punctuation as a guide to what the character is feeling and to how you should read the response.

MECHANICS

CHAPTER

13

Punctuation
Underlining (Italics), Quotation Marks, Apostrophes, Hyphens, Parentheses

1.0 Written and Oral English Language Conventions
Students write and speak with a command of standard English conventions appropriate to this grade level.

Diagnostic Preview

A. Proofreading Sentences for the Correct Use of Underlining (Italics) and Quotation Marks

Each of the following sentences contains at least one error in the use of underlining (italics) or quotation marks. Rewrite each sentence correctly.

EXAMPLE
  1. The recent movie of Shakespeare's "Hamlet" is true to the original play.

  1. *The recent movie of Shakespeare's Hamlet is true to the original play.*

1. "The next short story we will be reading is called All Summer in a Day," Mr. Willis told us.

2. My younger brother learned how to play the song "Yesterday" on the piano.

3. Isn't your favorite poem "The Unicorn"?

4. "Wasn't that a song?" asked Carrie.

5. "I think a folk singer wrote it," answered Tony.

6. Juanita said that "she would hum a bit of it."

7. Brad commented, "I think my parents have a copy of it."

8. "Can you bring it to class?" Elena asked.

9. "Who said, 'Time is money'?" Gerald asked.

10. "Benjamin Franklin wrote it," answered Karen, "in a book called Advice to a Young Tradesman."

11. "I think," said Theo, "that you're right."

12. "Into the Woods" is a musical comedy in which characters from several different fairy tales meet in the same forest.

13. Kelly's favorite episode of *Star Trek: Voyager* is titled "Message in a Bottle."

14. Sean often wonders what makes van Gogh's painting "Twelve Sunflowers in a Vase" so interesting.

15. Melba built a model of the Merrimack for extra credit in social studies.

7. [13g]
8. [13h]
9. [13k, h]
10. [13a]
11. [13c]
12. [13a]
13. [13l]
14. [13a]
15. [13b]

B. Proofreading Sentences for the Correct Use of Apostrophes, Hyphens, and Parentheses

Each of the following sentences contains at least one error in the use of apostrophes, hyphens, or parentheses. Rewrite each sentence correctly.

EXAMPLE   1. We havent finished dinner yet.
            1. *We haven't finished dinner yet.* The ⌄ symbol indicates a hyphen.

16. John F. Kennedy(1917–1963)was the youngest person to be elected President of the United States.

17. Each classroom has thirty-one desks.

18. This recipe I'm trying calls for fresh greens, potatoes, carrots, and onions.(It's a vegetarian dish.)

19. The assembly featured a speech by the president-elect of the student council.

20. Who's going to sample this dish?

21. Don't forget the soy sauce.

22. The two chefs' dishes(all were original recipes)were delicious.

23. Jiro's last name has two I's.

24. It is not healthy to eat high-fat foods every day.

25. In the quiet early evening, we could hear the flapping of the geese's wings.

16. [13x]
17. [13u]
18. Parentheses are optional for this item. [13t(1), x]
19. [13w]
20. [13r]
21. [13r]
22. [13o, x]
23. [13s]
24. [13v]
25. [13n]

and to use quotation marks with titles of short works. The following section explains the use of apostrophes in possessives, in contractions, and in the plural forms of letters, numerals, symbols, and words used as words. The next section focuses on the use of hyphens. The final section explains the use of parentheses with information of minor importance and the use of brackets to enclose an explanation added to quoted or parenthetical material.

■ The chapter concludes with the **Chapter Review,** including a **Writing Application** that asks students to use apostrophes correctly in writing a personal letter.

■ For help in integrating this chapter with writing assignments in *Holt Literature and Language Arts,* use the **Teaching Strands** chart on pp. T22–T23.

ASSESSING

Entry-Level Assessment
Diagnostic Preview. To avoid unnecessary reteaching, you may want to analyze students' responses to the **Diagnostic Preview** and assign specific sections to individuals or groups. For students who do exceptionally well on the **Diagnostic Preview,** you may want to assign only **Reviews A, B,** and **C** within the chapter, the **Chapter Review,** and the **Writing Application.**

MECHANICS

Differentiating Instruction

■ *Lesson Plans for Language Development*

■ *Supporting Instruction in Five Languages*

Assessment

■ *Progress Assessment for the Holt Handbook,* pp. 25–26, 41

■ *Test Generator (One-Stop Planner CD-ROM)* 🎧

Other Language Resources

■ *Spelling Lessons & Activities*

■ *Vocabulary Development*

■ *Daily Language Activities Transparencies*

Lesson Starter

Prior Knowledge. On the chalkboard, write the sentences *Brian just finished reading the short story "The Dragon Slayer"* and *Ella thinks* <u>Sounder</u> *is a good book.* Then, ask volunteers to explain the meaning of the quotation marks and the underlining in the titles and the reason that the two titles are punctuated differently. Point out that titles of other artistic works also have special punctuation, and ask for volunteers to list examples.

Underlining (Italics)

Rules 13a, b *(pp. 290–292)*

OBJECTIVE

■ To use underlining (italics) correctly in sentences

Modeling and Demonstration

Underlining (Italics). Model how to use underlining (italics) correctly in sentences by using the example *I deliver* The Dallas Morning News. First, ask what *The Dallas Morning News* is. [*title of a newspaper*] Next, ask whether newspaper titles should be underlined (italicized). [*yes*] Then, ask whether the word *the* is part of the newspaper's title. [*yes, according to the chart on page 290*] Therefore, *the* should be underlined (italicized) and capitalized. Point out that when *the* is part of the sentence and not part of the title, it should not be underlined (italicized) or capitalized. Now, have a volunteer use an example from this chapter to demonstrate how to use underlining (italics) correctly.

COMPUTER TIP

If you use a computer, you may be able to set words in italics yourself. Most fonts can be set in italic type.

MEETING THE CHALLENGE

Write the following categories in a column: book, play, newspaper/magazine, movie, television series, painting, long musical work. Next to each category, write the title of your favorite work. Then, make up a sentence using each of your favorite titles. After you have finished, check your work against the examples given in **Rule 13a.**

ANSWERS
Answers will vary, but students should mark answers with underlining (italics) according to the guidelines in **Rule 13a.**

Reference Note
For examples of **titles that require quotation marks** instead of italics, see page 297.

Underlining (Italics)

Italics are printed letters that lean to the right—*like this*. When you handwrite or type, you show that a word should be italicized by underlining it. If your writing were printed, the typesetter would set the underlined words in italics. For example, if you wrote

Zora Neale Hurston wrote <u>Mules and Men</u>*.*

the sentence would be printed like this:

`Zora Neale Hurston wrote` *`Mules and Men`*`.`

13a. Use underlining (italics) for titles and subtitles of books, plays, periodicals, films, television series, works of art, and long musical works.

Type of Name	Examples
Books	*Number the Stars*
	To Kill a Mockingbird
	Tibet: Through the Red Box
Plays	*Song of Sheba*
	Romeo and Juliet
	Life with Father
Periodicals	*Sioux City Journal*
	The Dallas Morning News
	Highlights for Children
Films	*Babe: Pig in the City*
	The Wizard of Oz
	Oliver & Company
Television Series	*Under the Umbrella Tree*
	Fun with Watercolors
	Reading Rainbow

Underlining (Italics)
Practice

■ *Language & Sentence Skills Practice,* pp. 260–261, 266–267, 277, 280

■ *Developmental Language & Sentence Skills,* pp. 111–112

Type of Name	Examples
Works of Art	*The Old Guitarist*
	Mona Lisa
	Confucius and Disciples
Long Musical Works	*The Pirates of Penzance*
	The Nutcracker Suite
	A Little Night Music

Generally, use italics for titles of works that stand alone, such as books, CDs, and television series. Use quotation marks for titles of works that are usually part of a larger work, such as short stories, songs, and episodes of a television series.

NOTE An article (*a, an,* or *the*) before the title of a magazine or a newspaper is not italicized or capitalized when it is part of a sentence rather than part of the title.

EXAMPLES I deliver **the** *Evening Independent.* [*The* is part of the sentence, not part of the title.]

Is that the latest issue of ***The*** *New Yorker*? [*The* is part of the magazine's title.]

13b. Use underlining (italics) for names of trains, ships, aircraft, and spacecraft.

Type of Name	Examples
Trains	*Stourbridge Lion*
	Best Friend of Charleston
Ships	*Lusitania*
	USS *Lexington*
Aircraft	*Solar Challenger*
	Hindenburg
Spacecraft	*Landsat-7*
	Discovery

┌HELP─

If you are not sure whether an article is part of a title, check the periodical's masthead (the section that lists the publisher, owners, editors, etc.) or the table of contents to find out the official title.

MECHANICS

Exercise 1

DISTRIBUTED REVIEW

Point out to students that the titles in sentences 1 and 4 in **Exercise 1** are appositives. Ask why the title in sentence 1 is not set off by commas, while the title in sentence 4 is. [*In sentence 1, the title is necessary to the meaning of the sentence. There are many magazines, and the title* Popular Science *tells which one. The title in sentence 4 is not necessary to the meaning of the sentence. The Wright brothers had only one first airplane, the* Flyer.]

Quotation Marks
Rules 13c–l *(pp. 292–299)*

OBJECTIVES

- To use punctuation and capitalization correctly in quotations
- To rewrite indirect quotations as direct quotations
- To use single and double quotation marks correctly in sentences

DIRECT TEACHING

Modeling and Demonstration

Quotation Marks. Model how to punctuate and capitalize quotations by using the incorrect example *Juan said, the bus is late*. First, ask whether the example contains Juan's exact words. [*yes; the bus is late*] Point out that since the word group *the bus is late* represents Juan's exact words, the word group is a direct quotation. Then, ask where quotation marks should be placed. [*before* the *and after the period following* late] Ask whether the first word in the direct quotation should be capitalized. [*yes; capitalize* the] Now, have a volunteer use another example to demonstrate how to punctuate and capitalize quotations.

| STYLE | TIP |

Now and then, writers will use italics (underlining) for emphasis, especially in written dialogue. Read the following sentences aloud. Notice that by italicizing different words, the writer can change the meaning of the sentence.

EXAMPLES
"Are you going to wear the *red* shoes?" asked Ellen. [Will you wear the red shoes, not the blue ones?]

"Are *you* going to wear the red shoes?" asked Ellen. [Will you, not your sister, wear them?]

"Are you going to *wear* the red shoes?" asked Ellen. [Will you wear them, or are you just trying them on?]

Italicizing (underlining) words for emphasis is a handy technique that should not be overused. It can quickly lose its impact.

Exercise 1 **Using Underlining (Italics) Correctly**

For each of the following sentences, write <u>each word or item that should be printed in italics</u> and underline it.

EXAMPLE **1.** We saw Rodin's famous statue The Thinker.

     1. The Thinker

1. The magazine <u>Popular Science</u> reports news about science.
2. Have you ever seen the movie <u>The Shaggy Dog</u>?
3. My favorite painting is <u>Morning of Red Bird</u> by Romare Bearden.
4. The Wright brothers built their first airplane, the <u>Flyer</u>, in 1903.
5. We read the play <u>You're a Good Man, Charlie Brown</u>.
6. On his famous voyage in 1492, Christopher Columbus acted as captain of the ship named the <u>Santa Maria</u>.
7. Which newspaper do you read, the <u>Chicago Sun-Times</u> or the <u>Chicago Tribune</u>?
8. My sister watches <u>Sesame Street</u> every day.
9. Aboard <u>Vostok 1</u>, Yuri A. Gagarin orbited Earth.
10. The book <u>Stuart Little</u> is by E. B. White.

Quotation Marks

13c. Use quotation marks to enclose a *direct quotation*—a person's exact words.

Be sure to place quotation marks both before and after a person's exact words.

EXAMPLES Our team leader says, "I try to practice every day."

"Let's go home," Jeanne suggested.

Do not use quotation marks for an *indirect quotation*—a rewording of a direct quotation.

DIRECT QUOTATION Juan said, "The bus is late." [Juan's exact words]

INDIRECT QUOTATION Juan said that the bus was late. [not Juan's exact words]

RESOURCES

Quotation Marks
Practice
- *Language & Sentence Skills Practice,* pp. 262–267, 277, 280
- *Developmental Language & Sentence Skills,* pp. 111–114

DIRECT QUOTATION	Juan asked, "Is the bus late?" [Juan's exact words]
INDIRECT QUOTATION	Juan asked whether the bus was late. [not Juan's exact words]

13d. A directly quoted sentence begins with a capital letter.

EXAMPLES   Mrs. Talbott said, "**P**lease get a pencil."

Kristina asked, "**I**s it my turn?"

13e. When an expression identifying the speaker interrupts a quoted sentence, the second part of the quotation begins with a lowercase letter.

EXAMPLE   "Will you take care of my lawn and my pets," asked Mr. Franklin, "**w**hile I'm on vacation next month?"

When the second part of a divided quotation is a new sentence, it begins with a capital letter.

EXAMPLE   "Yes, we will," I said. "**W**e can use the extra money."

13f. A direct quotation can be set off from the rest of the sentence by a comma, a question mark, or an exclamation point, but not by a period.

(1) If a quotation comes at the beginning of a sentence, a comma, question mark, or exclamation point usually follows it.

EXAMPLES   "Dogs make better pets than cats do**.**" said Frank.

"Have you ever had a cat**?**" Donna asked.

"No, and I never will**!**" he replied.

(2) If a quotation comes at the end of a sentence, a comma usually comes before it.

EXAMPLE   Maria asked**,** "What makes you say that?"

(3) If a quoted sentence is divided, a comma usually follows the first part and comes before the second part.

EXAMPLE   "Oh**,**" Donna commented**,** "he's probably just saying that because he's never had a cat."

┌HELP─

To set off means "to separate."

DIFFERENTIATING INSTRUCTION

English-Language Learners

Spanish and Vietnamese. Although quotation marks are not unheard of in Spanish and Vietnamese, it is far more common to use dashes to set off quotations. For example:

—No—he said—I don't believe you.

When quotation marks are used, they look like this: « ».

Special Education Students

Some students may have difficulty identifying an unpunctuated direct quotation, especially if it is interrupted by explanatory or declarative text. Have these students copy an exercise sentence that contains a direct quotation. Next, pair each student having difficulty with a partner who can read the sentence aloud, emphasizing the quoted words. Tell the student having difficulty to repeat only the quoted words.

Learners Having Difficulty

Some students may be able to create dialogue but may not know how to punctuate it. You might pair these students with students who have a good grasp of punctuation. Have each student who has difficulty dictate some dialogue to the other student. Then, have the other student punctuate the dialogue and discuss the punctuation with the student who has difficulty. Finally, you may wish to have students switch roles so that the student who has difficulty can practice punctuating quotations offered by his or her partner.

Quotation Marks

Activity. Some students will learn punctuation rules more easily if sentences are broken into parts. For this activity, you may want to use sentences 1, 2, 4, 8, and 9 from **Exercise 2,** which require only punctuation and not additional capitalization. Have a volunteer write parts of each sentence on pieces of stiff cardboard; one or two pieces will contain the quotation itself (depending on whether or not the quoted sentence is divided), and the other piece will contain the text identifying the speaker(s). For example, for sentence 8 the words *That means* should be written on one card, the words *said Barbara* on another, and the words *that the water will be cold* on the last card. Then, the volunteer should create a set of cards with eight punctuation marks: two large opening quotation marks, two large closing quotation marks, two large commas, one large question mark, and one large period. Finally, select students to come to the front of the class and arrange the cards correctly for each sentence. (The one set of cards of punctuation marks can be reused for each sentence.)

13g. A period or a comma should be placed inside the closing quotation marks.

EXAMPLE   "I can't wait to see Shirley Caesar's new video**.**" James said. "It's supposed to come out next week**.**"

13h. A question mark or an exclamation point should be placed inside closing quotation marks when the quotation itself is a question or an exclamation. Otherwise, it should be placed outside.

EXAMPLES   "What time will you be home from work, Mom**?**" asked Michael. [The quotation is a question.]

Who said, "All the world's a stage"**?** [The sentence, not the quotation, is a question.]

"Stop**!**" yelled the crossing guard. [The quotation is an exclamation.]

What a surprise to hear Susana say, "We're moving back to Puerto Rico in June"**!** [The sentence, not the quotation, is an exclamation.]

Exercise 2 Punctuating and Capitalizing Quotations

Rewrite the following sentences, using commas, end marks, quotation marks, and capital letters where they are needed. If a sentence is already correct, write *C*.

EXAMPLE   1. We're going tubing next Saturday said Carlos.
     1. *"We're going tubing next Saturday," said Carlos.*

1. May I go with you I asked.
2. We'd like to go, too added Barbara and Tranh.
3. Barbara asked who will bring tubes for everyone?
4. Jim said I'll bring them.
5. I offered to bring sandwiches and lemonade. 5. C
6. My dad will drive said Carlos he has a van.
7. Tranh told us that the river is fed by a glacier. 7. C
8. That means said Barbara that the water will be cold.
9. It should feel good I pointed out if Saturday is as hot as today is.
10. Carlos told all of us to meet him at his house at 8:30 A.M.   10. C

Exercise 3 **Punctuating and Capitalizing Quotations**

Rewrite each of the following sentences correctly, using
punctuation and capitalization as needed.

EXAMPLE   **1.** Clementine Hunter was born in 1887 said María
            and she died in 1988.

           *1. "Clementine Hunter was born in 1887," said María,
              "and she died in 1988."*

1. Staci said here is a photograph of this self-taught
   American artist.
2. Clementine Hunter was born in Natchitoches, Louisiana
   Staci remarked.
3. She started working on a plantation when she was only
   fourteen María added.
4. When she was fifty-three years old said Staci Hunter
   decided to do what she loved most—paint.
5. Staci continued she began painting on almost any surface that would hold the paint!
6. Her early pieces were painted on brown paper bags and
   cardboard boxes María remarked and then on canvas,
   wood, and paper.
7. Hunter used bright colors Mike explained to paint everyday scenes like this one, called *Wash Day.*
8. It may surprise you to
   learn added Mike that her
   paintings sold for as little
   as twenty-five cents fifty
   years ago!
9. María asked Mike didn't
   you say that her paintings
   are now worth thousands
   of dollars?
10. Moreover Staci concluded
    Clementine Hunter's
    paintings have been
    exhibited throughout the
    United States.
9. [*or* María asked Mike,
   "Didn't you . . ."]

Clementine Hunter (c. 1945). Photo from the Mildred Bailey Collection, Natchitoches, Louisiana.

Clementine Hunter, *Wash Day.* The collection of Thomas N. Whitehead, courtesy of the Association
for the Preservation of Historical Natchitoches, Louisiana, Melrose Plantation.

Quotation Marks   **295**

MECHANICS

CONTENT-AREA CONNECTIONS

Social Studies

Writing About the Old South. In her
paintings, the artist Clementine Hunter portrayed African American life on a Southern
plantation. Numerous plantation houses still
exist in the South, and many of those houses
have been restored. Some of the houses are
now historical sites, and their histories
have been thoroughly documented. Have
students research an aspect of plantation
life in the Old South or the history of a
specific plantation house. Then, have students write a one-page report including at
least one quotation about their subject.

MECHANICS

Exercise 4 Revising Indirect Quotations to Create Direct Quotations

ANSWERS

Revisions may vary.

1. The cashier replied, "I'm not allowed to make change unless a purchase is made."
2. "I need a new pen," I said.
3. "It costs seventy-nine cents," the cashier told me.
4. I said, "I will give you $1.79."
5. "I can give you change for a dollar," she told me.
6. "How do you want the change?" the cashier asked.
7. I said, "Three quarters, two dimes, and a nickel would be good."
8. "I do not have any more dimes in my cash register," she replied.
9. "Then," I said, "I will gladly take four quarters."
10. "That's okay, but why do you want change?" she said.

APPLICATION

Direct and Indirect Quotations

Activity. Distribute to each student a short newspaper or magazine article that uses direct and indirect quotations. Then, have each student circle direct quotations and underline indirect quotations in his or her article. Afterward, have students trade articles with partners and check each other's work.

HELP

You will need to change some pronouns and verb forms in Exercise 4.

Exercise 4 Revising Indirect Quotations to Create Direct Quotations

Revise each of the following sentences to change the indirect quotation to a direct quotation. Be sure to use capital letters and punctuation marks where they are needed.

EXAMPLE 1. I asked the cashier for change for a dollar.
1. *"May I please have change for a dollar?" I asked the cashier.*

1. The cashier replied that she was not allowed to make change unless a purchase was made.
2. I said that I needed a new pen.
3. The cashier told me that it cost seventy-nine cents.
4. I said that I would give her $1.79.
5. She told me she could give me change for a dollar.
6. The cashier asked how I wanted the change.
7. I said that three quarters, two dimes, and a nickel would be good.
8. She replied that she did not have any more dimes in her cash register.
9. Then I said that I would gladly take four quarters.
10. She said that was okay but asked why I wanted change.

13i. When you write dialogue (conversation), begin a new paragraph every time the speaker changes.

EXAMPLE   In Khanabad, Mulla Nasrudin was sitting in a tea house when a stranger walked in and sat down beside him.
    The newcomer said:
    "Why is that man over there sobbing his heart out?"
    "Because I have just arrived from his hometown and told him that all his winter camel fodder was lost in a fire."
    "It is terrible to be a bearer of such tidings," said the stranger.
    "It is also interesting to be the man who will shortly tell him the good news," said Nasrudin. "You see, his camels have died of a plague, so he will not need the fodder after all."

    Idries Shah, "Camel Fodder"

13j. When a quotation consists of several sentences, put quotation marks only at the beginning and the end of the whole quotation.

EXAMPLE   "Will Bao help with the play? Zachary has offered to make costumes," Aaron said.

13k. Use single quotation marks to enclose a quotation within a quotation.

EXAMPLE   "Mrs. Engle distinctly said, 'Your book reports are due Thursday,'" Krista told me.

13l. Use quotation marks to enclose the titles of short works such as short stories, poems, newspaper or magazine articles, songs, episodes of television series, and chapters and other parts of books.

Type Of Name	Examples
Short Stories	"The Stone" "All Summer in a Day"
Poems	"Jetliner" "Song of the Sky Loom"
Articles	"Celebrating Our Heritage" "The Giants of Easter Island"
Songs	"Georgia on My Mind" "America the Beautiful"
Episodes of Television Series	"Kali the Lion" "The Trouble with Tribbles"
Chapters and Other Parts of Books	"Energy from the Stars" "I Go to Sea"

NOTE   Titles that appear in quotation marks are set in single quotation marks when they appear within a quotation.

EXAMPLE   Kris said, "Our class learned 'America the Beautiful' today."

⌐TIPS & TRICKS⌐

In general, the title of a work that can stand alone (for instance, a novel, a TV series, a collection of poems) is in italics. The title of a work that is usually part of a collection or series (for instance, a chapter of a book, an episode of a television series, a poem) is in quotation marks.

Reference Note

┌ For examples of **titles that require italics** instead of quotation marks, see page 290.

EXTENSION

Relating to Literature

Some excellent dialogue for discussion can be found in the "Riddles in the Dark" chapter of J.R.R. Tolkien's *The Hobbit*. To illustrate how Tolkien uses dialogue for characterization, read aloud several examples and ask your students to identify the speaker as Bilbo or Gollum. Ask students to identify places where Tolkien's use of punctuation contributes to meaning.

APPLICATION

Quotation Marks or Underlining?

Activity. Divide the class into groups of five, and give each group a list of books, plays, stories, articles, and poems taken from the table of contents of a literature textbook. Have each group member take responsibility for one of the five types of works. Each member should decide for each title in his or her category whether it should be underlined or placed in quotation marks. Then the five members should correctly write their titles on poster board, noting to the side of each title the relevant rule from this chapter (**Rules 13a** or **13l**). Ask a volunteer from each group to present the group's poster to the rest of the class.

MECHANICS

Punctuating Quotations and Titles

Rewrite the following sentences, adding single and double quotation marks where they are needed.

EXAMPLE
1. I just finished the chapter The Circulatory System in our health book, Dell told me.

1. "I just finished the chapter 'The Circulatory System' in our health book," Dell told me.

1. Diane is learning the song "This Little Rose" for her recital.
2. "Angelo, can we meet after school tomorrow? We need to practice our presentation," Sam said.
3. "I'm sure I heard the announcer say, 'Schools are closed because of the storm," I said.   3. storm,'"
4. "I can pronounce all the words in Lewis Carroll's poem Jabberwocky," Nina told Lou.   4. 'Jabberwocky,'"
5. Ted said, "My dad will pick us up on Saturday at 7:30 A.M. After the race, he is taking us to Lucy Chang's for lunch. Do you like Chinese food?"
6. "The weather should be nice tomorrow. Let's plan on hiking in the woods," Eric said.
7. Mrs. Banister said, "'The Fun They Had' is a good short story, don't you think?"
8. "Have you read 'The Toaster'? Sue May asked. "It's the funniest poem I know."
9. One article in the newspaper this morning is titled "Black Scientists Make History."
10. "Strong's new song is 'Be True, Not Blue,' and it's great!" Marcie said.

┌ HELP ─
All of the punctuation marks already in Review A are correct.

Review A **Punctuating Paragraphs in a Dialogue**

Rewrite the following paragraphs, using capital letters as well as quotation marks and other marks of punctuation where they are needed.

EXAMPLE
[1] What are you writing my grandfather asked.
1. "What are you writing?" my grandfather asked.

[1] "Grandpa," I said, "I'm writing a report about your hero, Octaviano Larrazolo. Can you tell me how he helped Mexican Americans?"

Learning for Life

Keeping a Journal. Personal journals give writers a window into their pasts. A writer can look back on journal entries to recall important events or favorite artistic works or moments. Have students compose journal entries about their favorite books, magazines, music, movies, television programs or series, short stories, and poems. Explain that in a few years they will be able to read about some of the things that were important to them in the sixth grade.

In writing these journal entries, students

[2] Grandpa got out his scrapbook."Octaviano did many things for our people,"he began."In 1912, New Mexico became a state. Octaviano and other Hispanic leaders wanted to be sure that Mexican Americans could hold political office. They wanted to make certain that they would always be allowed to vote. When New Mexico's new constitution was written, Octaviano and the other leaders fought for these rights."

[3]"How did Mr. Larrazolo know how to protect the rights of people?"I said.

[4] Grandpa replied,"he had studied law. His knowledge of the law helped him understand the constitution. It also helped him later when he became interested in politics."

[5]"When did Mr. Larrazolo become involved in politics?" I asked.

[6]"In 1916, he campaigned for Ezequiel Cabeza de Baca for governor,"said Grandpa."De Baca was elected, but he died a month later. Another election was held, and Larrazolo became New Mexico's governor."

[7] I asked,"what are some things that Mr. Larrazolo felt strongly about?"

[8] He answered,"Octaviano believed that public schools should teach children about Mexican American culture. He also was in favor of both English and Spanish being spoken in schools. Here is a picture of him with his daughters."

[9]"What else should I know about Octaviano Larrazolo?"I asked Grandpa.

[10]"Octaviano was elected to the United States Senate in 1928,"Grandpa said."He continued to work hard for the rights of Hispanic Americans until he died. If you want to read more about him, I have a copy of an article,"Octaviano Larrazolo: New Mexico's Greatest Governor,"here in my scrapbook."

Photo: Wesley Bradfield. Courtesy Museum of New Mexico, #47660.

Quotation Marks **299**

should correctly underline (or italicize if they complete this assignment using a computer) or place in quotation marks titles of their favorite works.

Apostrophes, Hyphens, and Parentheses

Rules 13m–x *(pp. 300–312)*

OBJECTIVES

- To use apostrophes to write the singular and plural possessives of nouns
- To use apostrophes correctly in the possessive forms of personal pronouns and indefinite pronouns
- To use apostrophes correctly in contractions
- To form correctly the plurals of numbers, letters, words used as words, and symbols using apostrophes
- To use hyphens correctly
- To use parentheses correctly

MECHANICS

DIRECT TEACHING

Modeling and Demonstration

Apostrophes. Model how to use apostrophes correctly by using the incorrect examples *Heidis comb,* *mens clothing,* and *boxes lids.* Ask what is being expressed in the phrase *Heidis comb.* [*possession*] Ask where the apostrophe should be placed to show possession. [*before the* s *in* Heidis] Next, ask how to form the possessive of *men.* [*men's clothing*] Then, ask how to form the possessive of *boxes.* [*boxes' lids*] Point out that plural nouns that do not end in *s* form the possessive by adding an apostrophe and an *s,* and that plural nouns that end in *s* form the possessive by adding just an apostrophe. Now, have a volunteer use another example from this chapter to demonstrate how to use apostrophes to show possession.

Apostrophes

Possessive Case

The ***possessive case*** of a noun or a pronoun shows ownership or possession.

EXAMPLES **Heidi's** comb no **one's** fault

his jacket **two weeks'** vacation

our dog **my** stepbrother

13m. To form the possessive case of a singular noun, add an apostrophe and an *s.*

EXAMPLES a student**'s** grant Tanaka**'s** store

the child**'s** toy Tess**'s** painting

NOTE A proper noun ending in –*s* may take only an apostrophe to form the possessive case if adding –'*s* would make the name awkward to say.

EXAMPLES the Netherlands**'** climate

Ms. Andrews**'** class

Exercise 6 Using Apostrophes for Singular Possessives

For each of the following sentences, identify the word that needs an apostrophe. Then, correctly write the word.

EXAMPLE 1. Kenyans celebrate 1963 as the year of their countrys independence.

1. *country's*

1. Soon that young nations athletes were setting records in international sports.
2. Leading Kenyas world-class distance runners was Kipchoge Keino, shown on the next page.
3. Keino increased his endurance by running many miles in his homelands mountains.
4. In 1965, he burst into his sports top ranks by setting world records for both the 3,000-meter and the 5,000-meter races.

RESOURCES

Apostrophes
Practice
- *Language & Sentence Skills Practice,* pp. 268–273, 278, 280
- *Developmental Language & Sentence Skills,* pp. 115–116

5. Training in the mountains helped Keino win a gold medal at Mexico City's 1968 Olympics.
6. His record in that year's 1,500-meter race stood until 1984.
7. In fact, the Kenyan team's runners took home a total of eight medals in 1968.
8. In the 1972 Olympics, Keino's performance won him a second gold medal, this time for the 3,000-meter steeplechase.
9. A silver medal in the 1,500-meter race marked his career's remarkable completion.
10. His victories won Keino the world's praise and set new standards for all runners.

13n. To form the possessive case of a plural noun that does not end in s, add an apostrophe and an s.

EXAMPLES   geese**'s** feathers   men**'s** clothing

children**'s** books   feet**'s** bones

13o. To form the possessive case of a plural noun ending in s, add only the apostrophe.

EXAMPLES   boxes**'** lids   ten minutes**'** time

beetles**'** shells   the Ozawas**'** address

NOTE   In general, you should not use an apostrophe to form the plural of a noun.

INCORRECT   Two boy's left their books here.

CORRECT   Two **boys** left their books here.

Exercise 7   **Writing Plural Possessives**

For each of the following sentences, identify the word that needs an apostrophe. Then, correctly write the word.

EXAMPLE   1. Wild creatures survival depends on their ability to adapt.
    1. creatures'

1. Animals' ways of dealing with cold are fascinating.

Reference Note

For information about **using apostrophes to form the plurals of letters, numerals, symbols, and words used as words,** see page 307.

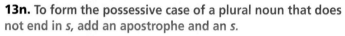
English-Language Learners

Romance Languages. Some students who speak Spanish or French may have difficulty using possessive nouns in English because their native languages do not have a possessive ending that resembles –'s. The most common way of expressing possession in those languages is with the preposition *de*, which means "of." Students may, therefore, generate phrases such as *the book of Lisa*, or they may use correct English word order but simply omit the possessive suffix, resulting in *Lisa book*. You may want to create an exercise such as the following one.

1. That pen belongs to Felipe. [*That is Felipe's pen.*]

2. This suitcase belongs to Martha. [*This is Martha's suitcase.*]

Special Education Students

Making It Real. Select or borrow several specific, recognizable objects from members of the class. For example, you might choose a backpack, a jacket, and so forth. Be sure that students will recognize who owns each object. Then, hold the objects up in front of the students and have them write down the name of each object and its owner. Have students use the possessive form of the name with the item, for example, *Roberto's backpack*.

MECHANICS

English-Language Learners

Hmong. Because written Hmong relies upon a possessive noun classifier to indicate possession, the language does not include the use of the possessive apostrophe. Therefore, Hmong speakers may find the mark confusing in both translation and use. Be sure to offer extra time for review and practice in using the apostrophe as a possessive signifier, and assist with any difficulties with translation.

2. At night, chickadees feathers are fluffed over the soft down next to their skin.
3. In addition, the birds breathing rates and heartbeats slow, and their body temperatures fall, saving energy.
4. Deer's winter coats, made of hollow hairs filled with air, keep body heat from escaping. **4.** [*or* Deers']
5. Soft undercoats of fine hair are many animals thermal underwear.
6. In the picture on the left, you can see how squirrels tails, flattened against their backs and necks, keep them warm when they leave their nests.

7. The picture on the right shows how red foxes tails are used as muffs curled around their heads while they sleep.
8. Even though their fur is white, polar bears skin is black for absorbing heat from the sun.
9. In cold weather, fur grows on the bottom of snowshoe hares feet for protection.
10. Some wild creatures survival during freezing temperatures and snow depends on traits like these.

Review B **Writing Possessives**

Rewrite each of the following expressions by using the possessive case. Be sure to add apostrophes where they are needed.

EXAMPLE **1.** the speeches of the politicians
    1. the politicians' speeches

1. the books of the children **1.** the children's books

2. the prize of the winner   **2.** the winner's prize

3. the bed of the kittens   **3.** the kittens' bed

4. the home of my friend   **4.** my friend's home

5. the streets of the city   **5.** the city's streets

6. the fish of the teacher   **6.** the teacher's fish

7. the cars of the women   **7.** the women's cars

8. the dens of the foxes   **8.** the foxes' dens

9. the fables of Aesop   **9.** Aesop's fables

10. the medal of Rowan   **10.** Rowan's medal

11. the hiding place of the mice   **11.** the mice's hiding place

12. the idea of the boss   **12.** the boss's idea

13. the plans of the builders   **13.** the builders' plans

14. the diet of moose   **14.** the moose's diet

15. the climate of the Cook Islands   **15.** the Cook Islands' climate

16. the lawnmower of the Barkers   **16.** the Barkers' lawnmower

17. the shoes of the girls   **17.** the girls' shoes

18. the elephants of the zoo   **18.** the zoo's elephants

19. the roads of the cities   **19.** the cities' roads

20. the computer of the company   **20.** the company's computer

21. the desks of the students   **21.** the students' desks

22. the driveway of the neighbor   **22.** the neighbor's driveway

23. the tail of the dog   **23.** the dog's tail

24. the stories of Mark Twain   **24.** Mark Twain's stories

25. the history of Texas   **25.** Texas's history [*or* Texas' history]

13p. Do not use an apostrophe with possessive personal pronouns.

EXAMPLES   Is this pencil **yours** or **mine**?

Our apartment is smaller than **theirs**.

Her enchiladas are spicier than **his**.

13q. To form the possessive case of many indefinite pronouns, add an apostrophe and an *s*.

EXAMPLES   either's topic

everyone's favorite

somebody's notebook

Reference Note

For more information about **possessive personal pronouns**, see page 177. For more information about **indefinite pronouns**, see page 34.

Apostrophes   **303**

DIRECT TEACHING

Possessive Personal and Indefinite Pronouns

Activity. Rules **13p** and **13q** explain the use of apostrophes with possessive pronouns. To help students distinguish between the punctuation of possessive personal pronouns and that of possessive indefinite pronouns, give them the practice exercise below and ask them to insert apostrophes where needed. Remind students that possessive personal pronouns do not require apostrophes, whereas many possessive indefinite pronouns do.

theirs	anybodys ['s]
everyones ['s]	ours
his	everybodys ['s]
yours	eithers ['s]
someones ['s]	hers
nobodys ['s]	anothers ['s]

MINI-LESSON **Usage**   **Continued on p. 304**

Personal Pronouns. You might want to review briefly common usage problems involving possessive pronouns. Some usage problems are discussed in **Chapter 10: A Glossary of Usage,** p. 220. Ask students to choose the correct word to complete each of the following sentences.

  1. Rafael and Lisha forgot to bring (*they're, their*) project to class this morning. [*their*]

Apostrophes   **303**

EXTENSION

Relating to Literature

Select an example of literary dialogue from your textbook or from a story such as Gary Soto's "La Bamba" or Isaac Asimov's "The Fun They Had." Be sure that the passage contains several contractions. Read the passage aloud as it is written. Then, read it aloud again, reading the contractions as separate, complete words. For example, say *are not* for *aren't*. Ask students which version they prefer and why they prefer it. Discuss with students the importance of representing oral language realistically in dialogue.

STYLE		TIP

Some people consider contractions informal. Therefore, it is generally best not to use them in formal writing and speech.

Oral Practice **The Possessive Case of Personal Pronouns and Indefinite Pronouns**

Read each of the following expressions aloud. Then, change each expression so that it uses the possessive case, and say the new version aloud. Finally, say which expressions need an apostrophe when they are written.

EXAMPLE   **1.** the speeches of everybody
     1. everybody's speeches

1. the wishes of everyone **1.** everyone's wishes
2. the fault of him **2.** his fault
3. the answer of no one **3.** no one's answer
4. the album of someone **4.** someone's album
5. the guess of me **5.** my guess
6. the job of neither **6.** neither's job
7. the color of something **7.** something's color
8. the deal of anyone **8.** anyone's deal
9. the sweaters of them **9.** their sweaters
10. the notebook of you **10.** your notebook

Contractions

13r. Use an apostrophe to show where letters, numerals, or words have been left out in a contraction.

A **contraction** is a shortened form of a word, a numeral, or a group of words. The apostrophe in a contraction shows where letters, numerals, or words have been left out.

Common Contractions	
I am . . . . I'm	they have . . . . they've
1999 . . . . '99	here is . . . . here's
let us . . . . let's	you are . . . . you're
of the clock . . . . o'clock	she is . . . . she's
movie is . . . . movie's	Bill has . . . . Bill's
he would . . . . he'd	you will . . . . you'll

    The word *not* can be shortened to *n't* and added to a verb. The spelling of the verb usually does not change.

MINI-LESSON **Usage**   *Continued from p. 303*

2. May Donna borrow (*your, you're*) pencil? [*your*]

3. The cat licked (*its, it's*) paws. [*its*]

4. (*Whose, Who's*) book is this? [*Whose*]

EXAMPLES

is not	isn**'**t	has not	has**n**'t
are not	are**n**'t	have not	have**n**'t
does not	does**n**'t	had not	had**n**'t
do not	do**n**'t	should not	should**n**'t
was not	was**n**'t	would not	would**n**'t
were not	were**n**'t	could not	could**n**'t

EXCEPTIONS   will not ...... **won't**   cannot .... **can't**

Do not confuse contractions with possessive pronouns.

Contractions	Possessive Pronouns
It's [*It is*] raining. **It's** [*It has*] been a long day.	**Its** tires are flat.
Who's [*Who is*] your coach? **Who's** [*Who has*] been in my room?	**Whose** watch is this?
You're [*You are*] welcome.	**Your** sister won.
They're [*They are*] late.	**Their** house is next door.
There's [*There is*] the bell.	That car is **theirs**.

Exercise 8   Using Apostrophes in Contractions

For the following sentences, write the <u>word or numeral that requires an apostrophe</u> and insert the apostrophe. If a sentence is already correct, write *C*.

EXAMPLE   **1.** Well be leaving soon.

      1. We'll

1. You<u>'</u>ve been a big help.
2. You<u>'</u>d better hurry up.
3. Whose umbrella is this?   **3.** C
4. We<u>'</u>re having a fund-raiser for the homeless.
5. I can<u>'</u>t find my skateboard.
6. He promised he<u>'</u>d wear his seat belt.
7. Let<u>'</u>s get tickets to see the concert.

┌HELP─────

To avoid the common error of confusing *it's* for *its*, proofread your work carefully. When you come to the contraction *it's*, substitute *it is* or *it has*. If the sentence sounds right with the substitution, the contraction is probably correct. If it doesn't sound right, the possessive pronoun *its* is probably correct.

EXAMPLES

It's your turn. [*It is your turn* makes sense. The contraction for *It is* is correct.]

I like our new car, but it's trunk is very small. [. . . *but it is trunk is very small* does not make sense; the possessive pronoun *its* is needed in this sentence.]

DIRECT TEACHING

Contractions and Possessive Pronouns

Activity. Have students prepare a poster or a display with the pairs of confusing possessive pronouns and contractions shown in the chart on this page.

Contractions	Pronouns
it's	its
who's	whose
you're	your
they're	their
there's	theirs

Tell students to refer to this display when they are completing exercises or writing.

PRACTICE

Guided and Independent

Exercise 8   You may wish to use the first ten items of **Exercise 8** as guided practice. Then, have students complete the exercise as independent practice.   **HOMEWORK**

DIRECT TEACHING

Correcting Misconceptions

Contractions and Possessive Pronouns. Some students may mistakenly think that the apostrophe in the contraction *it's* indicates possession and thus use that word instead of the correct possessive pronoun *its*. Tell students they can remember which form stands for two words (*it is*) by remembering that the apostrophe in *it's* separates the word into two parts. The form that is in two parts stands for the form that is two words. Two parts equals two words.

English-Language Learners

Hmong. Since written Hmong does not use apostrophes, Hmong speakers may find English contractions confusing. Remind students that English uses apostrophes in contractions to indicate missing vowels. Have students practice forming contractions: *Do not, don't; I am, I'm.*

8. It's time to leave for the party.
9. Its wings are painted blue. 9. C
10. I'll wash the car tomorrow morning.
11. Daniel asked the decoration committee who's going to be in charge.
12. Isn't this the book we need?
13. Remember to give your dog fresh water. 13. C
14. Stephanie said she'll bring a cardboard box from home.
15. This is a picture of my parents in '99, the year before my half-brother was born.
16. If that hummingbird returns to the feeder, I'm going to take a picture.
17. Theirs will be the last band to perform. 17. C
18. The cold weather doesn't bother Jeremy much.
19. We should be back to school by three o'clock.
20. Have you found out yet if you're on the team?

Exercise 9 **Writing Contractions**

For each of the following sentences, write the contraction of the italicized word or words.

EXAMPLE   1. *We will* see a performance of the puppet theater when we visit the Japan America Theatre in Los Angeles.
             1. *We'll*

1. *Have not* you always wondered what goes on backstage at a puppet show? 1. Haven't

2. *Here is* an illustration that takes you behind the scenes at a seventeenth-century puppet theater in Japan. **2.** Here's

3. The audience *cannot* see all the backstage action because of the curtain. **3.** can't

4. The men *who are* handling the puppets in the picture are very highly trained. **4.** who're

5. They *do not* speak the characters' lines, though. **5.** don't

6. *It is* the man sitting on the right on the platform who narrates the play. **6.** It's

7. As you can see, *he is* accompanied by a musician. **7.** he's

8. On the right are more puppets; *they have* been hung there for future use. **8.** they've

9. In the box at the top, *that is* the Japanese word that means "puppet." **9.** that's

10. As *you will* notice, the Japanese system of writing is very different from ours. **10.** you'll

Plurals

13s. Use an apostrophe and an *s* to form the plurals of letters, numerals, and symbols, and of words referred to as words.

EXAMPLES I think the word *Mississippi* has four *i*'s, four *s* 's, and two *p*'s.

Your *1*'s and *7*'s look alike.

You wrote +'s instead of *x*'s in these math problems.

Try not to use so many *you know* 's when you talk.

Exercise 10 Forming Plurals by Using Apostrophes

Correctly form the plural of each of the following items.

EXAMPLE   **1.** *9*
          1. *9*'s

1. *I*'s	6. #'s	11. *14*'s	16. *B*'s	21. $'s
2. *t*'s	7. *A*'s	12. %'s	17. *3*'s	22. *'s
3. @'s	8. *.com*'s	13. *at*'s	18. +'s	23. *uh oh*'s
4. *it*'s	9. *too*'s	14. *?*'s	19. *!*'s	24. ='s
5. *6*'s	10. *thou*'s	15. *and*'s	20. *of*'s	25. /'s

DIRECT TEACHING

Apostrophes with Plurals

Activity. Ask students to suggest sentences that include the plurals of letters, numerals, symbols, or words referred to as words while you write the sentences on the chalkboard. As you write the sentences, query students about the correct way to write the plural forms of letters.

Then, ask two or three volunteers to come to the chalkboard and, using the first example sentence under **Rule 13s** as a model, write sentences that describe how many times each letter of the alphabet appears in the name of their school, town, state, or region; or in the name of a family member, friend, or famous person. The volunteers should choose a name that has at least one letter that appears more than once. When volunteers have finished writing their sentences, ask the rest of the class whether the writers have used apostrophes correctly.

Using Hyphens to Divide Words

Activity. Place students in small groups. Give each group a list of ten words. Have the groups determine which words can be divided and then divide them correctly with hyphens. Possible words are *carpet, kitchen, basketball, desk, poster, sweater, friend,* and *football.* Include one or two one-syllable words, which cannot be divided, on each list. Provide a dictionary for each group of students.

Relating to Literature

Poetry. In his poetry, E. E. Cummings often uses hyphens and compound words to contribute to his meaning. For example, in "hist whist" he makes up the compound *ghostthings* and uses hyphens in the words *tip-toe, twinkle-toe,* and *hob-a-nob.* If this poem is available in your library, read it aloud to your students, carefully quickening your speed when you get to these words to indicate the poet's intention to emphasize the poem's rhythm. Then, ask students what effect the poet achieves by using these hyphenated words.

┌HELP─

You may need to look up words in a dictionary to be sure of how to divide them into syllables.

┌STYLE━━━━━━TIP┐

Hyphens are often used in compound names. In such cases, the hyphen is thought of as part of the spelling of the name.

EXAMPLES
 Margaret Bourke-White
 Kung-sun Lung
 Terry-Jo
 Edward Levy-Lawson

If you are not sure whether a compound name is hyphenated, ask the person with that name, or look up the name in a reference source.

Hyphens

13t. Use a hyphen to divide a word at the end of a line.

When you divide a word at the end of a line, remember the following rules:

(1) Divide a word only between syllables.

INCORRECT	Uncle Payat, Aunt Nina, and Ayita will jou-rney eighty miles to join us.
CORRECT	Uncle Payat, Aunt Nina, and Ayita will jour-ney eighty miles to join us.

(2) Do not divide a one-syllable word.

INCORRECT	They are bringing a salad, ham, and rye bre-ad.
CORRECT	They are bringing a salad, ham, and rye bread.

(3) Do not divide a word so that one letter stands alone.

INCORRECT	Is that your family's brand-new car parked a-cross the street?
CORRECT	Is that your family's brand-new car parked across the street?

13u. Use a hyphen with compound numbers from *twenty-one* to *ninety-nine.*

EXAMPLE   Until 1959, the United States had only forty-eight stars in its flag.

13v. Hyphenate a compound adjective when it comes before the noun it modifies.

EXAMPLES   an activity that is well planned

a **well-planned** activity

a flavor that is long lasting

a **long-lasting** flavor

Some compound adjectives are always hyphenated, whether they come before or after the nouns they modify.

RESOURCES

Hyphens
Practice
■ *Language & Sentence Skills Practice,* p. 274, 276, 279–280

EXAMPLES   a **brand-new** bicycle

a bicycle that is **brand-new**

an **up-to-date** encyclopedia

an encyclopedia that is **up-to-date**

13w. Use a hyphen with the prefixes *all–, ex–, great–, self–,* and with the suffixes *–elect* and *–free.*

EXAMPLES   all-purpose   self-confidence

ex-students   governor-elect

great-grandfather   sugar-free

Exercise 11 **Using Hyphens Correctly**

Write each of the following words. Add hyphens to show where the word may be divided at the end of a line or where they are needed in a compound word. If a word should not be hyphenated, write *do not hyphenate.*

EXAMPLES   **1.** tomorrow
1. *to-mor-row*   The ⌄ symbol indicates a hyphen.

2. self aware
2. *self-aware*

3. theme
3. *do not hyphenate*

1. loose **1.** d.n.h.
2. all-star
3. temporary
4. ex-wife
5. children
6. elect **6.** d.n.h.
7. principal
8. decorate
9. self-help
10. through **10.** d.n.h.
11. immediately
12. fat-free
13. seize **13.** d.n.h.
14. broomstick
15. great-aunt
16. piano
17. preferred
18. grammar
19. lint-free
20. among **20.** d.n.h.

---HELP---

If you are not sure whether a compound adjective is always hyphenated, look up the word in a dictionary.

---HELP---

The prefix *half–* often requires a hyphen, as in *half-life, half-moon,* and *half-truth.* However, sometimes *half* is used without a hyphen, either as a part of a single word (*halftone, halfway, halfback*) or as a separate word (*half shell, half pint, half note*). If you are not sure how to spell a word containing *half,* look up the word in a current dictionary.

Word breaks are based on *Webster's New World College Dictionary, Third Edition.*

PRACTICE

Guided and Independent

Exercise 11 You might want to use the first ten items of **Exercise 11** as guided practice. Then, have students complete the exercise as independent practice. You might want to provide a dictionary so that each student can check that he or she has hyphenated the words correctly.

HOMEWORK

MECHANICS

COMPUTER TIP

Some word-processing programs will automatically divide a word at the end of a line and insert a hyphen. Sometimes the program will divide a word at the wrong place. Always check a printout of your writing to see how the computer has hyphenated words at the ends of lines. If a hyphen is used incorrectly, move the word to the next line or divide the word yourself by correctly inserting a "hard" hyphen (one that the computer will not move).

Exercise 12 Using Hyphens in Numbers and in Compound Words

In the following sentences, identify each word or word group that needs a hyphen. Then, write the words or word groups correctly, using the required hyphens. If all words in a sentence are correct, write *C*.

EXAMPLE   1. My brother will be twenty one next week.

1. *twenty-one*   The ‸ symbol indicates a hyphen.

1. The ex‸mayor is now running for governor.
2. Are your information sources up‸to‸date?
3. The movie was well produced and well acted.   **3.** C
4. My sister, who is twenty‸seven, is getting married in March.
5. Gretchen's great‸grandmother came to the United States from the Netherlands.
6. Tree‸ripened peaches taste much better than peaches that are picked green.
7. To keep your photographs in good condition, put them in scrapbooks that are made with acid‸free paper.
8. When John was named an all‸American, his parents were very pleased.
9. That kind of flower is self‸pollinating, isn't it?
10. Six of the twenty‸six students in my class have hyphenated names.

Review C Using Apostrophes and Hyphens Correctly

Correctly write the word or letter that needs an apostrophe or a hyphen in each of the following sentences.

EXAMPLE   1. Wheres my history book?

1. *Where's*   The ‸ symbol indicates a hyphen.

1. Do you know where the atlases and the two diction‸aries are?
2. There are two r's in *tomorrow*.
3. The last speaker was the ex‸president of the Town Council.
4. The tiger cubs aren't on view yet.
5. Is that one of Bessie Smith's songs?

6. Someone's gold bracelet is on the counter in the bath‸room.
7. Forty‸nine students signed the get-well card.
8. Is that salad dressing fat‸free?
9. Who's going to the fair this weekend?
10. It's almost time to leave.

Parentheses

13x. Use parentheses to enclose material that is added to a sentence but is not considered of major importance.

EXAMPLES   The Civil War **(**1861–1865**)** is also known as the War Between the States.

My sister bought a beautiful lace mantilla **(**often pronounced man til´ə**)** when she was in Mexico.

Text enclosed in parentheses may be as short as a single word or as long as a short sentence. A short sentence in parentheses may stand alone or be contained within another sentence. Notice that a parenthetical sentence within a sentence is not capitalized and has no end mark.

EXAMPLES   Please be quiet and respectful during the ceremony. **(**Turn off your cell phones.**)**

The first metal-framed skyscraper **(**it was ten stories tall**)** was built in Chicago in 1885.

Exercise 13 **Correcting Sentences by Adding Parentheses**

Insert parentheses where they are needed in the following sentences.

EXAMPLE   1. My new computer my old one needed a new disk drive is amazingly fast.

1. *My new computer (my old one needed a new disk drive) is amazingly fast.*

1. Thomas Alva Edison (1847–1931) invented the phonograph and the electric light bulb.

STYLE  **TIP**

Parenthetical expressions are usually set off by commas or parentheses. Some parenthetical elements, however, need stronger emphasis. In such cases, a **dash** is used.

EXAMPLES

Central Park, by the way, has a wonderful bird sanctuary.

Central Park (it's two and a half miles long) is a New York City attraction.

We went to Central Park for a picnic—it was such fun—on Sunday afternoon.

DIRECT TEACHING

Modeling and Demonstration

Parentheses. Model how to use parentheses correctly by using the incorrect example *The Civil War 1861–1865 is also known as the War Between the States.* First, ask what the most important part of the example sentence is. [*The Civil War is also known as the War Between the States.*] Then, ask what has been added that is part of the sentence but is not of major importance. [*the dates, 1861–1865*] Next, ask what kind of punctuation marks are used to set off material that is part of the sentence but not of major importance. [*parentheses*] Last, ask where the parentheses should be placed. [*before* 1861 *and after* 1865] Now, have a volunteer use another example from this chapter to demonstrate how to use parentheses to set off information of minor importance in a sentence.

MECHANICS

RESOURCES

Parentheses (Dashes, Brackets)
Practice
■ *Language & Sentence Skills Practice*, p. 275–276, 279–280
■ *Developmental Language & Sentence Skills*, pp. 117–118

2. Edison did not have a formal education (his mother taught him at home), but he became a millionaire before he was fifty.

3. Some of the first incandescent (pronounced in•kən•des´ənt) bulbs used bamboo filaments.

4. Parentheses are optional for this item.

4. Until most homes and businesses had electricity, the light bulb was only a novelty. (Few places had electricity in 1880.)

5. Edison built the first electric power plant (it was known as the Pearl Street Station) in 1882 in New York City.

6. Electricity became widespread during the industrialism of the United States (1870–1916).

7. Edison's work (his inventions and his business practices) helped the United States to become an industrial power.

8. Edison invested in companies that manufactured other electrical equipment (lighting fixtures, generators, and power cables).

9. These companies (the electrical equipment manufacturers) joined with other companies to form General Electric in 1892.

10. Edison was friends with several other industrial leaders, including Henry Ford (automobiles) and Harvey Firestone (tires).

NOTE Use brackets to enclose an explanation added to quoted or parenthetical material.

EXAMPLES In his speech, the ambassador to Australia said, "I wish to thank you and the wonderful, friendly people of your great country for this [the award]." [The words are enclosed in brackets to show that they have been inserted into the quotation and are not the words of the speaker.]

The Mississippi River and its tributaries drain most of the land that lies between the Rocky and the Appalachian Mountains. (See p. 647 for a map [Diagram A] of the drainage area.)

MECHANICS

13

Numerals in brackets refer to rules tested by the items in the Chapter Review.

1. [13n]
2. "The Siamese Cat." [13l]
3. [13c, j]
4. [13m, a]
5. [13x, r]
6. [13m]
7. [13c, f(1), h]
8. [13c, u, f(1)]
9. its [13p]
10. [13o, x]
11. "The Standing Stones of Wales and Brittany." [13l]
12. [13b]
13. [13a]
14. [13c, f(1), g]
15. [13q, x, v]
16. noon.'"[13c, m, f(3), k, r, g]
17. [13l]
18. [13a]
19. [13r, s]
20. exer- cise *or* ex- ercise [13r, t(1), x]

Chapter Review

A. Using Underlining (Italics), Quotation Marks, Apostrophes, Hyphens, and Parentheses

Each of the following sentences contains at least one error in the use of underlining (italics), quotation marks, apostrophes, hyphens, or parentheses. Write each sentence correctly.

1. The children's bikes were in the driveway.
2. Chapter Two is called *The Siamese Cat.*
3. "I remember making a barometer in the fourth grade. "I had to start over twice before it would work," I said.
4. John read Robert Louis Stevenson's novel Treasure Island.
5. While in the shower, I sometimes(only when my family isn't around to complain) sing very loudly.
6. Washington's largest city is named for Chief Seattle.
7. "Will you please show me how to make a weather vane?" begged Todd.
8. "It took me only forty-five minutes to make a sundial," Carlos remarked.
9. We built a model airplane, but it crashed on it's test flight.
10. All students' projects (both science and art) are due Friday.
11. Ray read an interesting article called *The Standing Stones of Wales and Brittany.*
12. Be sure to visit the USS "Lexington" in Corpus Christi.
13. Which newspaper do you prefer, The New York Times or Newsday?
14. "Next time, please be prompt, Al," said Ms. Li as I walked in late.
15. Everyone's report(the two-page book report)is due Friday.
16. "Bill's exact words," said Sean, "were 'I'll be back at noon.'"
17. In her English class, Janice is reading the Dylan Thomas poem "Fern Hill."
18. Have you seen the magazine "Highlights for Children"?
19. Please don't use so many *like*'s when you speak.
20. Isn't twenty questions the average length for an exe-rcise of this kind? (It's the last exercise in the chapter.)

ASSESSING

Monitoring Progress

Chapter Review. To assess student progress, you may want to compare the types of items missed on the **Diagnostic Preview** to those missed on the **Chapter Review.** If students have not made significant progress, you may want to refer them to **Chapter 15: Correcting Common Errors, Exercises 27–29,** for additional practice.

MECHANICS

RESOURCES

Punctuation

Review

■ *Language & Sentence Skills Practice,* pp. 277–280

Assessment

■ *Progress Assessment for the Holt Handbook,* pp. 25–26, 41

■ *Test Generator (One-Stop Planner CD-ROM)*

Chapter Review

B. Revising Indirect Quotations to Create Direct Quotations

POSSIBLE ANSWERS

21. "You cannot take any breaks during the exam," our teacher warned us.
22. "I will call you at eight o'clock," Lisa said.
23. "Don't be late," Mom told us.
24. "Will you wait behind the fence?" the police officer asked us.
25. "Where is the *Mona Lisa*?" I asked the museum guard.
26. "Two hours should be long enough," Taylor said.
27. "I will be in the city for five days," Stephanie replied.
28. Dr. Grizzard reminded us, "Take your vitamins every day."
29. Wendy asked her father, "Will you drive me to the library?"
30. "I have never been so surprised in my life!" Giulio exclaimed happily.

C. Punctuating a Dialogue

[31]¶"Oh, Travis," said Lucy, "when are you leaving?" [32]¶"I told you, Lucy," replied Travis. "I'm planning to leave soon. At around ten o'clock." [33]¶"Oh," said Lucy. "Listen, Trav, I'm afraid I won't be able to come with you after all. Something has come up." [34]¶"Well, Grandma will certainly be disappointed," remarked Travis. "She's been looking forward to seeing her two grandkids on her birthday." [35]¶"Yes, but that's just it," said Lucy. "I haven't bought anything for her birthday yet. I just haven't had the time." [36]¶"Well, guess what, Sis. I took care of that yesterday." Travis went over to the desk and took something out of the drawer. [37]"Your present to Grandma is this framed photograph of me." [38]¶"You're kidding," said Lucy. [39]¶"And," continued Travis, "my present to her is this framed photograph of you. What do you think?"[40]¶"I think you're crazy, but we can discuss that on the way there. Let's go!"

B. Revising Indirect Quotations to Create Direct Quotations

Revise each of the following sentences by changing the indirect quotation to a direct quotation. Be sure to use capital letters and punctuation marks where they are needed.

21. Our teacher warned us that we could not take any breaks during the exam.
22. Lisa said that she would call me at eight o'clock.
23. Mom told us not to be late.
24. The police officer asked us to wait behind the fence.
25. I asked the museum guard where the *Mona Lisa* was.
26. Taylor said that two hours should be long enough.
27. Stephanie replied that she would be in the city for five days.
28. Dr. Grizzard reminded us to take our vitamins every day.
29. Wendy asked her father if he would drive her to the library.
30. Giulio exclaimed happily that he had never been so surprised in his life.

C. Punctuating a Dialogue

Rewrite the following dialogue, using quotation marks and other marks of punctuation where they are needed. Remember to begin a new paragraph every time the speaker changes.

[31] Oh, Travis, said Lucy, when are you leaving? [32] I told you, Lucy, replied Travis. I'm planning to leave soon. At around ten o'clock. [33] Oh, said Lucy. Listen, Trav, I'm afraid I won't be able to come with you after all. Something has come up. [34] Well, Grandma will certainly be disappointed, remarked Travis. She's been looking forward to seeing her two grandkids on her birthday. [35] Yes, but that's just it, said Lucy. I haven't bought anything for her birthday yet. I just haven't had the time. [36] Well, guess what, Sis. I took care of that yesterday. Travis went over to the desk and took something out of the drawer. [37] Your present to Grandma is this framed photograph of me. [38] You're kidding, said Lucy. [39] And continued Travis, my present to her is this framed photograph of you. What do you think? [40] I think you're crazy, but we can discuss that on the way there. Let's go!

—HELP—

You will need to change some pronouns and verb forms in Part B.

21.–30. [13c, d, e, f(1–3), g, h]

31.–40. [13c–j]

MECHANICS

Writing Application
Using Apostrophes in a Letter

Contractions and Possessives You have been so busy at summer camp that you have not had time to write to your best friend. Write your friend a letter telling about your first week at camp. Be sure to use apostrophes correctly to make your meaning clear.

Prewriting If you have never been to a summer camp, ask a friend or relative who has been to one to tell you about it. Write down some notes on your activities at summer camp. Use your experience or your imagination to describe activities such as sports, crafts, and hiking trips. Also, make some notes about the camp itself.

Writing Include specific details about the natural setting and special or daily activities at the camp. Tell your friend what you have enjoyed most. Try to give your friend a clear, vivid picture of your first week.

Revising Ask a friend or a family member to read your letter. Can he or she imagine the activities you have described? If not, revise your letter to make it clearer and more descriptive.

Publishing Be sure you have used the correct form for personal letters. As you proofread your letter, take extra care with apostrophes. Check your use of contractions and pronouns like *its, it's, your, you're, their,* and *they're.* Also, look for any other errors in grammar, spelling, and punctuation. Exchange letters with a classmate, and see how your camp experiences, real or imagined, are similar and how they are different.

MECHANICS

CHAPTER

14

Spelling
Improving Your Spelling

1.0 Written and Oral English Language Conventions
Students write and speak with a command of standard English conventions appropriate to this grade level.
1.5 Spell frequently misspelled words correctly (e.g., *their, they're, there*).

STANDARDS FOCUS

Grade-Level Standards
(Boldface indicates concepts that are taught and tested in this chapter.)

- Language Convention 1.0: **Students write and speak with a command of standard English conventions appropriate to this grade level.**

- Spelling 1.5: **Spell frequently misspelled words correctly (e.g., *their, they're, there*).**

Prerequisite/Review Standard

- Spelling 1.5: Spell roots, suffixes, prefixes, contractions, and syllable constructions correctly.

Standard Coming Up in the Next Grade Level

- Spelling 1.7: Spell derivatives correctly by applying the spellings of bases and affixes.

▼

INTRODUCING THE CHAPTER

- The chapter begins with a discussion of the methods students can use to improve their spelling. It then presents a series of basic spelling rules, including rules for adding prefixes and suffixes and for forming the plurals of nouns. Exercises are provided to reinforce the understanding of the spelling rules. The chapter also contains lists of homonyms and other words that are often confused and concludes with a list of spelling words.

(continued)

Numerals in brackets refer to rules tested by the items in the Diagnostic Preview.

1. happiest [14f]
2. chairs [14h(1)]
3. neighbor [14a]
4. blueberries [14h(3)]
5. driving [14d]
6. changeable [14d]
7. women [14h(7)]
8. truly [14e]
9. bravely [14e]
10. potatoes [14h(6)]

Diagnostic Preview

A. Proofreading Sentences for Correct Spelling

Correctly write the word that is ~~misspelled~~ in each of the following sentences.

EXAMPLE   1. The dog is diging in the flower garden again.
    1. digging

1. The children are ~~happyest~~ when swimming in the pool on a hot afternoon.
2. The porch ~~chaires~~ look newer than the tables.
3. Our ~~nieghbor~~ was born in Texas, I believe.
4. The Tolbys bought ~~blueberrys~~ for the party.
5. Uncle Steven is ~~driveing~~ through seven foreign countries on his trip.
6. Is the weather in Arizona ever ~~changable~~?
7. Five ~~womans~~ auditioned for the leading role in the Broadway production.
8. I think the Peter, Paul, and Mary folk songs of the sixties are ~~truely~~ delightful.
9. Matthew and Kim ~~bravly~~ rescued the baby raccoon from the muddy ditch.
10. Would you kindly dig up the ~~potatos~~ and let them dry in the cellar?

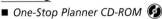

CHAPTER RESOURCES

Internet
- go.hrw.com (keyword: HLLA)

go. hrw .com

Planning
- One-Stop Planner CD-ROM 💿
- On Course: Mapping Instruction
- At Home: A Guide to Standards Mastery, p. 35

Practice & Review
- *Language & Sentence Skills Practice,* pp. 286–301; 302–305
- *Developmental Language & Sentence Skills,* pp. 119–130

Application & Enrichment
- *Language & Sentence Skills Practice,* pp. 306, 309; 285, 307–308

B. Proofreading Sentences to Correct Spelling Errors

Choose the correct word or words from the choices in parentheses in each of the following sentences.

EXAMPLE **1.** Please give (*you're*, *your*) book orders to me today.
  1. *your*

11. Angela is taking five (*courses*, *coarses*) this semester.
12. Nora said she was (*already*, *all ready*) for the banquet.
13. "Please pass me a (*peace*, *piece*) of bread," Gary said.
14. The (*altar*, *alter*) at the Spanish mission is marble.
15. The (*plain*, *plane*) to Ontario is ahead of schedule.
16. People often (*loose*, *lose*) pennies in stores and on streets.
17. We saw the (*principal*, *principle*) pass by twice.
18. Whose (*stationery*, *stationary*) has initials at the top?
19. (*There*, *Their*) shop sells shirts, dresses, and scarves.
20. "You'd better get these (*breaks*, *brakes*) fixed right away," the mechanic said.

11.–20. [Words Often Confused]

Good Spelling Habits

The following techniques can help you spell words correctly.

1. **To learn the spelling of a word, pronounce it, study it, and write it.** Pronounce words carefully. Mistakes in speaking can cause mistakes in spelling. For instance, if you say *ad•je•tive* instead of *ad•jec•tive*, you will be more likely to spell the word incorrectly.

   - First, make sure that you know how to pronounce the word correctly, and then practice saying it.
   - Second, study the word. Notice any parts that might be hard to remember.
   - Third, write the word from memory. Check your spelling.
   - If you misspelled the word, repeat the three steps of this process until you can spell the word correctly.

2. **Use a dictionary.** If you are not absolutely sure about the spelling of a word, look it up in a dictionary. Do not guess about the correct spelling.

─HELP─

If you are not sure how to pronounce a word, look it up in a dictionary. In a dictionary, you will usually find the pronunciation given in parentheses after the word. The information in parentheses will show you the sounds used, the syllable breaks, and any accented syllables or word breaks. A guide to the pronunciation symbols is usually found at the front of a dictionary.

Good Spelling Habits **317**

- A **Chapter Review** on pp. 341–343 includes a **Writing Application** asking students to use correct spelling in a personal letter.
- For help in integrating this chapter with writing assignments in *Holt Literature and Language Arts,* use the **Teaching Strands** chart on pp. T22–T23.

MECHANICS

ASSESSING

Entry-Level Assessment
Diagnostic Preview. You may wish to use the **Diagnostic Preview** to determine what kinds of spelling problems your students have. Keep in mind that students may have a variety of such problems. You could use the results of the preview to decide which lessons to teach to the entire class and which lessons to assign to small groups.

Good Spelling Habits and Spelling Rules
Rules 14a–g *(pp. 317–324)*

OBJECTIVES

- **To spell correctly words that contain the letters *ie* or *ei***
- **To add prefixes and suffixes to words**
- **To proofread sentences for correct spelling**

Differentiating Instruction
- *Lesson Plans for Language Development*
- *Supporting Instruction in Five Languages*
- *At Home: In Five Languages*

Assessment
- *Progress Assessment for the Holt Handbook,* pp. 27–28, 41

- *Test Generator (One-Stop Planner CD-ROM)*

Other Language Resources
- *Spelling Lessons & Activities*
- *Vocabulary Development*
- *Daily Language Activities Transparencies*

PRETEACHING

Lesson Starter

Prerequisite Skills. Choose one of the words from the spelling word list at the end of the chapter, and pronounce the word carefully for the class. For example, you might want to use *varied, political, constitution,* or *reconstruction.* Ask a volunteer first to repeat the pronunciation carefully and then to write the word on the chalkboard, making sure to spell the word as it sounds. If a volunteer misspells the word, ask him or her to divide the word into syllables. Then, pronounce the word again slowly and ask the volunteer to match sounds in the pronunciation to each syllable of the word. Lead the class to see that pronouncing a word correctly may help in spelling it correctly.

DIRECT TEACHING

Spelling by Syllables

Activity. To help students syllabicate words for their spelling notebooks, explain that words can be divided after a vowel if the vowel is long (an **open syllable**) and after a consonant if the vowel is short (a **closed syllable**). Students might use the following list of words as examples: be-come, co-bra, de-tail (open) be*ck*-on, co*p*-per, de*t*-o-nate (closed).

STYLE	TIP

In some names, marks that show how to pronounce a word are considered part of the spelling.

PEOPLE
Muñoz Søren Fauré

PLACES
Neuchâtel Košice
Cap-Haïtien

If you are not sure about the spelling of a name, ask the person with that name or look it up in a dictionary or other reference source.

---

3. Spell by syllables. A *syllable* is a word part that can be pronounced as one uninterrupted sound.

EXAMPLES   ear•ly [two syllables]

av•er•age [three syllables]

Instead of trying to learn how to pronounce and spell a whole word, break it into its syllables whenever possible. It is easier to learn a few letters at a time than to learn all of them at once.

4. Keep a spelling notebook. Divide each page into four columns:

COLUMN 1   Correctly spell any word you have misspelled. (Never enter a misspelled word.)

COLUMN 2   Write the word again, dividing it into syllables and indicating which syllables are accented or stressed. (You will probably need to use a dictionary.)

COLUMN 3   Write the word once more, circling the spot that gives you trouble.

COLUMN 4   Write down any comments that might help you remember the correct spelling.

Here is an example of how you might make entries for two words that are often misspelled.

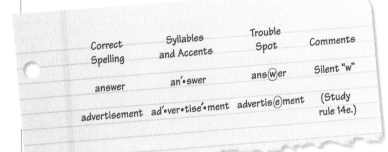

Correct Spelling	Syllables and Accents	Trouble Spot	Comments
answer	an'•swer	ans(w)er	Silent "w"
advertisement	ad'•ver•tise'•ment	advertis(e)ment	(Study rule 14e.)

5. Proofread for careless spelling errors. Re-read your writing carefully, and correct any mistakes and unclear letters. For example, make sure that your *i*'s are dotted, your *t*'s are crossed, and your *g*'s do not look like *q*'s.

RESOURCES

Good Spelling Habits and Spelling Rules
Practice
- *Language & Sentence Skills Practice,* pp. 286–293, 302
- *Developmental Language & Sentence Skills,* pp. 119–122

Spelling Rules

ie and *ei*

14a. Write *ie* when the sound is long *e*, except after *c*.

EXAMPLES   ch**ie**f, bel**ie**ve, br**ie**f, rec**ei**ve, c**ei**ling

EXCEPTIONS   **ei**ther, n**ei**ther, prot**ei**n, s**ei**ze

    Write *ei* when the sound is not long *e*, especially when the sound is long *a*.

EXAMPLES   n**ei**ghbor, w**ei**gh, r**ei**ndeer, h**ei**ght, for**ei**gn

EXCEPTIONS   fr**ie**nd, f**ie**rce, anc**ie**nt, misch**ie**f

Exercise 1   Writing Words with *ie* and *ei*

Complete the following letter by adding *ie* or *ei* to each numbered word.

EXAMPLE   I wrote Aunt Hannah a **[1]** br____f thank-you note.

     1. brief

December 12, 2003

Dear Aunt Hannah,

    Thank you very much for the **[1]** sl_ei_gh you recently sent me. I **[2]** rec_ei_ved it on the **[3]** _ei_ghth of this month, just in time for our first big snowstorm. My new **[4]** fr_ie_nds and I have great fun pulling each other across the **[5]** f_ie_lds in it. The **[6]** n_ei_ghbor's dog races alongside us, barking **[7]** f_ie_rcely all the way.

    So far, I like living here in Vermont, but I can't quite **[8]** bel_ie_ve how different everything is from life in California. Thank you again for your gift.

         Your loving **[9]** n_ie_ce,

         Mai

P.S. If only we had some **[10]** r_ei_ndeer to pull us!

┌HELP┐

This verse may help you remember the *ie* rule:

   I before *e*
   Except after *c,*
   Or when sounded like *a,*
   As in *neighbor* and *weigh.*

If you use this rhyme, remember that "*i* before *e*" refers only to words in which these two letters are in the same syllable and stand for the sound of long *e*, as in the examples under Rule 14a.

DIRECT TEACHING

Modeling and Demonstration

***ie* and *ei*.** Model how to spell words with *ie* and *ei* by using the examples *field, receive,* and *neighbor*. First, ask what sound *ie* makes in *field*. [*long e*] Then, ask whether the vowel pair *ie* comes directly after a *c*. [*no*] Therefore, *field* is spelled with an *ie*. Next, ask what sound *ei* makes in *receive*. [*long e*] Ask what letter appears just before the *ei*. [*c*] Point out that after *c*, the long *e* sound is spelled *ei*. Then, ask what sound *ei* makes in *neighbor*. [*long a*] Point out that when the *ei* vowel combination makes a long *a* sound, the correct spelling is *ei*. Now, have a volunteer use another example in this chapter to demonstrate how to spell a word with *ie* or *ei*.

DIRECT TEACHING

Correcting Misconceptions

Spelling. Some students may have the misconception that correct spelling is unimportant in contemporary life. Ask students to jot down a list of reasons why correct spelling is important. Ask students whether correct spelling may be less important sometimes, such as when taking class notes or writing in personal diaries. Lead students to understand that always using correct spelling is good practice. Doing so helps break bad spelling habits and prevents such poor habits from developing.

MECHANICS

Exercise 3 **Spelling Words with Prefixes**

ANSWERS
Words and sentences will vary. Here are some possibilities:

1. unable—The cat was unable to catch the mouse.

2. misplace—My parents sometimes misplace their keys.

3. overdo—Some athletes overdo their workouts.

4. discover—I wonder what secrets the scientist will discover.

5. replace—Please replace the air filter when it gets clogged.

6. disable—My sister is careful to disable the lawn mower before storing it.

7. undo—It is difficult to undo the damage a lie does.

8. prejudge—Be careful not to prejudge a situation before you know all the facts.

9. overpay—Sir, did you overpay the utility bill for which you got a refund?

10. misinformed—We were misinformed about the time for the picnic.

MEETING THE CHALLENGE

Base words (*part, take*) can stand alone or combine with other word parts to make new words (*partly, mistake*). A root is the main part of the word. It carries the word's meaning. Word roots (*–dict–, –vis–*), like prefixes and suffixes, cannot stand alone and are combined with other word parts to form words (*dictionary, visible*).

Form new words by adding a prefix, a suffix, or both to the following base words and word roots.

BASE WORDS
   cycle, graph, gram, verse

WORD ROOTS
   –crit–, –fer–, –gest–, –loc–

ANSWERS
Answers will vary. Here are some possibilities:
BASE WORDS: *recycle, graphic, kilogram, universe*
WORD ROOTS: *critical, transfer, digestible, relocate*

Prefixes and Suffixes

Prefixes

A *prefix* is a letter or a group of letters added to the beginning of a word to create a new word that has a different meaning.

14b. When adding a prefix to a word, do not change the spelling of the word itself.

EXAMPLES   dis + satisfy = dis**satisfy**

               mis + lead = mis**lead**

               un + done = un**done**

               pre + view = pre**view**

               a + typical = a**typical**

Exercise 2 **Spelling Words with Prefixes**

Combine each of the following prefixes and words to create a new word.

EXAMPLE   **1.** mis + place
              1. misplace

1. fore + word 1. foreword   **6.** im + patient 6. impatient

2. un + natural 2. unnatural   **7.** pre + historic 7. prehistoric

3. in + dependent 3. independent **8.** mis + spell 8. misspell

4. mis + use 4. misuse   **9.** dis + satisfied 9. dissatisfied

5. un + common 5. uncommon **10.** re + assert 10. reassert

Exercise 3 **Spelling Words with Prefixes**

Create ten different words by combining the prefixes given below with the words listed beside them. (You may use a prefix or word more than once.) Check each of your new words in a dictionary. Then, use each word in a sentence.

Prefixes			Words			
un–	mis–	dis–	able	do	judge	place
pre–	over–	re–	cover	trust	pay	informed

EXAMPLE   *1. repay—I'll repay you when I get my allowance.*

Exercise 3

DISTRIBUTED REVIEW
For each sentence, ask students to circle and identify the part of speech of each word they created from the chart. In the example sentence, the word *repay* is a verb.

Suffixes

A *suffix* is a letter or a group of letters added at the end of a word to create a new word that has a different meaning.

14c. When adding the suffix *–ness* or *–ly* to a word, do not change the spelling of the word itself.

EXAMPLES   kind + ness = **kind**ness

tough + ness = **tough**ness

sincere + ly = **sincere**ly

slow + ly = **slow**ly

EXCEPTIONS   For most words that end in *y,* change the *y* to *i* before adding *–ly* or *–ness.*

happy + ly = happ**ily**

friendly + ness = friendl**iness**

14d. Drop the final silent *e* before adding a suffix that begins with a vowel.

Vowels are the letters *a, e, i, o, u,* and sometimes *y.* All other letters of the alphabet are *consonants.*

EXAMPLES   cause + ing = **caus**ing

reverse + ible = **revers**ible

strange + er = **strang**er

adore + able = **ador**able

PEANUTS reprinted by permission of United Feature Syndicate, Inc.

English-Language Learners

Vietnamese. Modern Vietnamese spelling uses a Romanized alphabet (ABC's) and is phonetic. Some Vietnamese students find English spelling complex because it lacks consistency. Since mispronunciation may hinder spelling ability, have students repeat new words orally and check for correct pronunciation.

Hmong. The Hmong language's Romanized Popular Alphabet uses unvoiced final consonants as tonal markers whose only purpose is to indicate a word's stress and pitch. Therefore, when reading, Hmong students may have a tendency to leave English end consonants unvoiced. Because pronunciation is so crucial to spelling, this tendency may result in dropped final consonants on the part of Hmong spellers. Have students practice reading aloud, emphasizing final consonants as they read, until they begin to voice end consonants regularly.

MECHANICS

Exercise 4 Spelling Words
with Suffixes

ANSWERS

1. activity
2. surely
3. statement
4. location
5. courageous
6. silliness
7. suspenseful
8. littlest
9. decorated
10. traceable

MECHANICS

RETEACHING

Adding a Suffix

Activity. Ask for volunteers to come to the front of the class and use their arms and legs to form the shapes of letters needed to spell a word ending in a consonant plus *y* (such as *thirsty, happy,* or *cozy*). The person whose body is to form the *y* should hold up his or her arms like a football referee signaling a good extra-point kick. Have another student write the suffixes *–ness* and *–ly* on two pieces of poster board. Have that student then move to the side of the student representing *y* and hold up either the card with *–ness* or *–ly.* The person representing the *y* should then drop his or her arms to the side, forming the shape of an *i.* Use this demonstration to point out to students that, for words that end in a consonant plus *y,* the *y* should be changed to *i* when the suffix *–ly* or *–ness* is added. You might want to use a similar technique to demonstrate other spelling rules in this section.

┌ HELP ─

Some words that end with a silent *e* can either keep the *e* or drop it when a suffix is added.

EXAMPLES

judge + ment = judg**ment** *or* judg**ement**

acknowledge + ment = acknowledg**ment** *or* acknowledg**ement**

love + able = lov**able** *or* lov**eable**

┌ TIPS & TRICKS ┐

When you proofread your own writing, you will find more spelling errors by looking at each word separately. To focus on each word, try using a piece of paper to hide some of the nearby words or lines. You can even cut a slit in a sheet of paper and move it over your writing to show just a few words at a time.

EXCEPTIONS   Keep the silent *e* in words ending in *ce* and *ge* before adding a suffix beginning with *a* or *o.*

manage + able = manag**eable**

courage + ous = courag**eous**

notice + able = notic**eable**

14e. Keep the final silent *e* before adding a suffix that begins with a consonant.

EXAMPLES   hope + less = hop**eless**

place + ment = plac**ement**

EXCEPTIONS   argue + ment = argu**ment**

true + ly = tru**ly**

Exercise 4 Spelling Words with Suffixes

Combine each of the following words and suffixes to create a new word.

EXAMPLE   1. sudden + ness
　　　　　　　　1. *suddenness*

1. active + ity
2. sure + ly
3. state + ment
4. locate + ion
5. courage + ous

6. silly + ness
7. suspense + ful
8. little + est
9. decorate + ed
10. trace + able

14f. For words that end in a consonant plus *y,* change the *y* to *i* before adding a suffix.

EXAMPLES   cry + ed = cr**ied**   lonely + est = lonel**iest**

pretty + er = prett**ier**   lazy + ness = laz**iness**

EXCEPTION   Keep the *y* if the suffix begins with an *i.*

carry + ing = carry**ing**

NOTE   Keep the *y* if the word ends in a vowel plus *y.*

EXAMPLES   stay + ed = sta**yed**   key + ed = ke**yed**

EXCEPTIONS   day + ly = daily   pay + ed = paid

14g. Double the final consonant before adding *–ing*, *–ed*, *–er*, or *–est* to a one-syllable word that ends in a single vowel followed by a single consonant.

EXAMPLES   beg + ing = be**gging**   sad + er = sa**dder**

   chat + ed = cha**tted**   big + est = bi**ggest**

When a one-syllable word ends in two vowels followed by a single consonant, do not double the consonant before adding *–ing*, *–ed*, *–er*, or *–est*.

EXAMPLES   sleep + ing = slee**ping**   cool + er = coo**ler**

   treat + ed = trea**ted**   fair + est = fai**rest**

Exercise 5 **Spelling Words with Suffixes**

Combine each of the following words and suffixes to create a new word.

EXAMPLE   **1.** creep + er
   1. creeper

1. say + ing **1.** saying
2. slim + er **2.** slimmer
3. squeak + ing **3.** squeaking
4. rainy + est **4.** rainiest
5. steady + ness **5.** steadiness
6. beat + ing **6.** beating
7. rely + ing **7.** relying
8. easy + ly **8.** easily
9. chop + ed **9.** chopped
10. play + ed **10.** played

Review A **Proofreading Sentences for Correct Spelling**

Most of the following sentences contain a ~~misspelled~~ word. Write each misspelled word correctly. If a sentence is already correct, write *C*.

EXAMPLE   **1.** My grandma often says, "Let sleeping dogs lie."
   1. sleeping

1. It's ~~unnusual~~ weather for this time of year. **1.** unusual
2. In 1991, Lithuania regained its independence from the Soviet Union. **2.** C
3. With Sacagawea's help, the explorers Lewis and Clark ~~maped~~ out the Northwest. **3.** mapped
4. Now that Bao Duc is on the team, our ~~hiting~~ has improved. **4.** hitting

HELP

In Review A, none of the proper nouns are misspelled.

MECHANICS

5. Serita and I can ~~easyly~~ make enough rice for the class. 5. easily

6. We visited my grandmother in the Dominican Republic during the ~~rainyest~~ month of the year. 6. rainiest

7. Please ~~resstate~~ the question. 7. restate

8. My sister has the loveliest voice I've ever heard. 8. C

9. Former astronaut Sally Ride earned recognition for her courage and ~~steadyness~~. 9. steadiness

10. The temperature has ~~droped~~ at least ten degrees.
10. dropped

Review B **Proofreading a Paragraph for Correct Spelling**

ANSWERS

1. truly

2. neighbors

3. getting; dissatisfied

4. Fortunately

5. C

6. loving; receive

7. closing; putting

8. happily

9. retrieves; dropped

10. joking; writing

DIFFERENTIATING INSTRUCTION

English-Language Learners

Cantonese. Cantonese students may find English spelling complex. Problems arise from not applying spelling conventions (*letter* spelled *leter*), from the number of exceptions in English (including silent letters and various spellings of similar sounds), and from incorrect pronunciation (including not pronouncing all syllables). Write words on the chalkboard as often as you can, and have students pronounce them with you. Frequently point out unusual spellings (as in the word *Wednesday*).

HELP
Some sentences in Review B contain more than one misspelled word.

Review B **Proofreading a Paragraph for Correct Spelling**

For each sentence in the following paragraph, correctly write the word or words that are ~~misspelled~~. If a sentence is already correct, write *C*.

EXAMPLE   [1] My cousin Chris was very couragous after she was baddly hurt in a car accident.
1. *courageous; badly*

[1] After the accident, Chris found that she ~~truely~~ needed other people. [2] Her friends, family, and ~~nieghbors~~ gladly helped her. [3] However, Chris liked the idea of ~~geting~~ along on her own as much as she could, so she was ~~disatisfied~~. [4] ~~Fortunatly~~, she was able to join an exciting program called Helping Hands. [5] This program provides monkeys like this one as friends and helpers for people with disabilities. [6] Chris said that the baby monkeys are raised in ~~loveing~~ foster homes

for four years and then they go to Boston to ~~recieve~~ special training. [7] There, they learn how to do tasks on command, such as opening and ~~closeing~~ doors, turning lights on and off, and ~~puting~~ tapes into a VCR or tape player. [8] Chris has been ~~happyly~~ working with her own monkey, Aldo, for six months now. [9] Aldo ~~retreives~~ anything that Chris has ~~droped~~, works the TV remote control, and even scratches Chris's back when it itches! [10] Chris is always ~~jokeing~~, "Pretty soon Aldo will be ~~writting~~ my book reports for me!"

Forming the Plurals of Nouns

14h. Follow these rules for spelling the plurals of nouns:

(1) To form the plurals of most nouns, add *s*.

SINGULAR	snack	oven	Juliet	breeze	umbrella
PLURAL	snack**s**	oven**s**	Juliet**s**	breeze**s**	umbrella**s**

> **NOTE** Make sure that you do not confuse the plural form of a noun with its possessive form. In general, you should not use an apostrophe to form the plural of a word.
>
> INCORRECT   The boy's stayed after school for choir practice.
>
> CORRECT   The **boys** stayed after school for choir practice. [plural]
>
> CORRECT   The **boys'** choir has practice today. [possessive]

(2) Form the plurals of nouns ending in *s, x, z, ch,* or *sh* by adding *es*.

SINGULAR	glass	fox	buzz	itch	bush	Jones
PLURAL	glass**es**	fox**es**	buzz**es**	itch**es**	bush**es**	Jones**es**

Oral Practice   Giving the Plurals of Nouns

Read each of the following nouns aloud. Then, say and spell the plural form of each noun.

EXAMPLES   **1.** scratch
              1. scratches

              2. ax
              2. axes

1. night 1. nights
2. dish 2. dishes
3. address 3. addresses
4. lens 4. lenses
5. box 5. boxes
6. branch 6. branches
7. loss 7. losses
8. peach 8. peaches
9. waltz 9. waltzes
10. Smith 10. Smiths
11. complex 11. complexes
12. faucet 12. faucets
13. cobra 13. cobras
14. doctor 14. doctors
15. ditch 15. ditches
16. Sanchez 16. Sanchezes
17. tax 17. taxes
18. glue 18. glues
19. occurrence 19. occurrences
20. radish 20. radishes

Reference Note

For a discussion of **possessive forms of nouns,** see page 300. For information on using an apostrophe and an *s* to form **plurals of letters, numerals, symbols, and words used as words,** see page 307.

HELP

Some one-syllable words ending in *z* double the final consonant when forming plurals.

EXAMPLES
quiz   fez
qui**zz**es   fe**zz**es

Forming the Plurals of Nouns

Rule 14h *(pp. 325–329)*

OBJECTIVE

- To spell the plural and singular forms of nouns

DIRECT TEACHING

Modeling and Demonstration

Spelling Plurals of Nouns Ending in *s, x, z, ch,* or *sh*. Model how to form the plurals of nouns ending in *s, x, z, ch,* or *sh* by using the example *fox*. First, ask what the ending letter of *fox* is. [*x*] Next, ask how the plural of a noun ending in *x* is formed. [*by adding* es] Then, add *es* to *fox* to form the plural *foxes*. Now, have a volunteer use another example in this chapter to demonstrate how to form the plurals of nouns ending in *s, x, z, ch,* or *sh.*

MECHANICS

RESOURCES

Forming the Plurals of Nouns
Practice
- *Language & Sentence Skills Practice,* pp. 294–297, 302
- *Developmental Language & Sentence Skills,* pp. 123–124

(3) Form the plurals of nouns that end in a consonant plus *y* by changing the *y* to *i* and adding *es.*

| SINGULAR | country | mummy | berry |
| PLURAL | countr**ies** | mumm**ies** | berr**ies** |

EXCEPTION   With proper nouns, just add *s.*

the Shelby**s**   the Mabry**s**   the O'Grady**s**

(4) Form the plurals of nouns that end in a vowel plus *y* by adding *s.*

| SINGULAR | boy | turkey | holiday | Riley |
| PLURAL | boy**s** | turkey**s** | holiday**s** | Riley**s** |

(5) Form the plurals of nouns that end in a vowel plus *o* by adding *s.*

| SINGULAR | rodeo | patio | kangaroo | Romeo |
| PLURAL | rodeo**s** | patio**s** | kangaroo**s** | Romeo**s** |

(6) Form the plurals of nouns that end in a consonant plus *o* by adding *es.*

| SINGULAR | tomato | echo | veto | torpedo |
| PLURAL | tomato**es** | echo**es** | veto**es** | torpedo**es** |

EXCEPTIONS   auto—auto**s**   Latino—Latino**s**   Soto—Soto**s**

─HELP─

Form the plurals of most musical terms ending in *o* by adding *s.*

SINGULAR
piano   trio
soprano   cello

PLURAL
piano**s**   trio**s**
soprano**s**   cello**s**

Exercise 6   Spelling the Plurals of Nouns

Spell the plural form of each of the following nouns.

EXAMPLE   **1.** story

1. *stories*

1. toy 1. toys
2. apology 2. apologies
3. valley 3. valleys
4. try 4. tries
5. piano 5. pianos
6. potato 6. potatoes
7. emergency 7. emergencies
8. chimney 8. chimneys
9. radio 9. radios
10. video 10. videos

11. journey 11. journeys
12. stereo 12. stereos
13. county 13. counties
14. hero 14. heroes
15. delay 15. delays
16. scenario 16. scenarios
17. agony 17. agonies
18. solo 18. solos
19. O'Malley 19. O'Malleys
20. zoo 20. zoos

(7) The plurals of a few nouns are formed in irregular ways.

SINGULAR   woman   mouse   foot   man   child
  PLURAL   wom**en**   m**ice**   f**ee**t   m**en**   child**ren**

(8) Some nouns are the same in the singular and the plural.

SINGULAR AND PLURAL   fowl   sheep   spacecraft   Sioux

(9) Form the plurals of numerals, letters, symbols, and words referred to as words by adding an apostrophe and *s*.

SINGULAR   1990   *A*   +   *and*
  PLURAL   1990**'s**   *A*'**s**   +**'s**   *and***'s**

Exercise 7 Spelling the Singular and Plural Forms of Nouns

Spell the singular form and the plural form of each italicized word in the following sentences.

EXAMPLES   **1.** We use strong line to fish for *salmon*.
       1. salmon—singular; salmon—plural

       2. Field *mice* invaded the food supplies in the tent.
       2. mouse—singular; mice—plural

1. Our guide, Robert Tallchief, a *Sioux*, knows all about the animals called llamas.
2. Robert and his father use llamas like the ones shown below to carry equipment people need for hiking and for catching *fish*.
3. The trips are very popular with both men and *women*.

EXTENSION

Critical Thinking

Metacognition. Ask students how they know that the italicized words in **Exercise 7** are singular or plural when both forms are spelled the same. [*The sentence's context indicates whether the word is singular or plural.*]

Exercise 7 Spelling the Singular and Plural Forms of Nouns

ANSWERS
1. Sioux—singular; Sioux—plural
2. fish—singular; fish—plural
3. woman—singular; women—plural

MECHANICS

MINI-LESSON Mechanics

Apostrophes. You might want to review with students the use of apostrophes to show possession. Ask students to rewrite the following expressions by using the possessive case. Remind them to add apostrophes in the appropriate places.

1. the A's of the students [*the students' A's*]
2. the highways of the state [*the state's highways*]
3. the jacket of Roger [*Roger's jacket*]
4. the books of the class [*the class's books*]

Exercise 7 Spelling the Singular and Plural Forms of Nouns

ANSWERS continued

4. child—singular; children—plural

5. tooth—singular; teeth—plural

6. Japanese—singular; Japanese—plural

7. moose—singular; moose—plural

8. deer—singular; deer *or* deers—plural

9. sheep—singular; sheep—plural

10. goose—singular; geese—plural

DIFFERENTIATING INSTRUCTION

Special Education Students

Learning-disabled students typically have difficulty learning to spell contractions and words that are not spelled as they sound. For most students, repeated exposure through reading enhances spelling ability. To improve students' spelling abilities, copy misspelled words taken from their writing assignments. Ask students to write each word correctly at least three times and to use the words in sentences. Constant repetition in writing, as well as increased exposure to silent reading, can enhance spelling ability.

4. *Children* especially are fascinated and amused by the sure-footed llamas.

5. However, the llama has one very disagreeable habit—if upset, it bares its *teeth* and spits.

6. The Tallchiefs' llama trips have attracted tourists from all over the world, including many *Japanese*.

7. One highlight of these trips is viewing *moose* in their natural habitat.

8. *Deer* thrive in this area of the Northwest.

9. In addition, families of mountain *sheep* clamber up the steep cliffs.

10. Most people who go on the llama trips take many pictures of the wild *geese.*

Review C Proofreading Sentences for Correct Spelling

For each of the following sentences, correctly write the word or words that are misspelled. If a sentence is already correct, write *C.*

EXAMPLE   **1.** Aunt Dorothy's old-time sayings are echos of her childhood.

   1. echoes

1. Aunt Dorothy Kelly talks mostly in expressions from the 1930's and earlyer.

2. If we get into mischeif, she exclaims, "You little monkies!"

3. When my brother's run through the house, she shakes her head and mutters, "Boys will be boys."

4. Every time she can't find her eyeglasses, Aunt Dorothy says, "I've beaten the bushes, looking for them."

5. Aunt Dorothy believes that there are only two things in life that are certain: death and taxs.

6. We've heard her say "There's no use crying over spilled milk" and "Wishs won't wash dishs" about a thousand times apiece.

7. When we want something because our friends have it, Aunt Dorothy says we're trying to keep up with the Jones'.

8. Sometimes we get tired of hearing these little bits of folk wisdom, especially when Aunt Dorothy and all the little Kellies come over to visit for the holidays.

┌HELP─

Some sentences in Review C have more than one misspelled word.

1. earlier
2. mischief/monkeys
3. brothers
4. C
5. taxes
6. Wishes/dishes
7. Joneses
8. Kellys

9. However, Aunt Dorothy is so sweet that we just smile and listen to her proverbs and ~~storys~~.
   9. stories
10. Sometimes she says something really worthwhile, like "There are only two things that money can't buy—true love and home-grown ~~tomatos~~."
   10. tomatoes

Words Often Confused

People often confuse the words in each of the following groups. Some of these words are **homonyms.** They are pronounced the same, but they have different meanings and spellings. Other words in this section have the same or similar spellings, but have different meanings.

already	[adverb] *at an earlier time* The show has *already* begun.
all ready	[adjective] *all prepared; completely prepared* The floats are *all ready* for the fiesta.
altar	[noun] *a table or stand used for religious ceremonies* My uncle Chee wove the cloth for the *altar.*
alter	[verb] *to change* A flood can *alter* a riverbed.
altogether	[adverb] *entirely* I'm *altogether* lost.
all together	[adjective] *in the same place;* [adverb] *at the same time or place* Is everyone *all together*? Let's sit *all together* at the movie.
brake	[noun] *a device to stop a machine* The front *brake* on my bike squeaks.
break	[verb] *to fracture; to shatter;* [noun] *a fracture; an interruption; a rest* Try not to *break* your promises. Let's take a five-minute *break.*

Reference Note

In the Glossary of Usage in Chapter 10, you can find many other words that are often confused or misused. You can also look them up in a dictionary.

Words Often Confused **329**

Words Often Confused
(pp. 329–340)

OBJECTIVE

- To identify often-confused words and to use them correctly

MECHANICS

DIRECT TEACHING

Modeling and Demonstration

Words Often Confused. Model the correct use of often-confused words with the examples *The show has already begun* and *The floats are all ready for the fiesta.* First, point out that correct use often can be determined by asking what these words mean in a sentence. Ask what *already* means in the first example. [*tells when*] Since *already* modifies the verb *has begun,* it is an adverb and should be used only as an adverb in other sentences. Next, ask what *all ready* does in the second example. [*describes the floats*] Since *all ready* modifies the noun *floats,* it is an adjective and should be used only as an adjective in other sentences. Now, have a volunteer use another example from this chapter to demonstrate the correct use of words often confused.

DIFFERENTIATING INSTRUCTION

Advanced Students

Authors often use phonetic misspellings and nonstandard grammar to represent a character's dialect. Have students read Zora Neale Hurston's retelling of the African American folk tale "How the Snake Got Poison" and discuss at least five examples of phonetic misspellings used to indicate dialect.

Words Often Confused **329**

RESOURCES

Words Often Confused

Practice

- *Language & Sentence Skills Practice,* pp. 298–301, 303–305
- *Developmental Language & Sentence Skills,* pp. 125–130

DIFFERENTIATING INSTRUCTION

English-Language Learners

General Strategies. Homonyms might seem strange to many English-language learners whose native languages have few or no such pairs of confusing words. Ask the students to find in their native languages the equivalent words of the English homonyms that give them trouble. The corresponding words in their native languages may serve as mnemonics to help them remember which homonym to use.

Learners Having Difficulty

Homonyms. Some students might need extra help to master homonyms. Write the following pairs of words on the chalkboard, and ask volunteers to circle the letters that differentiate each pair. Ask other volunteers to look up the words in dictionaries and to report on the different definitions.

1. compliment, complement [*i, e*]
2. stationary, stationery [*a, e*]
3. their, there [*ir, re*]
4. threw, through [*ew, ough*]
5. weak, week [*a, e*]
6. capital, capitol [*a, o*]

⌐ TIPS & TRICKS ⌐

Here's a way to remember the difference between *capital* and *capitol*. There's a d**o**me on the capit**o**l.

Exercise 8 **Choosing Between Words Often Confused**

For each of the following sentences, choose the correct word or words from the pair in parentheses.

EXAMPLE   **1.** Can the artist (*altar, alter*) the design?
          1. alter

1. Did you help (*brake, break*) the piñata, Felipe?
2. Who arranged the flowers on the (*altar, alter*)?
3. I've (*all ready, already*) seen that movie.
4. My mom was (*all together, altogether*) pleased with my report card.
5. Don't forget to set the emergency (*brake, break*) when you park on a hill.
6. Our family will be (*all together, altogether*) at Thanksgiving this year.
7. "Will you (*altar, alter*) this sundress for me, Mom?" Angie asked.
8. You were (*all together, altogether*) right about the show times for the movie.
9. The Great Circus Parade is (*already, all ready*) to begin.
10. Unfortunately, handblown glass figurines (*break, brake*) very easily.

capital	[noun] *a city; the location of a government* Havana is the *capital* of Cuba.
capitol	[noun] *a building; statehouse* Our state *capitol* is made of granite.
choose	[verb, rhymes with *shoes*] *to select* Did you *choose* the movie for today?
chose	[verb, past tense of *choose*, rhymes with *shows*] Who *chose* the movie yesterday?
cloths	[noun] *pieces of cloth* My aunt brought these kente *cloths* home from Ghana.
clothes	[noun] *wearing apparel* Bob irons his own *clothes*.

coarse	[adjective] *rough; crude; not fine* Some cities still use *coarse* salt to melt snow on streets and roads.
course	[noun] *a path of action; a series of studies;* [also used in the expression *of course*] What *course* should we follow to accomplish our goal? The counselor suggested several *courses* for us to take. I can't, *of course*, tell you what to do.
desert	[noun, pronounced des'•ert] *a dry, sandy region; a wilderness* Plants and animals of the *desert* can survive on little water.
desert	[verb, pronounced de•sert'] *to abandon; to leave* Don't *desert* your friends when they need you.
dessert	[noun, pronounced de•sert'] *the final, sweet course of a meal* What's for *dessert* tonight?

Exercise 9 **Choosing Between Words Often Confused**

For each of the following sentences, choose the correct word from the pair of words in parentheses.

EXAMPLE   **1.** The sand on the beach is (*coarse, course*).

        1. coarse

1. The Mojave (*Desert, Dessert*) is located in California.
2. Juan packed lightweight (*clothes, cloths*) to wear on his trip.
3. The sailor set a (*coarse, course*) for the port of Pago Pago.
4. When was the (*capital, capitol*) built, and how long has the state legislature been meeting there?
5. For (*desert, dessert*) we had pears and cheese.
6. Each team must (*choose, chose*) a captain.
7. The polishing (*cloths, clothes*) are by the wax on the shelf.
8. "Of (*coarse, course*) you may go!" Mr. Vance said.
9. The (*capital, capitol*) is the second-largest city in the state.
10. The cooking (*coarse, course*) lasted six weeks last summer.

Words Often Confused

Mnemonics. The following memory tricks can help some students learn to remember words often confused.

1. dessert—When *dessert* is served, we often want two (two *s*'s).
2. hear—We *hear* with our *ears*.
3. piece—A *pie* contains a *piece*.
4. stationery—You might write a *letter* on *stationery*.
5. Tell students to remember the round *o* in *capitol* by thinking of the rotunda, a large round room that lies under a domed roof in many *capitol* buildings.

EXTENSION

Words Often Confused

Divide the class into groups of three or four students. Have each group compose a short poem, a series of cartoons, or song or rap lyrics that use three or four sets of confusing words from the charts in this section. Each group's project can be serious or funny, but students must correctly use or illustrate each word in their sets of words. The group should first decide on the theme or topic for their project. Then, each student in the group should be responsible for writing lines or creating illustrations for one set of words. One student should be responsible for arranging the group's work onto a piece of poster board or large sheet of paper. Invite groups to share their completed projects with the rest of the class.

MECHANICS

Review D Proofreading
Sentences for Words Often
Confused

ANSWERS

1. desert
2. all ready
3. all together
4. course
5. break
6. clothes
7. altars
8. alter
9. capital
10. dessert

TECHNOLOGY **TIP**

You might want to discuss the use of spellchecking features for students who use word processors. Explain that the computer will search for words not in its dictionary, highlight the words, and suggest alternative spellings. Remind students that they cannot depend entirely on computers for spelling. Most spellchecking programs will not recognize the misuse of a homonym. Tell students that they must carefully proofread in addition to using spellchecking features.

Review D Proofreading Sentences for Words
Often Confused

For each of the following sentences, correctly write the word
that is ~~misused~~.

EXAMPLE   1. The students are already for the Fall Festival.
            1. *all ready*

1. Throughout history, most societies and cultures, from the hot ~~dessert~~ regions to the cold northern regions, have celebrated the harvest.
2. The Jewish celebration of Sukkot marks the time when the harvest was gathered and the people were ~~already~~ for winter.
3. The most important tradition of Sukkot called for the family to live ~~altogether~~ in a temporary shelter called a sukkah.
4. Today, of ~~coarse~~, many Jews still celebrate Sukkot but simply eat a meal outdoors under a shelter like the one pictured below.
5. Native Americans believed that without the help of the gods, there would be a ~~brake~~ in their good fortune.
6. During their planting ceremonies, most Native Americans, like the ones at left, dressed in special ~~cloths~~.
7. To thank their harvest gods, the Chinese and Japanese placed wheat on ~~alters~~.
8. Today, the Japanese do not ~~altar~~ this tradition much.
9. In most Japanese cities, including the ~~capitol~~, the people hold parades to thank the ocean for the food it provides.
10. Many families in the United States celebrate Thanksgiving by sharing a meal, often with pumpkin pie for ~~desert~~.

CONTENT-AREA CONNECTIONS

Geography
Writing About Geography. Challenge pairs of students to describe various parts of the world using as many words as they can from the "Words Often Confused" section. Students should circle each target word that they use and note in the margin the word with which it is often confused, for example, *The Spree River flows* through *Berlin, the* capital *of Germany. The* course *of the Spree River takes it across the North German* Plain. (*threw, capitol, coarse, plane*) Students may need to use encyclopedias and other classroom and library resources.

hear	[verb] *to receive sounds through the ears* When did you *hear* the news?
here	[adverb] *in this place* The mail is *here.*
its	[possessive form of *it*] *belonging to it* You should not judge a book by *its* cover.
it's	[contraction of *it is* or *it has*] *It's* your turn, Theresa. *It's* been a long day.
lead	[verb, rhymes with *need*] *to go first; to be a leader* Will you *lead* the singing, Rachel?
led	[verb, past tense of *lead*, rhymes with *red*] *went first; guided* The dog *led* its master to safety.
lead	[noun, rhymes with *red*] *a heavy metal; graphite used in pencils* *Lead* is no longer used in household paints. Use a pencil with a softer *lead* if you want to draw dark, heavy lines.
loose	[adjective, rhymes with *goose*] *not tight* A *loose* wheel on a bike is dangerous.
lose	[verb, rhymes with *shoes*] *to suffer loss* That sudden, loud noise made me *lose* my place.

Exercise 10 **Choosing Between Words Often Confused**

For each of the following sentences, choose the correct word from the pair of words in parentheses.

EXAMPLE 1. Rabbi Epstein (*lead, led*) our group during our tour of Israel.

    1. *led*

1. We could (*hear, here*) the patter of the rain on the (*lead, led*) roof from a block away.
2. A kimono is a (*loose, lose*) Japanese garment with short, wide sleeves and a sash.
3. Mom said that (*its, it's*) your turn to wash the dishes.

Compiling a Thesaurus of Words Often Confused

Class Project. For a class project, have students compile a thesaurus from some of the words often confused listed in this chapter. Divide the class into teams of two or three, and assign each team several words often confused from this chapter. You may want to give students the option of adding their own homonyms to their team's list.

Give each team a stack of index cards. Instruct the teams to write one word on each card, followed by synonyms found in a dictionary, a usage book, or a thesaurus.

Once the cards have been completed, proofread, and corrected, ask for volunteers to alphabetize the cards. Enter the words on a word processor, and print a copy of the finished thesaurus for each member of the class.

MECHANICS

DIFFERENTIATING INSTRUCTION

Advanced Students

British English. Tell students that some English words have two spellings, depending on whether the word is written in British English or American English. For example, *labor* is spelled *labour* in British English. Ask students if they know other words that are spelled differently by U.S. and British writers. [*color, colour; curb, kerb; jail, gaol*]

┌ TIPS & TRICKS ┐

Here's a way to remember the difference between *peace* and *piece.* You eat a pi**e**ce of **pie.**

┌ TIPS & TRICKS ┐

To remember the spelling of *principal*, use this sentence: The princi**pal** is your **pal.**

4. (*Hear, Here*) is a good article about Black History Month.
5. I hope the team doesn't (*loose, lose*) its opening game.
6. Who will (*lead, led*) the team to victory tomorrow?
7. "Wait (*hear, here*) while I open the door," Peter ordered.
8. The weights were as heavy as (*led, lead*).
9. (*Its, It's*) taken too long to respond to your letter.
10. The (*lead, led*) in this mechanical pencil is almost gone.

passed	[verb, past tense of *pass*] *went by* We *passed* you on the way to school.
past	[noun] *time that has gone by;* [preposition] *beyond;* [adjective] *ended* You can learn much from the *past.* The band marched *past* the school. The *past* week was a busy one.
peace	[noun] *quiet, order, and security* People all over the world long for *peace.*
piece	[noun] *a part of something* I had a delicious *piece* of spinach pie at the Greek festival.
plain	[adjective] *simple; common;* [noun] *a flat area of land* Raul's directions were *plain* and clear. The coastal *plain* was flat and barren.
plane	[noun] *a flat surface; a tool; an airplane* A rectangle is a four-sided *plane* with four right angles. Wood shavings curled from the *plane* to the workshop floor. The *plane* flew nonstop to Atlanta.
principal	[noun] *the head of a school;* [adjective] *chief, main* The vice *principal* is at the high school. The committee's *principal* task is preserving the park.
principle	[noun] *a rule of conduct; a basic truth* Freedom of speech is one of the *principles* of democracy.

Exercise 11 Choosing Between Words Often Confused

For each of the following sentences, choose the correct word from the pair of words in parentheses.

EXAMPLE   1. The (*passed, past*) president served two terms, not three.

1. *past*

1. The Old Order Amish wear (*plain, plane*) clothes.
2. Many Americans believe that the golden rule is a good (*principal, principle*) by which to live.
3. Mark likes the (*piece, peace*) and quiet of the country.
4. One (*piece, peace*) of the puzzle was missing.
5. Komako used a (*plain, plane*) to smooth the rough edge of the door.
6. We flew in an enormous Singapore Airlines (*plain, plane*) to Frankfurt, Germany.
7. By studying the (*passed, past*), we understand the present.
8. She was (*principal, principle*) of the school for years.
9. Gail Devers quickly (*passed, past*) the other runners.
10. The trees are just (*passed, past*) their lovely fall colors.

Review E Proofreading a Paragraph to Correct Errors in Words Often Confused

For the sentences in the following paragraph, correctly∧write each ~~incorrect~~ word.

EXAMPLE   [1] Often, people don't know how precious something is until they loose it.

1. *lose*

[1] Several months ago, my aunt had what we all thought was a ~~plane~~ old cold. [2] In the ~~passed~~, her doctor had told her there was no cure for a cold, so my aunt didn't even seek treatment. [3] No one knew that she had an ear infection that would ~~led~~ to a hearing loss in one ear. [4] Very soon, my aunt realized that she was hearing only ~~peaces~~ of conversations and could no longer hear out of her left ear. [5] When she went to the doctor, he explained that an infection had caused her to ~~loose~~ hearing in that ear. [6] The doctor gave her a chart showing the ~~principle~~ types of hearing aids. [7] He suggested

1. plain
2. past
3. lead
4. pieces
5. lose
6. principal

7. it's
8. Its
9. course
10. hear

the in-the-canal hearing aid because ̲i̲t̲s̲ barely noticeable
when in place. [8] ̲I̲t̲'̲s̲ small size really surprised me. [9] The
doctor told my aunt that, of ̲c̲o̲a̲r̲s̲e̲, new advances in hearing
technology are being made every day now. [10] Some people
who could not ̲h̲e̲r̲e̲ at all before can now be helped.

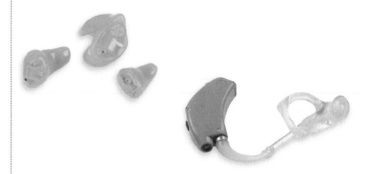

TIPS & TRICKS

Here is an easy way to
remember the difference
between *stationary* and
stationery. You write a
lett**er** on station**er**y.

stationary	[adjective] *in a fixed position* The desks are *stationary,* but the chairs can be moved.
stationery	[noun] *writing paper* Sarah designs her own *stationery.*
their	[possessive form of *they*] *belonging to them* *Their* pitcher struck out six players.
there	[adverb] *at or to that place;* [also used to begin a sentence] I'll see you *there.* *There* are more than two million books in the Harold Washington Library in Chicago.
they're	[contraction of *they are*] *They're* right behind you.
threw	[verb, past tense of *throw*] *tossed* Zack *threw* the ball to me.
through	[preposition] *in one side and out the other* Let's walk *through* the park.

MECHANICS

Exercise 12 Choosing Between Words Often Confused

For each of the following sentences, choose the correct word from the choices in parentheses.

EXAMPLE **1.** (*Their, They're, There*) goes the space shuttle!

1. There

1. The 100-yard dash will begin over (*their, there, they're*) by the fence.
2. In a flash, the girls (*threw, through*) everything into (*their, there, they're*) lockers and ran onto the field.
3. The planet earth was once thought to be (*stationary, stationery*) in space.
4. (*Threw, Through*) the door bounded a large dog.
5. Are you sure (*their, there, they're*) not coming?
6. "Who (*through, threw*) the pass that led to the touchdown?" Jill asked.
7. I think that the red envelopes do not go with the pink (*stationery, stationary*) at all.
8. (*They're, Their*) planning to see a new science fiction movie sometime this weekend.
9. We drove (*threw, through*) Kansas and Oklahoma on the way to Texas.
10. (*Their, There*) is a Cajun band playing in the park this afternoon until 4:00.

to	[preposition] *in the direction of; toward* We drove *to* Carson City.
too	[adverb] *also; more than enough* Am I invited, *too*? Your poem has *too* many syllables to be a haiku.
two	[adjective or noun] *one plus one* Ms. Red Cloud's last name is *two* separate words. *Two* of the pandas woke up then.
weak	[adjective] *feeble; not strong* People with *weak* ankles have difficulty ice-skating.
week	[noun] *seven days* The club meets once a *week*.

(continued)

DIFFERENTIATING INSTRUCTION

Learners Having Difficulty

If students are having problems finding misspelled words as they proofread, suggest that they go over their work starting at the end of a sentence and working backward in order to look at words out of context. Tell them to pay attention to each word and to circle any word about which they are uncertain. After they have gone over their papers, they should check each circled word in a dictionary.

MECHANICS

| COMPUTER TIP

A computer can help you catch spelling mistakes. Remember, though, that a computer's spellchecker cannot point out homonyms that are used incorrectly. Learn how to proofread your own writing. Never rely entirely on a spellchecker.

Learning for Life

Continued on pp. 338–339

Writing a Yearbook Article. Tell students that one of the most treasured mementos of some students is the school yearbook. Students who serve on a yearbook staff gather photographs and write articles about events that occurred during a particular school year.

Have each student imagine that he or she is writing an article for a class yearbook for the current academic year at your school. Each student should write a short article about a particular event in which his or her

(continued)

who's	[contraction of *who is* or *who has*] *Who's* wearing a watch? *Who's* seen Frida Kahlo's paintings?
whose	[possessive form of *who*] *belonging to whom* I wonder *whose* backpack this is.
your	[possessive form of *you*] *belonging to you* Rest *your* eyes now and then when you read.
you're	[contraction of *you are*] *You're* next in line.

Exercise 13 **Choosing Between Words Often Confused**

For each of the following sentences, choose the correct word from the choices in parentheses.

EXAMPLE **1.** I wonder (*who's, whose*) won the election.

    1. who's

1. (*Who's, Whose*) story did you like best?
2. Walking (*to, too*) the grocery store, he began to feel (*weak, week*).
3. Does (*your, you're*) dad work for the newspaper, (*to, too, two*)?
4. It took me a (*weak, week*) to complete my project for history class.
5. If (*your, you're*) not making that noise, (*who's, whose*) making it?
6. "Is there (*too, two*) much flour in the tortilla dough?" Alinda asked.
7. Always fasten (*you're, your*) seat belt when (*you're, your*) riding in a vehicle.
8. They asked (*who's, whose*) painting was chosen (*to, too*) be entered in the contest.
9. (*Too, Two*) of the foreign exchange students are from southern India.
10. "See you next (*weak, week*)!" the ballet teacher said to the students cheerfully.

Learning for Life *Continued from p. 337*

class has been involved. Students might write about a class play, a special program, a field trip, a band or choir concert, or another interesting event. Students should keep in mind that their articles will serve collectively as a record of events that occurred during the school year.

Tell students to make sure they use correct spelling in writing their articles. They should use at least one word spelled with an *ie* or an *ei* and other words that have prefixes or suffixes. If possible, students also should

Review F   **Choosing Between Words Often Confused**

For each of the following sentences, choose the correct word or words from the choices in parentheses.

EXAMPLE   **1.** Don't (*loose, lose*) your house key.

      1. lose

1. Oh, Rebecca, which of these (*to, too, two*) boxes of (*stationary, stationery*) do you like better?

2. The Israelis and the Palestinians met in Madrid, the (*capital, capitol*) of Spain, for the (*peace, piece*) talks.

3. (*Principal, Principle*) Wong raised his hand for silence, and the students waited to (*hear, here*) what he would say.

4. These curtains will likely be hard to (*altar, alter*) because the fabric is so (*coarse, course*).

5. (*Its, It's*) (*all together, altogether*) too easy to confuse similar words.

6. Ruth vowed to (*lead, led*) the life of an exile rather than to (*desert, dessert*) Naomi.

7. Can that (*plain, plane*) (*brake, break*) the sound barrier?

8. We're (*all ready, already*) for the big game against our rivals this (*weak, week*).

9. (*Your, You're*) next chore is to dust; the dust (*clothes, cloths*) are on the counter.

10. The two friends (*passed, past*) the time pleasantly reading (*there, their, they're*) books.

Review G   **Proofreading a Paragraph to Correct Spelling Errors and Errors in Words Often Confused**

For each sentence in the following paragraph, correctly∧write each ~~misspelled or misused word~~. If a sentence is already correct, write *C*.

EXAMPLE   **[1]** Its time to test you're knowledge of South American history.

      1. It's; your

[1] Starting about A.D. 1200, people known as the Incas began ∧too take over the western portion of South America. [2] Look at the map on the next page, and you'll see that ~~thier~~∧

      1. to

      2. their/deserts

include in their articles a plural numeral, letter, or symbol. Finally, each article should include at least five of the words often confused listed in this chapter. After students have completed their articles, they should circle words that have homonyms and write the homonym for each word in the margin.

    You might want to make copies of the articles so students can collect them in special folders or notebooks to serve as their class yearbooks.

3. capital
4. their
5. developed
6. principal
7. C
8. living
9. 1500's [*or* 1500s]
10. break

territory included mountains, seacoasts, river valleys, and ~~desserts~~. [3] The ~~capitol~~ of the Incan empire was Cuzco. [4] The Incas created an impressive road system that connected Cuzco with the rest of ~~there~~ empire. [5] These hard-working people also built storehouses and ~~developped~~ large irrigation projects. [6] To help them manage their huge empire, they used a device called a quipu as their ~~principle~~ method of keeping records. [7] The quipu (shown below) is a series of knotted, colored cords. [8] With it, the Incas recorded such information as the number of people ~~liveing~~ in an area, the movements of the planets, and the amount of goods in storage. [9] The Incan civilization lasted until the Spanish arrived in the mid- ~~1500s'~~. [10] In only a short time, Spanish conquistadors were able to defeat the Incas and ~~brake~~ up their empire.

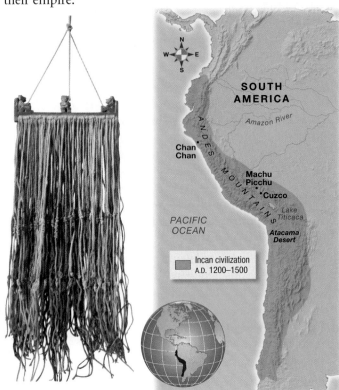

14

Chapter Review

A. Proofreading Sentences for Correct Spelling

┌HELP┐
No proper nouns in the Chapter Review are misspelled.

Terms and numerals in brackets refer to concepts and rules tested by the items in the Chapter Review.

1. chief [14a]
2. brief [14a]
3. Breathing [14d]
4. geese [14h(7)]
5. argument [14e]
6. *I*'s [14h(9)]
7. laziness [14f]
8. countries [14h(3)]
9. stereos [14h(5)]
10. tomatoes [14h(6)]
11. children [14h(7)]
12. branches [14h(2)]
13. itches [14h(2)]
14. pianos
   [14h(6)–Help: musical terms]
15. ancient [14a]
16. dissatisfied [14b]
17. friendliness [14f]
18. biggest [14g]
19. slimmer [14g]
20. Strawberries [14h(3)]

For each of the following sentences, correctly write the word that is misspelled.

1. The company's cheif accountant wrote the schedule.
2. Mr. Santander gave a breif speech before the ceremony.
3. Breatheing hard, we finally reached the summit.
4. Chickens and gooses are common fowl.
5. We changed the subject to avoid having an arguement.
6. How many Is did you use in your letter to Irene?
7. Mom and Dad have no tolerance for lazyness.
8. Spain and Portugal are two countrys I have always wanted to visit.
9. The new store on the corner will sell computer disks, computers, and stereoes.
10. My grandmother's recipe calls for half a clove of garlic and two garden tomatos.
11. Three small, active childs came running out of the house.
12. We cut several large branchs off the pine tree.
13. After she ran through the patch of stinging nettles, Alice had itchs up and down her legs.
14. We were surprised to see two pianoes on the stage instead of only one.
15. I am very interested in the history of anceint Egypt.
16. "The last thing we want," said the new sales manager, "is a disatisfied customer."
17. The first thing you notice in San Miguel is the friendlyness of the people.
18. That dinosaur skeleton must have been the bigest thing in the whole museum.
19. Aunt Rina has lost weight; she looks much slimer than she has in a long time.
20. Strawberrys are my favorite fruit.

Chapter Review **341**

B. Choosing Between Words Often Confused

For each of the following sentences, choose from each pair in parentheses the word that will make the sentence correct.

21.–30. [Words Often Confused]

21. Nothing would persuade him to (*altar*, *alter*) his plans.
22. Berlin is the (*capitol*, *capital*) of Germany.
23. Sometimes the wisest (*course*, *coarse*) of action is to do nothing.
24. Samantha tried on the new (*cloths*, *clothes*) she received on her birthday.
25. For (*desert*, *dessert*) we had red grapes, strawberries, frozen yogurt, and melon.
26. The vast (*planes*, *plains*) of Patagonia stretch from the mountains to the ocean.
27. "Your cousins are over (*their*, *there*)," said Mr. Octavius. "I think this is (*there*, *their*) luggage."
28. In all the confusion, it was difficult to tell (*whose*, *who's*) things belonged to whom.
29. We were somewhat surprised when an overloaded pickup truck (*past*, *passed*) us going uphill.
30. On their way (*too*, *to*) the train station, they were held up in the (*stationary*, *stationery*) traffic.

C. Proofreading a Paragraph to Correct Spelling Errors

For each sentence in the following paragraph, correctly write the word or words that are misspelled. If a sentence is already correct, write *C*.

[31] Dublin, the capitol of Ireland, has a beautiful locateion between the sea and the mountains. [32] The city has a rich and interesting passed. [33] The Viking's established Dublin in the mid-800's, though a small settlement had existed previously on the site. [34] Norman soldiers from England captured Dublin in 1170 and built St. Patrick's Cathedral and Dublin Castle their. [35] The castle remained the center of British rule in Ireland throughout the next 700 years. [36] War and piece came and went. [37] By the 1700's, Dublin was growing fast. [38] It's cultural life flourished, and manufacturing and trade increased.

31. capital/location [Words Often Confused/14d]
32. past [Words Often Confused]
33. Vikings [14h(1)]
34. there [Words Often Confused]
35. C [Good Spelling Habits]
36. peace [Words Often Confused]
37. C [14h(9)]
38. Its [Words Often Confused]

MECHANICS

[39] ~~Unfortunatly~~, between 1916 and 1922, much property was destroyed during the war of independence and a civil war.
[40] Today, Dublin is growing and prosperous and is ~~faceing~~ the challenges common to most modern big ~~citys~~.

39. Unfortunately
[14c]
40. facing/cities
[14d/14h(3)]

Writing Application

Using Correct Spelling in a Personal Letter

Following Spelling Rules   You are writing a letter to congratulate your cousin Mary, who has been awarded first prize in a spelling bee. Write a paragraph expressing your congratulations and saying how important you think it is to use correct spelling. In your paragraph, use at least five words often confused.

Prewriting   Jot down a list of reasons correct spelling is important. You might mention making a good impression and making communication easier. Also, compose sentences about how difficult it must be to remember correct spelling in front of an audience and how impressed you are that Mary managed to do so.

Writing   Begin your rough draft by stating how hard it is to spell correctly in English and how important it is to continue developing that skill. Then, congratulate Mary on her award and say that her success will inspire you to continue working hard at learning correct spelling.

Revising   Have a friend or classmate read your draft. Have you clearly stated the importance of correct spelling? Is your pleasure at your cousin's success clearly described?

Publishing   Make sure you have not used any homonyms incorrectly. Then, proofread your letter for any errors in grammar, punctuation, and spelling. You and your classmates may wish to post your letters on a class bulletin board or Web page.

Writing Application
Revising Tip. In writing and evaluating their letters, students need to be aware of their audience. As students work in pairs to evaluate and revise their letters, tell them to pretend to be the people who are receiving the letters. The letters should explain why proper spelling is so important.

Scoring Rubric. While you will want to pay particular attention to students' spelling and use of words often confused, you will also want to evaluate overall writing performance. You may want to give a split score to indicate development and clarity of the composition as well as mechanics skills.

MECHANICS

TEACHING TIP

In the **Spelling Words** list, the numbers of the word groups correspond to lessons in the *Spelling* workbook.

Lesson 1: OBJECTIVE
■ To spell words that demonstrate these sound-letter relationships: /a/a; /e/e; /i/i; /o/o; /u/u

Lesson 2: OBJECTIVE
■ To spell words that have a long vowel sound

Lesson 3: OBJECTIVE
■ To spell words that demonstrate these sound-letter relationships: /ou/ou; ô/o, a, au, aw; /o͞o/ou, oo, u

Lesson 4: OBJECTIVE
■ To spell words that demonstrate these sound-letter relationships: /är/ar; /âr/ar, are; /ôr/oar, ar, our; /ûr/ur, or, er

Lesson 6: OBJECTIVE
■ To spell words that include unusual spellings of the short *i*, short *u*, long *a*, and long *o* vowel sounds

Lesson 7: OBJECTIVE
■ To spell words that include the vowel combination *ei* or *ie*

Lesson 8: OBJECTIVE
■ To spell open, closed, and hyphenated compound words

Lesson 9: OBJECTIVE
■ To spell homophones

Lesson 10: OBJECTIVE
■ To spell words that sound similar and have spellings that are somewhat alike

Lesson 12: OBJECTIVE
■ To spell words ending with consonant plus *y* in which *y* changes to *i* before *es* or *ed* is added

Lesson 13: OBJECTIVE
■ To spell words that demonstrate these sound-letter relationships: /ər/er; /əl/al; /ən/en, an

MECHANICS

Spelling Words

1.
- contact
  contract
  advance
  depth
  comment
  summit
  sketch
  nonsense
  splendid
  ethnic
  liquid
  impulse

2.
- globe
  grove
  slope
  slice
  roast
  spike
  choke
  praise
  squeeze
  breathe
  gross
  thigh

3.
- shout
  youth
  amount
  pounds
  mountain
  thousands
  proof
  crawled
  account
  launched
  rumors
  saucer

4.
- turtle
  nightmare
  burnt
  curb
  purse
  declare

scarce
inserts
sparkling
source
nervous
warrant

6.
- enough
  though
  straight
  rough
  courage
  eighth
  system
  although
  sleigh
  boulder
  biscuit
  dough

7.
- freight
  foreign
  receive
  receiver
  belief
  relief
  weighed
  reins
  fierce
  heights
  thieves
  achieve

8.
- grandfather
  fairy tales
  bedtime
  cupboard
  upright
  teenager
  thunderstorm
  barefoot
  middle-class
  middle-aged
  bodyguard
  so-called

9.
- grown
  groan
  guest
  guessed
  creek
  creak
  weather
  whether
  sore
  soar
  stake
  steak

10.
- angle
  angel
  costume
  custom
  affect
  effect
  adopt
  adapt
  device
  devise
  decent
  descent

12.
- varied
  centuries
  colonies
  applies
  occupied
  identified
  enemies
  activities
  denied
  allied
  industries
  qualified

13.
- beaten
  musical
  rotten
  German
  Indian
  Roman

explorer
stretcher
critical
criminal
political
original

14.
- escape
  gotten
  velvet
  engine
  insist
  admire
  index
  intense
  further
  frantic
  convince
  instinct

15.
- agent
  evil
  local
  eager
  famous
  fiber
  razor
  vital
  rival
  basis
  cheetah
  scenic

16.
- speaking
  spelling
  wondered
  bragged
  healed
  scrubbed
  answered
  threatened
  admitted
  committed
  referring
  preferred

Lesson 14: OBJECTIVE
■ To spell two-syllable words that contain a vowel-consonant-consonant-vowel pattern (VCCV)

Lesson 15: OBJECTIVE
■ To spell two-syllable words that contain a vowel-consonant-vowel pattern (VCV)

18.
- insurance
- conference
- ambulance
- absence
- instance
- audience
- allowance
- intelligence
- assurance
- appearance
- obedience
- presence

19.
- activity
- ability
- argument
- personality
- electricity
- championship
- community
- majority
- responsibility
- curiosity
- necessity
- authority

20.
- approach
- accuse
- applause
- affection
- accompany
- assign
- appreciate
- accurate
- association
- apparent
- accustomed
- assistance

21.
- continued
- commander
- commit
- constitution
- confusing
- commence

- commotion
- commercial
- communicate
- communities
- communication
- committee

22.
- elephant
- confident
- instant
- element
- servant
- excellent
- opponent
- permanent
- assistant
- innocent
- significant
- sufficient

24.
- talent
- novel
- treason
- comic
- profit
- token
- weapon
- gopher
- pleasant
- siren
- frigid
- spiral

25.
- habit
- display
- clever
- gather
- empty
- chaos
- suspense
- Saturn
- oval
- orphan
- fatal
- crystal

26.
- media
- fungi
- bacteria
- stimulus
- stimuli
- larvae
- radius
- nucleus
- nuclei
- species
- salmon
- hippopotamus

27.
- curious
- tremendous
- enormous
- obvious
- delicious
- mysterious
- executive
- creative
- fabulous
- legislative
- negative
- sensitive

28.
- unpredictable
- disagreement
- renewal
- unemployment
- unexpectedly
- unfortunately
- unusually
- reproduction
- reconstruction
- disagreeable
- unsuccessful
- uncomfortable

30.
- wonderfully
- thoughtfully
- relationship
- respectively
- naturally
- nervously

- gracefully
- actively
- joyfully
- beautifully
- successfully
- accidentally

31.
- illegal
- impolite
- impossible
- invisible
- irregular
- inexpensive
- impure
- inability
- impatient
- indigestion
- indefinite
- incredible

32.
- descriptive
- description
- prescribed
- inspector
- spectacle
- spectacular
- scribbled
- inscription
- subscription
- spectrum
- spectators
- transcripts

33.
- erupt
- abrupt
- bankrupt
- inject
- disrupting
- disruption
- eject
- reject
- rejected
- rupture
- corrupt
- interrupt

MECHANICS

CHAPTER

15

STANDARDS FOCUS

Grade-Level Standard

- Language Convention 1.0: Students write and speak with a command of standard English conventions appropriate to this grade level.

▼

INTRODUCING THE CHAPTER

- This chapter provides application and review of some aspects of grammar, usage, and mechanics that cause students particular difficulty. You may find this chapter useful in a variety of ways. You could use the exercises and tests in this chapter as diagnostic tests, judging by student scores which areas need most attention; as a resource for reteaching and remediation, providing extra practice for concepts you feel need added emphasis; as a review of key concepts, helping to prepare students for standardized tests of language skills mastery; or in any combination of these ways.

1.0 Written and Oral English Language Conventions
Students write and speak with a command of standard English conventions appropriate to this grade level.

┌HELP┐
The exercises in this chapter test your knowledge of the rules of **standard, formal English.** These are the rules you should follow in your schoolwork.

Reference Note
For more information about **standard** and **nonstandard English** and **formal** and **informal English,** see page 221.

Correcting Common Errors

Key Language Skills Review

This chapter reviews key skills and concepts that pose special problems for writers.

- **Sentence Fragments and Run-on Sentences**
- **Subject-Verb Agreement**
- **Pronoun-Antecedent Agreement**
- **Verb Forms**
- **Pronoun Forms**
- **Comparison and Placement of Modifiers**
- **Double Negatives**
- **Standard Usage**
- **Capitalization**
- **Punctuation—Commas, End Marks, Semicolons, Colons, Quotation Marks, and Apostrophes**
- **Spelling**

Most of the exercises in this chapter follow the same format as the exercises found throughout the grammar, usage, and mechanics sections of this book. You will notice,

---

CHAPTER RESOURCES

Internet
- go.hrw.com (keyword: HLLA)

**go.
hrw
.com**

Planning
- *One-Stop Planner CD-ROM* 💿
- *On Course: Mapping Instruction*

Practice & Review
- *Language & Sentence Skills Practice,* pp. 311–340; 341–343
- *Developmental Language & Sentence Skills,* pp. 131–142

Application & Enrichment
- *Language & Sentence Skills Practice,* pp. 344, 347; 310; 345–346

however, that two sets of review exercises are presented in standardized test formats. These exercises are designed to provide you with practice not only in solving usage and mechanics problems but also in dealing with these kinds of problems on standardized tests.

Exercise 1 Identifying Sentences and Sentence Fragments

Identify each of the following word groups as a *sentence* or a *sentence fragment*. If a word group is a sentence, rewrite it correctly, using a capital letter at the beginning and adding an end mark.

EXAMPLES
1. the squirrel hopped across the branch
1. sentence—The squirrel hopped across the branch.

2. Jeremy's collection of comic books
2. sentence fragment

1. near the door of the classroom   1. frag.
2. all members of the safety patrol   2. frag.
3. sumo wrestling is popular in Japan.   3. sent.
4. please pass me the fruit salad.   4. sent.
5. will become a member of Junior Achievement   5. frag.
6. after school Sonya repaired her backpack.   6. sent.
7. what an active puppy that is!   7. sent.
8. lived in British Columbia for many years   8. frag.
9. do you like the sound of ocean waves?   9. sent.
10. on the top shelf of the refrigerator   10. frag.
11. ate goat cheese every day in Norway   11. frag.
12. that's a fantastic idea!   [or .]   12. sent.
13. because rap music is still popular   13. frag.
14. not everyone wants to play the game.   14. sent.
15. a tree was placed on top of the completed building.   15. sent.
16. when the armadillos enter another state   16. frag.
17. stopped traffic for half an hour   17. frag.
18. John the plumber around noon   18. frag.
19. please return the books by tomorrow afternoon.   19. sent.
20. plugged in the computer and nothing happened   20. frag.

Reference Note

For information on **sentences** and **sentence fragments,** see pages 4 and 386.

Exercise 1

OBJECTIVE

■ To distinguish complete sentences from sentence fragments and to punctuate complete sentences correctly

COMMON ERRORS

Differentiating Instruction
■ *Lesson Plans for Language Development*
■ *Supporting Instruction in Five Languages*
Assessment
■ *Progress Assessment for the Holt Handbook,* pp. 29–30, 41

■ *Test Generator (One-Stop Planner CD-ROM)*
Other Language Resources
■ *Spelling Lessons & Activities*
■ *Vocabulary Development*
■ *Daily Language Activities Transparencies*

Exercise 2

OBJECTIVE

- To identify and correct sentence fragments

Exercise 2 Revising Sentence Fragments

ANSWERS

Answers may vary. Sample responses are given.

1. The book is titled *The Case of the Missing Cutthroats.*
2. It is a book for young detectives who love nature.
3. S
4. S
5. Most people thought cutthroat trout had died out where she was fishing in the Snake River.
6. S
7. They are puzzled by the presence of a cutthroat trout.
8. S
9. Spinner and her cousin Al go on an adventure.
10. They hope to find clues that will help them solve the mystery.

Exercise 3

OBJECTIVE

- To revise run-on sentences by making two sentences or adding a comma and a coordinating conjunction

Reference Note

For information on **sentence fragments,** see pages 4 and 386.

┌ HELP ┐

Most of the sentences in Exercise 3 can be correctly revised in more than one way. You need to give only one revision for each sentence.

Reference Note

For information on **run-on sentences,** see page 389.

Exercise 2 Revising Sentence Fragments

Some of the following word groups are sentence fragments. First, identify the fragments. Then, make each fragment a complete sentence by adding (1) a subject, (2) a verb, or (3) both. You may need to change the punctuation and capitalization, too. If the word group is already a complete sentence, write *S.*

EXAMPLE
1. Finished reading an exciting book by Jean Craighead George.
1. *I finished reading an exciting book by Jean Craighead George.*

1. Titled *The Case of the Missing Cutthroats.*
2. A book for young detectives who love nature.
3. In the book, a girl named Spinner goes fishing.
4. During the trip, she catches a giant cutthroat trout.
5. Thought cutthroat trout had died out where she was fishing in the Snake River.
6. Both she and her family are surprised by her catch.
7. Puzzled by the presence of a cutthroat trout.
8. What has happened to the cutthroat trout?
9. Spinner and her cousin Al on an adventure.
10. Hope to find clues that will help them solve the mystery.

Exercise 3 Identifying and Revising Run-on Sentences

Decide which of the following word groups are run-on sentences. Then, revise each run-on sentence by (1) making two separate sentences or (2) using a comma and a coordinating conjunction. You may have to change the punctuation and capitalization, too. If the word group is already a complete sentence, write *S.* Revisions will vary. Sample responses are given.

EXAMPLE
1. Both girls enjoy playing soccer one is usually the goalie.
1. *Both girls enjoy playing soccer, and one is usually the goalie.*

or

Both girls enjoy playing soccer. One is usually the goalie.

1. Puffins are shorebirds, they have brightly colored beaks and ducklike bodies.

2. Cement is a fine powder, it is mixed with sand, water, and small rocks to make concrete.

3. Alicia collects birth dates, she has recorded the birthdays of all her friends and of her favorite movie stars.

4. We may go to the Zuni arts and crafts fair on Saturday, we may wait until next weekend.   4. or

5. The band placed first in regional competitions, it did not win at the state contests.   5. but

6. I plan to go to the Florida Keys someday, I want to skin-dive for seashells.   6. for

7. Kerry is having a party tomorrow night, we are planning to go.   7. and

8. The school board could vote to remodel the old cafeteria, or they may decide to build a new one.   8. S

9. My brother would like to live on a space station someday, I would, too.   9. and

10. These rocks are too heavy for me to lift, I asked Christy to help me move them.   10. so

Exercise 4 — Identifying and Revising Run-on Sentences

Identify which of the following word groups are run-on sentences. Then, revise each run-on sentence by (1) making two separate sentences or (2) using a comma and a coordinating conjunction. You may have to change the punctuation and capitalization, too. If the word group is already a complete sentence, write *S*. Revisions will vary. Sample responses are given.

EXAMPLE   1. The Navajo woman allowed the children to try on jewelry, it was made out of silver and beautiful turquoise.

1. *The Navajo woman allowed the children to try on jewelry. It was made out of silver and beautiful turquoise.*

1. Sheila liked a ring with one stone in the middle, it didn't fit her finger.   1. but

2. She found another ring with three small stones, it was a perfect fit for her.   2. and

HELP

Most of the sentences in Exercise 4 can be correctly revised in more than one way. You need to give only one revision for each sentence.

Reference Note

For information on **run-on sentences,** see page 389.

Exercise 4

OBJECTIVE

■ To revise run-on sentences by separating them into two sentences or by adding a comma and a coordinating conjunction

COMMON ERRORS

Grammar and Usage   **349**

3. Aaron picked out a turquoise watchband, and he also found a ring with blue stones and fire agates.   **3.** S

4. The watchband had little pieces of turquoise in the shape of a star. he really wanted to buy it.

5. Both Maria and Francine spied a necklace a rough chunk of turquoise was hung from a silver chain.

6. Thad may spend his allowance on a turquoise ring he may save up his money for a watchband.   **6.** or

7. Several children had never seen turquoise before, they wanted to know if the stones were real.   **7.** and

8. The saleswoman's arms were covered with bracelets every-one noticed her.   **8.** so

9. Ruben put six bracelets on his arms, and then he couldn't get all of them off.   **9.** S

10. The group wanted to see more turquoise jewelry the woman had sold many pieces earlier in the day.   **10.** but

---

Exercise 5 **Correcting Run-on Sentences and Sentence Fragments**

Decide which of the following word groups are run-on sentences and which are sentence fragments. Then, revise each word group to make one or more complete sentences. Remember to use correct capitalization and punctuation. If a word group is already a complete sentence, write *S*.

EXAMPLES   **1.** Do you like brightly colored art you should see Faith Ringgold's paintings.

   1. Do you like brightly colored art? You should see Faith Ringgold's paintings.

   2. Uses color boldly and imaginatively.

   2. Ringgold uses color boldly and imaginatively.

Revisions may vary. Sample responses are given.

1. Ringgold was born in Harlem in 1930. at a young age, she knew she wanted to be an artist.

2. Today her artwork in museums around the world.   **2.** is

3. Paints on fabric and sometimes uses fabric to frame her paintings.   **3.** She

4. Her creativity led her to invent a whole new art form she decided to call it the "story quilt."

5. Story quilts blend storytelling with painting.   **5.** S

Exercise 5

OBJECTIVE

■ To correct run-on sentences and sentence fragments

COMMON ERRORS

┌─HELP─

Most of the sentences in Exercise 5 can be correctly revised in more than one way. You need to give only one revision for each sentence.

Reference Note

For information on **sentence fragments,** see pages 4 and 386. For information on **run-on sentences,** see page 389.

6. One of Ringgold's series of story quilts about an African
   American woman in Paris.   **6.** is
7. Much of her work represents her African American roots.   **7.** S
8. Ringgold's painting *Tar Beach* is based on her childhood
   experiences she completed the work in 1988.   **9.** *Tar Beach*
9. Shows a playground on the roof of an apartment building.
10. Behind the rooftop lies the George Washington Bridge, a
    bridge with a string of lights that reminded Ringgold of a
    diamond necklace.   **10.** S

Reference Note
For information on **verb forms,** see page 147. For information on **subject-verb agreement,** see page 124.

Exercise 6 **Choosing Verbs That Agree in Number with Their Subjects**

For each of the following sentences, choose the form of the verb in parentheses that agrees with the subject.

EXAMPLE   **1.** Everyone except my twin sisters (*want, wants*) to go
to the powwow.

   1. wants

1. Here (*come, comes*) the marching bands in the parade!
2. Several of my friends (*has, have*) trail bikes.
3. I (*don't, doesn't*) like to swim when the water is cold.
4. Neither the guinea pigs nor the hamster (*is, are*) awake yet.
5. (*Has, Have*) Mr. Baldwin and Sherry been talking long?
6. One of the scientists (*was, were*) Isaac Newton.
7. Thunderstorms usually (*don't, doesn't*) bother me.
8. (*Is, Are*) the Chinese cookbooks still on sale?
9. All of the movie (*was, were*) filmed in Vietnam.
10. The boy in the red shoes (*run, runs*) fast.

Exercise 7 **Proofreading Sentences for Correct Subject-Verb Agreement**

Reference Note
For information on **subject-verb agreement,** see page 124.

Most of the following sentences contain a verb that does not
agree in number with its subject. If a verb form is incorrect,
write the correct form. If a sentence is already correct,
write *C*.

EXAMPLE   **1.** A carved slice of potato make a good stamp.

   1. makes

1. Images from this type of stamp are called potato prints.   **1.** C

Exercise 6

OBJECTIVE

- To choose verbs that agree in number with their subjects

Exercise 7

OBJECTIVE

- To write correct verb forms

COMMON ERRORS

Grammar and Usage   **351**

Exercise 8

OBJECTIVE

- To choose pronouns that agree with their antecedents

2. Both my cousins and my younger brother Michael ~~creates~~ potato prints.   **2.** create

3. It ~~don't~~ cost much to make these prints.   **3.** doesn't

4. A firm potato, a knife, paint, a paintbrush, and paper ~~is~~ the necessary supplies.   **4.** are

5. My friend James ~~find~~ unique shapes and patterns in his mother's old magazines.   **5.** finds

6. He then carves these designs on the flat surfaces of cut potatoes.   **6.** C

7. Next, each carved design on the potato slices ~~are~~ coated with paint.   **7.** is

8. Pieces of fabric or a sheet of paper ~~offer~~ a good surface for stamping.   **8.** offers

9. Each of my cousins ~~like~~ to make greeting cards with stamped designs.   **9.** likes

10. Other uses for a potato stamp ~~includes~~ making writing paper and wrapping paper.   **10.** include

Reference Note

For information on **pronoun-antecedent agreement,** see page 137.

Exercise 8 **Choosing Pronouns That Agree with Their Antecedents**

For each of the following sentences, choose the pronoun in parentheses that agrees with its antecedent.

EXAMPLE   **1.** The engineers showed (*his, their*) plans for the new bridge.

   1. their

1. J. W. and I hope to have (*our, their*) skits ready in time for the talent show.

2. Two boys and one girl have received honors, and all of (*her, their*) parents are very proud.

3. During the last serve, with the crowd watching, Danny's tennis racket flew out of (*his, our*) hand.

4. We treated (*ourselves, themselves*) to Chinese noodles and stir-fried vegetables for supper.

5. The table is made of oak and is quite solid, but one of (*his, its*) legs is broken.

6. The members of the Asian Students Club asked to have (*its, their*) picture taken with the school mascot.

7. Neither Jack nor Charles wants to have (*his, their*) hair cut by Lisa.

8. Arlene asked Samuel to go on the picnic, but (*he, she*) hasn't given an answer yet.

9. The squirrels and the rabbits play in the yard; (*they, it*) seem to have a lot of fun.

10. Each of the girls will receive (*their, her*) own directions.

Exercise 9 **Proofreading for Pronoun-Antecedent Agreement**

Most of the following sentences contain a pronoun that does not agree with its antecedent. Write each ~~incorrect pronoun~~ and then the‸correct form. If a sentence is already correct, write *C*.

EXAMPLES 1. The asteroids will not hit Earth, but it will come close.

1. *it—they*

2. Each of the boys thought that their independent project was the best one.

2. *their—his*

1. Dad wrote out the check to the painters although‸~~he~~ had not finished the painting job for him.   **1.** they

2. Tom Sawyer tricked his friends into doing his work, but they enjoyed it.   **2.** C

3. Jesse Owens, Willie Mays, and Joe Louis were sports stars in their day, and many people still remember‸~~him~~.   **3.** them

4. Have you ever noticed how the bears at the zoo really enjoy sunning‸~~itself~~?   **4.** themselves

5. Several of the men in our town plan to donate‸~~his~~ time to Habitat for Humanity.   **5.** their

6. Each of the girls wanted to read‸~~their~~ report first.   **6.** her

7. Did Randy or Tomás finish cleaning‸~~their~~ desk first?   **7.** his

8. Our grandparents gave us a surprise party when we came home from camp.   **8.** C

9. Either José or Andrew will arrive early so that‸~~they~~ can help us finish the posters.   **9.** he

10. Each of the cats was chasing‸~~their~~ toys.   **10.** its

Reference Note

For information on **pronoun-antecedent agreement,** see page 137.

COMMON ERRORS

Grammar and Usage   **353**

Exercise 10

OBJECTIVE

■ To use the principal parts of regular verbs

┌─**HELP**─

Some sentences in Exercise 10 may have more than one correct answer. You need to give only one answer for each sentence.

Reference Note

For information on **regular verb forms,** see page 148.

1. climbed
2. joking
3. shopped
4. filled
5. entering
6. watching
7. called
8. measured
9. loaded [*or* load]
10. jumped
11. laughed [*or* laugh]
12. fixing
13. washed
14. played
15. walked
16. talking
17. hammered [*or* hammers]
18. observing
19. helped
20. dressing [*or* dressed]

Exercise 10 **Using the Principal Parts of Regular Verbs**

Give the form of the italicized verb that will correctly complete each of the following sentences.

EXAMPLE   1. *roll*   The dog ____ on its back for us to pet it.
                 1. rolled
                    or
                    rolls

1. *climb*   Yesterday the cat ____ the tree.
2. *joke*   I can never tell when Bob is ____.
3. *shop*   My friend and I once ____ all day at a mall in Bloomington, Minnesota.
4. *fill*   Have the fans ____ the auditorium yet?
5. *enter*   Too many cars are ____ the parking lot.
6. *watch*   The class is ____ a video about the ancient Incan culture in Peru.
7. *call*   Who ____ my name a few seconds ago?
8. *measure*   My mother has ____ the space for the new bookcase.
9. *load*   Two men ____ our furniture into the truck.
10. *jump*   A deer has ____ over the fence.
11. *laugh*   We ____ for a long time over Ira's joke.
12. *fix*   Steven is ____ the computer.
13. *wash*   Cora's brother has ____ his new car at least a dozen times.
14. *play*   Have you ____ the soundtrack from that movie for Isaac yet?
15. *walk*   Mother and I ____ three miles on the county road yesterday morning.
16. *talk*   The young boys are ____ about starting their own soccer team.
17. *hammer*   The carpenter ____ the nails into the crossbeam in almost no time at all.
18. *observe*   Benjamin's family is ____ Yom Kippur in the traditional way.
19. *help*   Regular exercise has ____ many people to stay physically fit.
20. *dress*   Are you ____ up for the banquet tonight?

Exercise 11 Using Irregular Verbs

For each italicized verb, give the past or the past participle form that will correctly complete the sentence.

EXAMPLE   **1.** *drink*   The guests ____ all of the raspberry tea.

           1. *drank*

1. *blow*   The wind has ____ the kite out of the tree!

2. *shrink*   The boy in the movie had ____ to the size of a squirrel.

3. *steal*   "I've never ____ anything in my life," Abe declared in his defense.

4. *drive*   Pat and Justin ____ go-carts at the park.

5. *freeze*   The water in the birdbath has ____.

6. *sink*   The toy boat has ____ in the sudsy bath water.

7. *throw*   Each athlete has ____ the javelin twice.

8. *sing*   The choir ____ at the celebration last night.

9. *swim*   Have you ever ____ in warm mineral water?

10. *burst*   The balloon ____ when the cat clawed it.

11. *teach*   Mrs. Randall has ____ at Rosenwald Middle School for years.

12. *give*   Last year I ____ part of my allowance to the United Way.

13. *run*   Our car is old and unattractive, but it has ____ well for many years.

14. *eat*   Sharon baked two small potatoes and ____ both of them.

15. *fly*   "That hawk has ____ over the yard twice," Justin said.

16. *write*   Many people have ____ about the Mexican myth of Quetzalcoatl.

17. *begin*   It has ____ to snow, but the flakes are very small and dry.

18. *come*   "Who ____ to Dad's surprise birthday party?" Miriam asked.

19. *speak*   Lin and Jeff have ____ about their tickets to everyone in class.

20. *do*   It's a good feeling to know that you have ____ your best.

Reference Note

For information on **irregular verb forms,** see page 150.

1. blown
2. shrunk [*or* shrunken]
3. stolen
4. drove
5. frozen
6. sunk
7. thrown
8. sang
9. swum
10. burst
11. taught
12. gave
13. run
14. ate
15. flown
16. written
17. begun
18. came
19. spoken
20. done

Exercise 11

OBJECTIVE

- To complete sentences by supplying the past or past participle form of given irregular verbs

COMMON ERRORS

Exercise 12

OBJECTIVE

- To proofread sentences for errors in irregular verbs

Reference Note

For information on **irregular verb forms,** see page 150.

1. did
2. brought
3. began
4. came
5. saw
6. C
7. took
8. chose
9. gave
10. C
11. bought
12. broke
13. drunk
14. C
15. gone
16. fell
17. lent

Exercise 12 Proofreading for Errors in Irregular Verbs

Most of the following sentences contain incorrect verb forms. Identify each ~~error~~, and ∧write the correct form of the verb. If the sentence is already correct, write *C*.

EXAMPLE   1. We have went to the African art exhibit two weekends in a row.

　　　　　1. *went—gone*

1. Sarah ~~done~~ well at yesterday's track meet.
2. My stepfather ~~brung~~ me a stuffed animal when I was in the hospital.
3. Nickelodeon movie theaters ~~begun~~ to be quite popular in the United States around 1905.
4. Manuel's grandfather ~~come~~ to the United States forty years ago.
5. We ~~seen~~ the Rio Grande when we drove through the state of New Mexico.
6. Chris knew that a basement was a good place to take shelter during a tornado.
7. Judy ~~taked~~ a few minutes to decide what to say.
8. Maria's team ~~choosed~~ the oak tree in her front yard as home base.
9. The poison ivy in the woods ~~gived~~ me a rash.
10. Dr. Seuss wrote the poem "The Sneetches."
11. The blue pitcher that my godparents ~~buyed~~ for me in Denmark is on the table in the living room.
12. Do you remember what running records Carl Lewis ~~breaked~~?
13. The girls on the front porch have ~~drank~~ their lemonade too quickly.
14. My shirt and pants tore on the barbed wire as I climbed through the fence.
15. Jina's mother and stepfather have ~~went~~ to the same church for thirty-five years.
16. A raccoon ~~felled~~ from the roof of our house, but it was not injured.
17. In a very generous mood, Marsha ~~lended~~ her favorite scarf to Natalie.

18. The family made the giant scarecrow to scare away the grackles from their backyard garden.
19. The young artist ~~drawed~~ a lovely picture of the waves and rocks on the Oregon coast.
        ∧
20. Gwen ~~catched~~ the ball even though Craig threw it fast and high.
        ∧

18. C
19. drew
20. caught

Reference Note

For information on **verb forms,** see page 147.

Exercise 13 Using the Past and Past Participle Forms of Verbs

For the italicized verb in each of the following sentences, give the past or past participle form that will correctly complete the sentence.

EXAMPLE   **1.** *establish*   Robert D. Ballard, a marine geologist, _____ the JASON Foundation for Education.

               1. established

1. *create*   JASON, an underwater robot, was _____ for
1. created   scientific research.

2. *build*   JASON was _____ to dive much deeper than
2. built   humans can dive.

3. *sink*   More than 1,600 years ago, the Roman ship
3. sank   *Isis* _____ in the Mediterranean Sea.   **3.** [or sunk]

4. *know*   Ballard _____ that students would want to share
4. knew   in the exploration of the wrecked ship.

5. *make*   A network of satellites _____ it possible for many
5. made   students to see JASON explore the wreck.

6. *see*   Some 250,000 schoolchildren _____ JASON on
6. saw   giant video screens.

7. *ask*   While JASON searched the ship, students _____
7. asked   questions of Ballard and his team.

8. *take*   Ballard has _____ students on some amazing
8. taken   electronic field trips by televising himself working with JASON.

9. *give*   He has _____ much of his time and energy to
9. given   involving students in scientific discoveries.

10. *write*   Ballard has _____ about finding the *Isis* and
10. written   about the 1985 discovery of the *Titanic*, which sank in 1912.

COMMON ERRORS

OBJECTIVE

■ To choose correct pronoun forms

Reference Note

For information on **pronoun forms,** see page 177.

Exercise 14 Choosing Correct Pronoun Forms

Choose the correct form of the pronoun in parentheses in each of the following sentences.

EXAMPLE   1. The catcher gave (*she, her*) the signal.
         1. *her*

1. The winners may be you and (*her, she*).
2. Gregory asked (*her, she*) to the dance.
3. The ending of the movie really amazed Andrew and (*us, we*)!
4. Should Emily and (*they, them*) make the spaghetti?
5. The bus driver gave (*he, him*) a warning.
6. The competition is really between Mario and (*I, me*).
7. Who bought (*her, she*) that opal necklace?
8. The best player on our team is (*him, he*).
9. The next step for Michael and (*them, they*) is to check with the principal.
10. My cousin and (*me, I*) are learning to do origami in our class at the community center.
11. You and (*I, me*) can work together on a report about American Indians of the Southwest.
12. The physical education teacher designed a special exercise program for (*her, she*).
13. The ones who asked to see our pictures from the Miami zoo are (*they, them*).
14. (*Us, We*) always enjoy the plays at the children's theater, especially when they are performed outdoors.
15. (*He, Him*) plays the guitar quite well and has performed in a band.
16. Ms. Ruel asked Kei and (*I, me*) to recite the French nursery rhyme.
17. "I'd like to go to the movies with (*they, them*)," Thi said after meeting Carmela and Tony.
18. Aunt Edna is buying new backpacks for Carl and (*I, me*).
19. Last week (*them, they*) began taking tennis lessons after school.
20. Will you or (*I, me*) be the first one with the correct answer?

Exercise 15 Proofreading for Correct Pronoun Forms

Most of the following sentences contain a pronoun that has been used incorrectly. Identify each ~~incorrect pronoun~~. Then, write the correct form. If a sentence is already correct, write *C*.

EXAMPLE   1. Cassie sat between Melissa and I at the concert.
          1. *I—me*

1. ~~Who~~ did you meet at the skating rink last night?
2. You and ~~them~~ are the only ones who are going on the hike.
3. My pen pal in Vietnam will soon receive another letter from me.
4. Just between you and ~~I~~, the other book was much easier to understand.
5. One of the actors in that play was ~~her~~.
6. The pencils, paints, and colored paper belong to Kimiko and ~~he~~.
7. Matthew has invited you and ~~I~~ to his party next weekend.
8. Either ~~her~~ or I will make a poster for Black History Month.
9. Who is the fastest runner on the baseball team?
10. They and ~~us~~ went swimming in Lake Travis.

Reference Note
For information on **pronoun forms,** see page 177.

1. Whom
2. they
3. C
4. me
5. she
6. him
7. me
8. she
9. C
10. we

Exercise 16 Choosing Correct Regular and Irregular Modifiers

Choose the <u>correct form of the adjective or adverb</u> in parentheses in each of the following sentences.

EXAMPLE   1. The stars tonight look (*more bright, brighter*) than usual.
          1. *brighter*

1. This puzzle book is (*difficulter, more difficult*) than the other one.
2. Kevin is the (*taller, tallest*) of the four Sutherland brothers.
3. The (*most exciting, excitingest*) day of our trip to Indonesia was still to come.
4. I like drawing, but I like painting (*best, better*).
5. If you blend strawberries, bananas, and yogurt really (*good, well*), you'll have a great drink.
6. Felicia had the (*worst, worse*) case of chickenpox of anyone in the sixth grade.

Reference Note
For information on **using modifiers correctly,** see Chapter 9.

Exercise 15

OBJECTIVE

■ To proofread for correct pronoun forms

Exercise 16

OBJECTIVE

■ To choose the correct forms of adjectives or adverbs to fit sentences

COMMON ERRORS

Exercise 17

OBJECTIVE

■ To correct errors in the use of modifiers

Exercise 17 Correcting Errors in the Use of Modifiers

POSSIBLE ANSWERS

1. Ernest runs very well, but William can run even better.

2. Katherine is the most curious of the four Matsuo children.

3. Which flavor of frozen yogurt do you think would be worse, cheddar or carrot?

4. Tell me, did you do better on this week's spelling test than on last week's?

5. Annie brings to her friends homegrown tomatoes that she picks from her garden.

6. The astronaut who had commanded a mission aboard the space shuttle met with children.

7. Gloria became more worried as the storm grew worse.

8. Of the Amazon, Nile, and Mississippi rivers, the Nile is the longest.

9. At the video store we rented that scary movie from which the filmmakers spun off a television series.

10. Have you ever read *Fahrenheit 451*, the novel by Ray Bradbury about book burning?

Reference Note

For information on **using modifiers correctly,** see Chapter 9.

7. My brothers and I were taught how to wash, iron, and mend clothes, and we are (*gladder, glad*) that we were.

8. Rachel can't decide which of the two wallpaper patterns would look (*prettier, prettiest*) in her room.

9. Our schoolyard has been (*cleanest, cleaner*) since the Ecology Club asked people not to litter.

10. I am going to practice American Sign Language until I sign (*good, well*) enough to communicate easily.

Exercise 17 Correcting Errors in the Use of Modifiers

Rewrite each of the following sentences, correcting any errors in the use or placement of modifiers.

EXAMPLE 1. Do you like Western boots or hiking boots most?
 1. *most—more*

1. Ernest runs very good, but William can run even better.

2. Katherine is the more curious of the four Matsuo children.

3. Which flavor of frozen yogurt do you think would be worser, cheddar or carrot?

4. Tell me, did you do gooder on this week's spelling test than on last week's?

5. Annie brings homegrown tomatoes to her friends that she picks from her garden.

6. The astronaut met with children who had commanded a mission aboard the space shuttle.

7. Gloria became more worriedly as the storm grew worse.

8. Of the Amazon, Nile, and Mississippi rivers, the Nile is the longer.

9. We rented that scary movie at the video store from which the filmmakers spun off a television series.

10. Have you ever read *Fahrenheit 451*, the novel about book burning by Ray Bradbury?

11. After carefully rehearsing several times, Toni felt confidently about giving her speech.

12. Vincente made a cover for his textbook with his initials on it.

13. Janelle found a recipe for broiling catfish in a cookbook.

14. If you look close at the painting, you can see how tiny the brush strokes are.
15. We looked through the old photo album in the kitchen that we had just found in the attic.
16. It was a large crop, and it grew good, too.
17. Icarus foolish flew nearer to the sun than he should have.
18. In different parts of the world, we have read about unusual customs.
19. Aunt Dee and Uncle Mike enjoyed the CD of the symphony in their living room.
20. We found the sheet music for songs your mother used to sing in the piano bench.

Exercise 18 Correcting Double Comparisons and Double Negatives

Revise each of the following sentences to∧correct the ~~double comparison or double negative.~~ Answers may vary.

EXAMPLE
1. Grandma thought learning to swim would be more harder than it was.

1. *Grandma thought learning to swim would be harder than it was.*

1. My sister gave me her soccer ball because she never plays soccer∧~~no more~~.
2. You can get a ~~more~~ clearer idea of what the trail is like by looking at this map.
3. We∧~~couldn't~~ hardly believe our eyes when we saw what was under the rock!
4. You shouldn't stand∧~~nowhere~~ around a tall tree during a thunderstorm.
5. Keisha's uncle Anthony just adopted the ~~most~~ strangest pet I've ever seen.
6. My little sister∧~~can't~~ scarcely reach the doorknob without standing on tiptoe.
7. I'm not going to put off practicing my bongo drums ∧~~no more~~.
8. That was the ~~most~~ worst movie we've ever seen.

Reference Note

For information on **double comparisons** and **double negatives,** see pages 206 and 209.

1. anymore
3. could
4. anywhere
6. can
7. anymore

POSSIBLE ANSWERS CONTINUED

11. After carefully rehearsing several times, Toni felt confident about giving her speech.
12. Vincente made a cover with his initials on it for his textbook.
13. In a cookbook, Janelle found a recipe for broiling catfish.
14. If you look closely at the painting, you can see how tiny the brush strokes are.
15. In the kitchen, we looked through the old photo album that we had just found in the attic.
16. It was a large crop, and it grew well, too.
17. Icarus foolishly flew nearer to the sun than he should have.
18. We have read about unusual customs in different parts of the world.
19. In their living room, Aunt Dee and Uncle Mike enjoyed the CD of the symphony.
20. In the piano bench, we found the sheet music for songs your mother used to sing.

Exercise 18

OBJECTIVE

■ To correct double comparisons and double negatives

COMMON ERRORS

Exercise 19

OBJECTIVE

- To identify correct usage

Exercise 20

OBJECTIVE

- To correct errors in usage

COMMON ERRORS

9. either

9. Didn't ~~neither~~ of the books have the information you
      ^needed?

10. I've read that potbellied pigs learn ~~more~~ faster than
      dogs do.

Reference Note

For information on
common usage errors,
see Chapter 10.

Exercise 19 **Identifying Correct Usage**

For each of the following sentences, choose the <u>word or word</u>
<u>group in parentheses</u> that is correct according to the rules of
formal, standard English.

EXAMPLE   **1.** My aunt Claire was working in Athens, Greece,
                (*then, than*).

            1. then

1. Everyone from the volleyball team is here (*accept, <u>except</u>*)
      Roseanne.
2. Steve said he thought the new batting lineup looked
      (*alright, <u>all right</u>*).
3. The two friends felt (*<u>bad</u>, badly*) after arguing.
4. The children helped (*theirselves, <u>themselves</u>*) to the curry.
5. Do you know (*<u>whose</u>, who's*) sunglasses these are?
6. The boys will (*<u>try to</u>, try and*) finish painting today.
7. Be sure to (*bring, <u>take</u>*) your lunch when you go to the park.
8. The ten students in the art class divided all of the con-
      struction paper and markers (*between, <u>among</u>*) themselves.
9. (*<u>Who's</u>, Whose*) going to show them how to dance?
10. Heat lightning occurs too far from people for them to hear
      (*<u>its</u>, it's*) accompanying thunder.

Reference Note

For information on
common usage errors,
see Chapter 10.

Exercise 20 **Correcting Errors in Usage**

Each of the following sentences contains an error in the use of
formal, standard English. Identify each ~~error~~, and then write
                                                    ^
the correct usage.

EXAMPLE   **1.** Them fish are called sea horses.

            1. Them—Those

1. Where are sea horses found ~~at~~?
2. Sea horses are found in tropical and temperate waters—
      not ~~anywheres~~ that is very cold.   2. anywhere
         ^

3. Baby sea horses often use ~~they're~~ curved tails to hold on to each other.   **3.** their

4. That ~~there~~ sea horse used its tail to grasp some seaweed.

5. Don't you think that ~~it's~~ head looks amazingly like a tiny horse's head?   **5.** its

6. The little fin on a sea horse's back moves so fast that you ~~can't~~ hardly see it.   **6.** can

7. Several students asked the teacher ~~how come~~ the eyes of a sea horse work independently of each other.   **7.** why

8. My stepsisters and I ~~use~~ to look for sea horses when we lived near the coast in California.   **8.** used   **9.** take

9. The teacher reminded us to ~~bring~~ home a parental approval form for the field trip to the city aquarium.

10. When ~~your~~ at the aquarium, remember to stop by the sea horse exhibit.   **10.** you're

Exercise 21 **Proofreading Sentences for Correct Usage**

Each of the following sentences contains an error in English usage. Identify each ~~error~~. Then, write the correct usage.

EXAMPLE   **1.** Do you all ready know about the Pantanal?

   1. all ready—already

1. The Pantanal is the largest wetland ~~anywheres~~ on earth.
2. To get an idea of ~~it's~~ size, imagine an area about the size of Arkansas.
3. Most of the Pantanal is located ~~inside of~~ Brazil.
4. The area contains ~~a~~ enormous wealth of wildlife.
5. Our science teacher is ~~learning~~ us about the jaguar, the giant anteater, and other animals that live there.
6. The Pantanal may be more important for wading birds such as storks ~~then~~ any other place in South America.
7. In addition, ~~alot~~ of other birds, such as toucans and macaws, live there.
8. The Pantanal has swamps that sometimes have absorbed heavy rains that otherwise might ~~of~~ flooded nearby areas.
9. However, the Pantanal ~~ain't~~ all swamps; it also contains forests.
10. Although the Pantanal is a long ~~ways~~ from where I live, I hope to have a chance to explore it someday.

Reference Note

For information on **common usage errors,** see Chapter 10.

1. anywhere
2. its
3. inside
4. an
5. teaching
6. than
7. a lot
8. have
9. isn't
10. way

Exercise 21

OBJECTIVE

■ To proofread sentences for correct usage

COMMON ERRORS

TEACHING TIP

Using the Grammar and Usage Tests. A Correcting Common Errors Test Answer Sheet that students may use for these **Grammar and Usage Tests** is provided in the ancillary *Progress Assessment for the Holt Handbook.*

Students may benefit from reading "Test Smarts" (pages 434–439 of their textbook) before they take the **Grammar and Usage Tests.**

Grammar and Usage Test: Section 1

DIRECTIONS   In each of the following sentences, a word group is underlined. Using the rules of formal, standard English, choose the answer that most clearly expresses the meaning of the sentence. If there is no error, choose A. Indicate your response by shading in the appropriate oval on your answer sheet.

EXAMPLE   **1.** The fish smelled badly, so we didn't buy any.

  (**A**) smelled badly
  (**B**) smells badly
  (**C**) smelled bad
  (**D**) smelling bad

ANSWER   **1.**   A   B C   D

1. Roz and I catched fireflies in a jar.
  (**A**) I catched
  (**B**) me catched
  (**C**) I caught
  (**D**) me caught

2. Fun hiking in the wilderness preserve.
  (**A**) Fun hiking in the wilderness preserve.
  (**B**) While having fun hiking in the wilderness preserve.
  (**C**) Hiking in the wilderness preserve was fun.
  (**D**) Have had fun hiking in the wilderness preserve.

3. The election resulted in a runoff between he and I.
  (**A**) he and I
  (**B**) him and me
  (**C**) him and I
  (**D**) he and me

4. In bowling, a strike is when a bowler knocks down all ten pins on the first throw in a frame.
  (**A**) is when
  (**B**) occurs when
  (**C**) is where
  (**D**) is because

5. Have you heard of Lawrence and Lorne <u>Blair, two brothers who traveled in Indonesia for ten years?</u>
    (A) Blair, two brothers who traveled in Indonesia for ten years?
    (B) Blair? Two brothers who traveled in Indonesia for ten years.
    (C) Blair, two brothers whom traveled in Indonesia for ten years?
    (D) Blair and two brothers who traveled in Indonesia for ten years?

6. <u>Is this here</u> drill bit the right size?
    (A) Is this here
    (B) Is that there
    (C) Is this here kind of
    (D) Is this

7. <u>Here your car keys.</u>
    (A) Here your car keys.
    (B) Here are your car keys.
    (C) Here's you're car keys.
    (D) Here is your car keys.

8. <u>The dog barked the baby awoke.</u>
    (A) The dog barked the baby awoke.
    (B) The dog barked, the baby awoke.
    (C) The dog barked, and the baby awoke.
    (D) The dog barking and the baby awoke.

9. I <u>shouldn't of</u> waited to start my essay.
    (A) shouldn't of
    (B) shouldn't have
    (C) ought not to of
    (D) oughtn't not to have

10. Mrs. Levine asked <u>how come Darnell and he aren't</u> ready to leave yet.
    (A) how come Darnell and he aren't
    (B) how come Darnell and him aren't
    (C) why Darnell and he isn't
    (D) why Darnell and he aren't

Grammar and Usage Test: Section 2

DIRECTIONS Read the paragraph below. For each of the numbered blanks, select the word or word group that best completes the sentence. Indicate your response by shading in the appropriate oval on your answer sheet.

EXAMPLE Two species of elephant today: the African elephant and the Asian elephant.

    1. (A) does exist
       (B) exists
       (C) have been existing
       (D) exist

ANSWER   **1.**   Ⓐ   Ⓑ   Ⓒ   **Ⓓ**

> Each of these species has own unique features; for example, the African elephant has **(2)** ears and tusks than the Asian elephant does. Although different in some ways, both species of elephant **(3)** strong, intelligent, and social. Both have poor sight and are colorblind but can smell and hear quite **(4)** . Elephants can detect the scent of **(5)** human who is over a mile away. **(6)** hearing is so good that they can communicate over distances of more than two miles, using sounds **(7)** any that humans can hear. Unfortunately, human population growth, farming, industry, and illegal hunting **(8)** a decline in the elephant population. For instance, poachers have killed thousands of African elephants for their ivory tusks; in fact, from 1979 to the early 1990s, the number of elephants in Africa **(9)** from 1,300,000 to fewer than 600,000. **(10)** protect elephants, the trade of ivory was outlawed worldwide in 1989.

1. (A) it
    (B) its'
    (C) it's
    (Ⓓ) its

2. (Ⓐ) larger
    (B) more larger
    (C) the more larger
    (D) the most largest

3. (A) they are
    (Ⓑ) are
    (C) are being
    (D) is

4. (Ⓐ) well
    (B) good
    (C) better
    (D) best

5. **(A)** a
   (B) an
   (C) the
   (D) this

6. **(A)** They're
   (B) There
   (C) Their
   (D) They

7. **(A)** more lower than
   (B) lower than
   (C) more low then
   (D) lower then

8. **(A)** will have caused
   (B) causes
   (C) are causing
   (D) is cause

9. **(A)** shrinks
   (B) shrank
   (C) shrinked
   (D) is shrinking

10. **(A)** 2
    (B) Too
    (C) Two
    (D) To

COMMON ERRORS

Exercise 22 Correcting Errors in Capitalization

Each of the following word groups contains at least one error in capitalization. Correct the errors either by changing capital letters to lowercase letters or by changing lowercase letters to capital letters.

EXAMPLE   1. abilene, texas
            1. *Abilene, Texas*

1. the smoky mountains
2. rutherford B. hayes
3. *Alice In Wonderland*
4. university of kansas
5. labor day
6. near lake Placid
7. it's already tuesday!
8. english or Art II
9. washington monument
10. marta Hinojosa, m.d.
11. neptune and other planets
12. second day of hanukkah
13. my Uncle Jack
14. an airplane called *spirit of st. louis*
15. a river running South
16. Bryce canyon national park
17. 912 valentine st.
18. president Cleveland
19. "i'm home!"
20. newbery medal

Exercise 23 Correcting Errors in Capitalization

Correct the capitalization errors in the following sentences either by changing capital letters to lowercase letters or by changing lowercase letters to capital letters.

EXAMPLE   1. i went to see a play last saturday.
            1. *I went to see a play last Saturday.*

1. Our drama teacher, ms. soto, took us to see it.
2. the new play was first performed by the south Texas performance company.

3. this theater group's founder and director is the translator, playwright, and theater scholar joe rosenberg.

4. He has established an exchange program for theater students from the united states, mexico, and south america.

5. In addition, mr. rosenberg has written a full-length play titled *saturday stranger,* which was published in germany.

6. Mr. Rosenberg has also edited a Book called *¡aplauso! hispanic Children's theater.*

7. the book includes plays by héctor santiago, roy conboy, and lisa loomer, among others.

8. the plays are printed in both english and spanish.

9. these plays draw on hispanic literary traditions native to such places as mexico, puerto rico, and cuba.

10. Next month the southwest middle school drama club plans to perform one of the plays from this book.

Exercise 24 Using Periods, Question Marks, and Exclamation Points Correctly

For each of the following sentences, write each letter or word that should be followed by a period, question mark, or exclamation point, and add the proper punctuation.

EXAMPLE   1. Senator Jackson, can you meet with our class at 8:15 A M

    1. *A.M.?*

1. Please follow me.
2. Will you please help me carry my books?
3. Where in the downtown library is the new display of Peruvian pottery?
4. Watch out for that car!   4. [*or* car.]
5. Dr. Williamson taught me to fly a model helicopter.
6. Anthony asked Rose whether her favorite cartoonist was Charles M. Schulz.
7. One fossil recently discovered in these mountains dates back to three million B.C.
8. What a surprise that was!
9. Have you ever brought your skateboard to school?
10. The letter addressed to 4613 Sleepy Hollow Blvd, Kingston, NY 12401, must be for Mrs. C. R. Smith.

Reference Note

For information on **using end marks,** see page 263.

HELP

Some sentences in Exercise 24 need more than one punctuation mark.

Exercise 24

OBJECTIVE

■ To use periods, question marks, and exclamation points correctly

Exercise 25

OBJECTIVE

■ To proofread sentences for correct use of commas

Reference Note

For information on **using commas,** see page 268.

Exercise 25 Proofreading Sentences for the Correct Use of Commas

Each of the following sentences is missing at least one comma. Write the word or numeral that should be followed by a comma, and add the comma. Optional commas are underlined.

EXAMPLE   1. Oh I hope we win the track meet when we go to Salina Kansas next week.
   1. *Oh, Salina, Kansas,*

1. Sheila ran laps on Monday. Tuesday. and Wednesday.
2. On February 20. 1999. my family had a reunion in San Juan. Puerto Rico.
3. Yes. that is the dog they adopted from the animal shelter.
4. Because my father is going to teach me to play the guitar soon. he is showing me how to tune one now.
5. No. I have never read *The Hobbit*.
6. Scissors. pins. tacks. and other sharp items should be kept out of the reach of young children.
7. Athena. the Greek goddess of crafts. wisdom. and war. is often shown with an owl on her shoulder.
8. Douglas never leaves shopping carts in parking spaces set aside for people who have disabilities. and neither should anyone else.
9. My aunt and I bought nails. lumber. and paint for the birdhouses we plan to build.
10. Professor Chang. will you explain the differences between these two kinds of cells?

Reference Note

For information on **using semicolons and colons,** see pages 279 and 281.

Exercise 26 Using Semicolons and Colons Correctly

The following sentences lack necessary colons and semicolons. Write the words or numerals that come before and after the needed punctuation, and insert the proper punctuation.

EXAMPLE   1. My grandmother is coming to visit we will meet her at the airport.
   1. *visit; we*

1. We picked subjects for our reports. I chose sea turtles.
2. Our school day used to start at 8:15. now it starts at 8:00.

Exercise 26

OBJECTIVE

■ To use semicolons and colons correctly

3. The following items will be needed for the new playground: swings, slides, and picnic tables.
4. The rain just ended; maybe we will get a chance to see a double rainbow.
5. We can save water in these ways: turning off the faucet while brushing our teeth, pouring only as much as we plan to drink, and taking showers instead of baths.
6. At the farmers' market, shoppers were discussing the recent election; they were discussing the weather, too.
7. "Dear Sir or Madam:" is one proper way to begin a business letter, but not the only way.
8. Plains Indians include the following peoples: Comanche, Osage, Pawnee, Crow, and Blackfeet.
9. At 6:30 A.M. my alarm went off; I couldn't believe it was time to get up.
10. My wish list is as follows: a mountain bike, better grades, and a kitten.

Exercise 27 **Punctuating and Capitalizing Quotations**

Revise the following numbered items, using quotation marks, other marks of punctuation, and capital letters where needed. If a sentence is already correct, write *C*.

EXAMPLE   **1.** I admire Marian Wright Edelman said Paul she has worked hard for children's rights.

    1. "I admire Marian Wright Edelman," said Paul. "She has worked hard for children's rights."

1. "In 1973, Edelman founded the Children's Defense Fund, a nonprofit organization that has helped many people," said Mr. Knepp.
2. Paul commented that just the other day he had read an article titled "Edelman: The Children's Defender."
3. Justin said, "I'd like to work to protect children's rights, too, one day."
4. "Edelman was born in 1939," Paul told us. "She grew up in Bennettsville, South Carolina."
5. Mr. Knepp said that Marian Wright Edelman is one of our country's greatest civic leaders.   **5.** C

┌HELP─

Some sentences in Exercise 27 may be correctly revised in more than one way. You only need to give one revision for each sentence.

Reference Note

For information on **using quotation marks,** see page 292. For information on **using capital letters,** see Chapter 11.

Exercise 27

OBJECTIVE

■ To punctuate and capitalize quotations correctly

COMMON ERRORS

6. "Please tell me more about Edelman's career as a lawyer," Ashley said.
7. "She graduated from Yale Law School in 1963," he said. "And soon became the first African American woman licensed to practice law in Mississippi."
8. Mr. Knepp added, "Edelman has handled many civil rights cases and has always made community service a priority."
9. "did Edelman say that she had been taught as a child to make service a central part of her life?" Justin asked.
10. "Yes," Ashley answered. "I remember reading that in her autobiography, *The Measure of Our Success: A Letter to My Children and Yours*." 10. [*or* "Yes," Ashley answered. " I . . .]

Reference Note

For information on **punctuating dialogue,** see page 296.

Exercise 28 Punctuating Dialogue

Revise the following dialogue, adding quotation marks and other marks of punctuation and replacing lowercase letters with capital letters where necessary. Remember to begin a new paragraph each time the speaker changes.

EXAMPLE   **[1]** The legend of Greyfriars Bobby is so moving, Jennifer exclaimed, that I'll never forget it!

    1.   *"The legend of Greyfriars Bobby is so moving," Jennifer exclaimed, "that I'll never forget it!"*

[1] Bobby was a special dog, Jennifer said, and extremely loyal to his master. [2] Tony asked, "can you believe that Bobby actually lived by his master's grave for fourteen years?" [3] Jennifer said, My cousin went to Edinburgh, Scotland, and saw Bobby's grave. [4] It is in Greyfriars churchyard, near his master's grave. [5] When did Bobby die? Tony asked. [6] He died in 1872, Jennifer replied. [7] "the people in the town fed Bobby and cared for him until his death."

[8] "Bobby slept during the day, Tony recalled because, before his master died, they had worked together at night."

[9] Jennifer said, "yes, his master, old Jock, guarded cattle that were sold at the market." [10] Tony said, In Edinburgh there is a statue of Greyfriars Bobby on top of a drinking fountain for dogs.

COMMON ERRORS

Exercise 28

OBJECTIVE

■ To punctuate dialogue correctly

Exercise 28 Punctuating Dialogue

ANSWERS

1. "Bobby was a special dog," Jennifer said, "and extremely loyal to his master."

2. ¶Tony asked, "Can you believe that Bobby actually lived by his master's grave for fourteen years?"

3. ¶Jennifer said, "My cousin went to Edinburgh, Scotland, and saw Bobby's grave. **4.** It is in Greyfriars churchyard, near his master's grave."

5. ¶"When did Bobby die?" Tony asked.

6. ¶"He died in 1872," Jennifer replied. **7.** "The people in the town fed Bobby and cared for him until his death."

8. ¶"Bobby slept during the day," Tony recalled, "because, before his master died, they had worked together at night."

9. ¶Jennifer said, "Yes, his master, old Jock, guarded cattle that were sold at the market."

10. ¶Tony said, "In Edinburgh there is a statue of Greyfriars Bobby on top of a drinking fountain for dogs."

Exercise 29 Using Apostrophes Correctly

Rewrite the following word groups, inserting an apostrophe wherever one is needed.

EXAMPLE
    1. the womens class
      1. the women's class

1. if they've gone
2. no one's fault
3. that statue's condition
4. so let's try
5. since you're going home
6. that giant's castle
7. theirs weren't faded
8. the Rockies' highest peak
9. when there isn't time
10. these books' authors
11. Arkansas' governor
12. if everybody's there
13. made all A's in school
14. one pueblo's history
15. the five camels' saddles
16. born in '84
17. and there's the dog
18. the sheep's wool
19. when you'll find out
20. two o's in the word *igloo*
21. aren't able to
22. the one who's late
23. when I'm tired
24. around 10 o'clock
25. those two books' pages

Exercise 30 Correcting Spelling Errors

Most of the following words are misspelled. If a word is not spelled correctly, write the correct spelling. If a word is already spelled correctly, write *C*.

EXAMPLE
    1. mispeak
      1. misspeak

1. percieve
2. disolve
3. gladest
4. charging
5. comedies
6. sillyness
7. taxs
8. tryed
9. potatos
10. traceing
11. classes
12. sleigh
13. matchs
14. videoes
15. funnyer
16. toyes
17. schoolling
18. wieght
19. loosness
20. Gomezs
21. managable
22. unatural
23. ladys
24. runing
25. finaly

Reference Note
For information on **using apostrophes,** see page 300.

Reference Note
For information on **spelling rules,** see page 319.

Exercise 29

OBJECTIVE

■ To use apostrophes correctly

Exercise 30

OBJECTIVE

■ To correct errors in spelling

Exercise 30 Correcting Spelling Errors

ANSWERS

1. perceive
2. dissolve
3. gladdest
4. C
5. C
6. silliness
7. taxes
8. tried
9. potatoes
10. tracing
11. C
12. C
13. matches
14. videos
15. funnier
16. toys
17. schooling
18. weight
19. looseness
20. Gomezes
21. manageable
22. unnatural
23. ladies
24. running
25. finally

COMMON ERRORS

Exercise 31

OBJECTIVE

- To choose correctly between words often confused

Reference Note

For information on **words often confused,** see page 329.

Exercise 31 **Choosing Between Words Often Confused**

For each of the following sentences, choose the word or word group in parentheses that will make the sentence correct.

EXAMPLE   1. Matthew suggested that I (*altar, alter*) the first paragraph of my story.

        1. *alter*

1. Have you (*all ready, already*) finished your latest painting?
2. (*Your, You're*) pets need good food, clean water, warm shelter, and loving attention.
3. Be careful not to (*lose, loose*) any of those puzzle pieces, or we'll have to buy a new puzzle.
4. Chuckwallas are harmless lizards that may grow to be two feet long and live in rocky (*desserts, deserts*) in the United States and Mexico.
5. Manuel dreamed of finding a sunken ship and (*it's, its*) treasure chest.
6. The school (*threw, through*) away tons of paper and cardboard before the recycling program was started.
7. (*Whose, Who's*) planning to bring food and drinks to the fiesta tomorrow?
8. We drove (*passed, past*) the park, across the bridge, and around the lake to the dock.
9. Marcie's enthusiasm for playing in the marching band was (*plain, plane*) to see.
10. The guide (*lead, led*) the scouts through the museum.
11. Former President Jimmy Carter has been greatly involved in efforts to bring (*piece, peace*) to various countries all over the world.
12. In less than one (*weak, week*), Sandra's mother will begin her new job as editor-in-chief of the newspaper's new Washington bureau.
13. (*There, Their*) are many kinds of trees in our neighborhood, and they provide plenty of shade.
14. The gravel in the driveway is (*coarse, course*), but it still feels good on my bare feet.
15. The flagpole itself was (*stationary, stationery*), but the flag flapped in the breeze.

16. "The lamp may (*brake*, *break*) if you try to carry it on its side and with one hand," Dad cautioned.
17. What is the (*capital*, *capitol*) of Puerto Rico?
18. Mr. Edgars is a good man whose (*principles*, *principals*) include honesty and fairness.
19. When we sit outside on the porch, we can't (*hear*, *here*) the phone ring.
20. We read (*threw*, *through*) Gary Soto's book of poetry and picked out some poems to memorize.

Exercise 32 **Proofreading Sentences for Errors in Spelling and Words Often Confused**

For each of the following sentences, ~~identify~~ and ^correct any error in spelling or usage. If a sentence is already correct, write *C*.

EXAMPLE   **1.** The Iroquois people's name for themselfs means "we longhouse builders."

        1. *themselfs—themselves*

1. In our American history ^~~coarse~~, we learned that the Iroquois constructed large dwellings called longhouses.
2. Years ago, nearly all Iroquois lived in forests and built ^~~they're~~ longhouses out of logs and strips of bark.
3. Several individual ^~~familys~~ lived in each of these longhouses.
4. When a couple ^~~marryed~~, the husband would move into the longhouse of his wife's extended family, called a clan.
5. Each family had ^~~it's~~ own separate area with a sleeping platform that was raised about a foot above the ground.
6. They kept the longhouse neat by storing many of their belongings on ^~~shelfs~~ above their sleeping platforms.
7. Fires were made in hearths in a central corridor, and smoke rose ^~~threw~~ holes cut in the longhouse roof.
8. When it rained or snowed, ^~~slideing~~ panels were used to close the holes.
9. The ^~~bigest~~ longhouses measured more than two hundred feet in length.
10. Such large longhouses could shelter ten or more individual families at a time.

Reference Note

For information on **spelling rules,** see page 319. For information on **words often confused,** see page 329.

1. course
2. their
3. families
4. married
5. its
6. shelves
7. through
8. sliding
9. biggest
10. C

Exercise 32

OBJECTIVE

■ To proofread sentences for errors in spelling and in words often confused

COMMON ERRORS

Exercise 33

OBJECTIVE

■ To proofread a paragraph for errors in mechanics

Exercise 34

OBJECTIVE

■ To proofread a business letter for correct grammar, usage, and mechanics

┌HELP──
Many of the sentences in Exercise 33 contain more than one error.

Exercise 33 Proofreading a Paragraph for Errors in Mechanics

For the sentences in the following paragraph, correct each error in mechanics. If a sentence is already correct, write *C*. Optional commas are underlined.

EXAMPLES 1. Have you ever seen the movie *the Wizard of Oz*?
          1. *The Wizard of Oz*

          2. You may not know that its based on a book.
          2. *it's*

[1] The book was written by l. frank Baum. [2] He was born on May 15, 1856, in the state of New York. [3] When he was a teenager, he was interested in the theater; his father, a wealthy oilman, gave him several theaters to manage. [4] In 1881, he wrote *The maid of Arran*, a successful play. [5] For many years, he worked at several jobs, including storekeeper, newspaper reporter, and traveling salesman. [6] In 1900, he published a children's book called *The Wonderful Wizard of Oz*, which was a bestseller for two years in a row. [7] Baum adapted the book into a successful play, and he even made several silent movies about Oz. [8] Baum died in Hollywood, California, in 1919; after twenty years, the famous film starring Judy Garland as Dorothy was made in the same city. [9] During the making of the film, the actor who played the wizard discovered that L. Frank Baum's name was sewn into the lineing of the wizard's coat. [10] According to Baum's wife, it really was Baum's old coat; the movie studio's wardrobe department had bought it at a secondhand clothing shop.

7. C

9. lining

┌HELP──
Most items in Exercise 34 contain more than one error.

Exercise 34 Proofreading a Business Letter for Correct Grammar, Usage, and Mechanics

Correct the errors in grammar, usage, and mechanics in the numbered items in the following letter.

EXAMPLE [1] 254 Thirty second street
         1. *254 Thirty-second Street*

254 Thirty-second Street
Syracuse, NY 13210
[1] November 5 2003

Ms. Susan Loroupe
[2] *Syracuse daily times*
598 Seventh Avenue
Syracuse, NY 13208

[3] Dear Ms Loroupe

[4] Thank you for taking time during you're busy workday to show the Van Buren Middle School Journalism Club around the Newspaper's offices.

[5] Us club members are glad to have had the chance to see how newspaper articles are wrote and printed. [6] Especially enjoyed seeing the presses—even more then talking with the design artists and editors! [7] We were surprised that the presses were so loud and we were impressed by how quick and efficient everyone worked. [8] Please thank the artists, to, for showing us how they use computer's to arrange the art and photos on the pages.

Sincerely,

Carlos Lopez

Carlos Lopez
[9] journalism club Secretary
[10] Van Buren middle school

Exercise 34 Proofreading a Business Letter for Correct Grammar, Usage, and Mechanics

ANSWERS
Underscores in text below show corrections.

1. November 5, 2003
2. *Syracuse Daily Times*
3. Dear Ms. Loroupe:
4. Thank you for taking time during your busy workday to show the Van Buren Middle School Journalism Club around the newspaper's offices.
5. We club members are glad to have had the chance to see how newspaper articles are written and printed.
6. The club especially enjoyed seeing the presses—even more than talking with the design artists and editors! [Answers may vary.]
7. We were surprised that the presses were so loud, and we were impressed by how quickly and efficiently everyone worked.
8. Please thank the artists, too, for showing us how they use computers to arrange the art and photos on the pages.
9. Journalism Club Secretary
10. Van Buren Middle School

COMMON ERRORS

Mechanics Test: Section 1

DIRECTIONS   Each numbered item below contains an underlined word
or word group. Choose the answer that shows the correct capitalization,
punctuation, and spelling of the underlined part. If there is no error,
choose answer D (Correct as is). Indicate your response by shading in
the appropriate oval on your answer sheet.

EXAMPLE   **[1]** Quincy, MA 02158

(A) Quincy, Mass. 02158

(B) Quincy MA, 02158

(C) Quincy, M.A. 02158

(D) Correct as is

ANSWER   1.   (A)   (B)   (C)   (D)

---

147 Hickory Lane
Quincy, MA 02158
[1] May 11 2003

The Hobby Shop
[2] 2013 forty-First Street
Los Angeles, CA 90924

[3] Dear Mr. Shaw

While I was visiting **[4]** my aunt Laura, who's
house is near your store, she bought a model
airplane from you. **[5]** Two of my freinds have
[6] already tryed to help me get the plane to
fly, but we haven't been able to. **[7]** Putting
the plane together was not difficult; the
problem is that the engine will not start.
Also, I found no stickers in the box when I
opened **[8]** it and the box says that there
should be stickers for the plane's wings. I
have enclosed the engine and my **[9]** aunt's
reciept. I hope that **[10]** youre able to send
me stickers and a new engine soon.

Sincerely,

Timothy Martin

Timothy Martin

---

1. (A) May, 11 2003
   (B) May 11, 2003 ⊛
   (C) May, 11, 2003
   (D) Correct as is

2. (A) 2013 Forty First Street
   (B) 2013 Forty-first street
   (C) 2013 Forty-first Street ⊛
   (D) Correct as is

3. (A) Dear Mr. Shaw,
   (B) Dear Mr. Shaw: ⊛
   (C) Dear mr. shaw:
   (D) Correct as is

4. (A) my aunt Laura, whose ⊛
   (B) my Aunt Laura, whose
   (C) my Aunt Laura, who's
   (D) Correct as is

5. (A) Two of my friends ⊛
   (B) To of my freinds
   (C) Too of my friends
   (D) Correct as is

6. (A) all ready tryed
   (B) already tried ⊛
   (C) all ready tried
   (D) Correct as is

7. (A) Puting the plane
   (B) Puting the plain
   (C) Putting the plain
   (D) Correct as is ⊛

8. (A) it and the box says that their
   (B) it, and the box says that their
   (C) it, and the box says that there ⊛
   (D) Correct as is

9. (A) aunt's receipt ⊛
   (B) Aunt's receipt
   (C) aunts' reciept
   (D) Correct as is

10. (A) your
    (B) you're ⊛
    (C) your'
    (D) Correct as is

Mechanics Test: Section 2

DIRECTIONS   Each of the following sentences contains an underlined word or word group. Choose the answer that shows the correct capitalization, punctuation, and spelling of the underlined part. If there is no error, choose answer D (Correct as is). Indicate your response by shading in the appropriate oval on your answer sheet.

EXAMPLE   1.   Today the school librarian Mr. Woods will show us a video.

(A) librarian, Mr. Woods
(B) librarian, Mr. Woods,
(C) librarian Mr. Woods,
(D) Correct as is

ANSWER   1.   A B C D

1. I wonder what the capital of Spain is?
   (A) capital of Spain is.
   (B) capitol of Spain is.
   (C) capitol of Spain is?
   (D) Correct as is

2. The mouses' nest may be in the garage.
   (A) mouses
   (B) mices
   (C) mice's
   (D) Correct as is

3. "What did you see at the park?" asked my grandfather.
   (A) see at the park"? asked my grandfather.
   (B) see at the park," asked my grandfather?
   (C) see at the park? asked my grandfather."
   (D) Correct as is

4. Felix, you've been a naughty kitten this passed week!
   (A) passed weak
   (B) past weak
   (C) past week
   (D) Correct as is

5. Aisha exclaimed, "see how much these crystals have grown!"
   (A) exclaimed, "See
   (B) exclaimed! "See
   (C) exclaimed "see
   (D) Correct as is

6. The Olympic team waved at the crowd, the audience cheered.
   (A) crowd; the audeince
   (B) crowd: the audience
   (C) crowd, and the audience
   (D) Correct as is

7. The <u>Kalahari Desert</u> is in southern Africa.
- **(A)** Kalahari Dessert
- **(B)** kalahari desert
- **(C)** Kalahari desert
- **(D)** Correct as is

8. <u>"Its snowing,"</u> observed Mrs. Daniels.
- **(A)** "It's snowwing,"
- **(B)** "It's snowing,"
- **(C)** Its snowing,
- **(D)** Correct as is

9. The Red Cross is asking <u>for: blankets,</u> sheets, and pillows.
- **(A)** for; blankets,
- **(B)** for, blankets,
- **(C)** for blankets,
- **(D)** Correct as is

10. Robert Frost's <u>poem The Road Not Taken</u> is famous.
- **(A)** poem *The Road Not Taken*
- **(B)** poem "The Road Not Taken"
- **(C)** poem "the Road not Taken"
- **(D)** Correct as is

RESOURCES

Correcting Common Errors

Assessment

- *Progress Assessment for the Holt Handbook,* pp. 29–30, 41
- *Test Generator*
  (One-Stop Planner CD-ROM*)*

PART 2 Sentences

16 Writing Effective Sentences

17 Sentence Diagramming

go.
hrw
.com

GO TO: go.hrw.com
KEYWORD: HLLA

Sentences   **383**

CHAPTER

16

Writing Effective Sentences

Sentences will vary; word group identification will not.

1. frag.—Elizabeth was riding a beautiful, black Arabian horse.
2. sent.
3. run-on—Dinner was great; Dad cooked my favorite dish.
4. sent.
5. run-on—When I wake up, I do a few exercises. Then I shower.

Answers may vary.
6. I collect interesting rocks, and my sister collects pressed flowers.
7. Robert read a book that Sara had already read.

Diagnostic Preview

A. Identifying Sentences, Sentence Fragments, and Run-on Sentences

Identify each of the following word groups as a *sentence*, a *sentence fragment*, or a *run-on sentence*. Rewrite fragments to make complete sentences. Rewrite run-ons to make one or more complete sentences. Use correct capitalization and punctuation.

EXAMPLE **1.** We visited Arkansas, my aunt lives there now.
  1. run-on—We visited Arkansas. My aunt lives there now.

1. Riding a beautiful, black Arabian horse.
2. If you don't mind, I'd like to rest a minute.
3. Dinner was great, Dad cooked my favorite dish.
4. Is Tony my first cousin?
5. When I wake up, I do a few exercises, then I shower.

B. Combining Sentences

Combine the two sentences in each of the following items to make a single sentence by adding connecting words, inserting words or phrases, or using compound or complex sentences.

EXAMPLE **1.** We went to the state fair. We had a good time.
  1. We had a good time when we went to the state fair.

6. I collect interesting rocks. My sister collects pressed flowers.
7. Robert read a book. Sara had already read it.

CHAPTER RESOURCES

Internet
■ go.hrw.com (keyword: HLLA)   go. hrw .com

Planning
■ *One-Stop Planner CD-ROM*
■ *On Course: Mapping Instruction*
■ *At Home, A Guide to Standards Mastery*, p. 36

Practice & Review
■ *Language & Sentence Skills Practice*, pp. 349–358; 361–370, 359–360, 371–374
■ *Developmental Language & Sentence Skills*, pp. 133–142

Differentiating Instruction
■ *Lesson Plans for Language Development*

8. When you go, turn out the lights. Please also lock the door.
9. Snails are mollusks. Slugs are also mollusks.
10. The painting shows a waterfall. The waterfall is beautiful.

C. Revising Stringy Sentences and Sentences with Passive Voice

Revise each stringy or awkward sentence so that it is clear and so that each verb is in the active voice.

EXAMPLE   **1.** Dinner was ready, so we all gathered around the table, and then dinner was eaten.

     1. When dinner was ready, we all gathered around the table and ate.

11. I had asked my little sister to help me set the table, so that had been done already.
12. My brother likes potatoes, and the kind that he likes best is mashed potatoes.
13. I made the salad, and I made the side dish of carrots.
14. The main dish was made up of noodles with mushrooms and red sauce, and it was enjoyed by everyone.
15. That we eat together as many nights a week as we can is what is preferred by my parents.

D. Using Transitions

Rewrite the following paragraph, adding transitions that make the meaning clearer and make the paragraph easier to read.

EXAMPLE   Ari had the idea that he was forgetting something. He didn't know what it could be.

     Ari had the feeling that he was forgetting something; however, he didn't know what it could be.

```
    Ari set out to walk to soccer prac-
tice. He knew that he would have to
hurry. He had waited until later than
usual to leave. Ari had gone a few
blocks. He realized that he had forgot-
ten his jersey. He would not be able to
get it and still get to practice on
time. He decided to go on without his
jersey. Ari remembered that he needed
his jersey. The coach had said there
```

8. When you go, please turn out the lights and lock the door.
9. Snails and slugs are mollusks.
10. The painting shows a beautiful waterfall.

Answers may vary.
11. I had asked my little sister to help me set the table, so she had set it.
12. The kind of potatoes my brother likes best is mashed potatoes.
13. I made the salad and the side dish of carrots.
14. Everyone enjoyed the main dish of noodles with mushrooms and red sauce.
15. My parents prefer that we eat together as many nights a week as we can.

Revisions will vary.
   When Ari set out to walk to soccer practice, he knew that he would have to hurry because he had waited until later than usual to leave. When Ari had gone a few blocks, he realized that he had forgotten his jersey. Since he would not be able to get it and still get to practice on time, he decided to go on without his jersey.

Diagnostic Preview **385**

ASSESSING

Entry-Level Assessment
Diagnostic Preview. You may want to use the **Diagnostic Preview** to identify areas in which students need instruction and practice in writing effective sentences. You could use the results of the test to decide which lessons to teach to the entire class and which ones to assign to small groups.

PRETEACHING

Lesson Starter

❝ **Writing is exploration. You write to find out what you're writing.**❞
(E. L. Doctorow, 1931– , American writer and editor)

Motivating. After you write the quotation on the chalkboard, ask students to respond to Doctorow's idea. In what ways do writers find out what they are writing about when they are drafting? [*Often, ideas lead from one to the next and give the writers new ways to explore their material.*]

❝ **You've got to know when to turn around.**❞
(John Roskelley, 1950– , mountain climber)

Discuss with students how this quotation relates to writing sentences. [*The time for a writer to "turn around" may be when he or she needs to revise.*] Explain that writers often write quickly to get an idea down on paper. As a result, the idea may come out as a sentence fragment or as a run-on or stringy sentence.

- *Supporting Instruction in Five Languages*
- *At Home: In Five Languages*
Assessment
- *Diagnostic & Summative Assessments, End-of-Year Test*
- *Progress Assessment for the Holt Handbook*, pp. 31–34, 41

- *Test Generator (One-Stop Planner CD-ROM)* 🎧
Other Language Resources
- *Spelling Lessons & Activities*
- *Vocabulary Development*
- *Daily Language Activities Transparencies*

Writing Clear Sentences

(pp. 386–396)

OBJECTIVES

- To identify and revise sentence fragments

- To identify and revise run-on sentences

- To identify and revise stringy sentences

- To identify and use verbs in the active and passive voice

DIRECT TEACHING

Modeling and Demonstration

Sentence Fragments. Model how to determine whether a group of words is a sentence or a sentence fragment and how to revise a fragment by using the incorrect example *Wanted a hamster.* First, ask students whether the group of words has a subject. [*no*] Then, ask whether the group of words has a verb. [*yes; Wanted*] Point out that we don't know who wanted a hamster, and ask what subject could make the group of words a sentence. [*Answers will vary.*] Finally, ask whether the word group expresses a complete thought, now that a subject has been added. [*yes*] Now, have a volunteer use another example from this chapter to demonstrate how to identify and correct a sentence fragment.

Then, Ari remembered that he needed his jersey because the coach had said there would be team pictures tonight. Finally, Ari stopped at a friend's house and called his sister to ask her to bring his jersey to the field.

```
would be team pictures tonight. Ari
stopped at a friend's house and called
his sister to ask her to bring his jer-
sey to the field.
```

Writing Clear Sentences

Your goal in writing should always be to communicate clearly with your reader. A clear sentence gives your reader just enough information. It does not leave out any important pieces, and it does not run together or string together too many ideas at once. Clear sentences make it easier for your reader to understand what you are saying. In this chapter you will learn about three enemies of clear writing: *sentence fragments, run-on sentences,* and *stringy sentences.*

Sentence Fragments

What kind of sentence could you write about this picture? You might write something like this:

> The high jumper flips backwards over the bar.
>
> *or*
>
> How high the bar is!
>
> *or*
>
> How does she know where to jump?

These groups of words say different things, but they have something in common. Each is a *complete sentence.* A **complete sentence** is a group of words that expresses a complete thought and that has a subject and a verb.

A part of each thought is expressed by the verb: *flips, is, does know.* Another part is expressed by the subject: *high jumper, bar, she.*

A **sentence fragment** is a part of a sentence that is punctuated as if it were a complete sentence. A fragment is confusing because it does not express a complete thought. The following

RESOURCES

Writing Clear Sentences
Practice

- *Language & Sentence Skills Practice,* pp. 349–360, 373–374
- *Developmental Language & Sentence Skills,* pp. 133–136

word groups are the example sentences—with some important words left out. Notice how unclear the word groups are when written as fragments.

Flips backwards over the bar. [The subject is missing. *Who or what* flips?]

How high the bar! [The verb is missing. *What about* how high the bar?]

Where to jump. [This word group does not express a complete thought. *What about* where to jump?]

Use this simple three-part test to help you decide whether a word group is a sentence fragment or a complete sentence.

1. Does the group of words have a *subject*?
2. Does the word group have a *verb*?
3. Does the word group express a *complete thought*?

You know the word group is a complete sentence if you answer "yes" to all three questions above. If you answer "no" to a question, the word group is a sentence fragment.

Oral Practice **Recognizing Fragments**

Read each of the following word groups aloud, and say whether it is a sentence fragment or a sentence. Remember that a complete sentence meets three requirements: It has a subject, it has a verb, and it expresses a complete thought.

EXAMPLE 1. Wanted a hamster.
    1. *sentence fragment*

1. We visited the pet shop in the mall. **1.** S
2. A bright-eyed hamster chewing on pieces of carrot. **2.** F
3. Named him Mustard. **3.** F
4. Has pouches inside each fat cheek. **4.** F
5. The pouches are for carrying food. **5.** S
6. Newspaper in lots of little shreds. **6.** F
7. Making his cage quite comfortable. **7.** F
8. He is plump and has white and tan fur. **8.** S
9. A diet of mostly fruit, vegetables, and grain. **9.** F
10. If you decide to raise hamsters. **10.** F

┌─────────────────────┐
│ TIPS & TRICKS │
└─────────────────────┘

Sometimes a fragment is really a part of a nearby sentence. You can correct the fragment by attaching it to the sentence that comes before or after it.

SENTENCE WITH FRAGMENT
Mark is practicing his hook shot. Because he wants to try out for the basketball team.

SENTENCE
Mark is practicing his hook shot **because he wants to try out for the basketball team.**

When you attach a fragment to a sentence, be sure to check your new sentence for correct punctuation and capitalization.

DIFFERENTIATING INSTRUCTION

Learners Having Difficulty
Students may benefit from copying the three numbered questions on this page onto index cards and then referring to the cards as they complete the **Oral Practice** and **Exercise 1.**

EXTENSION

Relating to Literature
Fragments in Poetry. Poets may use fragments in their writing. They are using "poetic license"—breaking the rules of formal writing to achieve an effect. Encourage students to look through books of poetry for examples of sentence fragments. Have students share their examples with the class. Ask students what effect the poets might have been trying to achieve by using sentence fragments. [*to create rhythm or rhyme; to evoke a mood by focusing on sensory words and phrases; to emphasize key ideas through repetition*]

Exercise 1 Revising
Fragments

ANSWERS

Here are sample revisions.

1. I was watching TV alone.
2. I was watching a movie about aliens invading from space.
3. S
4. I had to light a candle because the batteries in the flashlight were dead.
5. I heard a strange noise in the backyard.
6. After our dog started to bark, I wondered what was outside.
7. I crept slowly to the door and looked out.
8. I saw two small, glowing eyes in the dark.
9. I laughed when I saw it was just the cat from next door.
10. S

DIFFERENTIATING INSTRUCTION

Advanced Learners

To help students see that there are many ways to revise sentence fragments, you may want to let selected pairs of students work on **Exercise 1.** Have each pair produce two revised versions of each fragment, with each student responsible for one of the versions.

| COMPUTER TIP

If you are using a computer, you can use a word-processing program to help eliminate sentence fragments. Using the cut and paste commands, you can easily try attaching a fragment to both the sentence before it and the sentence after it. Doing so will allow you to see which sentence makes more sense. Check your writing for correctness and completeness after making changes.

Exercise 1 **Revising Fragments**

Some of the following word groups are sentence fragments. First, identify the fragments. Then, revise each fragment by (1) adding a subject, (2) adding a verb, or (3) attaching the fragment to a complete sentence. You may also need to change the punctuation and capitalization in your revised sentence. If a word group below is already a complete sentence, write *S* on your paper.

EXAMPLE
1. It a stormy Wednesday night.
   1. *It was a stormy Wednesday night.*

1. Was watching TV alone.
2. A movie about aliens invading from space.
3. Suddenly, the lights went out on the whole block.
4. Because the batteries in the flashlight were dead.
5. A strange noise in the backyard.
6. After our dog started to bark.
7. Crept slowly to the door and looked out.
8. Two small, glowing eyes in the dark.
9. When I saw it was just the cat from next door.
10. Maybe I should stop watching scary movies.

Run-on Sentences

A **run-on sentence** is actually two or more sentences run together with no punctuation between them or with only a comma between them. It is often hard to tell where one idea in a run-on ends and the next one begins.

Using Fragments. Explain to students that sentence fragments appear often in newspapers, advertisements, and TV commercials; on street signs and the Internet; at bus stops; and in subway stations and airports. Ask students to give examples of sentence fragments in these places. [*a street sign that says "Parking 9:00 A.M. to 5:00 P.M. only"; an advertisement that says "Because you care"; a subway sign that says "Tokens*

Like sentence fragments, run-on sentences usually appear in your writing because you are in a hurry to get your thoughts down on paper. There is more than one way to revise a run-on sentence. You can break the run-on into two complete sentences, or you can link the two ideas with a comma and a coordinating conjunction such as *and*, *but*, or *or*.

RUN-ON   In 1962 John Glenn became the first American to orbit Earth, he made his second space flight on the space shuttle *Discovery* in 1998, when he was 77 years old.

CORRECT   In 1962 John Glenn became the first American to orbit Earth. **H**e made his second space flight on the space shuttle *Discovery* in 1998, when he was 77 years old.
[The sentence has been broken into two complete sentences.]

or

In 1962 John Glenn became the first American to orbit Earth, **and** he made his second space flight on the space shuttle *Discovery* in 1998, when he was 77 years old.
[Two complete ideas have been linked by a comma and the word *and*.]

NOTE   A comma alone is not enough to link two complete ideas in a sentence. If you use just a comma between two complete ideas, you create a run-on sentence.

RUN-ON   Sally Ride was the first American woman in space, she was a member of a shuttle crew.

CORRECT   Sally Ride was the first American woman in space. **S**he was a member of a shuttle crew.

Exercise 2   Identifying and Revising Run-on Sentences

Decide which of the following groups of words are run-ons. Revise each run-on by (1) making it into two separate sentences, or (2) using a comma and a coordinating conjunction. You may have to change the punctuation and capitalization, too. If the group of words is already correct, write *C*.

EXAMPLE   1. People in business and in school use the Internet on a daily basis, they can use the Internet at home, too.

1. *People in business and in school use the Internet on a daily basis. They can use the Internet at home, too.*

Reference Note
For more information about using **commas with coordinating conjunctions,** see page 270.

┌HELP┐

You can also use semicolons to correct run-on sentences.

RUN-ON
I am interested in space exploration, in fact, I would like to be an astronaut.

CORRECTED
I am interested in space exploration; in fact, I would like to be an astronaut.

Reference Note
For more information on **using semicolons,** see page 279.

DIRECT TEACHING

Run-on Sentences
Students may overuse one method of revising run-ons, such as dividing them into separate sentences. To help students avoid overusing one strategy, remind them that good writing contains a variety of sentence structures. Some run-ons will be better divided into separate sentences (when the ideas are not closely related), while others will be better joined in one sentence by a comma and a coordinating conjunction or by a semicolon (when the ideas are closely related).

Writing Clear Sentences   **389**

here"] Have students discuss why fragments are used in these cases. [*Fragments are used when there is limited space and when people in a hurry need just basic information.*]

Emphasize that while sentence fragments are acceptable in these contexts, they are not acceptable in formal writing because they may confuse a reader.

EXTENSION

Critical Thinking

Metacognition. After students have completed **Exercise 2,** read aloud each item and ask students how they determined whether or not the sentence was a run-on. Some strategies that students might have used are identifying subjects and verbs, using a mental checklist, or mentally crossing out words. Ask a student to take notes on the strategies mentioned by the class and read the complete list aloud when you complete the review.

Review A Revising
Sentence Fragments and Run-on Sentences

ANSWERS
Here are some sample revisions.

1. C
2. fragment; Some animals see only light and dark shapes.
3. run-on; Squids and octopuses have very advanced eyes. They see almost as well as humans.

Here are possible revisions.

1. and **1.** People constantly search for faster ways to communicate, the Internet is one tool that helps people share information quickly.

2. C **2.** The earliest form of the Internet was designed over thirty years ago, and it was created to be used by the military.

3. ⊙ **3.** The Internet has changed a great deal since then now it can be used by almost anyone who uses a computer.

4. ⊙ **4.** The first e-mail program was invented in 1972, e-mail is a way to send messages from one computer to another.

5. C **5.** Twenty years later, scientists in Switzerland created the World Wide Web, and *Internet* quickly became a household word.

6. , but **6.** The scientists planned to use the Web to share research with scientists in other parts of the world, the new invention soon interested businesses and government organizations.

7. , but **7.** The programs that make the Internet and the World Wide Web work are very complicated they are not hard to use.

8. C **8.** Many schools and libraries have computers that are connected to the Internet and the World Wide Web.

9. C **9.** The World Wide Web began with four newsgroups in 1991, but it soon included millions of sites.

10. ⊙ **10.** Many sites on the World Wide Web focus on school subjects, news, and hobbies, these sites can be useful sources of information.

Review A Revising Sentence Fragments and Run-on Sentences

Decide which of the following word groups are fragments and run-ons. Then, revise each of these word groups to make it clear and complete. Remember to add correct capitalization and punctuation. If a word group is already correct, write *C*.

EXAMPLE **1.** Most humans see very well, they often assume other life forms see as they do.

1. run-on—Most humans see very well, and they often assume other life forms see as they do.

1. Not all animals see the world in the same way humans see the world.
2. See only light and dark shapes.
3. Squids and octopuses have very advanced eyes they see almost as well as humans.

4. The jeweled squid lives deep underwater in the Indian Ocean, it has white, blue, and red lights around its eyes to help it see in the dark water.

5. Several other sea creatures have their own "headlights," these lights are sometimes produced by helpful bacteria, which the fish store in special skin pouches.

6. Some owls can catch mice in total darkness by hearing alone others can find a mouse by the light of one candle placed nearly a quarter of a mile away from the mouse.

7. Grazing animals must have a wide field of vision so that they will know when an enemy is coming.

8. Rabbits and deer eyes on the sides of their heads.

9. Mammals that hunt other animals for food must be able to judge distance well, therefore their eyes are usually located toward the front of their faces.

10. Most apes do not hunt other animals for food, their eyes are in much the same position as human eyes, apes also see the same range of colors humans see.

Stringy Sentences

For variety, you will sometimes want to join sentences and sentence parts with *and*. If you string many ideas together with *and*, though, you create a ***stringy sentence.*** Stringy sentences ramble on and on. They do not give the reader a chance to pause between ideas.

STRINGY   The ostrich is the largest living bird, and it stands nearly eight feet tall, and it weighs over three hundred pounds when it is fully grown, and this speedy bird can run up to forty miles an hour!

Review A   Revising
Sentence Fragments and Run-on Sentences

ANSWERS continued

4. run-on; The jeweled squid lives deep underwater in the Indian Ocean. It has white, blue, and red lights around its eyes to help it see in the dark water.

5. run-on; Several other sea creatures have their own "headlights." These lights are sometimes produced by helpful bacteria, which the fish store in special skin pouches.

6. run-on; Some owls can catch mice in total darkness by hearing alone. Others can find a mouse by the light of one candle placed nearly a quarter of a mile away from the mouse.

7. C

8. fragment; Rabbits and deer have eyes on the sides of their heads.

9. run-on; Mammals that hunt other animals for food must be able to judge distance well. Therefore, their eyes are usually located toward the front of their faces.

10. run-on; Most apes do not hunt other animals for food. Their eyes are in much the same position as human eyes. Apes also see the same range of colors humans see.

BETTER   The ostrich is the largest living bird. It stands nearly eight feet tall, and it weighs over three hundred pounds when it is fully grown. This speedy bird can run up to forty miles an hour!

In the revised version, only two ideas are linked by *and*. These ideas can be combined into one sentence because they are closely related. Notice that a comma is used before the word *and*. The comma is also necessary to show a slight pause between the two complete ideas.

Exercise 3 **Identifying and Revising Stringy Sentences**

Revise each of the following stringy sentences by breaking it into two or more sentences.   Possible revisions follow.

EXAMPLE   **1.** Raccoons look like cute, mischievous animals wearing a mask, and they are often seen in residential areas, and they frequently eat pet food left outside.

   1. *Raccoons look like cute, mischievous animals wearing a mask. They are often seen in residential areas, and they frequently eat pet food left outside.*

Thomas and José were playing softball at school and Thomas hit the ball very hard, and then he saw it roll under the steps of the library. Thomas peered under the dark steps to recover his ball and when he reached for it, he saw a giant raccoon and Thomas wasn't sure what to do next! José told Thomas that raccoons are fierce fighters, and then José warned him not to anger the raccoon and by this time, other softball players had gathered to offer advice. Thomas finally rolled the ball out from under the steps with a baseball bat and the raccoon stayed completely still, but it hissed and looked fiercely at the group and then Thomas saw why the raccoon was behaving so strangely. Five baby raccoons were hiding behind the mother and they were too small to protect themselves and the mother raccoon was trying to frighten the softball players away!

Active and Passive Voice

A verb in the **active voice** expresses an action done *by* its subject. A verb in the **passive voice** expresses an action done *to* its subject.

ACTIVE VOICE   The band teacher **instructed** us. [The subject, *teacher,* performs the action.]

PASSIVE VOICE   We **were instructed** by the band teacher. [The subject, *We,* receives the action.]

ACTIVE VOICE   **Did** we **play** the march well? [The subject, *we,* performs the action.]

PASSIVE VOICE   **Was** the march **played** well by us? [The subject, *march,* receives the action.]

In a passive sentence, the verb phrase always includes a form of *be* and the past participle of the main verb. Other helping verbs may also be included.

ACTIVE   The artist **had used** oils for the painting.

PASSIVE   Oils **had been used** by the artist for the painting.

Reference Note

For more information on **past participles,** see page 147.

Exercise 4   Identifying Active and Passive Voice

For each of the following sentences, tell whether the verb is in the *active voice* or the *passive voice.*

EXAMPLE   1. The truck was filled with dirt by the workers.
         1. *passive*

1. The new play was reviewed favorably by the critics.
2. The firefighters finally have put out the forest fire.
3. The flight attendant described the safety features of the plane.
4. The unhappy baby was comforted by his mother.
5. Did Dan misplace his car keys again?
6. The campfire had not been extinguished by the campers.
7. Mary Beth was chosen as the team leader.
8. The free tickets will be raffled on Tuesday.
9. Did the strong wind blow the leaves off the trees?
10. Have the cabinet members been named by the new president?

1. passive
2. active
3. active
4. passive
5. active
6. passive
7. passive
8. passive
9. active
10. passive

Using the Passive Voice

The passive voice emphasizes the person or thing receiving the action. The passive voice is useful when you do not know who performed the action or when you do not want to reveal the performer of the action.

EXAMPLES   The territory **was explored** in the early 1700's. [The person who explored the territory is unknown.]

"A bad choice **was made** for the location of the party," said Marie. [The speaker does not want to reveal who made the choice.]

Although you may want to use the passive voice in situations like those above, the active voice is stronger and more direct. The passive voice generally requires more words to express a thought than the active voice does, and too many passive sentences can cause your writing to sound weak or awkward. It is generally best to avoid using the passive voice except in the situations described above.

Exercise 5 **Using Verbs in the Active Voice and the Passive Voice**

For each of the following sentences, tell whether the verb is in the *active voice* or the *passive voice*. Then, revise each sentence that contains a verb in the passive voice so that the verb is in the active voice.

EXAMPLE   **1.** My book report was just completed.

1. passive—I just completed my book report.

1. active
2. active
3. passive—On Monday, the recycling company will pick up our old newspapers, glass, and aluminum cans.
4. passive—The orthodontist adjusted Tod's braces.
5. active
6. passive—The technician repaired the copier in just one hour.
7. active

1. Marta hung the wet laundry on the clothesline.
2. Have you read today's newspaper?
3. On Monday, our old newspapers, glass, and aluminum cans will be picked up by the recycling company.
4. Tod's braces were adjusted by the orthodontist.
5. For the last two days, the geese have been flying south.
6. The copier was repaired by the technician in just one hour.
7. Would Gail have left the party so soon?

8. We had been searching the stores for an antique oak table and chairs.
9. On Wednesday, art projects will be displayed by the sixth-graders.
10. Have the tall bushes in front of the post office been pruned by the gardeners?

8. active
9. passive—On Wednesday, the sixth-graders will display art projects.
10. passive—Have the gardeners pruned the tall bushes in front of the post office?

Review B Revising Stringy Sentences and Sentences Containing Passive Voice

Some of the following sentences are stringy sentences, and some sentences have verbs in the passive voice. First, identify which sentences are stringy and which have verbs in the passive voice. Then, rewrite each stringy sentence as two or more clear sentences. Rewrite each sentence with a verb in passive voice so the verb is in active voice.

EXAMPLE 1. Jim's new bicycle was ridden by him on his very first try.
1. *passive—Jim rode his new bicycle on his very first try.*

1. Our family planned a picnic for Saturday, and the day started off sunny and bright, and suddenly it started to rain, and we ate in the car.
2. A fine nest of twigs and string was built in the apple tree by the pair of robins.
3. When we visited my grandmother, we took a taxi to the airport, and we flew to Chicago, and then we drove for four hours, and we arrived just in time for supper.
4. The printer for my computer made an odd noise, and the paper jammed, and we couldn't remove the jam, and we finally took the printer to the shop for repair.
5. According to this morning's newspaper, the election ballots had been counted before the deadline by the workers at the polls.
6. The fine, dry snow had been blown into drifts three feet high by the strong, north wind.
7. Rachel planned every detail of the party, and then she invited the guests, and she cleaned the house, and she prepared all of the food.
8. The fifty miles of county roads were cleaned and maintained by a crew of only two workers.

Writing Clear Sentences **395**

Review B Revising Stringy Sentences and Sentences Containing Passive Voice

ANSWERS
Answers may vary.

1. stringy—Our family planned a picnic for Saturday. The day started off sunny and bright, but suddenly it started to rain. We ate in the car.
2. passive—The pair of robins built a fine nest of twigs and string in the apple tree.
3. stringy—When we visited my grandmother, we took a taxi to the airport and flew to Chicago. Then we drove for four hours. We arrived just in time for supper.
4. stringy—The printer for my computer made an odd noise, and the paper jammed. We couldn't remove the jam, so we finally took the printer to the shop for repair.
5. passive—According to this morning's newspaper, the workers at the polls had counted the election ballots before the deadline.
6. passive—The strong, north wind had blown the fine, dry snow into drifts three feet high.
7. stringy—Rachel planned every detail of the party. Then she invited the guests, cleaned the house, and prepared all of the food.
8. passive—A crew of only two workers cleaned and maintained the fifty miles of county roads.

Review B · Revising Stringy Sentences and Sentences Containing Passive Voice

ANSWERS continued

9. passive—The mother cat weaned the eight-week-old kittens before Eileen adopted them.

10. stringy—Reid trained every day and was in excellent condition. He competed in many track meets and won many medals.

Combining Sentences

(pp. 396–408)

OBJECTIVES

- To combine sentences by inserting words and groups of words
- To combine sentences by joining subjects and verbs
- To combine complete sentences
- To identify transitional words and phrases in a passage

TIPS & TRICKS

To get ideas for a variety of ways to organize your ideas into sentences, look at sentences written by professional authors. Try imitating the style of a favorite author by using similar sentence structures in your own sentences or paragraphs.

9. The eight-week-old kittens were weaned by the mother cat before they were adopted by Eileen.

10. Reid trained every day, and he was in excellent condition, and he competed in many track meets, and he won many medals.

Combining Sentences

Good writers usually use some short sentences, but they don't use them all the time. An entire paragraph of short sentences makes writing sound choppy. For example, notice how dull and choppy the following paragraph sounds.

> Quicksand is really just sand. The sand is wet. The sand is loose. You can sink in quicksand. It will not actually suck you down. You might get caught in quicksand. You can lie on your back. You can float. Then you can roll or wriggle. Your movements must be slow. You can get to solid ground this way.

Now, see how the writer has revised the paragraph by combining some of the short sentences. Notice how sentence combining has helped to eliminate some repeated words and ideas. The result is a smoother paragraph that has much more variety.

> Quicksand is really just wet, loose sand. You can sink in quicksand, but it will not actually suck you down. If you are caught in quicksand, you can lie on your back and float. Then you can slowly roll or wriggle to solid ground.

You can combine sentences in several different ways. Sometimes you can insert a word or a group of words from one sentence into another sentence. Other times you can combine two related sentences by using a connecting word.

RESOURCES

Combining Sentences
Practice

- *Language & Sentence Skills Practice*, pp. 361–372, 373–374
- *Developmental Language & Sentence Skills*, pp. 137–142

Inserting Words

One way to combine two sentences is to pull a key word from one sentence and insert it into the other sentence. Sometimes you can just add the key word to the first sentence and drop the rest of the second sentence. Other times you will need to change the form of the key word before you can insert it.

ORIGINAL   Dr. Martin Luther King, Jr., was a civil rights leader. He was an American.

COMBINED   Dr. Martin Luther King, Jr., was an **American** civil rights leader. [The noun *American* was inserted as an adjective to modify *civil rights leader*.]

ORIGINAL   He was famous for his brilliant speeches. His fame was international.

COMBINED   He was **internationally** famous for his brilliant speeches. [The adjective *international* was changed to the adverb *internationally* and was inserted to modify *famous*.]

ORIGINAL   Dr. King led the civil rights movement in the early 1960's. The movement was growing.

COMBINED   Dr. King led the **growing** civil rights movement in the early 1960's. [The verb form *growing* was inserted as a participle to modify *civil rights movement*.]

> **TIPS & TRICKS**
>
> When you change the forms of key words, you often add endings such as *–ed, –ing, –ful,* and *–ly* to make adjectives and adverbs.
>
> EXAMPLES
> skill → skill**ed**
> crash → crash**ing**
> use → use**ful**
> quiet → quiet**ly**

Exercise 6 Combining Sentences by Inserting Words

Each of the following items contains two sentences. Combine the two sentences by taking the italicized key word from the second sentence and inserting it into the first sentence. The directions in parentheses will tell you how to change the form of the key word if you need to do so.

EXAMPLE   **1.** Chief Joseph was a Nez Perce Indian chief who fought for his people. He was a *brave* fighter. (Add *–ly*.)

1. *Chief Joseph was a Nez Perce Indian chief who fought bravely for his people.*

Combining Sentences   **397**

> ### DIRECT TEACHING
>
> **Modeling and Demonstration**
>
> **Combining Sentences.** Model how to combine sentences by using the example *Chief Joseph was a Nez Perce Indian chief who fought for his people. He was a brave fighter.* First, ask whether the two sentences are about the same subject. [*yes; Chief Joseph*] Next, ask whether the two sentences repeat any information. [*yes; he fought; he was a fighter*] Point out that when information is repeated in two sentences, it is often possible to take information from one sentence and insert it into the other sentence. Next, ask what information could be moved from the second sentence to the first sentence. [*what kind of fighter Chief Joseph was*] Ask which word can be used. [*brave*] Point out that the sentences could be combined in at least two ways—*Chief Joseph was a brave Nez Perce Indian chief who fought for his people* or *Chief Joseph was a Nez Perce Indian chief who fought bravely for his people.* To make the second revision, students would have to add an *–ly* to the adjective *brave* to turn it into the adverb *bravely.* Now, have a volunteer use another example from this chapter to demonstrate how to combine two sentences by inserting a word.

DIFFERENTIATING INSTRUCTION

Learners Having Difficulty

To help students grasp the importance of sentence combining to strong writing, ask them what a rock concert would be like if the band played everything in one key and at the same tempo or beat. What would students think of the performance? Then, point out that if a writer repeats the same patterns and words in short, choppy sentences, the writing can be as dull as a one-note song. Remind students that combining sentences eliminates repetition and improves the flow and rhythm in writing.

English-Language Learners

Spanish. Adding key words that are adjectives may be confusing to some Spanish speakers. In Spanish, descriptive adjectives usually follow the nouns they modify. In addition, when an adjective appears before the noun, it often has a different meaning. Working through **Exercise 6** orally can help focus attention on the placement of adjectives in relation to the nouns they modify. You might point out that the words *retreating* and *moving* in sentences 6 and 10 are verb forms called participles and are used as adjectives.

1. The name Joseph was given to his father by ⌃missionaries. ~~The missionaries were *Christian*.~~ **1.** Christian
2. Chief Joseph's ⌃name, Hin-mah-too-yah-lat-ket, means "thunder rolling down the mountains." ~~That is his *Nez Perce* name.~~ **2.** Nez Perce
3. The United States government ordered the Nez Perce to move from their ⌃homeland. ~~The homeland was *beloved* by the Nez Perce.~~ **3.** beloved
4. The government wanted to open the ⌃Wallowa Valley in Oregon to white settlers. ~~The valley was *beautiful*.~~ **4.** beautiful
5. Chief Joseph ⌃fought the United States Army to defend his people's homeland. ~~The fighting was *fierce*.~~ (Add *–ly*.) **5.** fiercely
6. When he realized he could not win, he led the ⌃Nez Perce band more than one thousand miles. ~~The band was in *retreat*.~~ (Add *–ing*.) **6.** retreating
7. The ⌃Nez Perce thought that they had escaped. ~~They were *weary*.~~ **7.** weary
8. The ⌃soldiers quickly marched two hundred miles to catch the Nez Perce. ~~The soldiers were *determined*.~~ **8.** determined
9. The soldiers easily defeated the ⌃Nez Perce band. ~~The Nez Perce band had been *weakened*.~~ **9.** weakened
10. Chief Joseph's ⌃surrender speech is famous. ~~The speech is *moving*.~~ **10.** moving

Inserting Groups of Words

Often, you can combine two related sentences by taking an entire group of words from one sentence and adding it to the other sentence. When the group of words is inserted, it adds detail to the information in the first sentence.

Reference Note

For more information on **prepositional phrases**, see page 63.

| ORIGINAL | The first known baseball game was played in 1846. It was played in Hoboken, New Jersey. |
| COMBINED | The first known baseball game was played in 1846 **in Hoboken, New Jersey.** [The prepositional phrase *in Hoboken, New Jersey* was inserted to modify the verb phrase *was played*.] |

CONTENT-AREA CONNECTIONS

Science
Writing About Water Conservation.
Consider using the following activity to give students another opportunity to practice sentence combining. Ask students to collect information on water conservation from their science textbooks or from science magazines. Then, have them work in randomly

ORIGINAL	The game ended with a score of 23–1. It was played by the New York Baseball Club and the Knickerbockers.
COMBINED	**Played by the New York Baseball Club and the Knickerbockers,** the game ended with a score of 23–1. [The participial phrase *Played by the New York Baseball Club and the Knickerbockers* was inserted to modify the noun *game*.]
ORIGINAL	The players were all amateurs. They were in the first organized baseball league.
COMBINED	The players **in the first organized baseball league** were all amateurs.
ORIGINAL	The All-American Girls Professional Baseball League had ten teams at its 1948 peak. The league was the subject of a 1992 movie.
COMBINED	The All-American Girls Professional Baseball League, **the subject of a 1992 movie,** had ten teams at its 1948 peak. [The appositive phrase *the subject of a 1992 movie* was inserted to identify or rename the subject, *The All-American Girls Professional Baseball League*.]
ORIGINAL	Many people around the world play baseball. They play baseball so they can exercise and have fun.
COMBINED	Many people around the world play baseball **to exercise and have fun.** [The infinitive phrase *to exercise and have fun* was inserted. It is used as an adverb, modifying *play*.]

After you combine two sentences, be sure to read your new sentence carefully. Then, ask yourself the following questions:

- Is my new sentence clear?
- Does it make sense?
- Does it sound better than the two shorter sentences?

If you answer "no" to any of the above questions, try to combine the sentences in a different way. Then, ask yourself the questions again.

Combining Sentences   **399**

DIRECT TEACHING

Using Commas with Groups of Inserted Words
Students may have trouble understanding when to set off appositive phrases with commas. Point out that commas are used to set off word groups that can be left out of the sentence without affecting its meaning.

Use these examples to explain the rule.

- My cousin Al pitches for the Flyers. (Commas are not needed here because I have more than one cousin and must use Al's name to identify him.)
- Al, an enthusiastic player, hopes to pitch all nine innings. (Commas are needed here because *an enthusiastic player* is not essential to the meaning of the sentence. The pitcher has already been identified by name.)

RETEACHING

Inserting Groups of Words
You may make sentence combining easier for students by supplying them with sentences and asking them to break the sentences down into basic concepts. Then, have students recombine the concepts into new sentences. Below is an example.

Sentence: The yellow butterfly floated gracefully on the gentle breeze.

Basic Concepts:

The butterfly was yellow.
The butterfly floated on the breeze.
The butterfly floated gracefully.
The breeze was gentle.

New Sentence: On the gentle breeze, the yellow butterfly floated gracefully.

SENTENCES

selected groups of three or four to prepare a list of suggestions for conserving water at home. Encourage students to include both sentences and fragments in their lists. Each group should then pass its list to another group, who will write a paragraph that combines the items in the list using the techniques learned in class.

Exercise 7

DISTRIBUTED REVIEW

Ask students to rewrite **Exercise 7** as a paragraph that includes complete and varied sentences. Remind students to check for commas after introductory elements, in compound sentences, and with nonessential phrases.

Exercise 7 Combining Sentences by Inserting Word Groups

Combine each pair of sentences by taking the underlined word group from the second sentence and inserting it into the first sentence. Be sure to add commas if they are needed.

EXAMPLE
1. Jorge read *Storm Chaser: Into the Eye of a Hurricane* for his science report. Jorge is <u>a boy in my class</u>.

1. *Jorge, a boy in my class, read* Storm Chaser: Into the Eye of a Hurricane *for his science report.*

1. by Keith Elliot Greenberg

2. directly into dangerous storms

3. Trained in the study of weather,

4. for years

5. of only 1,500 feet

6. , which includes high winds, heavy rain, hail, and severe air currents

7. Using computers and other machines,

8. While the aircraft flies through the hurricane, [Answers may vary.]

9. Called "hurricane hunters,"

10. , such as predicting the amount of snowfall for the Winter Olympics

1. *Storm Chaser* is an exciting book. ~~It is by Keith Elliot Greenberg.~~
2. The book is a true story about a pilot named Brian Taggart, who flies a P-3 aircraft. ~~He flies the aircraft directly into dangerous storms.~~
3. Taggart works for the National Oceanic and Atmospheric Administration. ~~He is trained in the study of weather.~~
4. He also trained to learn to fly the P-3 at low altitude through hurricanes. ~~He trained for years to learn this skill.~~
5. The low altitude is very dangerous because there is little time to react to violent wind gusts. ~~The pilots often fly at an altitude of only 1,500 feet.~~
6. Before the pilots reach the calm eye of the storm, they must fly through dangerous weather. ~~This weather, which includes high winds, heavy rain, hail, and severe air currents, is very dangerous.~~
7. Scientists aboard this P-3 collect information about hurricanes. ~~The scientists collect this information using computers and other machines.~~
8. The weather instruments record information about wind speed and barometric pressure changes. ~~The instruments collect this information while the aircraft flies through the hurricane.~~
9. Pilots like Brian help weather forecasters predict where and when a storm will hit land. ~~These pilots are called "hurricane hunters."~~
10. During the non-hurricane season, the P-3 pilots work on other weather-related projects. ~~Other weather-related projects include interesting work such as predicting the amount of snowfall for the Winter Olympics.~~

Using *And, But,* and *Or*

Another way you can combine sentences is by using connecting words called *conjunctions.* Conjunctions allow you to join closely related sentences and sentence parts.

Joining Subjects and Verbs

Sometimes two sentences are so closely related that they have the same subjects or verbs. If two sentences have the same subject, you can combine them by making a *compound verb.* If the sentences have the same verb, you can combine them by making a *compound subject.*

The conjunction you use is important. It tells your reader how the two subjects or verbs are related to one another.

- Use *and* to join similar ideas.

ORIGINAL   The Sun Dance is an American Indian tradition. The Spirit Dance is an American Indian tradition.

COMBINED   **The Sun Dance and the Spirit Dance** are American Indian traditions. [compound subject]

- Use *but* to join contrasting ideas.

ORIGINAL   Mike will cook the main course. Mike will buy the dessert.

COMBINED   Mike **will cook** the main course **but will buy** the dessert. [compound verb]

- Use *or* to show a choice between ideas.

ORIGINAL   Sara Tallchief may be elected president of the student council. Frances O'Connor may be elected president of the student council.

COMBINED   **Sara Tallchief or Frances O'Connor** may be elected president of the student council. [compound subject]

> **Exercise 8** **Combining Sentences by Joining Subjects and Verbs**

Use *and, but,* or *or* to combine each of the following pairs of sentences. If the sentences have the same verb, make one sentence with a compound subject. If the sentences have the same

Reference Note

For information about and practice using **conjunctions,** see page 66.

┌─HELP─┐

Coordinating conjunctions such as *and, but,* and *or* are used to join words or word groups that are closely related. This joining of words or word groups is called **coordination.**

┌─HELP─┐

When you use the conjunction *and* to link two subjects, your new compound subject will be plural. Remember to make the verb plural, too. A verb must agree with the subject in number.

EXAMPLE
Carlos and Hannah play on the same team. [The plural subject *Carlos and Hannah* takes the plural verb *play.*]

SENTENCES

DIRECT TEACHING

Joining Subjects and Verbs

Agreement. Students may need a reminder that a compound subject joined by *and* usually takes a plural verb. You may wish to review the two exceptions to this rule as well. (Two subjects that refer to one thing, such as *peanut butter and jelly,* or two subjects preceded by *each* or *every,* such as *each door and window,* require a singular verb.) You may also point out that in a sentence like the first combined example on this page, the predicate nominative *traditions* is plural to agree in number with the compound subject *Sun Dance and Spirit Dance.*

Combining Sentences   **401**

> **MINI-LESSON** | **Grammar** | *Continued on p. 402*

Identifying Subjects and Verbs. Review with students the definitions of *subject* and *verb.* Then, ask students to identify the <u>sub-</u>jects and **verbs** in the following sentences.

   1. <u>Clowns</u> **are** just people in funny makeup.

2. <u>Each</u> **creates** his or her special face.
3. Using white greasepaint, <u>clowns</u> **paint** over their faces.
4. Then <u>they</u> **draw** a lot of red around the mouth.

Exercise 8 Combining Sentences by Joining Subjects and Verbs

ANSWERS

1. Climbing fish and mudskippers have side fins that work much like feet.

2. Mudskippers walk on mud flats and even climb trees.

3. Mudskippers use their pectoral fins to move themselves along the ground but use their tails to launch themselves into the air.

4. The mudskippers absorb oxygen from water filtered through their skin and also absorb oxygen from the air.

5. Adult mudskippers dig a hole in the mud in which to lay their eggs and dig another hole in which to live.

6. Mudskippers can hop more than a yard at a time and can catch insects as the insects fly.

7. Walking catfish are native to the East Indies but have been seen in Florida.

8. Walking catfish or climbing perch might be found in warm, muddy water.

9. Fish farm owners in areas that have walking catfish must protect their fish ponds or lose many fish to the walking fish with the big appetite.

10. Walking catfish will live in a large aquarium but will eat smaller fish in the same tank.

---

subject, make one sentence with a compound verb. The hints in parentheses will help you.

EXAMPLE 1. The climbing perch is a fish that can walk. The mudskipper is a fish that can walk. (Join with *and*.)

   1. *The climbing perch and the mudskipper are fish that can walk.*

1. Climbing fish have side fins that work much like feet. Mudskippers have side fins that work much like feet. (Join with *and*.)

2. Mudskippers walk on mud flats. Mudskippers even climb trees. (Join with *and*.)

3. Mudskippers use their pectoral fins to move themselves along the ground. They use their tails to launch themselves into the air. (Join with *but*.)

4. The mudskippers absorb oxygen from water filtered through their skin. They also absorb oxygen from the air. (Join with *and*.)

5. Adult mudskippers dig a hole in the mud in which to lay their eggs. They dig another hole in which to live. (Join with *and*.)

6. Mudskippers can hop more than a yard at a time. Mudskippers can catch insects as the insects fly. (Join with *and*.)

7. Walking catfish are native to the East Indies. They have been seen in Florida. (Join with *but*.)

8. Walking catfish might be found in warm, muddy water. Climbing perch might be found in warm, muddy water. (Join with *or*.)

9. Fish farm owners in areas that have walking catfish must protect their fish ponds. They can lose many fish to the walking fish with the big appetite. (Join with *or*.)

MINI-LESSON | **Grammar** | *Continued from p. 401*

5. Because of the mouth's importance, <u>clowns</u> **pay** special attention to it.

6. The <u>mouth</u> **reveals** a clown's personality.

7. Many <u>clowns</u> often **wear** a rubber nose.

8. <u>They</u> **may** also **wear** wigs on their heads.

9. A <u>wig</u> **can make** them appear bald or **can give** them a mop of curly blue hair.

10. Baggy <u>pants</u> and floppy <u>shoes</u> **complete** the costume.

Review the answers as a class.

10. Walking catfish will live in a large aquarium. They will eat smaller fish in the same tank. (Join with *but*.)

Joining Sentences

Sometimes you may want to combine two related sentences that express equally important ideas. You can connect the two sentences by using a comma and *and, but,* or *or*. The result is a *compound sentence.*

ORIGINAL	A group of frogs is called an *army*. A group of turtles is called a *bale*.
COMBINED	A group of frogs is called an *army***, and** a group of turtles is called a *bale*.

Other times you may want to combine two sentences that are related in a special way. One sentence helps explain the other sentence by telling *who, what, where, when, why,* or *how*. A good way to combine these sentences is to add a connecting word that shows the special relationship. In this kind of sentence combining, you create a *complex sentence.*

ORIGINAL	The drawbridge was pulled up. The enemy knights could not get into the castle.
COMBINED	**When** the drawbridge was pulled up, the enemy knights could not get into the castle.

ORIGINAL	Their leader had not counted on the princess. The princess knew how to operate the drawbridge.
COMBINED	Their leader had not counted on the princess, **who** knew how to operate the drawbridge.

Some connecting words that you can use to create complex sentences are given below. The word that you choose will depend on what you want your sentence to say.

after	before	so that	when	who
although	how	that	whether	whom
as	if	until	which	whose
because	since	what	while	why

Reference Note

For more about **complex sentences,** see page 99.

HELP

The words in the chart to the left are *subordinating conjunctions.* Using a subordinating conjunction to create a complex sentence is called *subordination.*

Combining Sentences   **403**

DIRECT TEACHING

Correcting Misconceptions

***Who, Which,* and *That*.** Students might think they always can use the relative pronoun *who* when creating complex sentences. Tell them that *who* refers to people only, *which* refers to things only, and *that* may refer to either people or things. Point out that the category *things* includes animals, organizations, and places. Use the following examples as models.

- Larry is the man <u>who</u> will deliver our new heater. [*person*]
- We needed to replace our old heater, <u>which</u> we have had for fifteen years. [*thing*]
- Toxic Waste Get-a-Ways, <u>which</u> is a volunteer group, removed the heater today. [*organization*]
- He is the salesperson <u>that</u> helped us choose the new heater. [*person*]
- It is a heater <u>that</u> will last a long time. [*thing*]

APPLICATION

Combining Sentences

Activity. To give students additional practice in combining sentences, have students work in groups of two or three to combine some of the simple sentences from familiar children's stories. Suggest that students try to use each of the methods they've studied for combining sentences. Representatives from each group may then take turns reading their revised sentences to the class. Discuss with students why children's stories are written mainly in short, simple sentences.

Exercise 9 Combining Complete Sentences

SENTENCES

ANSWERS

Here are sample answers.

1. I would like to learn more about stars because they are interesting and beautiful.

2. Planets do not give off light of their own, but stars do.

3. Some stars are fainter than our sun, and some are many times brighter.

4. The sun is just a medium-sized star, but it is close enough to the earth to look larger than all the other stars.

5. Even the largest stars look like little points of light because they are millions of miles away.

6. On a clear night, a person without a telescope can see about 3,000 stars, while a person using a three-inch-diameter telescope can see about 600,000 stars.

7. After the sun changes hydrogen into helium and energy, this energy escapes from the sun in the form of light.

8. Although the sun was formed about five billion years ago, it has enough hydrogen to last many more years.

9. While our sun will change, the change will be slow.

10. We must continue to study the stars and planets so that we will understand how we fit into our vast universe.

MEETING THE CHALLENGE

When you want to express complicated ideas and show how they fit together, use a compound-complex sentence. A compound-complex sentence has two or more independent clauses and at least one subordinate clause. Try combining the short sentences in each item below into a compound-complex sentence.

1. The marching band began to play the first piece. The trumpets were featured in that piece. The trumpet players were at the front of the band's formation.

2. People go on vacation every summer. They pay me for my service. I mow lawns, water plants, and collect mail.

ANSWERS

1. The trumpets were featured in the first piece that the marching band began to play, and the trumpet players were at the front of the band's formation.

2. I mow lawns, water plants, and collect mail for people who go on vacation every summer, and they pay me for my service.

Exercise 9 Combining Complete Sentences

Following are ten pairs of short, choppy sentences that need improving. Make each pair into one sentence by using the connecting word given in parentheses. Be sure to change the capitalization and the punctuation where necessary.

EXAMPLE 1. Planets move quickly. Stars move slowly. (*but*)
1. Planets move quickly, but stars move slowly.

1. I would like to learn more about stars. They are interesting and beautiful. (*because*)
2. Planets do not give off light of their own. Stars do. (*but*)
3. Some stars are fainter than our sun. Some are many times brighter. (*and*)
4. The sun is just a medium-sized star. It is close enough to the earth to look larger than all the other stars. (*but*)
5. Even the largest stars look like little points of light. They are millions of miles away. (*because*)
6. On a clear night, a person without a telescope can see about 3,000 stars. A person using a three-inch-diameter telescope can see about 600,000 stars. (*while*)
7. The sun changes hydrogen into helium and energy. This energy escapes from the sun in the form of light. (*after*)
8. The sun was formed about five billion years ago. It has enough hydrogen to last many more years. (*although*)
9. Our sun will change. The change will be slow. (*while*)
10. We must continue to study the stars and planets. We will understand how we fit into our vast universe. (*so that*)

Using Transitions

Carefully written sentences help make a reading passage clear and understandable. Sometimes, though, those sentences need some help to show how the ideas are related. If you are telling a story, the reader needs to know what comes first, next, and so on. If you are explaining an idea or how something works, the reader needs to know how the different parts relate to each other—how they connect.

The words that help show how ideas are related are called *transitional words and phrases.* They act as signposts to the reader, pointing out relationships between ideas, between sentences, and between paragraphs. They can show similarities and differences; they can show causes and effects; and they can show time, place, and importance. The following chart lists some common transitional words and phrases.

Transitional Words and Phrases		
Showing Similarities	also in addition and	another like too
Showing Differences	although but	however instead
Showing Causes and Effects	as a result because	since so
Showing Time	after before finally first	next second then when
Showing Place	above nearby	here there
Showing Importance	first last	mainly most important

Exercise 10 Identifying Transitional Words and Phrases

Read the following passage and identify the type of transition that each underlined word or phrase expresses. Write *sim.* for similarity, *dif.* for difference, *C/E* for cause and effect, *time* for time, *place* for place, and *import.* for importance.

EXAMPLE   1. Preparation for a hike is <u>more important</u> than any other detail.
1. *import.*

DIFFERENTIATING INSTRUCTION

English-Language Learners

Vietnamese. In Vietnamese, an introductory clause may be followed by a "balancing" word in the main clause.

English: ***Because*** he runs fast, he is on the track team.

Vietnamese: ***Because*** he runs fast, ***therefore,*** he is on the track team.

Some Vietnamese speakers may omit the subordinating word and use just the balancing word. Others may use *also* as a balancing word with a range of uses: *Even if I had a bike, I would also not ride to school.*

Show students that they usually need only one subordinating conjunction, or connecting word, to form a complex sentence. Have them locate connecting words in sample sentences, and check their writing for correct usage.

Cantonese. Cantonese sentences are sometimes patterned in ways that allow an adverbial clause to act as a coordinating rather than a subordinating element: *Although I worked on homework, but I did not finish.*

Show students that complex sentences that begin with a subordinating conjunction, or connecting word, cannot also have *and* or *but* between clauses.

1. time	[**1**] <u>Before</u> you begin a hike, you must choose a route.
2. time	[**2**] <u>First</u>, study the map, and then determine how far you want
3. sim.	to hike. [**3**] <u>In addition to</u> getting a map if the route is new
	to you, be sure to talk to someone who has hiked the route
4. dif.	before. Maps are very informative, [**4**] <u>but</u> the knowledge an
5. time	experienced hiker can share is even more valuable. [**5**] <u>Then</u>,
6. dif.	gather your supplies. [**6**] <u>Although</u> you may have hiked your
	chosen route in the spring, a summer hike requires more
	water and, probably, a hat. [**7**] <u>Another</u> requirement is addi-
7. sim.	tional sunscreen. You don't want to have an accident on the
8. C/E	trail [**8**] <u>since</u> many trails are remote. You are not likely to find
9. place	a doctor [**9**] <u>nearby</u>, so brush up on your safety training. Plan
	to rest occasionally, too, instead of hiking the route all at one
10. C/E	try. [**10**] <u>As a result</u> of your preparation, you are sure to have a
	great time.

Review C Revising a
Paragraph by Combining
Sentences

ANSWERS
Here is a sample revision.

Some of the world's oldest cities have been found in Sumer, the land between the Tigris and the Euphrates rivers. These early cities began as farm villages. Eventually, Sumerian merchants began to trade with their neighbors in the mountains. The Sumerians sold the mountain people grains, and the mountain people sold them lumber, stone, and copper. Over five thousand years ago, Sumerians invented a system of writing to keep track of their trading. We know much about how ancient Sumerians lived because they left us many written records.

Review C Revising a Paragraph by Combining
Sentences

The following paragraph sounds choppy because it has too many short sentences. Use the methods you have learned in this section to combine some of the sentences. After you have revised the paragraph, read the choppy version and the new version aloud. You will notice how much better the paragraph sounds after you have revised it.

EXAMPLE   Ancient cities provide information. The information is about how people lived.
Ancient cities provide information about how people lived.

```
    Some of the world's oldest cities
have been found in Sumer. Sumer is
the land between the Tigris and the
Euphrates rivers. These early cities
began as villages. The villages were
made of farms. Sumerian merchants began
to trade with their neighbors in the
mountains. The Sumerians sold the moun-
tain people grains. The mountain people
sold the Sumerians lumber, stone, and
```

copper. Over five thousand years ago,
Sumerians invented a system of writing.
They invented their writing system to
keep track of their trading. We know
much about how ancient Sumerians lived.
They left us many written records.

Review D **Writing Clear Sentences**

The following paragraph is hard to read because it contains
some sentence fragments and run-on sentences as well
as choppy and stringy sentences. Identify **two** fragments by
underlining them; identify **one** run-on sentence by double
underlining it; and identify **two** stringy sentences by putting
brackets around them. Then, revise those sentences using the
methods you have learned. Also, combine sentences in at least
two other places, and identify **three** transitional words or
phrases by circling them.

EXAMPLE   Have you ever seen a sumo wrestling match? A style
            of Japanese wrestling. A goal is to eject the opponent
            from the ring, another goal is to make the opponent
            touch the ground with some part of his body other
            than his feet.

            Have you ever seen a sumo wrestling match? Sumo is
            a style of Japanese wrestling. *The goal is to eject the*
            opponent from the ring or to make the opponent
            touch the ground with some part of his body other
            than his feet.

    Sumo wrestling is an unusual sport,
not only because of the unique and
impressive appearance of the athletes.
On average weigh 330 pounds and dress
in traditional loincloths. Sumo is
based in myth. It is also based in ritual. There is a myth that the Japanese
people gained control of Japan when a
god won a sumo match with another
leader. From a rival group. The earliest sumo matches, dating back over 1500
years, were rituals performed to ensure

ANSWERS
Sentences 2 and 6 are sentence
fragments. Sentence 8 is a run-on
sentence. Sentences 7 and 13 are
stringy sentences. Transitional words
are in boldface type.

Here is a sample revision.

    Sumo wrestling is an unusual sport
because of the unique and impressive appearance of the athletes, who
on average weigh 330 pounds and
dress in traditional loincloths. Sumo
is based in myth and ritual. There is
a myth that the Japanese people
gained control of Japan **when** a god
won a sumo match with a leader
from a rival group. The earliest sumo
matches, dating back over 1500
years, were rituals performed to
ensure a good harvest. Sumo **later**
became a way to entertain royalty.
Japan **then** entered a time of military
rule, **and** sumo wrestlers were used
in fighting. **When** peace returned,
sumo became entertainment again
and came to be known as the
national sport of Japan. The ritual
elements of early sumo remain today.
At tournaments, each day opens with
a colorful and exciting ritual performed by the wrestlers. The ritual is
called *dohyo-iri,* which means "entering the ring." In this ceremony the
wrestlers enter the ring, **and then**
the highest ranked wrestler formally
claps and stomps on the ground.
When he is finished, the other highly
ranked wrestlers repeat the clapping
and stomping. The ceremony, which
the world got to see at the 1998
Winter Olympics opening ceremony
in Nagano, Japan, symbolically drives
evil spirits away.

a good harvest, and sumo later became a way to entertain royalty, and Japan then entered a time of military rule, and sumo wrestlers were used in fighting. When peace returned, sumo became entertainment again, it came to be known as the national sport of Japan. The ritual elements of early sumo remain today. At tournaments, each day opens with a colorful and exciting ritual performed by the wrestlers. The ritual is called *dohyo-iri*. *Dohyo-iri* means "entering the ring." In this ceremony the wrestlers enter the ring, and then the highest ranked wrestler comes into the ring, and he claps and stomps on the ground in a very formal way, and when he is finished other highly ranked wrestlers repeat the clapping and stomping. The ceremony symbolically drives evil spirits away. The world got to see this ceremony when it was part of the 1998 Winter Olympics opening ceremony in Nagano, Japan.

Chapter Review

A. Identifying Sentences, Sentence Fragments, and Run-on Sentences

Identify each of the following word groups as a *sentence*, a *sentence fragment*, or a *run-on sentence*. If a word group is a sentence fragment, rewrite it to make a complete sentence. If a word group is a run-on sentence, rewrite it to make it one or more complete sentences. Remember to use correct capitalization and punctuation.

EXAMPLES
1. Because you know the difference between those kinds of birds.

    1. frag.—Because you know the difference between those kinds of birds, you should make the captions for the photos.

2. Marion left.

    2. sent.

3. The temperature is dropping, I think it will freeze tonight.

    3. run-on—The temperature is dropping. I think it will freeze tonight.

1. The best movie of all the ones showing.
2. I know the person who painted the mural at the downtown library.
3. Stop.
4. Drive two miles, after the water tower, turn left.
5. Went with Georgia to the store for more eggs and flour.
6. That is my uncle, he is a member of the school board.
7. Because Lloyd and Joan have already sold their house.
8. I will go to the orthodontist tomorrow she is going to fit me for a new retainer.
9. The computer crashed again, so I restarted it.
10. Before I had saved enough money to buy a new bicycle.

Chapter Review **409**

Sentences will vary; word group identification will not.

1. frag.—That is the best movie of all the ones showing.
2. sent.
3. sent.
4. run-on—Drive two miles. After the water tower, turn left.
5. frag.—She went with Georgia to the store for more eggs and flour.
6. run-on—That is my uncle. He is a member of the school board.
7. frag.—Because Lloyd and Joan have already sold their house, they will be ready to move before the first of the month.
8. run-on—I will go to the orthodontist tomorrow. She is going to fit me for a new retainer.
9. sent.
10. frag.—Before I had saved enough money to buy a new bicycle, I changed my mind about what I wanted.

ASSESSING

Monitoring Progress

Chapter Review. To assess student progress, you may want to compare the types of items missed on the **Diagnostic Preview** to those missed on the **Chapter Review.** If students have not made significant progress, you may want to provide them with additional practice.

CHAPTER RESOURCES

Writing Effective Sentences
Review
- *Language & Sentence Skills Practice,* pp. 359–360, 371–374

Assessment
- *Progress Assessment for the Holt Handbook,* pp. 31–34, 41
- *Test Generator* (One-Stop Planner CD-ROM)

B. Combining Sentences

Each of the following items contains two complete sentences. Combine these sentences to make a single sentence that is clearer and more interesting. To combine the sentences, you can add connecting words, insert words or phrases, or use compound or complex sentences.

EXAMPLE   1. The ant carried a large leaf across the sidewalk. Then it carried the leaf up the tree trunk.

1. *The ant carried a large leaf across the sidewalk and up the tree trunk.*

Answers may vary.

11. I save money in a savings account at my mother's credit union.

11. I save money. I have a savings account at my mother's credit union.

12. Taylor will write Grandmother a thank-you note for the new sweater she sent.

12. Taylor will write Grandmother a thank-you note. Grandmother sent Taylor a new sweater.

13. Please remember to give your parents the permission slip and to return it tomorrow after they have signed it.

13. Please remember to give your parents the permission slip. Return it tomorrow after they have signed it.

14. Will you paint your room light blue or yellow?

14. Will you paint your room light blue? Or will you paint it yellow?

15. Mr. Byrd, the principal, asked Jonah to help arrange the desks.

15. Mr. Byrd asked Jonah to help arrange the desks. Mr. Byrd is the principal.

C. Revising a Passage to Improve Sentence Style

The passage below contains stringy sentences, sentences containing awkward uses of the passive voice, and sentences that need transitions between them. Rewrite the passage to make it clearer and to improve the sentences.

EXAMPLE   What do you do during the summer? Vacation plans are made in some families by the entire family, and vacation plans are made in other families by just the parents, and the children wait excitedly to hear about those plans.

What do you do during the summer? In some families, the entire family makes vacation plans. In other families, just the parents make vacation plans while the children wait excitedly to hear about those plans.

We take a weeklong vacation in the summer, and we sometimes visit my mother's best friend, Barbara. She lives in a small house on an island just off the coast of Florida. She says she likes living there because the beach changes all the time, and it is always new and interesting to her. We were there, and we went for a walk on a very long fishing pier, and a huge sea turtle was seen by several of us. The water was very clear. We could see how big the turtle was. I think its shell was about four feet across. It came up for air, and its head looked almost the size of a human head. Barbara was asked several questions about the turtle. Barbara said that at that beach more turtles are seen now than in earlier years. She said that turtle eggs are sometimes laid in nests in the sand, and people mark where the nests are, and people try not to walk where the nests are, and the baby turtles hatch during a full moon and make their way to the water.

Revisions will vary. Here is a sample revision.

When we take a weeklong vacation in the summer, we sometimes visit my mother's best friend, Barbara. She lives in a small house on an island just off the coast of Florida. She says she likes living there because the beach changes all the time; therefore, she finds it always new and interesting. When we were there, we went for a walk on a very long fishing pier where several of us saw a huge sea turtle. Because the water was very clear, we could see how big the turtle was. I think its shell was about four feet across, and when it came up for air, its head looked almost the size of a human head. When we asked Barbara several questions about the turtle, she said that people see more turtles at that beach now than in earlier years. She also said that turtles sometimes lay their eggs in nests in the sand. People mark where the nests are and try not to walk there. During a full moon, the baby turtles hatch and make their way to the water.

Sentence Diagramming

1.0 Written and Oral English Language Conventions
Students write and speak with a command of standard English conventions appropriate to this grade level.
1.1 Use simple, compound, and compound-complex sentences.

Reference Note

For more about **subjects** and **verbs,** see page 7.

The Sentence Diagram

A *sentence diagram* is a picture of how the parts of a sentence fit together. It shows how the words in the sentence are related.

Subjects and Verbs

To diagram a sentence, first find the simple subject and the simple predicate, or verb, and write them on a horizontal line. Then, separate the subject and verb with a vertical line. Keep any capital letters, but leave out sentence punctuation.

EXAMPLES   Dogs bark.

Dogs	bark

Children were singing.

Children	were singing

The preceding examples are easy because each sentence contains only a simple subject and a verb. Now, look at a longer sentence.

EXAMPLE   My older brother is studying Arabic in school.

To diagram the simple subject and the verb of this sentence, follow these three steps:

Step 1: Separate the complete subject from the complete predicate.

complete subject	complete predicate
My older brother	is studying Arabic in school.

Step 2: Find the simple subject and the verb.

simple subject	verb
brother	is studying

Step 3: Draw the diagram.

brother	is studying

Exercise 1 Diagramming Simple Subjects and Verbs

Diagram the simple subject and verb in each of the following sentences.

EXAMPLES   **1.** Aunt Carmen is teaching me to cook.

1. | Aunt Carmen | is teaching |

2. The dog sleeps in the garage.

2. | dog | sleeps |

1. My family goes to the store together every Saturday.
2. We shop at the grocery store at the corner of our street.
3. I select the red beans, rice, meat, and cheese.
4. Grandma López must have written the shopping list.
5. Rosita is buying the chile peppers and cilantro.

┌─HELP─
Remember that simple subjects and verbs may consist of more than one word.

Exercise 1 Diagramming Simple Subjects and Verbs

ANSWERS

1. | family | goes |

2. | We | shop |

3. | I | select |

4. | Grandma López | must have written |

5. | Rosita | is buying |

Reference Note
For more about **compound subjects,** see page 13.

Compound Subjects

To diagram a compound subject, put the subjects on parallel lines. Then, put the connecting word (the conjunction, such as *and, but,* or *or*) on a dotted line between the subject lines.

EXAMPLE   **Koalas** and **kangaroos** are found in Australia.

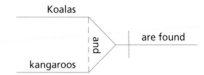

Compound Verbs

Reference Note
For more about **compound verbs,** see page 14.

To diagram a compound verb, put the two verbs on parallel lines. Then, put the conjunction on a dotted line between the verbs.

EXAMPLE   Callie **washes** and **dries** the dishes after dinner.

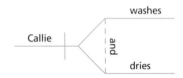

Compound Subjects and Compound Verbs

A sentence with both a compound subject and a compound verb combines the two patterns you just learned.

EXAMPLE   The **cat** and her **kittens ate** and then **slept**.

Exercise 2 Diagramming Compound Subjects and Compound Verbs

Diagram the simple subjects and verbs in the following sentences.

┌HELP┐

Sentences in Exercise 2 may contain compound subjects, compound verbs, or both.

EXAMPLE   1. Brittany and La Tonya skated and skied last winter.

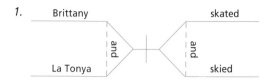

1. Ursula LeGuin and Nicholasa Mohr are my favorite authors.
2. Ms. Sanchez and Mr. Charles teach Spanish.
3. Bill Russell first played and later coached in the NBA.
4. My friends and I hurried home and told our parents the good news.
5. The students and the teacher visited the museum but did not have time for a complete tour.

Questions

To diagram a question, first make the question into a statement without changing or dropping any words. Then, diagram the sentence.

EXAMPLE   Can all insects fly? [question]
           All insects can fly. [statement]

Notice that the diagram uses the capitalization of the original sentence.

Understood Subjects

In an imperative sentence (a request or command) the subject is always understood to be *you*. Place the understood subject *you* in parentheses on the horizontal line.

EXAMPLE   Look over there.

Reference Note

For more information about **questions,** see page 18.

┌─HELP─┐

Remember that in a diagram, the subject always comes first, even if it does not come first in the sentence.

Reference Note

For information about **imperative sentences** and **understood subjects,** see page 18.

Exercise 2 Diagramming Compound Subjects and Compound Verbs

ANSWERS

1.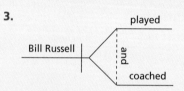

2.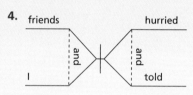

3.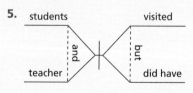

4. friends   hurried
   I   told

5. students   visited
   teacher   did have

The Sentence Diagram   **415**

Exercise 3 Diagramming Questions and Commands

ANSWERS

1.
| (you) | Eat |

2.
| you | Do know |

3.
| driver | is going |

4.
| (you) | help |

5.
| they | are standing |

Reference Note
For more information about **adjectives,** see page 38.

Exercise 3 Diagramming Questions and Commands

Diagram the simple subjects and verbs in the following sentences.

EXAMPLE   **1.** Please wash the dishes.

1.
| (you) | wash |

1. Eat the rest of your jambalaya.
2. Do you know much about the Jewish holidays?
3. Where is the driver going?
4. Please help me with these cartons.
5. Why are they standing in line?

Adjectives and Adverbs

Adjectives and adverbs are written on slanted lines connected to the words they modify. Notice that possessive pronouns are diagrammed in the same way adjectives are. Also notice that the articles *a*, *an*, and *the* are included as adjectives.

Adjectives

EXAMPLES   **yellow** bird   **her best** blouse   **a playful** puppy

  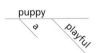

Exercise 4 Diagramming Sentences with Adjectives

Diagram the subjects, verbs, and adjectives in the following sentences.

EXAMPLE   **1.** A strong, cold wind blew all night.

1.

1. My favorite singer is coming to town.
2. The long, grueling hike tired us.
3. Red, ripe tomatoes grow there.
4. The two brave astronauts stepped into space.
5. Is a funny movie playing downtown?

Adverbs

When an adverb modifies a verb, the adverb is placed on a slanted line below the verb.

EXAMPLES   wrote **quickly**   walked **there slowly**

When an adverb modifies an adjective or another adverb, it is placed on a slanted line connected to the word it modifies.

EXAMPLES   **incredibly** large poster   runs **very** fast

Reference Note
For more about **adverbs,** see page 59.

Exercise 5 Diagramming Sentences with Adverbs

Diagram the subjects, verbs, adjectives, and adverbs in the following sentences.

EXAMPLE   **1.** We almost always recycle newspapers.

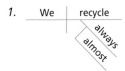

1. Gloria Estefan recently recorded that song.
2. That new band plays very loudly.
3. Her two brothers visited Chinatown yesterday.

Exercise 4 Diagramming Sentences with Adjectives

ANSWERS

1.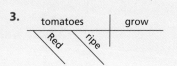

2.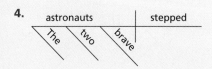

3.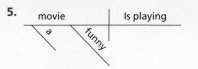

4.

5.

Exercise 5 Diagramming Sentences with Adverbs

ANSWERS

1.

2.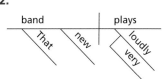

4. The busy librarian almost never rests.
5. An extremely unusual program will be broadcast tonight.

3.

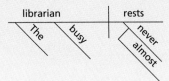

4.

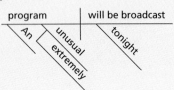

5.

Reference Note
For more information about **prepositional phrases,** see page 63.

Reference Note
For more about **adjective phrases,** see page 79.

Reference Note
For more about **adverb phrases,** see page 83.

Prepositional Phrases

Prepositional phrases are diagrammed below the words they modify. Write the preposition on a slanting line. Then, write the object of the preposition on a horizontal line connected to the slanting line. Notice that the slanting line extends a little beyond the horizontal line.

Adjective Phrases

EXAMPLES   time **of day**   several **in a row**

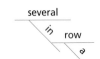

Adverb Phrases

EXAMPLES   walked **on the moon**   are ready **for the test**

moves quickly **for an old dog**

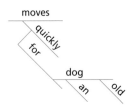

Exercise 6 **Diagramming Sentences with Prepositional Phrases**

Diagram the following sentences.

EXAMPLE   **1.** The freighter slowed for the first lock.

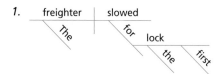

1. Tamales are wrapped in corn husks.
2. The soccer team from Brazil ran onto the field.
3. My friend from India skis very well.
4. The students in his class went to the library.
5. Catherine Zeta-Jones and Will Smith may star in that new movie.

Direct and Indirect Objects

Direct Objects

A direct object is diagrammed on the horizontal line with the subject and verb. A short vertical line separates the direct object from the verb.

Reference Note
For more about **direct objects,** see page 107.

EXAMPLE   We have been playing **CD's.**

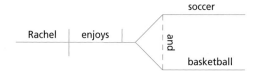

Compound Direct Objects

Reference Note
For more information about **compound direct objects,** see page 107.

EXAMPLE   Rachel enjoys **soccer** and **basketball.**

Exercise 6 **Diagramming Sentences with Prepositional Phrases**

ANSWERS

1.

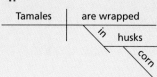

2.

3.

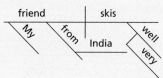

4.

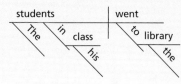

5.

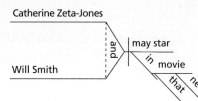

SENTENCES

Exercise 7 Diagramming Direct Objects and Indirect Objects

A N S W E R S

1.

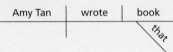

2.

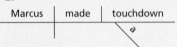

3.

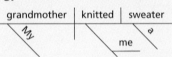

4.

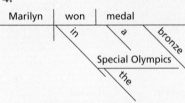

5.

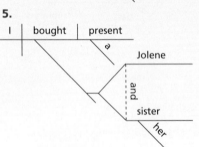

Reference Note

For more about **indirect objects,** see page 109.

Reference Note

For more information about **compound indirect objects,** see page 110.

─**HELP**─

Not every sentence in Exercise 7 contains an indirect object.

Indirect Objects

The indirect object is diagrammed on a horizontal line beneath the verb. The verb and the indirect object are joined by a slanting line.

EXAMPLE   Dad fixed **us** some spaghetti.

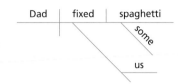

Compound Indirect Objects

EXAMPLE   Marisa gave her **brother** and **me** some grapes.

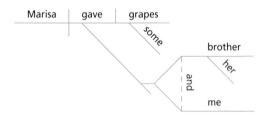

Exercise 7 Diagramming Direct Objects and Indirect Objects

Diagram the following sentences.

EXAMPLE   **1.** He handed her the report.

1. Amy Tan wrote that book.
2. Marcus made a touchdown.
3. My grandmother knitted me a sweater.
4. Marilyn won a bronze medal in the Special Olympics.
5. I bought Jolene and her sister a present.

Subject Complements

A subject complement is diagrammed on the horizontal line with the subject and the verb. The complement comes after the verb. A line slanting toward the subject separates the subject complement from the verb.

Predicate Nominatives

EXAMPLE   Mickey Leland was a famous **congressman** from Texas.

Reference Note

For more information about **predicate nominatives,** see page 112.

Compound Predicate Nominatives

EXAMPLE   Aaliyah is a **singer** and a **dancer.**

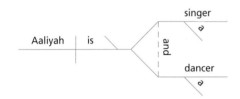

Reference Note

For more information on **compound predicate nominatives,** see page 113.

Predicate Adjectives

EXAMPLE   The guitarist was very **skillful.**

Reference Note

For more information on **predicate adjectives,** see page 114.

The Sentence Diagram   **421**

Exercise 8 Diagramming Sentences with Subject Complements

ANSWERS

1.

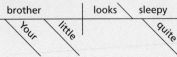

2.

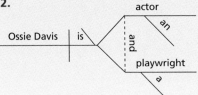

3.

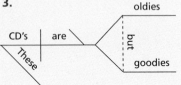

4.

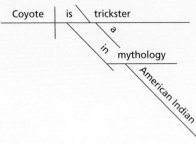

5.

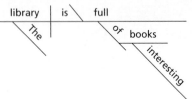

Reference Note
For more about **compound predicate adjectives,** see page 115.

Compound Predicate Adjectives

EXAMPLE   They were **weary** but **patient.**

Exercise 8 Diagramming Sentences with Subject Complements

Diagram the following sentences.

EXAMPLE   1. Ms. Chang is an excellent teacher and a fine lawyer.

1.

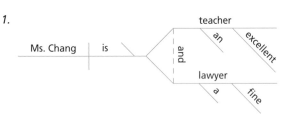

1. Your little brother looks quite sleepy.
2. Ossie Davis is an actor and a playwright.
3. These CD's are oldies but goodies.
4. Coyote is a trickster in American Indian mythology.
5. The library is full of interesting books.

Subordinate Clauses

Adjective Clauses

Diagram an adjective clause by connecting it with a broken line to the word it modifies. Draw the broken line between the relative pronoun and the word to which it relates. The adjective clause is diagrammed below the independent clause.

Reference Note
For more information about **independent clauses,** see page 89. For more about **adjective clauses,** see pages 91 and 214. For more about **relative pronouns,** see pages 37 and 214.

EXAMPLE   Certain land crabs **that are found in Cuba** can
           run fast.

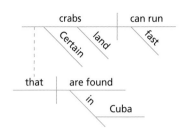

┌─HELP────
The words
who, whom, whose, which,
and *that* are often used as
relative pronouns.

Adverb Clauses

Diagram an adverb clause by using a broken line to connect
the adverb clause to the word it modifies. Place the subordinating conjunction that introduces the adverb clause on the
broken line. The adverb clause is diagrammed below the
independent clause.

Reference Note
For more information
about **adverb clauses,**
see page 93. For a list of
**subordinating conjunc-
tions,** see page 90.

EXAMPLE   **When Halley's Comet returns,** I will be a very
           old man.

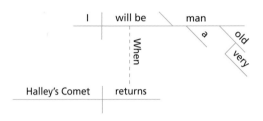

┌─HELP────
The words
*after, because, if, since,
unless, when,* and *while*
are often used as subordinating conjunctions.

PEANUTS reprinted by permission
of United Feature Syndicate, Inc.

The Sentence Diagram   **423**

Exercise 9 Diagramming Sentences with Adjective Clauses and Adverb Clauses

ANSWERS

1.
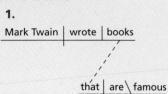

2.
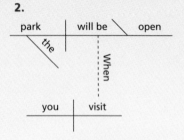

3.
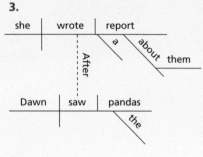
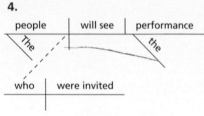

4.

5.
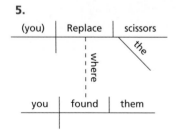

Exercise 9 Diagramming Sentences with Adjective Clauses and Adverb Clauses

Diagram the following sentences.

EXAMPLE   **1.** If you go to the library, will you return this book?

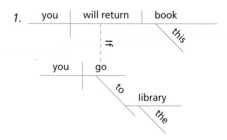

1. Mark Twain wrote books that are famous.
2. When you visit, the park will be open.
3. After Dawn saw the pandas, she wrote a report about them.
4. The people who were invited will see the performance.
5. Replace the scissors where you found them.

The Kinds of Sentence Structure

Simple Sentences

A simple sentence contains one independent clause.

Reference Note

For more about **simple sentences,** see page 96.

EXAMPLE   The coach gave Alfonso a pat on the back. [one independent clause]

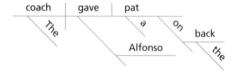

Compound Sentences

A compound sentence contains at least two independent clauses. The second independent clause in a compound sentence is diagrammed below the first and is joined to it by a coordinating conjunction.

EXAMPLE   Ostriches walk in a funny way, but they can run fast.
[two independent clauses]

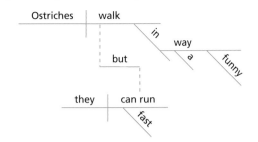

NOTE   The coordinating conjunctions are *and, but, for, nor, or,*
so, and *yet.*

Exercise 10 **Diagramming Compound Sentences**

Diagram the following compound sentences.

EXAMPLE   **1.** Genna went to the mall, but I stayed home.

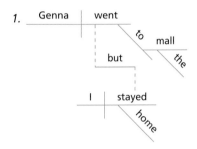

1. Lisa likes soccer, but I prefer basketball.
2. Gabriela Mistral is a poet, but she has also written essays.
3. Cactuses are desert plants, yet they can grow in milder
   climates.
4. I can give Jewel the news tonight, or you can call her now.
5. Chinese immigrants worked on the railroad in the West,
   but Irish immigrants built the railroad in the East.

Reference Note

For more information about **compound sentences,** see page 97. For more about **coordinating conjunctions,** see page 66.

Exercise 10 **Diagramming Compound Sentences**

ANSWERS

1.
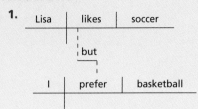

2.
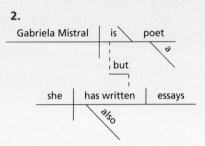

3.
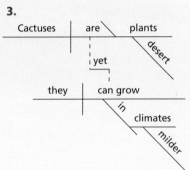

4.
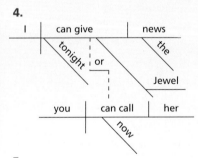

5.
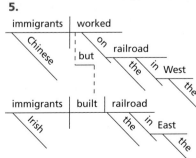

SENTENCES

The Sentence Diagram   **425**

Complex Sentences

A complex sentence contains one independent clause and at least one subordinate clause.

Reference Note

For more about **complex sentences,** see page 99.

EXAMPLE   Leon received a letter that was mailed from Germany.
[one independent clause and one subordinate clause]

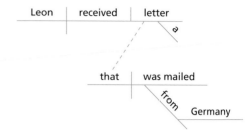

Compound-Complex Sentences

A compound-complex sentence contains two or more independent clauses and at least one subordinate clause.

Reference Note

For more about **compound-complex sentences,** see page 100.

EXAMPLE   After we rehearse this scene, we will move to another room, and the stage crew will work on the set. [two independent clauses and one subordinate clause]

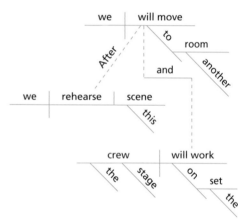

Exercise 11 Diagramming Complex and Compound-Complex Sentences

Diagram the following complex and compound-complex sentences.

EXAMPLE **1.** If the Bulldogs win their last two games, they will finish in first place.

1. Hector walked to school because his bicycle had a flat tire.
2. Rosa was the contestant who knew the correct answer.
3. Unless the rain stops soon, the umpire will cancel the game.
4. As the lights dimmed, the audience grew quiet.
5. The student that designs the best cover receives a free yearbook, so many students will be entering designs.

Exercise 11 Diagramming Complex and Compound-Complex Sentences

ANSWERS

1.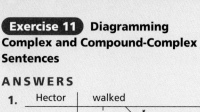

2.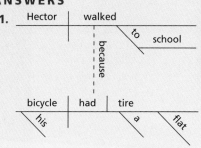

3.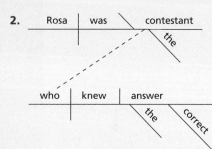

4.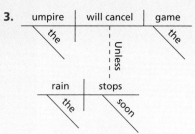

5.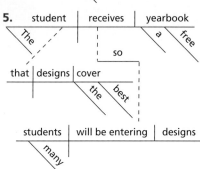

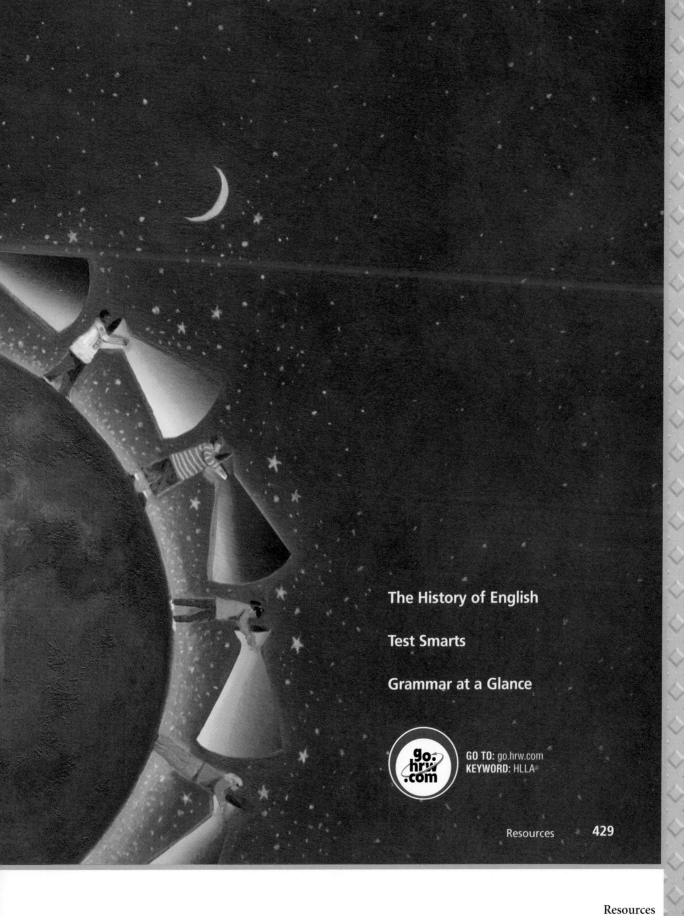

The History of English

Test Smarts

Grammar at a Glance

GO TO: go.hrw.com
KEYWORD: HLLA

Resources 429

The History of English

Origins and Uses

A Changing Language

No one knows exactly when or how English got started. We do know that English and many other modern-day languages come from an early language that was spoken thousands of years ago. The related languages still resemble that parent language, just as you resemble your parents. For example, notice how similar the words for *mother* are in the following modern-day languages.

ENGLISH mother   FRENCH mère
SPANISH madre   ITALIAN madre
SWEDISH moder

Over 1,500 years ago, a few small tribes of people invaded the island that is now Britain. These tribes, called the Angles and Saxons, spoke the earliest known form of English, called **Old English.** Old English was very different from the English we speak.

English continued to evolve through a form known as **Middle English.** While our language has always changed and grown, some of our most basic words have been around since the very beginning.

EARLY WORD
hand   dohtor   andswaru   hleapan

PRESENT-DAY WORD
hand   daughter   answer   leap

Changes in Meaning   It may be hard to believe that the word *bead* once meant "prayer." Many English words have changed meaning over time. Some of these changes have been slight. Others have been more obvious. Below are a few examples of words that have changed their meanings.

naughty—In the 1300s, *naughty* meant "poor or needy." In the 1600s, the meaning changed to "poorly behaved."

lunch—In the 1500s, a *lunch* was a large chunk of something, such as bread or meat.

caboose—*Caboose* entered the English language in the 1700s when it meant "the kitchen of a ship."

Even today the meanings of words may vary depending on where they are used. For example, in America a *boot* is a type of shoe, but in Great Britain, a *boot* may refer to the trunk of a car.

Changes in Pronunciation and Spelling

If you traveled back in time a few hundred years, you would probably have a hard time understanding spoken and written English.

■ **Changes in pronunciation** English words used to be pronounced differently from the way they are pronounced today. For example, in the 1200s, people pronounced *bite* like *beet* and *feet* like *fate*. They also pronounced the vowel sound in the word *load* like our word *awe*.

You may have wondered why English words are not always spelled as they sound. Changes in pronunciation help account for many strange spellings in English. For example, the *w* that starts the word *write* was not always silent. Even after the *w* sound that started the word *write* was dropped, the spelling stayed the same. The *g* in *gnat* and the *k* in *knee* were once part of the pronunciations of the words, too.

■ **Changes in spelling** The spellings of many words have changed over time. Some changes in spelling have been accidental. For example, *apron* used to be spelled *napron*. People mistakenly attached the *n* to the article *a*, and *a napron* became *an apron*. Here are some more examples of present-day English words and their early spellings.

EARLY SPELLING

| jaile | locian | slæp | tima |

PRESENT-DAY SPELLING

| jail | look | sleep | time |

■ **British vs. American spelling and pronunciation** Pronunciations and spellings still vary today. For instance, the English used in Great Britain differs from the English used in the United States. In Great Britain, people pronounce *bath* with the vowel sound of *father* instead of the vowel sound of *cat*. The British also tend to drop the *r* sound at the end of words like *copper*. In addition, the British spell some words differently from the way people in the United States do.

AMERICAN

| theater | pajamas | labor |

BRITISH

| theatre | pyjamas | labour |

Word Origins

English grows and changes along with the people who use it. New words must be created for new inventions, places, or ideas. Sometimes, people borrow words from other languages to create a new English word. Other times, people use the names of people or places as new words.

■ **Borrowed words** As English-speaking people came into contact with people from other cultures and lands, they began to borrow words. English has borrowed hundreds of thousands of words from French, Hindi, Spanish, African languages, and many other languages spoken around the world. In many cases, the borrowed words have taken new forms.

FRENCH ange	HINDI champo
ENGLISH angel	ENGLISH shampoo
KIMBUNDU mbanza	SPANISH patata
ENGLISH banjo	ENGLISH potato

■ **Words from names**   Many things get their names from the names of people or places. For example, in the 1920s, someone in Bridgeport, Connecticut, discovered a new use for the pie plates from the Frisbie Bakery. He turned one upside down and sent it floating through the air. The new game sparked the idea for the flying plastic disk of today.

Dialects of American English

You probably know some people who speak English differently from the way you do. Different groups of people use different varieties of English. The kind of English we speak sounds most normal to us even though it may sound unusual to someone else. The form of English a particular group of people speaks is called a *dialect*. Everyone uses a dialect, and no dialect is better or worse than another.

Ethnic Dialects   Your cultural background can make a difference in the way you speak. A dialect shared by people from the same cultural group is called an ***ethnic dialect.*** Because Americans come from many cultures, American English includes many ethnic dialects. One of the largest ethnic dialects is the Black English spoken by many African Americans. Another is the Hispanic English of many people whose families come from places such as Mexico, Central America, or Cuba.

Regional Dialects   Do you *make* the bed or *make up* the bed? Would you order a *sub* with the *woiks* or a *hero* with the *werks*? In the evening, do you eat *supper* or *dinner*? How you answer these questions is probably influenced by where you live. A dialect shared by people from the same area is called a ***regional dialect.*** Your regional dialect helps determine what words you use, how you pronounce words, and how you put words together.

Not everyone from a particular group speaks that group's dialect. Also, an ethnic or regional dialect may vary depending on the speaker's individual background and place of origin.

Standard American English

Every dialect is useful and helps keep the English language colorful and interesting. However, sometimes it is confusing to try to communicate using two different dialects. Therefore, it is important to be familiar with ***standard American English.*** Standard English is the most commonly understood variety of English. In this textbook you can find some of the rules for using standard English. Language that does not follow these rules and guidelines is called ***nonstandard English.*** Nonstandard English is considered inappropriate in many formal situations.

NONSTANDARD   I don't want no more spinach.

STANDARD   I don't want **any** more spinach.

NONSTANDARD   Jimmy was fixing to go hiking with us.

STANDARD   Jimmy was **about** to go hiking with us.

Formal and Informal   Read the following sentences.

Many of my friends are excited about the game.

A bunch of my friends are psyched about the game.

Both sentences mean the same thing, but they have different effects. The first sentence is an example of *formal English,* and the second sentence is an example of *informal English.*

Formal and informal English are each appropriate for different situations. For instance, you would probably use the formal example if you were talking to a teacher about the game. If you were talking to a friend, however, the second sentence might sound natural. Formal English is frequently used in news reports and in schools and businesses.

■ **Colloquialisms**   Informal English includes many words and expressions that are not appropriate in more formal situations. The most widely used informal expressions are *colloquialisms.* *Colloquialisms* are colorful words and phrases of everyday conversation. Many colloquialisms have meanings that are different from the basic meanings of words.

EXAMPLES
I wish Gerald would *get off my case.*
Don't get *all bent out of shape* about it.
We were about to *bust* with laughter.

■ **Slang**   *Slang* words are made-up words or old words used in new ways. Slang is highly informal language. It is usually created by a particular group of people, such as students or people who hold a particular job, like computer technicians or artists. Often, slang is familiar only to the groups that invent it.

Sometimes slang words become a lasting part of the English language. Usually, though, slang falls out of style quickly. The slang words in the sentences below will probably seem out of date to you.

That was a really *far-out flick.*
Those are some *groovy duds* you're wearing.
I don't have enough *dough* to buy a movie ticket.

Test Smarts
Taking Standardized Tests in Grammar, Usage, and Mechanics

Becoming "Test-Smart"

Standardized achievement tests, like other tests, measure your skills in specific areas. Standardized achievement tests also compare your performance to the performance of other students at your age or grade level. Some language arts standardized tests measure your skill in using correct capitalization, punctuation, sentence structure, and spelling. Such tests sometimes also measure your ability to evaluate sentence style.

The most important part of preparing for any test, including standardized tests, is learning the content on which you will be tested. To do this, you must

- listen in class
- complete homework assignments
- study to master the concepts and skills presented by your teacher

In addition, you also need to use effective strategies for taking a standardized test. The following pages will teach you how to become test-smart.

General Strategies for Taking Tests

1. **Understand how the test is scored.** If no points will be taken off for wrong answers, plan to answer every question. If wrong answers count against you, plan to answer only questions you know the answer to or questions you can answer with an educated guess.

2. **Stay focused.** Expect to be a little nervous, but focus your attention on doing the best job possible. Try not to be distracted with thoughts that aren't about the test questions.

3. **Get an overview.** Quickly skim the entire test to get an idea of how long the test is and what is on it.

4. **Pace yourself.** Based on your overview, figure out how much time to allow for each section of the test. If time limits are stated for each section, decide how much time to allow for each item. Pace yourself, and check every five to ten minutes to see if you need to work faster. Try to leave a few minutes at the end of the testing period to check your work.

5. **Read all instructions.** Read the instructions for each part of the test carefully. Also, answer the sample questions to be sure you understand how to answer the test questions.

6. **Read all answer choices.** Carefully read *all* of the possible answers before you choose an answer. Note how each possible answer differs from the others. You may want to make an *x* next to each answer choice that you rule out.

7. **Make educated guesses.** If you do not know the answer to a question, see if you can rule out one or more answers and make an educated guess. Don't spend too much time on any one item, though. If you want to think longer about a difficult item, make a light pencil mark next to the item number. You can go back to that question later.

8. **Mark your answers.** Mark the answer sheet carefully and completely. If you plan to go back to an item later, be sure to skip that number on the answer sheet.

9. **Check your work.** If you have time at the end of the test, go back to check your answers. This is also the time to try to answer any questions you skipped. Make sure your marks are complete, and erase any stray marks on the answer sheet.

Strategies for Answering Grammar, Usage, and Mechanics Questions

The questions in standardized tests can take different forms, but the most common form is the multiple-choice question. Here are some strategies for answering that kind of test question.

Correcting parts of sentences

One kind of question contains a sentence with an underlined part. The answer choices show several revised versions of that part. Your job is to decide which revised version makes the sentence correct or whether the underlined part is already correct. First, look at each answer carefully. Immediately rule out any answer in which you notice a grammatical error. If you are still unsure of the correct answer, try approaching the question in one of these two ways.

- **Think how you would rewrite the underlined part.** Look at the answer choices for one that matches your revision. Carefully read each possible answer before you make your final choice. Often, only tiny differences exist between the answers, and you want to choose the *best* answer.

■ **Look carefully at the underlined part and at each answer choice, looking for one particular type of error, such as an error in capitalization or spelling.** The best way to look for a particular error is to compare the answer choices to see how they differ both from each other and from the underlined part of the question. For example, if there are differences in capitalization, look at each choice for capitalization errors.

After ruling out incorrect answers, choose the answer with no errors. If there are errors in each of the choices but no errors in the underlined part, your answer will be the "no error" or "correct as is" choice.

EXAMPLE

Directions: Choose the answer that is the **best** revision of the underlined words.

1. My neighbor is painting his <u>house and my brother helped him.</u>

   A. house; and my brother is helping him.
   B. house, and my brother had helped him.
   C. house, and my brother is helping him.
   D. Correct as is

Ⓐ Ⓑ Ⓒ Ⓓ

Explanation: In the example above, the possible answers contain differences in punctuation and in verb tense. Therefore, you should check each possible answer for errors in punctuation and verb tense.

   A. You can rule out this choice because it has incorrect punctuation.
   B. This choice creates inconsistent verb tenses, so you can rule out this answer.
   C. This choice has correct punctuation and creates consistent verb tenses.
   D. You can rule out this choice because the original sentence lacks correct

punctuation between the clauses.
   Answer: Choice C is the only one that contains no errors, so the oval for that answer choice is darkened.

Correcting whole sentences This type of question is similar to the kind of question previously described. However, here you are looking for mistakes in the entire sentence instead of just an underlined part. The strategies for approaching this type of question are the same as for the other kind of sentence-correction questions. If you don't see the correct answer right away, compare the answer choices to see how they differ. When you find differences, check each choice for errors relating to that difference. Rule out choices with errors. Repeat the process until you find the correct answer.

EXAMPLE

Directions: Choose the answer that is the **best** revision of the following sentences.

1. After Brad mowed the lawn, he swept the sidewalk and driveway, then he took a shower. And washed his hair.

   A. After Brad mowed the lawn, he swept the sidewalk and driveway. Then he took a shower and washed his hair.
   B. After Brad mowed the lawn, he swept the sidewalk and driveway. Then he took a shower, and washed his hair.
   C. After Brad mowed the lawn. He swept the sidewalk and driveway; then he took a shower and washed his hair.
   D. Correct as is

Ⓐ Ⓑ Ⓒ Ⓓ

Explanation: The original word groups and answer choices have differences in sentence structure and punctuation, so you should check each answer choice for errors in sentence structure and punctuation.

    A. This choice contains two complete sentences and correct punctuation.

    B. This choice contains two complete sentences and incorrect punctuation.

    C. This choice begins with a sentence fragment, so you can rule it out.

    D. You can rule out this choice because the original version contains a sentence fragment.

Answer: Choice A is the only one that contains no errors, so the oval for that answer choice is darkened.

Identifying kinds of errors

This type of question has at least one underlined part. Your job is to determine which part, if any, contains an error. Sometimes, you also may have to decide what type of error (capitalization, punctuation, or spelling) exists. The strategy is the same whether the question has one or several underlined parts. Try to identify an error, and check the answer choices for that type of error. If the original version is correct as written, choose "no error" or "correct as is."

EXAMPLE

Directions: Read the following sentences and decide which type of error, if any, is in the underlined part.

1. Marcia, Jim, and Leroy are participating in <u>Saturday's charity marathon. they</u> are hoping to raise one hundred dollars for the new children's museum.

    A. Spelling error

    B. Capitalization error

    C. Punctuation error

    D. Correct as is

Explanation: If you cannot tell right away what kind of error (if any) is in the original version, go through each answer choice in turn.

    A. All the words are spelled correctly.

    B. The sentences contain a capitalization error. The second sentence incorrectly begins with a lowercase letter.

    C. The sentences are punctuated correctly.

    D. The sentences contain a capitalization error, so you can rule out this choice.

Answer: Because the passage contains a capitalization error, the oval for answer choice B is darkened.

Revising sentence structure

Errors covered by this kind of question include sentence fragments, run-on sentences, repetitive wording, misplaced modifiers, and awkward construction. If you don't immediately spot the error, examine the question and each answer choice for specific types of errors, one type at a time. If you cannot find an error in the original version and if all of the other answer choices have errors, then choose "no error" or "correct as is."

EXAMPLE

Directions: Read the following word groups. If there is an error in sentence structure, choose the answer that best revises the word groups.

1. Mary Lou arranged the mozzarella cheese and fresh tomatoes. On a platter covered with lettuce leaves.

   A. Mary Lou arranged the mozzarella cheese and fresh tomatoes on a platter covered with lettuce leaves.

   B. Mary Lou arranged the mozzarella cheese and fresh tomatoes, on a platter covered with lettuce leaves.

   C. Mary Lou arranged the mozzarella cheese and fresh tomatoes; on a platter covered with lettuce leaves.

   D. Correct as is

Explanation: The original word groups and answer choices have differences in sentence structure and punctuation.

   A. This choice is correctly punctuated and contains a correct, complete sentence.

   B. This choice contains an incorrect comma, so you can rule it out.

   C. This choice contains an incorrect semicolon, so you can rule it out.

   D. The original word groups contain a sentence fragment, so D cannot be correct.

Answer: Choice A is the only one that contains no errors, so the oval for that answer choice is darkened.

Questions about sentence style

These questions are often not about grammar, usage, or mechanics but about content and organization. They may ask about tone, purpose, topic sentences, supporting sentences, audience, sentence combining, appropriateness of content, or transitions. The questions may ask you which is the *best* way to revise the passage, or they may ask you to identify the *main* purpose of the passage. When you see words such as *best*, *main*, and *most likely* or *least likely*, you are not being asked to correct errors; you are being asked to make a judgment about style or meaning.

If the question asks for a particular kind of revision (for example, "What *transition* is needed between sentence 4 and sentence 5?"), analyze each answer choice to see how well it makes that particular revision. Many questions ask for a general revision (for example, "Which is the *best* way to revise the last sentence?"). In such situations, check each answer choice and rule out any choices that have mistakes in grammar, usage, or mechanics. Then, read each choice and use what you have learned in class to judge whether the revision improves the original sentence. If you are combining sentences, be sure to choose the answer that includes all important information, that demonstrates good style, *and* that is grammatically correct.

EXAMPLE

Directions: Choose the answer that shows the **best** way to combine the following sentences.

1. Jacques Cousteau was a filmmaker and author. Jacques Cousteau explored the ocean as a diver and marine scientist.

   A. Jacques Cousteau was a filmmaker and author; Jacques Cousteau explored the ocean as a marine scientist.

   B. Jacques Cousteau was a filmmaker and author, he explored the ocean as a diver and marine scientist.

   C. Jacques Cousteau was a filmmaker

and author who explored the ocean as a diver and marine scientist.

D. Jacques Cousteau was a filmmaker, author, diver, and scientist.

 A B **C** D

Explanation:

A. Answer choice A is grammatically correct but unnecessarily repeats the subject *Jacques Cousteau* and leaves out some information.

B. Choice B is a run-on sentence, so it cannot be the correct answer.

C. Choice C is grammatically correct, and it demonstrates effective sentence combining.

D. Choice D is grammatically correct but leaves out some information.

Answer: Because answer choice C shows the best way to combine the sentences, the oval for choice C is darkened.

Fill-in-the-blanks This type of question tests your ability to fill in blanks in sentences, giving answers that are logical and grammatically correct. A question of this kind might ask you to choose a verb in the appropriate tense. A different question might require a combination of adverbs (*first, next*) to show how parts of the sentence relate. Another question might require a vocabulary word to complete the sentence.

To approach a sentence-completion question, first look for clue words in the sentence. *But, however,* and *though* indicate a contrast; *therefore* and *as a result* indicate cause and effect. Using sentence clues, rule out obviously incorrect answer choices. Then, try filling in the blanks with the remaining choices to determine which answer choice makes the most sense. Finally, check to be sure your choice is grammatically correct.

EXAMPLE

Directions: Choose the words that **best** complete the sentence.

1. When Jack _____ the dog, the dog _____ water everywhere.

    A. washes, splashed
    B. washed, will be splashing
    C. will have washed, has splashed
    D. washed, splashed

 A B C **D**

Explanation:

A. The verb tenses (present and past) are inconsistent.

B. The verb tenses (past and future) are inconsistent.

C. The verb tenses (future perfect and present perfect) are inconsistent.

D. The verb tenses (past and past) are consistent.

Answer: The oval for choice D is darkened.

Using Your Test Smarts

Remember: Success on standardized tests comes partly from knowing strategies for taking such tests—from being test-smart. Knowing these strategies can help you approach standardized achievement tests more confidently. Do your best to learn your classroom subjects, take practice tests if they are available, and use the strategies outlined in this section. Good luck!

Grammar at a Glance

A

┌─HELP─

Grammar at a Glance is an alphabetical list of special terms and expressions with examples and references to further information. When you encounter a grammar or usage problem in the revising or proofreading stage of your writing, look for help in this section first. You may find all you need to know right here. If you need more information, **Grammar at a Glance** will show you where in the book to turn for a more complete explanation. If you do not find what you are looking for in **Grammar at a Glance,** turn to the index.

abbreviation An abbreviation is a shortened form of a word or a phrase.

■ **capitalization of** (See page 250.)

TITLES USED WITH NAMES	**M**r.	**D**r.	**J**r.	**Ph.D.**
KINDS OF ORGANIZATIONS	**C**o.	**I**nc.	**D**ept.	**C**orp.
PARTS OF ADDRESSES	**B**lvd.	**A**ve.	**S**t.	**P.O. B**ox
NAMES OF STATES	[without ZIP Codes]		**K**y.	**W**yo.
			Wis.	**N.J.**
	[with ZIP Codes]		**KY**	**WY**
			WI	**NJ**
TIMES	**A.M.**	**P.M.**	**B.C.**	**A.D.**

■ **punctuation of** (See page 265.)

WITH PERIODS	(See preceding examples.)
WITHOUT PERIODS	VCR UN PBS NASA
	DC (D**.**C**.** without ZIP Code)
	kg ft lb yd cm
	[Exception: in.]

action verb An action verb expresses physical or mental activity. (See page 52.)

EXAMPLES Stefan **rode** the bike over the bridge.

Teresa **trimmed** the hedge and **raked** the leaves.

I **thought** about the problem.

active voice Active voice is the voice a verb is in when it expresses an action done by its subject. (See page 393. See also **passive voice**.)

EXAMPLE   He **ran** his first marathon last year.

adjective An adjective modifies a noun or a pronoun. (See page 38.)

EXAMPLE   **The** Nobles live in **a beautiful, old** house.

adjective clause An adjective clause is a subordinate clause that modifies a noun or a pronoun. (See page 91.)

EXAMPLE   The woman **who directs the City Ballet** is from Romania.

adjective phrase A prepositional phrase that modifies a noun or a pronoun is called an adjective phrase. (See page 79.)

EXAMPLE   Fruit **from Mr. Park's market** always seem fresher than the produce **in the grocery store.**

adverb An adverb modifies a verb, an adjective, or another adverb. (See page 59.)

EXAMPLE   **Occasionally,** when he's feeling **especially** energetic, Dino goes ice-skating.

adverb clause An adverb clause is a subordinate clause that modifies a verb, an adjective, or an adverb. (See page 93.)

EXAMPLE   **Before I watch TV,** I have to do my homework.

adverb phrase A prepositional phrase that modifies a verb, an adjective, or an adverb is called an adverb phrase. (See page 83.)

EXAMPLE   **At the shore,** Trish and Sandy played volleyball.

affix An affix is a word part that is added before or after a base word or root. (See **prefix** and **suffix.**)

EXAMPLES   dis + like = **dis**like

un + wind = **un**wind

complete + ly = complete**ly**

say + ing = say**ing**

agreement Agreement is the correspondence, or match, between grammatical forms. Grammatical forms agree when they have the same number and gender.

■ **of pronouns and antecedents** (See page 137.)

SINGULAR **Marcie** could not check out the book because **she** did not have **her** library card with **her**.

PLURAL **Readers** who do not have **their** library cards with **them** cannot check out books.

SINGULAR Every afternoon, **each** of the students is given time to write in **his or her** journal.

PLURAL Every afternoon, **all** of the students are given time to write in **their** journals.

■ **of subjects and verbs** (See page 124.)

SINGULAR That **box** of blankets **is** for the homeless shelter.

PLURAL The **blankets** in that box **are** for the homeless shelter.

SINGULAR **Mixed vegetables, roasted potatoes, or rice pilaf comes** with any seafood entree.

PLURAL **Rice pilaf, mixed vegetables, or roasted potatoes come** with any seafood entree.

SINGULAR **Each** of these books **was written** by Amy Tan.

PLURAL **All** of these books **were written** by Amy Tan.

SINGULAR **Neither Eli nor Leo wants** to go skateboarding.

PLURAL **Both Eli and Leo want** to go skateboarding.

SINGULAR Here **is** my **collection** of baseball cards.

PLURAL Here **are** the most valuable baseball **cards** in my collection.

SINGULAR	Where **is** my **wallet?**
PLURAL	Where **are** the **tickets?**

SINGULAR	**He doesn't** know how to play jai alai.
PLURAL	**They don't** know how to play jai alai.

antecedent An antecedent is the word or word group that a pronoun stands for. (See page 30.)

EXAMPLE   **Patricia** told **Aunt Sally** and **Uncle Ted** that **she** was thinking of **them.** [*Patricia* is the antecedent of *she. Aunt Sally* and *Uncle Ted* are the antecedents of *them.*]

apostrophe

■ **to form contractions** (See page 304. See also **contraction.**)
  EXAMPLES   hasn't   you'll   let's   o'clock   '01

■ **to form plurals of letters, numerals, symbols, and words used as words** (See page 307.)
  EXAMPLES   *a*'s, *e*'s, *i*'s, *o*'s, and *u*'s

              A's, *I*'s, and *U*'s

              v's and *w*'s

              1900's

              UFO's

              +'s and −'s

              using *and*'s instead of *&*'s

■ **to show possession** (See page 300.)
  EXAMPLES   the astronaut's spacesuit

              the astronauts' spacesuits

              someone's book bag

              Kim's and Mariah's math projects

              Kim and Mariah's math project

appositive An appositive is a noun or a pronoun placed beside another noun or pronoun to identify or describe it. (See page 272.)

EXAMPLE   The manager, **Max,** always brought his lunch to work.

appositive phrase An appositive phrase consists of an appositive and its modifiers. (See page 272.)

EXAMPLE   Claude Baker, **the manager of our local branch,** has been in banking for ten years.

article The articles, *a, an,* and *the,* are the most frequently used adjectives. (See page 38.)

EXAMPLE   **The** jetliner, **a** new model, had **an** eventful voyage.

B

bad, badly (See page 223.)

NONSTANDARD   This tuna salad smells badly.

STANDARD   This tuna salad smells **bad.**

base A base word can stand alone or combine with other word parts to make new words. Prefixes and suffixes can be added to a base to create many different words. (See page 320.)

EXAMPLES   light   trade   civil

twi**light**   **trade**-off   un**civil**

lighting   **trade**r   **civil**ly

base form The base form, or infinitive, is one of the four principal parts of a verb. (See page 147.)

EXAMPLE   Lee helped me **lift** the heavy box.

brackets (See page 312.)

EXAMPLES   Joshua read from the newspaper, "On Saturday [December 1], Mayor Johnston resigned due to poor health."

Refer to the chart (page 485 **[**Section D**]**) for other causes of pollution.

C

capitalization

■ **of abbreviations** (See page 250. See also **abbreviation.**)

■ **of first words** (See page 239.)

EXAMPLES **I**n Norse mythology, Thor is the god of thunder, war, and strength.

His sister asked him, "**H**ave you already fed our goldfish today?"

Dear Mrs. Yellowfeather:

Yours truly,

■ **of proper nouns and proper adjectives** (See pages 26 and 40.)

Proper Noun	Common Noun
Col. **C**urtis **L. B**rown, **J**r.	astronaut
Charles the **W**ise	leader
North **A**merica	continent
Argentina	country
Elk **P**oint, **S**outh **D**akota	city and state
Kodiak **I**sland	island
Yukon **R**iver	body of water
Guadalupe **P**eak	mountain
Cheyenne **M**ountain **Z**oological **P**ark	park
Siuslaw **N**ational **F**orest	forest
Luray **C**averns	caves
the **S**outhwest	region
Twenty-**f**ourth **S**treet	street
World **H**ealth **O**rganization (**WHO**)	organization
Federal **A**viation **A**dministration (**FAA**)	government body
North **C**arolina **S**tate **U**niversity (**NCSU**)	institution
Klondike **G**old **R**ush	historical event
Ice **A**ge	historical period
Little **L**eague **W**orld **S**eries	special event
Hana **M**atsuri, or **F**lower **F**estival	holiday
February, **M**ay, **A**ugust, **N**ovember	calendar items
winter, **s**pring, **s**ummer, **f**all (**a**utumn)	seasons
Nez **P**erce	people
Islam	religion

(continued)

(continued)

Proper Noun	Common Noun
Protestant	religious follower
God (*but* the Greek **g**od **A**pollo)	deity
Rosh **H**ashanah	holy days
Koran	sacred writing
Joshua **T**ree **N**ational **M**onument	monument
Metropolitan **M**useum of **A**rt	building
Caldecott **M**edal	award
Uranus	planet
Canopus	star
Delphinus, or **D**olphin	constellation
HMS *L*eopard	ship
Lunar Prospector	spacecraft
Physical **S**cience **I** (*but* **p**hysical **s**cience)	school subject
Cherokee	people or language

■ **of titles** (See page 253.)

EXAMPLES   **M**ayor Maria Sanchez [preceding a name]

       Maria Sanchez, the city's **m**ayor [following a name]

       Welcome, **M**ayor. [direct address]

       Uncle Darnell [*but* our **u**ncle Darnell]

       *T*he *C*all of the *W*ild [book]

       *S*aved by the *B*ell [television series]

       *A*mahl and the *N*ight *V*isitors [musical composition]

       "**O**ver the **R**ainbow" [song]

       "**T**he **S**mallest **D**ragonboy" [short story]

       "**I A**m of the **E**arth" [poem]

       *R*eader's *D*igest [magazine]

       *T*he *W*ashington *P*ost [newspaper]

       *R*ose *I*s *R*ose [comic strip]

case of pronouns Case is the form a pronoun takes to show how it is used in a sentence. (See page 177.)

NOMINATIVE Louis and **she** were the finalists in the spelling bee. [part of the compound subject of the verb *were*]

The only sixth-graders in the contest were Felicia and **he.** [part of the compound predicate nominative referring to the subject *sixth-graders*]

We volunteers spent Saturday afternoon making piñatas for the fiesta. [subject followed by the noun appositive *volunteers*]

Who painted *Cow's Skull: Red, White and Blue*? [subject of the verb *painted*]

Who is the author of *Yolanda's Genius*? [predicate nominative referring to the subject *author*]

OBJECTIVE On Friday, Ms. Yabuuchi took **them** on a field trip to the planetarium. [direct object of the verb *took*]

Gwen sent **me** an invitation to her family's Kwanzaa party. [indirect object of the verb *sent*]

I went with Carla and **her** to a Japanese tea ceremony. [part of the compound object of the preposition *with*]

The judge awarded each of **us** contestants a certificate of achievement. [object of the preposition *of,* followed by the noun appositive *contestants*]

Whom did the coach select as the captain of the team? [direct object of the verb *did select*]

In the last line of the poem, to **whom** is the speaker referring? [object of the preposition *to*]

POSSESSIVE **Your** birthday is the same day as **mine** is. [*Your* is used as an adjective before the subject *birthday; mine* is used as the subject of the verb *is.*]

clause A clause is a group of words that contains a subject and a verb and that is used as part of a sentence. (See page 89. See also **independent clause** and **subordinate clause.**)

INDEPENDENT CLAUSE   she stripped the walls of the living room

SUBORDINATE CLAUSE   before I painted them

colon (See page 281.)

■ before lists

EXAMPLES   Amber's favorite fables by Aesop are as follows: "Belling the Cat," "The Fox and the Grapes," and "The Frogs Who Wished for a King."

I need to get a few items at the pet shop: a bag of colored gravel for the aquarium, a small mirror for the birdcage, and a new collar for my pet Chihuahua.

■ in conventional situations

EXAMPLES   9:15 A.M.   Genesis 4:1–16

State Names, Seals, Flags and Symbols: A Historical Guide

Dear Dr. Kawabata:

comma (See page 268.)

■ in a series

EXAMPLES   Dad made chicken quesadillas and topped them with a relish of diced tomatoes, onions, and chilies.

The book is a collection of stories that tell about the daring exploits of Heracles, King Arthur, Gilgamesh, and fourteen other heroes of ancient times.

■ in compound sentences

EXAMPLES   My neighbor Mr. Kim owns a hardware store, and occasionally he hires me to restock the shelves.

We should leave now, or we may not get home before curfew.

■ with introductory elements

EXAMPLES   Well, were you able to get Sammy Sosa's autograph after the ballgame?

Yes, here's the baseball that he autographed!

■ with interrupters

EXAMPLES   The Jaw-Dropper, the world's fastest roller coaster, is at the amusement park near my house.

On Saturday afternoon, Tyrone, let's play miniature golf after we finish our chores.

■ **in conventional situations**

EXAMPLES San Antonio, Texas, is the home of the Alamo.

I was born on July 17, 1988, in Des Moines, Iowa.

Is 483 Cottonwood Way, Columbia, SC 29250-3840, your current address?

comparison of modifiers (See page 199.)

■ **comparison of adjectives and adverbs**

Positive	Comparative	Superlative
sharp	sharp**er**	sharp**est**
friendly	friendl**ier**	friendl**iest**
loyal	**more** loyal	**most** loyal
cheerfully	**less** cheerfully	**least** cheerfully
good/well	**better**	**best**

■ **comparing two**

EXAMPLES These red grapes are **sweeter** than those.

Jiro speaks the language **more fluently** than Anzu does.

■ **comparing more than two**

EXAMPLES Of the nine planets, Mercury is **nearest** the sun.

Of a gazelle, a cheetah, and an ostrich, which animal can run **most swiftly**?

Alaska is the **largest** of all the U.S. states.

complement A complement is a word or word group that completes the meaning of a verb. (See page 105. See also **direct object, indirect object, predicate nominative** and **predicate adjective**.)

EXAMPLES Ed gave **Martha** a **nod**.

Rei is the **leader** because he is so **organized**.

complex sentence A complex sentence has one independent clause and at least one subordinate clause. (See page 99.)

EXAMPLES   Two of my favorite writers are Katherine Paterson, who wrote *Bridge to Terabithia,* and Beverly Cleary, who wrote *Dear Mr. Henshaw.* [one independent clause and two subordinate clauses]

When Jason and I were stargazing last night, we clearly saw the planets Venus, Mars, Jupiter, and Saturn. [one subordinate clause and one independent clause]

compound-complex sentence A compound-complex sentence has two or more independent clauses and at least one subordinate clause. (See page 100.)

EXAMPLES   Most people think of dolphins as gentle, playful creatures, but as the documentary film shows, they can become fiercely aggressive predators in the wild. [one subordinate clause between two independent clauses]

When we were in Boston last summer, we visited The Computer Museum; we were especially impressed by the exhibit called The Giant Walk-Through Computer. [one subordinate clause followed by two independent clauses]

compound sentence A compound sentence has two or more independent clauses and no subordinate clauses. (See page 97.)

EXAMPLE   This Saturday, the Library Club at our school will hold a book fair; the price of each hardcover book will be one dollar, and the price of each paperback will be fifty cents. [three independent clauses]

compound subject A compound subject is made up of two or more subjects that are connected by a conjunction and have the same verb. (See page 13.)

EXAMPLES   **Spaghetti** or **lasagna** will be served at the banquet.

Do **Alma, Kelsey,** and **Liz** want to join us for lunch?

compound verb A compound verb consists of two or more verbs that are joined by a conjunction and have the same subject. (See page 14.)

EXAMPLES   My aunt Martha **grows** her own vegetables and **shares** them with her neighbors.

               Lane **tumbled** and **slid** down the steep incline.

conjunction A conjunction joins words or groups of words. (See page 66.)

EXAMPLE   **Both** Sy **and** Ben went to the Chinese restaurant, **but** they had to wait before being served, **for** the power was out.

contraction A contraction is a shortened form of a word, a numeral, or a group of words. Apostrophes in contractions indicate where letters or numerals have been omitted. (See page 304. See also **apostrophe.**)

EXAMPLES   **we'd** [we had *or* we would]   **it's** [it is *or* it has]

            who's [who is *or* who has]   **won't** [will not]

            '98 [a year ending in *98*]   **o'clock** [of the clock]

coordinating conjunction A coordinating conjunction joins words or word groups that are used in the same way. (See page 66.)

EXAMPLES   You can have strawberries **or** peaches for dessert.

               The squirrels chattered **and** barked at the blue jays.

coordination Coordination is the use of a conjunction to link ideas of approximately equal importance. (See page 401. See also **coordinating conjunction.**)

EXAMPLES   **Apricots and raspberries** are my favorite fruits.

               Dan likes **canoeing** on Inks Lake **and camping.**

dashes (See page 311.)

EXAMPLES   That CD—thanks for letting me borrow it—has become one of my favorites.

               I thought I hung my coat on the—oh, there it is.

D

declarative sentence A declarative sentence makes a statement and is followed by a period. (See page 18.)

EXAMPLE Birmingham is the second-largest city in the United Kingdom**.**

dependent clause (See **subordinate clause.**)

direct object A direct object is a word or word group that receives the action of the verb or shows the result of the action. A direct object answers the question *Whom?* or *What?* after a transitive verb. (See page 107.)

EXAMPLE Ms. Echavarría saw **John** and **Peter.**

double comparison A double comparison is the nonstandard use of two comparative forms (usually *more* and *–er*) or two superlative forms (usually *most* and *–est*) to express comparison. In standard usage, the single comparative form is correct. (See page 206.)

NONSTANDARD King's Holly, a shrub growing in Tasmania, is considered the world's most oldest living plant.

STANDARD King's Holly, a shrub growing in Tasmania, is considered the world's **oldest** living plant.

double negative A double negative is the nonstandard use of two or more negative words to express a single negative idea. (See page 209.)

NONSTANDARD Without her eyeglasses, Ally couldn't hardly read the letters in the bottom line of the eye chart.

STANDARD Without her eyeglasses, Ally **could hardly** read the letters in the bottom line of the eye chart.

end marks (See page 263.)

■ **with sentences**
EXAMPLES At the state fair, we rode in a hot-air balloon**.** [declarative sentence]

Have you ever ridden in a hot-air balloon**?** [interrogative sentence]

Wow**!** [interjection] What a thrilling adventure that was**!** [exclamatory sentence]

Don't be afraid to look down**.** [imperative sentence]

■ **with abbreviations** (See **abbreviation.**)

EXAMPLES   Your tae kwon do class begins at 7:00 P**.**M**.**

Doesn't your tae kwon do class begin at 7:00 P**.**M**.?**

exclamation point (See **end marks.**)

exclamatory sentence An exclamatory sentence expresses strong feeling and is followed by an exclamation point. (See page 19.)

EXAMPLE   How kind you are**!**

fragment (See **sentence fragment.**)

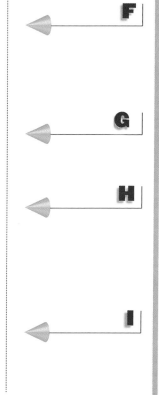

future perfect tense (See **tense of verbs.**)

future tense (See **tense of verbs.**)

good, well (See page 204.)

EXAMPLES   Doreen is a **good** saxophone player.
Doreen plays the saxophone **well** [not *good*].

hyphen (See page 308.)

■ **to divide words**

EXAMPLE   The bright star Sirius is part of the constella-tion Canis Major.

■ **in compound numbers**

EXAMPLE   In a leap year, February has twenty-nine days.

imperative sentence An imperative sentence gives a command or makes a request and is followed by either a period or an exclamation point. (See page 18.)

EXAMPLES Please close the window. [request]
Close the window! [command]

indefinite pronoun An indefinite pronoun refers to a person, place, thing, or idea that may or may not be specifically named. (See page 34.)

EXAMPLES We ate **all** of the soup for lunch.

Everyone was ready to go to the museum.

independent clause An independent clause (also called a main clause) expresses a complete thought and can stand by itself as a sentence. (See page 89.)

EXAMPLE After you get home, **please water the plants.**

indirect object An indirect object is a word or word group that often comes between a transitive verb and its direct object and that tells to whom or to what or for whom or for what the action of the verb is done. (See page 109.)

EXAMPLE Give the **dog** a bath.

infinitive An infinitive is a verb form, usually preceded by *to*, that is used as a noun, an adjective, or an adverb. (See page 147.)

EXAMPLE Sharon and I agreed **to study** together.

interjection An interjection expresses emotion and has no grammatical relation to the rest of the sentence. (See page 68.)

EXAMPLE **Wow,** look at that sunset!

interrogative sentence An interrogative sentence asks a question and is followed by a question mark. (See page 18.)

EXAMPLE Is Clay Regazzoni still racing**?**

intransitive verb An intransitive verb is a verb that does not take an object. (See page 55.)

EXAMPLE The crowd **laughed,** but Bob only **smiled.**

irregular verb An irregular verb is a verb that forms its past and past participle in some way other than by adding *–d* or *–ed* to the base form. (See page 150. See also **regular verb.**)

Base Form	Present Participle	Past	Past Participle
be	[is] being	was, were	[have] been
begin	[is] beginning	began	[have] begun
bring	[is] bringing	brought	[have] brought
burst	[is] bursting	burst	[have] burst
fall	[is] falling	fell	[have] fallen
go	[is] going	went	[have] gone
make	[is] making	made	[have] made

italics (See **underlining.**)

its, it's (See page 228.)

EXAMPLES **Its** [the snow leopard's] scientific name is *Panthera uncia.*

It's [It is] considered an endangered species.

It's [It has] been overhunted for **its** fur.

lie, lay (See page 168.)

EXAMPLES Anxious about his first day at a new school, Harry **lay** awake most of the night. [past tense of *lie*]

Aunt Una **laid** the map on the table and showed us the route we would travel. [past tense of *lay*]

linking verb A linking verb connects the subject with a word that identifies or describes the subject. (See page 53.)

EXAMPLE Cousin Marty **became** a clarinetist.

misplaced modifier A misplaced modifier is a word, phrase, or clause that seems to modify the wrong word or words. (See page 211.)

MISPLACED	Ms. Osaka said on Friday the sixth-grade students would elect class officers. [Does the phrase *on Friday* modify the verb *said* or the verb phrase *would elect*?]
REVISED	**On Friday,** Ms. Osaka said the sixth-grade students would elect class officers. [The phrase *On Friday* clearly modifies the verb *said.*]
REVISED	Ms. Osaka said the sixth-grade students would elect class officers **on Friday.** [The phrase *on Friday* clearly modifies the verb phrase *would elect.*]

modifier A modifier is a word or word group that makes the meaning of another word or word group more specific. (See page 197.)

EXAMPLE   **The loud** chirping **of sparrows** filled **the** air.

noun A noun names a person, place, thing, or idea. (See page 25.)

EXAMPLE   During the **drive, Ms. Washington** asked **Tommy** and **Sarah** to sing their **version** of the **song.**

number Number is the form a word takes to indicate whether the word is singular or plural. (See page 124.)

EXAMPLES   The **dove** dipped **its head** as **it** drank.
                The **doves** dipped **their heads** as **they** drank.

object of a preposition An object of a preposition is the noun or pronoun that ends a prepositional phrase. (See page 63.)

EXAMPLE   Do you have any books about **elephants**? [*About elephants* is a prepositional phrase.]

parentheses (See page 311.)

EXAMPLES   Lincoln Ellsworth **(**1880–1951**)** discovered the highest mountain on the continent of Antarctica.

          Let's meet in Conference Room 245 **(**directly across from the library**)**.

participial phrase A participial phrase consists of a participle and any complements and modifiers it has. (See page 399.)

EXAMPLE   Marcy is the only sixth-grader **running this race.**

participle A participle is a verb form that can be used as an adjective. (See page 397.)

EXAMPLE   Elena tickled the **smiling** baby.

passive voice The passive voice is the voice a verb is in when it expresses an action done to its subject. (See page 393. See also **active voice.**)

EXAMPLE   The tire **was punctured** in three places.

past perfect tense (See **tense of verbs.**)

past tense (See **tense of verbs.**)

period (See **end marks.**)

phrase A phrase is a group of related words that does not contain both a verb and its subject and that is used as a single part of speech. (See page 76.)

EXAMPLE   Marcia **is designing** a dress **for her cousin Francine's wedding.** [*Is designing* is a verb phrase. *For her cousin Francine's wedding* is a prepositional phrase.]

predicate The predicate is the part of a sentence that says something about the subject. (See page 9.)

EXAMPLES   She **is waiting for the bus.**

Does Walter **know Rebecca?**

predicate adjective A predicate adjective is an adjective that completes the meaning of a linking verb and that modifies the subject of the verb. (See page 114.)

EXAMPLE   At the farm, the cows looked **sleek** and **healthy.**

predicate nominative A predicate nominative is a noun or pronoun that completes the meaning of a linking verb and identifies or refers to the subject of the verb. (See page 112.)

EXAMPLE   The first passengers to exit were **Ron** and **Dee.**

prefix A prefix is a word part that is added before a base word or root. (See page 320.)

EXAMPLES   un + solved = **un**solved

im + mature = **im**mature

dis + satisfied = **dis**satisfied

preposition A preposition shows the relationship of a noun or a pronoun to some other word in a sentence. (See page 62.)

EXAMPLE   **At** the market, Tancredo bought green peppers, cheese, and tomatoes **for** the meal he was planning.

prepositional phrase A prepositional phrase is a group of words that includes a preposition, an object of the preposition, and any modifiers of that object. (See page 63.)

EXAMPLE   A book **of swashbuckling adventure** is *Treasure Island,* **by Robert Louis Stevenson.**

present perfect tense (See **tense of verbs.**)

present tense (See **tense of verbs.**)

pronoun A pronoun is used in place of one or more nouns or pronouns. (See page 30.)

EXAMPLE   Julie told Mom and Dad **she** would be happy to drive **them** to the airport.

question mark (See **end marks.**)

quotation marks (See page 292.)

■ **for direct quotations**

EXAMPLE   "On our vacation in Mexico," said Mrs. Tamayo, "we visited Chichén Itzá, where we saw the ruins of pyramids and temples that the Maya had built."

■ **with other marks of punctuation** (See also preceding example.)

EXAMPLES   "In what year was the first Earth Day celebration held?" asked Megan.

Who is the main character in Gary Soto's story "The No-Guitar Blues"?

The teacher asked, "What do you think Benjamin Franklin meant when he wrote the proverb 'Hunger is the best pickle'?"

■ **for titles**

EXAMPLES   "Amigo Brothers" [short story]

"Madam and the Rent Man" [short poem]

"Under the Sea" [song]

regular verb A regular verb is a verb that forms its past and past participle by adding –*d* or –*ed* to the base form. (See page 148. See also **irregular verb.**)

Base Form	Present Participle	Past	Past Participle
ask	[is] asking	asked	[have] asked
drown	[is] drowning	drowned	[have] drowned
move	[is] moving	moved	[have] moved
risk	[is] risking	risked	[have] risked
suppose	[is] supposing	supposed	[have] supposed
use	[is] using	used	[have] used

rise, raise (See page 166.)

EXAMPLES   When the sun **rose,** the restless scouts were still awake. [past tense of *rise*]

The orchestra conductor **raised** the baton to begin the concert. [past tense of *raise*]

root A root is the main part of the word. It carries the word's meaning. Prefixes and suffixes can be added to a root to create new words. (See page 320. See also **base.**)

EXAMPLES   –act–   –log–   –ped–

             action   bio**log**y   **ped**icure

             re**act**   geo**log**ical   bi**ped**

run-on sentence A run-on sentence is two or more complete sentences run together as one. (See page 388.)

RUN-ON   Nishi and I have been computer pen pals for two years she lives in Tokyo, Japan I live in Omaha, Nebraska.

REVISED   Nishi and I have been computer pen pals for two years**;** she lives in Tokyo, Japan**, and** I live in Omaha, Nebraska.

REVISED   Nishi and I have been computer pen pals for two years**.** **S**he lives in Tokyo, Japan**, and** I live in Omaha, Nebraska.

semicolon (See page 279.)

EXAMPLE   In 1993, Ramon Blanco from Spain became the oldest person to scale Mount Everest**;** he was sixty years old at the time.

sentence A sentence is a group of words that contains a subject and a verb and that expresses a complete thought. (See page 4.)

                       S   V

EXAMPLE   The fish swam lazily in the clear water.

sentence fragment A sentence fragment is a group of words that is punctuated as if it were a complete sentence but that does not contain both a subject and a verb or that does not express a complete thought. (See pages 4 and 386.)

FRAGMENTS   Hera, the queen of the Greek gods, casting a spell on Hercules. Because she was jealous of him.

SENTENCE   Hera, the queen of the Greek gods, cast a spell on Hercules because she was jealous of him.

simple sentence A simple sentence has one independent clause and no subordinate clauses. (See page 96.)

EXAMPLE   On the Internet, Milo and I accessed a search page and searched for information about King Tutankhamen. [one independent clause with a compound subject and a compound verb]

sit, set (See page 165.)

EXAMPLES   Carmen **sat** on the bench, anxiously waiting for Coach Engle to send her back into the game. [past tense of *sit*]

Anthony **set** the box of dominoes on the table, hoping that someone in his family would play the game with him. [past tense of *set*]

stringy sentence A stringy sentence is a sentence that has too many independent clauses. Usually, the clauses are strung together with coordinating conjunctions like *and* or *but*. (See page 391.)

STRINGY   One day, the gods Jupiter and Mercury decided to come down to the earth to test the people of Phrygia for their hospitality, so the gods disguised themselves as peasants who were in desperate need of food and shelter, and they stopped at hundreds of houses, and at each one the "peasants" were turned away, but finally, they came to the very small house of a poor, elderly couple named Baucis and Philemon.

REVISED   One day, the gods Jupiter and Mercury decided to come down to the earth to test the people of Phrygia for their hospitality. The gods disguised themselves as peasants who were in desperate need of food and shelter. They stopped at hundreds of houses, and at each one the "peasants" were turned away. Finally, they came to the very small house of a poor, elderly couple named Baucis and Philemon.

subject The subject tells whom or what a sentence is about. (See page 7.)

EXAMPLE   The **geraniums** bloomed early this year.

subject complement A subject complement is a word or word group that completes the meaning of a linking verb and identifies or describes the subject. (See page 112. See also **predicate adjective** and **predicate nominative**.)

EXAMPLES   My cousin Brian is a **software technician.**

The art room was **messy.**

subordinate clause A subordinate clause (also called a *dependent clause*) does not express a complete thought and cannot stand alone as a sentence. (See page 90. See also **adjective clause** and **adverb clause**.)

EXAMPLE   **After I read that article,** I changed my opinion.

subordination Subordination is the use of dependent clauses to express ideas of less importance than those expressed in independent clauses. (See page 403. See also **subordinate clause.**)

EXAMPLES   You can bring the book back **whenever it is convenient.**

The writer **who reviewed the new movie** was very positive.

If we leave by seven o'clock, we will be on time.

suffix A suffix is a word part that is added after a base word or root. (See page 321.)

EXAMPLES   steady + ly = steadi**ly**
forgive + ness = forgive**ness**
obey + ing = obey**ing**
adore + able = ador**able**
shop + ing = shop**ping**

syllable A syllable is a word part that can be pronounced as one uninterrupted sound. (See page 318.)

EXAMPLES   sleep [one syllable]

en • gine [two syllables]

di • a • gram [three syllables]

tense of verbs The tense of verbs indicates the time of the action or of the state of being that is expressed by the verb. (See page 160.)

T

Present Tense

I do	we do
you do	you do
he, she, it does	they do

Past Tense

I did	we did
you did	you did
he, she, it did	they did

Future Tense

I will (shall) do	we will (shall) do
you will (shall) do	you will (shall) do
he, she, it will (shall) do	they will (shall) do

Present Perfect Tense

I have done	we have done
you have done	you have done
he, she, it has done	they have done

Past Perfect Tense

I had done	we had done
you had done	you had done
he, she, it had done	they had done

Future Perfect Tense

I will (shall) have done	we will (shall) have done
you will (shall) have done	you will (shall) have done
he, she, it will (shall) have done	they will (shall) have done

their, there, they're (See pages 229 and 336.)

EXAMPLES Candace and Ruben moved **their** desks closer to the window. [*Their* tells whose desks.]

Grammar at a Glance**463**

We stood **there** in the cold rain until the bus arrived. [*There* tells where we stood.]

There are five days left until the end of school. [*There* begins the sentence but does not add to the meaning of the sentence.]

They're planning a surprise birthday party for Emily. [*They're* is a contraction of *They are*.]

transitions Transitions are words or word groups that help show how ideas and details in words, phrases, sentences, and paragraphs are related. (See page 405.)

EXAMPLES **In addition** to tomatoes, we also grow lettuce. [*In addition* shows similarities.]

The sky is mostly gray; **however,** there are some small patches of blue. [*However* shows differences.]

I left the game at 5:00 P.M. **because** I was meeting a friend at 5:30. [*Because* shows cause and effect.]

transitive verb A transitive verb is an action verb that takes an object. (See page 55.)

EXAMPLE   Their dog **chased** our cat.

underlining (italics) (See page 290.)

■ **for titles**

EXAMPLES   *The Way to Rainy Mountain* [book]

National Geographic World [magazine]

Sleeping Gypsy [work of art]

Duke Bluebeard's Castle [long musical composition]

■ **for names of vehicles**

EXAMPLES   *Orient Express* [train]

Air Force One [aircraft]

verb A verb expresses an action or a state of being. (See page 49.)

EXAMPLE   Evelyn **wore** a blue blazer.

Is the desert nearby?

verb phrase A verb phrase consists of a main verb and at least one helping verb. (See page 50.)

EXAMPLES The helicopter **should have been** here by now.

I **have** never **heard** Michael Bolton sing.

voice (See page 393. See also **active voice** and **passive voice**.)

well (See *good, well.*)

who, whom (See page 188.)

EXAMPLES **Who** was the first astronaut to walk in space?
[nominative form used as the predicate nominative referring to the subject *astronaut*]

Whom have you invited to your bat mitzvah party?
[objective form used as the direct object of the verb phrase *have invited*]

INDEX

with personal pronouns, 303
with plurals, 307, 327, 443
with possessives, 300–303, 443
Appositive phrases, 272–73, 444
Appositives, 190, 272–73, 443–44
"April Rain Song" (Hughes), 239
Articles
a, an, the, 38, 444
capitalizing in titles, 256
underlining (italicizing) in titles, 291
Artwork
capitalization of names of, 255
underlining (italicizing) names of, 290–91
At, 223
Audiotapes, capitalization of, 255
Auxiliary verbs. *See* Helping verbs.
Awards, capitalization of, 247

Bad, badly, 223, 444
Base form, 147, 148, 444
Base words, 320, 444
B.C., 266
Be. See also Helping verbs; Irregular verbs.
conjugation of, 162–63
as linking verb, 53, 114
overuse of, 114, 115
Become, **principal parts of,** 151
Begin, **principal parts of,** 151
Between, among, 223
Blow, **principal parts of,** 151
Books, underlining (italicizing) titles of, 290
Brackets, 312, 444
Brake, break, 329
Brand names, capitalization of, 246
Break, **principal parts of,** 151
Bring, **principal parts of,** 152
Bring, take, 225
British English, spelling and pronunciation, 431
Buildings and other structures, capitalization of, 247
Businesses, capitalization of, 246
Business letters, punctuation of, 276, 281
But, **combining sentences with,** 401, 403
Buy, **principal parts of,** 152

Calendar items, capitalization of, 244
"Camel Fodder" (Shah), 296
Capital, capitol, 330
Capitalization, 239–56
of abbreviations, 250–51, 440

of aircraft, 247
of animal names, 241
of audiotapes, 255
of awards, 247
of brand names, 246
of buildings and other structures, 247
of businesses, 246
of calendar items, 244–45
of compact discs, 255
of constellations, 248
of deities (specific), 247–48
of directions, 243
of directly quoted sentences, 293
of family relationships, 253
of first words, 239, 444–45
of geographical names, 242–43
of government bodies, 244
of heavenly bodies, 248
of historical events and periods, 245
of holidays, 244
of holy days and celebrations, 247
of institutions, 244
in letter salutation and closing, 240
of memorials, 247
of monuments, 247
of musical compositions, 255
of nationalities, 246
of organizations, 244
of peoples, 246
of personal names, 241
of planets, 248
of pronoun *I,* 240
of proper adjectives, 40, 250, 445
of proper nouns, 26, 241, 445–46
of publications, 255
of races, 246
of religions and followers, 247
of sacred writings, 247
of school subjects, 250
of ships, 247
of spacecraft, 247
of special events, 244
of stars, 248
of teams, 244
of television programs and movies, 255
of titles and subtitles of works, 254–56, 446
of titles of persons, 253, 446
of trains, 247
of video games, 255
of videos, 255
of works of art, 255
Case forms
nominative case, 177, 447
objective case, 177, 447
possessive case, 300–301, 303, 447
Choose, **principal parts of,** 152
Chose, choose, 330

Names. *See* Capitalization; Personal names; Titles (personal); Titles (works); Underlining (italics).
Nationalities, capitalization of, 246
–ness, 321
Neuter pronouns, 137–38
Nominative case, 177, 447
Nonstandard English, 221, 432–33
Nor, or
    joining singular and plural subjects with, 132
    pronoun-antecedent agreement and, 139–40
Not, never, 12
Not **and contraction** *–n't,* 304–305
    as adverbs, 50
Noun(s). *See also* Pronouns.
    as appositives, 190
    common nouns, 26, 241
    compound nouns, 25
    definition of, 25, 456
    of direct address, 274
    plurals, 300–301, 325
    possessive case of, 300–301
    proper nouns, 26, 241, 300
    spelling plurals of, 325–27
Nowheres, 223
Number (grammar)
    definition of, 124, 456
    indefinite pronouns and, 129–30
    phrases between subject and verb and, 127–28
    pronoun-antecedent agreement in, 138–39
    subject-verb agreement and, 124–25
Numbers (numerals)
    contractions and, 304
    hyphenation of, 308, 453
    plurals of, 307, 327
    punctuation of, 263

Objective case, 177, 447
Object form, of personal pronouns, 177–78, 183–87
Objects of prepositions. *See also* Prepositions.
    definition of, 63–64, 77, 456
    indirect objects compared with, 110
    placement in sentences, 63
    pronouns as, 187
Objects of verbs
    definition of, 55
    direct objects, 107–108, 113, 183, 184, 419, 452
    indirect objects, 109–10, 185, 420, 454

Of, 229
Off of, 229
One-word modifiers, 197–98
Or, **combining sentences with,** 401, 403
Or, nor
    joining singular and plural subjects with, 132
    pronoun-antecedent agreement and, 139–40
Organizations (groups)
    abbreviations of names of, 265
    capitalization of names of, 244
Ought to of, 225
Outside of, 229

Parentheses, 311–12, 456
Participial phrases, 457
Participles, 457
Parts of speech
    adjectives, 38–41
    adverbs, 59–60
    conjunctions, 66–67
    determining parts of speech, 70
    interjections, 68
    nouns, 25–26
    prepositions, 62–65
    pronouns, 30–37
    verbs, 49–56
Passed, past, 334
Passive voice, definition of, 393–94, 457
Past participle, 147, 148, 150–52
Past perfect progressive tense, 162
Past perfect tense, 160, 161, 163, 463
Past progressive tense, 162
Past tense, 147, 148, 160, 162, 463
Pay, **principal parts of,** 154
Peace, piece, 333
Peoples, capitalization of names of, 246
Periodicals, underlining (italicizing) titles of, 290
Periods, 263, 264
    with abbreviations, 265
    with quotations, 294
Personal letters, commas used in salutations, 276
Personal names
    capitalization, 241
    hyphens in, 308
    punctuating abbreviations in, 265
Personal pronouns, 31–32
    antecedent of, 138
    forms of, 177–78
    object form, 177–78, 183–87
    possessive form, 177–78, 303
    as predicate nominative, 181
    subject form, 177–81

Verb(s)
 action verbs, 52, 53, 54, 112, 114, 440
 active voice and, 393
 agreement with subjects, 124–35
 compound verbs, 14, 15–16, 401, 414, 451
 definition of, 49, 464
 diagramming and, 412–13
 helping verbs, 49–50, 147, 161
 infinitives, 78, 147, 454
 intransitive verbs, 55–56, 454
 irregular verbs, 148, 150–52, 154–55, 455
 lie, lay, 168
 linking verbs, 53–54, 56, 112, 205, 455
 main verbs, 49–50
 objects of verbs, 107–108
 participles, 457
 passive voice and, 393–94, 457
 principal parts of, 147–55
 progressive forms of, 161–62
 regular verbs, 148, 459
 rise, raise, 166
 sit, set, 165
 tenses of, 160–64, 463
 transitive verbs, 55–56, 464
Verb phrases, 50
 definition of, 11, 465
 not, never and, 12
Videos and video games, capitalization of, 255
Vocabulary. *See also* English language.
 word origins, 431–32
Voice, active and passive, 393–94

Wash, **principal parts of,** 148
Way, ways, 232
Weak, week, 337
Wear
 conjugation of verb, 160–61
 principal parts of, 147, 155
Well, good, 204–205, 225–26, 453
When, where, 232

Who, whom, 188–89, 465
Whose, who's, 232, 338
Word division, 308, 453
Words
 base words, 444
 borrowed, 431–32
 commonly misspelled, 344–45
 contractions, 304–305
 from names, 432
 often confused (homonyms), 329–38
 plurals of words referred to as words, 307, 327
 punctuation of introductory, 274–75
 roots of, 460
 word origins, 431–32
Word order, inverted, 134
Would of, 225
Write, **principal parts of,** 155
Writing applications
 agreement (subject-verb) in instructions, 145
 apostrophes in a personal letter, 315
 capital letters in an essay, 261
 complements in a paragraph, 120–21
 correct pronoun forms in writing, 195
 correct spelling in a personal letter, 343
 end marks in a screenplay, 287
 formal English in a letter, 237
 negative words in description, 219
 prepositional phrases in a story, 103
 pronouns in a plot summary, 47
 sentence variety in a comic strip, 23
 using verbs in a description, 175
 using verbs in lists, 73
Written works, underlining (italicizing) titles of, 290–91

Your, you're, 232, 338

ZIP Codes
 use of punctuation and, 251, 276

ACKNOWLEDGMENTS

For permission to reprint copyrighted material, grateful acknowledgment is made to the following sources:

Alfred A. Knopf, Inc.: "April Rain Song" from *Collected Poems* by Langston Hughes. Copyright ©1994 by the Estate of Langston Hughes.

The Octagon Press, Ltd., London: "Camel fodder" from *The Subtleties of the Inimitable Mulla Nasrudin* by Idries Shah. Copyright ©1983 by The Octagon Press, Ltd.

PHOTO CREDITS

Abbreviations used: (t)top, (tl)top left, (tc)top center, (tr)top right, (l)left, (lc)left center, (c)center, (rc)right center, (r)right, (bl)bottom left, (bc)bottom center, (br)bottom right.

AUTHOR ESSAYS: Amy Benjamin (Dylan Griffin/HRW Photo), Brock Haussamen (Dylan Griffin/HRW Photo), Rei Noguchi (Henry Blackham/HRW Photo), Billy Boyar (John Langford/HRW Photo).

TABLE OF CONTENTS: Page v (lc), Rod Planck/Photo Researchers, Inc.; vii, Image Copyright ©2001 PhotoDisc, Inc.; viii, H. Knaus/SuperStock; ix, Photograph by Franko Khoury, National Museum of African Art, Eliot Elisofon Photographic Archives, Smithsonian Institution; x, Mike Okoniewski /The Image Works; xiii, Fred Bavendam/Peter Arnold, Inc.; xv, Carl Purcell/Photo Researchers, Inc.

CHAPTER 1: Page 5, SuperStock; 9, Russel Dian/HRW Photo; 10, Comstock; 15, David Allen/CORBIS; 20, Spencer Swager/Tom Stack & Associates.

CHAPTER 2: Page 27, Orion Press, Japan; 29, Image Copyright ©2001 PhotoDisc, Inc.; 30, Bob Daugharty, AP/Wide World Photos; 36, Photograph by Franko Khoury, National Museum of African Art, Eliot Elisofon Photographic Archives, Smithsonian Institution; 39, Peter Gridley/FPG International; 42, Image Copyright ©2001 PhotoDisc, Inc.; 43, SuperStock.

CHAPTER 3: 52, Jerry Jacka Photography/Courtesy: The Heard Museum, Phoenix, Arizona; 55, Johnson Publishing Company, Inc.; 57, Image Copyright ©2001 PhotoDisc, Inc.; 58 (bc), Dr. Ronald H. Cohn/ The Gorilla Foundation/Koko.org; 58 (l), Image Copyright ©2001 PhotoDisc, Inc.; 61, Lionel Delvigne/ Stock Boston; 69, Linda Kelen.

CHAPTER 4: Page 1931, True Fresco, 22'7" x 29'9", San Francisco Art Institute. Photo Credit: David Wakely; 85, Michael Newman/Photo Edit; 87 (br), Katherine Feng/Viesti Collection; 87 (c), Lowell Georgia/Photo Researchers, Inc.; 98, ©1994 J. Lotter Gurling/Tom Stack & Associates; 99, Michele Burgess/Stock Boston.

CHAPTER 5: Page 111, Image Copyright 2001 Photodisc, Inc.; 117, H. Knaus/SuperStock.

CHAPTER 6: Page 126, Bruce Davidson/Animals Animals; 128, CORBIS/W. Perry Conway; 134, Joe Viesti/Viesti Collection; 137, Bob Couey/Seaworld Inc. © 1998. All rights reserved. Reproduced by permission.; 142, Image Copyright ©2001 PhotoDisc, Inc.

CHAPTER 7: Page 150, Hampton University Museum, Hampton, Virginia; 157, Bettmann/CORBIS; 171, ©1997 Radlund & Associates for Artville.

CHAPTER 8: Page 179, National Museum of American Art, Washington DC/Art Resource, NY; 183 (b), Mike Okoniewski/ The Image Works; 183 (t), Joe Jaworski/HRW Photo; 190, Image Copyright ©2001 PhotoDisc, Inc.

CHAPTER 9: Page 208 (bl), Giraudon/Art Resource, NY.; 208 (br), Gianni Dagli Orti/CORBIS.

CHAPTER 10: Page 228, Image Copyright ©2001 PhotoDisc, Inc.; 234, Photo Image Technologies.

CHAPTER 11: Page 249, SuperStock; 258, Margaret Sulanowska/Woods Hole Oceanographic Institution.

CHAPTER 12: Page 265, Carl Purcell/Photo Researchers, Inc.; 267, Michael Newman/Photo Edit; 273, Giraudon/Art Resource, New York; 278, Eastcott/Momatiuk/Animals Animals.

CHAPTER 13: Page 295, Clementine Hunter, (c.1945). Photo from the Mildred Bailey Collection, Mildred H. Bailey, Natchitoches, Louisiana; 301, Keystone/Sygma; 302 (lc), Rod Planck/Photo Researchers, Inc.; 302 (rc), Gordon and Cathy Illg/Animals Animals/Earth Scenes; 319, Aaron Horowitz/CORBIS.

CHAPTER 14: Page 324, Chris Brown/SIPA Press; 327, A. Ramey/Photo Edit; 332, Photo Edit; 336 (tc), Aaron Haupt/ Photo Researchers, Inc.; 336 (tr), Aaron Haupt/Photo Researchers, Inc.; 340, Werner Forman Archive/Museum fur Volkerkunde, Berlin/Art Resource, NY; 350, Richard Weiss/ HRW Photo.

CHAPTER 15: Page 357, News Office, Woods Hole Oceanographic Institution; 363, Fred Bavendam/Peter Arnold, Inc.; 369, Courtesy of Joe Rosenberg; 372, Robert Trippett/ SIPA Press.

CHAPTER 16: Page 386, Jim Corwin/Stock Boston; 391 (bl), Patti Murray/Animals Animals/Earth Scenes; 391 (bc), SuperStock; 391 (br), Toni Angermayer/Photo Researchers, Inc.; 392, Image Copyright ©2001 PhotoDisc, Inc.; 397, Huntington Library/SuperStock; 399, Bettmann/CORBIS; 402, Zigmund Leszczynski/Animals Animals/Earth Scenes.

ILLUSTRATION CREDITS

All work, unless otherwise noted, contributed by Holt, Rinehart & Winston.

Page 78, Rich Lo; 82, Rondi Collette; 126, Ortelius Design; 170, Chris Ellison; 202, Rondi Collette; 211, Rondi Collette; 230, Tom Gianni; 233, Ortelius Design; 234, Leslie Kell; 249, Ortelius Design; 306, Rondi Collette; 340, Ortelius Design.